The Network Architecture
Design Handbook

Taylor Networking Series

Multiplatform Network Management, 0-07-063295-2

McGraw-Hill Internetworking Command Reference, 0-07-063301-0

The McGraw-Hill Internetworking Handbook, Second Edition,
0-07-063399-1

Network Architecture Design Handbook, 0-07-063333-9 (hardcover)
0-07-063362-2 (softcover)

The Network Architecture Design Handbook

Data, Voice, Multimedia, Intranet, and Hybrid Networks

Ed Taylor

McGraw-Hill

New York   San Francisco   Washington, D.C.   Auckland   Bogotá
Caracas   Lisbon   London   Madrid   Mexico City   Milan
Montreal   New Delhi   San Juan   Singapore
Sydney   Tokyo   Toronto

Library of Congress Cataloging-in-Publication Data

Taylor, Ed.
   The network architecture design handbook : data, voice,
multimedia, intranet, and hybrid networks / Ed Taylor.
      p.   cm.—(Taylor networking series)
   Includes index.
   ISBN 0-07-063333-9 (hardcover).—ISBN 0-07-063362-2 (softcover)
   1. Computer networks—Management. 2. Computer network
architectures. I. Title. II. Series: Taylor, Ed, date. Taylor
networking series.
   TK5105.5.T396 1997
   004.6—dc21   97-34694
                                                 CIP

McGraw-Hill

*A Division of The **McGraw·Hill** Companies*

*The sponsoring editor for this book was Steven Elliot and the
production supervisor was Pamela Pelton. It was set in Century
Schoolbook by North Market Street Graphics.*

Printed and bound by R. R. Donnelley & Sons Company.

McGraw-Hill books are available at special quantity discounts to use as
premiums and sales promotions, or for use in corporate training programs. For more information, please write to the Director of Special
Sales, McGraw-Hill, 11 West 19th Street, New York, NY 10011. Or contact your local bookstore.

This book is printed on recycled, acid-free paper containing a
minimum of 50% recycled, de-inked fiber.

Dedicated to:

God

The Master Architect

Contents

Preface   xv
Acknowledgments   xvii

Chapter 1. Perspective, Principles, and Operations   1

    1.1   Fallacies and Misperceptions   2
    1.2   Signal Characteristics   10
    1.3   Data Representation   15
    1.4   Summary   18

Chapter 2. Network Architecture Basics   19

    2.1   Transmission Topics   19
    2.2   Communication Terms and Concepts   26
    2.3   Signal Distortion   34
    2.4   Types of Transmission Media   36
    2.5   Communication Links   40
    2.6   Summary   42

Chapter 3. Network Architecture: Insights from Experience   43

    3.1   How to Learn Architectures   43
    3.2   Perspective on Technology   44
    3.3   Practical Learning Tools   61
    3.4   Summary   63

Chapter 4. Network Architecture Analysis   65

    4.1   Personal Computing   65
    4.2   Personal Computer Architecture   67
    4.3   Network Architecture   73
    4.4   Summary   81

Chapter 5. Network Design Considerations   83

    5.1   Design Needs   83
    5.2   Physical Considerations   85

5.3   Electrical Considerations   86
5.4   The Human Factor   89
5.5   Evolution   92
5.6   Technical Factors   93
5.7   Summary   93

Chapter 6. Network Design and Components, Part 1   **95**

6.1   Network Design   95
6.2   Component Overview   97
6.3   Personal Computers   97
6.4   Rack Enclosure   99
6.5   Electrical Test Equipment   102
6.6   Network HUBs   105
6.7   Patch Panel and Wiring   106
6.8   Power Protection   109
6.9   Communication Equipment   112
6.10 Summary   117

Chapter 7. Network Design and Components, Part 2   **119**

7.1   Communication Equipment   119
7.2   Operating System Software   124
7.3   Network Printer   132
7.4   Network Security   135
7.5   Multimedia Components   138
7.6   Network Analyzer   140
7.7   Miscellaneous Devices and Tools   142
7.8   Summary   143

Chapter 8. Network Architecture, Operation, and Maintenance   **145**

8.1   Communication Equipment   145
8.2   Network Architecture Design and Implementation   149
8.3   Network Operation   162
8.4   Your Network and the Y2K Problem   164
8.5   Network Maintenance   168
8.6   Summary   169

**Chapter 9. Network Architecture and Asynchronous
Transfer Mode (ATM)**   **171**

9.1   A Perspective on ATM   171
9.2   ATM Layer Structure   172
9.3   ATM Adaptation Layer (AAL) Functions   174
9.4   ATM Cell Structure   175
9.5   ATM Interface Types   176
9.6   ATM Concepts   177

9.7   A Perspective on ATM Implementation   179
9.8   A Perspective on ATM Physical Layer Architecture   181
9.9   ATM Terminology   186
9.10 Where to Find Additional Information   187
9.11 Summary   188

**Chapter 10. Data, Voice, and Integrated Services Digital
Network (ISDN) Technology   189**

10.1   What Is ISDN?   190
10.2   ISDN Channels   192
10.3   Signaling System 7 (SS7)   195
10.4   ISDN Interfaces and How They Are Used   197
10.5   Practical Uses of ISDN   198
10.6   Summary   200

Chapter 11. Data, Multimedia, Voice, and Frame Relay   201

11.1   Voice, Data, and Frame Relay   203
11.2   Frame Relay Frame Components   205
11.3   Multimedia and Virtual Circuits   206
11.4   Access Devices   207
11.5   Consumer Tips   210
11.6   Additional Information   210
11.7   Summary   211

Chapter 12. Managing Data, Voice, and Multimedia   213

12.1   Data, Voice, and Multimedia Considerations   214
12.2   Management Philosophies   218
12.3   Multiprotocol Management   220
12.4   Information Attained via Management   222
12.5   Summary   224

Chapter 13. File Structures   225

13.1   Perspective   226
13.2   Apple   226
13.3   Multiple Virtual Storage (MVS)   227
13.4   UNIX   231
13.5   OS2/400   232
13.6   Virtual Machine (VM)   235
13.7   Open/VMS   239
13.8   Virtual Storage Extended (VSE)   241
13.9   S/38   243
13.10 MS-DOS   244
13.11 S/36   244
13.12 Summary   248

Chapter 14. Network Architecture and TCP/IP Network Design   251

14.1   TCP/IP Perspective   251
14.2   TCP/IP Growth   251
14.3   TCP/IP Layers   255
14.4   Planning and TCP/IP Network Design   258
14.5   Internet Protocol (IP)   259
14.6   Internet Control Message Protocol (ICMP)   262
14.7   Address Resolution Protocol (ARP)   263
14.8   Reverse Address Resolution Protocol (RARP)   267
14.9   Router Protocols   268
14.10 TCP: A Perspective   273
14.11 Establishing TCP Connections   275
14.12 TCP Connection Termination   281
14.13 TCP and Data Communication   283
14.14 User Datagram Protocol (UDP)   286
14.15 TCP/IP Addressing   287
14.16 Popular TCP Applications   291
14.17 Popular UDP Applications   301
14.18 Summary   308

Chapter 15. TCP/IP Network Design and IP Version 4   309

15.1   IP Functions   309
15.2   IP Operation   311
15.3   IP Terminology   314
15.4   Routers and IP   316
15.5   IP Header Format   317
15.6   Internet Timestamp   326
15.7   Interfaces and IP Version 4   334
15.8   Summary   339

Chapter 16. TCP/IP Network Design and IP Version 6   341

16.1   IPv6 Terminology   342
16.2   IPv6 Header Format   343
16.3   IPv6 Extension Headers   343
16.4   Extension Header Order   345
16.5   IPv6 Options Header (Hop-by-Hop)   347
16.6   IPv6 Routing Header   349
16.7   IPv6 Fragment Header   353
16.8   IPv6 Destination Options Header   357
16.9   IPv6 No Next Header   358
16.10 IPv6 Packet Size Considerations   358
16.11 IPv6 Flow Labels   359
16.12 IPv6 Packet Priority   362
16.13 IPv6 and Upper-Layer Protocols   362
16.14 IPv6 Addressing Types   366
16.15 IPv6 Addressing   367

16.16   Address Type Representation   368
16.17   Unicast Addresses   369
16.18   IPv6 Addresses and IPv4 Addresses   371
16.19   Anycast Addresses   373
16.20   Multicast Addresses   375
16.21   Node Address Requirement   378
16.22   Summary   379

Chapter 17. Designing Networks That Use DHCP   381

17.1   Introduction   381
17.2   DHCP Terms   384
17.3   DHCP Protocol   385
17.4   DHCP Configuration Parameters Repository   388
17.5   Network Address Dynamic Allocation   388
17.6   Client/Server Protocol   389
17.7   DHCP Messages and Meanings   390
17.8   DHCP Client/Server Protocol Specification   392
17.9   DHCP Server Function   396
17.10   DHCP Client Function   402
17.11   Summary   406

Chapter 18. Network Design and the Domain Name System   407

18.1   DNS Design Goals   408
18.2   Assumptions About DNS Usage   409
18.3   Elements of DNS   411
18.4   Domain Name Space and Resource Records   412
18.5   DNS Name Syntax   415
18.6   DNS Queries   416
18.7   Standard DNS Queries   417
18.8   DNS Name Servers   418
18.9   DNS Resolvers   423
18.10   DNS Summary   425
18.11   DNS References   425

Chapter 19. Designing NetWare Networks   429

19.1   Perspective   429
19.2   NetWare Protocols: An Orientation   431
19.3   Open Data Interface (ODI) Concepts   436
19.4   Internet Packet Exchange (IPX)   439
19.5   Sequence Packet Exchange (SPX)   442
19.6   NetWare Core Protocol (NCP)   443
19.7   Service Advertising Protocol (SAP)   446
19.8   Routing Information Protocol (RIP)   448
19.9   Error, Echo, and NetBIOS Protocols   450
19.10   System Fault Tolerance (SFT)   451

19.11   NetWare Implementations   452
19.12   Summary   456

Chapter 20. Designing Networks with Windows NT   459

20.1   Perspective   459
20.2   NT Architecture   460
20.3   Architectural Analysis   461
20.4   Workstation and Server Commonalities   466
20.5   Topics of Interest   467
20.6   The Registry   469
20.7   Network Configuration   470
20.8   High-Speed Server Connections   472
20.9   General Considerations   476
20.10   Summary   477

Chapter 21. Designing Networks with Bridges   479

21.1   Functionality Within a Network   479
21.2   Theory of Operation   481
21.3   Bridges by Protocol   483
21.4   Bridges by Geographic Location   487
21.5   Source Routing and Transparent Bridges   490
21.6   Source Routing Theory of Operation   493
21.7   Summary   496

Chapter 22. Network Design with Routers   497

22.1   Understanding Routers   497
22.2   Types of Routers   498
22.3   Router Function   499
22.4   Reasons to Use Routers   501
22.5   Types of Routing   503
22.6   Bandwidth-on-Demand Routing   511
22.7   Router Advantages in Brief   511
22.8   Multiprotocol Routers   516
22.9   Summary   521

Appendix A. Network Architecture Study Questions   525

Appendix B. Trademarks   539

Appendix C. Network Architecture Acronyms and Abbreviations 543

Appendix D. Network Architecture: Well-Known Ports   575

Appendix E. Network Architecture: TCP/IP RFC Reference   577

Appendix F. Open Shortest Path First (OSPF) with Digital Signatures   657

    F.1   OSPF and Current Operation   657
    F.2   Implementation of Digital Signatures   658
    F.3   Signed LSA Processing   659
    F.4   Router Public Key LSA   660
    F.5   MaxAge Processing   661
    F.6   Identifying Keys   662
    F.7   Identification of TE Public Keys   663
    F.8   Signing Keys   663
    F.9   Trusted Entity (TE) Requirements   664
    F.10   Trusted Entity Key Replacement   666
    F.11   Flexible Cryptographic Environments   667
    F.12   Multiple Trusted Entities   667
    F.13   Compatibility with Standard OSPF V2   668
    F.14   Special Considerations and Restrictions for the ABR/ASBR   669
    F.15   LSA Formats   669
    F.16   Router Public Key Certificate   669
    F.17   Signed LSA   670
    F.18   Area Border Routers (ABRs)   671
    F.19   Internal Routers   672
    F.20   Autonomous System Border Routers (ASBRs)   672

Bibliography   755
Glossary   673
Index   761

Preface

Purpose of This Book

The reason I wrote this book is because no other book is like it. A need existed for a book to present basic information that is common to most network architectures used today.

In this book I have included fundamental datacommunication information. I have also provided a real-world example network that I designed, as they say, from scratch. The fact is, some of the network's original design came from my notes on a markerboard in the garage— for that is where some design ideas came to mind.

Throughout the book I have included a variety of information that is sometimes required when working with networks. Having this information in a single source is valuable. I hope you enjoy it.

If you like, you can contact me:

Internet	IWIinc@aol.com
	IWIinc@ibm.net
	IWIinc@msn.com
	Edtaylor@aol.com
	zac0002@ibm.net
AOL	IWIinc
	Edtaylor
Compuserve	72714, 1417

How to Use This Book

You can read it from front to back. You can use it as a reference. It can be used to teach network architecture design principles. The questions in the back of the book can be used to reinforce the principles presented in the book.

Acknowledgments

MJH

IBM

Creative Labs

3Com USR

SMC

Hubbell

Tripp Lite

Bud Industries

Fluke Instruments

Hewlett Packard

McAfee

Altec Lansing

Wagner Edstrom

Microsoft

SMS Data Products, Inc.

Sony Corporation

SnapOn Tools

Information World, Inc.

Adaptec Corporation

Iwao Matsushita

Steve Elliot

Donna Namorato

Jane Palemeri

The International Group

DHL

Airborne

Emery Airfreight

Federal Express

United Parcel Service (UPS)

Roadway

United States Post Office

Perspective, Principles, and Operations

Network design has evolved in the past 20 years to emerge as an important aspect in the technological arena. When local area networks (LANs) began to take off in the early 1980s, design and planning was mostly after the fact. Network design was rudimentary, involving little more than determining what device would be located where. During the mid- to late 1980s, this began to shift.

Because of rapid invention, creation, and manufacturing, and rapidly increasing consumer awareness and consumption, most technology was deployed without much planning. Certainly this was not true in every case or for large networks, but it does reflect the norm of operation for medium- to small-size environments where technology was utilized. In the timeframe from the early to mid-1990s, a shift began to occur in the technical community concerning the planning or design of networks.

By the mid-1990s, sources of all types, such as newspapers, employment agencies, consulting firms, and others, had identified an occupational skill set with the title of *network architect*. Little consensus exists even today around what a network architect is able to do. Designing a network involves many different disciplines. In a sense, network design is as complex, or more so, than the architectural design of buildings.

Beginning in this chapter, a variety of perspectives are presented for the reader to consider regarding network architecture. The best place to begin is with the basics—and in this case, that means addressing those ideas that need adjustment, removal, or deeper consideration.

1.1 Fallacies and Misperceptions

Many different networking technologies were created and brought to market during the 1980s and early 1990s. Bringing technology to market has been the order of the day for some time. But many anomolies have emerged in some instances of integrated technologies. Think about how much computer and network technology has been created, developed, and brought to market since 1980. In anybody's statistics, it is a profound amount. Because this is true, few people before then had the ability to work with multiple technologies at the same time for the sake of research or to gain pure knowledge.

Generally speaking, prior to the 1980s, most professionals devoted much of their careers to one or another type of network technology. For example, it was normal to devote years to learning and working with COBOL, Fortran, C, or another programing language.

Similarly, working with technology on a larger scale, one generally spent years working with IBM's Systems Network Architecture (SNA) or the public domain's Transmission Control Protocol/Internet Protocol (TCP/IP) or even Digital Equipment's DECnet architecture. In the mid-1980s, professionals in many locations began to work with multiple network technologies, integrating them in various ways. At first this was unusual, because that had formerly been left to those groups of researchers in primarily academic settings.

In merely a decade or so, many professionals were attempting to master multiple technologies. For example, one would learn TCP/IP and SNA simultaneously. Not too long prior to the mid-1980s this would mostly have been laughed at. Today this type of focus in multiple areas is *expected*.

The topic of network fundamentals is not new. However, the vast array of topics now included in the arena of network fundamentals is radically different than it was 20 or 25 years ago. Network fundamentals in the past traditionally focused on hardware and software. Basically, this meant that one studied and worked with hardware and understood its inner workings. Conversely, software designers focused upon the design and results of programs.

A further delineation could be made that data network fundamentals were segmented by vendor. For example, one who studied SNA fundamentals would typically not be thought of as one who would also study Digital Equipment's Digital Network Architecture (DNA). In the mid-1970s, TCP/IP was being nurtured, and it was not formally acknowledged in a significant way until 1983 when the U.S. government required that supplying vendors be (or become) compliant with TCP/IP. In the 1980s, Apple computer brought AppleTalk to market. NetWare was brought to market in the 1980s as well.

With these facts as a backdrop, consider the following explanation of some common fallacies and misperceptions about network architecture.

Architecture

Network architecture has not had a lot of attention until the not-too-distant past. This is interesting, to say the least, because the underlying or inner architecture of anything is the infrastructure that supports things built on that architecture. For example, everything in your house is built (directly or indirectly) upon the architectural design that was created before any piece of dirt was moved to build the house. So it is with networks—the larger and more complex the network, the more important it is to design an adequate architecture to support the original purpose of the network's design.

Not too many years ago, some approached network architecture with the following thoughts:

- How much does it cost?
- Who will install it?
- What will we do with it?
- How many of these widgets do we need?
- What are the installation requirements?
- Can it do thus and so?

Dear reader, do not laugh. I have been in numerous meetings where this was the extent of network design put into equipment and infrastructure that cost untold amounts of money.

Network design requires more than a simple understanding of technology. Some who work with network design are pre-*PC* thinkers! This is not inherently bad. But a commonality of thought that seems to lurk among the pre-PC people is: "It can be changed or modified later." This is true. Unfortunately, the costs of doing so are generally very high.

Once a network architecture is in place, with most of its functional components built in, its daily operation commences. The typical result is that the network is taken for granted—quickly. If the network has not been well thought out during the planning phase, with contingencies for real-world scenarios, then chaos generally results when the network fails.

Notice, I said "*when* the network fails." That's right—the question is *when*, not *if*. Even the best-designed networks fail. What sets these networks apart from others is how much forethought went into making the network architecture transparent to the user. What I mean here is that the best networks are not "seen," they are *used*—without the user realizing the complexities.

Who designed the network?

Different philosophies exist for network design. At one time many joked that people who worked in the network industry were similar to those in religious groups. Some were of the *IBM* group, others were from the *DEC* group, while still others were hard-core *Apple* people! (No pun intended.) The significance of this should not be dismissed. Many networks have been designed and created that parallel an affiliation between people for no significant technical reason.

For example, in times past some networks predominantly used one particular vendor's equipment. However, today this is not the norm. In some situations, having predominantly the same vendor's equipment for all aspects of a network is not necessarily good or bad, but today it is increasingly difficult for any given vendor to supply all the components of a network.

Beyond the notion of which vendor's equipment dominates the network is the idea of what the primary motives driving the design of the network were. Sometimes it is fairly easy to determine that a chief financial officer (CFO) has had the most influence on the design of a network. With all due respect to CFOs, generally speaking, the most inexpensive components are not necessarily the best when it comes to using them in a network. My grandmother used to say, "Don't be penny wise and pound foolish."

My experience tells me that the best networks include input from all aspects of a business when network design is the issue at hand. All companies (no exceptions) are like a three-legged chair. Leg number one is the investors (typically stock holders). Leg number two is the customers. Leg number three is the employees. Remove any one of these components, and the company will be on life support until it fades away or dies. The idea here is that a network's design objectives should include meeting the customers' needs, fitting into the investment budget, and being capable of being maintained and enhanced by the employees. All this should be viewed against the backdrop of designing a network for the longest period of time in which it can be used. Some argue this point today.

Network design is like building a house. When one builds a house, foundational matters are all one-time decisions—like how much iron is in the concrete, how much concrete is used, what size water pipe is used, what size drainage pipe is used, what size wiring is used, and other matters such as how the joists are put together and how the roof is attached to the frame. Once the architect determines the size of water pipe to be put in the foundation of the house and the pipe is installed in the foundation and the house is built, then there is practically only one way to change the size of the water pipe. You guessed it—destroy the house, tear up the foundation, and replace the pipe! Not many do this. Why? Because to tear a house down to change the water pipes is not sensible at all. Since this is true, decisions about water-pipe size are made before any ground is broken to build the house. Similar concepts are true with networks.

Good network design includes not only consideration of immediate needs, but also determining needs and building in capacity for as far into the future as every participant in the design phase can see. If the reader thinks this is too theoretical, then consider the other side of the coin—that is, damage control when the network reaches saturation in one or more areas.

Common fallacies

Fallacies in network design include the following thoughts:

1. Distance (of operations) is not too important.
2. The vendor supplying the equipment does not matter.
3. The more bandwidth the better.
4. This _____ technology (insert whatever technology is popular this week) is best.
5. Topology and architecture are synonymous.
6. Little is more.
7. The fewer employees the better.
8. Ongoing training is not very important; on-the-job training is most important.
9. Income is more important than investment in technology.
10. Technical people make unwise decisions when network design is the topic.

I can name people in the business community who have said each one of these 10 items. However, to protect the innocent from their own ignorance, I will not. Suffice it to say, fallacies of this magnitude still exist in the marketplace. Other fallacies of thinking exist in regard to network design; these are just a few I have encountered.

In fairness, there are some people in the networking industry today who recognize that past problems resulted from a lack of planning and have begun to invest in professionals who understand how to design networks. The trend is toward more planning and less de facto implementation because of the raw costs of not planning ahead; that is, ignorance. Most people do not build a house without having architectural plans to work with.

Hardware

Hardware alone does not a network architecture make. Unfortunately, in the past many data networks have been built around hardware and not architecture. This line of thinking reflects concentration upon the lower levels of network operation—primarily routing or moving signals from place to place. Some people tend to think that hardware alone is the core of a network architecture. It is not. Hardware is just one part of the network. It seems this widespread misconception is the case because hardware is visible and, therefore, people tend to be able to relate to it. For some reason, it seems that more people are able to relate to things that are tangible than to things that are not tangible. So, it stands to reason that some people tend to relate to the hardware part of a network rather than to the operational nature of it, which is abstract. In the final analysis, both the physical and the logical aspects come together to make a network operational.

Hardware should not be the only consideration in designing a network architecture. Sometimes topologies can be thought of as the entire network architecture. Topologies such as a bus, a star, a ring, and other variations are part of network architecture. Consider Fig. 1.1, which shows the logical view of a bus topology.

Figure 1.1 shows multiple devices connected to the network. The illustration depicts a *thick-net* implementation utilizing Ethernet protocol. Granted, this illustration best depicts many networks of the 1980s more than of the 1990s, but it is still valid to show the logical construction of bus topology. The reason Fig. 1.1 is considered *logical* is because, in reality, bus topologies do not appear this way. Normally, cables and other parts of the network are obscured and not so neat as this illustration depicts.

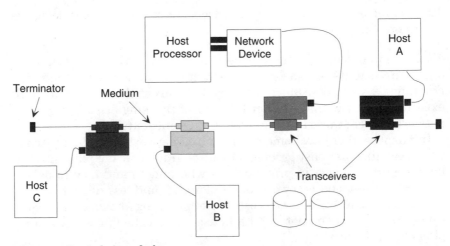

Figure 1.1 Logical view of a bus.

Figure 1.2 shows a physical implementation of a HUB-based network.

This type of topology is a star configuration and is generally seen this way in reality. Lower-layer protocols may function either as broadcast (not connection-oriented at the data link) or as some form of token passing (connection-oriented at the data link layer).

A physical HUB topology can be achieved by a small box or a rackmount device. Figure 1.2 depicts a 10base-T, HUB-based connection. This example implies Ethernet as a lower-layer protocol; hence, broadcast technology is used, not a form of token passing.

Figure 1.3 depicts a physical view of a star implementation. It is rather simplistic. However, the protocols that utilize this technology are not necessarily simple.

Figure 1.4 depicts the operational characteristics of a star implementation using ring technology.

Figure 1.5 shows another example of a star topology with a ring implementation.

After hardware components are connected, the logical operation of data movement becomes a focus. Logical network operation is the result of hardware abilities and inabilities and how the hardware is integrated, software characteristics and how the software is configured, and any environmental considerations that could affect the network.

Software

Both physical and logical architectures exist within networks. Once network hardware is in place, the software is the part that provides network characteristics; thus, a network actually exhibits a behavior.

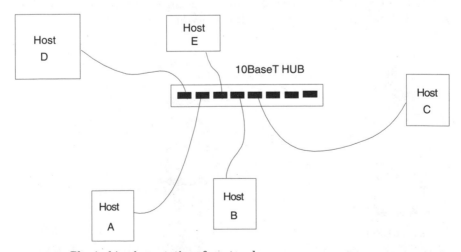

Figure 1.2 Physical implementation of a network.

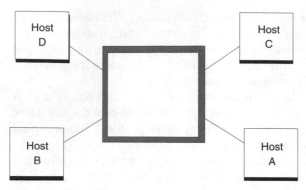

Figure 1.3 Physical view of a star network.

Software determines network aspects such as routing, which applications can be used, and what network functions can be performed. For example, the latter could be software configuration used in a SNA that permits TCP/IP routing through SNA.

Software works with hardware to determine abilities and limitations within networks. Assume that an infinite amount of hardware is available in a network. Assume that a database software application is used. Unless the software application is able to *address* the number of physical hardware devices used for storage, the combination of software and hardware does not provide a viable network architecture. They are contingent on each other to a degree.

Post hoc network design

Many networks created in the past two decades were assembled, and what was created was discussed and was drawn on marker boards—and in some lucky instances, the network was documented. This

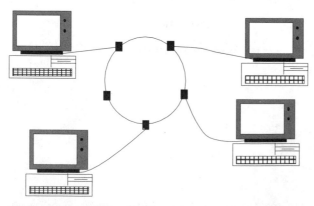

Figure 1.4 Star implementation using ring technology.

sounds like a backward way to create a network—and it is. Not all networks designed over the past couple of decades were created this way; however, you might be shocked to know how many were.

In the past two decades a tremendous amount of network technology was designed, developed, and brought to market. Fifteen years ago, LANs as they are known today were embryonic. Some network devices that seem to be taken for granted today have been recently developed with regard to a technological development timeframe. If the reader will consider my personal insight, it will show a different view of technology in use today:

A topic I rarely hear is the discussion of technological development put into a context with time used as a backdrop for the discussion. Does anyone remember when the first PCs came to market? It was the early 1980s; yes, some existed before then. However, from a practical standpoint it was really the mid-1980s when PCs began to take hold and their market share began to expand. Think about it. Where were you in 1981? What were you doing? That year IBM introduced its first PC.

In 1975 the very idea of PCs was primarily found only in places of higher education, in think tanks, and in the minds of a few. Let me convey my thoughts about how fast technology has developed another way. Regardless of how long you believe the human race has existed, more technology has been created in the past 50 years than since the beginning of time. Lest you desire to argue with me, I have one final comment for you to think about. It has to do with my grandmother.

My grandmother was born in the late 1890s. She witnessed mankind's ability to travel go from horse and carriage to putting the space shuttle in orbit on a regular basis. The amount of technology that has been unleashed on the human race in the past 50 years is unprecedented.

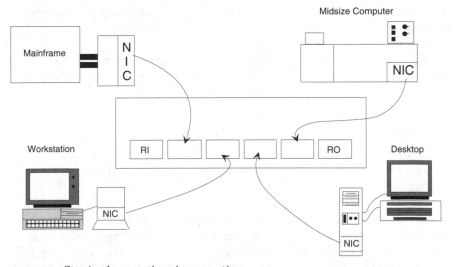

Figure 1.5   Star implementation ring operation.

Now, the point is that much technology was being implemented in the 1980s and early 1990s, and minimal understanding existed regarding network design. Implications of component integration were just beginning to be explored.

When technology became available to integrate upper-layer protocols, it brought an ability to merge networks that had been previously considered to be *incompatible*. Reality was a matter of degrees of operational ability—this was understood about some technology but not about all networking technology. In many cases realization of heterogeneous technology integration came after the fact.

A priori network design

By definition, this type of thinking means that one goes from a known or assumed case to a deduced conclusion. In network design this may or may not be the best approach. This view of network design reasons that such-and-such worked here, it worked there, so it must work *here!* Certainly, there is a degree of truth to a priori reasoning. However, network design should include post hoc thinking as well. Both should be tempered by common sense.

Some of the best approaches to network design include both a priori and post hoc thinking, because the latter does represent experience.

1.2   Signal Characteristics

Communication between entities is achieved through signals of some sort. This is true with humans or machines. Humans normally use speech, whereas networks, computers, and internetworking devices use electrical or optical signals. These signals have many characteristics and, to a degree, the signal type—electrical or optical—determines the characteristics of that signal.

This section explores signals and their characteristics. The details presented here are a reference for information needed to work at fundamental layers within a network.

Signal types

A signal can be defined or characterized in many ways; however, for purposes here, the difference between analog and digital signals is explained.

Analog.   An analog signal can be described by what it is not. It is not on or off, positive or negative, or other diametrically opposed positions. An example would be a dimmer switch used in electrical lighting. The function of the dimmer switch is to vary the light intensity without full intensity or being fully off (unless the latter two states of intensity are desired).

Digital.   A digital signal is best defined as being in either an on or an off state, with no in-between point. In datacommunications, a digital signal is a binary 1 or 0.

Signaling methods

Two signaling methods exist: baseband and broadband. *Baseband signaling* uses digital signal techniques for transmission, and *broadband signaling* uses analog signal techniques for transmission. Baseband signaling has a limited bandwidth in general, whereas broadband signaling has a large bandwidth potential.

Signaling characteristics

Signals, either analog or digital, are based on fundamental trigonometric functions. As a result, understanding some fundamental principles yields the benefit of being able to evaluate waveforms.

A baseline for evaluating waveforms is rooted in the Cartesian coordinate system. This system of measurement is mathematically unique for defining or locating a point on a line, on a plane, or in space. Fundamental to this coordinate system is numbered lines that intersect at right angles (see Fig. 1.6).

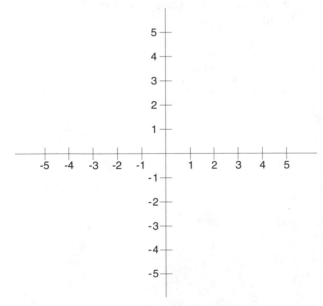

Figure 1.6   Cartesian coordinate system.

This coordinate system, along with other aspects of trigonometry, is used in signaling. Here, the focus is on certain characteristics of signals.

Signals in computers, in networking, or in datacommunications can be categorized as being analog or digital. Consequently, this coordinate system, along with the aid of other tools, makes the explanation of signals possible.

Analog and digital commonalities

Analog and digital signals have commonalities. Each can be evaluated by amplitude, frequency, and phase.

Amplitude.   The amplitude of a signal refers to its height in respect to a base line. Height may be a positive or negative voltage. The base line is a zero-voltage reference point. This amplitude value is proportional to the movement of the curve about the x axis of the coordinate system, as shown in Fig. 1.9.

Frequency.   Frequency is the number of cycles a wave makes per second. Specifically, frequency is measured in hertz (Hz), which is also known as a unit of frequency. A *cycle* is a complete signal revolution from zero to the maximum positive voltage, past zero to the maximum negative voltage, then back to zero. In the coordinate system this is a complete revolution from 0° to 360°. Figure 1.7 is an example of signal characteristics, showing one cycle of the signal in respect to time and amplitude, as well as its frequency.

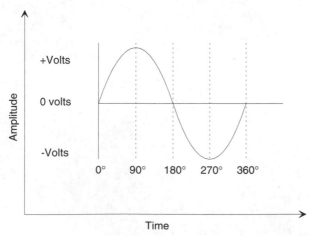

Figure 1.7   Signal characteristics.

Phase. Phase is normally measured in degrees that represent the location of a waveform. Another way of thinking about phase is that phase is a relative time of a signal with respect to another signal. A change of phase without the change of frequency or amplitude results in the scenario depicted in Fig. 1.8.

In Fig. 1.8 three waveforms are present—A, B, and C. In this example waveform A has a 20° phase angle or leads waveform B by 20°. Determination of the leading waveform is derived by visually ascertaining which waveform crosses the x axis first; in this case it is waveform A. Waveform C, on the other hand, is lagging waveform A by 20°.

Figure 1.9 shows an example of two signal waveforms (better known as *sine waves*) that have the same frequency but are out of phase with respect to each other.

In general, signals transmitted over a medium are subject to varying frequencies. Phase can be thought of as the distance a waveform is from its beginning point (which is 0°). This is particularly important when examining transmission characteristics of encoded signals. Explanation of encoded signaling characteristics is forthcoming; however, the significance of this information becomes real when one uses different measuring scopes to troubleshoot a line with varying frequencies.

Period. A period is best described as the length of a cycle. It is defined as the time required for signal transmission of a wavelength.

Waveforms

Waveforms come in many forms. Two are discussed here: the sine wave and the square wave.

Sine wave. A sine wave can be defined as a *periodic wave*. Characteristically, this is a wave's amplitude based upon the sine of its linear quantity of phase or time (see Fig. 1.10).

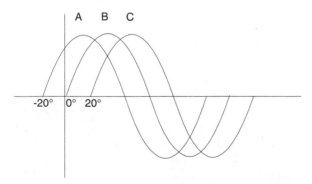

Figure 1.8 Example of a phase angle.

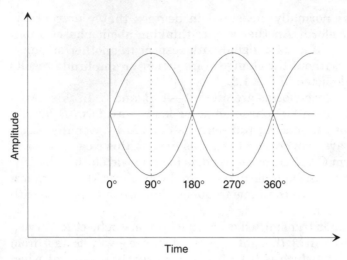

Figure 1.9   Phase differentiation.

Square wave.   A square wave is a wave with a square shape. It, too, has the same characteristics as the sine wave (see Fig. 1.11).

The square wave has similar characteristics to the sine wave except that its form has a *square* appearance, rather than the *wave* appearance of the sine wave.

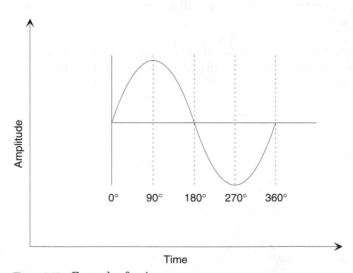

Figure 1.10   Example of a sine wave.

1.3   Data Representation

Before discussing characteristics of transmission, it is important to understand the ways that data are represented. Two methods of data representation are presented here: binary and hexadecimal.

Data networks

Data networks, as well as voice systems, represent data in a number of ways. The dominant ones are listed in the remaining part of this section.

Binary

Binary data representation uses 1s and 0s to represent alphanumeric characters within computer systems. Another way of approaching binary representation is the American Standard Code for Information Interchange (ASCII) method, which uses 128 permutations of arrangements of 1s and 0s.

With a computer using an ASCII character set, the letters, numbers, control codes, and other keyboard symbols have a specific binary relationship. Consider the following examples showing the correlation of a letter or number in the ASCII character set to its binary equivalent.

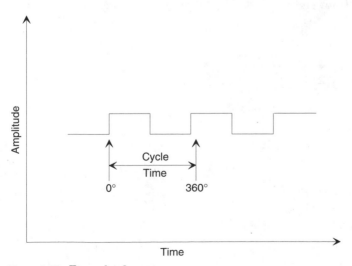

Figure 1.11   Example of a square wave.

Letter or Number	Binary Value
A	01000001
a	01100001
E	01000101
2	00110010
3	00110011
7	00110111
T	01010100
t	01110100
"	00100010
-	00101101

Each time a key is pressed on a keyboard, the equivalent binary value is generated (a string of 1s and 0s). This value is represented inside the computer as a voltage. That voltage is DC.

Computers, for the most part, are digital—that is, they register data as either a 1 or a 0. Hence, converting letters, numbers, or control codes to a numeric value is straightforward. When it comes to how computers work with data representation, consider what I told a friend: "Computers do not negotiate; they are binary, my dear Zac." At the most fundamental level within the representation of data, computers operate in a method similar to being in an *off state* or an *on state*.

A *bit* is a single digit, either 1 or 0. A *byte* is 8 bits. Hence, in the previous example a single letter or number is represented by a combination of 1s and 0s. The binary numbering system is based on powers of 2 and is counted from right to left. The following list shows examples.

Powers of 2	Value
2×0	1
2×1	2
2×2	4
2×3	8
2×4	16
2×5	32
2×6	64
2×7	128
2×8	256
2×9	512
2×10	1024
2×11	2048
2×12	4096

One byte is 2×0, which is 8 binary digits (either 1s or 0s).

Hexadecimal

Hex, as the term is used, refers to a numbering scheme that uses base 16 for counting. Hex is a shorthand notation for expressing binary values of characters. Consider the following examples:

Hexadecimal Value	Decimal Value
0	0
1	1
2	2
3	3
4	4
5	5
6	6
7	7
8	8
9	9
A	10
B	11
C	12
D	13
E	14
F	15

The following examples correlate a character with a binary representation and a hex expression of that value.

Letter or Number	Binary Value	Hex Value
A	01000001	41
a	01100001	61
E	01000101	45
2	00110010	02
3	00110011	03
7	00110111	07
T	01010100	54
k	01101011	6B
m	01101101	6D
z	01111010	7A

As this example indicates, it is easier to represent the letter *z* by its hex value 7A than by its binary representation.

Other methods of representation exist—*octal,* which uses base 8 for a numbering system, and *decimal.* Of these, binary and hex are prevalent, and understanding this binary representation is helpful with other datacommunication concepts.

A final word about data representation. IBM uses Extended Binary Coded Decimal Interchange Code (EBCDIC) as a prevalent method for representing data, alphanumerics, and control codes. EBCDIC uses an arrangement of 256 1s and 0s to make this possible. And, it should be noted that ASCII and EBCDIC are not one-for-one interchangeable.

1.4 Summary

Network architecture can be summed up in at least three categories: (1) hardware, (2) software, and (3) all of a network's collective components that interact directly or indirectly.

Designing a network architecture requires an understanding of a broad variety of technology and how it is implemented. This means that fundamental knowledge, such as presented here, should be understood because this level of knowledge is elementary in a network's architecture.

To design a network requires good thought processes. An old saying once existed: "One can judge a book by its cover." Well, in the case of a network one can judge the depth of thought that went into its planning by its functionality, reliability, and manageability. De facto networks are, at best, problematic. Networks that are planned stand a much greater probability of functioning with heavy loads and stresses from outside sources.

2

Network Architecture Basics

Network architecture does have identifiable *basics.* Just as a house is nothing more than isolated components put together in such a way as to be a house, so a network consists of components that are put together in such a way that a network (of something) is created. Parts of any network are functions that can be identified by users and technicians alike.

This chapter presents topics that one will encounter in varying degrees. Those who seem to be best at network design tend to understand a wide breadth of technical topics—not just hardware and software.

2.1 Transmission topics

Communication is achieved through signals of some sort. This is true with humans or machines. Humans normally use speech, whereas networks, computers, and internetworking devices use electrical or optical signals. These signals have many characteristics. These and other topics are presented here.

Asynchronous transmission

Asynchronous transmission is also called *start / stop transmission.* It is characterized by character-oriented protocols. Data is transmitted asynchronously and is timed by the start and stop bits of the frame, primarily the start bit (see Fig. 2.1).

Figure 2.1 depicts a start bit, data bits, and a stop bit. In asynchronous transmission, the start bit notifies the receiving entity that data bits follow. Likewise, the stop bit signifies the end of data bits.

A problem exists with this method of communication if the last data bit and the stop bit are the same. If this occurs, the receiving

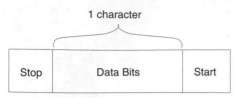

Figure 2.1 Example of an asynchronous frame.

entity is confused. Ironically, whether the last data bit and the stop bit are the same is relatively unimportant because this is overcome with parity.

Parity is achieved by the originating entity counting the number of bits and appending the outgoing character as necessary to achieve an even or odd parity. The receiver, on the other hand, calculates for parity against 7 data bits and compares it to the parity bit received (the parity bit is the eighth bit transmitted). If the parity sent and the computation on behalf of the receiver do not match, an error has occurred.

Terms normally used with parity are *odd* and *even*; they reflect an accurate representation of the transmission. However, the terms *mark* and *space* are sometimes used as well. When they are, they refer to parity as the bit setting of 1 and 0, respectively.

Ironically, asynchronous serial communication is a misnomer. In fact, the start bit actually synchronizes the following bits, whereas synchronous serial communication is synchronized by byte. Both are synchronized—asynchronous synchronization is performed on bits while synchronous synchronization is typically performed at the byte level, as is explained in the following subsection. The bottom line is that, theoretically, more overhead occurs with asynchronous communication than with synchronous communication.

Synchronous transmission

Basic to synchronous transmission is the intent to reduce the overhead inherent in *asynchronous* transmission and to provide more efficient error detection and correction. Perspectives of two categories of synchronous protocols are explained here: byte-oriented and bit-oriented.

Byte-oriented.   An example of a byte-oriented protocol used in synchronous transmission is IBM's *Binary Synchronous* (BISYNC) *Protocol*. Introduced by IBM in 1967, it is illustrated in Fig. 2.2.

Figure 2.2 shows the beginning field as the *synchronization* (SYN) character. This precedes all data, and a SYN control character may even be inserted in the middle of a long message to ensure synchronization.

S Y N	S I X	DATA	E T X	B C C

Figure 2.2 Byte-oriented protocol for synchronous transmission.

The *start of text* (STX) character indicates that data immediately follows.

Data codes supported in BISYNC are ASCII, EBCDIC, and a 6-bit transparent code.

The *end of text* (ETX) character follows data. If a BISYNC transmission is lengthy and divided into segments, only the last segment will have an ETX indicator.

The *block check character* (BCC) can be either a *longitudinal redundancy check* (LRC) or a *cyclic redundancy check* (CRC).

The byte-oriented protocol BISYNC is not dominant today as it was in the 1970s. Its code dependence and transparency implementation are not flexible enough to support popular needs today.

Bit-oriented. Two examples of bit-oriented protocols transmitted synchronously are *High Level Data Link Control* (HDLC) and *Synchronous Data Link Control* (SDLC). Figure 2.3 shows an example of a SDLC frame.

The beginning and ending flag has a reserved value and is always 01111110 (7E).

The address field in the SDLC frame contains addresses.

The control field (CF) in the frame indicates the type of frame it is— that is, control, information, or supervisory.

The data field contains the data being transmitted.

The frame check sequence (FCS) is implemented to determine if errors in transmission have occurred.

The last field is the ending flag.

SDLC supports code transparency because it was designed into the protocol. The result of this architecture is good performance with low overhead.

Synchronization of these byte- and bit-oriented protocols is achieved by performing error checks upon larger blocks of data, and the result is less overhead.

F l a g	Address	Control	Data	Frame Check Sequence	F l a g

Figure 2.3 Bit-oriented protocol used in synchronous transmission.

Interpreting bandwidth

Bandwidth is an interesting topic. Depending upon the company present for the conversation, one could find many different aspects to the discussion. For example, many think of an ability to connect between a given point *A* and point *B*. This is an appropriate consideration for bandwidth. However, before examining this line of discussion, *channel* needs to be defined. A *channel* is the medium used for transmission—be that data, voice, or even multimedia. A channel can also be defined as a path along which data can be moved—a path along which analog or digital signals can pass.

Another way to examine bandwidth is to realize that it is the difference between the highest and lowest frequency signal that can be sent simultaneously across the channel. Bandwidth directly reflects the data transfer rate of the channel. Obviously, the higher the bandwidth the higher the data rate. This poses an interesting scenario.

Say a given channel has a bandwidth value of x. That number, whatever it is, is fixed. Not true. Consider implementing a compression algorithm for the data to be moved through the channel. Assume that algorithm operates on an 8-to-1 ratio. This could mean that in most cases the amount of data denoted as a quantity of 1 going through a channel is actually 8 because of the compression algorithm.

In most instances today, networks of all sorts employ algorithms to compress data so that more can move through a channel. Many different compression utilities are available today, and some even come with systems in a preloaded package.

Understanding bandwidth encompasses more than how much data can move through a channel. In some instances a bandwidth problem exists on either end of a given channel. Where fiber medium is the channel, either end will generally have a problem keeping up *feeding* data to the channel or, the opposite problem, keeping up *receiving* the amount of data passing through the channel.

Still another twist on bandwidth is a focus on network devices. Some vendors provide network devices that operate as a concentrator or HUB, then pass data to a processor. Figure 2.4 shows an example of this idea.

Figure 2.4 depicts multiple devices connected to a HUB, which is connected to a processor. There is nothing inherently wrong with this configuration or implementation. When discussing bandwidth, however, one must discuss the bandwidth capacity of the HUB's backplane. Bandwidth of the device channels to the HUB is one matter; the capabilities of the backplane of this HUB is entirely different. To not discuss bandwidth of the HUB's backplane and the link to the processor is to address only one side of the bandwidth equation.

T
O

D
E
V
I
C
E
S

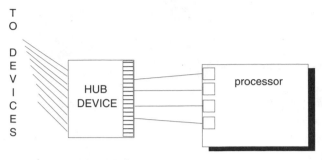

Figure 2.4   Bandwidth.

Interpreting channels

Different types of channels exist. They can be described categorically as voice, data, narrowband, wide- or broadband, and a variety of other terms. Today a wide variety of channels exists. There is a growing migration to fiber channels, and with encoding and compression techniques a channel can be exploited in ways not thought of just a few decades ago.

Generally, a channel is the pipe, so to speak, that moves data from point *A* to point *B*. The term itself is generic; however, IBM uses the term in a proprietary sense in referring to its Byte, Block, and Selector channels. IBM also uses the term to refer to ESCON (fiber) channels.

From a different perspective, some think of channels as referring to television, while still others use the term to refer to nonvisible channels such as microwave and radio frequencies. Furthermore, some online service providers now use the term *channel* to refer to accessible parts of their networks that can be easily identified, such as weather or news.

Serial transmission

Another transmission characteristic is how data is moved from one entity to another. Serial communication is bit-by-bit. An example of this is fiberoptic-based data transfer. In this example, photons are moved in serial fashion through the medium. Figure 2.5 shows an example of serial transmission.

Parallel transmission

Parallel transmission is movement of data along a channel path in byte form. An example of this is IBM's parallel channels. The essence of transmission is moving data in bytes rather than sequential bits. Figure 2.6 shows an example of parallel data transfer.

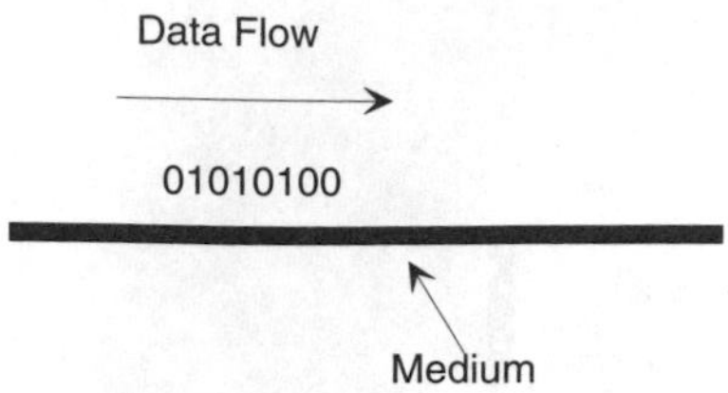

Data Flow

01010100

Medium

Figure 2.5   Serial transmission.

Simplex transmission

Simplex transmission is a reference to the direction that data can move at any given instance. Simplex transmission is best exemplified by the analogy of a radio station broadcasting and multiple receivers detecting the signal. Hence, the direction of data flow is one way.

Half duplex transmission

This reference to the direction of data flow means that data can flow in either of two directions, but only one direction at a time. An analogy of this is courteous communication between individuals. Normally, one speaks while another listens; then the reverse happens. Unfortunately, this does not have to be the case with humans, but it does with technology.

Full duplex transmission

This direction of data flow is both directions at the same time. The implication here is that simultaneous data transfer can occur and be interpreted by both parties. Each entity can send and receive at the same time.

Multiplexing

The idea behind multiplexing is the maximum utilization of a channel. Multiplexing can be accomplished a variety of ways; however, two are popular and are explained here.

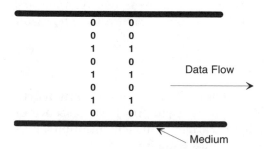

Figure 2.6   Example of parallel transmission.

Frequency division multiplexing (FDM). FDM is as its name implies—that is, the multiplexing of frequencies. This type of multiplexing can be readily used with analog transmission because frequencies are divided, then multiplexed onto the medium (see Fig. 2.7).

Figure 2.7 shows one medium and three devices connected to the medium. Each device transmits on a different frequency; in this hypothetical example the frequencies are 1, 2, and 3. These hypothetical frequencies could realistically be 10 to 14 kHz, 5 to 9 kHz, and 0 to 4000 kHz. The premise behind a FDM multiplexer is that each device uses a range of frequencies that stay within that range. The point is that the bandwidth of the medium is utilized effectively to accommodate multiple users communicating with different frequencies.

Time division multiplexing (TDM). TDM is, as its name implies, multiplexing data via time. Figure 2.8 illuminates this idea.

Time division multiplexing is the utilization of the medium by time-slicing devices attached to the multiplexer. Its premise for operation is this notion of data transfer based upon time. In Fig. 2.8, three devices are attached to the multiplexer and the multiplexer itself multiplexes signals from devices 1, 2, and 3 to maximize the channel. Though not shown, on the receiving end of the data path is another multiplexer that demultiplexes the data to its destination point.

Types of multiplexers. A number of types of multiplexers exists. For example, a network-based multiplexer may provide services for a variety of devices, each utilizing different transfer speeds. T1 multiplexers operate at T1 speeds (1.54 Mbps). Another type of T1 multiplexer is the

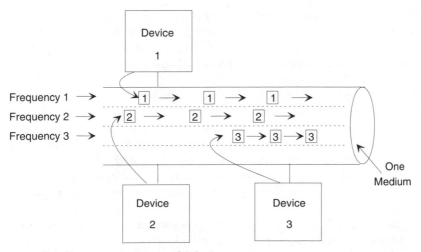

Figure 2.7 Frequency division multiplexing.

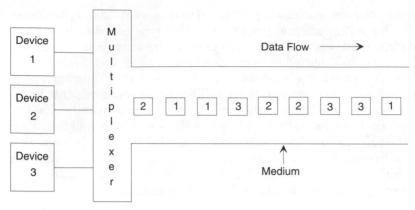

Figure 2.8 Time division multiplexing.

fractional T1. This type of multiplexer supports fractions of the T1 speeds, which are incremented in 56 or 64 kbps. Normally, 1 to 23 circuits can be derived from a fractional T1.

2.2 Communication Terms and Concepts

At the physical layer within a network numerous topics need consideration. A number of well-written books exist that focus on just this level within a network. Information here is focused and concise.

Interfaces

If defined from a perspective of networking and computers, an *interface* can be considered to be a point for common ground between independent systems. In the networking community two terms apply to this question about the interface: *data terminal equipment* (DTE) and *data circuit terminating equipment* (DCE).

A DTE is generally thought of as user-oriented, whereas a DCE is communications-oriented. Many conversations, be they verbal or printed, tend to separate the DTE and DCE. The DTE is generally referred to as a *terminal* or *personal computer,* and the DCE referred to as the *modem* or *communications device* (see Fig. 2.9).

The separation of the two does not have to be the case. Later in this text is an example of the DTE and DCE located in the same physical device in a large system.

For clarification's sake, the DTE is user-oriented and is concerned with communications higher up in a given system. The DCE is communications oriented and is concerned with signal transfer to and from

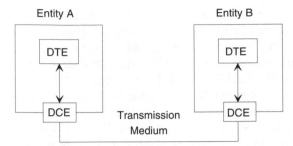

Figure 2.9 Conceptual view of the DCE and DTE.

the DTE and to and from another DCE. An organization called the International Telegraph and Telephone Consultative Committee (CCITT) has numerous specifications that cover DTE and DCE operations. Some of them are more common than others and are presented in this section, but before examining these details examining other information is beneficial.

An interface can also be thought of as a piece of hardware that is inserted into a personal computer, mainframe, or midrange computer. *Interface boards,* as they are called, have not only hardware logic but generally firmware, as well. *Firmware* is best understood as software instructions that perform specific functions, stored on a microchip. Other characteristics of interface boards are their connecting points (or connectors). These connectors have specifications that specify not only the number of pin-outs but also the protocol for communication through them.

Universal synchronous/asynchronous receiver/transmitter (USART)

The universal synchronous/asynchronous receiver/transmitter (USART) is responsible for numerous functions in communications with both DTEs and DCEs. Before exploring the basics of this component, its other names are provided.

Basic to the USART is the *universal asynchronous receiver/transmitter* (UART). The UART differs from the USART in that the UART handles only asynchronous communications. UARTs are also known by the terms *asynchronous communications element* (ACE) and *asynchronous communications interface adaptor* (ACIA).

The USART or UART performs the function of assembling and reassembling bytes of data. It also handles timing. Specifically, a UART handles both internal clocking of its operations and clocking to handle the receiver and transmitter sections.

The UART is also responsible for framing the serial data unit that is transmitted over a medium. It is responsible for parity, stop bits, start bits, and some error detection. Conversely, if the UART is on the receiving end it is responsible for unframing (disassembling) the serial data unit.

Another characteristic of the UART is that it is interrupt-driven. No polling occurs. Consequently, basic conditions that exist when an interrupt is generated are transmitter-, receiver-, or break-related. An interrupt can also be generated by a state change in an RS-232 input line.

This one chip on communication interface boards makes communications much easier. In addition, it takes some load off the processor. An additional note about UARTs is that they generally have some common input and output functions native to RS-232 built into them.

Bit rate

The bit rate is the number of bits transmitted per second, and is a term generally used with modems.

Baud rate

The baud rate is a measurement of the number of times per second a change occurs in the amplitude, frequency, or phase of a wave. One baud (Bd) is a change in one of the aforementioned. To calculate the number of bits per second the following equation can be used.

Determine the number of bits that equal one baud. This information is usually ascertainable though documentation sources from modem suppliers. Or, it can be obtained by referencing specifications for the modem. Next, multiply by the number of bauds per second the modem can transmit; the result will equal the number of bits per second for that modem.

The equation appears as follows:

Number Bd/s × 1 bit/Bd
  (or the appropriate amount according to specifications)
                                           = number bits/s

Modulation techniques

When data is transmitted over a channel via a modem, modulation is involved. *Modulation* is simply the conversion of digital signals into analog signals. Conversely, when this signal arrives at the destination, the modem performs reverse modulation—*demodulation.*

Three modulation techniques are popular. *Amplitude modulation* (AM) varies the amplitude of a signal without changing its frequency or phase. *Frequency modulation* (FM) changes the frequency to reflect the change in binary state but maintains the amplitude. *Phase modulation* (PM) varies the phase of the wave to reflect the binary value.

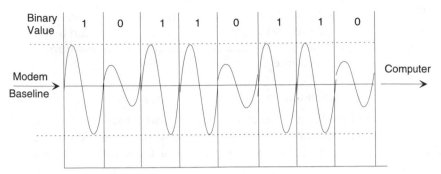

Figure 2.10 Amplitude modulation.

Amplitude modulation.

Amplitude modulation. Amplitude modulation is the use of a single-carrier frequency to convert the digital signals to analog. Figure 2.10 shows an example of this. The high wave amplitude indicates a binary one and a low wave amplitude indicates a binary zero.

Frequency shift key modulation

FSK, as it is frequently called, uses a constant amplitude carrier signal along with two additional frequencies so a mark and space can be differentiated between them (see Fig. 2.11).

This type of modulation technique is not prevalent among higher-speed modems because of the simplicity of its nature. Higher-speed baud rates require different modulation techniques.

Differential phase shift key modulation

This type of modulation technique uses a phase angle comparison of an input signal to the prior di-bit. The *di-bit* concept is where each phase angle represents 2 bit values (see Fig. 2.12).

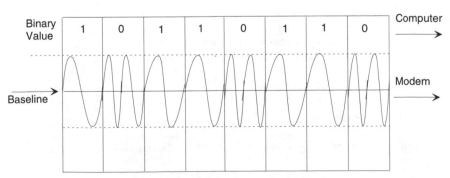

Figure 2.11 Frequency shift key modulation.

Figure 2.12 shows the comparison of the wave pattern and the square wave interpretation thereof. Actually, the modulation technique is a comparatively based modulation technique. Some medium-speed modems use this technique.

Phase shift key modulation

This method of modulation, comparative in nature to a degree, is where the phase of the signal is shifted at the baseline (transition point; see Fig. 2.13). It uses a phase shift relative to a fixed reference point. A

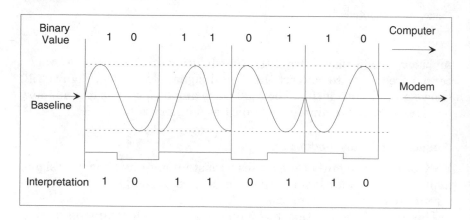

The illustration above assumes the phase change as shown below. (The reader is aware that phase change means phase difference between the prior di-bit and the current di-bit.)

Di-bit	0 0	0 1	1 0	1 1
Phase Change	0 degrees	90 degrees	180 degrees	270 degrees

Corresponding binary values as they relate to phase in the above illustration can be interpreted by the following chart.

Di-bit	1 0	1 1	0 1	1 0
Phase Change	180 degrees	270 degrees	90 degrees	180 degrees
Absolute Change	0 degrees	270 degrees	360 degrees (0 degrees)	180 degrees

Figure 2.12 Differential phase shift key modulation and assisting interpretation information.

modem using this type of modulation has an oscillator inside to determine a signal phase angle as it enters the modem. (An oscillator is basically a component that continuously generates an alternating signal. Its voltage, or current, is periodic relative to time.)

Encoding techniques

The term *encoding* refers to how signals are introduced onto the medium and how signals appear on the medium when examined. This idea is reflected in Fig. 2.14, which shows an example of what is called *non–return to zero encoding*. This type of encoding scheme uses each signal change to represent a bit.

Figure 2.15 represents a type of encoding known as *Manchester encoding*. This type of encoding scheme changes the polarity each bit time. This method of encoding results in good clocking performance and is widespread throughout local area network technology.

Other encoding schemes include *differential Manchester encoding,* which is a form of Manchester encoding. Differential Manchester encoding uses the previous bit time as a base reference point for interpretation of the signal. *Return to zero* is another scheme that utilizes two signals to represent one bit change. It is similar to Manchester in that polarity is changed each bit time.

Popular interface standards

Interface standards include such popular terms as RS-232, V.35, T1, and X.21. These interfaces and many others are prevalent throughout the marketplace. There are entire books devoted to explaining these and other interfaces.

Physical layer interfaces have protocols to transfer data just as the higher layers within a network. A particular interface specification identifies the protocols of its operation. Some examples follow.

RS-232. RS-232-D is the follow-up to RS-232-C. The fundamental difference between the two is that the RS-232-D is parallel with the V.24, V.28, and ISO 2110 specifications. The RS-232 standard comes from the Electronics Industry Association (EIA). It specifies the pin-outs of a 25-pin cable used for serial communications. Granted, most of them are not used for typical modem installations with PCs, but the 25 pins are nevertheless assigned.

V.35. This specification comes from the CCITT. It specifies modem operation of 48 kbps. It is typically implemented, however, at 56 kbps.

T1. T1 interfaces have the capability to move data up to 1.54 Mbps. T1 lines are comprised of 24 channels, each using 8 bits per channel. The

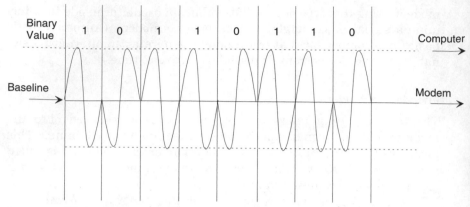

Figure 2.13 Phase shift key modulation.

result is that one T1 line uses a twisted pair for 24 voice signals. The result is a ratio of 24 to 1.

X.21. This CCITT specification is flexible in that different signaling rates are supported. For example, a given DTE and DCE may differ with respect to adherence to their specification. X.21 calls for synchronous operations with public data networks. An example of this scenario is X.25 using X.21 as the interface.

Many other interfaces exist. To list them here would require the remainder of the book, but the purpose is to get oriented as to what happens at the physical layer.

Regardless of the vendor, interfaces exists to provide a link between one system and another or between a system and the medium. The interface standard used may be vendor-specific, but in most cases vendors adhere to guidelines that the service providers offer.

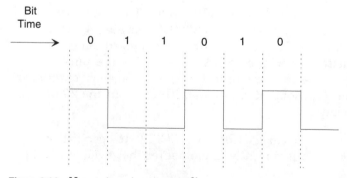

Figure 2.14 Non–return to zero encoding.

A final note about interfaces: they do not have to be physical in the sense that they are used to bridge cables or some tangible medium. For example, wireless networks require interfaces between network devices, transmitters, and receivers.

Types of links

A network can be described by its upper-layer protocols that comprise the network or make up the bulk of the network. Another usage of the phrase could be in reference to the lower-layer protocols within the network, or the prevalent ones. Still another usage could refer to the dominant media used throughout the network. Others exist, but these are dominant usages of the phrase.

Two terms are used to explain various aspects of networks and, sometimes, the network itself. Most references where the term *physical* is used mean something tangible; however, aberrations exist, as this text points out in later chapters.

Use of the term *logical* does not necessarily mean it specifically reflects sound reasoning. In many usages the term *logical* defines a function. For example, the SNA network protocol, which is explained in forthcoming chapters, uses these two words frequently.

In the case of the SNA protocol, multiple transmission lines may exist. These are literally physical, tangible objects. Put together, they can connect two devices. The transmission lines that form a transmission group may have data moving through a particular one for reasons of better throughput (see Fig. 2.16).

Figure 2.16 depicts two hosts, two devices, three physical lines (*A, B,* and *C*) connecting devices 1 and 2, and a circle around all three lines reflecting that they are collectively considered a group; it shows data flow over link C.

Reference to these three lines can be as follows. Three physical lines exist between device 1 and device 2, and the logical path where data

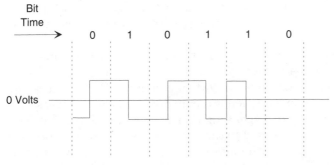

Figure 2.15   Manchester encoding.

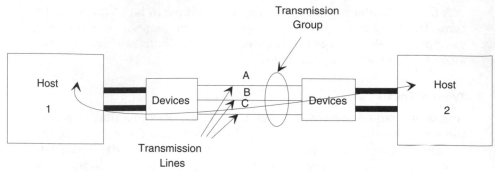

Figure 2.16   Physical and logical characteristics.

flows in this example is through line *C*. This is an example; theoretically, data could pass over lines *A* or *B*. Since the potential is there for data to flow through either *A, B,* or *C,* reference to the selected path is considered *logical*. This may not necessarily be the *best* route for data flow, but it is, by definition in this example, the logical path. In fact, it is not only logical, it is the physical path as well.

In most cases, something referred to as *logical* in a network maps to something physical. Exceptions may exist, but for most cases this applies. Therefore, understand that *logical* does not necessarily mean *reasonable,* or the best way for something to occur—it refers to a characteristic or aspect of an occurrence, or the potential thereof.

Conversely, *physical* does not always mean something tangible. In some usages of the term, *physical* refers to a function, service, or capability of a device. However, reality does set in—if it is logical it must have a basis in something physical, but just because it is physical does not necessarily make it logical.

2.3   Signal Distortion

Signal transmission involves a number of topics. As discussed previously, types of signals, how they are transmitted, the bandwidth used, the way data is represented, and a variety of other topics surround the topic of transmission.

Signal distortion is no trival matter. It occurs in most transmissions. For example, when lines originally designed for voice transmission are used for data transmission, some distortion can occur. Distortion can be filtered out by the human ear when it occurs during a voice conversation between two or more parties speaking over a given medium. This happens frequently; we become used to the *noise,* or distortion, and unless it is extreme enough to cause difficulty interpreting another's words it is typically dismissed. This is not always possible when data is transmitted. Because data is generally transmitted via machines of some sort, they have preprogrammed methods of dealing with distortion.

Delay is a type of distortion. Delay is the time it takes for a signal to arrive at its destination from its point of origin. Frequently, this type of delay is called *propagation delay*. It may seem trival to discuss delay in light of how fast current technology can transmit and receive signals, but consider the following example: if a signal is generated in Dallas, routed through local switches, transmitted to a satellite, and received in Paris, a considerable delay time is incurred. Granted, the delay may be milliseconds or seconds, but it is quite important. The significance of propagation delay is growing because of how technology is being implemented. An example of how propagation delay can affect day-to-day operations is easily conveyed. TCP/IP is the backbone protocol in the Internet. TCP/IP and certain devices encounter difficulty when delays occur in the transmission of data packets from point A to point B. When significant delay is introduced to the transmission, some devices cannot convey a data stream; thus, reliable transmission fails. This is a significant topic of concern in many technical arenas today.

Harmonic distortion is an older reference to a type of distortion. When a frequency is transmitted through a medium, other harmonics can be measured as a result of the main tone in the medium; these are generally referred to as *second* and *third harmonics*.

Nonlinear distortion is a current way to evaluate what has been traditionally viewed as harmonic distortion. A nonlinear distortion measurement is the value obtained from monitoring paired frequencies and the harmonics associated with them. The net effect of nonlinear distortion is the introduction of other symbols of some measurable magnitude that appear in low magnitude. This type of distortion is similar to harmonic distortion, but it has a twist that is different enough so that it can be compensated for, thus improving line quality.

Jitter refers to the phenomenon where a signal moves around the center of an axis upon which it is being transmitted. This is a frequency-oriented noise or distortion. Jitter has been a common type of distortion with analog signals. In the world of digital signal transfer, jitter causes problems with clocking an incoming signal on the receiving end of a transmission.

Cross-talk happens with analog signals when the lines carrying them are too close and there is literally cross-talk—a bleeding of one onto the other. Technically, this is a form of induction that generally occurs between two wires or other types of equipment in close proximity.

Fading is where a signal becomes weaker and weaker. Generally, this is due to atmospheric conditions. In microwave and satellite transmission, distortion is an effect of atmosphere. Rain, snow, ice, and other atmospheric phenomena, such as ozone and particulates, create distortion of signals transmitted through space. Different times of the year and even different seasons affect some signals differently.

Other types of distortion exist. Many interferences occur when signal transmission occurs, regardless of whether the signal is transmitted over a physical line, through space, or by other means. These types of distortion are examples of the difficulties encountered with signal transmission. Degradation of signals is not a trival topic—in fact, it is a core topic to those entities that provide services that carry signals from place to place.

2.4   Types of Transmission Media

Networks use transmission media to communicate; this is common to all networks. The question is, "What type media are used to connect network devices?" Two categories of media types exist: hard and soft media.

Hard media

Twisted pair cable.   Hard media include a number of types of distinctly different media. For example, the simplest of the hard media is the twisted pair cable. Figure 2.17 shows an example of how this appears.

Twisted pair cabling is normally copper stranded cable. Normally, this type of cable has shielding on each stranded group. However, some twisted pair cables are collectively compounded together and benefit from a shield and an outer jacket housing all the individual shields.

Twisted pair cable is measured by gauge. The lower the gauge number, the larger the physical size of the cable, and the larger the amount of current it can support. Interpreting cable gauge is not arbitrary; formal definitions apply. For example, 20-gauge or higher cabling is typically found in networking scenarios. Cable gauges below 20 are increasingly larger. For example, 10- or 8-gauge twisted pair cable is common in electrical wiring. Each strand of this size twisted pair cable is about the size of an ordinary pencil, and it can accommodate considerable electrical voltage and current.

All twisted pair cabling, regardless of size, has a fundamental characteristic with respect to electric current—succinctly, resistance. Twisted pair cable's electrical capacity (be that alternating or direct current) is proportional to its length. The greater a cable's length, the greater the resistance; hence, greater signal loss.

Figure 2.17   Twisted pair cabling.

Tables are available that explain the amount of resistance incurred with different gauges of cable, but I have witnessed two scenarios. First, I have witnessed cases where signal loss was so great, due to cable length, that devices at the far end of the cable were not functional. Ironically, I have also witnessed the converse.

I have participated in wiring a terminal with twisted pair cable that far exceeded the cable specifications—and yet the terminal worked. The only answer to this paradox must be that, in fact, the maximum distance was not exceeded. The precise point (or length) at which a cable begins to show significant signal loss is contingent on at least two factors: the device driving the cable and the cable size. Another factor is the environment in which the cable is placed.

Coaxial cable. This type of cable is prevalent in many networks today. It is the same type of cable that is widespread in cable television installations. Figure 2.18 depicts a coaxial cable.

Coaxial cable has an outside covering called a *jacket*. Immediately inside the jacket is a *shield*. This is generally fine wire wrapped around the inner component; the shield typically serves as a ground. Just inside the shield is a plastic material that serves as *insulation*. Inside the insulating material is the *core* (the actual cable). The core is usually solid copper cable.

Coaxial cable also has a means of measurement. Its rating differs from that of twisted pair, but the idea is similar. The larger the core, the greater the length of cable that can be implemented. However, coaxial cable differs from twisted pair.

Coaxial cable has good resistance to outside interference because of its design. The cable core is insulated, shielded, and jacketed.

Fiberoptic cable. Fiberoptic cable, as Fig. 2.19 shows, has an outer covering called a *sheath*. Inside it, some cables have strands of string or other strengthening component. Next is the *cladding*. The cladding is glass or other transparent material surrounding the optical fibers. Inside the cladding is the *core,* the part of the cable that carries the signal.

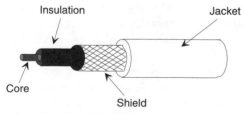

Insulation   Jacket

Core

Shield

Figure 2.18 Coaxial cable.

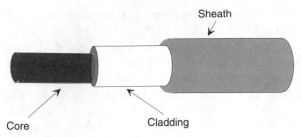

Figure 2.19   Fiberoptic cable.

Fiberoptic cable is distinctly different from any form of copper cable. Fiberoptic cable does not emit any electromagnetic properties, nor is it sensitive to these properties. Fiber can span much farther distances than copper-based cable before signal loss is a significant factor. However, length is not the only factor in the computation of signal loss—in fiberoptic cable, the *refractive index* is also important. The refractive index is the ratio of the speed of light in a vacuum to the speed of light in a material, such as optical fibers. *Pulse dispersion* is another factor in the equation used to calculate bandwidth and, hence, data loss. Simply, pulse dispersion is the spreading of pulses as they traverse fiber cable.

Fiber also has a rule for measurement. Numbers used to indicate the size of fiber reflect the core size and the cladding size. One example of size is a 50-μm core and 125-μm cladding (measured from side to side); this rating would appear as 50/125. Another example is a fiber with a core size of 62.5 μm and 125-μm cladding. Other sizes and types of fiber exist; however, fiber is used to move photons, not electrons.

Soft media

Soft media in fact use hard tangible components, but they move data through means other than a cable of some sort.

Satellite communication.   Satellite communication utilizes satellites in orbit around the earth. These satellites are geosynchronous—they orbit at approximately 36,000 km above the equator, and they remain stationary because they are synchronized with the earth's revolutions. These satellites remain in a fixed position relative to the ground, consequently permitting signals to be transmitted to and from earth stations. Figure 2.20 illustrates this idea.

Satellite communication is interesting in concept. Three satellites positioned 120° apart can cover the entire earth, from a communications standpoint. Using satellite communication means that a transmitter and receiver are needed at both the origination and destination points. Satellite communication, by definition, means a delay in trans-

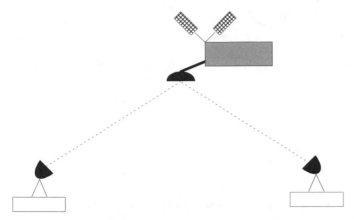

Figure 2.20 Satellite communication.

mission will occur. The delay may be measured in seconds or fractions of seconds, but it nevertheless occurs.

Infrared communication. This type of communication uses different hardware and frequency bands. Infrared communication is a *line-of-sight* method. This means that if anything physically interferes with it, the signal is impaired. At the time of this writing, infrared LANs are beginning to be introduced into the marketplace. Figure 2.21 conveys the idea behind infrared communication.

In this example, two devices are communicating. This could be implemented in physical plants where distances between two points of communication are long and clear.

Microwave communication. Microwave communication is similar to satellite communication in that transmitters and receivers must be located at both the origin and destination points. Microwave communications do not use orbiting devices in communications; however, they do use line-of-sight communication. Figure 2.22 illustrates this idea.

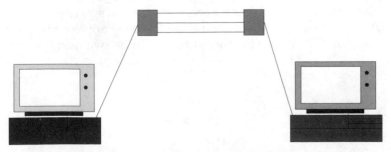

Figure 2.21 Conceptual view of infrared communication.

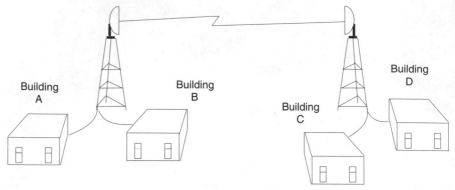

Figure 2.22   Conceptual view of microwave communication.

Microwave communication is possible between sites approximately 25 to 30 km apart. Microwave communication distance is restricted primarily because of the curvature of the earth. However, the transmitter and receiver tower height also affect this equation. Obviously, the terrain affects it as well. Microwave communications are popular in metropolitan areas and are an effective means for signal transmission to various locales outside a metropolitan area. Not only is microwave communication technically effective, but from a price standpoint it is cost-effective as well.

2.5   Communication Links

Physical links used in datacommunications can take on a variety of conformations. Technologies covered in this book use different implementations to achieve their purposes. This section explores some of the popular implementations.

Figure 2.23 shows an example of a point-to-point connection. A point-to-point connection is just that—from one place to another. This type of connection can be categorized in two ways: switched or dedicated.

Figure 2.24 depicts a switched connection. A *switched* communication line is best described as being in use when needed and not in use when not needed, hence its name. An excellent example of this is the ordinary telephone. It is used when necessary; that is, switched.

A *dedicated* point-to-point communication line may appear as either scenario shown in Fig. 2.25. The one on top could be two hosts in one

Figure 2.23   Point-to-point communication.

Figure 2.24   Switched point-to-point communication.

physical location with a line dedicated between the two. Or, in the second example with hosts C and D, a modem and what would be thought of as a switched connection are used. The difference between this connection and a switched one is that in this scenario, the line is dedicated. Analogously, the modems do not release the line; rather, the signal is maintained. This type of connection is typically referred to as a *leased line* because of the notion of having a circuit to accommodate this service. Leased connections are common with commercial companies in the United States.

Figure 2.26 depicts what is called a *multipoint* or *multidrop line.* In this example, one host is connected to multiple devices with one communication line. This is simple to understand. It is similar to a street with houses located on the street. At any given time the host may communicate with a device *downstream,* as it is called, and vice versa. The idea behind this type of communication is that there is one single path for data flow and multiple device accessibility. Scenarios similar to Fig. 2.26 are generally nonswitched.

Figure 2.27 depicts a *ring* or *loop* communication line configuration. These normally operate in what is considered a nonswitched mode, but in some implementations this type of line can have devices removed and inserted into the line without disruption to other devices on the line.

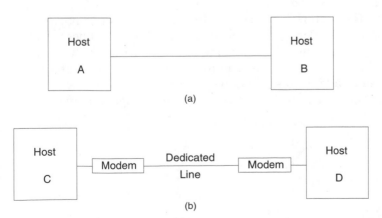

Figure 2.25   Dedicated point-to-point communication: (a) two hosts at one location, and (b) two hosts at remote location.

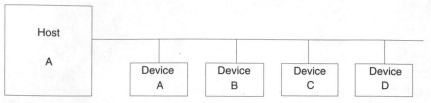

Figure 2.26   Multipoint communication line.

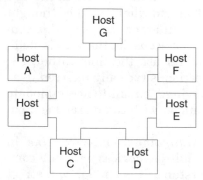

Figure 2.27   Ring or loop communication line.

2.6   Summary

Network architecture is a complex topic. Many different topics are presented and explained here. These topics form some of the foundation for understanding the fundamentals of any network architecture. Transmission, terms and concepts, signal distortion, types of transmission media, and types of communication links all play a major role in any network architecture.

In a sense, the material covered in this chapter can be analogously compared to words. Words themselves do not make sentences. Words are understood and then used in a particular way to convey meaning in a sentence. So it is with a network architecture. Many different components, concepts, and topics must be understood before the glue of understanding can be applied to produce a well-designed network.

3

Network Architecture: Insights from Experience

Network architecture is a complex topic. It is also relatively new, in the sense of being acknowledged in the marketplace. If it were possible to have all the readers of this book read only one chapter, it might be this one. This chapter contains insights from first-hand experience.

3.1 How to Learn Architectures

When I began to work in the computer networking industry, I asked numerous people what I should learn. I got almost as many different answers as questions I asked. However, one word kept recurring—*architecture*. It is only in retrospect that I can explain the impact that focusing on this word had on me.

In an industry that changes so fast, I knew there must be an area that had some stability. At the time, I didn't know what that was. I soon learned that the key to staying in the industry and not being run over by the volume of new technology is to learn the basics.

The first thing I had to learn was the definition of architecture. My entry into the field was early in 1986. That was an interesting time in the technical community. I found myself going back, and back, and back in order to get a good understanding of what was actually going on in the technical arena. It is important even in the technical field to understand more than the facts. The professional who harnesses the facts, mixes them with understanding gained through experience, and sees it all through hindsight, in the current day, and ahead is the one who stands in the technical community unmoved by daily change. Take time to comprehend the following section.

3.2 Perspective on Technology

Computing's origins are based in a *centralized* approach, and a brief look at the past can orient our perspective of technology today. Approximately one century ago (actually in 1890), a *tabulating device,* as it was called, computed the U.S. census at record speed. Created by Herman Hollerith, this device used punched cards to calculate the 1890 census in record time.

Prior to Hollerith's tabulating machine was a device known as an *analytical engine,* an idea conceived by a man named Charles Babbage. Although the analytical engine was never built, it was planned to replace the *differential engine* that Babbage toiled over for years.

Both Babbage and Hollerith, along with others during the nineteenth century, contributed greatly to the mechanical devices that were the forerunners of what we use today. Another man who made a significant contribution during the nineteenth century was George Boole. He invented *symbolic logic,* which some call *boolean algebra.* His works brought humankind the basis of what are called *logic gates* through the algebraic operations known as *AND, NOT,* and *OR.* These operands, and Boole's basic approach to logic, provided a structure for arriving at swift conclusions without verbiage. This, coupled with other inventions during the nineteenth century, laid the framework that shaped the direction of technical accomplishments in the early twentieth century.

By the 1930s the technology had evolved to vacuum tubes. Their prevalence took hold in the 1940s. However, in 1947 the transistor was invented. These technological strides, coupled with the contributions of John von Neumann, began to solidify a foundation that is now looked back on as some of the central roots of developments in the decades that immediately followed.

John von Neumann contributed the fundamentals of computers that hold true even today. He described the following as key components for computer architecture:

- Arithmetic logic unit
- Memory
- Input
- Output
- Central controlling unit (which became the CPU)

These components became the basis for computers decades ago and are the fundamental components of computers today. The question today concerning technological evolution is, "How are these and other components implemented?"

Centralized computing

From a critical analysis, it is certainly more reasonable to believe that computing was centralized before it was decentralized. The brief historical perspective just provided, coupled with an understanding of the basic history of technology over the past 50 years, is sufficient premise to believe that centralized computing came first.

Centralized computing could be used to categorically define the 1960s to a considerable degree. It was the technology of the 1960s and 1970s that brought together the fundamentals that began to make decentralized computing, as we have come to know it today, possible. Consider the origins of the first viable networks, in the late 1960s and early 1970s. At that time they were considered state-of-the-art, but by today's standards they are rudimentary. Much of the computing in the 1970s was centralized, by the popular definition of centralized computing today. It was in the mid- to late 1970s and the decade of the 1980s that technological advances began to make decentralized computing a reality.

Decentralized computing

In the 1980s, decentralized computing began to come into fruition. Technology, market forces, and a different philosophical approach to computing seemed to usher in what is now considered to be decentralized computing. A tremendous amount of technology was conceived and invented in the 1980s. Much of this technology provided the ability to utilize computers in ways not possible before—at least not to the degree made possible in the 1980s.

A few concise examples pave the way for exploration into this matter. From 1980 to 1985 the following technology was brought to market:

- Wordperfect version 1
- IBM Personal Computer (PC)
- Hayes 300 Smartmodem
- Compaq Computer PC compatible
- LOTUS 1-2-3
- Intel 286 microchip
- Apple IIe
- Apple Macintosh
- Novell NetWare file server
- Microsoft Word
- DOS operating system

- IBM Token Ring

- Intel 386 microchip

- Microsoft Windows version 1.0 (Yes, friends, not that long ago on the timeline.)

These examples are purposely personal computer–oriented. This very phenomenon began to revolutionize how computing was perceived. By the end of the decade, a glut of personal computer hardware and software was the order of the day. If the personal computer revolution was not enough to begin a change in how computers were viewed and used, consider other aspects of technology.

Local area networks (LANs) for practical purposes had their birth in the 1980s. Hardware and software making a variety of computing functions possible were brought to market. Devices making it possible to connect heterogeneous networks sprouted. All sorts of network-specific devices were introduced. Routers, bridges, servers, repeaters, and gateways were brought to market and made possible scenarios that are still being contemplated and implemented.

Distributed programming became a reality in the 1980s. Mixing computers and networks from different vendors became the trend, and the notion of distributed heterogeneous networking became reality. A distinct aspect of the 1980s can be summarized by a philosophical shift in the *way* many thought about *how* computing, networking, and ultimately *work* would be performed.

Decentralized computing can be defined in many ways. Today, for some, it means that *where* they do their work is not very important anymore. In a sense, using computers is now similar to using telephones—the idea of having to go to a *place* to use either is becoming a matter of history.

Decentralized computing, for some, means that a corporation is no longer restricted to having just one physical location or having to duplicate equipment in another location to perform the same task. For others, decentralized computing means that a central repository for data can be maintained and used at will from practically anywhere. Decentralized computing also means that printing can be done in one facility (or city) and data entry in another, while the actual processing is done at a third location.

Defining decentralized computing is difficult at best, because the nature of the phrase lends itself to a wide category of definitions. In fact, centralized computing actually occurs when decentralized computing is implemented. The nature of implementing a decentralized computing environment means that *some* functions (computing) will be performed locally—wherever locally is.

Herman Hollerith, George Boole, Charles Babbage, and many others, such as John von Neumann, were the forerunners of where technology is today. Each made significant contributions in their own ways.

Herman Hollerith formed a company that later became International Business Machines (IBM). IBM's growth leaped during the 1940s, with World War II in progress. The contributions of this company cannot go without recognition. IBM has become, by various means of calculation, one of the largest companies ever known. Its contributions in the technical arena have left an imprint upon the technical community that is destined to last well into the twenty-first century.

George Boole approached reasoning from a different perspective than the Aristotelean approach. Boole's contributions have literally impacted technology everywhere. As a product of his work we have the following equation:

$$X = Y$$

$$Y = Z$$

Therefore,

$$X = Z$$

This equation, known as the *hypothetical syllogism,* is the foundation of the vast number of programs written for today's computers and networking technology.

Charles Babbage's contributions to the technical community include his papers and ideas on machines that could compute and print large amounts of numbers. Some of his ideas were implemented in variegated ways decades later and thus were eventually, though indirectly, achieved.

John von Neumann conceived the fundamental computer architecture used in the vast majority of personal computers today. In their own way, the components he defined as what a computer requires for fundamental operation shape the computer industry today.

Many other individuals contributed ideas, products, and pieces to the puzzle that has become known as the computer. Their contributions are nonetheless important.

Centralized and decentralized computing exists today. In a sense, decentralized computing is centralized computing. The notion that a singular task may be performed in a given location with other tasks performed in other locations is at the heart of decentralized computing.

Networks can be categorized by the geographical space they occupy. The idea of physical and logical phenomena presented the idea that all things logical are mapped to something physical; however, not all things that are physical are logical.

Topologies reflect the actual implementation of a network and also the way in which the human mind perceives it. Media of some sort are a common ground among all networks. Hard media include different types of cabling. Soft media include satellite transmission, microwave, and infrared. Communication lines can be categorized by the nature of their link operations. Multiple examples are presented in Sec. 2.5.

Conclusions about computers and networks can be made. Technology has come a long way in a short amount of time. In a sense, a time existed when humankind seemed to drive the technological engine, but today it is clear that technology is used to drive technology; the result is exponential change in design, manufacturing, and product delivery.

In 1890, when the punched card was first used to tabulate the census, people were able to compete in terms of time, but today the apparent time available continually decreases when, in reality, it is the devices used that have changed. Computers and networking of all sorts have ushered in a generational era—a considerable amount that is presupposed to be as constant as the elements is, in fact, not.

Computers and technology today have brought humankind where no person has been before in the history of the world. In a sense, technology has changed how business is conducted and lives are lived, and has put humankind in a position to achieve what has heretofore been unthinkable to some. In less than a century humankind has gone from horse-and-carriage transportation to putting people in space on a regular basis. In fact, in less than 15 years technology has advanced the devices that make computing and communication possible from having to be in a fixed physical location to mobility practically anywhere.

Another way to examine architecture is by associating it with the appropriate time of development. Architecture can be viewed as being the characteristic behavior presented by hardware, software, and the logical exponents of both. With this in mind, consider the following architectures.

Advanced Peer-to-Peer Architecture (APPN)

Advanced Peer-to-Peer Architecture (APPN) is a network solution offered by IBM. Its origin is in the 1983 timeframe. Since that time APPN has gone through two versions. As of this writing (late twentieth century), APPN is at version 2, according to the APPN architecture manual.

APPN is peer-oriented, whereas traditional SNA is hierarchical in nature. Simply put, APPN is designed for program communication between one computer and another, without an intervening entity to aid in this communication once tables have been established in the systems. Traditional SNA requires the Virtual Telecommunication Access Method (VTAM) to assist in session assignment between the communicating entities, normally called network accessible units (NAUs).

APPN is a proprietary networking technology. IBM has not made it so that other vendors can implement it in its fullness according to the APPN architectural manuals. But this does not preclude other vendors from reverse engineering.

Another characteristic of APPN is that some of its functions have been incorporated into SNA. Some of SNA's core components, namely the VTAM, began *official support* of some APPN functions with VTAM version 4 release 1. The indication of VTAM version 4 release 2 currently, general knowledge, seems to point more of an integration between SNA functionality and APPN. A pictorial of the architecture that APPN is based upon appears in Fig. 3.1.

Figure 3.1 shows an abstract of how a node (a piece of hardware) works. However, if the reader is interested, I wrote a detailed chapter in the *McGraw-Hill Internetworking Handbook* (2d ed., 1997) about the topic.

Both APPN and SNA are from IBM. Their philosophical intents are different. In fact, they emerged from two entirely different camps within the IBM Corporation. Their original functional differences kept them apart by design; however, in retrospect it does appear that they come somewhat closer in what they each can do. And, they have been positioned to meet different needs.

AppleTalk

AppleTalk is a protocol used to connect Macintosh computers together to make a network. AppleTalk is a proprietary protocol. The

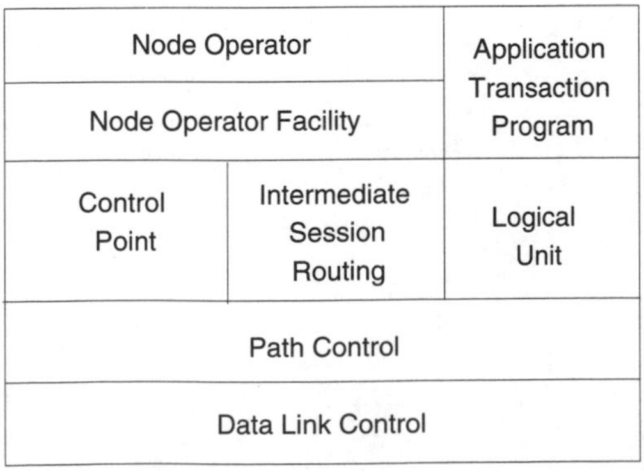

Node Operator	Application Transaction Program
Node Operator Facility	

Control Point	Intermediate Session Routing	Logical Unit

Path Control

Data Link Control

Figure 3.1 Conceptual view of APPN node structure.

Apple corporation had a line of Apple computers before the Macintosh line was introduced. In approximately 1984, the Macintosh was introduced. In many ways the rest is history—if you are familiar with Macintosh computers.

AppleTalk has had primarily two phases, or versions: Phase I and Phase II. Prior to the Macintosh, Apple did not have a networking solution for its computers. Figure 3.2 illustrates the AppleTalk protocol.

The fact that Apple did not have a networking solution prior to the Mac is not a negative statement—it is merely factual. In the late 1970s, basically three personal computers existed: the Apple, Tandy Corporation's TRS-80, and Commodore's Computer. As history reveals, that changed in 1981 when IBM introduced its first personal computer. So, the point is that at that time the world of networking was not prevalent in what now are considered personal computers.

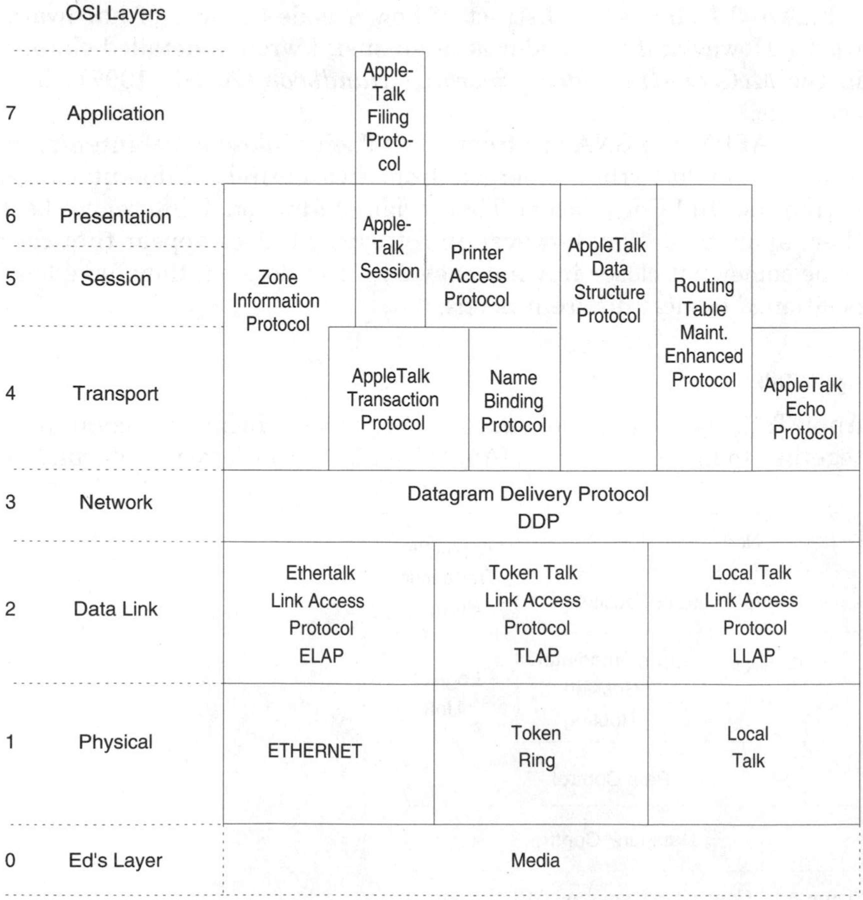

OSI Layers							
7	Application		Apple-Talk Filing Protocol				
6	Presentation	Zone Information Protocol	Apple-Talk Session	Printer Access Protocol	AppleTalk Data Structure Protocol	Routing Table Maint. Enhanced Protocol	
5	Session						
4	Transport		AppleTalk Transaction Protocol	Name Binding Protocol			AppleTalk Echo Protocol
3	Network	Datagram Delivery Protocol DDP					
2	Data Link	Ethertalk Link Access Protocol ELAP		Token Talk Link Access Protocol TLAP		Local Talk Link Access Protocol LLAP	
1	Physical	ETHERNET		Token Ring		Local Talk	
0	Ed's Layer	Media					

Figure 3.2   AppleTalk by layers.

Apple introduced Phase I of AppleTalk after the introduction of the Macintosh. Apple's solution to networking was simply to meet the needs of a local area where numerous Macintoshes might be located, as in a documentation department or such. This phase of AppleTalk used 8 bits to support defining a node. This alone meant that 254 nodes could be used—and remember, at that time that was a lot in a personal computing environment. The reason only 254 nodes were supported rather than 256 is because of how Appletalk used 2 bits in a reserved manner.

Phase II of AppleTalk is the latest at the time of this writing. The primary difference between it and Phase I is that Phase II supports more than 254 nodes because of the use of a network number that employs 16 bits; hence, a given node is identified by the network node number *and* the 8-bit node assignment. Another feature of Phase II is multiple zone support. A *zone*, according to Apple documentation, is the logical grouping of a subset of nodes on an internet (note that this refers to a *local* internet, not the big-I Internet).

One of the greatest strengths behind AppleTalk is its simplicity from a user's perspective. Another strength behind the protocol is the underlying architecture and how the software and hardware have been designed with AppleTalk. It is a peer-oriented protocol, and it does support multiple connections. It can be integrated into other networks with some effort—usually less than other network protocols.

Apple computers are interesting in the sense of their original design intent. Because AppleTalk is proprietary and so are Apple computers, including Macintoshes, a certain tendency seemed to have developed. Based upon observation, it seems Apple computers have evolved over the past decade to fit into a strata of organizations. And, it seems, as they evolve, the more integrated they become in a variety of organizations.

A simple point sums up the thought concerning Macintoshes (which use AppleTalk) and other vendors' personal computers that use network protocols—in the early years of Tandy, Apple, Commodore, and even IBM personal computers, the idea of networking them in the sense that is meant today was not a prevalent thought. Times have changed and so have personal computers from all vendors.

Digital Network Architecture (DNA)

The Digital Equipment Corporation basically supports the DNA Phase IV method of networking and *DECnet/OSI for OpenVMS*. This is Digital Equipment's implementation of OpenVMS, which includes:

- Support for OSI communication specifications
- Digital Network Architecture (DNA) Phase V, which is backward-compatible with Phase IV

- Compliance with CCITT standards
- Compliance with IEEE standards

According to Digital Equipment's documentation, this phase of its network offering supports more systems than previous versions of DNA, provides distributed management, and maintains a multivendor network support environment.

Digital Equipment's DNA network architecture is not new. According to Digital Equipment's documentation (*DECnet/OSA for OpenVMS Introduction and Planning,* 1993, part number AA-PNHTB-TE), the first phase of DNA was introduced in 1976. Since then Digital has revised it and made enhancements to bring it to Phase V. DNA Phase V is also called *DECnet/OSI.* But, whatever name may be attached, it is clear that the structure of Digital's network offering supports multiple protocols and is open to standards not previously available (see Fig. 3.3).

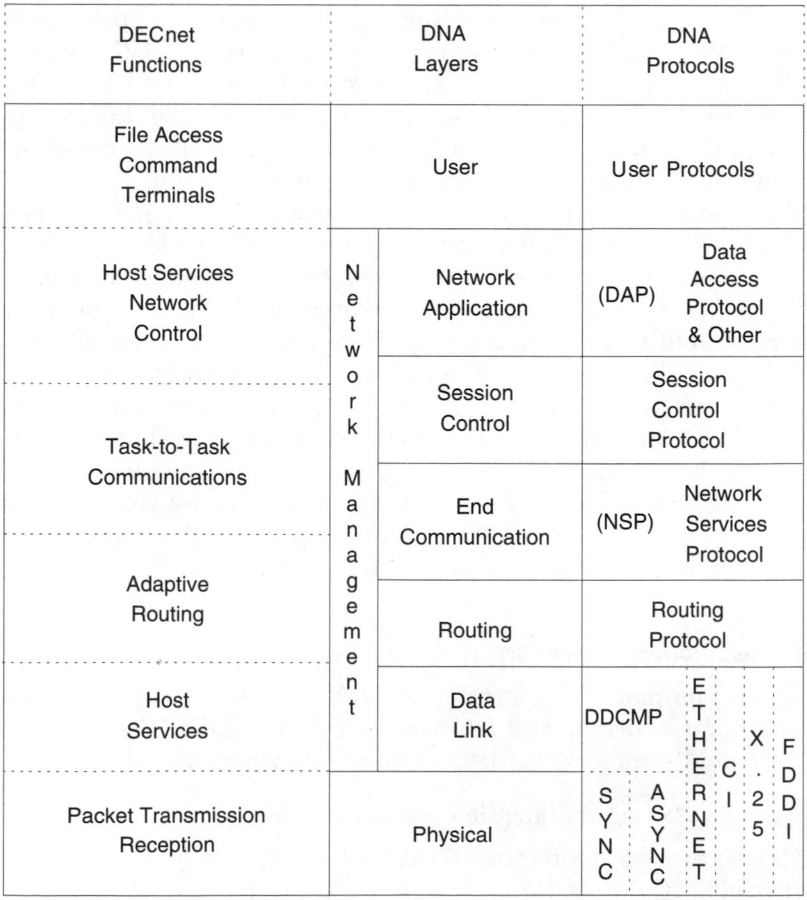

DECnet Functions	DNA Layers	DNA Protocols
File Access Command Terminals	User	User Protocols
Host Services Network Control	**N e t w o r k M a n a g e m e n t** — Network Application	(DAP) Data Access Protocol & Other
Task-to-Task Communications	Session Control	Session Control Protocol
	End Communication	(NSP) Network Services Protocol
Adaptive Routing	Routing	Routing Protocol
Host Services	Data Link	DDCMP ETHERNET X.25 FDDI
Packet Transmission Reception	Physical	SYNC ASYNC

Figure 3.3   DECnet by layers.

From a practical standpoint, Digital has managed to provide support for FTAM, CCR, Virtual Terminals, and OSI applications through the VAX OSI Application Kernel (OSAK). Multiple transport layer protocols are supported, along with OSI network layer addressing. At the data link layer, Digital's DECnet/OSI for OpenVMS supports Ethernet, HDLC, FDDI, and X.25, to name a few. At the physical layer, the appropriate drivers are available to support a variety of interfaces. Still another way of viewing DECnet and OSI support is shown in Fig. 3.4.

From a network management standpoint, DECnet/OSI for OpenVMS supports Digital's Enterprise Management Architecture (EMA).

The EMA defines a way to manage heterogeneous networking environments with distributed computing. This approach offers wide support for large enterprise environments.

Another feature of DECnet/OSI for OpenVMS is its scalar capability. It can meet the needs of small-based operations, or it can accommodate large mission-critical data centers that require large amounts of processing power and versatility.

NetWare

NetWare protocol is a product of the Novell Corporation. It began by offering print and file services and has evolved into a full network protocol that is now at version 4. NetWare has proliferated throughout the market for multiple reasons. First, it operates on PCs, and the Novell corporation has kept upgrading the product to make it as robust as possible. That is tough in today's marketplace with the increased pace of technical change.

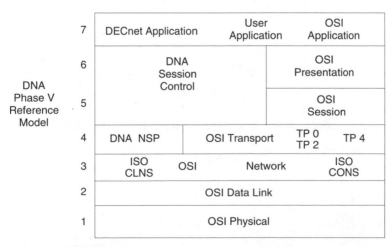

Figure 3.4   OSI layers.

Second, Novell ported NetWare to some UNIX operating platforms. This is significant because of the prevalence of UNIX throughout the marketplace today. A third reason for its popularity is its user-friendliness, comparatively speaking (no names mentioned). It operates as a peer environment, which makes some aspects of the installation easier to implement.

Another aspect of NetWare that keeps it in the circle of popularity is the protocol support it provides. For example, it supports FDDI, Token Ring, and Ethernet as data link protocols. It also supports connectivity into IBM's AS/400 series. In addition, Novell supports NetWare TCP/IP on a NetWare file server with services such as IP routing, tunneling, and Simple Network Management Protocol (SNMP). Figure 3.5 illustrates NetWare.

Beyond this, NetWare supports IBM's RISC/6000 AIX operating system, as well as OS/2. IBM included NetWare functionality in the Blueprint introduced in the spring of 1992. Even in NetWare's early years it was broad in scope. NetWare version 2.01 had support for Digital Equipment's Virtual Address eXtended (VAX) operating system.

NetWare is different from the other protocols mentioned because its original design intent was different. However, today it has evolved into a competitive upper-layer network protocol. It has grown in breadth to support large networks and a diverse mix of operating systems.

Open Systems Interconnection (OSI)

Open Systems Interconnection (OSI) is the culmination of work by the International Standards Organization (ISO). In approximately 1977, the ISO chartered a committee to create a standard for networking. They did, and it became known as the *OSI reference model.*

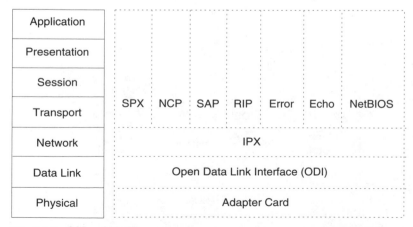

Figure 3.5   OSI and NetWare.

This OSI model identified seven layers that, at a minimum, should exist in a network. The committee defined what occurs at each layer, but did not define the layer that is the medium. Part of the rationale behind this was that different network protocols are capable of using different media types.

The ISO has come to embrace CCITT and some other specifications in its networking model. In a real sense, the OSI model is an example of a de jure standard. Some may disagree, but generally this is true. Figure 3.6 illustrates this model.

On a lighter note, I have often presented my own version of this model as an alternative, as shown in Fig. 3.7.

My rationale on the difference between the two is based on my own learning experience. Technically, OSI does define the media by default at layer 1. Unfortunately for me, it took a few passes around the explanation for this idea to get into my brain.

OSI products are implemented by vendors, because the ISO is an organization, not a company in the sense of production (at least at the time of this writing). Consequently, some companies are more involved in developing OSI-compliant offerings than others. Figure 3.8 sheds some insight on the implications of the media used.

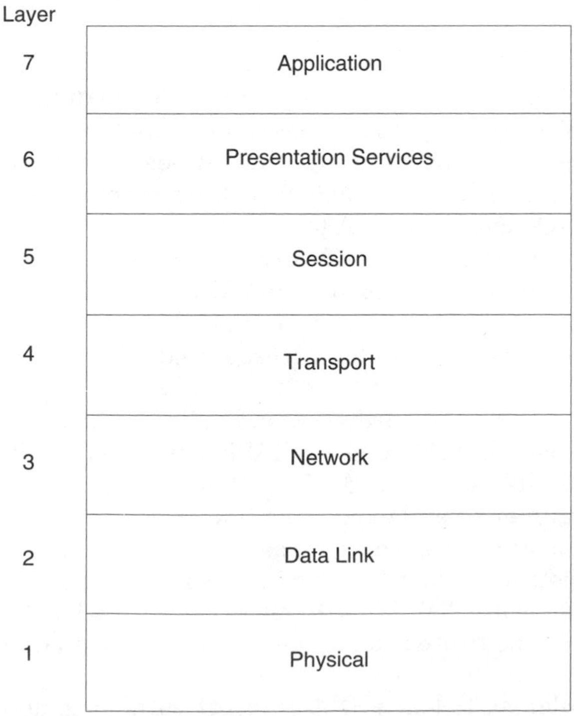

Layer

7	Application
6	Presentation Services
5	Session
4	Transport
3	Network
2	Data Link
1	Physical

Figure 3.6 Conceptual view of the OSI model.

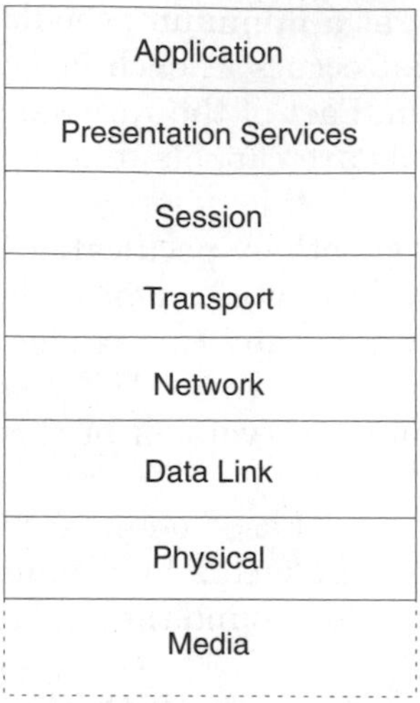

Application
Presentation Services
Session
Transport
Network
Data Link
Physical
Media

Figure 3.7   Ed's model.

Some parts of the adopted OSI protocols are used more than others. For example, the electronic mail and directory service protocols are more widespread than some other ISO OSI specifications.

Systems Network Architecture (SNA)

SNA, as it is typically called, is IBM's networking solution for medium to large networks. Its origins go back to 1974, when it was introduced, and it has been through many iterations since that time. It began as a layered network architecture which, until 1992, was IBM's primary networking solution. Figure 3.9 shows the SNA layers.

In the spring of 1992, IBM announced its *Networking Blueprint*. Figure 3.10 illustrates it. This announcement marked a radical break from the past with regard to IBM's approach to networking solutions. The Blueprint not only embraced SNA, but incorporated other protocols as well.

SNA is based on terms, concepts, hardware, and software architecture. Many of the terms used in SNA refer to IBM hardware and software and were coined and defined by IBM. Until 1993, IBM produced its own dictionary defining terms and explaining how they fit into the SNA environment. SNA is built upon concepts as well. These concepts are, for the most part, abstract. However, some SNA concepts are used in actual software and hardware definitions to make the network functional. IBM's hardware and software are the tangible components that SNA is built upon.

To learn SNA is a challenge. To learn SNA concepts without understanding the terms is difficult at best. On the other hand, to memorize terms and not attmept to understand the abstract concepts is little more than memorization. The best way to learn SNA is from a topical perspective. In time, as one learns topics (consisting of terms and concepts) a cumulative effect takes place, and the whole picture begins to come into perspective.

Transmission Control Protocol/ Internet Protocol (TCP/IP)

TCP/IP, as it is known in the technical community, traces its origins in time to 1975. It was then, and a little before, that TCP/IP's birth began. It was the follow-up to the Arpanet, which was government-related. In

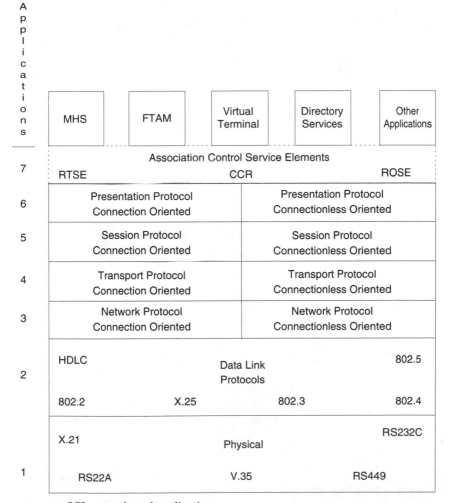

Figure 3.8 OSI protocols and applications.

7	Transaction Services
6	Presentation Services
5	Data Flow Control
4	Transmission Control
3	Path Control
2	Data Link Control
1	Physical Control

Figure 3.9   SNA traditional layers.

1978 a public demonstration of TCP/IP was given, and in 1983 the U.S. government made a statement to the effect that if connection was to be made to what had become known as the Internet, it must be done with the TCP/IP protocol suite.

TCP/IP has been refined and has been through many changes since 1975. It is unlike IBM's SNA in the sense that no particular corporation or entity charts its course and maintains proprietary aspects of it. TCP/IP is a prime example of a de facto–type network.

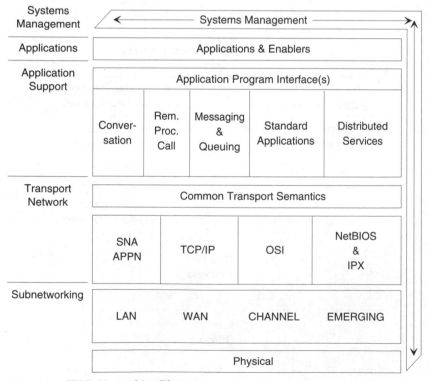

Figure 3.10   IBM's Networking Blueprint.

Even though TCP/IP has been funded by the U.S. government at times, its basic direction has come from citizens. TCP/IP is a *protocol suite*, a collection of protocols. The protocols have been the contributions and enhancements of individuals and corporations alike. Granted, an overseeing body does provide guidance and maintain order, but the protocols themselves that make TCP/IP what it is are not *owned* by any one body. This is commonly considered *public domain*.

Similarly to OSI, TCP/IP is implemented by corporations that chose to make their protocols available to prospective customers. If no other fuel was added to the growth of TCP/IP, the 1983 government mandate was enough motivation to get many vendors interested to the point of making protocols available to government agencies and other ancillary agencies.

TCP/IP is considered a *client/server* protocol. This terminology comes from the fact that two of the most popular applications in the TCP/IP protocol suite are client/server based. Clients initiate something; servers serve the requests of clients. In a sense, this concept is similar to the peer concept in APPN and peer capabilities in SNA.

TCP/IP is unique in one sense—it has as a part of the protocol specification a *windowing system*. Another interesting characteristic of TCP/IP and the windowing system is *hardware and software independence*. This means that TCP/IP can operate on practically any vendor's equipment. Granted, exceptions exists; for the most part, however, this is the case. Another aspect of TCP/IP is that it does not have to be implemented in a full protocol suite; pieces of it can be implemented.

Figure 3.11 shows a high-level perspective of the TCP/IP protocol stack. Note the location of the Hyper Text Protocol. It operates similarly to the X window system in that both it and X are protocols that use TCP for a transport mechanism, and both are also protocols in their own right. They do, however, function at a high level within the network.

Windows NT

Windows NT is a Microsoft product. Its origins date back to 1988. Some characteristics included in the original design intent were to be compatible among a variety of hardware platforms and operating systems, be easily adaptable to internationalization, be portable, and meet high security standards.

Windows NT originally started with a version number of 3.1. Some sources believe this was to provide an identity with Windows version 3.1. The fact is, applications that ran under Windows version 3.1 would also run under Windows NT version 3.1. Another characteristic of Windows NT's first release was that it was brought to market as two components: *Windows NT 3.1* and *Windows NT Advanced Server 3.1*.

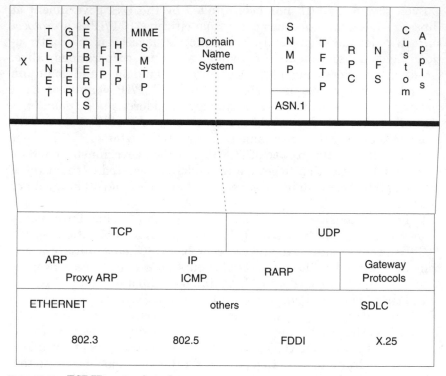

Figure 3.11 TCP/IP protocol stack.

Windows NT version 3.5 was released in the fall of 1994. The major advantages this version had over its predecessor included:

- Less memory required
- Point-to-point protocol support
- Changes to the TCP/IP protocol suite

Other enhancements were included in this revision as well. For example, IPX/SPX support was included, and the restrictions that kept file naming to 11 characters were removed by implementing the *NT File System*.

Windows NT version 4 was released during the 1995/1996 time-frame. Most opinions seem to agree that this version of NT could be the standard by which other operating systems are judged. From appearances, it has the look-and-feel interface of Windows 95. This version of NT has robust features. It is separated into the *NT Server* and the *NT Workstation*.

Some common characteristics between them include the following:

- Advanced file-handling systems
- Backup capabilities
- C2 security
- Graphical user interface tools
- Network capabilities
- Remote access capabilities
- TCP/IP

Other similarities exist between workstation and server. To better understand the architecture of Windows NT, consider Fig. 3.12.

Windows NT client/server design makes peer operation among desktop systems possible and relatively easy to implement.

The architectures presented here are the dominant network architectures in use today. Some have been around longer than others. However, the relative newness of some does not negate their capabilities.

3.3   Practical Learning Tools

Learning network architecture is not easy. People learn differently, and readers would benefit from self-analysis of their own learning methods. For example, I worked with a person for years who approaches most technology from a hands-on approach. I, on the other hand, would read and think about the same technology. Invariably, he and I would come to the same understanding over a period of time. After some years of working together, we realized that we learn differently.

Readers would probably benefit by attempting to understand their own learning styles. Some think hands-on is the best approach. Others think learning is best done by classroom, tutorial, and self-study work and the like. I believe significant insight exists to understand that theoretical networking topics are learned entirely differently than, say, a programming language. The latter always requires hands-on practice somewhere during the learning process. However, aspects of network architectural design require no hands-on work but, rather, demand that a person have good abstract reasoning capability.

My personal opinion is that a healthy mix of both is best. As for me, I work best by reading, thinking, being taught by others. Once I think I am ready, then I can begin the hands-on aspect. However, my personal interests are not in hands-on network design anyway. I prefer to work with logical network design when it is challenging.

At a minimum, I encourage all readers to obtain multiple dictionaries and read them. That's right—read the dictionaries. If you are serious, then do not forget the fundamentals. *Everything* we discuss is

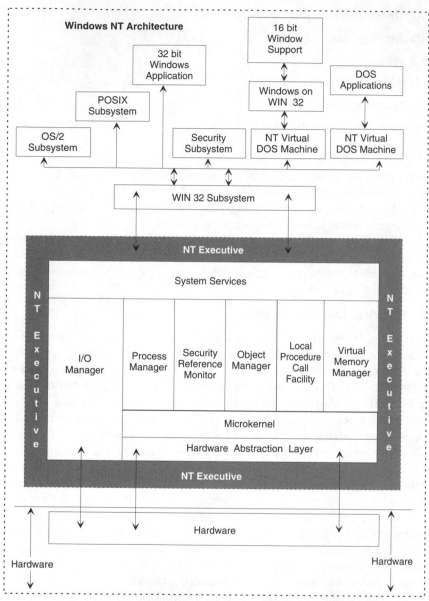

Figure 3.12   Windows NT architecture.

based on a language. Languages are based on words. So it is in the networking and computing community. My challenge to you (the reader) is
to look up words you cannot define or explain. Now, you are probably
thinking, "Ed, that is a tall order." Yes, it is. However, may I remind you
that professionals are always measured by the degree of precision they

obtain. Consequently, your vocabulary, and the accuracy thereof, is very important. McGraw-Hill publishes the *IBM Dictionary of Computing* (1994; ISBN #0-07-031488-8). I recommend it to all readers. Other dictionaries are available, as well. Sometimes the best source for documentation is the original equipment manufacturer.

There is no substitute for reading, videos, audio tapes, lectures, online information, classroom teaching, and thinking. It is not enough to have simple facts stored away in your brain; it is important to be able to synthesize thoughts. Learning to think and synthesize ideas is important to understanding and designing network architectures.

3.4 Summary

Network architecture is a complex topic. The information presented here is intended to show the differences and complexities in any given architecture. Mastering network architecture requires time and patience.

People learn differently. The computing and network industry uses hands-on skills as well as abstract thinking skills. Both are important. However, it is possible to be more focused in the hands-on arena than in working with abstract thoughts.

My encouragement is with you as you partake in the discipline of network architecture. Discouragement is easy, but determination in learning does pay off. Knowledge is something nobody can take away from you, so invest your time and efforts in the area of interest that you have.

Network Architecture Analysis

During the preparation of this book I thought about network architecture, computing, and networking in general for a number of months before I actually sat down to write. At some point I realized a parallel between the evolution of the personal computer (PC) and of networking as we have come to know it today. This chapter focuses upon the parallel development of computers and networks.

4.1 Personal Computing

People generally date the origins of the PC differently. For practical purposes, I identify the time period between 1977 and 1984 as the birth period of the personal computing and networking industry. Granted, other timeframes might be included; however, this time period saw the introduction of technology that did affect numerous areas beyond that of technology itself. Consider the following dates, products, technologies, and events from this timeframe:

1977   Commodore introduces the Personal Electronic Transactor.

1977   Apple Computer introduces the Apple II.

1977   Tandy introduces the TRS-80.

1978   Open Systems Interconnection is formulated by the Geneva,
       Switzerland–based International Organization for Standardization.

1978   Atari introduces the Atari 400 and the Atari 800.

1978   Epson introduces the dot matrix printer.

1978   Sony introduces the Beta format videotape recorder.

1979   Hayes Microcomputer introduces the Micromodem 100.

1979   Compuserve is founded.

1979   Intel introduces the 8088 chip.

1980   Cable Network News (CNN) begins broadcasting.

1980   *Infoworld* publishes its first issue.

1980   Satellite Software International (WordPerfect's precursor) introduces its first copy of WordPerfect for Data General computers (the IBM PC was yet to happen).

1981   The space shuttle is launched for the first time.

1981   IBM introduces the Personal Computer (PC).

1981   MS-DOS is used with the IBM PC.

1981   CD-ROM technology is introduced.

1982   Columbia Data Products introduces the first IBM clone.

1982   Norton Utility software for PCs is introduced.

1982   Intel introduces the 286 processor.

1982   Lotus 1-2-3 Spreadsheet is introduced to work with the IBM PC.

1983   Novell Corporation introduces the first file server–oriented Local Area Network.

1983   Microsoft introduces its Word wordprocessor.

1983   AT&T introduces UNIX System V.

1983   Hewlett Packard offers the first 8088-based machine with a touch screen.

1983   Compaq Computer introduces its PC clone.

1983   Microsoft announces Windows (but does not begin shipment until 1985).

1984   Apple Macintosh is introduced.

1984   The 3.5-in floppy is introduced.

1984   IBM introduces the AT version of its PC.

1984   Satellite Software International introduces WordPerfect for the IBM PC.

The significance of these and other happenings from 1977 to 1984 made a significant impact on the business community. My own introduction to the computer industry was by way of the Tandy TRS-80.

Recent conversations with Isaac May and Ted Taylor confirm that the first time I saw the TRS-80 in use was in either 1979 or 1980. At that time, Mr. Taylor was using a TRS-80 to calculate students' grades for a mathematics course he was teaching. I was unaware of his knowledge of or use of computers. Mr. May and myself were vacationing from college, when Mr. May came and said he wanted me to see something. When I saw how Mr. Taylor was using the computer to calculate grades, I literally thought to myself: "If this machine can do what I just saw it do, the personal computer is going to change the way business is conducted in my lifetime." I did not tell that to either Mr. Taylor or Mr.

May at the time, but later I did. I was right—the personal computer has changed the way business is conducted around the world.

Beyond the contributions PCs have made (and still make) to the business community, they have made an interesting contribution to the computing community. At one time, humankind was driving technology. Today, with the advent of the PC and networks, technology is driving technology. For example, 20 years ago technological advances were primarily being made by human effort. The same is true today—but factor in the contribution of the PC and network technology, and the equation is tilted. Personal computer software can create other computer software today. Some networks have been designed so that monitoring of various sorts can take place, thus providing real-time information that until recently had to be obtained in different ways. As this chapter presents, networks themselves are now similar to personal computer architecture of the 1980s.

4.2   Personal Computer Architecture

If we use 1981 and the IBM PC as a starting point for the examination of PC architecture, Fig. 4.1 adequately represents the PC architecture of that time.

Figure 4.1 shows the PC architecture of the PCs of the early to mid-1980s. This architecture is similar to the *mainframe* architecture of the early 1960s (see Fig. 4.2).

Figure 4.2 shows that the *mainframe* architecture of the 1960s is similar to early PC architecture. At that time, the processor actually housed the CPU and main storage. Figure 4.3 better illustrates the physical representation of some mainframes of that day.

Today, personal computer architecture is best illustrated by Fig. 4.4. Note that Fig. 4.4 shows multiple devices attached to the PC. Fifteen years ago, this was not the case. However, now multimedia and a variety of other peripherals work with an ordinary PC. This is partly due to the advances made in chip technology as well as in the software written to exploit those designs.

Figure 4.5 shows a typical PC architecture of today. The Extended Industry Standard Architecture (EISA) hardware bus is shown as well as the Peripheral Component Interconnect (PCI) bus.

Initially, PCs used the Industry Standard Architecture (ISA) bus technology. This architecture was *dumb,* meaning it could not detect any devices without manual configuration. (What is the old saying? Children must crawl before they can walk?) This ISA architecture, and cards, were also called *Legacy ISA cards.* The ISA architecture had no vendor, device ID, or class code identification. Software drivers for ISA cards were written specifically for those cards—no interchanging

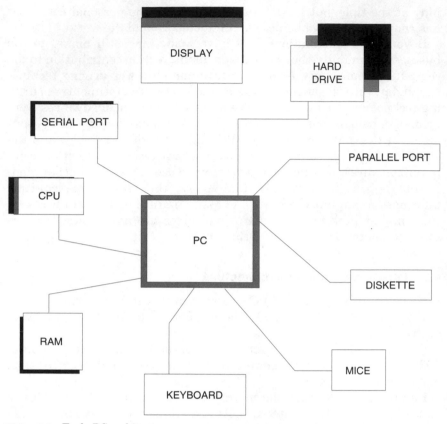

Figure 4.1 Early PC architecture.

existed. This type of architecture presupposes an incredible amount on behalf of a user or installer of such components.

Before the reader judges too quickly, let me address plug-and-play (PnP) ISA. First of all, Legacy ISA cards cannot operate with plug-and-play compatibility. The reason for this is that Legacy ISA cards do not have registers that are configurable to be read to or written from. Newer PnP-identified cards *can* operate with PnP technology.

ISA PnP cards (they have been out for a number of years) are capable of being configured. This configuration ability is the unique aspect of PnP. Some people may argue the hair-split here, but most configuration processes involve the following steps or functions (granted, more or fewer may well be included; these are the ones this author is aware of):

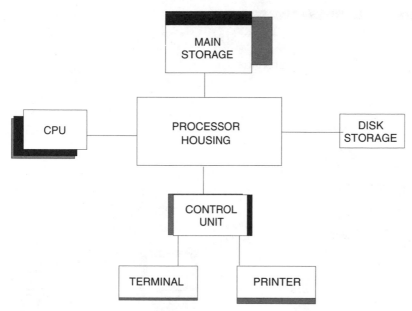

Figure 4.2   1960s mainframe architecture.

1. Card setup—preparing them to listen. This is a predefined key sequence.
2. A *read* is performed on each card in the system until one of them has been *isolated*. (Hope it's not lonely!)
3. A Card Select Number (CSN) is assigned to the isolated card.
4. The isolated card enters a configuration state.
5. The isolated card, which is in the configuration state, is interrogated concerning its requirements.
6. The isolated card is to *go-to-sleep.*
7. Functions 1 through 6 are performed on all cards.
8. Each card is placed into configuration mode by the configuration software, using the CSN number obtained.
9. Each card has registers written to it with resource addresses that do not conflict.
10. Each card is enabled until the process is complete.

A different interpretation of personal computers is to consider them in light of comparison and contrast, as Fig. 4.6 shows.

Figure 4.6 illustrates both early and present personal computer architecture. Since the introduction of the PC in the early 1980s, many

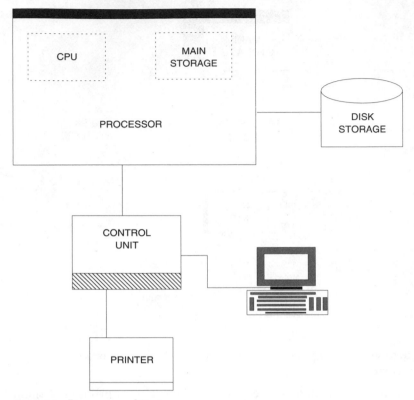

Figure 4.3 Processor architecture.

enhancements have been made. Some explanation of differences of board architecture was previously provided. In addition, more *things* have been made available via the PC.

Multimedia capability is now supported through hardware and software. Infrared capabilities also exist on many PC systems today. In most cases, infrared capabilities enable systems to receive file transfers and print capabilities from other systems. Other features, such as telephone and fax support, are also available in personal computers. Television feed can also be accommodated in personal computers today.

In every way, the PCs of today are more powerful and capable than their predecessors. In a real sense, PCs have undergone evolution, a revolution, and a transformation. The *evolution* is best understood when examining events in and around the PC industry of the 1980s. The *revolution* in the PC industry happened in the early 1990s. The revolution I refer to can be understood when one thinks of the software, microprocessor, hardware, and peripheral changes that occurred from around 1990 through the fall of 1995. Do we not still have Windows 95? Will it

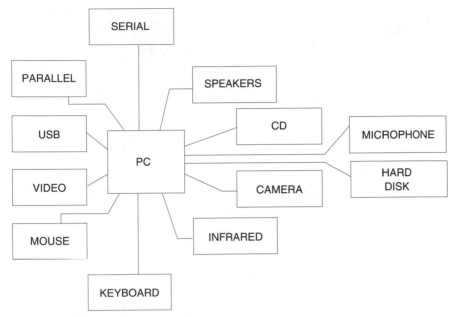

Figure 4.4   1990s personal computer architecture.

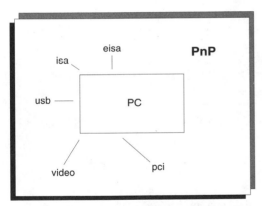

Figure 4.5   PC bus architecture.

not be around by default for some time? The transformation in the PC industry is still in the works. From one perspective, the PC transformation could be viewed in terms of the direct effect it has had on business.

Much more could be said about PC architecture, but a line has to be drawn somewhere. Lest the reader think the author is unaware of IBM's Microchannel architecture, I had better mention it. IBM knew the Legacy ISA architecture was amiss and needed enhancing in the

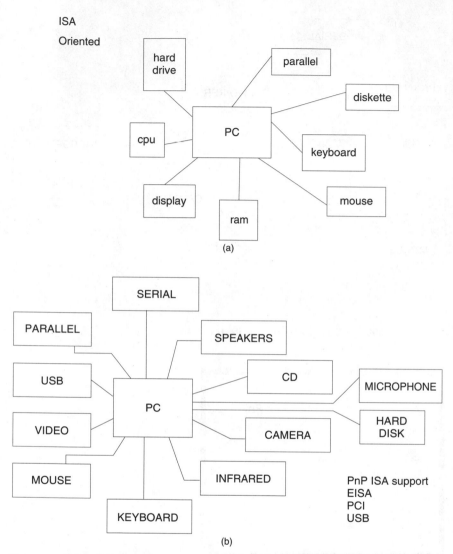

Figure 4.6 PC architecture: (a) past, and (b) present.

mid-80s. IBM's solution was Microchannel architecture. It was, shall I say, not the overwhelming success IBM wanted. The architecture itself was powerful. Technically, it was a great idea. However, sometimes marketing prevails and technical solutions do not—at least in the short run. IBM did not bring the peripheral items necessary to make Microchannel work. Yes, they did do a good job technically and, to be fair, the failure of Microchannel was not completely IBM's fault, if a fault is to be assessed—and I do not think it should be. The facts reveal that Microsoft was well under way with its marketing campaign, software rollout, and massive appeal to the general public when IBM was attempting to launch its Microchannel architecture. Consequently, Microchannel's lack of success could easily be explained by the fact of the overshadowing campaign on behalf of Microsoft and the lack of technical depth on the part of the consuming public.

4.3 Network Architecture

I hope the reader reflects upon earlier comments made in this book. In case the reader has not been reading this book in linear form, a few additional comments are in order.

The world in which we live is entirely different with regard to technology than it was a mere 30 years ago. So what, you say? Well, the impact of this change is felt in nearly every aspect of life. As a result of technical advances, jobs are now available that were not available 30 years ago. Business is conducted differently; both inter- and intrabusiness affairs are different than they were 30 years ago. Even business between consumers and providers is conducted differently.

I have said many times that what has occurred in the past 50 years is a *technical revolution,* not an information revolution; the latter is yet to come, but it is on the horizon. Thirty years ago there were no PCs, no automatic teller machines (ATMs), no local area networks (LANs) as there are today, no multimedia technology, no CD-ROM technology, no imaging as it is today, no digital telephone systems to speak of—and an entire list of other technology that is available today. So what, you may say. That is the point.

There has never before been technological advance as broad, deep, and wide as has occurred in the past 50 years. You say, "Ed, that is a strong statement." Yes, it is; I mean it to be that blunt because it is an indisputable truth. The significance of this technical revolution touches every aspect of the human race. You may think, "Well, not everyone has e-mail and a lot of technology like some do." This is true. So, consider the social ramifications (positive and negative) that the technical revolution has brought with it. Think of the other ramifications as a result of the technical advances of just the past 20 years.

In conclusion, consider the positive and negative effects that the technical revolution has imposed on those you know, within your circle of friends. Technology is neither inherently *good* nor *bad;* in fact, these emotive words do not apply to the evaluation of technology. However, the indirect impact technology brings with it does have advantages and disadvantages.

During the 1960s, much networking was centralized (see Fig. 4.7). Figure 4.7 illustrates the nature of networking as being a hard-wired connection, for the most part, between a terminal user (input device) and printers (output devices).

During the 1970s, networking began to appear in different ways. The implementations of the 1960s were still in use, but distributed networks began to show more presence (see Fig. 4.8).

Figure 4.8 shows the advent of a distributed communications controller and other devices in a physically different location communicating with what would have been considered at that time the *central* location.

During the 1980s, network architecture like that shown in Fig. 4.9 began to emerge. Figure 4.9 shows LANs with host systems connected across multiple physical locations. This phase of networking brought with it the ability of systems to communicate in multiple locations. It should be noted that this arrangement of network devices can be traced back many years prior to the mid-80s, but the dominant implementation of this type of architecture emerged in the 1980s.

Another insight into networks during the 1980s is shown by Fig. 4.10, which illustrates varieties of LAN implementations.

During the 1980s, network architecture was both centralized and decentralized. LANs began to change in the functional abilities that could be implemented. One might debate Fig. 4.10 as being a LAN. Actually, the illustration shows multiple LANs connected over a widely dispersed geographic distance; thus, a virtual WAN is created. Interaction of each LAN with the others has more to do with the logical configuration of the devices themselves than the distances between them.

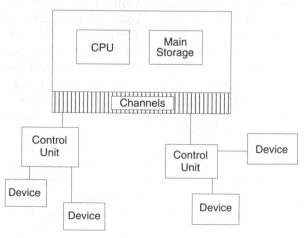

Figure 4.7   Centralized architecture.

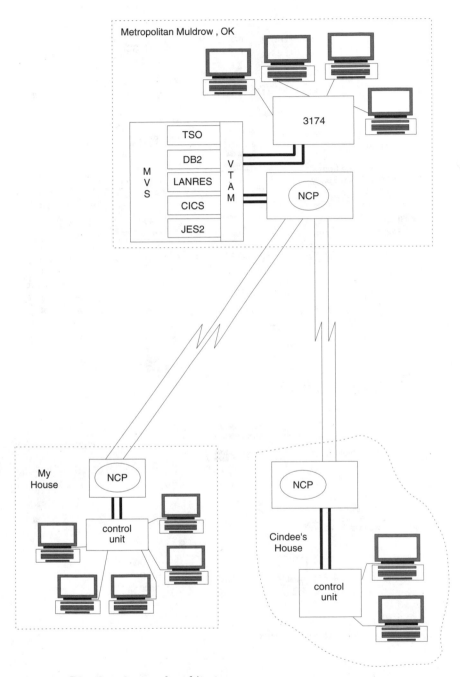

Figure 4.8 Distributed network architecture.

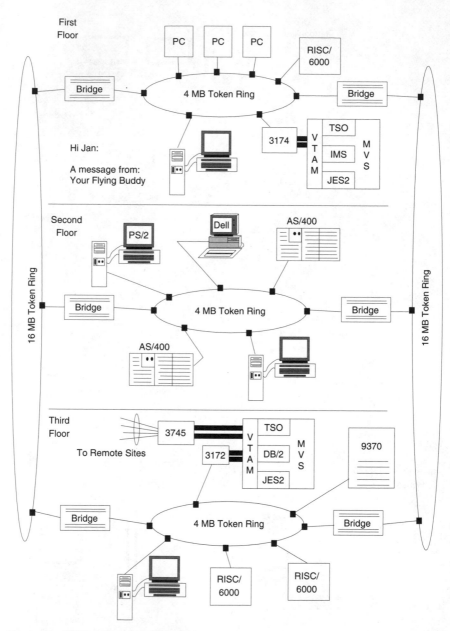

Figure 4.9   1980s network architecture.

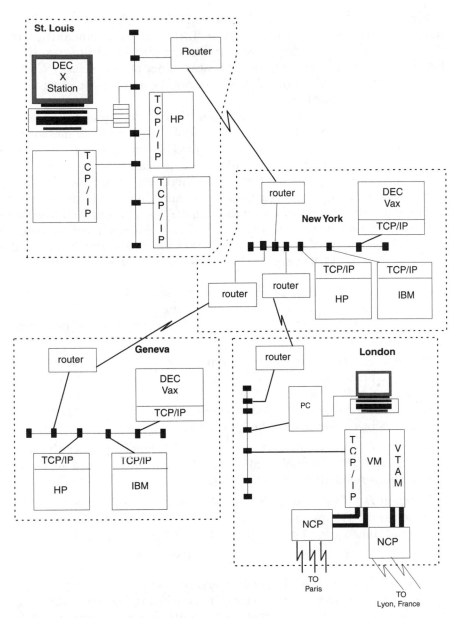

Figure 4.10   LAN implementations.

Figure 4.11 shows another addition to the network—a BRouter. This device enabled enhanced flexibility in LANs, and implementation of them increased in the early 1990s. In this sample illustration, multiple LANs are connected together to the central office of Information World, Inc. Even though this is an example, in reality many companies have architectures similar to it.

Figure 4.12 shows still another evolution of network architecture implementation that emerged in the 1980s, with multiple networks and multiple sites participating together. This variation on architecture also emerged in the 1980s and became prevalent in the 1990s.

Networks in many installations have increasingly become like that shown in Fig. 4.13, which illustrates how many different vendor computers and other pieces of hardware and software can be combined to make a diverse environment functional. The operation in this environment is a sequence of five functions performed by the dumb terminal user (no pun intended), user 1. These five functions are as listed:

Function A. The dumb terminal user (user 1) invokes the Telnet client inside the terminal server against the Convex host. The native Telnet server in the TCP/IP stack on the Convex answers the Telnet client request.

Function B. User 1 invokes the Telnet client on the Convex against the 3172 attached to the MVS host. The MVS host has TCP/IP running as an offload option, but as default a VTAM application. Hence, when user 1 invokes the Telnet client against the Telnet server on the MVS host, user 1 sees the VTAM banner screen.

Function C. User 1 performs a logon to ISPF editor under the control of TSO. The line mode option is selected, and user 1 invokes the FTP client resident on the MVS hos.

Function D. Even though TCP and IP is operating on the 3172, the Telnet and FTP applications are running indirectly as VTAM applications. Hence, user 1 can execute an FTP client against the SUN.

Function E. User 1 moves a file from MVS disk D to the SUN host.

Networks have evolved. Technology created in the 1980s is now prevalent in the marketplace. Increasingly, networks are becoming the company and users are the arms and mouthpieces of the corporate information infrastructure. The coming 10 to 20 years will be dominated by those companies, regardless of size, that have the best-architected networks. The amount and diversity of information has just begun to pick up momentum. Time will reveal those companies that invested in network design—those that did will reap manyfold rewards; those that did not will not.

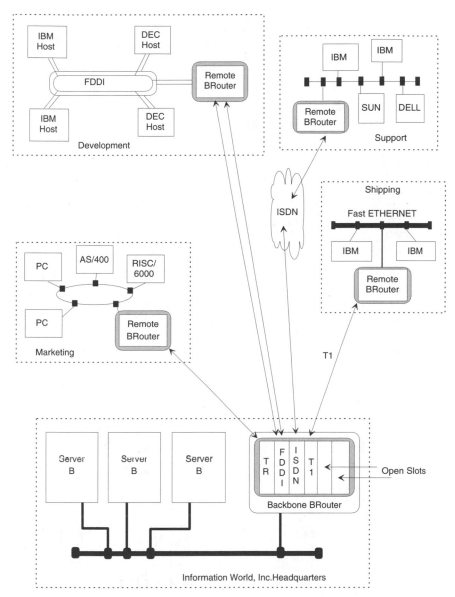

Figure 4.11   Distributed LAN architecture.

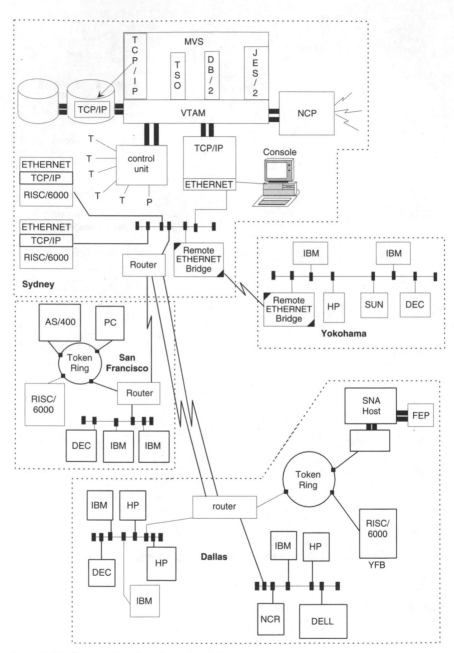

Figure 4.12   Internationally oriented architecture.

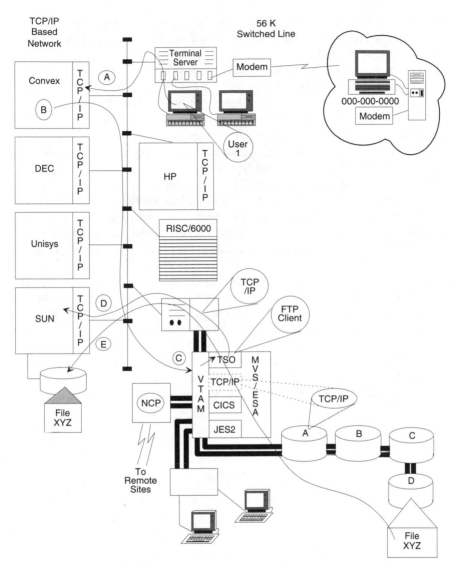

Figure 4.13 Integrated architecture.

4.4 Summary

Network architecture consists of software, hardware, and datacommunication and telecommunication equipment. The personal computer has evolved into a core aspect of most companies. The personal computer of the late 1970s and early 1980s did not begin with the design intent that it is being used for today. Nobody could have predicted what the personal computer has done to the business community. Similarly, in about two decades networks have evolved beyond anything anyone could have predicted.

Not even IBM understood what was about to happen when it released the PC in 1981—if it had, it surely would have staged a design plan to stay ahead of the technological curve. PCs and networks, generally, are central to my thinking when I say we are now at a point in time where technology is giving technology.

This chapter presents a brief insight to some aspects of PCs and networks. The Internet is not addressed, for it is a horse of a different color, as the old saying goes. The Internet is a prime example of humankind in this current generation. It is a worldwide network controlled by no government or single entity, and it breaks down barriers to communication around the globe. In a sense, the size of the Internet is difficult to understand; on the other hand, it is not too difficult to understand.

Some of the small, medium, and large networks employed in the world today are constituent components of the Internet. Businesses that use network technology would be wise to acknowledge with their wallets and words that their networks are their backbones—and that as go the people who run the networks, so go the companies.

Architectures change more slowly than next week's whiz-bang technology. Dear reader, if you are serious about going deep into technology, get into architecture—then the rest will be a piece of cake.

Chapter

5

Network Design Considerations

Designing a network goes beyond picking hardware and software, installing it, and hoping it works. Networks that have a lasting ability and quality during the heaviest loads have generally been well thought out. Success rarely *just happens* in the data communications and networking industry. As I told a friend, "One can be a few feet off landing a jet and not worry much; however, being a few *bits* off in the computing industry can bring down an entire network."

The remainder of this chapter provides practical insight, from experience, concerning network design.

5.1 Design Needs

When a company or a group of people decide a network is needed, a reason or two usually exists. In too many places I have seen networks that emerged to meet a need in various departments that eventually ended up crashing into the higher needs within a company.

Your company size, customer size, anticipated company size, and customer base should all factor into the equation that is the basis for building your network.

Internal needs

Each company, regardless of size, has internal needs. Bare-bones companies usually have shipping and receiving, sales, marketing, operations, support, financial, and personnel services. Granted, this is not all-inclusive, but it is a place to begin.

Internal needs may be subtle, but take time to examine the inner workings of the company. If technology is involved, then engineering, support, and sales may all need access to varying depths of information about the product or services the company offers. What does this mean for a network? At a minimum it means people in these departments will need to be able to access and, most likely, exchange information. The information may include graphics, internal reports, external feedback from potential or existing customers, and, possibly, a database of information.

Other internal information is most likely required for a given company to maintain some type of order. For example, online calendars are handy. This information is generally considered public within the company and may well be needed by shipping and receiving. For example, if Ms. Hoover is on vacation this month and multiple packages are received for her, the receiving department could take advantage of an online calendar to learn that she is out of the office and check whether any special instructions are standing regarding her absence.

Another help online calendars provide is in the scheduling of meetings. Fewer conference rooms might be needed if everyone in the company *knows* when a meeting is going to occur and what facility will be used to accommodate it. Parallel to this calendaring idea is the need for conference room services that affect the network. For example, are telephone services needed in the conference room? Are data network services needed in the conference room? If so, how will these services be provided? Will cabling exist for connecting portable computers? What will be the capacity of connections that can be made in the conference room at any given time? These and similar questions factor into the equation of network design. Overlook these points and you may well end up hiring a crew to tear part of a wall out to make something available that should have been included in the first place.

Many other *types* of information may need to be exchanged within a company. Regardless of what that may include, one should attempt to plan as far into the future as possible when adding this information into the network design equation. Granted, nobody can plan with a 100 percent ability to be on target 5 to 10 years out, but it is possible to plan for worst-case and best-case scenarios. Do this, and your work with datacommunication gear will be less painful. However, you would be wise to memorize the seven best words I have ever heard in this industry: "Comm gear ain't never gone in easy."

Words from experience.

External needs

Needs external to the company will also affect your network. For example, the way customers interact with the company is important. If there is a need for them to be able to access certain information, such as downloading files or reading certain information made available to the public, then this should be factored into the network design equation.

Beyond awareness of customer interaction with the company is the number of customers (current and planned) that will need this interactive ability. Circumstances may well justify an entirely separate network to meet the needs of the customer base. If so, then how this network will or will not interact with the network being designed is an important aspect to investigate.

The marketplace today is full of companies that cannot meet the demands placed upon them by customers. I hate to be the one to tell you, but this is typically due to a company's lack of attention to needs, unawareness that needs exist, or inability to cope with needs in a positive way. Too many times today, the philosophy of the day is "less is more." People who have this mentality are either on the way out of business or they already are. (Feel free to quote me on this.) Less never has been more, and in the datacommunications industry *more* is required to get *more* results. The point here is simple: be cognizant of the consumers; know their needs, desires, and requirements. Remember, the customer is one leg of the three-legged chair on which *all* companies are based.

5.2 Physical Considerations

This section's importance cannot be overstated. This chapter is most likely the most important in this entire book. When network design commences, hopefully it is done on paper first. I have a philosophy: if I cannot solve a problem or fix something on the marker board (or paper), then I cannot fix the problem in reality. It is easier to work through painstaking areas on the markerboard than through experience.

Consider the physical part of network design. Before we get to the technical part, we must address the fundamentals. Some say I am a master at understatement; in this case, though, enough cannot be said.

Assume that you have worked through the needs of the company and customers on paper. You are ready to begin ordering. In this case, assume that the physical location you are in is the location where the network will be built. The following should be used as a minimum rule-of-thumb checklist:

1. Is there enough free space so that when equipment begins to arrive it will not impede day-to-day operations?

2. Will any of the equipment arrive on pallets? If multiple pallets of equipment arrive, where will they initially be put for unloading, and then where will they be stored until the equipment is used?

3. Are stairs used to access the area where the equipment will be stored? If so, how many?

4. Can a forklift enter the location to unload and load equipment?

5. What is the estimated weight per square foot that the floor can sustain?

6. How wide are the doors?

7. Are your hand trucks capable of sustaining the weight of new equipment if it is shipped so that hand trucks are required to load or unload it?

8. Are elevators required to get to a location where the equipment will be stored? How accessible are they? Will using these elevators affect daily operations of your company or another company?

9. Will the location where the equipment is stored until implementation be secure?

10. Does the addition of the new equipment cause any code infringement with the fire or police departments, or with any other city, county, state, or federal government entity?

11. If any of the equipment is shipped on pallets or in large boxes, how do you plan to dispose of them?

12. Is any of the equipment sensitive to any environmental conditions in your location, such as temperature and humidity? Have you verified this with the manufacturer of the equipment?

13. Do you have a single point of contact with the company shipping equipment to you?

At a minimum, you should have clear, definible answers to these questions before you ever give the okay to receive the first shipment of equipment. Your particular location may require that additional questions be posed and answered. I encourage you to think the matter of your physical location through. It might even be helpful to have someone who knows the physical plant well enough go through this phase with you. Somebody should take responsibility for this task of physical premise evaluation and preperation—if this is not addressed prior to the receipt of equipment, one could learn about some matters the hard way. Then someone *will* take responsibility, like it or not.

5.3   Electrical Considerations

The importance of this section cannot be overstated. It is imperative that you, or the appropriate person, know the electrical capability of your physical location. Once you have determined the equipment that is to be deployed, then ascertain the specifications for each piece of equipment. When you create the logical network illustration, this information will be critical.

Should you not have personnel capable of performing a certified electrical evaluation, contact the following company, which does have the personnel to do so:

Information World, Inc.
8601 Mystic Trail
Suite S
Fort Worth, TX 76118

You may think, "We have plenty of electrical outlets, so we will not need additional sources." Here is where the problem begins. Most offices have multiple electrical outlets tied into one circuit breaker. Hence, a given room may have six outlets. Assume three are being used by a computer, a light, and a radio. To assume that one could add a mid-size photocopier to this room and plug it into an available wall outlet is, at the least, misguided. Even the addition of two laser printers could easily overload a single circuit breaker.

My thoughts on network design and electrical considerations begin with determining all pieces of equipment that require electricity. List all these on paper. Next, obtain from the manufacturers the amounts of watts, amps, and volts that the devices will consume upon power-up and in idle state. You could be in for a surprise.

Once you have obtained information about all devices, next determine how power conditioning will be included into the equation. Forthcoming chapters explain the network designed and used as an example in this text. This network uses Tripp Lite power protection equipment. Once electrical information was obtained about each device, information about each piece of Tripp Lite equipment was needed. Just because power protection equipment has multiple outlets on it does not mean that one can fill each one and expect power protection. In the case of Tripp Lite equipment, the specifications of each piece of equipment were adhered to during the installation phase of this network. In order for power protection equipment to operate the way it was designed to, one must use it the way the manufacturer designed it to be.

Many offices have 20-A circuit breakers for electrical outlets. Exceptions abound, but this is the general rule. My recommendation is, do not exceed 70 to 80 percent of the circuit breaker's capacity. For example, if you know that a given room has four outlets tied into one 20-A breaker and that none of these outlets are currently in use, then add equipment that will not exceed 15-A. Why? Because it is safe. Odds are that when you design your network and install equipment into this hypothetical office that does not exceed 70 to 80 percent of the circuit breaker's capacity, someone will come along behind you in a few weeks or months and add a few additional items that will use the remaining percentage of the circuit's capacity.

If no planning went into the electrical part of the location where the network will be installed, you are in for some extra work. Do not assume that you can superimpose a network into an existing site without coping with the electrical factor. If you do not, it will have a plan for you.

Some companies have computer rooms where the bulk of the computing and network equipment resides. This room is generally preplanned to handle computing and networking equipment. However, if you do not have such a room or designated area, then you must start from scratch. The best place to begin is by contacting the facilities manager, who usually will be able to get you in touch with electricians who can answer your questions or assist you in the planning phase.

The network designed, built, and explained in forthcoming chapters has two laser printers. This is a good example because it is typical of many scenarios—it could even be typical of what you intend to implement. Both laser printers are from IBM. Both have their power consumption stated explicitly on the appropriate plate as defined by national and international requirements. In addition, both have their power requirements stated clearly in the documentation shipped with them. These two printers use a single Tripp Lite spike and surge protector and voltage regulator. You may be surprised to learn that these two printers have a single dedicated 20-A circuit breaker (see Fig. 5.1).

Figure 5.1 shows the circuit breaker, wire size, Tripp Lite spike and line noise filter, voltage regulator, and the IBM printers. You may think, "Gee, Ed, this is overkill." Really? Now, what if I told you these two printers absorb 12.5 to 13.5 A when powered up simultaneously? Now, assume you have some additional equipment to be added to this outlet. What if you took this equipment and plugged it into the place you have the network printers connected? Would these additions work without overloading the circuit breaker? This level of detail needs to be obtained and factored into the network design equation.

While plans were formulated for the network, FLUKE test instruments were used to obtain results of existing power supplied to the facility. Consider Figs. 5.2a to 5.2e. Note the voltage differences among the illustrations. I monitored the AC for approximately a week. These show how much the incoming voltage varies at my location. Yours may be different; however, I suspect that you might find similar voltages. These voltages were obtained using a certified calibrated FLUKE 123 ScopeMeter. FLUKE includes software and cabling with a 123 ScopeMeter kit to interface it into a PC running Windows or Windows NT. This makes capturing real-time line voltages easy. The scopemeter

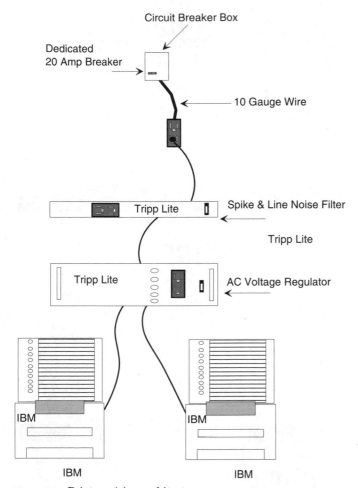

Figure 5.1   Printer wiring architecture.

itself and the software both enable capture functions to be performed and enable print-out capabilities. This level of information is critical in planning a network. This information is part of the foundation of the network. The better your measurements of what the electrical *reality* is in your facility, the more solid your network will be.

5.4   The Human Factor

Networks don't get built without people. Neither is it possible to maintain them without people. Some time back a movement occurred in the datacommunication and telecommunication industry to cut back on personnel. This mind-set was general in many companies of all sizes. Boomerangs happen.

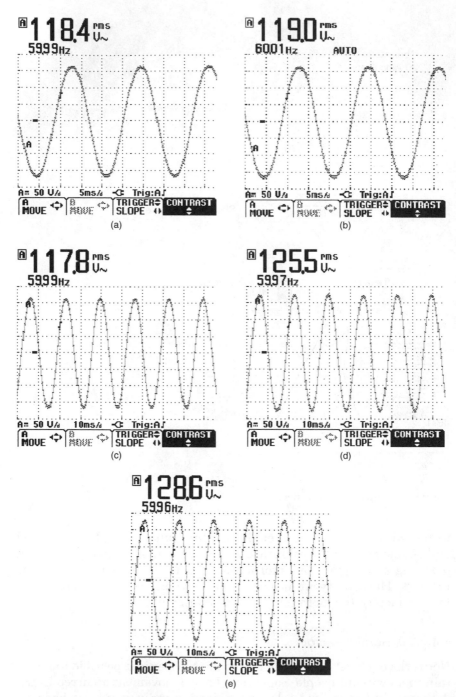

Figure 5.2 Voltage and cycle readings at the same location over a week: (*a*) first reading, (*b*) second reading, (*c*) third reading, (*d*) fourth reading, and (*e*) fifth reading.

It is most unfortunate for many companies that some managers think money is more important than people. I have seen companies that were cash-rich and brain-poor when it came to technical people. Companies exist that have incredible amounts of money but cannot keep good technical talent. It seems that some company management thinks the technical people are dispensable. Ironically, the past few years have dealt the management of many companies a great blow. Why is this important? No, I am not just expressing an opinion.

See, networks are either planned for or they are not. In the planning of a network one must factor into the equation the human factor. If one does not, then the defaults of *life* will override and will impose a decision. It takes more than good people with technical skills to design a network. It also takes representatives from every aspect of the company that will use the network to participate in the planning of it. You may think this is trite. Think again. Not too long ago, there was a great move to get networks and data centers to operate in *lights-out* mode—meaning as few people as possible operating them. Well, this too came to pass. Yes, I have seen some data centers go from lights-out operation to *everything-out* operation! The more advanced the networks and technology deployed, the more brains it takes to keep them running.

Education is not optional, and neither are people when it comes to network design and maintaining daily operations. If you happen to be the one responsible for network design, I encourage you to get together with the appropriate people and include (as best as possible) the skill sets required to keep the network operational. At the least you will have documented estimates of reality on paper, and ideally this phase of planning could attract the right attention and make life easier for many as network implementation begins.

My implication here is not to have an army of people for the sake of having people. The intended message is that I have yet to see any technology that created itself, maintained itself, and phased growth into itself. It is foolish to buy the best equipment available in the open market today and not pay to get *and to keep* reasonable technical skill to maintain it—it does not matter what a *business plan* says about this.

Another aspect of the human factor is education. In the late 1980s Derek Bok, a professor at Harvard University (if memory serves), was on the cover of *Time* magazine. Inside, an article quoted him to say, "If you think education is expensive, try ignorance." My thoughts exactly.

Go ahead and factor into the network equation continuing education across the board for all technical people who will be involved. Since most network implementations vary, I can only endorse a principle here. Train your people or have them trained.

5.5 Evolution

The network you are about to design, or are in the process of designing, will evolve. What I mean is that sooner or later someone will suggest that this or that be added to the network, and it probably will be. As the network evolves, be sure to document all additions and changes to the existing architectural layout of the network.

More than likely, as time goes by some people will leave the company for a variety of reasons; these could be due to personal health or family illness, death, accident, promotion, transfer or otherwise. Try to plan as best as possible for this. This is part of the evolution the network will experience.

It seems that most networks tend to reflect the personalities of those who have designed and worked with them, directly and indirectly. As the network changes, do not lose sight of the original design intent of the network. This is critical. Yes, this is critical. Again, I have seen many people argue this or that for or against a network's operation. Typically, these situations are squashed when the questions, "What was the original design intent of the network? Is it meeting that intent?" are asked. Unfortunately, some people maintain the bizarre notion that "If it is not doing this or that, *it* is not *right.*" These situations can be easily resolved—simply ask, "Why is it that the modem will never print laser-quality reports?" You are probably laughing, but you get my point. Sometimes it takes holding a mirror up to the mind of some for them to realize their own lack of thought about a situation.

A real-life experience is a good fit here. In the past year I was at a certain location with about a half dozen professionals who were designing a network. I came onto the scene a little late. Many aspects of the network had been penciled in on paper.

As I was being briefed about the network, its purpose, the size, and the plan for implementation, I read through the notes of what had been done so far. The network was large. It was fairly costly. As I examined the preliminary design I could not believe it. I must have had some facial expression as I was reading through the materials, for someone asked, "What is the matter? Is there something that needs changing?" That is when I really got concerned. Here is why.

I explained, "This network design is going to break. It is not a matter of *if,* it's merely a matter of *when.*" One could have heard a pin drop. I will leave it at that. My point here is that some group of people had made a preliminary design of a network around a single point of failure. This type of thinking is either intentional or those with this mindset need to be doing something other than designing networks.

So, when designing, factor in evolution. Please do not even think about designing a network that has a single point of failure. However, if that is the only way a design can be achieved, then design in redundancy—an alternative architecture (with real equipment) that will kick in *when* the first one fails. You will probably get a raise or promotion if you do.

5.6 Technical Factors

During the penciling phase of network design, include a detailed examination of the following factors. Your actual checklist may vary, but at the minimum you should look into these areas and estimate the impact they will have on the network.

1. Telephone line capabilities, or lack thereof.
2. Heating considerations once all the equipment is in place.
3. Cooling considerations once all the equipment is in place.
4. Backup contingencies for electrical power, telephone lines, and operations.
5. Electromagnetic field interference.
6. Radio frequency (RF) interference.
7. Cable lengths (maximums for AC, DC, voice, and data).
8. Cable locations.
9. Service accessibility for all equipment.
10. Hot-site location for backup operational plans, architectural design plans, emergency procedures, and so on.
11. Identified chain of command (technical people) to execute plans in case of emergency.
12. Labeling cables (data, voice, video, AV, DC, etc.).
13. Checklist for testing *all* cables prior to use with any equipment— especially if they are new.
14. Plan for 10 worst-case technical scenarios and have a detailed action plan ready to implement for any variation of need.
15. Know your security—physical and logical.
16. Categorize technical needs into critical, urgent, and as-soon-as-possible categories; remember, most things are not urgent.

Your site may require a variation on this list; however, I have used it in many places with networks of all sizes.

5.7 Summary

This chapter presents information to assist you in the planning of your network. The examples of my experience are real. May it be that you profit from them.

Network design includes electrical, cooling and heating, and weight, height, width, and storage considerations, as well as knowing component functions. Forthcoming chapters present additional information that goes hand-in-hand with that presented in this one. This book as a whole provides the foundation you will need to begin a solid network design.

6

Network Design and Components, Part 1

This chapter presents the logical network design I created prior to obtaining any equipment. After the design is explained, further sections in this and the following chapter explain the components that comprise the network.

6.1 Network Design

I began this network design the same way as I have all others—that is, literally at the drawing board. I use a marker board to work out my ideas. This can take days, sometimes weeks, as I sift through the requirements, my thoughts, and variations of what equipment is needed and how it fits into the overall design scheme.

The network design explained in this chapter and those ahead is based more on principle than on a given piece of technology. The purpose of the network design here is to meet current needs and sustain growth. Let me repeat: the original design intent of this network is to do what I want it to do now and be flexible enough to change and accommodate growth in the near future. It is not designed for anyone else's criteria.

Before examining the components of the network, consider the logical network design as shown in Fig. 6.1.

Note that Fig. 6.1 shows numerous network components. Some are not shown as well, such as the network interface cards, particular wiring details, and so on. However, the figure does show the overall logical design of the network. Close inspection of the figure may tend to imply a single point of failure in a given place, but redundancies have been built into the design.

The reason this is the logical network design is because it was driven by user requirements. This network enables users to exchange files, e-mail, and remote logons to systems such as servers, and even to use network printing. The remaining sections in this chapter explain the components of the network.

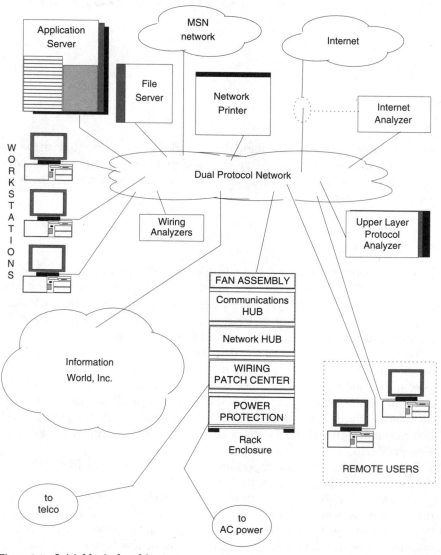

Figure 6.1   Initial logical architecture.

6.2   Component Overview

Before examining each component, this section provides a list of what is part of this network. The list includes a variety of components—for example, wire testers, phone line testers, and utility programs, to name a few. The list here is in no particular order; it is, however, a list of the vendor components used in this network.

- Bud Industries rack enclosure
- SMC Ethernet network HUBs
- SMC SNMP management board for network HUBs
- Hubbell Premise Wiring 48-port inline panel
- Hubbell 10base-T wire for all interface cards
- Hubbell patch cables for patch panel
- Fluke 123 ScopeMeter
- Fluke Model 41B Power Analyzer
- Fluke 685 Enterprise LANMETER
- Microsoft software
- McAfee software suite
- Tripp Lite power protection
- IBM network printer
- Hewlett-Packard Internet Advisor and Upper Layer Protocol Analyzer
- 3Com USR Enterprise network HUB
- IBM personal computers
- Creative Labs multimedia support
- Miscellaneous equipment

These components, and others presented forthwith, have been put together to make the network possible.

6.3   Personal Computers

IBM personal computers are used in this network. The commercial desktop series used include the PC350 and PC365 series. A typical example of the general specifications for the base system units (model 350s) used in this network include:

200-MHz Pentium MMX processor

2.6-GB hard disk

16-MB Nonparity EDO Memory

3.5-in floppy disk drive

Units used in this network employ a PCI Busmaster controller and SMART capabilities. These systems include PCI Enhanced IDE hard drives, Universal Serial Bus ports, infrared, 64-bit PCI graphics, and wake-on-LAN capability.

Functionality of the Universal Serial Bus (USB) makes peripheral connectivity easier. The hot-connect ability enables peripheral devices to be connected in seconds. Such devices can be added or removed without reconfiguring or rebooting. Each USB port permits up to 127 USB-capable devices.

Some of the PCs used in this network have the capability for symmetrical multiprocessing (SMP) when dual processors are used. An L2 external CPU cache of 256 K and also a Pipeline burst L3 cache are used. The BIOS type is 256-K Flash, SurePath.

The systems can accommodate up to 192 MB RAM at a speed of 60 ns, deployed by 72-pin SIMMs. Their hard disk average seek time is 12 µs with a latency of approximately 5.8 µs. They support RAID and hot-swappable drive bays.

The graphic capabilities of these systems employ an S3 Trio64 V+Graphics-type chipset. The result is SVGA graphics and data width of 64-bit video RAM. Graphic resolution with the standard video RAM is 1280 × 1024 with 16 colors. The maximum resolution (with a maximum video RAM) is 1280 × 1024 with 65,536 colors. The graphics bus interface uses PCI architecture.

The systems have a 200-W power supply for either 110 or 220 V, with a universal manual switch. The heat and sound emissions are 48 dB. The typical weight of each cabinet is 28 lb, with a height of 6.3 in, width of 16.5 in, and depth of 17.6 in.

Systems used in this network include the following security features:

- Boot sequence control
- Boot without keyboard or mouse
- Cover key lock
- Diskette boot inhibit
- Diskette write protect (switch)
- Diskette I/O control
- Hard disk I/O control
- Parallel I/O control
- Power-on password
- Secure fixed DASD

- Secure removable media
- Serial I/O control
- Setup utility password (administrator password)
- U-bolt tie-down support

The systems specifications used in this network also include the following product approvals and/or certifications, according to IBM: BABT (U.K.); CE; CISPR-22 Class B; CSA C22.2 No. 950 (Canada); DEMKO (EN 60950); EIF (SETI) (EN 60950); Energy Saving Law (refer to N-B 1-9174-001); FCC Class B (U.S.); IECEE CB Certificate and report to IEC-950 Second Edition; ISO 9241-3 Compliant; JATE; NEMKO (EN 60950); NS/G/1234/J/100003 (Telecommunications Safety only: no approval mark); OVE (EN 60950); Power Line Harmonics (refer to N-B 2-4700-017); SEMKO (EN 60950); TUV-GS (EN 60950); TUV-GS—ZH1/618; UL-1950 First Edition; VCCI Class 2 (Japan).

In addition, IBM's current warranty is limited warranty period and Type 3: three-year (first year on-site, second/third years carry-in), 3 years parts and labor.

The IBM desktop systems used in this network came with preinstalled software. Some of these systems were reconfigured to meet the needs of the network. However, all legal and ethical respect was given to manufacturers of hardware and software products. Each system used in this network either is covered by a site license or has a dedicated piece of software for each system, and each system has one user. In the case of servers, workstations or otherwise, each manufacturer's legal guidelines were followed. I strongly recommend that these matters be factored into the design of any network. Simply put: using an unpaid piece of software, unless it is clear that it is freeware, is stealing. It is no different than stealing a tangible item. Consider this when you design your network.

For more information on IBM products, contact:

International Business Machines
Department M7FE, Bldg. 003G
P.O. Box 1900
Boulder, CO 80301
Internet: www.ibm.com

6.4 Rack Enclosure

A Bud Industries rack enclosure is used in this network. This enclosure includes industry standard 19-in rack mounts in the front and rear. Figure 6.2 illustrates it.

Figure 6.2 shows a front view of the rack enclosure. The enclosure used has a 42-in rack capability inside. When the rack enclosure is

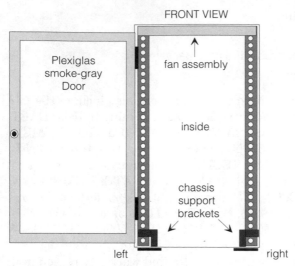

FRONT VIEW

Plexiglas
smoke-gray
Door

fan assembly

inside

chassis
support
brackets

left   right

Figure 6.2   Bud Industries rack enclosure chassis.

assembled, with casters on, its total height is 48 in. Figure 6.3 shows a rear view of the Bud rack enclosure.

Figure 6.3 is similar to Fig. 6.2; however, the chassis support brackets run the length of the cabinet. Note that the rear view shows that the chassis support brackets are mounted beneath the fan assembly at the top as well as on the bottom. As Figs. 6.2 and 6.3 show, there are vertical panel mounting rails in the front and the rear of the enclosure. It is possible to mount equipment in the enclosure without rear vertical panel mounting rails and chassis support brackets. This is a judgment call you need to make. The enclosure is sturdy enough to hold considerable weight.

Bud Industries has a variety of options that can be used in its cabinets. My decision to use front and rear vertical mounting rails was due to weight concerns regarding the equipment to be mounted in the enclosure. Your situation could differ; however, having front and rear vertical rails with chassis support brackets connecting them makes the enclosure even stronger. It is an added strength.

The enclosure has a very unique benefit. Both sides can be removed without any tools. Both sides of the enclosure are vented to assist in air circulation. The front and rear doors are both keyed and lockable—and they are also removable. This flexibility makes the cabinet accessible from every side. The top has a circle of machined holes to aid in air circulation. In addition, Bud ships the fan assembly unassembled, which is a great advantage. The orientation of the fans inside the fan assembly determines the direction of air flow. This is very important, because the equipment to be mounted in the cabinet for this example also has fans mounted inside. Consequently, because the Bud enclosure's fan orientation can be changed, everything can circulate air in the same direction.

The Bud enclosure arrived at the location where the network was being physically assembled. It arrived by way of tractor-trailer, on a pallet. The pallet weighed in at approximately 250 lb. Bud included all the required parts to assemble the enclosure with the least number of tools. A Phillips screwdriver, a wrench to tighten the nuts and bolts on the casters, and pliers were required.

If you desire more information about rack enclosures, regardless of your size requirements, contact:

Bud Industries, Inc   or   BUD WEST
4605 East 355th Street   P.O. Box 41190
P.O. Box 998   Phoenix, AZ 85080
Willoughby, OH 44094   Internet: www.budind.com

This enclosure is a good example of what I mentioned earlier about having a facility capable of accommodating equipment. In fact, this pallet arrived within a day of another pallet of equipment. Together they weighed over 600 lb and required approximately 10 ft^2 of floor space.

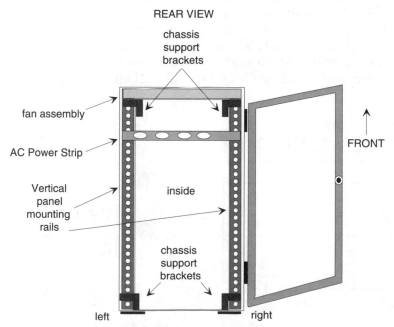

Figure 6.3 Bud Industries rack enclosure chassis support brackets, rear view.

6.5 Electrical Test Equipment

Knowing the electrical requirements for all network equipment is not optional. Neither is knowing the electrical capacity of the environment in which the equipment will be installed. Someone needs to be well trained to perform electrical testing prior to, during, and after the installation of each piece of equipment. In addition, this person should be able to analyze the power supply at the site, factor in the various components to be used, and convey what changes need to be made, if any.

Personally, my background includes training in electricity. It also includes training in test equipment. Fluke instruments were used in this network. Actually, FLUKE equipment was used prior to any piece of equipment being powered up so that a baseline reading and capacity measurement could be obtained.

The Fluke analyzers were calibrated and tested for mechanical and electrical function. This is important. Those of you who understand analyzers know the purpose of calibration. For those unfamiliar with this, calibration puts the analyzer at a *known* position to begin. A reference point must be obtained for any analyzer or meter to be reliable (see Figs. 6.4 and 6.5).

Figures 6.4 and 6.5 show the readings at the electrical outlet prior to any equipment being connected. They are typical readings. These readings were viewed in real time by a Fluke 41B Power Analyzer and were captured with Fluke software on a PC. The PC in this case was an IBM ThinkPad using batteries, so no skewed readings here!

Consider Figs. 6.6, 6.7, 6.8, and 6.9. After the initial readings (and information regarding which outlets were wired to which breaker) were obtained, additional readings were taken. Figure 6.6 is a snap-

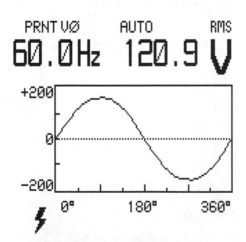

Figure 6.4 Reference reading.

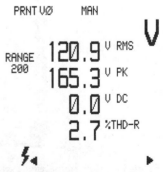

Figure 6.5 Reference reading.

shot of a Tripp Lite voltage regulator with an IBM network printer attached. Note that the figure shows the voltage and amperage. In this case the amperage reading is 0.81 A. Note as well that the duty cycle is 60.0, displayed in the lower left of the figure. Figure 6.7 shows the same FLUKE instrument and the same Tripp Lite voltage regulator, with the same IBM network printer. Examine the figure again. Note that the amperage used is 5.12. The printer is drawing this current for its heating element. Now note Fig. 6.8. This snapshot was taken seconds after Fig. 6.7. The amperage is back down to 0.39. Look at Fig. 6.9, where the current drawn is 8.11 A.

The significance of these readings is as follows. Assume you intend to install two network printers. Assume both *can* draw 8.11 A when required. That is a total of 16.22 A. Now, assume these printers are plugged into a 20-A circuit breaker. This scenario would be fine, but a word of caution is due. If such a scenario is used, be aware that the circuit utilization is approximately 65 percent of capacity.

The significance of this section is to show you a principle. When you are designing your network you need to get this specific before the equipment is deployed. Then once it is deployed, you need to verify your prior estimates. Electricity requires respect—violate that respect and consequences are certain; the only question is how severe they will be. Electricity is not anything to play with or to guess about. You may think I am pushing the point here—and I am, because I understand what electricity can do. Network equipment is sensitive. A considerable amount of equipment can easily overload circuits if one is not careful. Unfortunately, this oversight is common.

When you are addressing the electrical considerations for your network, rely on qualified expertise. Should you have that expertise in house and need equipment, Fluke can be reached at:

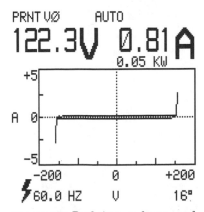

Figure 6.6 Real-time voltage and amperage.

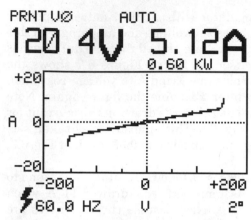

Figure 6.7   Real-time voltage and amperage.

Internet: www.fluke.com

or

Fluke Corporation   or   Fluke Europe B. V.
P.O. Box 9090   P.O. Box 680
Everett, WA 98206   7600 AR, Alemelo
                                             The Netherlands

After you have performed preliminary testing, and testing during the installation phase of network design, you will need to continue to monitor electrical considerations day by day. This part of network maintenance works hand-in-hand with power protection, which is addressed later in this chapter.

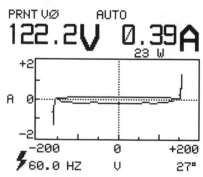

Figure 6.8 Spot check of volts and amps.

6.6   Network HUBs

Most networks have some form of HUB or device that serves as the vehicle for the lower-layer network protocols. In this case Standard Micro Systems (SMC) Network Interface Cards (NICs) were selected for both the desktop systems and the notebook computers. SMC network HUBs were also chosen.

The NICs can accommodate 10base-T or BNC conectors. The exposed end of the card (where the cables connect) have LEDs showing the link and transmit/receive status of the board. These boards support SNMP; therefore, management at the lower-layer interface board level is possible.

SMC PCMCIA cards are used with notebook computers. They have the same functionality as the NICs used in the desktop systems.

The SMC NICs in this network are 10base-T 14-port stackable, rackmount enclosures. This particular HUB (the Elite 3812TP) is configurable and stackable to accommodate up to a maximum of 112 ports. Figure 6.10 illustrates how these appear inside the rack enclosure.

Figure 6.10 shows two HUBs with two SCSI ports on the front of each. A cable is used to daisy chain these together to make them stackable. In this case two are used; therefore one cable is used to connect them, and each HUB has a terminator that is supplied by SMC in order to close the connection.

The rear of the HUBs is where the network device cabling is connected (see Fig. 6.11).

The rear of each HUB has 10base-T connection points. Though not shown in Fig. 6.11, the rear of each HUB has LEDs indicating the status of links, sources, and partitions.

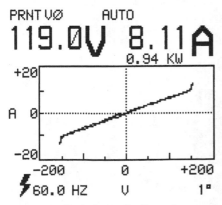

Figure 6.9   Spot check of volts and amps.

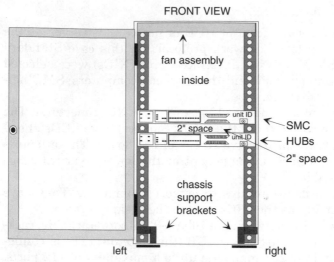

Figure 6.10   Network HUB mounting.

6.7   Patch Panel and Wiring

Wiring any network is either planned, or chaos exists. Believe me, I speak from experience of walking through layers of unlabeled cable behind equipment. With that thought in mind, the design for wiring in this network was examined from multiple angles. First, the reliability

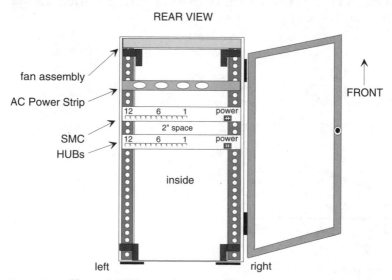

Figure 6.11   Network HUB access.

of the cable maker. Second, the actual implementation: Would it be easy to reconfigure equipment once installed? How would one *know* which cables go where? With this level of thought and multiple designs on the markerboard, the determination was made to use Hubbell equipment for the rack enclosure as well as the wiring.

Note that Fig. 6.12 shows an inside view of the enclosure from the rear. The figure shows that the inline panel has RJ-45 female connectors on what is considered its back side.

Figure 6.13 shows a front and rear view of the inline panel. The significance of this inline panel will become very clear forthwith. Rackmount panels are available that have RJ-45 female connectors on the front but the rear has a 110 connector. This is neither good nor bad. Some environments require this type of rear connection point for each connection. However, in this case it is different.

Hubble offers a patch panel with all connection points wired straight through. So what, you say? Well, with a rack enclosure full, would you like to work inside the rear or be able to work with all the equipment from the front? That's what I thought. Now, consider Fig. 6.14.

Figure 6.14 shows a side view of the rack enclosure. Note that there is a 3Com USR Enterprise network HUB, two SMC network HUBs, and the Hubbell inline panel. Look closely at the area of the dotted-line rectangular box. This illustrates that any combination of connections can be achieved from the front of the enclosure. How? All equipment is connected into the rear of the inline panel. Actual physical configuration is then made via patch cables from the front. In this network a 48-port inline panel is used; however, Hubbell has larger panels as well.

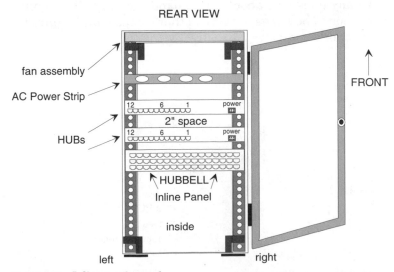

Figure 6.12 Inline patch panel.

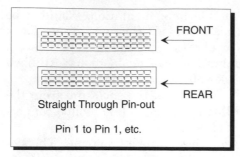

FRONT

REAR

Straight Through Pin-out

Pin 1 to Pin 1, etc.

Figure 6.13   HUBBELL inline panel.

This example of component and wiring design is what I mean by designing ease of use, flexibility, and expandability into the network from the outset. Go one step further with Fig. 6.14 and consider this: with a Fluke 685 LANMETER any cables can be tested *from the front of all equipment* with relative ease. The same is true for troubleshooting or monitoring upper-layer protocols. The Hewlett-Packard Internet Advisor can be easily connected to the inline panel to monitor network traffic and other operating parameters. To make life even better, Hubbell wiring is color-coded. During the installation of this equipment, colors, numbers, and labels were assigned to all ports, equipment, and other entry points to the network. There is no reason why a network design should not be documented completely from the very beginning. A well-designed network will be such that anyone who understands the technology would be able to perform any applicable work function.

If you have any questions about inline panels, wiring, fiber connections, surface mount housings, jacks, or other components required to design your network, contact:

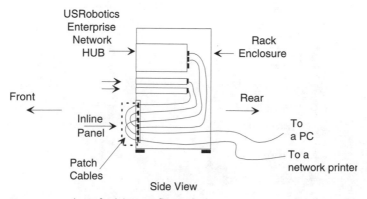

Figure 6.14   Actual wiring configuration.

Hubbell
Corporate Headquarters
14 Lord's Hill Road
Stonington, CN 06378
Phone: 800-626-0005
Internet: www.hubbell-premise.com
or www.hubbell-canada.com

Hubbell Ltd.
Ronald Close, Woburn Road
Industrial Estate
Kempston, Bedford, England
MK42 7SH
Phone: 44-1234-855444

Hubbell-Taian Co., Ltd.
12 Floor, 66, Sec. 2, Chien-Kuo
North Road
Taipei, Taiwan
Phone: 886-2-515-0855

Hubbell Canada, Inc.
870 Brock Road South
Pickering, Ontario, Canada L1W 1Z8
Phone: 905-839-1138

6.8 Power Protection

Power protection in any computing, network, or peripheral equipment is not optional. I have a standard reply when asked if such-and-such needs to be protected with power protection equipment: "If you can afford to throw away any or all of your equipment, replace it, and not be negatively impacted by downtime, then don't use power protection equipment." With that in mind, let us examine the power protection equipment used in this network.

Tripp Lite power protection equipment is used. A wide variety of both rack-mount and non-rack-mount equipment is used. It is easiest to list the equipment used, then address its functionality in the network.

- Isotel Premium surge suppressor with fax/modem protection
- Surge Alert plus tel
- Internet Series uninterruptible power supplies (UPS)
- BC Pro Series (UPS)
- Data Shield parallel dataline surge suppressors
- Data Shield 10base-T surge suppressors
- Data Shield dial-up line surge suppressors
- Data Shield AUI 802.3 surge suppressors
- Data Shield DB9 surge suppressors
- Data Shield DB-25 serial surge suppressors
- SmartPro rack-mount 1050 UPS
- LCR 2400 rack-mount line conditioner (also called a voltage regulator)
- IBAR 12 rack-mount surge suppressors

All power protection in this list is integrated into the network at the appropriate place. The rack-mount pieces appear as shown in Fig. 6.15.

The rack enclosure houses the 1050 UPS, voltage regulator, and two spike and line noise filters. Two spike and line noise filters were needed because of the number of low-amperage devices requiring AC power. Another voltage regulator is used, but not shown. It is external to the rack enclosure. A voltage regulator is used for the network printer.

The Data Shield protectors are used at all points in the network. These inline devices are used with serial, parallel, 10base-T, AUI, modem cable, and DB-9 connections. In addition, various electrical protection equipment also has telephone line spike and surge protection that is used to protect all incoming telephone lines. Figure 6.16 shows the protection design I used.

Figure 6.16 shows AC wall outlets, spike and surge protection, and then either a voltage regulator, a UPS, or another spike and surge protector. Next, other equipment connects to the second phase of power protection. This is two-stage power protection. I consider this the minimum acceptable level.

In addition to the equipment shown in the figures and explained, some of the remaining power protection equipment was used in the following way. Each IBM P70 monitor has a dedicated UPS connected to a dedicated line and noise supressor, and the latter is connected into an

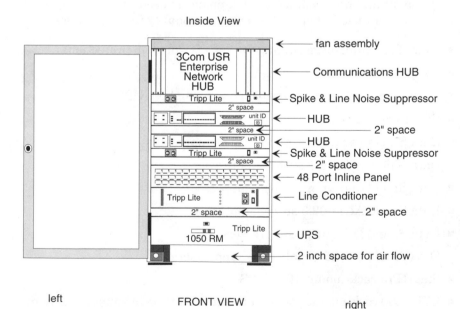

Figure 6.15 Equipment mounting.

isolated wall outlet. In this case the isolated wall outlets are concentrated into a particular circuit breaker. The notebook computers each have a dedicated UPS connected into a spike and surge protector when they use AC power.

Tripp Lite monitoring software provides administrators the ability to monitor and control power protection equipment in a remote location. One example of the power behind the monitoring software included with Tripp Lite power protection is the ability to log information events. The following is an excerpt from a log of the network where this equipment is used.

```
DATE        TIME    INFORMATION
06/21/97 - 14:45 - UPS monitoring started.
06/21/97 - 14:45 - Unable to communicate with UPS!
06/21/97 - 15:43 - UPS monitoring started.
06/21/97 - 15:43 - Unable to communicate with UPS!
06/21/97 - 15:47 - Unable to communicate with UPS!
06/21/97 - 15:50 - Communications reestablished with UPS.
06/21/97 - 15:50 - The UPS is operating on battery power.
06/21/97 - 15:50 - The utility power has been restored.
```

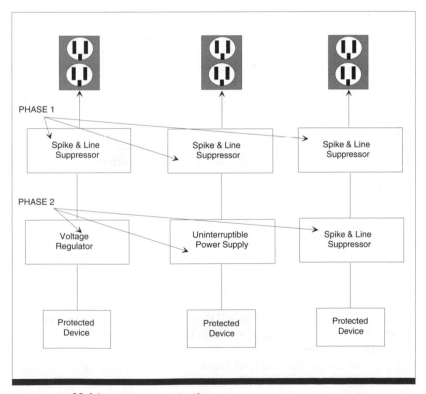

Figure 6.16 Multistage power protection.

```
06/21/97 - 15:50 - Self-test has passed.
06/21/97 - 15:58 - UPS monitoring terminated.
06/21/97 - 16:00 - UPS monitoring started.
06/21/97 - 16:28 - UPS monitoring started.
06/21/97 - 16:29 - UPS monitoring terminated.
06/21/97 - 16:35 - UPS monitoring started.
06/21/97 - 16:36 - UPS monitoring terminated.
06/22/97 - 20:33 - UPS monitoring started.
06/22/97 - 20:33 - Unable to communicate with UPS!
06/22/97 - 20:34 - UPS monitoring terminated.
06/22/97 - 21:04 - UPS monitoring started.
06/22/97 - 21:05 - Unable to communicate with UPS!
06/22/97 - 21:06 - Communications reestablished with UPS.
06/22/97 - 21:07 - Unable to communicate with UPS!
06/22/97 - 21:07 - Communications reestablished with UPS.
06/23/97 - 10:30 - UPS monitoring started.
06/23/97 - 10:31 - Unable to communicate with UPS!
06/23/97 - 10:31 - Communications reestablished with UPS.
06/23/97 - 20:10 - Unable to communicate with UPS!
06/23/97 - 20:29 - UPS monitoring terminated.
06/24/97 - 09:07 - UPS monitoring started.
06/24/97 - 09:07 - Unable to communicate with UPS!
06/24/97 - 09:13 - UPS monitoring terminated.
06/24/97 - 16:10 - UPS monitoring started.
06/24/97 - 16:10 - Unable to communicate with UPS!
06/24/97 - 16:36 - Communications reestablished with UPS.
```

This information was captured by the Tripp Lite software monitoring the Smart 1050 UPS. The software is capable of providing formatted data for print as well as file.

Tripp Lite has an entire line of power protection equipment that can be monitored by LAN equipment. For more information on Tripp Lite products, contact:

Tripp Lite
500 North Orleans
Chicago, IL 60610
Phone: (312) 755-5400
Internet: www.tripplite.com

6.9 Communication Equipment

A 3Com USR Enterprise network HUB was selected for use in this network. Datacommunication equipment is the single most critical link in any network. This is true because it is the central point of attachment between remote users and the backbone network, regardless of the size of the backbone or the location. It is also true if all users are in the same physical locaiton. Datacommunication equipment is central to networks—as they go, so goes the network. At one time, *remote computing* meant having a device in one location and a terminal attached to it by a wire. 3Com USR revolutionized that definition by designing the Enterprise network HUB. This device, explained in greater detail forthwith, is powerful.

Consider Fig. 6.17, which illustrates the network designed here in Dallas, and remote users and a remote network, both located in Chicago.

Note that remote users are connecting directly into the Dallas network via the communications HUB. In this case the remote users use their modems and connect directly to the HUB.

When remote users or remote networks are a concern, multiple issues must be considered during the design phase. The following issues, at minimum, must be reviewed during your plans:

- Security
- Reliability
- Maintenance
- Ease of use
- Internal protocol compatibility
- Expandability
- Internal design architecture
- Interface standard compatibility

Security has become the single most important topic in networking, regardless of the type of network or location. Networks can have a considerable degree of security built into their design if proper components are used that implement security. Where datacommunication equipment is concerned, having a device that can provide a security firewall is best (see Fig. 6.18).

Figure 6.18 shows a secure firewall implemented in the communications HUB. Remote users in this illustration are required to sign on to the HUB. It is a point of isolation. Other devices on the network require sign-ons and passwords, as well.

The 3Com USR communication HUB used in this network has three possible configurations regarding its function in the network. 3Com USR refers to these as *gateway application cards*. 3Com USR uses the following terminology and explanations:

- X.25 card
- NETServer card
- API card

According to 3Com USR, the *X.25 card* provides access capability to packet-switched networks. This card uses a EIA-232/V.35 interface connection point.

The *NETServer card* functions as either a router, a terminal server, or both. Ethernet and Token Ring NICs can be used with it. 3Com USR

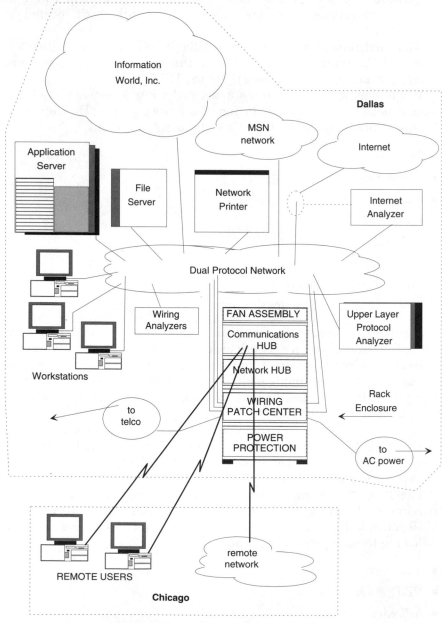

Figure 6.17 Architectural view of datacommunications gear.

refers to this card as the *EdgeServe card*. This card has Windows NT loaded onto it; more is explained later about the functionality this card provides.

Third, an *API card* can be used. This card is designed to let customers design their own applications by way of 3Com USR software development kits. Figure 6.19 illustrates the Enterprise HUB.

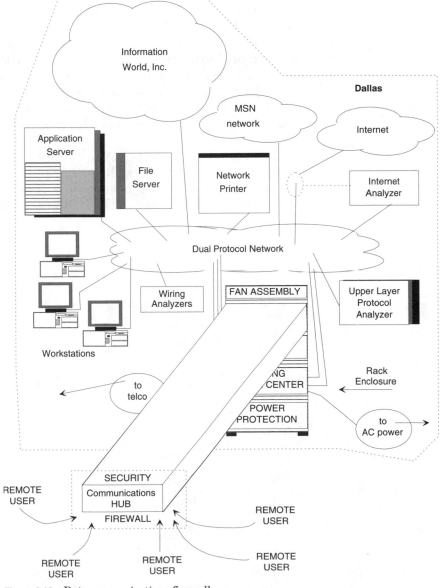

Figure 6.18   Datacommunications firewall.

Note that Fig. 6.19 shows the HUB with blank face panels. These panels can be removed and other cards inserted. A total of 17 slots exist. Slot 1 is the T1 card. Beginning with slot 2 are analog or digital quad modem cards. These cards have the equivalent of four modems on them. Slots 15 and 16 are the EdgeServer location. Slot 17 is where the network management card is located. The remaining slots house two power supplies. Though not shown in this illustration, the undercradle portion of the HUB houses approximately 16 fans to cool the components.

Reliability is another important factor for any communication equipment. The design of the 3Com USR HUB has reliability built into it. One example supports this observation: the HUB has two power supplies; however, only one is required to operate the unit. Redundancy is built in even to the level of the power supply unit.

Maintenance is another part of the equation for communication equipment. The HUB used in this network has remote management capability, local management capability, and easy access to those components that may need removal.

Any communication device requires skill to use. Most require fairly advanced levels of skill to maximize use. The capability of any communication device has little to do with its ease of use. *Ease of use* is a design issue. Ease of use is designed into the HUB used in this network. Ease

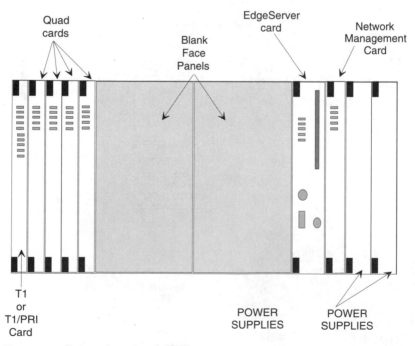

Figure 6.19   Enterprise network HUB.

of use can be measured in communication equipment by how thorough and detailed the documentation provided is, by accessibility to configure ports, and by the equipment's ability to be used in a partially failed state (should that occur). My rule of thumb is that the more complex functions a device offers, the simpler the documentation should be. The simple fact is that datacommunication equipment is complex enough without humans adding another layer of complexity to it.

Another factor to analyze with datacommunication equipment is the *protocol compatibility*. This includes evaluation of upper- and lower-layer protocols. Because this HUB has the EdgeServer card in it, Net-BEUI, TCP/IP, and IPX upper-layer protocols are supported. Token Ring and Ethernet lower-layer protocols are supported as well. An author's note regarding the 3Com USR HUB used in this network: use of Token Ring and Ethernet is more than sufficient, because these two protocols are the dominant lower-layer protocols used in networks today.

Expandability is very important with datacommunication equipment. The design of the 3Com USR Enterprise network HUB is such that any size network can be built around it. This is true because of how the equipment has been architected. With the 3Com USR equipment, it is possible to start a network with one or two Enterprise HUBs and then continue to add them until the racks are filled with them.

Internal design architecture is also very important in datacommunication equipment. The internal architecture of datacomm gear is the proverbial pivot upon which all communication transactions hinge. The internal communications bus and the incoming port architecture are the foundation of the device. These should be capable of handling a complete load on the device without causing hangs or system slowdowns.

Interface standard compatibility is another matter to examine when you are evaluating datacommunication equipment. In this network, the HUB has flexibility regarding how certain connections are made. In some instances, options exist to make a connection. This alone makes for ease of use, installation, and maintenance. It also means that some existing equipment at your site may be usable. That can save money.

6.10 Summary

This is the first chapter of two that present information about network design and the components used in the network I designed. It is important to do most of the work on markerboard or paper. Once this is done, one can begin to acquire equipment and build the network.

The next chapter continues to list and explain the components used in this network. All this equipment is integrated in such a way that the network yields benefits beyond the benefits of each single piece.

7

Network Design and Components, Part 2

The previous chapter begins explaining considerations and components regarding network design. This chapter concludes the presentation of that information.

7.1 Communication Equipment

The last section in the previous chapter begins to explain the role of communication equipment in networks. This section continues with that explanation and completes it.

The 3Com USR Enterprise network HUB has the EdgeServer card installed in it. This card has the following features:

- 1.44 floppy drive
- Mouse port
- Keyboard port
- Display port
- SCSI port
- Minimum 800-MB hard drive
- Minimum 100-MHz processor
- 10base-T capability

The EdgeServer card also has Microsoft Windows NT Server 4.0 installed on it. Conceptually, the card and some of its functionality appear as shown in Fig. 7.1.

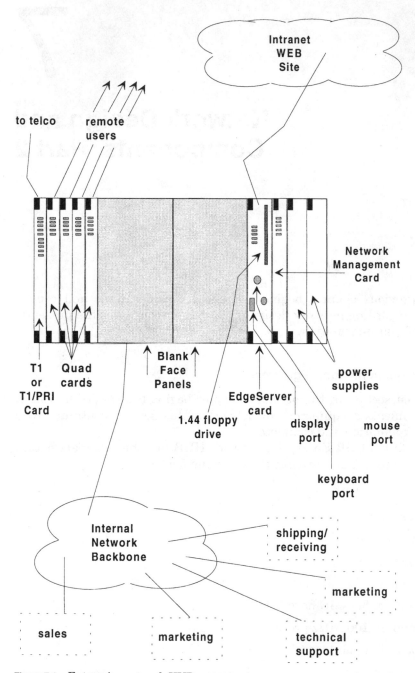

Figure 7.1 Enterprise network HUB components.

The advantages of having NT Server on the EdgeServer card are manyfold. First, when remote users access the communications HUB for information purposes only, they can be stopped there and not allowed to access other systems that are part of the network. Second, remote users who require access to other systems can use the Edge-Server as a *gateway,* if you will, to access the network behind it. The EdgeServer card can function as an excellent firewall to protect the assets behind it while permitting access to them.

Still another powerful feature of the EdgeServer card is the SCSI port it has located on the back. This feature makes it possible to connect a CD-ROM drive to it. Documentation is provided with the Enterprise network HUB, but it is also provided via CD, which makes it convenient to access when manuals are not easily accessible.

A network management card is also part of the HUB's component configuration. The card supports Ethernet and Token Ring as lower-layer protocols. It is a separate card, and it provides a console port that can be used for the following purposes:

1. *Remote access.* It can be dialed into from a remote site.

2. *Local access.* Management access locally with an RJ-45 and DB-25 cable with a null-modem adapter provided with the HUB.

3. *Software download.* Can be used to aid in the management aspect of the HUB.

The network management card supports 10base-T, 10base-5, and 10base-2 connection points for Ethernet cable flexibility. Token Ring cable support includes shielded twisted pair (also called *IBM type 1*) and unshielded twisted pair (also called *IBM type 3*).

The network management card does not run SNMP management agents directly on the card; however, the support for SNMP is not compromised. The network management card technically functions as a proxy agent, but the functionality and management ability with SNMP operation features the same support.

The Enterprise HUB used in this network has a T1 card. It operates as a primary rate interface (PRI). The T1 card is managed by what is called *Total Control Manager* (TCM). It is SMP-based and works with Windows. The card itself is easily configurable. A dumb terminal, remote PC, LAN PC, or direct connect PC can work with configuration management parameters. Its operands function within the SNMP MIB standards; both GET and SET operations can be issued against the T1 card.

The T1 front panel includes LEDs to indicate the operational status of the card. Those LEDs include the following:

ALARM: This LED is activated upon the occurrence of any of the following states: alarm indication signal, frame slip, out of frame condition, excessive CRC errors, change of frame alignment, line format violation, or frame alignment error.

CARRIER: This LED indicates whether a carrier is present; an unframed signal LED indicates an out of frame condition; indicates a loss of signal condition; and indicates if a signal is reported "not present."

LOOPBACK: This LED indicates that a test is in operation, initiated from the local telephone company.

RUN/FAIL: This LED indicates the operational mode of the T1 card; that is, whether it is operating in normal or in critical mode due to a hardware or software failure.

The Enterprise network HUB modems are either analog or digital. Figures 7.2 and 7.3 illustrate this.

Figure 7.2 shows the Enterprise network HUB with analog modems (Quad cards) connected to analog telephone lines. The gateway interface card in this illustration shows a generic connectivity to a network. The gateway connectivity portion of the Enterprise network HUB does

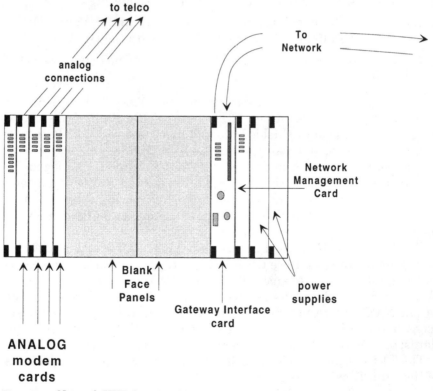

Figure 7.2   Network HUB functionality.

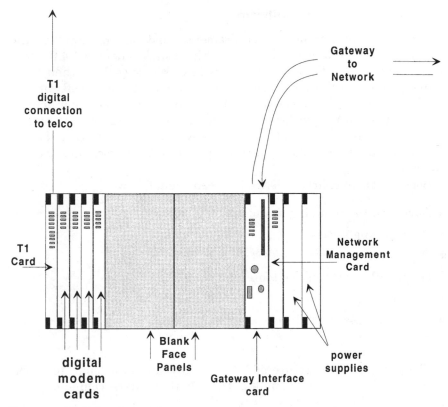

Figure 7.3   Digital modem cards.

not necessarily require Windows NT Server; however, this implementation is popular.

Figure 7.3 shows a different HUB implementation—a T1 link to the telephone company. It also shows the digital modems that users use after a signal is in the HUB. The gateway aspect of the HUB indicates that users can have access outbound to a network if such is configured. Technically, the network access that a remote user has is configurable for either analog or digital modem connectivity.

The Enterprise network HUB is but one of many products offered by 3Com USR. For additional information, contact them at:

3Com USR
Corporate Systems Division
8100 North McCormick Blvd.
Skokie, IL 60076
Internet: www.usr.com

7.2   Operating System Software

After a consideration of the requirements made on the network, the operating system software chosen was Microsoft Windows NT 4.0 Workstation and Server. Some workstations have Windows 95 as their operating system, but those are being upgraded to workstation software.

Windows NT version 4 could be the standard by which other operating systems are judged for some time to come. From appearances, it has the look-and-feel interface of Windows 95. This version of NT has robust features, and it is separated into the *NT Server* and the *NT Workstation*.

Some common characteristics between them follow:

- Advanced file-handling systems
- Backup capabilities
- C2 security
- Graphical user interface tools
- Network capabilities
- Remote access capabilities
- TCP/IP

The physical architecture of NT is its division into separate Workstation and Server components. Though they share commonalities, they operate independently of each other.

The NT Workstation is basically a standalone operating system. It does not require NT Server to operate (see Fig. 7.4).

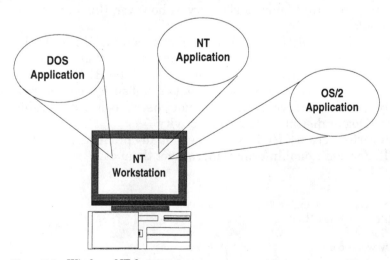

Figure 7.4   Windows NT features.

NT Workstation can function in different modes to support a variety of software applications. It comes with the networking component integrated into it, and it can easily be configured to operate in a networked environment.

NT Server software is capable of supporting a variety of workstations in a networked environment (see Fig. 7.5).

Figure 7.5 shows a hypothetical example of two segments of an intranet. In this example, each department can operate independently from the other. However, they are connected via a fiber connection. If required, workstations in segment 1 can access the NT Server in Segment 2 and vice versa. In addition, each NT workstation can operate independently of the others.

Generally speaking, NT is capable of supporting a significant amount of resources. For example, NT currently supports 4 GB of RAM per system. It also supports 2 GB of virtual memory and it can address up to 402 million terabytes (TB) of storage.

Windows NT architecture is considered modular because it contains multiple components (see Fig. 7.6).

Figure 7.6 shows four distinct components of NT. These four components include the following:

- Application Environment Subsystems
- Hardware Abstraction Layer (HAL)
- Kernel
- NT Executive Services

The *Application Environment Subsystem* is that part above the *WIN 32 Subsystem* as shown in Fig. 7.6. The WIN 32 Subsystem is the main subsystem for NT. It includes WIN 32-bit Application Program Interfaces (APIs). Beyond support for 32-bit programs, the WIN 32 Subsystem supports application programs for other operating environments as well.

NT Executive is the highest order of control within the operating system. In addition, the NT Kernel is part of the executive as well. The kernel basically dispatches and schedules threads used in the operating system. For those new to the terminology of *thread* as used in this context, the following definition is adequate: *thread* is an executable object that belongs to a process. An *object* can be something as concrete as a device port or application.

The *Hardware Abstraction Layer* (HAL) is a Dynamic Load Library (DLL) used between a system's hardware and the operating system software. The purpose of HAL is to keep NT from being concerned with I/O interrupts, thereby making NT easily portable. It is because of HAL that NT is considered portable between different types of operating

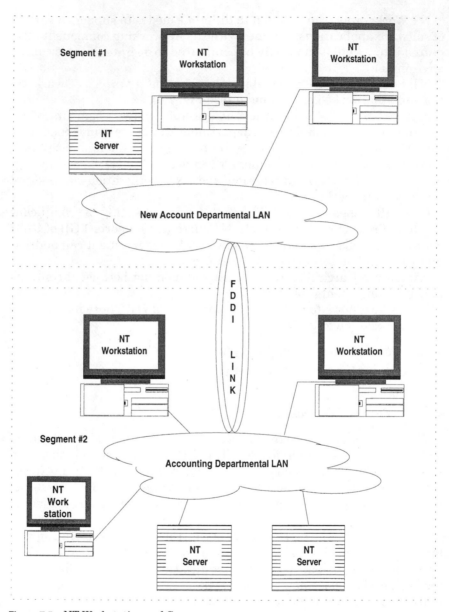

Figure 7.5 NT Workstation and Server.

systems. It also provides support for Symmetrical Multi-Processing
(SMP). The result is that NT can be used on Intel, MIPS, Alpha, and
other processors.

The *input/output* part of NT handles input and output processing.
The I/O manager coordinates all system I/O: drivers, installable file
systems, network directors, and caching memory management.

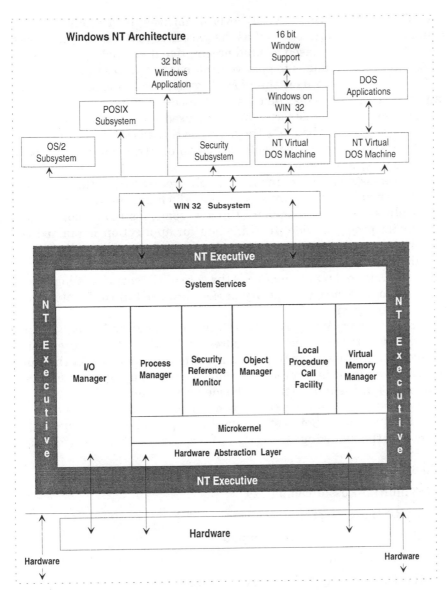

Figure 7.6 NT architecture.

The *Local Procedure Call* (LPC) functions as an interface between all clients and servers on an NT system. Functionality of LPC is similar to that of the Remote Program Call (RPC) facility. However, LPC and RPC are not equals because LPC permits exchange of information between two thread processes on a local machine.

The *microkernel* is part of the NT Executive. It operates in kernel mode. The microkernel runs in kernel mode and communicates with the NT Executive via very low-level primitives. In a crude way, one could think of the microkernel as the part that controls the entire system. Because NT is based around preemptive multitasking, it controls time slices and manages to pass control to other processes.

The NT Executive uses the *object manager* to manage objects. The object manager creates, deletes, and modifies objects. Objects are nothing more than abstract data types used as operating system resources. Objects can be ports (physical) or threads (logical). The object manager also works in the system to clean up stray objects that could exist if a program crashes.

The *process manager* is involved in all processes and threads. General consensus defines a *process* as that which has an identifiable virtual address space, one or more threads, some system resources, and executable program code. In NT, when an application is started the object manager is called to create a process, which sequentially creates an initial thread.

The *security reference monitor* is the core of NT security. A logon process and local security authority process are used in the implementation of security with NT.

Virtual Memory Manager (VMM) translates a system's process memory address into actual memory addresses. In short, it manages virtual memory. Virtual memory in personal computers operates on the same principles as in large computers. Some aspects may be augmented or enhanced, but the foundation of the idea is the same.

NT's modular design makes it robust. It has a great degree of hardware independence. Some of the hardware platforms NT can operate on include the following:

- X86 uniprocessor computers
- X86 multiprocessor computers
- AXP RISC architecture
- AXP RISC multiprocessor computers
- MIPS RISC architecture
- MIPS RISC multiprocessor architecture
- Motorola PowerPC

Another powerful aspect of NT is its use of *unicode* rather than ASCII for a character set. Unicode is based on 16 bits, meaning this character set can represent 65,536 characters. Hence, its unicode is more powerful than its ASCII counterpart, which uses 8 bits that yield only 256 characters. The inherent meaning of this is that multinational characters are supported, such as Japanese, Chinese, Russian, and Swedish, among others.

Windows NT is clearly delineated into two distinct parts. Both workstation and server use what are considered advanced file systems. NT supports the NT File System (NTFS) and the file allocation table (FAT). NTFS supports long file names, file-level compression, file data-forking support (required for Macintosh systems), international file-names, software-level sector support for fault tolerance, and file-level security permissions.

FAT support makes NT backwards-compatible with DOS. Floppy drives use FAT, and RISC systems using NT use FAT in the boot partition.

Both workstation and server support TCP/IP. NetBIOS is also supported, as defined in RFCs 1001 and 1002. This means logical naming at a session level is possible. The NetBIOS interface also supports Dynamic Data Exchange (DDE). DDE enables sharing data embedded within documents.

NT Workstation and Server also share a Dynamic Host Configuration Protocol (DHCP) client. This means an NT station can participate in an environment to obtain DNS addresses, IP addresses, gateway addresses, and netmasks.

NT provides support for SNMP. This makes workstations and servers capable of participating in environments that use management tools such as OpenView, SunNet Manager, and SystemView.

Both support Remote Access Service (RAS). In NT version 4, this is a point-to-point tunneling protocol. This function of NT enables a virtual network to be created over a wide distance. NT data encryption makes this part of NT popular.

Both workstation and server provide support for C2-level security. Protecting data on a system is achieved by Access Control Lists (ACLs). This enables directory- and file-level security maintenance.

NT Workstation and Server are administered in the same way. Some of the tools with which this is done include the following:

- DHCP manager
- Disk manager
- Event viewer
- Performance monitor
- RAS administrator
- Server manager
- User manager
- WINS manager

The *DHCP manager* is used to configure the station to obtain required information upon startup. In addition to the DHCP manager is the *DHCP server service;* this permits remote control of DHCP servers.

The *disk manager* is the tool with which disk partitions, mirrored disks, and volume set disk partitions are created.

The *event viewer* enables a user to view events on local and remote systems. Information such as the system log, security log, and application log can be obtained.

The *performance monitor* provides a method for real-time monitoring. The performance monitor also makes it possible to send administrative alerts to remote systems, monitor performance counters, and maintain performance logs.

The *Remote Access Service (RAS) administrator* is a configuration tool used to designate certain users privileged to gain access to a network node. RAS administrator can also be used to configure remote stations.

The *server manager* tool is used to create domain systems for workstations, standalone servers, and domain controllers. It is also used to determine the status of servers and users that are logged on.

The *user manager* enables the creation and management of user accounts. When used on a domain controller, interdomain trust relationships are set up by this tool. It is the tool used to set up user rights, systemwide passwords, and auditing functions.

The *Windows Internet Name Service (WINS) manager* is used to manage the WINS server service. This function of NT can be used to manage a local host or remote host. The basic purpose of WINS is dynamic name resolution.

NT security is probably the best of any operating system to date to show itself operable on a PC. More than one method can be used with NT security. One way to implement security in NT is with a logon and password; this is commonly referred to as *simple system access*. The next level, or way, of security implementation is through resource access security. This method of security implementation is a double-edged sword; that is, security can be tight, but then it is equally difficult to maintain. The next level, or way, of implementing security is by creating groups. For example, users in ABC group can access all files and programs in ABC group; on the other hand, they cannot access files or programs in, say, group DEF.

NT security is powerful and flexible. Once a site is set up with whatever security policy is in place, I recommend making records of the way it is set up and documenting changes as they are made to the system.

Domains are used with NT. Microsoft considers a *domain* as a secure workgroup with centralized maintenance. With a little thought it is easy to understand how this can become complex, if a site is large.

Within the *microsoft* domain, as some say, there are domain controllers. These are systems that maintain critical information to keep the domain operational—for example, information such as resources, security access privileges, passwords, logins, and other information. Many sites run the primary domain controller and the secondary or backup domain controller. A thought one needs to remember with NT and domains is that the primary domain controller is actually made at the time of installation and cannot be changed later. The reason for this is because the domain controller must be configured during installation. This means that on any given network only one primary domain controller can exist. Should two or more domain controllers *think* they are the primary controller, a contention scenario will ensue. That means that the domain controller with the most *trust* relationships on the network will win the contention, and thus will be considered the primary domain controller.

A *trust* relationship among domains simply means that two or more domains trust each other. This does not mean that in this relationship all users in one domain will inherently have automatic access to resources in the other domain. Further definition of access is required. In addition, the notion of a *global domain* is required for operation wherein multiple domains exist. One could think of this loosely as "the great global domain in the sky." The purpose behind it is to facilitate coordination of domains and of users within various domains.

Another concept to remember about domains is that trust relationships among them are one-way, not two-way. For example, user *A* in domain *A* may trust resource *B* in domain *B;* this does not, however, mean that resource *B* in domain *B* trusts user *A* in domain *A*.

The simplest way to think of trust and domains is with the following three examples. First, where a master domain has domains that have trust relationships with it. Second, where two domains have bidirectional trust relationships. This could loosely be called peer-to-peer. Third, a scenario where three or more domains have multiple trust relationships with more than one domain.

NT users have attributes associated with them; hence, another powerful characteristic of the operating system. The following list reflects the attributes generally associated with users:

- Account
- Password
- Application access
- Logon capabilities
- Home directory
- Group memberships
- Profile
- Rights

- RAS capabilities
- Policies

This information is used by administrators to customize a wide variety of user profiles. Some users may have much broader abilities than others due to their work requirements. This degree of information in user profiles enables great control over user access and provides system security.

These features, functions, and design characteristics of NT Workstation and Server contributed heavily to the decision to use it as a PC operating system.

7.3 Network Printer

An IBM printer was selected to be the network printer. The Model 17 was determined to be the best fit. The following features and functions factored into that reasoning during the decision process. Before examining all the features and functions of this printer, first consider this list of its *standard* features and functions:

- 17-page-per-minute output
- 600 × 600 resolution
- Up to 5 addressable input trays
- 4 MB RAM (up to 66 MB optional)
- PCL5e standard language (postscript, IPDS, and SCS optional)
- Auto language switching with options
- Auto I/O switching
- Standard parallel with two network interface slots

The following options were added to the printer to make it capable of meeting the needs of all users on the network:

- 75-envelope feeder
- Ethernet interface
- Token Ring interface
- 24 MB RAM
- Postscript language option level 2
- 500-sheet second paper tray
- Duplex unit
- 10-bin secured mailbox unit

This printer arrived on a pallet, weighing in at approximately 250 lb. The printer itself, unpacked, weighs 40.9 lb (18.6 kg). With all options installed, its dimensions are: 31 in high, 25 in deep, and 17 in wide; it weighs about 65 lb. (These are my approximate measurements, including space for rear cabling, and so forth.)

This printer was chosen because of its flexibility and power. Note that it supports IPDS and SCS character strings. This is valuable—should the network need a system that uses either of these character strings for printing, the printer itself is already capable of handling it.

Intelligent Printer Data Stream (IPDS) is used between an IBM host and a printer; generally this refers to a SNA environment. This data stream is used with an all-points addressable printer. IPDS can intermix text and graphics—both vector- and raster-based. An *SCS character string* is a protocol used with printers and certain terminals in the SNA environment. LU1 and LU6.2 can use this data stream. One unique aspect of this data stream is its lack of data flow control functions. The significance of the Model 17 printer chosen for this network should not be overlooked—when the need arises for a host running MVS and VTAM, the *current* printer can be used with it. Here again is another example of architecting success into the network.

Because the printer is on the network, all network users can take advantage of it. If a user who is off-site desires to work on the network from a remote location and print something to someone while keeping that document secure, it is possible to do so (see Fig. 7.7).

Figure 7.7 shows a remote user connecting via a switched line to the network. The *network* in this example is viewed as the equipment in the rack enclosure. However, the network includes all devices participating in it. This example shows the remote user working with a file on the NT Server. The NT Server then sends the file to the printer. The printer prints it and sends it to bin #3, where the owner of bin #3 must enter a code to receive the print.

Users on-site where the printer is installed have free access to it, with the exception of those who require secured access through the mailbox feature.

Author's note: The IBM Model 17 printer arrived on a pallet as described previously. From time of delivery until the printer was operational, 1 working day elapsed. I estimate it took about 2 hours to unpack the printer and read the material IBM recommends before beginning. Assembling the various components (assessories) for the printer was easy. IBM designed the printer so that minimal tools are needed to install it. More than likely you, like myself, will require longer to configure it and integrate the network workstations and servers than to do the actual printer setup.

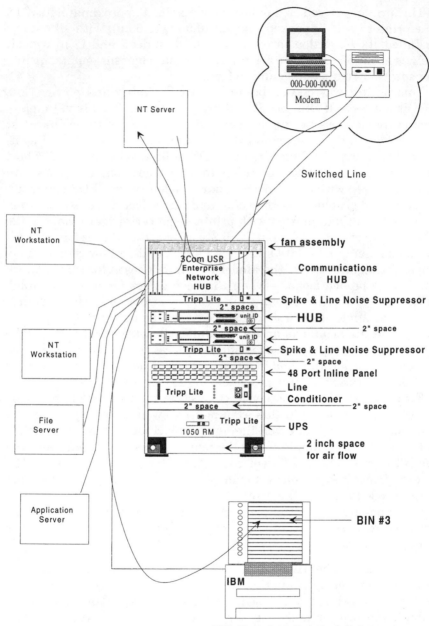

Figure 7.7   Remote user working on LAN and printing to another location.

IBM has a wealth of information that can assist in your network plans. You can reach IBM at:

Internet: www.ibm.com
International Business Machines
Department M7FE, Bldg. 003G
P.O. Box 1900
Boulder, CO 80301

7.4   Network Security

Computer and network security is probably the single most important issue today. I predict it will become three to five times as important as it is today. Viruses, bots, and all sorts of antidata objects exist within the Internet. Most people have no idea how vulnerable parts of the Internet are. Even service providers are more vulnerable than they will admit. The sad fact is that every company—yes, every company— that I know, of any size, has disinformation arsenals to make people feel secure. Management at the higher levels in most corporations operate in ignorance of these matters because it is legally safe and prudent for them to do so—ask and this statement will be denied, but remember where you read it. I point this out because I do not want you to be ignorant. There is no magic program or anything else that can make networks safe. Good programs exist—the ones chosen and implemented in this network are examples—however, no single program can make your network 100 percent immune.

Remember this during the design phase of your network: networks can have security designed into them from the outset. Security in your network needs to be factored into every area—electricity provision, telephone access, and every other aspect that categorizes your network.

A McAfee software suite was selected to meet the needs of this network. Part of the reason for this is the amount of antivirus programs and information included—and it works. The second reason for selecting McAfee was because of the frequency with which its antivirus software is updated. At present McAfee has over 250 highly technical documents available on viruses; likewise, McAfee claims to have information about the 1000 most common viruses. When the security analysis for this network was completed, the following software packages were selected for use in this network:

- VirusScan
- Desktop Security Suite
- Commuter

- QuickBackup
- McAfee Service Desk
- NetShield
- WEBScan
- PCCrypto

These products have been implemented to varying degrees on each system. Each program's benefits and highlights are presented here.

VirusScan

This program may well be the most popular antivirus software in the marketplace today. It operates with Windows 3.1 and 95, Windows NT 4.0, DOS, and OS/2. It is software that, once installed, operates automatically upon power-up. It can be used at will once a system is operational. This program requires minimal space but does a professional job. This program is NCSAA certified.

Desktop Security Suite

This program also operates with Windows 3.1, 95, and NT 4.0. This suite of programs includes antivirus software, backup capabilities, and encryption technology. The virus program is VirusScan. QuickBackup operates with ZIP, JAZ, the Internet, or rewritable CD-ROMs. The backup program enables hourly backup or on demand, whichever is best for you. The cryptographic part of the suite provides 160-bit encryption. This part of the suite enables users to encrypt files before they are sent over the Internet. The PC cryptographic part also permits network traffic to be encrypted between Windows-based computers and those running UNIX.

Commuter

Commuter is more than just communications software. It also includes virus protection, a desktop storage manager, electronic mail, a personal information organizer, a calendar, a to-do list, and a contact manager.

QuickBackup

This backup program works with Windows 95 and NT 4.0. It enables transparent backup of files to SCSI, ZIP, and JAZ drives. An icon-driven program makes for ease of use. The program installs quickly and works well. It provides encryption protection and Internet support.

Service Desk

The Service Desk product is powerful. It is actually multiple products in one box. It works with Windows 3.1, 95, and NT 4.0. The product lets customer support personnel have access to information about the customer and make a remote connection to a system reported with a problem. The package comes with the ability to distribute software. The package also includes a system diagnostic part for support personnel to use with customers.

NetShield

Netshield uses McAfee's proprietary code, called *Code Trace, Code Matrix,* and *Code Poly.* The product actually operates in an NT environment in native mode. The program takes full advantage of NT's server-client remote task distribution capability. The product supports real-time scanning while operations of other tasks run.

WEBScan

The WEBScan product is designed to detect viruses within a browser. It examines downloads and e-mail attachments, making it a powerful addition to any desktop or laptop system communicating in networks today. It also provides a cybersifter that blocks out unwanted websites and chatgroups. Coverage of the program includes examination of .doc, lzip., exe., zrc., arj., and other file types.

PCCrypto

PCCrypto is used to secure documents and other data files created by anyone using computers. It can encrypt graphics, spreadsheets, and text documents. It uses a 160-bit blowfish encryption mechanism. The package consumes a minimal amount of space and is one of the most powerful, if not the most powerful, tools of its kind on the market today.

Author's note: I recommend that you initially dedicate a system for testing software. Then I recommend installing McAfee VirusScan. Then scan each and every diskette you have, even new diskettes out of the box. That's right. It does not matter if it takes someone two months. Every diskette you receive from a manufacturer must be scanned. You say, "But Ed, isn't this going a little too far?" I'll say this. One year (I won't say when) I bought some software. It was new. It came from the original vendor in shrink-wrapped plastic. The shrink-wrapped diskettes were enclosed in a box with a seal on it. The box with a seal on it was shrink-wrapped. I didn't think a thing about it. Within 10 minutes after opening the software, it brought one of my systems to its knees. The diskette had a virus. How do I know? I checked it personally. How do I know the system it went into was clean? It was and is my benchmark system. Furthermore, those who know me know that nobody, not anyone, puts a disk in my systems except me. It took me two days to recover the system. Consider this the next time you stick a new program on diskette into your system. You can pay now or you can gamble, but remember—the odds are against you.

McAfee has other products that may meet your needs. I recommend you contact them. My experience with them has always been pleasant and their staff is very informative. They can be reached at:

Internet: www.mcafee.com

McAfee
2710 Walsh Avenue
Santa Clara, CA 95051
Phone: (408) 988-3832

McAfee Canada
178 Main Street
Unionville, Ontario
Canada L3R 2G9

McAfee France S. A.
50 rue de Londres
75008 Paris
France

McAfee (UK) Ltd.
Hayley House, London Road
Bracknell, Berkshire
GR12 2TH United Kingdom

McAfee Europe B. V.
Orlypein 81—Busitel 1
1043 DS Amsterdam
The Netherlands

McAfee Deutschland GmbH
Industriestrasse 1
D-82110 Germering
Germany

7.5 Multimedia Components

Creative Labs was chosen as the vendor for multimedia equipment. In the past, buying IBM compatibles, or clones, was not a problem. However, all things change. In the arena of multimedia, Creative Labs wrote the book on how to do it. Since multimedia is primarily add-on at this point in time, systems do not depend on multimedia like they do the hard disk or monitor, for example.

However, some multimedia clone products exist. Many of these products attempt to copy what Creative Labs has already designed. In the arena of multimedia, clones are the incorrect way to invest money. The operational nature of some multimedia software is such that multimedia clone equipment may not be able to execute all of the exploits of multimedia. This may sound strange, but it is true.

Today, systems typically have CD-ROMs, speakers, microphones, line outputs for amplifiers, line inputs for peripheral integration, and software that enables a user to create, play back, and listen to or see various data streams.

All the desktop systems in this network are IBM 350 series. I selected these because each one would be customized to deliver a robust workload. Another reason for choosing this series is the upgrade capability. So it is the same with Creative Labs equipment.

In each system, Creative Labs equipment is the multimedia hardware and software. One system has a package of multimedia equipment from Creative Labs. The system includes an interface board, speakers, necessary cabling, a microphone, CD-ROM, infrared remote control, software drivers, and various software titles for viewing and listening.

Creative Labs has designed the benchmark for multimedia systems. The significance of this should not be overlooked during the design phase of your network. Windows 95 and NT 4.0 acknowledges most, if not all, Creative Labs hardware and software. It is plug-and-play compatible. Another significant aspect of this equipment is its adaptability. Creative Labs is continually upgrading its equipment to stay in line with other vendors; however, it supports equipment and systems that are not this year's product.

Multimedia is more than a CD-ROM and speakers. Today multimedia typically encompasses a digital video disc (DVD) and enhanced display support. More than at any other time, displays need powerful drivers and memory to store the screen of information to be presented.

Creative Labs is based in California, but has offices around the world. I recommend contacting the one closest to you for additional information about multimedia.

Internet: www.soundblaster.com

Creative Labs
1901 McCarthy Blvd.
Milpitas, CA 95035

Creative Technology Ltd.
67 Ayer Rajah Crescent #03-18
Singapore 0513

Creative Labs Technical Support
1523 Cimarron Plaza
Stillwater, OK 74075

Creative Labs Ltd.
Blanchardstown Industrial Park
Blanchardstown
Dublin 15
Ireland

7.6   Network Analyzer

To design a network requires a certain type of skill, a marriage between the abstract and the practical, if you will. To keep a network operational at its peak is another thing altogether.

Obtaining information about an operational network is important. To be sure that the information is accurate is more important. It is important here to understand precisely what I mean. Examine Figure 7.8.

Figure 7.8 shows a conceptual view of network layers. At the lowest layer in the network is the *physical layer.* This layer is where the media connects to an interface board of some type. At this level you need a tester to check cables and verify they are in good working order.

At the *data link layer,* and below, data link–layer protocols operate. These include Ethernet, Token Ring, ATM, FDDI, Fast Ethernet, SDLC, SLIP, Frame Relay, ISDN, and others. At this layer, one needs an analyzer to analyze how the network is talking among nodes. In order to understand this, one needs to be fairly familar with the lower-layer protocol that operates in the network.

From the network layer up, upper-layer protocols operate. A sophisticated network analyzer is needed to accomplish this task. Network protocols at the upper layers include TCP/IP, Novell, APPN, SNA, DECnet, AppleTalk, and NetBIOS. You may think, well, Windows NT should be on the list. The fact is that Windows NT uses one of these protocols to achieve its task.

For this network the Hewlett-Packard Internet Advisor was selected. It can provide a single screen of real-time information about the network. Frame errors, events, and other vital statistics can be viewed through the Internet Advisor.

The Hewlett-Packard Internet Advisor used in this network includes Ethernet, Fast Ethernet, and Token Ring support. It provides a com-

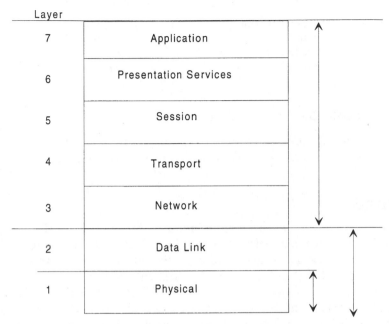

Figure 7.8　Conceptual view of network layers.

plete breakdown of the seven-layer protocol stack in the network. Results can be printed and/or saved to a file. A special feature of this device is its ability to select a single protocol and view it; even beyond this is its ability to select a single layer within a given protocol and view it.

One powerful aspect of the HP Internet Advisor is its ability to run in *promiscuous mode,* as I refer to it. It can literally tap into the network and provide a window into network operations, and users never know they are being watched. Of course, technical concerns are the only ones worth watching. The Internet Advisor itself is small but powerful. It has the ability to accommodate all the major interfaces today. The Internet Advisor supports V.35, RS-232, 10base-T, AUI, Token Ring, and other connectors.

The HP Internet Advisor comes from HP configured with the parts you need. The components that support Ethernet and Token Ring are combined, so this makes for easy operation in dual-protocol networks. A quick switch of undercradles makes operation in other network protocols easy. The device itself is very user-friendly.

I recommend your consideration of this particular device to maintain your network. The ease of use, documentation, and human support available make this device easy and fun to use. Contact Hewlett Packard at:

Hewlett-Packard Company
Colorado Communications Operation
5070 Centennial Boulevard
Colorado Springs, CO 80919-2497
Internet: www.hp.com/info/advisor
Phone: (800) 452-4844

7.7   Miscellaneous Devices and Tools

When you get into the design of your network you may realize what I did—that is, some things you will need have to be looked for extensively or created.

External CD-ROM

First, a need in this network existed for an external CD-ROM that could connect via SCSI connection to the 3Com USR HUB, the laptops, and the Hewlett-Packard Internet Advisor. Sometimes finding things to make the network run is like the proverbial witch-hunt.

I selected a Sony CD-ROM, model PRD-650. Whether this particular device will be available as you read this will be a different story. However, should this specific device not be available, I suppose some vendor will make a CD-ROM with SCSI connection available. This device works well. The technology is genuine Sony and Adaptec for the SCSI PCMCIA card. This device is a must-have for network installers and administrators.

Wire testers

Another device you will need is a cable tester. You need to be able to check AC cables, data cables of all sorts, RJ-45 wire, RJ-11 wire, RJ-11 wall connectors, and so forth. Do not assume that just because this-and-that is *new* it is *good*. I have seen perfectly new equipment come right out of a vendor's box bad. No equipment or any type of cable in this network was discovered to be bad, but that does not mean you should not test cables and connection points.

I selected Fluke meters to provide AC testing ability. This same equipment can be used to obtain amperage readings, test cable, and so on. I order two devices to specifically check cable—one for RJ-45 and the other for RJ-11 wire.

Breakout AC test cable

I make my own extension cords. Many ask why. If you saw them you would know why. Any single one of them could be used to supply voltage and current to multiple dryers, ovens, or other high-amperage devices. Electricity demands respect—you can give it or it will be taken.

Who knows if my breakout AC test wire is UL listed or not? They work. What I do is this: buy some 10-gauge SO-type wire—two conductors with ground. Connect a regular 110-V three-prong connector on one end. On the other end put one or two pairs of regular electrical outlets in a metal box with an enclosed top. Carefully, take about 6 to 8 in of outer sheath off the conductors. Three conductors should be exposed with insulation. Tape these ends where the cuts were made and presto! Now you can literally clamp an AMP probe on around the hot wire— without going into any danger areas—and get the amperage pull off the line. Am I recommending that you do this? Absolutely not. I'm telling you what I did and how I did it. This level of information assisted me in the design phase of the ground floor of the network. I had to go back and draw four clean lines to the breaker box to accommodate the new equipment.

Again, you better make it your business to know the electrical part of your network. If you do not have the education and background for this, then get somebody who does. You cannot afford to have this base uncovered.

7.8 Summary

This and the previous chapter cover just about all of the aspects of network design. Do not forget to factor in time for interacting with the companies you decide to do business with. If you have established relationships, that is all the better; if you have not, factor in additional time.

Remember: network design is similar to designing a house. Once the foundation is laid, things are in cement and are not easily moved. Do your homework. You should be able to work through the majority of your network on the markerboard or on paper first. If you do so, you may find it is a bit less expensive.

Network Architecture, Operation, and Maintenance

The previous two chapters explain considerations and components regarding network design. This chapter focuses upon the network architecture designed and implemented, and its operation and maintenance. First, this network's critical component is examined.

8.1 Communication Equipment

Chapters 6 and 7 begin to explain the role of communication equipment in networks. I cannot underscore enough how important the communication gear used in networks really is. If a single item were pinpointed as being the critical link in a network, it would be the communication gear.

The network designed and installed includes a 3Com USR Enterprise network HUB as the communication part of the network (see Fig. 8.1).

Figure 8.1 shows the fundamental architecture of the network designed. Consider the network backbone itself. Figure 8.1 shows a dual-protocol network. In this case Ethernet and Token Ring are used. This provides scalability to grow because support for both lower-layer protocols provides a path whereby the network, could one day be split into two different backbones (see Fig. 8.2).

Note that Fig. 8.2 shows a dual-backbone network. It also shows devices such as file and application servers being *multihomed;* that is, they are connected to both networks for equal access. This scenario provides growth ability and load balancing. This may not seem important in the initial phase of your network, but load balancing will become important down the road. This scenario provides flexibility to mix and

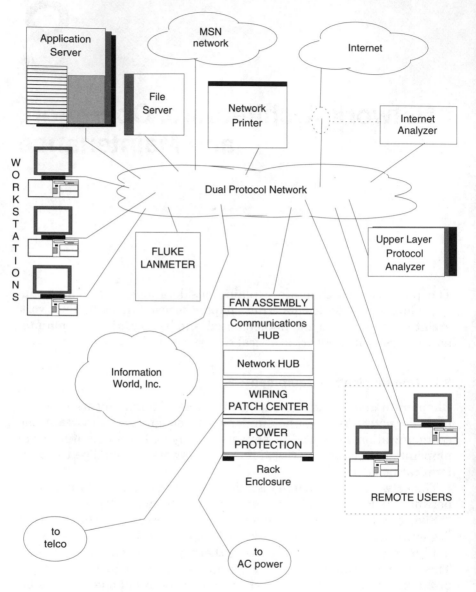

Figure 8.1 Network implementation.

match equipment for the best performance of equipment and user demand.

Another ability this network architecture provides is *scalability,* in that additional equipment can be added with relative ease (see Fig. 8.3).

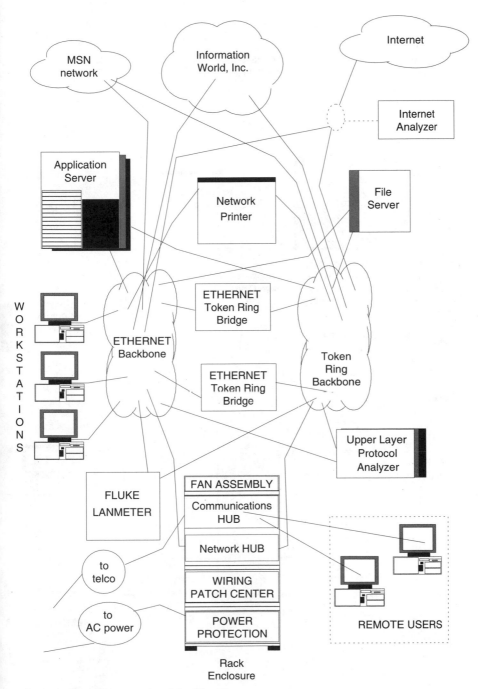

Figure 8.2 Contingency network backbone.

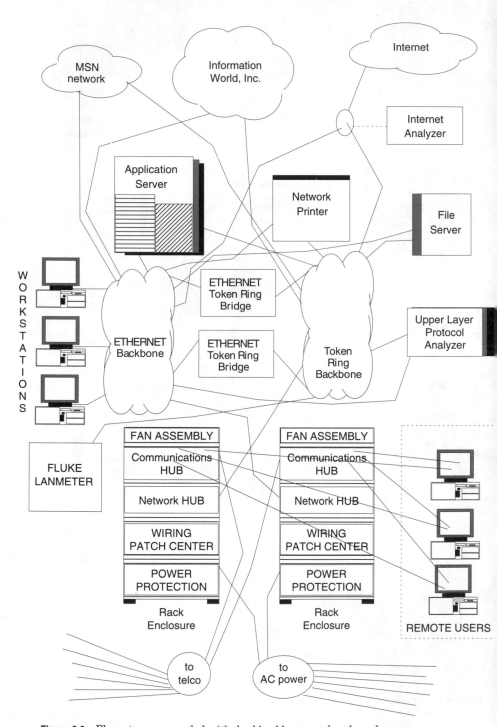

Figure 8.3 Phase two—expanded with dual backbones and rack enclosures.

Figure 8.3 shows dual backbones and dual rack-mount enclosures. This provides increased load balancing for scalability. This idea, conveyed in Figs. 8.2 and 8.3, can be augmented so that growth can continue.

At the heart of this architecture is the communication equipment. Figure 8.4 shows a highlighted view of the communication equipment in light of the overall basic network architecture.

Figure 8.4 shows the 3Com USR HUB highlighted. Multiple remote users are connecting to the network via this HUB. Figure 8.5 shows a closeup view of the HUB's components.

The Enterprise network HUB has the EdgeServer card installed in it. This card has the following features:

- 1.44 floppy drive
- Mouse port
- Keyboard port
- Display port
- SCSI port
- Minimum 800-MB hard drive
- Minimum 100-MHz processor
- 10base-T capability

The EdgeServer card also has Microsoft Windows NT Server 4.0 installed on it. Conceptually, the card and some of its functionality appear as shown in Fig. 8.6. This device can be expanded to accommodate additional incoming lines or T1 direct input via a PRI interface.

8.2   Network Architecture Design and Implementation

The network designed was done so based on the following premises. These are not in any particular order. They are the result of synthesized thought over a period of time during the initial network design—while the design characteristics were being written on a markerboard.

- Scalability
- Reliability
- Availability
- Maintenance

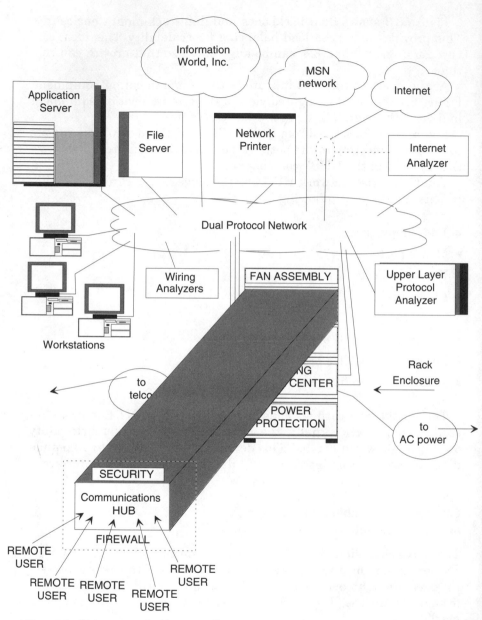

Figure 8.4   Datacommunication operation.

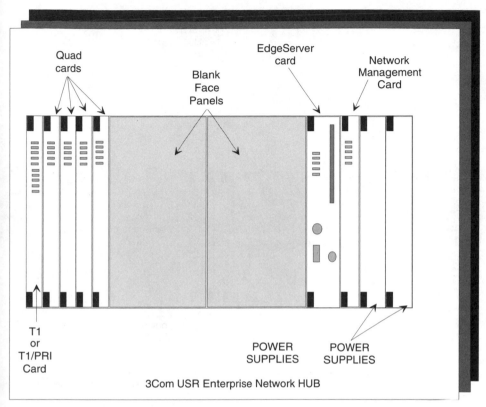

Figure 8.5   Enterprise network HUB.

Scalability

Scalability was one of the first characteristics determined to be needed by the network. Scalability is a singular characteristic that is difficult to change once a network foundation is laid. This involves more than merely adding another PC or printer; it cuts deep into the network architecture itself.

The notion of network scalability includes all aspects of the network (see Fig. 8.7).

The idea behind Fig. 8.7 is the ability to grow all aspects of the network as the need arises. This example shows how continual expansion is possible with even the most fundamental components. With the core components in place, the overall network size can continue to grow to whatever size the need presents.

Reliability

Reliability is another characteristic built into the network. At a fundamental level, AC power is required for all components (see Fig. 8.8).

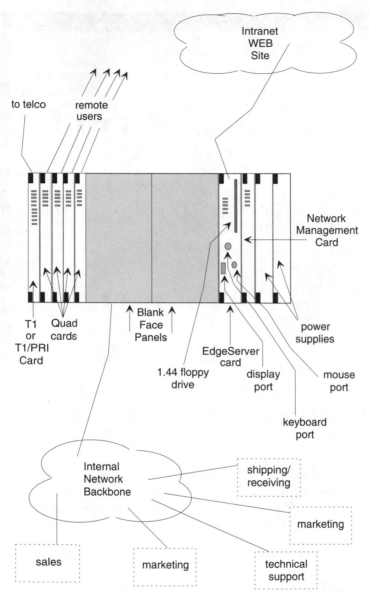

Figure 8.6 Conceptual view of the HUB's function.

In Fig. 8.8, devices are connected to a voltage regulator and it is connected to a Tripp Lite spike and surge protector. This level of protection makes the reliability of devices greater. When power surges or spikes occur they may not destroy a piece of equipment, but they do weaken the equipment on the receiving end. In essence, when spikes, surges, or

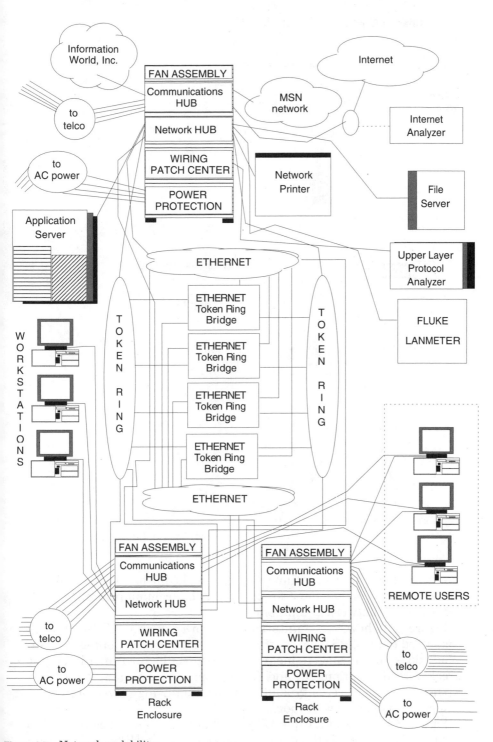

Figure 8.7 Network scalability.

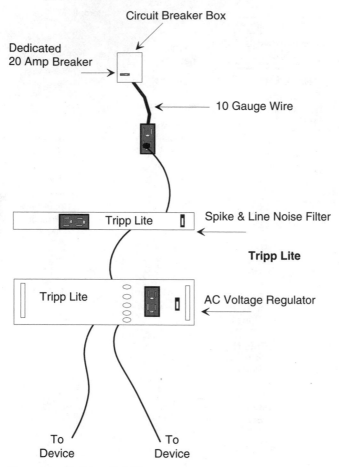

Figure 8.8 Design reliability.

overvoltage conditions continue, it shortens the life of some equipment. Voltage regulation is a must for computer, datacommunication, and all other sorts of network equipment.

Figure 8.9 shows an uninterruptible power supply (UPS). Devices connected to the UPS have continued power when power outages occur. What does this mean? It means that one could turn off the circuit breaker to the equipment, and the equipment connected to the UPS would not know it. This type of configuration using power protection equipment is money well spent.

Figure 8.10 shows multiple UPSs and multiple devices connected to them. In this case, all the devices connected to the UPSs will operate

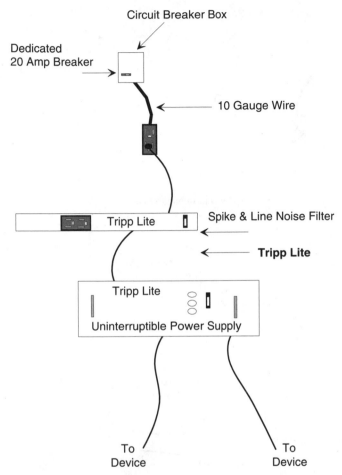

Figure 8.9 Two-stage power protection.

during a power outage. This alone is important enough for many companies so that operations can be sustained.

Availability

Availability is a characteristic of the network that was determined to be critical for network operation during the initial planning phases. Availability touches on the aspect of the power consumption of network devices, but it goes beyond that. For example, consider the SMC HUBs used in this network and the Hubbell inline wiring panel (see Fig. 8.11).

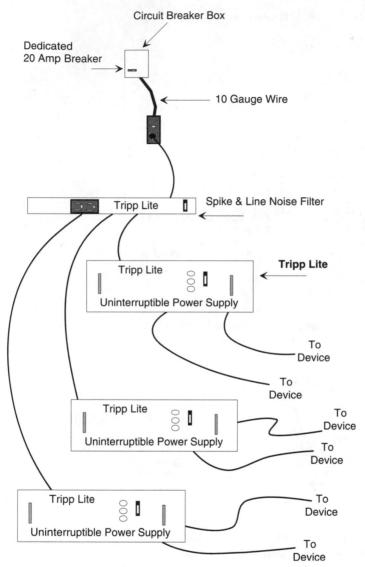

Figure 8.10 Two-stage power protection for multiple devices.

Figure 8.11 shows a front view of two network HUBs used in this network. The connectors on the front are used for stacking HUBs together; hence, planned and implemented appropriately, there can be a level of redundancy and expandability. Figure 8.12 shows the rear view of the HUBs, where network devices literally connect.

Figure 8.13 shows the inline panel and HUBs from the rear. The HUBs connect to the rear of the inline panel. Hence, from the front of HUB 1, port 1 can be switched by jumper cable to port 2, or any other

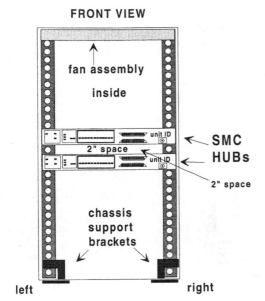

FRONT VIEW

Figure 8.11 Easy access design.

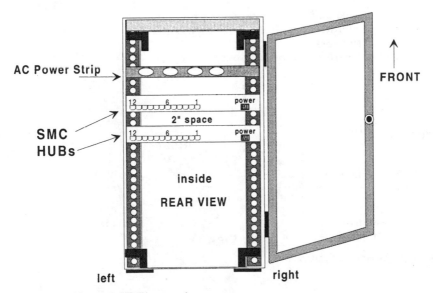

Figure 8.12 Network HUB's rear view.

viable port. Many other configurations of HUB ports and network devices are possible, because of the power the inline panel provides to the network administrator. Consider Fig. 8.14.

Figure 8.14 shows a side view of the rack enclosure. Note the flexibility provided by the inline panel. Network devices connect to it, as do the

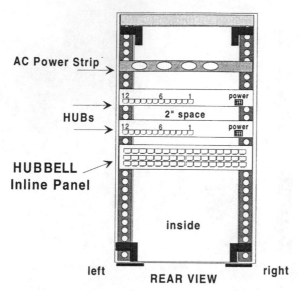

Figure 8.13 Patch panel connection.

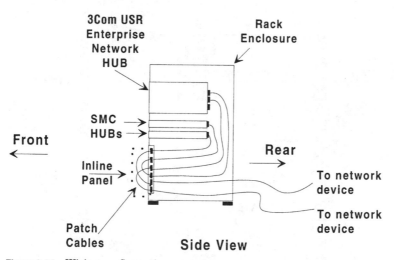

Figure 8.14 Wiring configuration.

network HUB and other devices, such as the communications server, which is in this case the 3Com USR HUB. The fundamental architectural design principle I used to create this scenario is as follows:

$$X = Y$$

$$Y = Z$$

Therefore,

$$X = Z$$

The formula is a hypothetical syllogism used in symbolic logic. It works quite well because, implemented as shown in Fig. 8.14, the SMC HUBs and 3Com USR communcation server are X; the inline panel is Y; and the network devices are Z. The hypothetical syllogism operates because of the distributed middle, Y.

Consequently, the degree of flexibility obtained is part of the maximum availability the design provided here offers. Availability is by way of front panel access, side panel access, and rear panel access. Availability is also manifest in that the inline panel provides a common point for hot swaps or quick changes. Redundancy can also be achieved through use of the inline panel.

Maintenance

Maintenance is also a consideration in any network. The easiest networks to maintain are those where maintenance was thought of during the design phase. Maintenance was planned for by including the following equipment:

- Fluke ScopeMeter
- Fluke 41B Power Analyzer
- Fluke LANMETER
- Hewlett-Packard Internet Advisor
- Tripp Lite power analysis software
- Cable testers

Figure 8.15 shows some readings obtained from the Fluke Power Analyzer. Figure 8.16 shows another reading obtained while a network printer drum was activated, thus drawing current as shown.

Figure 8.16 is an important example of the level of detail needed at different points for network evaluation and maintenance. It is necessary to know what the current levels are at different times in the life of the network. It is critical that this be known to the appropriate people when any network changes are made.

The following is information obtained from the Hewlett Packard Internet Advisor about the network. It is a simple snapshot of the network at a given point in time. However, the Internet Advisor can perform a complete seven-layer protocol analysis and an incredible number of other specific tests.

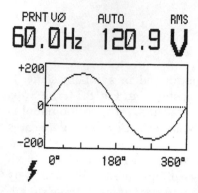

Figure 8.15 AC power waveform.

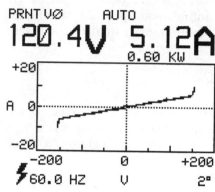

Figure 8.16 Laser printer power consumption.

	Protocol	DLL	Frames	Bytes	Errors	Ave Length
Jul 8 97	Netware IPX	E0	4558	39	30	9
Jul 8 97	IP DOD	0800	4498	13	0	10
Jul 8 97	Novell IPX	8137	650	10	0	13
Jul 8 97	NetBIOS	F0	1167	7	1	6

Note the date, upper-layer protocol type, DLL or SAP identifier, number of frames, number of bytes, the DLL errors that have occurred, and the average length.

The Internet Analyzer also provided the following details as a snapshot of the network at this given point in time.

"Ethernet Expert Analyzer"

Date	Time	Pro	#B/ sec	#/ stations	Warn- ings	Alerts	Utiliza- tion	Health	#F/ Missed
Jul 8 97	10:34	Network Total	0	5	0	0	" "	" "	0
Jul 8 97	10:34	IP	0	0	0	0			
Jul 8 97	10:34	Novell	0	1	0	0			
Jul 8 97	10:34	Other Protocols	0	2	" "	" "			
Jul 8 97	10:34	MAC Level	0	2	0	0			

This information is critical to network troubleshooters. It is important to plan during the design phase which devices will be used, where they will access the network, and how they will access the network.

Tripp Lite power protection equipment is used in this network. However, one of the reasons Tripp Lite was chosen as the power protection provider during the planning phase was due to the ability it has in providing software to monitor the network—even from a remote location. Consider the following information about a UPS from the software included with the equipment.

```
DATE        TIME      INFORMATION
06/21/97 -  14:45  -  UPS monitoring started.
06/21/97 -  14:45  -  Unable to communicate with UPS!
06/21/97 -  15:43  -  UPS monitoring started.
06/21/97 -  15:43  -  Unable to communicate with UPS!
06/21/97 -  15:47  -  Unable to communicate with UPS!
06/21/97 -  15:50  -  Communications reestablished with UPS.
06/21/97 -  15:50  -  The UPS is operating on battery power.
06/21/97 -  15:50  -  The utility power has been restored.
06/21/97 -  15:50  -  Self-test has passed.
06/21/97 -  15:58  -  UPS monitoring terminated.
06/21/97 -  16:00  -  UPS monitoring started.
06/21/97 -  16:28  -  UPS monitoring started.
06/21/97 -  16:29  -  UPS monitoring terminated.
06/21/97 -  16:35  -  UPS monitoring started.
06/21/97 -  16:36  -  UPS monitoring terminated.
06/22/97 -  20:33  -  UPS monitoring started.
06/22/97 -  20:33  -  Unable to communicate with UPS!
06/22/97 -  20:34  -  UPS monitoring terminated.
06/22/97 -  21:04  -  UPS monitoring started.
06/22/97 -  21:05  -  Unable to communicate with UPS!
06/22/97 -  21:06  -  Communications reestablished with UPS.
06/22/97 -  21:07  -  Unable to communicate with UPS!
06/22/97 -  21:07  -  Communications reestablished with UPS.
06/23/97 -  10:30  -  UPS monitoring started.
06/23/97 -  10:31  -  Unable to communicate with UPS!
06/23/97 -  10:31  -  Communications reestablished with UPS.
06/23/97 -  20:10  -  Unable to communicate with UPS!
06/23/97 -  20:29  -  UPS monitoring terminated.
06/24/97 -  09:07  -  UPS monitoring started.
06/24/97 -  09:07  -  Unable to communicate with UPS!
06/24/97 -  09:13  -  UPS monitoring terminated.
06/24/97 -  16:10  -  UPS monitoring started.
06/24/97 -  16:10  -  Unable to communicate with UPS!
06/24/97 -  16:36  -  Communications reestablished with UPS.
```

This information was captured by the Tripp Lite software monitoring the Smart 1050 UPS. The software is capable of providing formatted data for print as well as file. This level of information, as well as more in-depth information, is critical to the maintenance of power protection equipment.

Various cable testers are needed for network maintenance as well. You should have a policy that no cable be used without first being tested. A complete set of cable testing equipment should be obtained. This includes fiberoptic testing equipment if fiber cabling is used.

Other considerations should be included during the markerboard phase of network design. These include training, how the network will be documented, how the network equipment will be inventoried, who is responsible for what, and other applicable topics.

One last item, but *I consider this to be critical to network maintenance:* list and identify the 10 worst-case scenarios for your network (or parts of it) and provide written, detailed responses as to how, who, when, and where these contingency plans will be employed. If you don't do this, don't say I didn't tell you. I have seen companies literally so concerned with network security at an application level that they were totally oblivious to the fact that one could bring down an entire country's network operations with a $59.99 bolt cutter by cutting the telephone cabling on the side of a building. This is to be ignorant and not know it! Please, please look for the obvious and plan for the worst.

8.3   Network Operation

Network operation is very important. If it doesn't work, you have a problem. The network operation, or how it operates, should be written out on paper or markerboard long before you ever get to the point of implementing equipment.

I suggest building your network plans around the following questions:

- How does printing occur?
- Where does printing occur?
- Is printing secure?
- How many users will use the communications server?
- How many users will use the network simultaneously?
- What time of day/night does peak usage occur?
- When can software upgrades be performed?
- How do software upgrades happen?
- Are the operating systems compatible?
- When, where, how, and who will run network analysis?

- How many hours can the network run without power?
- Is the operational load inside the facility where the majority of the equipment is located, or is it in a remote location, thus requiring communication HUB usage, and so on?
- Are file transfers performed; how are they performed?
- Is remote printing possible?
- Is the communication equipment secure?
- How many security break points are there?
- When does the security program override users?
- When, how, where, and how often are security procedures changed? By whom?
- Do the file servers have RAID ability?
- Where is the single or close-to-single point of failure in the network?
- Does the network equipment operate so that no EMI, RF, or other distubances occur with the equipment?
- How well does the network operate without air conditioning?

You may be able to add to or subtract from this list to better fit your network. The operation of this network includes the following capabilities:

- Complete hot AC power backup (UPSs)
- Redundant telephone circuits through different telephone junction circuits throughout the city and cellular hot switch
- Remote access
- File sharing
- Printer sharing
- Application sharing
- Private e-mail
- Secure network printing
- Remote network printing
- Remote power monitoring
- Dual-protocol network backbone
- Real-time network traffic monitoring
- Real-time AC power monitoring
- Real-time remote user login monitoring

- Multimedia support
- Cryptographic application control on each system
- Intranet WEB
- 3270 WEB server access

8.4   Your Network and the Y2K Problem

Please don't tell me you aren't aware of the Year 2000 (Y2K) problem! Unfortunately, many are not as aware of it as they think. The problem is complex. As of this writing, most—as in over 80 percent, by conservative estimate—of all those I hear addressing this problem do so from a single mind-set; that is, it is mostly an application software problem. Other fallacies people maintain about the Y2K problem include the following:

- It (generally speaking) can be fixed.
- It is a software (application-oriented) problem.
- The impact of the problem won't be large.
- It won't affect my life.
- Enough technically oriented companies have the talent to fix these problems.

The single biggest illusion people have about Y2K is that they understand it. The size of the problem is so large that I cannot begin to say I completely understand it. The Y2K problem is most often discussed in such broad generalities that it amazes me. I have often thought, "How can such technical people be so obtuse?" The technology they are attempting to explain and fix is multifaceted and detailed to an incredible degree of precision. What do I mean?

Well, first of all, the Y2K problem is not just an application problem. Yes, the Y2K problem is going to affect many applications written in programming languages that are date-dependent and that have not been changed to accommodate the turn of the century. How big is this? Well, in my opinion, it is so big that it gets most of the attention, if not all of it. This problem is like a burning house. Many look on from the street and say the house is burning. This is true. Then someone comes along and says the living room is on fire, and this is true. Then someone starts explaining what is burning in the living room and the consequences of not having a couch to sit on. This is all good and fine, except I have a question: why doesn't anyone notice that the entire house is one fire? That means the living room is burning, the kitchen, the dining room, all the bathrooms, the garage, the attic, the den, the closets, and everything that is part of the house. Now, let me transfer the analogy to the technical arena.

In the world of computing and networking, more exists than simple applications. Applications are written to operating systems; these, in turn, are written to firmware and hardware. The hardware is controlled by programmed chips and firmware instructions. Suffice it to say that every part of a computer, network, and anything that uses a programmed instruction is suspect. This may blow you off your chair. Well, it is true. Consider Fig. 8.17.

You may know this model well enough to teach it. If you do, then you should be able to teach this. At every layer in the network a computer and/or network component can be identified. These are not merely abstract layers in some drawing. For example, applications appear at layer 7. Routers operate at layer 3 and below. Repeaters work at layer 1. Presentation of how data is formatted appears at layer 6. The point is that all layers in a given computer, network, LAN, WAN, telephone system, or any other technological device are susceptible to the Y2K problem.

Is it possible to fix all the layers in any given network by working on just one? Absolutely not. One can do all one can to fix a problem at layer 7, but if the layers below it are not examined to see if a potential problem exists there, then what value is it to fix layer 7's problem? See my point?

So, the Y2K problem has really already happened; it simply has not manifested itself into the reality that we have experienced. It is com-

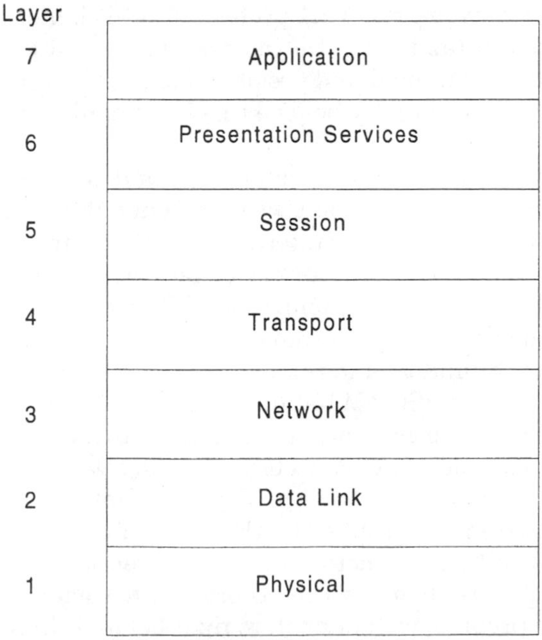

Layer

7	Application
6	Presentation Services
5	Session
4	Transport
3	Network
2	Data Link
1	Physical

Figure 8.17 Network layers.

ing. It is nonnegotiable. It is impossible to believe that the Y2K problems can be fixed before that date because of its breadth and magnitude. The reality of the matter is that from now on it is a matter of damage control. How much damage will be done? Nobody knows yet.

Many speculators, from *Newsweek* to *BusinessWeek* and *PC week* to *I-am-weak,* speak about the problem. Ironically, the best presentations I have heard on the problem come from people who are primarily not technically oriented, but who have enough understanding to ask questions. If you think I am saying this to add pages to the book, hang around—your life is going to be affected.

I have had many dismiss what I say, laugh at it, not believe it, discount it, and even attempt to argue with it. However, the greater the mind I encounter, the less resistance I receive about this. So what can you do? That is a very good question. First, be aware that you may not be able to do anything that will significantly change your environment.

In the world of networking just about everything is one big API, so to speak. The entire heart and soul of networking is built around a hypothetical syllogism—the one I have presented previously. Consequently, remove one piece of it, and, like dominos, things start to fall.

Am I trying to scare you? No. Why would I want to do that? What would be my motive? My own ignorance? Let me address the problem from another end of the spectrum.

Assume it is possible to gather all the technical talent this world has to offer (and it is not). Now assume it is possible to coordinate all of this talent into a single force to work on the Y2K problem (and it is not). Now assume money is no object (and it is). Do you really think all the technology in the world can be examined and possibly fixed by the year 2000? Be real for a moment. Do you really believe this is humanly possible?

What if you make your entire company's computers and network Y2K-proof? Assume you do. Your interaction with the outside world will hit you from all sides. What about your interaction with the Internet? What about your interaction with online service providers? What about your interaction with the telephone companies? What about the facility you work in? Do you control the internal operation of the environmental controls (air, heat, humidity, and temperature)? Do you control the water coming into your facility? What do you control? See my point? You may say, "Well, Ed, the entire world is not coming to an end." No, it is not—yet—but the pain of the Y2K problem is going to be felt far, deep, and wide. That you can count on. Actually, I am optimistic. Once the world has had its attention grabbed by the scope of the problem, maybe some programs and infrastructures will be better off.

Another fact about the Y2K problem is this: there are not enough people who understand the problem well enough to fix it before it happens. For example, there is a county in this nation that is prepared. They did their homework, worked out the bugs and have solutions and preemptive plans. Unfortunately, or fortunately, not all the counties in this nation sing the same song—let alone sing in the same key. The way your county manages data in a given arena is most likely not the way a county, say, halfway across the United States manages it. You mean there are no standards enforced on data management? That is exactly what I am saying. Let me be blunt: there is very little standardization when it comes to networking, computing, and other areas. Technology itself has exploded in the past 30 years; not even companies like IBM, DEC, and others can control it. A perfect example of this is the Internet. Who controls it? Nobody. So, you tell me: is the Internet going to be affected by the Y2K problem? If so, to what degree? I would be happy to hear your opinion—remember, everybody has one.

Recently, a friend of mine said, "Well, Ed, what is going to happen to your systems?" This friend was attempting to catch me in the proverbial corner. I responded, "I have no idea." I don't with some of them, because I simply use a word processor and drawing package—neither of which are date-dependent! This caught him off guard. I told him to give me enough money and some months' time, and I would let him know. However, the network designed with the equipment mentioned in this book has been Y2K-proofed.

When is the magic date and hour? Well, my opinion is this: probably a window of time from one or two months prior to the end of 1999 to the first one or two months of 2000 is going to be the most painful. The reason for this is simple: there is no master clock. The Y2K will ring in around the world, at different times, presenting different problems at every turn. What could be affected? Anything with a computer chip that relies on dates. Are you ready to head for the farm?

I would be suspicious of anyone who denies this. However, I have met people who will argue that water is not wet. What will happen to your VCR come the first day of the year 2000? Will your clock show 2000 or 00? That's what I thought—you don't know! I was born in 1958. I wonder if, according to the U.S. Social Security computer, I will be 58? See, if the program is programmed to read only the last two digits, I will be 58 years old. This could be true because such a program would reflect time from a reference point of 0000. This makes life somewhat more interesting.

In all seriousness, the Y2K problem is real and, generally speaking, cannot be fixed before the turn of the millennium. I do not believe the world is going to end, but I do believe the pain of modern technology will be felt as it has not been felt before. In all seriousness, the question remains: will enough deep technical people care enough to want to take jobs to fix Y2K problems worldwide?

8.5   Network Maintenance

Planning for network maintenance is no accident. There are simply two ways to maintain a network—proactively or de facto—and the latter is painful. During the early stages of planning this network I determined that the following equipment would be used to monitor the network and therefore contribute to its maintenance.

- Hewlett-Packard Internet Advisor
- Fluke 123 ScopeMeter
- Fluke 41B Power Analyzer
- Custom-built AC cable testing equipment
- Cable testers
     RJ-45
     RJ-11
     Token ring
     AUI
     BNC
- Tripp Lite Power Protection software analyzer
- Microsoft's NT Administration software
- Fluke temperature sensors
- Fluke LANMETER for local HUB maintenance

Much of this equipment has already been presented in explanation.

Another part of network maintenance that is not optional is education. Since you are reading this book, you probably agree. However, since education is not optional, you can elect to do it or it will happen to you by default—and then you can only hope it ain't your fault!

Maintenance includes system backups. As presented in earlier sections, McAfee's products are used to make this aspect of the network more easily managed and maintained. An additional aspect of maintenance is having off-site data protection. My recommendation is to have a minimum of one site, preferably two.

Network maintenance includes being prepared for disaster. This includes personnel plans, equipment plans, location plans, operational plans, and restoration plans. In reality, it means that you test these plans.

Network maintenance means that you document everything that is important about your network and keep it in a location where all appropriate people can access it.

Plan for laser printer maintenance. Plan for monitor maintenance. Plan for each system's maintenance. Plan for dot matrix printer maintenance. Plan for telecommunication line maintenance.

Plan your maintenance to avert and avoid brownouts, blackouts, spikes, surges, continued low voltages, continued overvoltage conditions, electromagnetic interference, ion storm interference, earthquakes, electrical storms, wind, hail, and fire. Of course you don't have to be this serious—just be as serious as your reputation and business will permit.

8.6 Summary

Your network should incorporate some of the information provided in this chapter. The purpose of it is to show you the significance of the communication equipment; of the network designed and implemented here, along with some of its characteristics; of network operation; and of network maintenance.

The overall purpose of this chapter, as of previous ones, is to get you thinking about your network. To the degree that you plan, that degree of success will be ensured.

Network Architecture and Asynchronous Transfer Mode (ATM)

Many networks today are using ATM technology. Some carrier services use this technology and many private networks are using it because of the amount of data it can move in such a short amount of time. ATM is a good technology choice for data, voice, and multimedia networks.

ATM technology has not been on the market very long compared to other technologies. However, credit is due to researchers at Bell Laboratories for their work in this area long before it came to the forefront of media attention in the late 1980s and early 1990s. ATM actually began to take shape in the late 1980s; the driving force behind its development was a need for a fast switching technology that could support data, voice, video, and multimedia in general. This chapter explores various aspects of ATM and serves to orient the reader to it. Just before the summary, a section listing CCITT specifications is provided for more in-depth information.

9.1 A Perspective on ATM

Asynchronous Transfer Mode (ATM) is a cell-switching technology. Specifically, it uses a 53-byte cell. It consists of a *header* with routing and other network-related information and an *information field* for data, images, voice, and video. A major thrust behind ATM is its capability to support multimedia and to integrate these services along with data into a single transmission method. Heretofore this was attainable but awkward, and timing problems, along with other significant issues, hindered it.

ATM can be implemented at the enterprise level (privately), in public networks, or both. In reality, this is the way it is implemented. Realization of ATM throughout a dispersed network environment is twofold. First, it is implemented at the local level, as in a given organization or corporation. Second, it is implemented at the public level (or service provider). ATM usage capabilities can be customized to meet a given environment's needs, and it is application-transparent; therefore, integration of multimedia and data does not cause problems.

As of this writing ATM is not new, but neither is it seasoned with regard to implementations. Some trade magazines, forums, and other technical communications predict that ATM will dominate LANs, WANs, and public service providers in the not-too-distant future. ATM growth has been rapid over the past few years. Many vendors are in some phase of support for ATM. Some have ATM products to offer today, while other companies are beginning to create ATM products. The technology itself is being defined, and it appears that the process of refining ATM will continue for some time to come.

9.2   ATM Layer Structure

Many network protocols are compared and contrasted against the OSI model. ATM does not fit the structure of the OSI model, except for the physical layer. Figure 9.1 shows ATM network technology in light of a layered approach.

The physical layer of the ATM model can be divided into two sublayers: the *physical media dependent* (PMD) sublayer and the *transmis-*

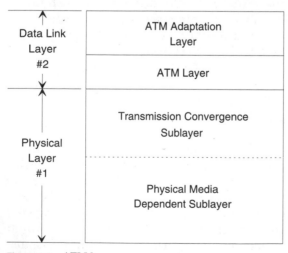

Figure 9.1 ATM layers.

sion convergence sublayer. The PMD performs two primary functions: *bit timing* and *line coding*. The function of the transmission convergence sublayer is contingent upon the interface used beneath it. Some interfaces supported include Synchronous Optical Network (SONET) at 155.52 MB/s, DS3 at 44.736 MB/s, multimode fiber at 100 MB/s, pure cells at 155 MB/s, and others.

Functions at the transmission convergence sublayer are contingent to the interface used. Some of the functions at this sublayer include performing header error correction (HEC), which covers the entire cell header (this includes generation and verification); multiplexing; frame generation and recovery; and mapping of the ATM cells onto DS3 facilities, if used, by the Physical Layer Convergence Protocol (PLCP). In addition, PLCP framing and delineation is performed, if DS3 is used. In addition to these functions, others are performed relative to the interface in use.

ATM layer functions include switching, multiplexing, routing, and congestion management. Above this layer is the *ATM adaptation layer* (AAL). Here different categories of functions are identifiable. Figure 9.2 shows the components at the PMD sublayer and interfaces supported, the transmission convergence sublayer, the ATM layer functional components, and the AAL.

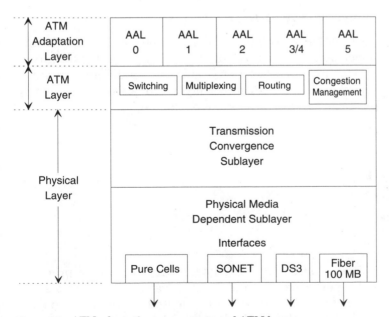

Figure 9.2   ATM adaptation components and ATM layer.

Figure 9.2 shows functions that occur at the ATM layer, and it also shows categories of functions that occur at the AAL. Details of the ATM adaptation layer functions are explained in Sec. 9.3, but the ATM layer is the focus here.

The ATM layer also defines two virtual connections. First, a *virtual channel connection* (VCC) between two ATM VCC endpoints. This may be either point-to-point or point-to-multipoint. Second, multiple virtual channel connections carried through *virtual path connection* (VPC) endpoints. This connection will be either point-to-point or point-to-multipoint.

This layer also translates the *virtual path indicators* (VPIs) and the *virtual channel indicators* (VCIs). It is responsible for cell multiplexing and demultiplexing.

The ATM adaptation layer (AAL) is responsible for mapping data from higher layers within a network onto cell fields and conversely. This layer operates on functions that are end-to-end functions.

The connection-oriented or connectionless conversion protocol incorporates the broadband data service and includes the B-ISDN, Integrated Switching Data Network (ISDN) standard. B-ISDN supports interactive service, including conversational, such as video, voice, and sounds, as well as document messaging for electronic mail, and multimedia. It also specifies the way text, data, sound, pictures, and video are transmitted and received. (ISDN technology is presented in Chap. 10.)

9.3   ATM Adaptation Layer (AAL) Functions

The AAL layer has been explained as that protocol layer itself that maps upper-layer protocols onto ATM. Devices that use this terminate signals. This layer provides functional support for different types of traffic (signals) that come from upper-layer protocols. Consequently, the following categories of functions are explained:

- AAL Type 0
- AAL Type 1
- AAL Type 2
- AAL Type 3–4
- AAL Type 5

AAL Type 0

AAL Type 0 is considered a place holder when customer premises equipment (CPE) performs required functions at this layer. In a sense it is a pass-through capability for cell-oriented services. Figure 9.3 shows a detailed view at the ATM adaptation layer.

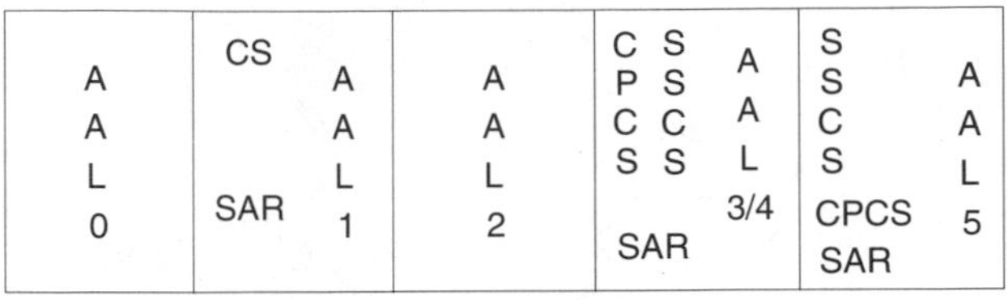

AAL 0	AAL 1	AAL 2	AAL 3/4	AAL 5
	CS		CPCS SSCS	SSCS
				CPCS
	SAR		SAR	SAR

Figure 9.3   Conceptual view of functions at the ATM adaptation layer.

AAL Type 1

AAL Type 1 functions provide constant bit rate services. This is also known as unstructured circuit transport between points. This type of function is connection-oriented. The *CS* component in AAL 1 in Fig. 9.3 is called the *convergence sublayer*. It modulates differences that may occur in the differences of physical interfaces. The *SAR* function performs *segmentation and reassembly* upon data as it moves through AAL 1.

AAL Type 2

This service specifies support for isochronous service with varying bit rates. An example of such a user of this function is compressed or packetized video.

AAL Type 3–4

AAL Type 3–4 functions support local area network (LAN) traffic. It supports a variable bit rate. Both connection-oriented and connectionless-oriented connections are supported. The *SSCS* is the *service-specific convergence sublayer*. One of its functions is data translation. It also maps upper-layer services to the ATM layer. *CPCS* is the *common part convergence sublayer*. This part works in conjunction with switched multimegabit data service. SAR is again the component that performs segmentation and reassembly.

AAL Type 5

Type 5 is designed for variable bit rate services. It is similar to Type 3–4, but it differs in that it is easier to implement. Most ATM local area network devices support this type.

9.3   ATM Cell Structure

The components of an ATM cell, as it appears at the user network interface (UNI), are shown by Fig. 9.4.

Figure 9.4 ATM cell structure at the UNI.

ATM cell structure

The cell structure shown in Fig. 9.4 contains 5 bytes of header information and 48 bytes of user information. The contents of the cell are defined as follows.

The *generic flow control* (GFC) field controls data traffic locally and can be used to customize a local implementation. The bit value in this field is not moved from end to end. Once the cell is into the network, ATM switches overwrite the fields.

The next two fields are the *virtual path identifier* (VPI) and the *virtual channel identifier* (VCI) bits. Information stored in these fields performs routing functions. The number of bits here varies because the bits used for virtual channel identifiers for user-to-user virtual paths are negotiated between the users of each virtual path. These two fields constitute the way nodes communicate.

The *payload type* (PT) field indicates if the data being carried is user data or management-related information. The field is also used to indicate network congestion.

The *cell loss priority* (CLP) field is used to explicitly indicate the cell priority. In short, it indicates whether the cell is a candidate for discarding if network congestion occurs.

The *header error control* (HEC) field is used by the physical layer. This field is used to detect errors in the header and to correct bit errors within the header, as well.

The *user data* field contains the user data from upper layers within the network. This is a 48-byte field. This field does not have error checking performed upon it.

The other cell type, known as the *network node interface* (NNI), is similar to Fig. 9.4, with the exception that a difference is indicated in the header portion of the cell.

9.4   ATM Interface Types

As indicated in the previous section, two types of nodes are recognized. The user network interface (UNI) can be divided into two groups: private and public.

Private UNIs can best be described by function. They are typically used to connect an ATM user with an ATM switch to which both are considered local and part of the site. The switch itself may be referred to as private and be considered to be *customer premises equipment* (CPE). CPE is ATM equipment that is located on a customer site and is not in the public arena. An ATM user may be a device, such as a router or workstation. The ATM switch is a private ATM switch. This ATM switch is what connects the *private* user to the *public* interface.

The *public UNI* is the interface used to connect an ATM user to an ATM switch in the domain of the public service provider (see Fig. 9.5).

Figure 9.5 shows private CPE and the public ATM switch. The functionality of the ATM switches (both private and public) utilize the same functionality at the physical layer; however, different media may be implemented.

The network node interface refers to the ATM switches in the public service provider network that communicate with one another to achieve routing and, thus, end-to-end service (see Fig. 9.6).

Figure 9.6 shows the network nodes implemented in a public ATM network, ATM users, an ATM switch, and, implicitly, the boundaries between the public ATM network and the private ATM switch.

9.5   ATM Concepts

Three concepts are used with ATM. These include:

- Transmission path
- Virtual path
- Virtual circuit

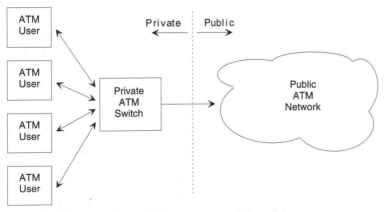

Figure 9.5   Conceptual view of the user network interface.

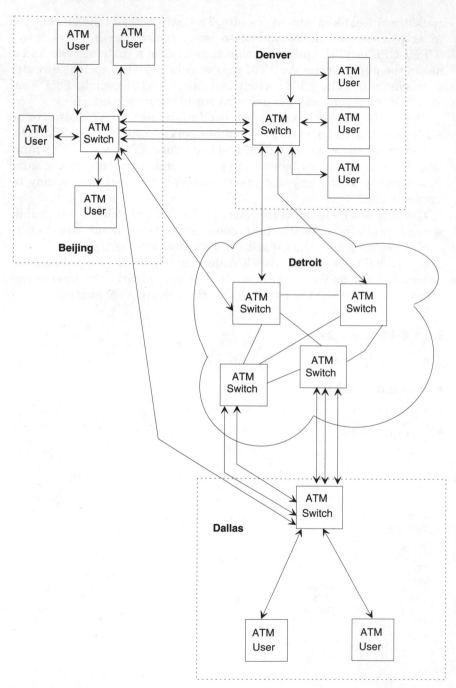

Figure 9.6 Public ATM network.

These three concepts are generally found together because they are part of ATM operation.

The *transmission path* is a physical connection between ATM-supported devices. These paths may have different characteristics, but they nevertheless exist. The physical transmission path between entities is what connects the virtual concepts and the usage to which they are mapped.

The idea of a *virtual path* is derived from having a transmission path on which it can be mapped. The virtual is mapped to the physical. Figure 9.7 shows an example of this concept.

The notion of a *virtual circuit* exists. The virtual circuit (some refer to this as a *virtual channel*) is mapped to both a virtual path and a transmission path (physical path).

The concepts of transmission path, virtual path, and virtual circuit are implemented at the physical layer in the ATM model. This is merely another method of multiplexing. This structure is part of the intricate nature of the ATM physical layer and is part of the robust nature of ATM.

9.6   A Perspective on ATM Implementation

Where and how ATM is implemented are valid questions. Because its support is versatile and it can accommodate high speeds, multiple possibilities exist as to how and where it is implemented. This section explores four distinct instances of how and where ATM is implemented. These include:

- Local router and ATM backbone
- ATM-based LANs
- ATM backbone nodes
- ATM LANs and ATM backbone

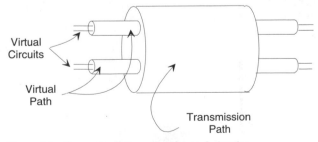

Figure 9.7   Conceptual view of paths and circuits.

Local Router and ATM Backbone

This type of implementation uses routers that support ATM in a local geographical area. Here a LAN exists with other lower-layer protocols and network devices, but a router with an ATM interface is used to connect the LAN into the ATM backbone that serves a much larger geographical area (see Fig. 9.8).

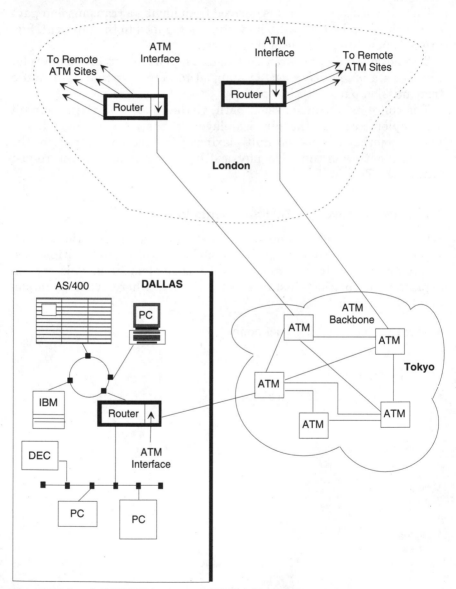

Figure 9.8 Local ATM HUB/router and ATM backbone.

Figure 9.8 is a real example of an ATM implementation. It illustrates a router with an ATM interface in a local implementation, along with devices attached to it directly or indirectly. It also indicates the local router with an ATM interface connected to an ATM backbone by which other sites connect. The ATM backbone consists of ATM devices. This is one of the simplest examples discussed in this section.

ATM backbone LANs

The notion of ATM backbone LANs is as its name implies—the LAN is built around ATM equipment (see Fig. 9.9).

In Fig. 9.9, three ATM-based LANs are shown. One is located in Atlanta, one is located in New York, and one is located in Los Angeles. All the local LANs have interconnections to other LANs in other cities; hence, a virtual LAN or WAN exists.

ATM backbone nodes

ATM backbone nodes are typically implemented in public environments (in contrast to a private enterprise). Many ATM nodes working together constitute an ATM backbone. Figure 9.10 shows multiple ATM nodes, creating a wide area network backbone.

Figure 9.10 also includes a network attached to the ATM node in Salt Lake City. The Salt Lake City network enters the ATM network via a router. A similar scenario could be repeated in the other sites shown in Fig. 9.10.

ATM LANs and ATM backbone

The notion of ATM LANs and an ATM backbone is an example of complete ATM implementation (see Fig. 9.11).

Figure 9.11 shows ATM nodes comprising the backbone of the ATM network and the focal points of the networks in Boise and Syracuse. This example shows maximum utilization of ATM both locally and in a WAN sense. Note the SNA environment located in Mexico City; it is connected to the Boise location. An additional ATM LAN is located in San Francisco and is participating in the overall WAN.

Variations of the last four figures are possible. These are representative of likely implementations. Other *hybrid* ways of implementing ATM are possible, depending heavily upon the site.

9.7 A Perspective on ATM Physical Layer Architecture

In Sec. 9.2, Fig. 9.2 shows the details of interfaces supported by the physical media dependent sublayer. Some of those are presented here:

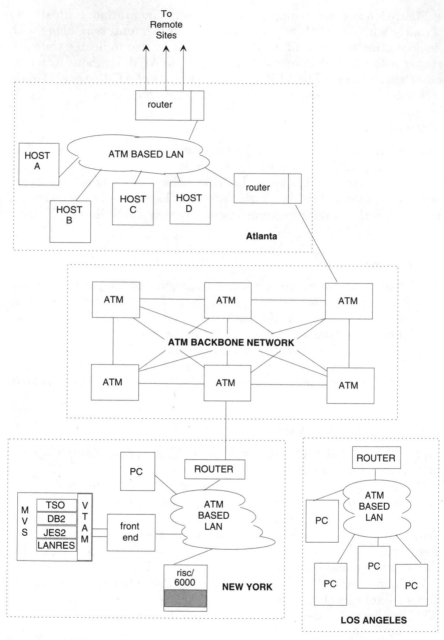

Figure 9.9   ATM backbone.

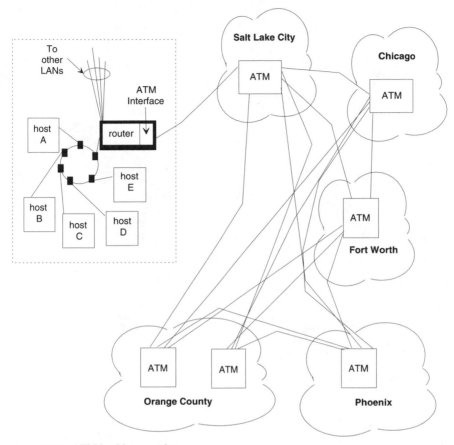

Figure 9.10   ATM backbone nodes.

- SONET
- DS3
- Fiber 100 MB

The interfaces and their provided technical characteristics are explained here.

SONET

Synchronous Optical Network (SONET) is one of the supported interfaces shown in Fig. 9.2. Its data rate transfer can accommodate speeds up to 155.52 MB/s. SONET frame structure is such that it can easily accommodate ATM. SONET support for ATM is achieved by mapping ATM cells, aligned by row, correlating to the structure of every SONET

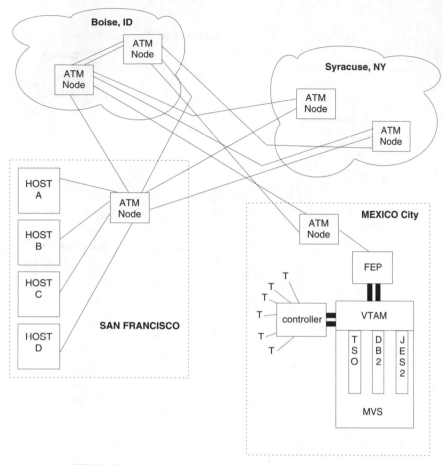

Figure 9.11   ATM LANs.

byte structure. Figure 9.12 shows an example of how SONET, ATM, and other technology can merge together.

Figure 9.12 shows an ATM device connecting into a SONET interface. In turn, an ATM LAN is attached to the ATM device. This implementation utilizes speeds through the SONET interface.

DS3

DS3 can be used as an interface to carry ATM cells. The data rate of DS3 is 44.7 MB/s. If this is used a Physical Layer Convergence Protocol (PLCP) must be defined. Once this is complete, then ATM cells are merely mapped to the DS3 PLCP frame. Figure 9.13 shows an example of this.

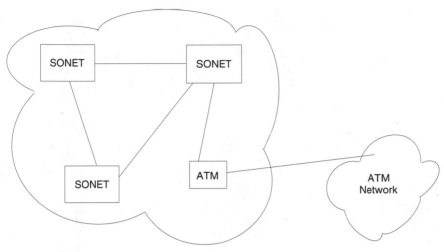

Figure 9.12   SONET and ATM.

Fiber 100 MB

This interface supports speeds up to 100 MB/s. The physical link is between the equipment at a given site, which connects it to a private ATM switch. This specification calls for the current FDDI implementation. Figure 9.14 shows an example of this.

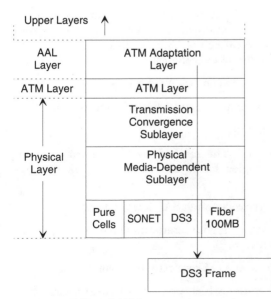

Figure 9.13   DS3 and ATM.

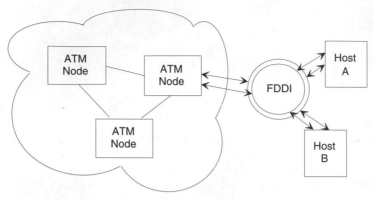

Figure 9.14   FDDI and ATM.

Other interfaces are supported in the ATM environment; these are good illustrations of how ATM works with other protocols.

9.7   ATM Terminology

ATM has a highly specialized vocabulary. Some ATM terms are presented here to serve as a specific ATM reference source.

AAL CONNECTION: The establishment of an association between ATM adaptation layer (AAL) or higher entities.

ATM: A fast-packet switched, cell-based method of moving voice, data, video, and other data and telecommunication-oriented information from one location to another. The ATM cell is 53 bytes in length, 5 bytes of header information and 48 bytes of user information.

ATM LAYER LINK: A connection between two ATM layers.

ATM LINK: A virtual path or a virtual circuit (channel) connection.

CELL: An ATM protocol data unit.

CONNECTION ADMISSION CONTROL: The method used to determine if an ATM link request can be accepted, based upon the origin's and destination's attributes.

CONNECTION ENDPOINT: A layer connection SAP termination.

CONNECTION ENDPOINT IDENTIFIER: A characteristic of an endpoint used to identify a service access point (SAP).

END SYSTEM: The place where an ATM connection is terminated.

HEADER: That control information which precedes the user information in an ATM cell.

FAIRNESS: The meeting of all specified quality-of-service requirements through control of active connections across an ATM link.

METASIGNALING: A way of managing virtual circuits and different types of signals.

NETWORK NODE INTERFACE: The ATM interface as it relates to the network node.

SEGMENT: An ATM link, or group of links, that comprises an ATM connection.

SERVICE ACCESS POINT (SAP): An addressable endpoint at a given layer within a network.

SUBLAYER: The division of a layer logically.

SWITCHED CONNECTION: A connection established via a signaling method.

SYMMETRIC CONNECTION: A connection where both directions have the same bandwidth.

VIRTUAL CHANNEL: Also called a *virtual circuit*. That which an ATM cell can traverse.

VIRTUAL CIRCUIT: Also called a *virtual channel*. That which an ATM cell can traverse.

VIRTUAL PATH: The logical association of virtual circuits.

VIRTUAL PATH CONNECTION: A one-way joining of virtual path links.

VIRTUAL PATH LINK: The connection between points where a virtual path identifier is assigned.

VIRTUAL PATH TERMINATOR: The system that processes the virtual circuits (channels) after they are demultiplexed.

9.8 Where to Find Additional Information

Additional ATM information can be obtained from the CCITT. Some of this includes the following standards:

I.113	I.327	I.610
I.121	I.361	G.707
I.150	I.362	G.708
I.211	I.363	G.709
I.311	I.413	
I.321	I.432	

9.9 Summary

ATM is a cell-based, fast-packet switching technology. It can be implemented privately or publicly. Many public service providers are opting for ATM installations. ATM technology has received considerable attention since its entry into the technical arena in the late 1980s.

ATM conceptual structure does not correlate one-for-one with the OSI model. ATM layers begin with a physical layer that has two sublayers. The lowest sublayer is called the physical media dependent sublayer; above it is the transmission convergence sublayer. Next is the ATM layer, which includes four functions as explained previously. The ATM adaptation layer is above the ATM layer. Part of the ATM layer and the ATM adaptation layer make up layer 2. The ATM adaptation layer includes five types of functions.

ATM cells are unique because they are small and can handle voice, data, video, and other multimedia information. The ATM adaptation layer protocols are an interface between ATM and upper-layer protocols.

ATM utilizes a transmission path, a virtual path, and a virtual call as part of its implementation and method of passing information. Virtual paths and virtual calls are mapped to a transmission path.

The CCITT has a list of ATM specifications that are both directly and indirectly related to this subject.

10

Data, Voice, and Integrated Services Digital Network (ISDN) Technology

When ISDN is discussed, many times the topic of conversation never gets above layer 2 in the OSI model! Occasionally it does, and products are discussed. Bear in mind as you read this chapter that ISDN is a service that data and voice networks use. In fact, multimedia networks use it as well.

For example, earlier chapters discuss one of the components used in the network, a 3Com USR HUB. This device is capable of using a primary rate interface (PRI) connection. So, what does this mean, you ask? Well, PRI, as explained later in this chapter, is a way that certain devices connect to the telephone service provider. Technically, it is how a device operates with the telephone service provider. In this case, a PRI connection enables the 3Com USR HUB to operate digitally by way of the T1 card in the HUB.

The point is this: consider a 3Com USR HUB connected with a PRI connection using a T1 line. Say the network is mostly data, but some multimedia is designed into the software. Now, assume you are on the other end, at a given location connected to the network. Now, assume you have software that enables you to communicate with the 3Com USR HUB. Your computer delivers data and voice to you (the user). The sender of this information is the network I designed. What is going on here is that the 3Com USR HUB is the device most visible to people. It is the primary device that connects the network on one end to the telephone company service provider with another, similar device on the other end. The data and voice stuff you see and hear did not originate with the 3Com USR HUB—the HUB is merely a focal point between the network and the pipeline between locations *A* and *B*. Simply put, ISDN is the technology used to deliver the data and voice from point *A* to point *B*. The fact is that ISDN is prevalent in the United States today and seems to have a significant hold on the future of technology at the lowest layers in the network, as well.

ISDN is a very comprehensive topic that includes vast amounts of standards, protocols, and information contributed by a number of standards-making bodies. The purpose of this chapter is to orient the reader to ISDN. It begins by clarifying what ISDN is, presents some fundamental standards that it is based upon, explains some basic terms and concepts, and briefly explains Signaling System 7 (SS7). Interfaces used with ISDN and their functions are presented, in addition to some examples of practical services resulting from ISDN implementations. Both data and voice networks use ISDN. To attempt to segregate data and voice networks from ISDN is not prudent. Data and voice applications merely *use* ISDN technology.

10.1   What Is ISDN?

You may have asked this question to yourself or possibly others if your background is not related to this technology. The technology is not new in the sense that it was just invented a few years ago, but rather its implementation and use generally keep it one step removed from most except those who work with it directly.

Working definition

ISDN is an acronym for *Integrated Services Digital Network*. Practically speaking, it has more to do with functionality from the perspective of regional telephone company and service provider implementations than it does with isolated implementations. In fact, ISDN *users* realize its benefits and are typically not involved in its implementation. But clarification on this point is forthcoming.

For example, many telephone companies (in the United States and other countries) have implemented the ISDN technology in central offices, private digital systems, and private branch exchanges (PBXs). This is significant because the technology is based on digital, not analog, signals. Not only are digital signals fundamental to ISDN's foundations, but the fact that ISDN can support voice, data, video, electronic mail, and numerous other services integrated together make it a powerful technology to build upon. The result is the potential to offer services through the telephone network that were heretofore not possible. Figure 10.1 shows a conceptual view of the idea behind ISDN implementations.

ISDN realization requires more than the telephone system implementation. In fact, ISDN requires that the calling party, the network, and the destination party all implement ISDN technology. If these three conditions are not met, some ISDN capabilities are not possible. Further exploration into what this means from a practical standpoint is presented later.

CCITT recommendations

ISDN is a protocol. Its operation, standards, and recommendations have been defined by the CCITT. The *I* series of CCITT recommendations covers a broad range of ISDN technology. The *I* series is divided into groups of 100. The following list categorically describes the CCITT recommendations.

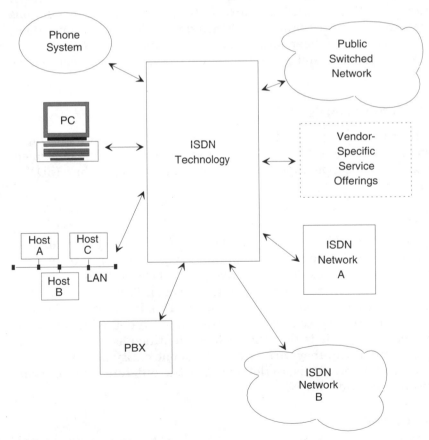

Figure 10.1   ISDN implementation.

CCITT Number	Function
I.100	This series contains general information such as terminology used, the structure of the *I* series of recommendations, and the basic capabilities of ISDN.
I.200	This series specifies ISDN service capabilities such as circuit, packet, and a variety of digital services.
I.300	This series includes the principles, protocols, and architecture of ISDN.
I.400	This series includes specifications of user interfaces and network layer functions.
I.500	This series includes interface standards, principles for internetworking ISDN networks, and related topics.
I.600	This series includes ISDN maintenance recommendations, including subscriber access, basic access, and primary rate access.

These recommendations, along with many others, detail ISDN according to the CCITT. The source of this series of recommendations is from my reference library, which includes CCITT recommendations. Any of these recommendations can be obtained from sources that provide standards and recommendations from entities such as the CCITT.

10.2   ISDN Channels

ISDN has basic concepts that are applicable in the majority of implementations. The question is, "What is used in a given ISDN implementation?" This section explains the terms and concepts that ISDN is built upon.

Channels

The term *channel* is frequently used in ISDN to convey the meaning of *service provided*. Channels are an integral part of ISDN technology, and, as this section explains, different types of channels exist.

Channels in general are physical or logical entities that data, voice, video, or other *information* travel through. This is important, because in ISDN different types of channels are defined. A definable characteristic about channels is that they can be identified as being digital or analog. Either way, they carry signals from one entity to another.

The remainder of this section explains the different types of channels available with ISDN.

The D channel

In ISDN the D channel is used to convey user signaling messages. This type of channel uses out-of-band signaling. This means that network-related signals are carried on a separate channel from user data. These signals transmitted over the D channel convey the characteristics of the service on behalf of the user. The name *out-of-band* arose because the network signal is out of band with the user signal.

The protocol used on the D channel defines logical connections between the terminal equipment (TE) and the local exchange (LE) via local loop termination equipment. In order to use this arrangement, customer premise equipment (CPE) that performs switching functions is required. Figure 10.2 shows a conceptual view of this idea.

The essence of understanding the D channel is knowing that it uses out-of-band signaling but carries user data. It operates at approximately 16 or 64 kbps and is used by user equipment to transmit requests and messages within the network. In summary, the D channel provides signaling service between a user and the network and provides packet-mode data transfer.

The B channel

The B channel carries voice, video, and data. This channel functions at a constant 64 kbps. This channel can be used for packet- and circuit-switching applications. The difference between the two is that packet-switching applications utilize a logical connection through a network and no dedicated facilities exist. This is generally referred to as a *store and forward* method of data transfer. Circuit switching differs because its switching technology is based upon devices that are connected via some resource for the extent of the call (or communication instance).

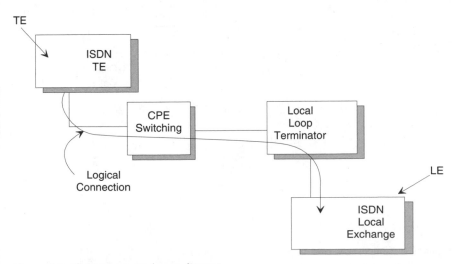

Figure 10.2 Customer premise equipment.

B and D channels work in harmony. The D channel is used to transfer requests for services that are delivered on a B channel. Figure 10.3 shows an example of B and D channel operation.

H channel

Multiple H channels exists. The basic differences between them are in the services they offer. As a general rule, H channels have a considerably higher transfer rate than B channels. These channels effectively meet the needs of real-time video conferencing, digital-quality audio, and other services requiring a much higher bandwidth.

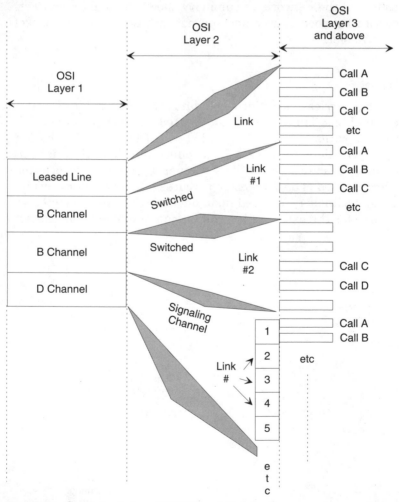

Figure 10.3 Conceptual view of ISDN B and D channels.

The basic H channel known as H_0 is comprised of one channel that can provide rates of 384 kbps. H_{11} channels can support throughput rates of approximately 1536 Mbps, and the H_{12} channel sustains rates of up to approximately 1920 Mbps. This type of channel is most suitable for a trunk where subdivision can be implemented to maximize the effective bandwidth.

10.3   Signaling System 7 (SS7)

SS7 is a standard being implemented by regional and long-distance telephone companies today. Its relationship to ISDN is important. Without SS7 implementation in the telephone systems, ISDN is somewhat inhibited. They are interrelated in many ways. The fundamental reason for this is that SS7 is digital by design, and its link capacity outstrips that of SS6.

SS7 is a protocol and method for networks of switching entities to communicate with one another. Though ISDN can be implemented without SS7, with the implementation of SS7 ISDN can be more comprehensive in scope.

Characteristics

SS7 is a complex standard. The CCITT has a series of recommended standards about the signaling system. Some highlights of SS7 characteristics include the following:

- It can accommodate digital communications in networks using digital channels.
- It can also operate with analog communication channels.
- It can be used domestically in the United States or internationally.
- It is a layered architecture.
- Speeds are 56 and 64 kbps.
- In regard to information transfer, it is considered reliable because it ensures sequential movement of signals through a network and provides a mechanism to prevent signal loss or duplicate signals.
- It can operate in point-to-point network implementations and can be used with satellite communications.
- Its method of handling routing and delivery of control messages is also considered reliable.
- It has built into it management capabilities, maintenance, and also a method for call control.

SS7 CCITT recommendations define packet-switched network functions but do not restrict implementation to specific hardware. According to CCITT recommendations, two signaling points are defined: a signaling point and a signaling transfer point. The *signaling point* is defined as a point in the network capable of handling control information. A *signaling transfer point* is identified as a entity where routing of messages can be achieved.

Protocol components

SS7 protocol can be categorized into three groups:

- Signaling connection control part (SCCP)
- Application
- Message transfer part (MTP)

The SCCP protocol specifies five classes of network service:

Class 0	Unsequenced connectionless
Class 1	Sequenced connectionless
Class 2	Connection-oriented
Class 3	Flow control connection-oriented
Class 4	Flow control connection-oriented with error recovery

The SCCP supports OSI addressing capabilities and, in a sense, functions to deliver messages intended for a specific user once the message reaches the destination signaling point. The SCCP works with the MTP to achieve OSI network layer support.

The MTP protocol has multiple layers of signaling. The first level corresponds to the physical layer of the OSI model. It functions as the signaling data link. The second level of the protocol operates at the data link layer of the OSI model. It is by design a bit-oriented protocol; consequently, it is robust in its capabilities. The third level corresponds roughly to the network layer of the OSI model. It is concerned with routing and link management.

SS7 application protocol correlates to the upper layers in the OSI model. The structure at this layer is divided into a telephone user part that focuses upon singaling processes required for voice communications. The data user part is related to requirements for circuit-oriented networks and has been usurped by the ISDN user part.

Additional information

The CCITT and ANSI standards for SS7 are comprehensive in scope. The following list is only a partial one, but it provides an excellent starting point for those who need additional information. A more complete list can be obtained from standard source suppliers who maintain lists of standards-making bodies like ANSI and CCITT.

ANSI T1.110 SS7 Overview

ANSI T1.111 Overview of the Message Transfer Part

ANSI T1.113 ISDN User Part

CCITT Q.700 SS7 Overview

CCITT Q.701 Message Transfer Part

CCITT Q.702 Signaling Data Link

CCITT Q.711–Q.716 Signaling Connection Control Part

CCITT Q.730 ISDN Supplementary Services

CCITT Q.761–Q.766 ISDN User Part

10.4 ISDN Interfaces and How They Are Used

Two ISDN user interfaces are explained in this section. They are the basic rate interface and the primary rate interface.

Basic rate interface

This is a way to access ISDN. It consists of two B channels and one D channel according to the CCITT I.430 recommendation. Hence, it is sometimes referred to as the 2B+D interface.

No specific protocol specification restrictions are applicable here. This interface utilizes circuit-switched transparent "pipes" to make a connection between two end users by way of the ISDN network. Examples of where this interface is implemented would be PBXs, individual terminals, video conference units, personal computers, and workstations.

Primary rate interface

This is also a way to access ISDN. This interface calls for one of the following implementations:

- 23 B channels and 1 D channel
- 24 B channels and 1 D channel
- 30 B channels and 1 D channel

These originate from the CCITT I.431 recommendation. In some ways, this is basically the bandwidth equivalent to T1s used in the United

States. This interface calls for point-to-point, serial, synchronous communications. A fundamental difference between the primary rate interface and the basic rate interface is that the primary rate interface can support H channels as well as B channels. As a result, bandwidth is greatly enhanced.

How interfaces are used

These two interfaces are used by a business, personal, or other user to connect directly to the local telephone company's central office. In large scenarios the basic rate interface is used to connect individual users to the organization's PBX, and, in turn, the PBX is connected to the local telephone central office. However, this could also be achieved by connecting this latter scenario to an interchange carrier via a broadband interface. The connection is made via an ISDN interface board, ISDN controller, or an external terminal adapter, and the connection is physically established.

10.5   Practical Uses of ISDN

Like many technologies used in networks that may not reside inside a user's workplace environment, ISDN is somewhat abstract. ISDN uses can be understood more easily than the internal operations by those who are not technically adept. This section hones in upon practical services that are based directly or indirectly on ISDN technology.

Automatic number identification (ANI)

ANI is a service that provides the telephone number of the caller prior to answering the call. This service is beneficial for a company that prides itself on customer service.

Just a telephone number and a well-designed and -implemented database can be a powerful tool for a company to better serve its customers. The examples below are based on the ANI service and an updated database. Consider the implications.

- Identification of the customer—name, address, phone number, and other information pertinent to serving the customer.
- Identification of the customer's language preference. Our diverse culture is a blend of individuals who speak different languages. This is important information for companies who have international customers and customers who do not speak English. With a good database and UNI, callers who speak a language other than English can be routed immediately to a service representative who speaks their native language. This in itself communicates to the customer that

the company cares enough about its customers to employ individuals who can communicate in a variety of languages.

- Ascertaining telephone numbers of callers who terminate a call before a representative can respond because they have been on hold for an inordinate length of time. Consequently, a representative can return the customer's call.

- Identifying callers in a particular category via their number and the database. For example, assume that a customer purchases large quantities of widgets and has been a long-standing account of a particular sales representative because that representative understands the needs of the caller. In this case the call and the caller's files can be directed to the appropriate representative.

- A customer's preferred method of payment can be determined from payment history data, therefore avoiding repeating the same numbers and information except to verify appropriate information.

These ANI-based services are available today for applications from large system computing to personal computer systems. Regardless of the implementation, the results of such a service generally make a positive impression upon a customer.

Electronic library interconnections

With the help of ISDN and supporting technology, it is possible for libraries in geographically remote parts of the country to utilize electronic information exhange that would have been impractical a decade ago.

Electronic manual access

Many companies, such as Philips, Apple Computer, Microsoft, and others, put manuals in electronic media and distribute them to databases through ISDN networks. These manuals span topics such as hardware maintenance, software changes, and a variety of other topics.

Image retrieval

A major advantage of ISDN and supporting systems is the ability to transmit images, full-motion video, text, graphics, data, and prerecorded video information. This is particularly significant in the realm of medicine. Now CAT scans can be moved in their entirety by participating ISDN customers in the medical community.

Other practical everyday uses of ISDN are not generally presented and explained in technical form to those who utilize its capabilities. Suffice it to say that ISDN is growing in vendor products, telephone system implementations, and is even coming close to the houses we live in.

Companies such as AT&T, Sprint, and MCI are implementing ISDN and variations thereof. The end result will be services via networks that a widespread customer base will be able to access.

10.6   Summary

Actual ISDN technology is removed from most users. The services of ISDN are the result of the implementation. ISDN services provide capabilities for moving voice, data, live video, text, imaging, and variations of multimedia technology from one location to another in real time.

CCITT and ANSI have numerous recommendations and proposed standards related to ISDN and supporting peripheral equipment. These standards are lengthy; my references on the topic consume many linear feet of shelf space. A list of CCITT and ANSI specifications is provided in Sec. 10.3 for the reader who needs additional information on the topic.

ISDN channels are explained. The B, D, and H channels are explained in light of their features and differences. SS7 characteristics and protocol components are presented, and references for additional information are also provided in Sec. 10.3.

ISDN basic rate interfaces and primary rate interfaces are explained. A brief explanation pertaining to how interfaces are used is also presented.

A section on the practical uses of ISDN is presented to help the reader understand some of the services that are directly or indirectly based in ISDN technology.

Data, Multimedia, Voice, and Frame Relay

Multimedia and voice networks require real-time transfer of data from both ends to each other. It is not enough for applications and systems to be designed to accommodate such transfer—the conduit between points must be able to provide such data transfer. Frame relay is a typical choice for multimedia end voice networks.

Frame relay provides real-time communication between end users. This is possible because frame relay serves as an interface into public and private networks. Frame relay networks pass frames from origin to destination without intermediate nodes performing packet assembly and disassembly. Frame relay is also considered to be a protocol. A frame relay control protocol is also defined, explaining how users make service requests in the network.

Frame relay is designed to support data in bursts and to provide high speeds. It is *not* a store and forward–based technology; rather, it is a bidirectional conversational method of communication. Most frame relay standards are concentrated at layers 1 and 2; however, standards do define the mechanism for upper-layer protocols to hook into frame relay.

For example, this means that frame relay operates between users— that is, between origin and destination *networks*. Figure 11.1 best conveys this concept of frame relay operation.

Three sites using frame relay as an interface are shown in Fig. 11.1. These sites are a dispersed frame relay network. In addition, frame relay is used to connect different networks in multiple geographical locations. This example shows each location implementing frame relay. Each physical location uses frame relay for an interface into what is considered a frame relay network.

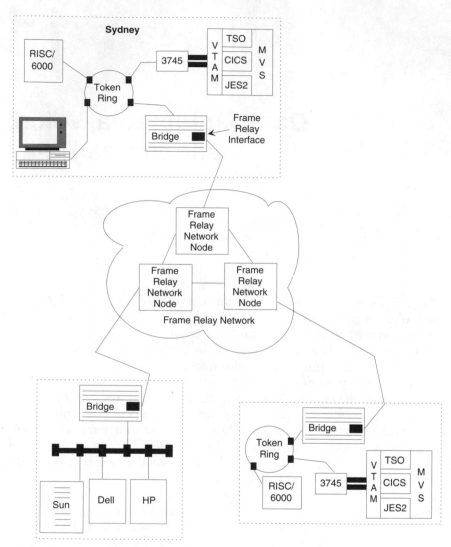

Figure 11.1 Conceptual view of frame relay.

Frame relay has been defined by at least three noted entities: ANSI, CCITT, and the Local Management Interface (LMI) group. ANSI has a list of specifications. These standards generally have the ISDN name within them. The CCITT has its list of CCITT recommendations. The CCITT has two groups of standards that relate to frame relay: the *I* group and the *Q* group. Last, the LMI standards were created by Cisco Systems, Digital Equipment Corporation, Northern Telecom, and StrataCom. These four vendors collectively created standards that parallel ANSI and the CCITT. Later in this chapter, additional information is included about what information comes from which source and how to obtain additional information.

The remainder of this chapter explains frame relay principles, frame structure, virtual circuits, and access devices. Consumer tips and a brief list of reference material are also provided.

11.1   Voice, Data, and Frame Relay

Frame relay operates upon mulitple principles. Some presented in this section include virtual links, permanent virtual connections, and the data link connection identifier, among others.

The virtual link

A basic frame relay principle is the *virtual connection*. The concept alone is interesting, because the virtual connection may differ with respect to the time that it exists. But practically, the connection is permanent in the sense that it remains as long as is necessary (see Fig. 11.2).

Figure 11.2 shows three hosts connected to a frame relay node, the physical links connecting each host to the node, the memory inside the frame relay device, and the connection mapping table within the frame relay node. Host #1's physical link supports two permanent virtual con-

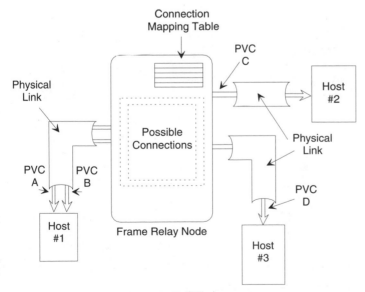

Figure 11.2   Enhanced view of a frame relay node.

nections (PVCs). However, host #2's and host #3's physical links support one PVC each.

The connection mapping table is at the heart of frame relay operations within the frame relay node shown in Fig. 11.2. The connections made are dynamic and are based upon requests from the incoming data stream. The connection mapping table is responsible for matching the request of the source to the destination; this constitutes a *route* or, in frame relay lingo, a *virtual connection*.

Figure 11.3 is similar to Fig. 11.2, but it shows the frames and a highlighted view of the mapping table. Note PVC A #1 and PVC B #5 originating at host #1. Figure 11.3 also shows these connecting to PVC C #3 and PVC D #7, respectively. To be more precise, mapping between A #1 and C #3 and B #5 and D #7 is performed inside the frame relay node.

Data link connection identifier (DCLI)

The inbound frame from host #1 via PVC A #1 contains a data link connection identifier (DCLI). The DCLI is the local address in a frame relay. The DCLI address is relevant in reference to the particular link. It identifies the frame and its type. This means that the same DCLI value could be used at both ends of the frame relay network where each host connects via a particular link. Differentiating the DCLI are the physical link that the frame traverses and the host. Hence, more than one identifying factor is used for frame identification.

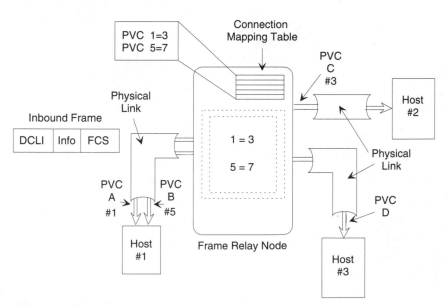

Figure 11.3 Highlighted view of the mapping table.

In the connection mapping table, each entry includes the following information:

- Node ID
- Link ID
- DCLI

Frame relay costs

Aside from the hardware and software required to implement a frame relay connection, additional fees are incurred—for example, the *committment information rate* (CIR), which is the bandwidth available from one end to another. Another factor is called the *port access rate*. This refers to access into the frame relay network. Finally, there is what is considered a *network access charge,* which reflects the costs of the line connecting a given site to the access point in the frame relay network.

Understanding these aspects of frame relay is important. For example, if data is transmitted in bursts, one must know what the burst data rate is. Another related factor to understand is the normal or average throughput required on a daily basis.

11.2   Frame Relay Frame Components

Frame relay frame components are shown in Fig. 11.4. Maximum frame size is 8250 bytes, and the minimum is generally considered to be 262 bytes.

Figure 11.4 is based upon the CCITT I.441 recommendation. Variations of this structure exist, primarily those with different methods of implementing addressing. A significant point to note about frame relay is that it utilizes the same standards as those of ISDN.

The *flag* field indicates the beginning of the frame.

The *address* field typically consists of the components in Fig. 11.5.

In Fig. 11.5, the *DLCI* fields identify a logical channel connection in a physical channel or port, thus identifying a predetermined destination. (Simply put, it identifies the connection.) The *CR* field contains a bit indicating a command response. The *EAB* field contains a bit set at either *1* or *0*. The field indicates extended addressing. The *FN* field is sometimes referred to as the *FECN* or forward explicit congestion noti-

Flag	Address Field	Control	Information	FCS	Flag

Figure 11.4   CCITT I. 441 Frame relay frame format.

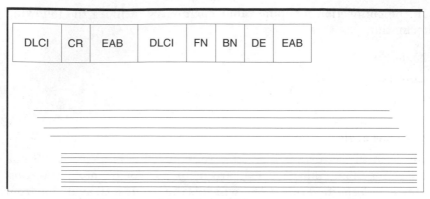

Figure 11.5 Highlighted view of the address field.

fication field. The bit in this field indicates whether or not congestion was encountered during the transfer from origin to destination. The *BN* field indicates that congestion was encountered on the return path. The *DE* field is the discard eligibility field. This field indicates whether or not the frame can be disposed of during transfer if congestion is encountered. A bit setting of *1* means a discard eligibility, whereas a bit setting of *0* indicates a higher setting for the frame, and it should not be discarded.

11.3   Multimedia and Virtual Circuits

Different frame types of virtual circuits have been defined for use with frame relay. As a result, this technology is good to use with multimedia. In a sense, these circuits represent different definable services. They include the following:

- Switched virtual circuit (SVC)
- Permanent virtual circuit (PVC)
- Multicast virtual circuit (MVC)

Switched virtual circuit (SVC)

This type of circuit is similar to telephone usage. When the circuit is needed, a request is made. When the circuit is not needed, the circuit is not used. Information is passed from origin to destination to set up the call and to bring it down. Some information provided in the call setup phase includes bandwidth allocation parameters, quality of service parameters, and virtual channel identifiers, to name a few.

Permanent virtual circuit (PVC)

This type of connection is considered point-to-point. It could be thought of as a leased line in that it is dedicated. This type circuit is used for long periods of time. Commands are still used to set up the call and to bring it down. The difference between the PVC and a SVC is duration.

Multicast virtual circuit (MVC)

MVCs are best described as being a connection between groups of users, through which individual users can use SVC connections as well as PVC connections. Technically, this type of connection is considered permanent. To date, this type of connection is generally considered a local management interface (LMI) extension.

11.4   Access Devices

Different devices can be used to connect devices into a frame relay environment. Some of those are examined here.

Switches

Frame relay networks can be accessed via different types of devices. For example, switches similar to those accommodating X.25 provide a way to access frame relay networks. However, these switches are typically implemented in the sense of creating a backbone. Figure 11.6 shows an example of this type of device implemented in three environments. It is a network backbone made up of three components—switches in Tanzania, Bogota, and Miami.

Network devices

A more focused view of Bakersfield is represented by Fig. 11.7, which shows a network device (specifically a bridge) connecting a Token Ring and Ethernet network into the frame relay environment.

Frame relay access devices (FRADs)

A frame relay access device (FRAD) is a particular piece of equipment that typically connotes capabilities including packet assembly and disassembly and speeds of DSO, T1, or fractional T1. Most FRADs can handle multiple protocols and can focus network traffic into a centralized managed facility, such as Fig. 11.8 shows.

FRADs can be the best components to concentrate multiple devices into a single unit. Vendors such as Wellfleet and Cisco Systems provide devices such as these.

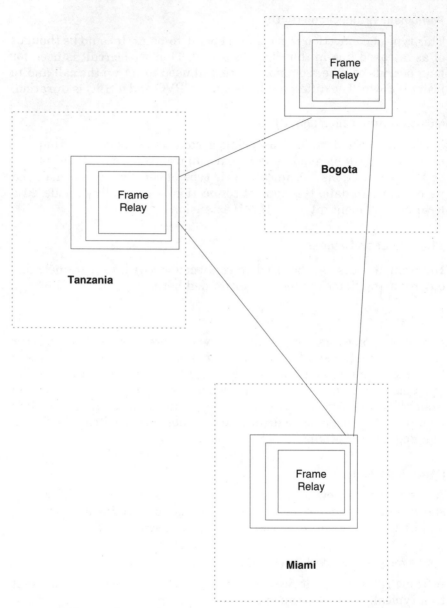

Figure 11.6   Frame relay switches.

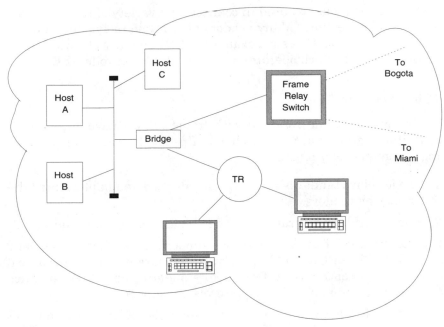

Figure 11.7 Frame relay implementation in Bakersfield.

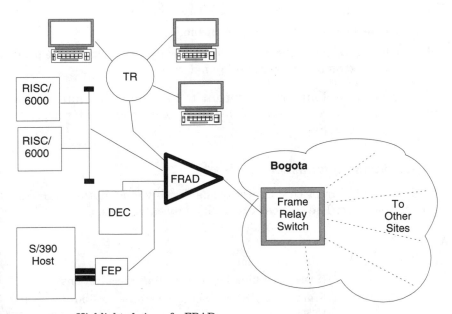

Figure 11.8 Highlighted view of a FRAD.

Other devices may be used in connecting a variety of resources into a frame relay network. Many vendors offer frame relay support as an additional function. One such example is IBM and its Network Control Program (NCP), which operates on a Front End Controller (FEP).

11.5   Consumer Tips

During my work and research with frame relay, I have encountered some information that provides handy tips for the consumer purchasing frame relay equipment.

1. Frame relay standards are still being defined and implemented differently by vendors.

2. When considering a frame relay device, ascertain what it does.

3. Determine if a frame relay device supports DCLI, header bits, and FCS, FECN, BECN, and DE bits within the frame. Also determine if congestion control is performed to standards, and if so, to which ones? Determine if multiple protocols are supported.

4. Find out in what way a given device supports FECN, BECN, and DE bits. How do they function in respect to congestion management? For example, one may say DE is supported, but what does this mean? Does it mean the bit is read or that it can be set? The latter is important.

5. Is link management supported, and if so, what type?

6. Does the device support transparent mode?

7. Is the device switch-oriented or is it primarily an access device used to provide access into a frame relay network?

This is but a preliminary list meant to help those beginning with frame relay. A more exhaustive list can developed from reference sources included in Sec. 11.6.

11.6   Additional Information

Here is a list of sources that contain considerably more detail than can be presented here. The sources are divided by categories.

ANSI

T1.601	Basic Access Interface
T1.602	ISDN Data Link Layer Signaling Specifications
T1S1/90-75	Frame Relay Bearer Service, Architectural Framework Description
T1S1/90-214	Core Aspects of Frame Protocol for Use with Frame Relay Bearer Service

T1S1/90-213	Signaling Specification for Frame Relay Bearer Service
T1.606	ISDN Architectural Framework
T1.607	Digital Subscriber Signaling Service
T1.617	Standards Concerning Customer Interface
T1.618	Standards Concerning Customer Interface
T1S1/90-051R2	Carrier to Customer Interface

CCITT

I.122	Q.920	1.320	X.25
I.233	Q.921	1.320	X.31
I.130	Q.922	1.430	X.134
I.441	Q.930	1.431	X.213
I.450	Q.931	1.462	X.300
I.451			

Four corporations.   The following corporations made considerable contributions to the development of frame relay standards, as previously mentioned. They should be the point of contact for further information about the LMI standards.

- Cisco Systems, Inc.
- Digital Equipment Corporation
- Stratacom
- Northern Telecom, Inc.

11.7 Summary

Frame relay principles are explained, including the concept of virtual links, the data link connection identifier, and the associated costs of frame relay beyond supporting hardware and software. Frame relay frame components are presented and the fields that comprise a frame are briefly explained.

The concept of virtual circuits is explained. The switched virtual circuit (SVC) is similar to a telephone; a permanent virtual circuit (PVC) is similar to a leased line arrangement; and a multicast virtual circuit (MVC) is where a group of users can be reached through one multicast.

Access devices used in frame relay networks are discussed. The basic function of a switch, a network-related device, and a frame relay access device are explained. Different implementations may use one or more of these devices.

A brief list of consumer tips is included for the consumer who is new to frame relay. A list of reference sources is included in Sec. 11.6 for those who desire more in-depth knowledge of this topic.

12

Managing Data, Voice, and Multimedia

When you begin to plan for your network, you should consider how it will be managed. Rather than isolate a given vendor's program and analyze whether or not it is to be used, this chapter explains the nature of network management. The principles explained in this chapter provide you with guidelines to consider when you begin to make network management decisions.

Data, voice, and multimedia networks now require management techniques that provide maximum information to the administrator. Therefore, programs and support provisions in hardware for data, voice, and multimedia need to be evaluated with a broad range of network management requirements in mind.

The notion of network management connotes different meanings to different people, depending upon their background and technical expertise. Some view network management as the means by which technical information is obtained about a network and conclusions are made to chart the future of the network or its technical aspects. For example, information can be obtained about networks to indicate where additional resources may be required to achieve a predefined desired result. Information can also be obtained to indicate placement of equipment to balance network loads, thus making a network cost-efficient. These and similar decisions are technical by nature and are the result of the technical philosophy of managing networks.

Another philosophy towards network management exists—that is, one rooted in a financial philosophy. Some people use network management tools to obtain information to substantiate financial decisions affecting the network. This group usually makes what seem to be financially good decisions at the time, but the eventual costs exceed the initial savings. If my grandmother were alive, she would call this penny-wise and pound-foolish. A trained technical eye can usually discern those corporations that have people who make decisions based mostly upon costs today rather than smart technical investment. An indicator of this is that decisions affecting the technical aspects of a network can impact it so negatively that it is obvious a trained technical person most likely did not make the decisions.

These two approaches to network management are prevalent in the marketplace. Granted, they are not advertised, but observation can reveal one or the other over time. In the best of environments, a healthy mix of the two exists.

12.1   Data, Voice, and Multimedia Considerations

Network management is a context-dependent term, and a solid definition of the term is debatable. "What can be managed in a network?" is not as important a question as "What is desired to be managed?" Most pieces of a network can be managed, regardless of the category a network component might fit into. The degree to which a network component is important within the context of a network generally dictates if it should be managed and, if so, to what degree.

For example, many networks consist of the following components:

- Hardware
- Core equipment
- Local resources
- Proprietary equipment
- Software
- Peripheral equipment
- Remote resources
- Nonproprietary equipment

To a degree, practically all networks consist of components from these categories. Some networks may have equipment concentrated in a few categories, whereas others may have numerous pieces of equipment compiled from most of the categories.

Hardware

Networks consist of hardware—the question is to what degree and how much. As of this writing, networks are predominately hardware and software. This combination consists of different types of each, performing different functions, therefore synthesizing the results of each into a whole that yields more than the pieces. That, in short, constitutes a network.

Hardware can be delineated into subcategories, such as the following:

- Processors
- Controllers
- Interfaces
- Telecommunication devices
- Physical links
- Network devices

These devices perform definable roles. The degree to which they are mixed is usually dictated by the needs which the network is intended to serve, by the capabilities of an individual product, and by the vendor. For example, some vendors have processors that can perform functions that other vendors' processors cannot merely because of the architecture.

Software

Software also can be delineated into categories. Some of these include:

- Operating systems
- Network operating systems
- User applications
- Software used to control or provide specialized services via network devices

Other categories may be definable, but the aforementioned exist to some degree in all networks. In some instances, an operating system can supply the capabilities required to perform certain network services, such as a network protocol. Software used to control and provide services for network devices is another example. This software could perform some type of protocol conversion or could aid in the connectivity of mulitple platforms that combine to create a network.

Core equipment

Core equipment can be defined as that equipment crucial to create a network and make it function. Usually, a processor, software, telecommunication equipment, user applications, and physical links combined comprise the minimum requirements for a network. What an individual might consider to be core equipment typically varies by vendor and the size of the network. For example, a network that spans multiple countries and time zones would most likely have different core equipment than a network that meet the needs of a single classroom in a geographically isolated location.

Peripheral equipment

This type of equipment varies greatly, typically by vendor. For example, IBM peripheral equipment might be required to aid in the functionality of terminals or printers. Another example, at the opposite extreme, could be an AppleTalk network utilizing a device to make printer sharing possible. Defining peripheral equipment in a network is difficult to do outside the confines of a vendor implementation.

Local resources

Most networks can have equipment identified as being local or remote. The former generally agreed as being in the same physical location to which reference is made. These resources may differ as to how they are managed and in the degree to which they need network management functions.

Local resources tend to be easier to manage in a network, if for no other reason than that they are local and that they are at or near the major portion of the network. Local resources are usually defined as those resources in close proximity to the main portion of a network, or at least to the part that is considered central.

Remote resources

These resources are not within the confines of the identified location of a network. *Remote* has multiple connotations. A remote resource may be across the street or halfway around the world. Conservatively, remote means not in the locale of the user (be it human or program).

A remote resource is considered to be one that is not at the processor or loaction of the user (be it human or program).

Proprietary equipment

It is possible to contruct a network with one vendor's equipment. This is becoming more unusual, but it nevertheless can be done. From a management perspective, this is becoming increasingly important. Some vendors that provide network equipment have their own ways of managing hardware and software. These vendors plan into the management scheme what components can and cannot be managed.

Many companies today claim to have compatible equipment. This can be misleading. When someone says something is compatible, I immediately wonder to what degree. Compatibility is a growing concern in the network industry today. And, just because someone says something is compatible does not mean it is 100 percent replaceable. So, the technical hairsplit becomes, wherein lies the incompatibility?

To a considerable degree, incompatibility is unimportant. A considerable amount of networking equipment at the time of this writing can be classified as compatible or not according to varying categories of compatibility. One area wherein compatibility is not clear is that of network management. In a broad sense, it is easy for a device or software to be compatible with network mangement tools, but the original question still applies: to what degree?

Despite popular opinion, there is an argument for maintaining proprietary vendor equipment. But it should be noted that just because a single vendor is the equipment provider, this does not guarantee that an entire network can be managed. Startling as it sounds, this is true.

Nonproprietary equipment

Probably the most difficult equipment to manage is a network that is a hodgepodge of vendors' equipment. Not that this is a *bad* thing, but it is difficult to manage. This is true because network management, just like any kind of management, implies agreement upon fundamental issues—not only what these issues are but also how they are managed.

The argument here is simple. The more diverse a network is by representation of vendors' equipment, the more likely it is that a degree of *unmanageability* will exist. A simpler way to say this is, "One size fits all." Those who have been around the block more than once know this is not the case in most instances. Unfortunately, it is the naive who are susceptible to such claims.

The idea of nonproprietary equipment in a network permeates the industry. A difficult concept to define is that which is nonproprietary. In today's market, vendors shun the notion of anything being proprietary; however, the idea of being nonproprietary carries equal adverse connotations. For example, if a piece of equipment is nonproprietary, then who (what vendor) is responsible for it? Suddenly, the notion of being nonproprietary becomes less popular.

These ideas bring us full circle to again ask the question, "What can be managed?" No exhaustive list exists explaining those devices that can be managed and those that cannot. A time may come when such a list does exist, but at present, partial listings and human recall of reality govern the industry. A better way to examine the question is by way of network protocol.

12.2   Management Philosophies

Two basic philosophies or methods of management can be used; in fact, both may be incorporated and employed within the confines of a singular network management program.

Poll-driven management

Poll-driven management can easily be understood by examining its function via analogy. Consider a cook, a kitchen, and three ovens. Each oven has a loaf of bread baking inside, but the loaves are not yet ready to be removed. One method of determining when a loaf of bread in a given oven is ready is by visual examination of each loaf.

This means that the cook examines each loaf of bread every so often to see if it ready to be removed. This examination is similar to polling. Here is an anology of a cook with multiple loaves of bread. This example of polling means that the cook examines ovens 1, 2, and 3 every so often, each time making a mental note of the condition of each loaf of bread; thus, there is a reference point for determining when each loaf of bread is ready. At some time, each loaf of bread is deemed *ready* and, hence, is removed from the oven.

This analogy may seem crude, but it is a good example of how polling operates—not only in management schemes, but also in other areas, such as data link protocols or other technological implementations. In the cook, bread, and oven example, some observations can be made.

First, the cook exerts tremendous energy opening and closing oven doors or peering through windows in each oven. Regardless of the method, time is required on behalf of the cook. *Time* is here considered to be that required by a cook to examine each loaf of bread (even though this amount of time may be minuscule) and to assimilate the visual information obtained by observing each loaf of bread.

Second, each loaf of bread may be at a different state of readiness. For example, just because the bread in oven 1 appears to be like that loaf of bread in oven 3 does not necessarily mean that it *is* identical. The difference between the two may be small, but that amount is nevertheless significant. If you do not think this is the case, expand your thoughts to include 100 ovens, 100 loaves of bread, and 1 cook! Get the point?

Third, the ovens are not the same. They may be made by the same vendor, manufactured to meet the same specifications, and checked to be at the same temperature, but differences nevertheless exist. If in no other difference than location, ovens differ. Even cooks attest to this!

The point is that each oven may differ by an insignificant amount, but multiplied by a considerable number of ovens, the difference becomes significant. Practically speaking, most agree that the ovens are the same. This agreement is a matter of degrees—no pun intended.

Event-driven management

Event-driven anything is just that. To put it bluntly, this is interrupt-driven. An *interrupt* in any environment is an interruption. A simplistic analogy of event-driven management comes by way of another example of ordinary life.

Consider how many times an individual visits an emergency medical facility. Normally, people visit these facilities only when emergency care is needed. In other words, their care is given on an as-needed basis.

This as-needed basis is problematic by design. One need only think on a global scale to realize the world's problems in the medical arena. The inherent problem of event-driven (on-demand) anything is that the greater number of events inversely affects the ability, at some point, to meet event requests. Think about it. The ability to meet the emergency needs of a given community effectively is inversely proportional to the number of individual demands placed on emergency medical clinics. Consider this: imagine one person going to an emergency clinic requiring care. Next, imagine 10 people needing immediate care in the same clinic. Then, imagine 100 people in the same clinic requiring care. Now, imagine 1,000 people entering an emergency clinic requiring immediate attention. I think the point is made.

The same is true for network management that utilizes this type of philosophy. The greater the number of devices in a given network, the greater the requirements to meet those needs become. And, at some point, there is a point of no return. It is one thing to have a designated host to manage another host, 10 hosts, or even 100 hosts, but consider the same host attempting to manage 1,000 hosts. The implications abound.

First, the implication of having a pipeline big enough to move data from the hosts requiring management to the management host either accommodates multiple hosts to be managed or a singular one; if the latter is the case, then increasing the number of hosts to be managed clearly implies that a saturation point will be reached in time. Furthermore, since this type of management is *event*-driven, it is similar to having a room of some 100 or 1,000 individuals listening to a mathematics lecture—the number of possible questions increases with each individual. At some point, multiple individuals will have questions simultaneously; how will this be handled?

12.3   Multiprotocol Management

Networks consisting of multiple upper- and lower-layer protocols are the order of the day. Maybe not to the user, but to those who must cope with the operational aspect of the network, multiple protocols lend themselves to complexity. Complexity in anything is, at best, difficult to manage. Ironically, it is the complexity that creates the user-friendly appearance to the end user.

Most upper-layer protocols have their own method of management. For example, the way Advanced Peer-to-Peer Networking is managed is different from that of Transmission Control Protocol/Internet Protocl (TCP/IP). The former is defined and maintained by IBM, whereas the latter is maintained by the Internet Engineering Task Force, which oversees those requests for comments (RFCs) that define how TCP/IP is managed.

As these two examples indicate, the origins of these network protocols differ, and so do their methods of management. Consequently, when both are integrated into a single environment, a multiplatform environment emerges. Hence, that which had been the norm for management no longer applies.

Systems network architecture (SNA)

SNA is IBM's networking architecture. It is one of IBM's networking solutions, and it is the oldest of those offered. SNA was launched in the 1970s and has continued gaining marketshare since. SNA is a complex architecture. It was designed that way so that it could accommodate a variety of implementations. Its dominance in the marketplace is due partially to this adaptability.

Managing SNA can be traced back to the 1970s. Network management then was not what it is today. At that time, the technology in the marketplace was barely one step above punched cards. The marketplace is singled out because in research environments, the space industry, and other engineering-intensive arenas, computing and networking was beginning to move into depths not to be reached in the marketplace in general for years to come. Now, some two decades removed from its inception, SNA continues to grow.

Advanced peer-to-peer networking (APPN)

APPN is another networking architecture from IBM. It differs from SNA because it is a peer-oriented rather than hierarchical SNA. It is not better; it is different.

APPN is managed differently than SNA. Though some of the aspects of management are similar, such as some network mangement protocols, others are different. They differ in that they exchange data differently—SNA in a hierarchical manner and APPN in a peer manner.

APPN networks can be managed by multiple management programs, one of which is *NetView. SystemView* can also be used to manage APPN networks.

Transmission control protocol/internet protocol (TCP/IP)

TCP/IP is generally managed today by *Simple Network Mangement Protocol* (SNMP). This management application is defined by the RFCs that specify TCP/IP protocol architecture and operations. SNMP is offered by different vendors; operationally, it works about the same regardless of vendor.

SNMP is built around a distributed system that employs multiple small programs that communicate with a centralized management program.

DECnet

Digital Equipment's DECnet can be managed in multiple ways. In the past DEC used *Polycenter,* which is a product that focuses upon collective network management. Because of the open nature of DEC's architecture, DECnet management today is more peer-oriented with regard to functions such as time service, record management services, and distributed name service, to name a few.

A product named *Six2View* also can be used to manage a DECnet environment. This product was created by Phoenix Network Technologies Inc. The product is built around Logical Unit 6.2 (LU6.2). Because of this architecture, the product is robust and capable of handling significantly sized DECnet sites and integrating them into NetView.

The end result of Six2View is that a NetView operator can use NetView to manage not only the SNA environment but also the DECnet environment.

NetWare

NetWare has management capabilities built into it. Because of NetWare's capabilities, some of its components may be managed from NetView—for example, if multiple NetWare environments connect into an SNA environment via a Local Area Network Resource (LANRES). If this is the case, management issues arise in the SNA network and in local NetWare networks as well.

AppleTalk

AppleTalk network management is similar to other network management systems. Particular devices, functions, or services are managed.

AppleTalk management can provide information about network security as well as system resource workloads.

Functions such as system or program backup can also be realized from AppleTalk. Servers can be managed and network performance can be viewed.

12.4   Information Attained via Management

With most networks, similar information is needed to make accurate assessments about the network. Some information that is typically desired by a network manager includes the following:

- Resource utilization requirements
- Link bandwidth
- Response time
- Resource status
- Application-specific information

Resource utilization requirements may come under the guise of a different name, but usually the information is similar. A fundamental question to this notion of resource utilization is, "What is a resource"? Technical hairsplits usually begin at this point. In large networks a resource can be a link, a software application, or a CPU. Smaller networks may identify a resource in more general terms, identifying applications, CPU, memory, and other requirements.

Regardless of the network, all networks have resource utilization requirements. Lest one think this is not the case, try loading a program onto a system that requires more disk space or memory than is available. Realization of resource utilization requirements will become clear. Stated more simply: when the number of users exceeds the amount of disk space required for a system to operate, most work comes to a halt. I have experienced this first-hand and have learned the importance of understanding resource utilization requirements.

Resource utilization requirements are obtained partly by science and partly by art. Precision in measuring resource requirements becomes a blur in most networks. It seems a place is reached that cannot always be predicted. The best resource utilization requirement tools should be used with this thought in mind. A fine line exists between mathematics and reality.

Link bandwidth

Link bandwidth is best calculated after obtaining two pieces of information: details of the actual link and an overall view of the surrounding network components. Once this information is acquired, a synthesis of both is best.

Link bandwidth is tricky to calculate. Many factors enter the picture when dealing with reality. In test-bed environments, where isolated conditions can be maintained, figures can be tabulated. In the real world, factors enter into the equation that seldom reach the eyes of those who write specifications, unless those individuals have come from the real world of implementation.

A realistic question about link bandwidth usually overrides other information. In a real implementation, the question "Where is the bottleneck?" is always sobering. Sometimes the bandwidth of the link is insignificant, because a bottleneck in another part of the network causes congestion. This is where the reality/cost equation kicks in.

A point exists in most implementations where adding additional bandwidth to the link is moot. It is similar to an analogy I gave a friend about driving the congested freeways of Dallas at rush hour: "Concerning movement, what does it matter if I have a Corvette or Honda? When traffic is moving 10 miles per hour, little is gained if I have a 300-horsepower engine." This is similar to networks.

Some networks today have bandwidth capabilities that outstrip the capability of the components that make up the network. When this occurs, a decision must be made; normally, the reality/cost equation dominates.

Response time

This is another topic that many network administrators prefer to avoid. Response time in a network is usually proportional to the number of users currently using the network, the location of the network components, and the complexity of the network. Response time can be elusive.

In most networks, *response time* refers to the amount of time it takes for input from a keyboard to reach the application and a response to be returned. Some networks, like SNA, have this as a straightforward measurement. It is best to realize that because of the customization possibilities in SNA—namely, NetView—understanding response-time mesaurement can be site-specific and relative at best. Response time can reflect different measurements according to the network.

Resource status

Resource status is nebulous. Some networks use different terms to identify a resource. Some networks identify an application, a processor, or even a link as a resource. Other networks identify processors as servers, therefore indirectly identifying them as a resource.

Explaining a resource status is a matter of degrees. One might be *active* or *inactive,* or a resource could be defined as *80 percent with regard to maximum usage.* Many variances exist. Normally, they reflect vendor interpretation of the idea.

Application-specific

Application-specific information can be ascertained by management programs. Applications generally are products of the environment they operate in, and they reflect that environment's characteristics to some degree. An application may be interactive or programmatic in nature. In today's world of networking, another category exists where both can be characteristic of an application.

Application-specific information generally falls into a couple of categories, such as percentage of utilization with regard to the number of users; and percentage of utilization with regard to amount of system resources, such as CPU, memory, disk space, and other information.

12.5   Summary

Managing a network today is difficult. Managing data, voice, and multimedia networks requires significant artistic talent as well an ability to implement the skills acquired through learning the science of management. Network management difficulty is usually proportional to the size of the network (number of users), the location, the complexity of tasks being performed in the network, and site-specific issues.

In little more than a decade, network management has exploded from gathering statistical information generally used by the elite to gathering information to be digested by technical and management personnel alike. Not only have networks themselves changed radically (conservatively speaking) in the past decade, the management tools used to understand them have done so as well.

Network management is best implemented with consideration to long-term consequences. Along with this thought is a reminder that it is best to remember that different network protocols usually have inherently different methods of management. Furthermore, just because a network is integrated does not necessarily mean that the sum will be more easily managed than the parts.

13

File Structures

Most likely, you will encounter file systems you are unfamiliar with during the design or implementation of your network. For that reason, I am including this chapter for your benefit. It will give you all the information you need to work with the majority of systems in use throughout the world today.

Vendors have traditionally not paid much attention to the compatibility of their file structures with other vendors' equipment. As with the number of operating systems, so there is a significant number of different file structures. For example, IBM's mainframes have different file structures than do Apple computers or UNIX systems.

Conversely, some operating systems from different vendors are compatible—for example, UNIX. IBM's version of UNIX is compatible with Hewlett-Packard's version; hence, compatibility among files.

Another anomaly exists with file structures. Differences exist among the same vendor's equipment. An ideal example of this is IBM. IBM's three major large-systems operating systems—Multiple Virtual Storage (MVS), Virtual Machine (VM), and Virtual Storage Extended (VSE)—are all different with respect to how they store data. Likewise, these three differ in structure when compared to the AS/400 operating system known as OS/400.

File structure takes on greater significance today because of the integration of heterogeneous computing equipment. Lack of understanding as to how different operating systems (and their respective storage methods) handle files and directories is naive at best when working in an integrated site. For example, if a file exists on a UNIX host and is moved (copied) to a MVS host, where does the file appear by default? And, what is the naming convention of the file under MVS after it is transferred? Not knowing this can cost time. Time, as always, has a price tag associated with it.

This chapter focuses upon the file and directory structures of the following environments:

- Apple
- MVS
- UNIX
- OS/400
- VM

- Open/VMS
- VSE
- S/38
- MS-DOS
- S/36

13.1 Perspective

File structures in different systems are neither good nor bad. They are merely different. If any observation could be made, it could be that this a prime example that we live in a de facto world. On the other hand, the organization of file and directory structures is not totally arbitrary. Some organizational structures were constructed to optimize system resources. System design is directly proportional to the efficiency of system performance. Herein lies a valid consideration.

Decentralization and *heterogeneous integration* are recent phenomena on the computing timeline. Historically, most individuals were not thinking of decentralization and heterogeneous integration as we have come to know them today.

Take, for instance, UNIX and MVS. Around 1973, few if any individuals would have considered integrating the two together in the marketplace. It may have been discussed in think tanks or other esoteric locations, but as few as 20 or so years ago this idea of integrating different vendors' equipment was for the most part anathema. Sometime since then, the idea that different computer equipment should communicate and share data began to evolve.

Without understanding different file and directory structures in *dissimilar* systems, productivity usually falls short of expectations. As I have said before, integration is not solely a technical matter. A site that implements VM, UNIX, Open/VMS, and Apple operating systems, is complex. Understanding how data is stored is a different issue altogether. To overlook this is to overlook one of the most fundamental concerns in a heterogeneous environment.

13.2 Apple

Apple's operating system uses a straightforward directory and file structure from the user's perspective. An Apple user needs to be familiar with three basic concepts: the icon representing a disk, the concept of a folder, and a file. (Granted, other topics are important, too, but the issue here is file and directory structures.)

Most Apple environments present a *menu bar,* a *trash can icon,* and a *hard disk icon* (and possibly an icon representing another disk or item) once the system is powered on.

Navigation and operation in this environment is somewhat intuitive. But, little commonality in naming conventions exists in some areas. On the other hand, the icon representing a disk drive is obvious in its representation.

If an icon of a hard disk appears on the display, and one double-clicks on that icon, the directory listing of that disk is displayed. However, other icons and their functions are not as straightforward. Take, for instance, the trash can. This is particular to the Apple environment.

Some think that if the icon of a file is moved to the trash can, and the trash can is expanded, the file is destroyed (deleted). This is not necessarily true. The file is deleted after the command is isssued via menu bar to *empty trash,* or the system is powered down (or other possible methods). Prior to the "empty trash" command, the file remains intact in the trash can.

A *folder* in an Apple environment is analogous to a file folder one might use in a filing cabinet. If a folder used in a filing cabinet is labeled, the label typically reflects the contents. The same concept holds true for folders in the Apple environment. For example, if a folder is labeled *engineering,* its contents would most likely contain drawings and other information related to that topic. But this does not have to be the case. The naming convention used can be totally arbitrary, bearing significance only to the individual creating it.

A double-click on the folder icon reveals a list of its files. These files may be of practically any type. For example, a single folder may have word processor files, database files, programming files, and others.

13.3 Multiple Virtual Storage (MVS)

MVS is one of IBM's operating systems for large processors. This operating system stores and retrieves data in what is called a *data set.* Data sets are a unit of storage, and multiple types of data sets exist. The data set's name normally reflects the arrangement of data in a particular way. But at least seven different types of data sets can be identified that have particular purposes. Two types of data sets are presented here because of their popularity in the user community.

Partitioned data set (PDS)

A Partitioned Data Set (PDS) is also called a *PARMLIB*. The terms are used synonymously in documentation and among users who work with MVS. Nevertheless, a PDS has three basic components:

- Directory listing
- Member listing
- Records

Figure 13.1 depicts a basic conceptual view of PDS structure and its components. It consists of three parts. First, the part that most consider to be the *directory* is a list of the members. The directory contains more information than the list of members, however.

The directory listing is just that—a listing of the members in the PDS. A *member* is the same as a file, practically speaking. The records contain the actual data stored.

Figure 13.2 shows detailed information included in a PDS directory (which is usually the first page of a printout or screen view). Two boxes of *general data* are included in Fig. 13.2. The organization listed in the first box indicates the organization of the records that make up the member. Records can be organized in different ways. Some records can be fixed-block, some variable, and some can use other arrangements of organization. The *volume serial* is the name given to the volume. In IBM lingo, particularly in the MVS environment, a *volume* is a disk.

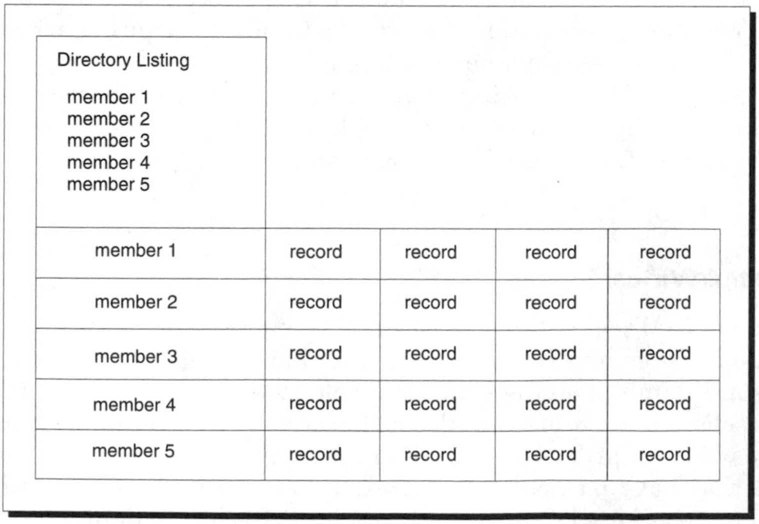

Directory Listing member 1 member 2 member 3 member 4 member 5				
member 1	record	record	record	record
member 2	record	record	record	record
member 3	record	record	record	record
member 4	record	record	record	record
member 5	record	record	record	record

Figure 13.1   Conceptual view of a PDS.

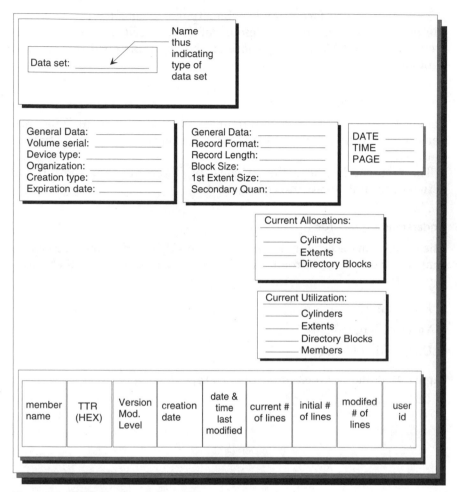

Figure 13.2   PDS directory information.

The other box includes the *record format,* which indicates the formatting of records of each member, and the *record length.* Records may have varying lengths. Because of this, it is important to know the designation.

Current allocations reflect specific disk information—namely, how the disk is utilized. The current utilization reflects real-time utilization of the disk with the data of this PDS.

Further specific information is provided about each individual member. For example, the *member name* is provided, and its *creation date,* the time it was *last modified,* the *current number of lines* in a particular member, and so forth—even the *user id* that created it.

This amount of information is exhaustive, but considering the size of the implementation and the amount of data stored in these environments, those troubleshooting those storage systems need this level of depth at times.

Sequential data set

Sequential data sets are popular in an MVS environment. They are basically a flat file. Figure 13.3 shows a conceptual view of this type of data set.

The member is like a file. It consists of records that contain the actual data that constitute the member.

Understanding records

The concept of records is dominant in the MVS environment. Records contain actual data. Three types of records are used in an MVS environment:

- Fixed length
- Variable length
- Unspecified length

Figure 13.4 shows an example of each type of record.

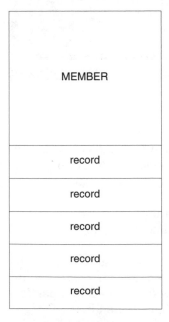

Figure 13.3 Sequential data set.

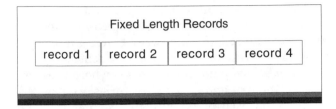

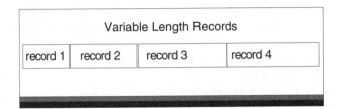

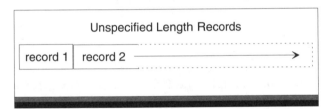

Figure 13.4 Types of record structures.

Record types are used in different circumstances for purposes that can sometimes maximize system storage. A *fixed-length* record has the same length as all other records to which it is physically or logically attached. *Variable-length* records have a length that is independent of other records to which they are physically or logically attached. *Unspecified-length* records have a length that is not defined. One way to describe this is that a single logical record makes up a physical record.

13.4 UNIX

The UNIX operating system uses directories, subdirectories, and files in much the same way as a DOS operating system implements these ideas. Some user tips are included in this section, but the primary focus here is upon directory and file structure.

In UNIX, a *forward slash* (/) separates directories and subdirectories. This is opposite from MS-DOS, which uses the *backslash* (\ ) to separate directores and subdirectories.

The UNIX directory structure is similar to an upside-down tree. At the top is the *ROOT* directory; beneath it are other directories, such as *bin* (for binary), *usr* (for user), and *etc* (for etcetera), to name a few.

Two additional items of interest are important to consider here. First, the notion of a *fully qualified path name.* This is where the complete directory listing from the root and all subdirectories are listed. A *partial qualified path name* is used to refer to the current working directory; that is, the subdirectory and the filename. An example of this could be */usr/myfile.*

Some variations of UNIX permits changing directories by entering the tilde (~) and a partial subdirectory, thus averting the need for much typing.

Conceptually, the structure of root directory and the first subdirectories appears as shown in Fig. 13.5.

Beyond the example in Fig. 13.5 is the typical working environment of many users, as shown in Fig. 13.6.

As Fig. 13.6 shows, multiple subdirectories exist in a typical working environment. Other subdirectories can be identified as text, binary, or other specific designators.

13.5 OS/400

OS/400 is the AS/400's operating system. OS/400 uses different concepts than other systems. For example, the OS/400 treats most items as objects. An *object,* to the AS/400, refers to anything that exists, occupies space, and can have operations performed on it.

Libraries

Libraries are used as a means of organizing objects. Consequently, different types of libraries exist. Some of them include the following:

QGPL   A general purpose library. It is the default library where files are stored, as are other objects, if no designation is specified.

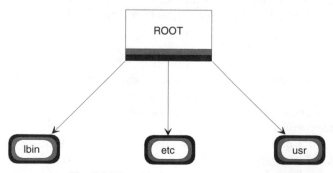

Figure 13.5 The ROOT and common directories immediately beneath it.

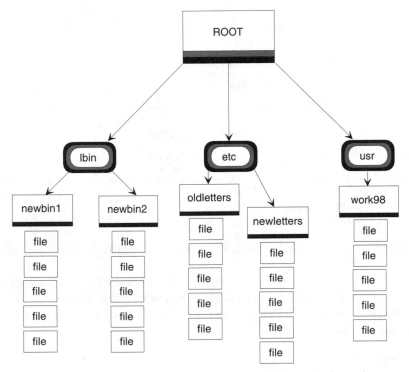

Figure 13.6   ROOT, first-level subdirectories, and subdirectories beneath.

QSPL   The spooling subsystem that contains objects required for the
          spooling of data.

QSYS   The library that contains IBM-supplied objects necessary to
          operate the system.

Practically speaking, libraries could be considered directories. But libraries are more than that; they may have pointers to objects that are not necessarily files.

Files

The AS/400 has two categories of files: physical and logical.

A *physical* file is made up of members, which in turn are made up of records—the actual data. Data in physical files are arranged by rows and columns. Figure 13.7 shows an example of a physical file.

File and directory structure in OS/400 is as follows:

Library   File   Member

In a loose sense, the library is a larger categorization of files. One way to look at the structure is to think of a file as similar to a directory

TEST FILE 1			
member 1	RECORD	RECORD	RECORD
member 2	RECORD	RECORD	RECORD
member 3	RECORD	RECORD	RECORD
member 4	RECORD	RECORD	RECORD
member 5	RECORD	RECORD	RECORD
member 6	RECORD	RECORD	RECORD

Figure 13.7   Physical file (conceptual view).

and a member as similar to a file. Consequently, multiple files can be part of a library.

A *logical* file reflects *how* data is viewed as a combination of one or more files or members. Logical files are ways of viewing data in different ways. The following lists four examples of logical files that are possible on the AS/400.

- Join logical files
- Multiple format logical files
- View logical files
- Simple logical files

A *join* logical file defines one record from a combination of fields, from multiple physical files.

A *multiple format* logical file allows access to multiple physical files, each having its own record format definition.

A *view* logical file can be created by an SQL *create view* declaration. This view logical file is one record definition comprised of fields from multiple physical and view logical files.

A *simple* logical file is the creation of a logical record definition with data mapped from one physical file.

OS/400 files have different characteristics. For example, there are binary, text, and other types of files. The diversity of the file structure in OS/400 should not be underestimated in terms of complexity.

I recommend acquiring the appropriate IBM manuals concerning the organization of file and library (directory) structure. The AS/400 system has a well-organized tutorial on these and other topics. I have viewed in excess of 50 tutorials and found them quite helpful. Another consideration is the commands used in the OS/400 environment.

13.6 Virtual Machine (VM)

VM is another IBM operating system used with large processors. VM is *unlike* MVS. VM has its own file structure, peculiar to the operation of VM.

It is helpful to examine other considerations before focusing upon VM field and directory structure. Fundamental to VM is the concept that multiple operating systems can run under VM. This concept is called *Multiple Preferred Guests* (MPGs). See Figure 13.8.

VM consists of multiple components. Two are of concern here—the *Conversational Monitoring System* (CMS) and the *Control Program* (CP). CMS is actually a user interface. Users enter commands to perform specific functions. CMS, in turn, operates under the control of CP.

CP communicates with hardware. It is easiest to think of these components as layers to understand their relationship to the actual machine. Consider Fig. 13.9, which depicts a logical view of an actual system, the hardware that CP interacts with, and CMS.

Figure 13.9 also shows DASD, which is controlled indirectly by the CP through the hardware. An MVS user in Fig. 13.9 would *see* DASD as if it were dedicated to that particular user. Note that this diagram shows that each MPG communicates with CP and CMS. CP handles

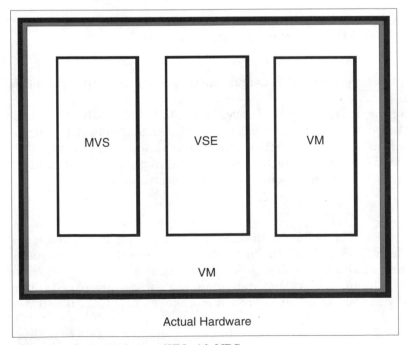

Figure 13.8 Conceptual view of VM with MPGs.

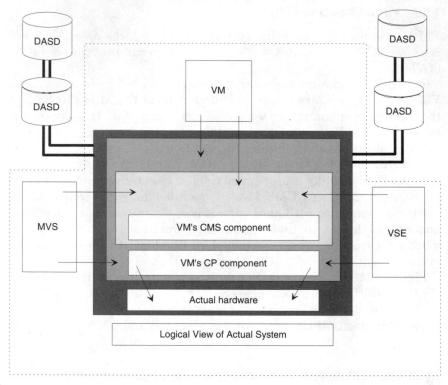

Figure 13.9   Two VM components and their interrelationship.

the hardware related requests and functions. Figure 13.10 depicts this idea.

CMS provides user-oriented services to MVS, VM, and VSE, respectively. A system directory in CMS is maintained and contains information such as users, user status, and a user's password, among other functions. This system directory can be used to produce a list of users and to shut the system down, to name two possibilities.

Disks

Each physical VM disk is partitioned into groups of tracks called *minidisks*. Each CMS disk volume has a *master file directory* that contains the names of all files on that disk. When a user accesses a particular minidisk, the file names that individual may access are paged into a *user file directory* residing in virtual storage. Figure 13.11 illustrates this idea.

The result is that a user thinks that each minidisk has its own directory of file names.

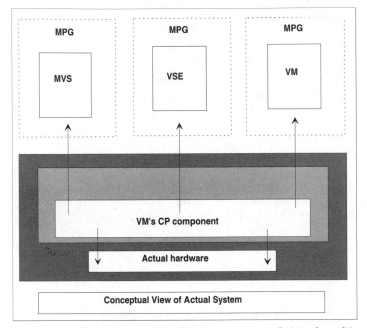

Figure 13.10   CP manages real hardware resources and virtual machines.

When a user updates a CMS file or creates a new file, information about the file is updated in the master file directory on the CMS disk and in the user file directory in virtual storage.

Minidisks are available to CMS users in two modes: read and write. This applies to files, collectively, on a particular minidisk—not on a file-by-file basis. For example, if a user has *read-only* privileges a file cannot be updated, but it can be browsed, copied, or executed. If a user

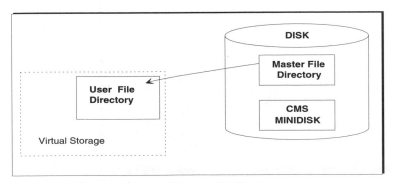

Figure 13.11   Conceptual view of the user file directory.

has *read and write* privileges for a particular minidisk, each time a file is updated the user file and master file directories are updated immediately. Normally, CMS users are allowed read and write privileges to access only one minidisk; this disk is called their *A* disk. Normally, all others are read-only minidisks. Each minidisk is known by a letter of the alphabet. Consequently, the maximum number of minidisks available to a user at a given time is 26.

Files

A file is the fundamental unit of data in a CMS environment. Even though VM/SP is a virtual machine capable of supporting MPGs, CMS disk files cannot be read or written to using other operating systems.

CMS files can be identified by the following attributes:

- Filename
- Filetype
- Filemode

The *filename* is part of what gives a CMS file its identity. The filetype is a naming convention used to group files according to some common characteristic—for example, assembler, executable, and others.

The *filemode* identifier consists of two characters. First, it indicates to CMS on which virtual minidisk the file resides. Second, it is used to assign certain access characteristics to a file. Consider Fig. 13.12 as an example of the file-naming convention.

Records

VM files consist of records. Records consist of a specified length and format; they can be fixed length or variable length.

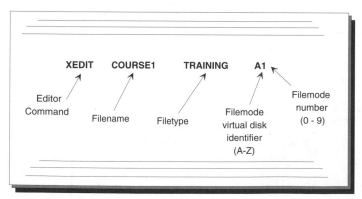

Figure 13.12 File-naming convention.

In a CMS, records constitute a line of data in a file. *Fixed-length* records in a CMS file means that if the line is not filled with data, CMS fills trailing positions to make all the records the same length. This amounts to less efficiency in disk capacity but allows faster processing speed. Figure 13.13 shows an example of this type of record organization.

Variable-length records in CMS do not fill the line so that all are the same length. This amounts to less overhead in storage, but causes slower processing speed (see Fig. 13.14).

13.7 Open/VMS

Digital Equipment's operating system, known as VMS, stores data on disks and tape. The following explores that structure and explains how a user can manipulate it.

Assuming a user has logged in and at the prompt enters *DIRECTORY* and presses return, the following will be displayed on the user's screen:

- The disk where that user's directory and files are located.

- The directory name.

- File names, types, and version numbers of files in that directory.

- The total number of files in the directory.

See Fig. 13.15.

Subdirectories

Subdirectories in VMS are similar to those in UNIX and DOS operating environments. They can be created for file organization. For example, consider Fig. 13.16.

Creating subdirectories presupposes that a user has the authorization to create a subdirectory in a given directory.

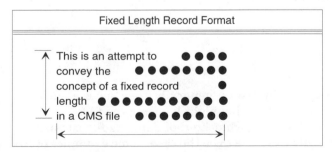

Figure 13.13   Fixed-length record format.

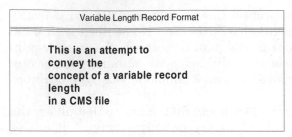

Figure 13.14   Variable length record format.

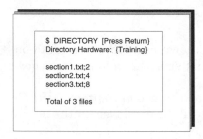

Figure 13.15   Example of entering *DIRECTORY*.

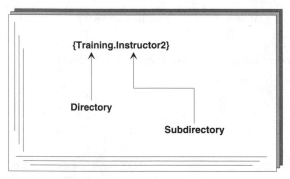

Figure 13.16   Example of a directory and subdirectory.

Files

Files are sets of data elements arranged in a manner significant to a user. Files are identified by:

- Filename
- Type
- Version number

Filenames are assigned by users; generally they have significant meaning to the user or to those who might be using the file.

A file *type* normally describes what kind of data the file consists of; however, this does not always have to be the case. Some examples of file types are listed in Fig. 13.17.

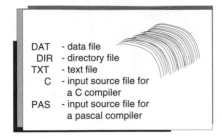

DAT - data file
DIR - directory file
TXT - text file
C   - input source file for
       a C compiler
PAS - input source file for
       a pascal compiler

Figure 13.17 Sample file types.

Files have *version numbers*. When a file is initially created, it is assigned a version number of 1. Anytime that file is edited the number is incremented by 1.

Full file specification

In VMS the concept of a full file specification exists. VMS needs this to locate a particular file; this may even require node identification if the VMS system is networked. Figure 13.18 shows an example of this.

Logical names

A logical name is a user-specified name for any portion or all of a file specification. In short, it is an abbreviation that can be used instead of entering the directory, filename, type, and version number. An example of this is shown in Fig. 13.19.

A logical table maintains the logical names and makes it possible to link them to the desired specification.

13.8   Virtual Storage Extended (VSE)

VSE is another IBM operating system used with relatively large processors. File structure here consists mainly of a user's *library* and its *members,* or files, as they are sometimes called.

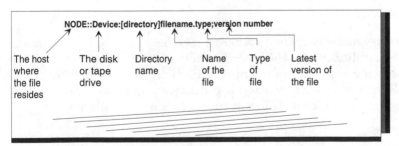

NODE::Device:[directory]filename.type;version number

| The host where the file resides | The disk or tape drive | Directory name | Name of the file | Type of file | Latest version of the file |

Figure 13.18 Example of a full file specification.

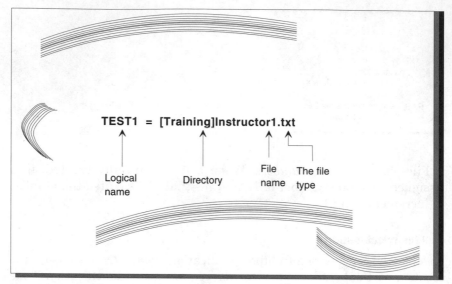

Figure 13.19   Example of a logical name.

Libraries

A group of programs manages libraries. Two types of libraries are the focus here: system and private. Each user has what is called a *private* library, meaning that it is user-owned and is separate from the system library. *System* libraries contain programs and other data necessary for system use.

Members

Members in a VSE environment are identified by:

- Library name
- Sublibrary name
- Member name
- Member type

The *library name* represents where a member is located. The same is true of the sublibrary. A *sublibrary* is a subset of the library. A *member name* is the name given to a member. VSE distinguishes *member types*.

In VSE, the member type used is contingent upon its contents. The following are examples of different types of member contents:

- DUMP
- OBJECT

- PHASE
- PROCEDURE
- SOURCE

Obviously, another type of member exists—that is, one that contains user data. Structure and use of data in the VSE environment is fairly straightforward. VSE itself has evolved into an operating system that is robust but not overly complex.

13.9 S/38

IBM's System/38 has been in the market for many years. Despite the opinion of some, there still is a significant presence of this system when the worldwide marketplace is considered. Hence, the reason for providing information here.

The S/38 has an object-oriented architecture. In many ways it is similar to the architecture of the AS/400. In fact, it was the forerunner of the AS/400. It, like the AS/400, implements the concept of *objects*. Figure 13.20 shows an example of an object's structure.

As Fig. 13.20 shows, two parts exist to any object: the *header* and the *object contents*.

Object classifications

Numerous classifications of objects exist in the S/38. Some of these include:

- Libraries
- Files

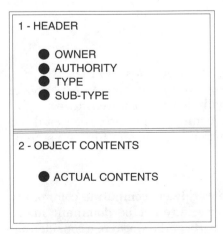

Figure 13.20 Example of an object's content.

- Classes
- Descriptions
- Programs
- Queues
- Tables
- Symbol Sets

Libraries

Libraries in the S/38 are similar to those in the AS/400. Upward compatibility exists between libraries in the S/38 and the AS/400. As in the AS/400, the libraries in the S/38 are used to group related objects.

Files

Two types of files exist within the S/38: physical and logical. *Physical* files contain actual data. *Logical* files are views of physical files. The structure here is similar to that of the AS/400.

13.10   MS-DOS

Most personal computers use either MS-DOS or PC-DOS; the former is a product of Microsoft and the latter is a product of IBM. However, a brand of DOS known as *DR-DOS* has market share. Most brands of DOS use the same file structure; little difference exists between them.

Personal computers (PCs) have the following structures for consideration:

- ROOT directory
- Directory
- Subdirectory
- Files

Figure 13.21 shows an example of these directories and files.

Figure 13.21 shows how *directories, subdirectories,* and *files* appear in a DOS environment. Files normally exist in the root directory as well. But a well-kept system will have minimum files in the root directory and directories of programs where programs and files are stored.

13.11   S/36

The S/36 still has a presence in the worldwide computing community. Though the presence of these systems may not be dominant in the United States, they are used in other parts of the world to a considerable degree. Because of this, understanding their structures is important.

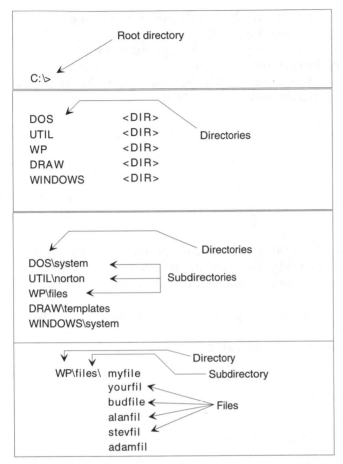

Figure 13.21   Example of DOS structures.

IBM's System/36 has three basic categories of organization:

- Files
- Libraries
- Folders

Each of these categories has its own method of organization. The rationale behind this is twofold. First, it results in efficient processing. Second, it provides flexibility in arrangement.

Files

A file is a set of related records that is treated as a single unit. Two popular types of files include: sequential and indexed.

A *sequential* file is one in which records are stored in the order by which they were entered (see Fig. 13.22).

An *indexed* file contains two parts: first, the *index,* which is a table containing an entry for each record. Each entry is called a *key.* This key is the part that identifies a record. The second part of the file is the *record.* The record is the data (see Fig. 13.23).

Libraries

For practical purposes, three types of libraries exist:

- System
- Program Product
- Application

A *system* library maintains information pertinent to the system itself. *Program product* libraries contain programs that users use. *Application* libraries contain applications and data that users need independently of other users.

A library consists of basically three components, as Fig. 13.24 depicts.

S/36 library *directory* contents include the following:

- Member name
- Time and creation date

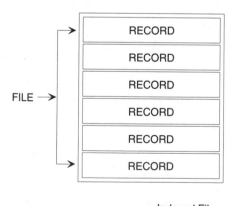

Figure 13.22 Example of S/36 sequential file.

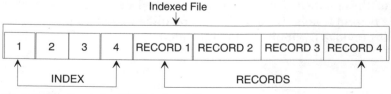

Figure 13.23   Example of S/36 indexed file.

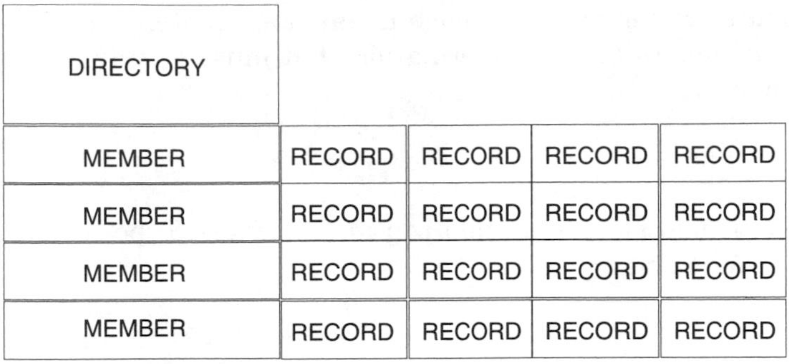

DIRECTORY				
MEMBER	RECORD	RECORD	RECORD	RECORD
MEMBER	RECORD	RECORD	RECORD	RECORD
MEMBER	RECORD	RECORD	RECORD	RECORD
MEMBER	RECORD	RECORD	RECORD	RECORD

Figure 13.24 Example of S/36 library format.

- Type of member
- Type of member subtype
- Size of member
- Attributes of the member
- Storage requirements
- Member reference number
- Number and length of the source statements in the procedure or source member
- The system program release level when the member was created or last changed

Member types

Members are collections of records that have a name, are treated as a single unit, and have a fixed length. Four types of members are the following:

- Source (S)
- Procedure (P)
- Load (L)
- Subroutine (S)

Source members contain statements that may be a part of a program or source specifications to be used by a compiler. Source statements for programs are the simplest examples.

Procedure members consist of necessary statements to perform a program. A set of Operation Control Language (OCL) statements provides an example.

Load members are comprised of machine language statements.

Subroutine members contain information that must be called by a program to be used.

Folders

Folders are areas in disk storage that contain members. Types of folders include the following:

- Mail
- Document
- Mail Log
- Data Dictionary

Mail folders are a designated area of storage used to store documents sent and received as mail.

Document folders are designated areas of storage used to store documents. The documents are lines of text that can be named and stored as members.

A *mail log* folder is also an area of storage. This area is used to record all mail sent and received by a user.

A *data dictionary* folder is an area of storage designated for recording a record field, a format, and file definitions.

Folder organization is hierarchical. It consists of directory, subdirectory, and member levels. The directory (also known as the *root*) contains the following:

- Subdirectories
- Member list
- Location of members

Folder *subdirectories* are a method of grouping related members. *Members* are named collections of statements. An example of a folder member is a *document*.

13.12   Summary

File structures differ according to vendor software and implementation. Understanding the differences of structure is important when files are moved between unlike systems. For example, if a file is moved from a UNIX system to an MVS system, the immediate question arises, "How will the file appear on the MVS system?" To know the answers to questions like this before actually using different systems can save the time that is usually spent coping with such questions after moving a file.

Each operating environment treats files differently. I recommend that the user acquire the original vendor's documentation describing the details of this topic.

14

Network Architecture and TCP/IP
Network Design

Many networks today use Transmission Control Protocol/Internet Protocol (TCP/IP). TCP/IP is an upper-layer network protocol that is in widespread use around the world. In fact, it may well be the most dominant upper-layer network protocol in use as of this writing. This chapter presents the core components of TCP/IP. Here is information that will help you in designing your network and planning to use TCP/IP.

14.1   TCP/IP Perspective

A good place to begin is in the late 1960s. An entity in the U.S. government called the Advanced Research Projects Agency (ARPA) was exploring technologies of all sorts. One of those technologies led to a need (or desire) to create a network based on packet-switching technology to help researchers experiment with what they built. It was also seen as a means whereby then-current telephone lines could be used to connect scientists and personnel in physically different locations in order to work together.

By late 1969, the necessary components had come together to create the *ARPAnet*. In short order, a few individuals had put together a network that was capable of exchanging data. Time passed; additions and refinements were made to the ARPAnet.

The 1970s

In 1971, the Defense Advanced Research Projects Agency (DARPA) succeeded ARPA. As a result, the ARPAnet came under the control of

DARPA. DARPA's forte was concentration on satellite, radio, and packet-switching technology.

During this same time period, the ARPAnet was using what was called a *network control program* (NCP). Since the NCP was so closely tied to the characteristics of the ARPAnet, it had limited capabilities for coping with the areas of research and other requirements. The protocols that ARPAnet utilized (namely the NCP) were characteristically slow, and there were periods when the network was not stable. Since the ARPAnet was now officially under DARPA's umbrella, and with the realization that a new approach to ARPAnet was needed, a different direction was taken.

In approximately 1974, DARPA sponsored development of a new set of protocols to replace the ones in use. This endeavor led to the development of protocols that were the basis for TCP/IP. The first TCP/IP began to appear in 1974 to 1975. While these technical matters were in full force, another phenomenon was occurring.

In 1975, the U.S. Department of Defense (DOD) put ARPAnet under the control of the Defense Communication Agency (DCA); the DCA was responsible for operational aspects of the network. It was then that the ARPAnet became the foundation for the *Defense Data Network* (DDN).

Time passed, and TCP/IP continued to be enhanced. Many networks emerged, working with and connecting to the ARPAnet with TCP/IP protocols. In 1978, TCP/IP was stable enough for a public demonstration from a mobile location connected to a remote location via satellite. It was a success.

The 1980s

From 1978 until 1982, TCP/IP gained momentum and was continually refined. In 1982, multiple strides were made. First, DOD made a policy statement adopting TCP/IP protocols and making it the overseeing entity for uniting distributed networks. The next year, 1983, the DOD formally adopted TCP/IP as the standard protocol to use when connecting to the ARPAnet.

Early 1983, when the DOD formally discontinued support for the NCP and adopted the TCP/IP protocol, marks the birth of the Internet. The term *Internet* was an outgrowth of the term *internetworking*, a technical term referring to the interconnection of networks. Nevertheless, the term *Internet* has maintained its association reflecting the multiple networks around the world today.

The 1990s

The Internet today consists of numerous interconnected networks. The National Research and Education Network (NREN) is a dominant part of the Internet today. Other networks that are part of the Internet include those of the National Science Foundation (NSF), NASA, the Department of Education (DOE), and many others, including those of educational institutions.

Commercial, educational, and other organizations of all types are connected to the Internet. An industry of service providers for the Internet seems to be emerging.

The twenty-first century

As we approach the twenty-first century, it is clear that TCP/IP will be a major network protocol. TCP/IP is deeply entrenched and, frankly, no serious protocol that can compete with it is on the horizon as of this writing (late 1990s). TCP/IP has literally become the de facto standard in networking.

Enhancements to the Internet Protocol have put TCP/IP in a much stronger position than even the rapid growth it enjoyed during the past 10 years had provided. IP version 6 is presented in Chap. 16 to provide solid reference information on this routing protocol.

With the advent of widespread use of Windows NT (even as a network protocol), TCP/IP is complemented. Windows NT appears to be the operating system of the early twenty-first century, and, by default, TCP/IP will be supported with it. As NT is currently configured, TCP/IP is actually an integral part of it. Therefore, TCP/IP has some assurance of built-in success in the early part of the twenty-first century due to the Windows NT scenario.

It seems most vendors in the networking community are either currently supporting TCP/IP as a part of daily operations, or they are planning for it. Either way, TCP/IP is going to continue to grow significantly in the coming century.

14.2   TCP/IP Growth

Technology

Section 14.1 provides some insight on technology surrounding TCP/IP and the Internet, but does not explain certain aspects of the Internet that might aid in understanding the technological impact it had on TCP/IP.

The Internet (big I) is based upon TCP/IP, as the U.S. government adopted it as the standard. The Internet is worldwide, and all sorts of entities are connected to it. Knowing this, we can deduce that these entities are using TCP/IP. This alone accounts for a tremendous amount of TCP/IP in the marketplace. And it is currently increasing at a rapid rate.

The 1980s can be characterized as a decade of rapid technological growth. Many companies capitalized on the U.S. government's endorsement of TCP/IP as the standard for the Internet, and began producing products to meet this need.

This influx of TCP/IP products nursed the need for additional products. For example, in the 1980s two technologies dominated, PCs and LANs. With the proliferation of PCs and LANs, an entirely new industry began to emerge. These technological forces seemed to propel TCP/IP forward because TCP/IP and PCs made a good match when implementing LANs. TCP/IP implemented on an individual basis is referred to as an *internet* (little *i*).

Market forces

A factor that contributed to the growth of TCP/IP in the market was corporate downsizing. This may seem strange, but during the 1980s I witnessed many cases where TCP/IP-based networks grew when others were shrinking. Granted, this was not the only reason for TCP/IP's healthy market share, but it did contribute to it.

For example, I witnessed the following scenario. A corporation (which I will not name) had its corporate offices in the northeast. This corporation had many (over 50) satellite offices around the nation. This corporation needed these satellite offices to have independence for daily operations and at the same time be connected to the corporate data center. They achieved this by implementing TCP/IP-based LANs in their satellite offices, then connecting them to the data center. This example is one of many I have seen.

Availability

TCP/IP could be purchased off the shelf at many computer stores by the end of the 1980s. This degree of availability says a lot for a product that was not readily available to end users at the beginning of the decade.

Another factor played a role in the availability of TCP/IP—the DOD not only encouraged the use of TCP/IP, it funded the Bolt, Deranek, and Newman company to port TCP/IP to UNIX. In addition, DOD encouraged UC Berkeley to include TCP/IP in its BSD UNIX operating system. This meant that by acquiring Berkeley UNIX, users got TCP/IP free. It was not long before TCP/IP was added to AT&T's System V UNIX operating system. I suppose this conveys how available it was becoming.

Individual knowledge

By the late 1970s, and surely into the 1980s, TCP/IP was in most colleges and many educational institutions. By the mid-1980s it was being shipped free with Berkeley UNIX and the availability was there; it became dominant in learning institutions. The obvious occurred; individuals were graduating from those educational institutions, and if their backgrounds included computer science, odds were they had been exposed to TCP/IP.

Granted that premise, consider this: these individuals entered the workplace and began penetrating the technical and managerial departments. When it came to contributing to a decision about a network protocol, which one would be the likely choice in many cases?

In the 1980s, the marketplace paid a premium for those who understood TCP/IP. Now, in the late 1990s, the market has a considerable number of individuals who have varying degrees of TCP/IP knowledge.

All these factors woven together, and surely others as well, have contributed to make TCP/IP as dominant as it is today. TCP/IP has become a prevalent upper-layer protocol worldwide.

14.3 TCP/IP Layers

In the early days of the Internet, the term *gateway* became commonplace. It generally meant a connection from a specific location into the Internet. This was adequate at the time; however, confusion now abounds on the use of this term.

According to the *American Heritage Dictionary,* the term *gateway* is defined as: "1. An opening, as in a wall or a fence, that may be closed by a gate. 2. A means of access." I believe the original intent of the term's meaning was "A means of access." This is fine, and you are probably wondering why it is even mentioned. Well, today an entire industry called *internetworking and integration* has appeared, and with it have come specialized devices. Once such device is a gateway.

A consensus among integrators and those who integrate heterogeneous networks exists regarding the definition of the term *gateway.* It is a device that, at a minimum, converts upper-layer protocols from one type to another. It can, however, convert all seven layers of protocols.

The purpose of explaining this here is simple. Throughout the presentation on TCP/IP, the term *gateway* may appear. The term has such a foothold in the TCP/IP community that it is still used. Ironically, the term *gateway* is used in many instances with TCP/IP and the Internet where technically the term should be *router.* More information on networking devices is presented in Chaps. 6 and 7 of this book. There these devices are explored in depth.

TCP/IP and the OSI model

TCP/IP is an upper-layer protocol. TCP/IP is implemented in software, although some specific implementations have abbreviated TCP/IP protocol stacks implemented in firmware. However, TCP/IP can operate on different hardware and software platforms, and it supports more than one data link layer protocol.

The OSI model is a representation of the layers that *should* exist in a network. Figure 14.1 shows TCP/IP compared to the OSI model.

Note that TCP/IP has three layers: network, transport, and the upper three layers combined functioning together as the application layer. TCP/IP is flexible when it comes to the lower two layers. It can be implemented in a variety of ways.

TCP/IP can operate with a number of data link layer protocols; some are listed in Fig. 14.1. The remainder of this section highlights popular components at each layer.

Network layer components and functions

Layer 3 of the OSI model is the network layer. In TCP/IP, it is the lowest layer in the protocol suite. TCP/IP network layer components include the following:

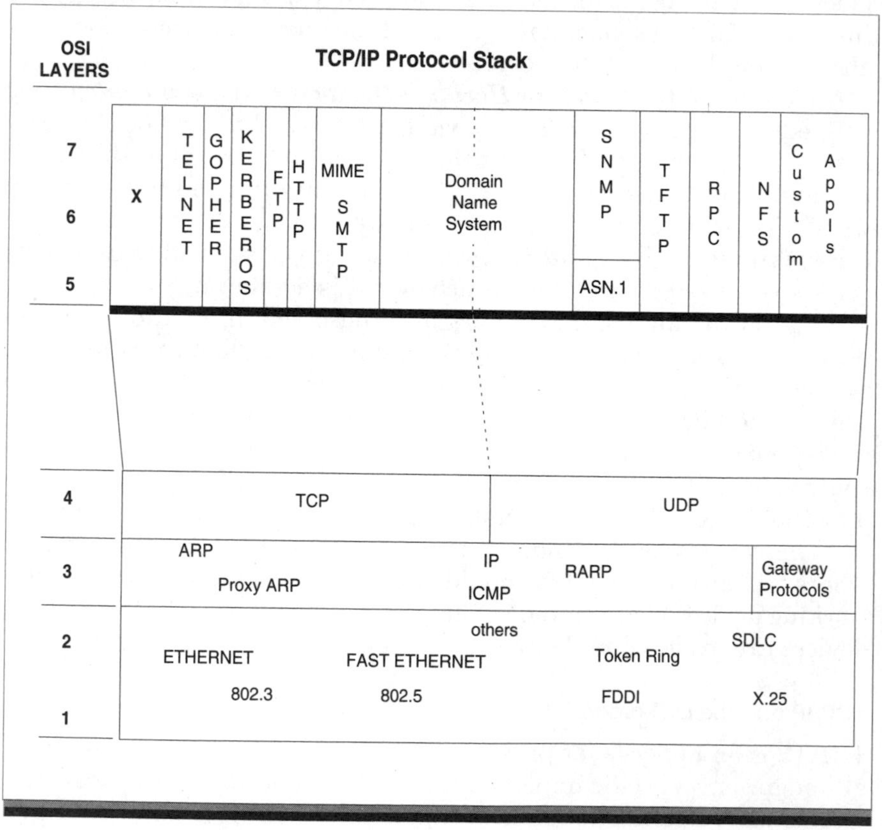

Figure 14.1   Comparison of TCP/IP and the OSI model.

Internet Protocol (IP). IP uses an addressing scheme to identify the host in which it resides. IP is involved in routing functions.

Internet Control Message Protocol (ICMP). ICMP is a required component in each TCP/IP implementation. It is responsible for sending messages through the network via the IP header.

Address Resolution Protocol (ARP). ARP dynamically translates IP addresses into physical (hardware interface card) addresses.

Reverse Address Resolution Protocol (RARP). RARP requests its host IP address by broadcasting its hardware address. Typically a RARP server is designated and responds.

Routing Information Protocol (RIP). RIP is a routing protocol used at the network layer. If implemented, it performs routing of packets in the host it resides within.

Open Shortest Path First (OSPF). OSPF is a routing protocol implemented at the network layer as RIP, but it utilizes knowledge of the internet topology to route messages by the quickest route.

Transport layer components and functions

Layer 4 of the OSI model is the transport layer. In TCP/IP it is the same. Transport layer components include the following:

TCP. This transport layer protocol is considered reliable and performs retransmissions if necessary.

UDP. This transport layer protocol is considered unreliable and does not perform retransmissions; this is left up to the application using its services.

Popular application layer offerings

A number of popular applications exist above the transport layer in TCP/IP. A list of these and brief explanations follows.

X. This is a windowing system that can be implemented in a multi-vendor environment.

TELNET. This application provides remote logon services.

HyperText Transfer Protocol (HTTP). This is a protocol used with World Wide Web technology. It enables transfer of various text, graphics, and other data using TCP as a transport mechanism.

File Transfer Protocol (FTP). This application provides file transfer capabilities among heterogeneous systems.

Simple Mail Transfer Protocol (SMTP).   This application provides e-mail services for TCP/IP-based users.

Domain Name Service (DNS).   This application is designed to resolve destination addresses in a TCP/IP network. This application is an automated method of providing network addresses without having to update host tables manually.

Trivial File Transfer Protocol (TFTP).   This UDP application is best used in initialization of network devices where software must be downloaded to a device. Since TFTP is a simple file transfer protocol, it meets this need well.

Simple Network Management Protocol (SNMP).   This is the way most TCP/IP networks are managed. SNMP is based on an agent and manager arrangement. The agent collects information about a host, and the manager maintains status information about hosts participating with agents.

Network File Server (NFS).   This is an application that causes remote directories to appear to be part of the directory system to the host that the user is using.

Remote Procedure Call (RPC).   This is an application protocol that enables a routine to be called and executed on a server.

Custom Applications.   Custom applications can be written using UDP as a transport layer protocol. By doing so, peer communications can be achieved between applications.

14.4   Planning and TCP/IP Network Design

Before exploring details of TCP/IP, the basic requirements for the functioning of a TCP/IP network should be known. For example, TCP/IP networks require that *all* participating hosts have TCP/IP operating on them, and they must be connected directly or indirectly to a common link. This may require some gateway functionality for some systems, but Fig. 14.2 shows an example of a typical TCP/IP network with different vendor's computers.

Figure 14.2 includes vendors whose operating systems are different. They also have different hardware platforms. However, if the link is established to the TCP/IP network, these computers can communicate effectively.

With this overview in mind, the remaining portion of this chapter presents detailed information about the TCP/IP protocols and applications.

14.5   Internet Protocol (IP)

IP resides at network layer 3. IP routes packets (units of data) from source to destination. Some individuals refer to a packet as a *datagram,* in the sense of IP. An IP datagram is a basic unit moved through a TCP/IP network.

IP is connectionless. It implements two basic functions, *fragmentation* and *addressing.* Fragmentation (and reassembly) is accomplished by a field in the IP header. Fragmentation is required when datagrams need to be smaller for passing through a small-packet-oriented network.

IP header format

The addressing function is also implemented in the IP header. The header includes the source and destination address. The IP header also includes additional information. Figure 14.3 shows an example of an IP header.

Following is a list of the components in the IP header and their definitions.

VERSION: The version field is used to indicate the format of the IP header.

IHL: IHL stands for *internet header length.* It is the length of the internet header in 32-bit words and points to the beginning of data.

TYPE OF SERVICE: The type of service field specifies how the datagram is treated during its transmission through the network.

TOTAL LENGTH: This field indicates the total length of the datagram, including the IP header and data.

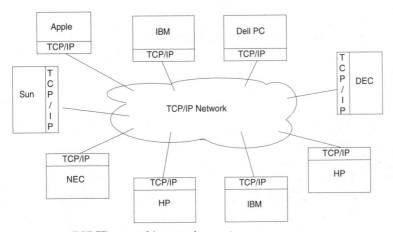

Figure 14.2   TCP/IP networking requirements.

FLAGS: The flag field has 3 bits. They are used to indicate if fragmentation is supported, not to fragment, and more to come or last fragment.

FRAGMENT OFFSET: This indicates where in the datagram the fragment belongs, assuming that fragmentation has occurred.

TIME TO LIVE: This indicates the maximum time a datagram is permitted to stay in the internet system (whether this is a local internet or the Internet). When the value equals 0 the datagram is destroyed. Time is measured in units per second, and each entity that processes the datagram must decrease the value by one even if the process time is less than a second.

PROTOCOL: This field determines whether the data should be sent to TCP or UDP in the next layer in the network.

HEADER CHECKSUM: This is a header checksum only. Some header fields change, and the header checksum is recomputed and verified every place the header is processed.

SOURCE ADDRESS: This is the originator of the datagram. It consists of 32 bits.

DESTINATION ADDRESS: This is target for the header and data. It, too, is 32 bits.

OPTIONS: Options may or may not appear in datagrams. Options must be implemented in IP modules; however, they may not be used in any given transmission. A number of variables in the options field exist. The following is a list of those variables, including a brief explanation.

NO OPTION: This option can be used between options to correlate the beginning of a following option on a 32-bit boundary.

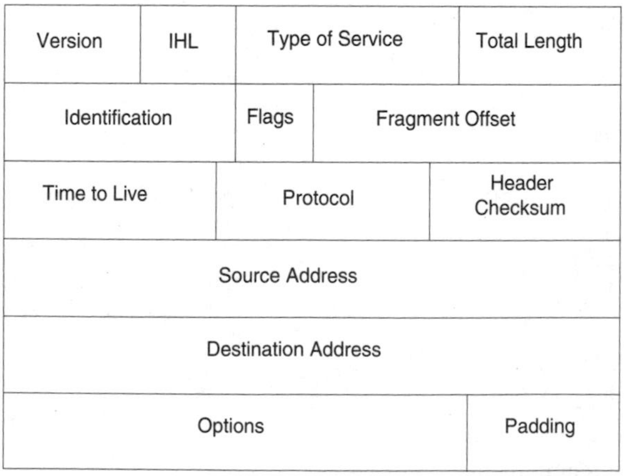

Version	IHL	Type of Service	Total Length
Identification		Flags	Fragment Offset
Time to Live		Protocol	Header Checksum
Source Address			
Destination Address			
Options			Padding

Figure 14.3   Conceptual view of an IP header.

SECURITY: Security is a mechanism used by DOD. It provides hosts a way to use security, by means of compartmentation, handling restrictions, and transmission control codes (TCCs). The compartmentation value is used when the information transmitted is not compartmented. Handling restrictions are defined by the Defense Intelligence Agency. TCC permits segregation of data traffic.

LOOSE SOURCE AND RECORD ROUTE: This provides a way for a source of a datagram to supply routing information to aid routers in forwarding the datagram. It also serves to record the route information.

STRICT SOURCE AND RECORD ROUTE: This option permits the source of a datagram to supply information used by routers and to record the route information.

RECORD ROUTE: This is simply a way to record the route of a datagram as it traverses the network.

STREAM IDENTIFIER: This provides a way for a stream identifier to be carried through networks that do not support the stream concept.

TIMESTAMP: This option includes a pointer, overflow, a flag field and an internet address. Simply put, this provides the time and date when a router handles the datagram.

PADDING: The padding is used to ensure that the header ends on the 32-bit boundary.

Network planning and the next IP

In June 1993 RFC 1475 was published, noted as having the status of a memo. Succinctly, this RFC explores the possibilities for the next generation of the Internet, particularly the IP addressing structure. However, other protocols in the TCP/IP protocol suite are also explored.

In brief, the RFC specifying Internet version 7 focuses upon four major areas, including:

- IP addressing to 64 bits

- A forward route identifier in each datagram to support increasingly fast data transfer speeds

- Increased speed capabilities for network path delays that TCP operates

- The addition of a numbering layer for administration and to provide more space for subnetting

Another way of comprehending the 64-bit addressing scheme (if it is adopted) is by attempting to understand it from a practical perspective. A 64-bit addressing scheme would mean, approximately, that each person on planet Earth would have more than 2 *billion* addresses available for their use!

Along with the idea of a 64-bit addressing scheme, another component would be added to the current 32-bit structure that accommodates space for network and host addresses. The 64-bit addressing scheme includes bits to identify an administrative domain. This domain identifies an administration that may be a service provider or other entity.

Much more information is available on the topic of the next Internet in RFC 1475. RFC 1475 is considered a *memo,* not a standard. It is approximately 35 pages and is a good reference source for this topic.

14.6   Internet Control Message Protocol (ICMP)

ICMP works with IP; it is also located at Layer 3 with IP. Since IP is connectionless, it has no way to relay messages or errors to the originating host. ICMP performs these functions on behalf of IP. ICMP sends status messages and error messages to the sending host.

ICMP utilizes IP to carry the ICMP data within it through a network. Just because ICMP uses IP as a vehicle does not make IP reliable; it just means that IP carries the ICMP message.

The structure of an ICMP message is shown in Fig. 14.4.

The first part of the ICMP message is the *type* field. This field has a numeric value reflecting its meaning; this field identifies its format, as well. The numeric values that can appear in the type field and their meanings are shown in Fig. 14.5.

The next field in the ICMP message is the *code* field. It, too, has a numeric value assigned to it. These numeric values have associated meanings, as shown in Fig. 14.6.

The *checksum* is computed from the ICMP message starting with the ICMP type.

Type
Code
Checksum
Not used or Parameters
IP Header and Original Data Datagram

Figure 14.4   ICMP message format.

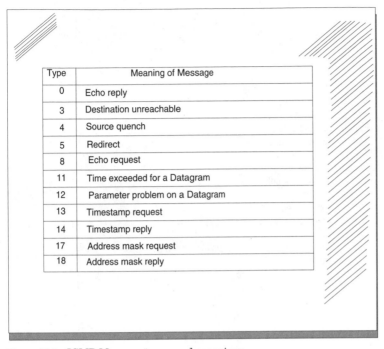

Figure 14.5   ICMP Message types and meanings.

The *not used* field means just that; I referenced RFC 792.

The next field is the *IP header and data datagram*.

ICMP is the source for many messages a user sees on the display. For example, if a user attempts a remote logon and the host is not reachable, then the user will see the message *host unreachable*. This message comes from ICMP.

ICMP detects errors, reports problems, and generates messages, as well. For IP to be implemented, ICMP must be part of it because of the design of IP.

14.7   Address Resolution Protocol (ARP)

ARP, as it is known, is located at Layer 3 along with IP and ICMP. ARP maps IP addresses to the underlying hardware address. Actually, ARP dynamically binds these addresses.

Since TCP/IP works at Layer 3 and above, it must have a mechanism to function with interface boards. When TCP/IP is implemented, it is done so in software. Each host participating on a TCP/IP network must have TCP/IP and have a unique IP address. This IP address is considered a software address since it is implemented at Layer 3 in software.

0	Network unreachable
1	Host unreachable
2	Protocol unreachable
3	Port unreachable
4	Fragmentation needed
5	Source route failed
6	Destination Network unknown
7	Destination Host unknown
8	Source Host isolated
9	Administrative restrictions to destination Network. Communication prohibited
10	Communication with destination Host prohibited by Administration
11	Network unreachable for service type
12	Host unreachable for service type

Figure 14.6 ICMP codes and meanings.

Because any one of many data link protocols could be used, IP requires a way to correlate the IP address and the data link address. Data link addresses are generally considered to be hardware addresses. For example, if TCP/IP is implemented with Ethernet, there is a 48-bit Ethernet address that must be mapped to the 32-bit IP address. Or, if Token Ring is used, a 12-digit hexadecimal address is used as the hardware address. Neither of these data link protocol addresses match the 32-bit IP address of TCP/IP. This is the reason for ARP.

ARP theory of operation

Using Ethernet for a data link, ARP can be explained in the following way. Assume that five hosts reside on an Ethernet network. Assume that a user on host A wants to connect to host E. Host A uses ARP to broadcast a packet that includes A's IP and Ethernet address and host E's IP address.

All five hosts on the network "hear" the ARP broadcast for host *E*. However, only host *E* recognizes its IP address inside the ARP request. Figure 19.7 depicts this.

When host *E* recognizes its hardware address, it replies back to host *A* with its IP address. Figure 14.8 shows an example of this process.

It is obvious that all hosts shown in Fig. 14.7 must examine the ARP request. This is expensive in regard to network utilization. To avoid this constant barrage, an *ARP cache* is maintained. This is a list of the network hosts' physical and IP addresses. As a result, this curbs the number of ARP packets on the network.

When a host receives an ARP reply, that host keeps the IP address of the other host in this ARP table. Then, when a host wants to communicate with another host on the network, it first examines its ARP cache for the IP address. If the desired IP address is found in the cache, there is no need to perform an ARP broadcast. The way the communication occurs is via hardware communication—for example, Ethernet boards communicating with one another.

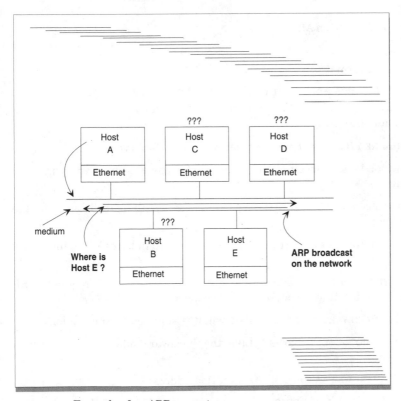

Figure 14.7 Example of an ARP request.

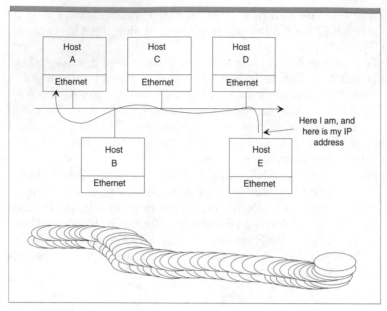

Figure 14.8 Analysis of an ARP response.

ARP message format

Figure 14.9 shows an example of the ARP message format.

Following is a list of the fields in the ARP packet with brief definitions of their meaning.

HARDWARE TYPE: Indicates the hardware interface type.

PROTOCOL TYPE: Specifies the upper-level protocol address the originator sent.

HARDWARE ADDRESS LENGTH: Specifies the length of the bytes in the packet.

PROTOCOL ADDRESS LENGTH: Specifies the length in bytes of the high-level protocol.

OPERATION CODE: Specifies one of the following: ARP request, ARP response, RARP request, or RARP response.

SENDER HARDWARE ADDRESS: If known, it is supplied by the sender.

SENDER PROTOCOL ADDRESS: Like the hardware address, it is sent if known.

TARGET HARDWARE ADDRESS: Destination address.

TARGET PROTOCOL ADDRESS: Contains the IP address of the destination host.

Physical Layer Header
Hardware Type
Protocol Type
Hardware Address Length
Protocol Address Length
Operation Code
Sender Hardware Address
Sender Protocol Address
Target Hardware Address
Target Protocol Address

Figure 14.9 ARP packet components.

Since ARP functions at the lowest layers within a network, the ARP request itself must be encapsulated within the hardware protocol frame because the frame itself is what physically moves through the network at this level. Conceptually, the frame carrying the ARP message and the frame appears as shown in Fig. 14.10.

ARP's dynamic address translation provides a robust method for obtaining an unknown address. The efficiency of ARP is in the utilization of the caching mechanism.

14.8 Reverse Address Resolution Protocol (RARP)

RARP is the reverse of ARP. It is commonly used where diskless workstations are implemented. When a diskless workstation boots, it knows its hardware address because it is in the interface card connecting it to the network. However, it does not know its IP address.

Devices using RARP require that a RARP server be present on the network to answer RARP requests. The question RARP requests ask is, "What is my IP address?" This is broadcast on the network and a designated RARP server replies by examining the physical address received in the RARP packet, comparing it against its tables of IP addresses, and sending the response back to the requesting host. Figure 14.11 shows an example of a RARP broadcast.

Figure 14.11 shows the RARP request going to all hosts on the network. It also shows a RARP server. Note in Fig. 14.12 that the RARP server answers the RARP request.

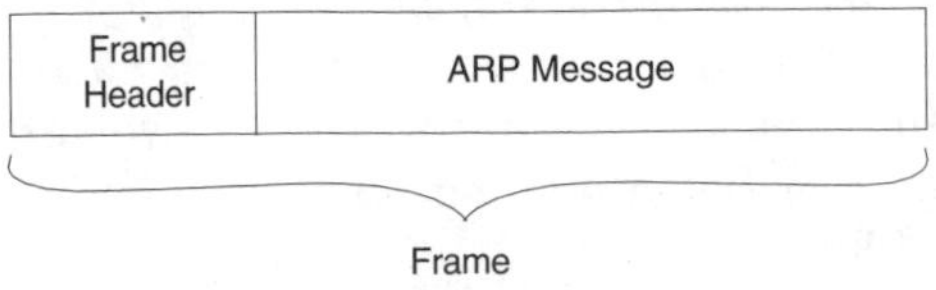

Frame Header	ARP Message

Frame

Figure 14.10 Conceptual view of the ARP frame and message.

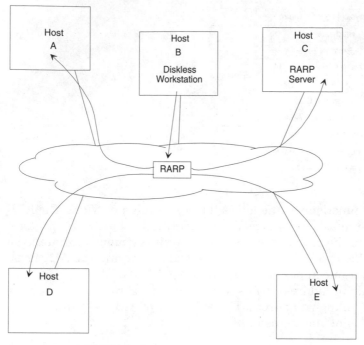

Figure 14.11   A RARP broadcast.

For RARP to be used in a network, a RARP server must exist. In most implementations, when RARP is used multiple RARP servers are used. One is designated as a primary server and another as a secondary server.

14.9   Router Protocols

Normally, this section would be called *gateway protocols,* but, as mentioned previously, this is incorrect if defined according to functionality. For the sake of clarity, this section covers the gateway protocols, but here they are called *routers* because that is what they do—*route.*

This section focuses upon *interior gateway protocols.* These are defined as routing protocols in an autonomous system. An autonomous system is a collection of routers controlled by one administrative authority and using a common interior gateway protocol. Two popular routing protocols exist in this category. They are the *Router Information Protocol* (RIP) and *Open Shortest Path First* (OSPF).

These protocols are used by such network devices as routers, hosts, and other devices normally implemented in TCP/IP software. However, it is feasable that these protocols can be implemented by firmware. This section explains RIP and OSPF.

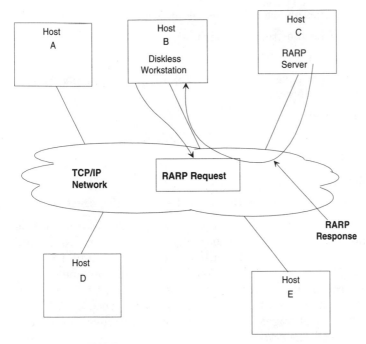

Figure 14.12   A RARP response.

Router Information Protocol (RIP)

RIP has its origins in Xerox's network systems protocol. At one time it was included in the software distribution of TCP/IP with Berkeley UNIX.

RIP is an example of a de facto protocol. It was implemented before a standard RFC existed. It was part of TCP/IP, it worked, and it was needed—all the ingredients to make a product popular! RFC 1058 brought RIP into a formal standard.

RIP header analysis

Consider Fig. 14.13, which shows an example of the RIP message format.
A brief description of each field in the RIP message format follows.

Command
Version
Zero
Address Family Identfier
Zero
IP Address
Zero
Zero
Distance to Net A

Figure 14.13 RIP message format.

COMMAND: Specifies an operation that could be a request or response.

VERSION: Identifies the protocol version.

ZERO: A blank field.

ADDRESS FAMILY IDENTIFIER: Used to identify the protocol family that the message should be interpreted under.

ZERO: A blank field.

IP ADDRESS: Usually has a default route attached to it.

ZERO: A blank field.

ZERO: A blank field.

DISTANCE TO NET n: A value indicating the distance to the target network.

RIP messages either convey or request routing information. RIP is based on broadcast technology. Periodically a router (or designated device) broadcasts the entire RIP routing table throughout the network, be that LAN or otherwise. This aspect alone has become a problem in some environments because of the lack of efficiency.

In addition to broadcasts and updates from that process, RIP also gets updates due to changes in the network configuration. These updates are referred to as *responses*.

Another characteristic of RIP is that it relies on other devices (adjacent nodes) for routing information for targets that are more than one hop away. RIP also calculates its distances by costs per hop. One hop is defined as a metric. The maximum number of hops that RIP can make along one path is 15.

RIP maintains tables with entries. This table is the one referred to previously that is broadcast throughout the network. Information contained in each entry in this table includes the following:

- The destination IP address
- The number of hops required to reach the destination
- The IP address for the next router in the path
- Any indication that the route has recently changed
- Timers along the route

RIP is still used today. Many vendors support it. In certain environments it may be a good gateway protocol to use. However, many vendors support Open Shortest Path First (OSPF).

Open Shortest Path First (OSPF)

The philosophy of OSPF differs from that of RIP. It was recommended as a standard in 1990, and by mid- to late 1991 OSPF version 2 was available. This is an example of its popularity. Some of the tenets that OSPF maintains include the following:

- Offers type of service routing
- Offers ability to define virtual networks
- Offers route distribution
- Offers minimized broadcasts
- Supports a method for trusted routers

Other tenets support OSPF and, depending upon the vendor, a variety of them may be implemented.

OSPF advertisements

OSPF uses what are called *advertisements* (not to be confused with television solicitations). These advertisements are ways that routers can inform other routers about paths. Four distinct types of advertisements include the following:

- *Autonomous.* Has information of routes in other autonomous systems.
- *Network.* Contains a list of routers connected to the network.
- *Router.* Contains information about given router interfaces in certain areas.
- *Summary.* Maintains route information outside a given area.

These advertisements enable a more focused approach to spreading information throughout a network. Besides the advertisements, OSPF uses a number of messages for communication. Some of these messages include the following:

- Hello
- Database Description
- Link State Request
- Link State Update
- Link State Acknowledgment

Two of these are presented and explained in detail to provide insight on the operation of OSPF. Additional information about OSPF is available from RFCs 1245, 1246, and 1247.

OSPF header analysis

The OSPF packet header is shown in Fig. 14.14.

Version
Type
Packet Length
Router ID
Area ID
Checksum
Authentication type
Authentication

Figure 14.14   OSPF packet header.

Following is a list of OSPF header fields with brief explanations.

VERSION: Indicates the protocol version.

TYPE: Indicates messages as one of the following:
1. Hello
2. Database Description
3. Link Status
4. Link Status Update
5. Link Status Acknowledgment

PACKET LENGTH: Indicates the length of the field, including the OSPF header.

ROUTER ID: Provides the sender's address.

AREA ID: Identifies the area from which the packet was transmitted.

CHECKSUM: Performed on the entire packet.

AUTHENTICATION TYPE: Identifies the authentication type that will be used.

AUTHENTICATION: Includes a value from the authentication type.

The *Hello packet* includes messages that are periodically sent on each link to establish if a destination can be reached. The Hello packet is shown in Fig. 14.15.

Following is a list of fields in the Hello packet with a brief explanation of each.

OSPF HEADER: This field is required.

NETWORK MASK: This field contains the network mask for the network from which the message originated.

DEAD TIMER: This field has a value (in seconds) that indicates a neighbor is dead if no response is received.

HELLO INTERVAL: This field has a value, in seconds, that reflects the amount of time before a router will send another Hello packet.

ROUTER PRIORITY: This field is used if a designated router is used as a backup.

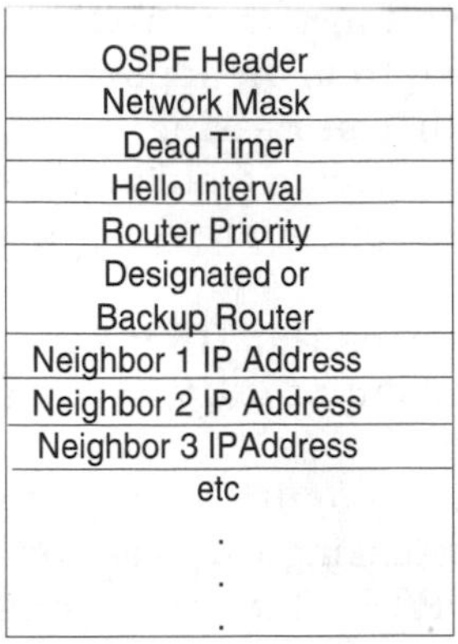

OSPF Header
Network Mask
Dead Timer
Hello Interval
Router Priority
Designated or
Backup Router
Neighbor 1 IP Address
Neighbor 2 IP Address
Neighbor 3 IPAddress
etc

Figure 14.15 Hello packet format.

DESIGNATED OR BACKUP ROUTER: This field identifies the backup router.

NEIGHBOR ROUTER ID: This field, and subsequent ones, indicates the IDs of routers that have recently sent Hello packets within the network.

The *Database Description* packet message includes an OSPF header and fields of information. These fields include information about messages received. They can be broken into smaller units. Information is also provided to indicate if information is missing. The packet also includes information about the type link and its ID. A checksum is provided to ensure that corruption has not occurred.

The *Link State* packet header includes an OSPF header and fields that provide such information as the router, network, link station type, and other information.

The essence of OSPF is that it reduces traffic overhead in the network because it performs individual updates rather than broadcasts that permeate the entire network. OSPF also provides an ability for authentication. Another strength of OSPF is that it can exchange subnet masks as well as subnet addresses.

14.10 TCP: A Perspective

TCP operates at Layer 4 and is a transport protocol. It takes data passed to it from its applications and places them in a send buffer. Then TCP divides the data into a segment. A *segment* is the application data and a TCP/IP header. This is necessary because data is delivered in datagrams.

Characteristics and functions

TCP treats data in different ways. For example, if a user enters a simple command and presses *Return,* TCP uses what it refers to as a *push* function to make it happen. This push ability is a function of TCP. On the other hand, if a large amount of data is passed from an application to TCP, it segments it and passes it to IP for further processing.

Applications that use TCP pass data to TCP in a stream fashion. This is in contrast to some protocols, where applications pass data down the protocol stack in byte fashion.

TCP is a connection-oriented protocol. This means that TCP keeps the state and status of streams passing into and out of it. It is TCP's responsibility to ensure reliable end-to-end service.

Two other major features that TCP provides are multiplexing and full duplex transmission. TCP is capable of multiplexing user sessions because of the addressing scheme used in TCP/IP. This addressing scheme is covered in Sec. 14.14.

TCP also performs a function called *resequencing*. It can perform this function because of the sequence numbers used for acknowledgments. This function manages segments if they reach the destination out of order.

TCP header analysis

Many of the aforementioned functions and others can be understood by examining the TCP header shown in Fig. 19.16.

Following is a list of the parts of the TCP segment with a brief description of each.

SOURCE PORT: Identifies the upper-layer application using the TCP connection.

Source Port
Destination Port
Sequence Number
Acknowledgment Number
Data Offset
Reserved
Urgent
Acknowledgment
Push
Reset
Synchronizer
Finished
Window
Checksum
Urgent Pointer
Options
Padding
Data

Figure 14.16   TCP header.

DESTINATION PORT: Identifies the upper-layer application using the TCP connection.

SEQUENCE NUMBER: Identifies the transmitting byte stream. This value is used during connection management operations.

ACKNOWLEDGMENT NUMBER: Reflects a value acknowledging data previously received.

DATA OFFSET: Determines where the field of data begins.

RESERVED: This field is reserved and the bits within it are set to zero.

URGENT: Indicates if the *urgent* pointer is used.

ACKNOWLEDGMENT: Indicates whether the acknowledgment field is significant.

PUSH: Indicates if the *push* function is used.

RESET: Indicates that the connection should be reset.

SYNCHRONIZE: Indicates that the sequence numbers are to be synchronized.

FINISHED: Indicates that the sender has no more data to send.

WINDOW: Indicates how much data the receiving host can accept. This value is contingent on the value in the acknowledgment field.

CHECKSUM: Performs a checksum on the 16-bit words in the segment.

URGENT POINTER: If used, indicates that urgent data follows.

OPTIONS: At the current time, three basic options are implemented in this field: *end-of-list, no operation,* and *maximum segment size.*

PADDING: Used to ensure that the header length equals 32 bits.

DATA: User data follows in this field.

TCP's reliable data transfer, connection-oriented nature, stream support for applications, multiplexing, full duplex transmission, push functions, flow control, and other characteristics make it a popular and *reliable* protocol.

14.11   Establishing TCP Connections

The *three-way handshake* is the procedure used to establish a connection. This procedure is normally initiated by one TCP and responded to by another TCP. The procedure also works if two TCPs simultaneously initiate the procedure. When simultaneous attempts occur, each TCP receives a *SYN* segment, which carries no acknowledgment after it has sent a SYN. Of course, the arrival of an old duplicate SYN segment can potentially make it appear, to the recipient, that a simultaneous connection initiation is in progress. Proper use of *reset* segments can disambiguate these cases. Although the examples do not show connection synchronization using data-carrying segments, this is perfectly legitimate, so long as the receiving TCP doesn't deliver the data to the user until it is clear that the data is valid—this means that the data must be buffered at the receiver until the connection reaches the *ESTAB-LISHED* state. The three-way handshake reduces the possibility of false connections. It is the implementation of a trade-off between memory and messages to provide information for this checking.

The simplest three-way handshake is shown in the illustration that follows. This should be interpreted in the following way.

Each line is numbered for reference purposes. Right arrows (--$>$) indicate the departure of a TCP segment from TCP *A* to TCP *B,* or the arrival of a segment at *B* from *A.* Left arrows ($<$--), indicate the reverse. Ellipses (. . .) indicate a segment that is still in the network (delayed). An *XXX* indicates a segment that is lost or rejected. Comments appear in parentheses. TCP states represent the state *after* the departure or arrival of the segment (whose contents are shown in the center of each line). Segment contents are shown in abbreviated form, with sequence number, control flags, and ACK field. Other fields, such as window, addresses, lengths, and text, have been left out in the interest of clarity.

```
  TCP A                                                        TCP B

1 CLOSED                                                       LISTEN
2 SYN-SENT --> <SEQ=100><CTL=SYN> -->                          SYN-RECEIVED
3 ESTABLISHED <-<SEQ=300><ACK=101><CTL=SYN,ACK><-              SYN-RECEIVED
4 ESTABLISHED -><SEQ=101><ACK=301><CTL=ACK>-->                 ESTABLISHED
5 ESTABLISHED-><SEQ=101><ACK=301><CTL=ACK><DATA>->             ESTABLISHED
```

In line 2 of the preceding illustration, TCP *A* begins by sending a SYN segment indicating that it will use sequence numbers starting with sequence number 100. In line 3, TCP *B* sends a SYN and acknowledges the SYN it received from TCP A. Note that the acknowledgment field indicates that TCP *B* is now expecting to hear sequence 101, acknowledging the SYN that occupied sequence 100. At line 4, TCP *A* responds with an empty segment containing an ACK for TCP *B*'s SYN; and in line 5, TCP *A* sends some data. Note that the sequence number of the segment in line 5 is the same as in line 4, because the ACK does not occupy sequence number space (if it did, we would wind up ACKing ACK's!).

Simultaneous initiation is only slightly more complex. Each TCP cycles from *CLOSED* to *SYN-SENT* to *SYN-RECEIVED* to *ESTAB-LISHED*.

```
   TCP A                                              TCP B

1  CLOSED                                             CLOSED
2  SYN-SENT--> <SEQ=100><CTL=SYN>                     ...
3  SYN-RECEIVED <-<SEQ=300><CTL=SYN><-                SYN-SENT
4  ... <SEQ=100><CTL=SYN>->                           SYN-RECEIVED
5  SYN-RECEIVED -><SEQ=100><ACK=301><CTL=SYN,ACK>     ...
6  ESTABLISHED <-<SEQ=300><ACK=101><CTL=SYN,ACK><-    SYN-RECEIVED
7  ... <SEQ=101><ACK=301><CTL=ACK> -->                ESTABLISHED
```

The principle reason for the three-way handshake is to prevent old duplicate connection initiations from causing confusion. To deal with this, a special control message, *reset,* has been devised. If the receiving TCP is in a nonsynchronized state (i.e., SYN-SENT or SYN-RECEIVED), it returns to *LISTEN* on receiving an acceptable reset. If the TCP is in one of the synchronized states (ESTABLISHED, FIN-WAIT-1, FIN-WAIT-2, CLOSE-WAIT, CLOSING, LAST-ACK, or TIME-WAIT), it aborts the connection and informs its user.

Consider the half-open connections shown in the following.

```
   TCP A                                              TCP B

1  CLOSED                                             LISTEN
2  SYN-SENT-><SEQ=100><CTL=SYN>                       ...
3  (duplicate) ... <SEQ=90><CTL=SYN>-->               SYN-RECEIVED
4  SYN-SENT <-<SEQ=300><ACK=91><CTL=SYN,ACK><-        SYN-RECEIVED
5  SYN-SENT-><SEQ=91><CTL=RST>->                      LISTEN
6  ... <SEQ=100><CTL=SYN>->                           SYN-RECEIVED
7  SYN-SENT<-<SEQ=400><ACK=101><CTL=SYN,ACK><-        SYN-RECEIVED
8  ESTABLISHED-><SEQ=101><ACK=401><CTL=ACK>->         ESTABLISHED
```

At line 3, an old duplicate SYN arrives at TCP *B.* TCP *B* cannot tell that this is an old duplicate, so it responds normally (line 4). TCP *A* detects that the ACK field is incorrect and returns a *RST* (reset) with its SEQ field selected to make the segment believable. TCP *B,* on receiving the RST, returns to the LISTEN state.

When the original SYN (pun intended) finally arrives at line 6, the synchronization proceeds normally. If the SYN at line 6 had arrived before the RST, a more complex exchange might have occurred, with RSTs sent in both directions.

Half-open connections and other anomalies

An established connection is said to be *half-open* if one of the TCPs has closed or aborted the connection at its end without the knowledge of the other, or if the two ends of the connection have become desynchronized owing to a crash that has resulted in loss of memory. Such connections will automatically become reset if an attempt is made to send data in either direction. However, half-open connections are expected to be unusual, and the recovery procedure is mildly involved.

If the connection no longer exists at site A, then an attempt by the user at site B to send any data on it will result in the site B TCP receiving a reset control message. Such a message indicates to the site B TCP that something is wrong and that it is expected to abort the connection.

Assume that two user processes, A and B, are communicating with one another when a crash occurs, causing loss of memory to A's TCP. Depending on the operating system supporting A's TCP, it is likely that some error recovery mechanism exists. When the TCP is up again, A is likely to start again from the beginning or from a recovery point. As a result, A will probably try to OPEN the connection again or try to SEND on the connection it believes to be open. In the latter case, it receives the error message "connection not open" from the local (A's) TCP. In an attempt to establish the connection, A's TCP will send a segment containing SYN.

After TCP A crashes, the user attempts to reopen the connection. TCP B, in the meantime, thinks the connection is open. Consider the following:

```
    TCP A                                    TCP B

1   (CRASH)                                  (send 300,receive 100)
2   CLOSED                                   ESTABLISHED
3   SYN-SENT-><SEQ=400><CTL=SYN>->           (??)
4   (!!)<-<SEQ=300><ACK=100><CTL=ACK><-      ESTABLISHED
5   SYN-SENT-><SEQ=100><CTL=RST>->           (Abort!!)
6   SYN-SENT                                 CLOSED
7   SYN-SENT-><SEQ=400><CTL=SYN>             -->
```

When the SYN arrives at line 3, TCP B, being in a synchronized state, and the incoming segment being outside the window, responds with an acknowledgment indicating what sequence it next expects to hear (ACK 100). TCP A sees that this segment does not acknowledge anything it sent and, being unsynchronized, sends a reset (RST) because it has detected a half-open connection. TCP B aborts at line 5. TCP A will continue to try to establish the connection; the problem is now reduced to the basic three-way handshake.

An interesting alternative case occurs when TCP A crashes and TCP B tries to send data on what it thinks is a synchronized connection. This is illustrated in the following example. In this case, the data arriving at TCP A from TCP B (line 2) is unacceptable because no such connection exists, so TCP A sends a RST. The RST is acceptable, so TCP B processes it and aborts the connection.

```
TCP A                                              TCP B

1  (CRASH)                                         (end 300,receive 100)
2  (??) <-<SEQ=300><ACK=100><DATA=10><CTL=ACK><-   ESTABLISHED
3  -><SEQ=100><CTL=RST>->                          (ABORT!!)
```

In the following illustration, two TCPs, *A* and *B*, with passive connections are waiting for SYN. An old duplicate arriving at TCP *B* (line 2) stirs *B* into action. A SYN-ACK is returned (line 3) and causes TCP *A* to generate a RST (the ACK in line 3 is not acceptable). TCP *B* accepts the reset and returns to its passive LISTEN state.

```
   TCP A                                           TCP B

1  LISTEN                                           LISTEN
2  ...<SEQ=Z><CTL=SYN>->                            SYN-RECEIVED
3  (??)<-<SEQ=X><ACK=Z+1><CTL=SYN,ACK><-            SYN-RECEIVED
4  -><SEQ=Z+1><CTL=RST>->                           (return to LISTEN!)
5  LISTEN                                           LISTEN
```

The old duplicate SYN initiates a reset on two passive sockets by the following rules for RST generation and processing.

Reset generation

As a general rule, reset (RST) must be sent whenever a segment arrives that is apparently not intended for the current connection. A reset must not be sent if it is not clear that this is the case. There are three groups of states:

1. If the connection does not exist (CLOSED), then a reset is sent in response to any incoming segment except another reset. In particular, SYNs addressed to a nonexistent connection are rejected by this means. If the incoming segment has an ACK field, the reset takes its sequence number from the ACK field of the segment; otherwise, the reset has sequence number 0 and the ACK field is set to the sum of the sequence number and segment length of the incoming segment. The connection remains in the CLOSED state.

2. If the connection is in any nonsynchronized state (LISTEN, SYN-SENT, or SYN-RECEIVED), and the incoming segment acknowledges something not yet sent (the segment carries an unacceptable ACK), or if an incoming segment has a security level or compartment that does not exactly match the level and compartment requested for the connection, a reset is sent.

If our SYN has not been acknowledged and the precedence level of the incoming segment is higher than the precedence level requested, then either raise the local precedence level (if allowed by the user and the system) or send a reset; or, if the precedence level of the incoming segment is lower than the precedence level requested, then continue as if the precedence matched exactly. (If the remote TCP cannot raise the precedence level to match ours, this will be detected in the next segment it sends, and the connection will be terminated then.) If our SYN has been acknowledged (perhaps in this incoming segment), the precedence level of the incoming segment must match the local precedence level exactly; if it does not, a reset must be sent.

If the incoming segment has an ACK field, the reset takes its sequence number from the ACK field of the segment; otherwise, the reset has sequence number 0 and the ACK field is set to the sum of the sequence number and segment length of the incoming segment. The connection remains in the same state.

3. If the connection is in a synchronized state (ESTABLISHED, FIN-WAIT-1, FIN-WAIT-2, CLOSE-WAIT, CLOSING, LAST-ACK, or TIME-WAIT), any unacceptable segment (out-of-window sequence number or unacceptable acknowledgment number) must elicit only an empty acknowledgment segment containing the current send-sequence number and an acknowledgment indicating the next sequence number expected to be received, and the connection remains in the same state.

If an incoming segment has a security level, or compartment, or precedence that does not exactly match the level, compartment, and precedence requested for the connection, a reset is sent and the connection goes to the CLOSED state. The reset takes its sequence number from the ACK field of the incoming segment.

Reset processing

In all states except SYN-SENT, all reset (RST) segments are validated by checking their SEQ fields. A reset is valid if its sequence number is in the window. In the SYN-SENT state (a RST received in response to an initial SYN), the RST is acceptable if the ACK field acknowledges the SYN.

The receiver of a RST first validates it, then changes state. If the receiver was in the LISTEN state, it ignores it. If the receiver was in the SYN-RECEIVED state and had previously been in the LISTEN state, then the receiver returns to the LISTEN state; otherwise, the receiver aborts the connection and goes to the CLOSED state. If the receiver was in any other state, it aborts the connection, advises the user, and goes to the CLOSED state.

14.12   TCP Connection Termination

CLOSE is an operation meaning "I have no more data to send." The notion of closing a full duplex connection is subject to ambiguous interpretation, of course, since it may not be obvious how to treat the receiving side of the connection. We have chosen to treat CLOSE in a simplex fashion. The user that CLOSEs may continue to RECEIVE until being told that the other side has CLOSED also. Thus, a program could initiate several SENDs followed by a CLOSE, and then continue to RECEIVE until signaled that a RECEIVE failed because the other side had CLOSED. We assume that the TCP will signal a user, even if no RECEIVEs are outstanding, that the other side has closed, so the user can terminate that side gracefully. A TCP will reliably deliver all buffers SENT before the connection was CLOSED, so a user that expects no data in return need only wait to hear that the connection was CLOSED successfully to know that all the data was received at the destination TCP. Users must keep reading connections they close for sending until the TCP says no more data.

Essentially, three cases exist:

1. The user initiates by telling the TCP to CLOSE the connection.

2. The remote TCP initiates by sending a FIN control signal.

3. Both users CLOSE simultaneously.

Case 1: Local user initiates the close

In this case, a FIN segment can be constructed and placed on the outgoing segment queue. No further SENDs from the user will be accepted by the TCP, and it enters the FIN-WAIT-1 state. RECEIVEs are allowed in this state. All segments preceding and including FIN will be retransmitted until acknowledged. When the other TCP has both acknowledged the FIN and sent a FIN of its own, the first TCP can ACK this FIN. Note that a TCP receiving a FIN will ACK but not send its own FIN until its user has CLOSED the connection also.

Case 2: TCP receives a FIN from the network

If an unsolicited FIN arrives from the network, the receiving TCP can ACK it and tell the user that the connection is closing. The user will respond with a CLOSE, upon which the TCP can send a FIN to the other TCP after sending any remaining data. The TCP then waits until its own FIN is acknowledged, whereupon it deletes the connection. If an ACK is not forthcoming, after the user timeout the connection is aborted and the user is told.

Case 3: Both users close simultaneously

A simultaneous CLOSE by users at both ends of a connection causes FIN segments to be exchanged. When all segments preceding the FINs have been processed and acknowledged, each TCP can ACK the FIN it has received. Both will, upon receiving these ACKs, delete the connection.

```
      TCP A                                                           TCP B

1     ESTABLISHED                                                     ESTABLISHED
2     Close FIN-WAIT-1-><SEQ=100><ACK=300><CTL=FIN,ACK>->   CLOSE-WAIT
3     FIN-WAIT-2<-<SEQ=300><ACK=101><CTL=ACK><-             CLOSE-WAIT
4     Close TIME-WAIT<-<SEQ=300><ACK=101><CTL=FIN,ACK><-    LAST-ACK
5     TIME-WAIT-><SEQ=101><ACK=301><CTL=ACK>->             CLOSED
6     2 MSL                                                           CLOSED

      TCP A                                                           TCP B

1     ESTABLISHED                                                     ESTABLISHED
2     Close                                                           Close
      FIN-WAIT-1-><SEQ=100><ACK=300><CTL=FIN,ACK>...       FIN-WAIT-1
      <--<SEQ=300><ACK=100><CTL=FIN,ACK><-                 ...
      <SEQ=100><ACK=300><CTL=FIN,ACK>->

3     CLOSING-><SEQ=101><ACK=301><CTL=ACK>...              CLOSING
      <-- <SEQ=301><ACK=101><CTL=ACK>                      <--
      ... <SEQ=101><ACK=301><CTL=ACK>                      -->

4     TIME-WAIT                                                       TIME-WAIT
      2 MSL                                                           2 MSL
      CLOSED                                                          CLOSED
```

Precedence and security

The intent is that connection be allowed only between ports operating with exactly the same security and compartment values and at the higher of the precedence levels requested by the two ports. The precedence and security parameters used in TCP are exactly those defined in the Internet Protocol (IP). Throughout this TCP specification the term *security/compartment* is intended to indicate the security parameters used in IP, including security, compartment, user group, and handling restrictions. A connection attempt with mismatched security/

compartment values or a lower precedence value must be rejected by sending a reset. Rejecting a connection due to too low a precedence only occurs after an acknowledgment of the SYN has been received. TCP modules that operate only at the default value of precedence will still have to check the precedence of incoming segments and possibly raise the precedence level they use on the connection.

The security parameters may be used even in a nonsecure environment (the values would indicate unclassified data); thus, hosts in nonsecure environments must be prepared to receive the security parameters, though they need not send them.

14.13   TCP and Data Communication

Once the connection is established, data is communicated by the exchange of segments. Because segments may be lost due to errors (checksum test failure), or network congestion, TCP uses retransmission (after a timeout) to ensure delivery of every segment. Duplicate segments may arrive due to network or TCP retransmission. As discussed in the section on sequence numbers, the TCP performs certain tests on the sequence and acknowledgment numbers in the segments to verify their acceptability.

The sender of data keeps track of the next sequence number to use in the variable $SND.NXT$. The receiver of data keeps track of the next sequence number to expect in the variable $RCV.NXT$. The sender of data keeps track of the oldest unacknowledged sequence number in the variable $SND.UNA$. If the data flow is momentarily idle and all data sent has been acknowledged, then the three variables will be equal. When the sender creates a segment and transmits it, the sender advances SND.NXT. When the receiver accepts a segment, it advances RCV.NXT and sends an acknowledgment. When the data sender receives an acknowledgment, it advances SND.UNA. The extent to which the values of these variables differ is a measure of the delay in the communication. The amount by which the variables are advanced is the length of the data in the segment. Note that once in the ESTABLISHED state, all segments must carry current acknowledgment information. The CLOSE user call implies a push function, as does the FIN control flag in an incoming segment.

TCP retransmission timeout

Because of the variability of the networks that compose an internetwork system and the wide range of uses of TCP connections, the retransmission timeout must be dynamically determined. One procedure for determining a retransmission timeout is given here as an illustration.

An example of a retransmission timeout procedure is to measure the elapsed time between sending a data octet with a particular sequence number and receiving an acknowledgment that covers that sequence number (segments sent do not have to match segments received). This measured elapsed time is the *round trip time* (RTT). Next, compute a *smoothed round trip time* (SRTT) as:

```
SRTT = (ALPHA*SRTT) + ((1-ALPHA)*RTT)
```

and, based on this, compute the retransmission timeout (RTO) as:

```
RTO = min[UBOUND,max[LBOUND,(BETA*SRTT)]]
```

where UBOUND is an upper bound on the timeout (e.g., 1 min), LBOUND is a lower bound on the timeout (e.g., 1), ALPHA is a smoothing factor (e.g., .8 to .9), and BETA is a delay variance factor (e.g., 1.3 to 2.0).

TCP communication of urgent information

The objective of the TCP *urgent* mechanism is to allow the sending user to stimulate the receiving user to accept some urgent data and to permit the receiving TCP to indicate to the receiving user when all the currently known urgent data has been received by the user. This mechanism permits a point in the data stream to be designated as the end of urgent information. Whenever this point is in advance of the receive sequence number (RCV.NXT) at the receiving TCP, that TCP must tell the user to go into *urgent mode;* when the receive sequence number catches up to the urgent pointer, the TCP must tell user to go into *normal mode.* If the urgent pointer is updated while the user is in urgent mode, the update will be invisible to the user.

The method employs an urgent field that is carried in all segments transmitted. The URG control flag indicates that the urgent field is meaningful and must be added to the segment sequence number to yield the urgent pointer. The absence of this flag indicates that there is no urgent data outstanding.

To send an urgent indication, the user must also send at least one data octet. If the sending user also indicates a push, timely delivery of the urgent information to the destination process is enhanced.

Managing the window

The window sent in each segment indicates the range of sequence numbers that the sender of the window (the data receiver) is currently prepared to accept. There is an assumption that this is related to the currently available data buffer space available for this connection.

Indicating a large window encourages transmissions. If more data arrives than can be accepted, it will be discarded. This will result in excessive retransmissions, adding unnecessarily to the load on the network and the TCPs. Indicating a small window may restrict the transmission of data to the point of introducing a round-trip delay between the transmission of each new segment.

The mechanisms provided allow a TCP to advertise a large window and to subsequently advertise a much smaller window without having accepted that much data. This so-called *shrinking the window* is strongly discouraged. The robustness principle dictates that TCPs will not shrink the window themselves, but will be prepared for such behavior on the part of other TCPs.

The sending TCP must be prepared to accept from the user and send at least one octet of new data, even if the send window is zero. The sending TCP must regularly retransmit to the receiving TCP, even when the window is zero. Two minutes is recommended for the retransmission interval when the window is zero. This retransmission is essential to guarantee that when either TCP has a zero window, the reopening of the window will be reliably reported to the other.

When the receiving TCP has a zero window and a segment arrives, it must still send an acknowledgment showing its next expected sequence number and current window (zero).

The sending TCP packages the data to be transmitted into segments that fit the current window, and may repackage segments on the retransmission queue. Such repackaging is not required, but may be helpful.

In a connection with a one-way data flow, the window information will be carried in acknowledgment segments that all have the same sequence number, so there will be no way to reorder them if they arrive out of order. This is not a serious problem, but it will, on occasion, allow the window information to be temporarily based on old reports from the data receiver. A refinement to avoid this problem is to act on the window information from segments that carry the highest acknowledgment number (that is, segments with acknowledgment numbers equal to or greater than the highest previously received).

Window management procedure has a significant influence on communication performance. The following comments are suggestions.

- Allocating a small window causes data to be transmitted in many small segments, whereas better performance is achieved by using fewer large segments.

- Another suggestion for avoiding small windows is for the receiver to defer updating a window until the additional allocation is at least X

percent of the maximum allocation possible for the connection (where X might be 20 to 40).

- Another suggestion is for the sender to avoid sending small segments by waiting until the window is large enough before sending data. If the user signals a push function, then the data must be sent even if it is a small segment.

Acknowledgments should not be delayed, or unnecessary retransmissions will result. One strategy is to send an acknowledgment when a small segment arrives (without updating the window information), and then to send another acknowledgment with new window information when the window is larger. The segment sent to probe a zero window may also begin a breakup of transmitted data into smaller and smaller segments. If a segment containing a single data octet sent to probe a zero window is accepted, it consumes one octet of the window now available. If the sending TCP simply sends as much as it can whenever the window is nonzero, the transmitted data will be broken into alternating big and small segments. As time goes on, occasional pauses in the receiver making window allocation available will result in breaking the big segments into a small and not-quite-so-big pair. And after a while, the data transmission will be in mostly small segments.

TCP implementations need to actively attempt to combine small window allocations into larger windows, since the mechanisms for managing the window tend to lead to many small windows in the simplest-minded implementations.

The TCP protocol is defined in RFC 793. Additional information can be obtained there if details are required.

14.14   User Datagram Protocol (UDP)

The user datagram protocol (UDP) resides at transport layer 4. In many ways it is the opposite of TCP. UDP is connectionless and unreliable. It does little more than provide a transport layer protocol for applications that reside above it.

UDP header analysis

The extent of information about UDP is brief compared to TCP. An example of the UDP datagram is shown in Fig. 14.17.

Following is a list of the components in the UDP datagram with brief descriptions.

SOURCE PORT: The value in this field identifies the origin port. (Ports are used in addressing and are discussed in detail in Sec. 14.15.)

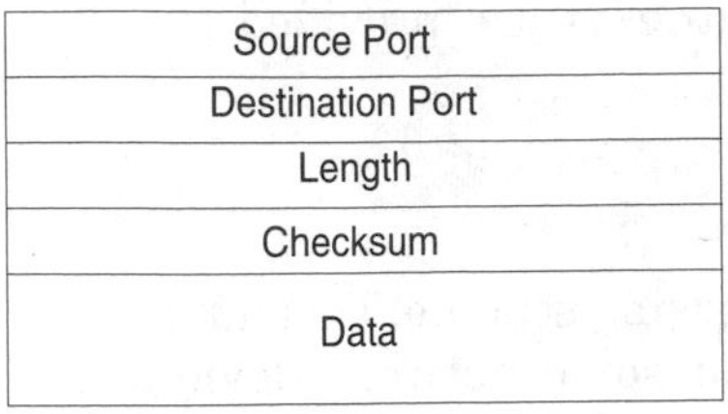

Source Port
Destination Port
Length
Checksum
Data

Figure 14.17 UDP datagram.

DESTINATION PORT: This identifies the recipient port for the data.

LENGTH: The value in this field indicates the length of the data sent, including the header.

CHECKSUM: This algorithm computes the psuedo-IP header, the UDP header, and the data.

DATA: The data field is the data passed from applications using UDP.

UDP applications

UDP is a useful protocol. Situations do exist where there is a need for a custom application. When this is the case, UDP is a good transport protocol to use to accomplish the task. Because UDP is unreliable, does not perform retransmissions, and lacks other services that TCP offers, the custom applications must perform these functions.

Because of UDP's nature, this leaves work for application programmers. But, these necessary operations can be achieved via the application; it merely requires more work on the part of the one creating the application.

Messages sent to UDP from applications get forwarded to IP for transmission. Some applications that reside on the UDP protocol pass messages directly to IP and ICMP for transmission.

14.15 TCP/IP Addressing

Addressing in TCP/IP consists of a variety of factors that work together to make TCP/IP a functioning upper-layer network protocol. Some of these factors include the following:

- IP addressing
- Address classifications
- Ports
- Well-known ports
- Port manipulation
- Sockets
- Hardware addresses

Each of these are presented and syntheses are provided to aid in understanding how they relate.

IP addressing

The Internet protocol uses a 32-bit addressing scheme. This addressing is implemented in software; however, in some network devices it is implemented in firmware and/or nonvolatile RAM.

Each host participating in a TCP/IP network is identified via a 32-bit IP address. This is significant because it is different from the host's hardware address.

The IP addressing scheme structure is shown in Fig. 14.18. There are five classes of IP addresses. The IP addressing scheme is dotted decimal notation. The class of address indicates how many bits are used for a network address and how many for a host address. Before examining these in detail, a word about how these addresses are assigned is beneficial.

As Fig. 14.18 shows, multiple classes of addresses exist. A reasonable question is, why? Two implementations of TCP/IP networks are possible: the Internet (big *I*) and internets (little *i*).

The Internet is a worldwide network that has thousands of entities connecting to it. An agency responsible for maintaining Internet addresses assigns IP addresses to entities connecting to the Internet; the entity itself has no say-so in the matter. On the other hand, if a TCP/IP network is implemented in a corporation, for example, then the IP addressing scheme is left up to the implementers responsible for that corporate network. In other words, it is *locally* administrated.

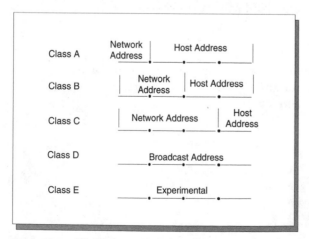

Figure 14.18   IP version 4 addressing scheme.

When the latter implementation is the case, it is best someone understands the ramifications of selecting an IP addressing scheme. Multiple issues should factor into the equation for selecting an IP addressing scheme.

Address classifications

In Fig. 14.18, five classes of addresses are shown. The following list explains the numerical meaning of the classes and how this affects hosts implemented with IP addresses.

Address Class	Assigned Numbers
A	0–127
B	128–191
C	192–223
D	224–239
E	240–255

Class A addresses have fewer bits allocated to the network portion (1 byte) and more bits (3 bytes) dedicated for host addressing. In other words, more hosts can be implemented than networks, according to the addressing scheme.

Class B addressing allocates equal amounts of bits for network addressing (2 bytes) and host addressing (2 bytes). This class is popular in locally administered implementations.

Class C addressing allocates more bits (3 bytes) to the network portion and fewer bits (1 byte) to the host portion.

Class D is generally used as a broadcast address. The numerical value in each of the 4 bytes is 255.255.255.255.

Class E networks are for experimental purposes. This author knows of no implemented class E networks.

Implementations of an internet use these addresses in conjunction with *aliases*. For example, an address assigned to a host would usually have a name associated with it. If a host had a Class B address, such as 137.1.0.99, its alias name might be RISC. This alias and internet address resides in a file on UNIX systems called /etc/hosts. Another related file is the /etc/networks file. These two files are normal in the configuration in a UNIX environment. Additional information is included in Sec. 14.16 regarding TCP/IP configuration in a UNIX environment.

Ports

Ports are the addressable endpoints at TCP and UDP. This is partially how applications atop TCP and UDP are addressed.

Well-known ports

TCP and UDP have popular applications that use them as transport protocols. Consequently, without some standardization of ports and relationships to applications, chaos could exist. As a result, TCP and UDP have applications that are assigned to well-known ports. Those working in the field of TCP/IP generally know this. It is a standardization to which most adhere. But flexibility does exist.

Port manipulation

Port numbers can be changed, but they usually are not. However, there is reason for this capability to exist. Sometimes port numbers are changed in gateways to achieve a given function.

Nevertheless, TCP and UDP applications can have their ports changed. Some port numbers are available for the development of custom applications. During the explanation of UDP in Sec. 14.14, the concept of custom applications is presented. This is an example where being able to use a "free" port number is required.

The downside of changing a port number is that if the application using that port is popular, it could cause problems in the network from a user perspective.

Sockets

A socket is the combination of an IP address and the port number appended to its end. Sockets are used in programming and are not normally of any concern to general users. However, in some instances it is important to understand the socket concept.

Hardware address

TCP/IP operates at Layers 3 and above in a network; therefore, it stands to reason that an interface of some type is needed for a TCP/IP host to participate in a network. The question then becomes, what is the lower-layer protocol used? If it is Ethernet, a 48-bit addressing scheme is used. If Token Ring, a 12-digit hexadecimal address is used, and so forth with the other lower-layer protocols—each has its own addressing scheme.

Understanding this addressing scheme is important, especially for those who troubleshoot networks. It is also important for those designing networks and for those implementers who have to make them work.

Synthesis

Understanding the previous information in this section is important for properly designing a TCP/IP network. The size of the network, the purpose for the network, and other site-specific parameters should be considered when selecting IP address classes and making decisions regarding other issues presented here. Planning, with the technical implications understood in the beginning, can save time and money in the long run.

14.16   Popular TCP Applications

In this section, popular applications that use TCP as a transport layer protocol are explained. Those presented in this section include the following:

- X Window system
- TELNET
- File Transfer Protocol (FTP)
- Simple Mail Transfer Protocol (SMTP)
- Domain Name System (DNS)

X window system

X, as it is known in the marketplace, is a distributed windowing system. At MIT in the early 1980s, developers were looking for a way to develop applications in a distributed computed environment. This was cutting-edge technology at the time. During their work they realized that a distributed windowing system would meet these needs very well.

MIT was given a considerable starting point to begin this endeavor after meeting and sharing information with individuals at Stanford who had been doing similar work. The Stanford group had dubbed this technology W, for windowing. The MIT group renamed it X, because that was the next letter in the alphabet. The name stuck.

By the late 1980s X commanded a considerable market share, specifically in the UNIX-based environment. One of the factors for its growth is its hardware and software independence. Suffice it to say that X is a dominant user interface in the UNIX environment, and it has spread into the MS-DOS and VMS environments, as well.

X is asynchronous and is based on a client/server model. It can manipulate two-dimensional graphics on a bitmapped display. Before examining some of the operational aspects of X, consider the layers of

X and its relationship to the TCP/IP protocol suite, as shown in Fig. 14.19.

Figure 14.19 shows the TCP/IP protocol suite, but the focus is upon X. The protocol suite is there to illustrate the relationship of X with TCP/IP. X is not a transport layer protocol; however, it uses TCP as a transport protocol.

X can be evaluated in two ways. From a TCP/IP perspective, it comprises Layers 5, 6, and 7. However, X itself has five layers. The names and functions of the layers in X include the following:

- *Protocol.* This is the lowest layer in X. It hooks into TCP. This includes the actual X protocol components.

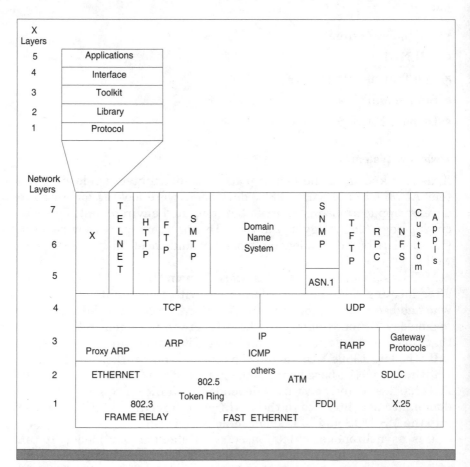

Figure 14.19 X and the TCP/IP protocol suite—A conceptual view of X layers with respect to TCP/IP.

- *Library.* The X library consists of a collection of C language routines based upon the X protocol. X library routines perform functions such as responding to the pressing of a mouse button.

- *Toolkit.* The X toolkit includes a higher level of programming tools. Examples of the support provided from this layer are the functions the tools provide in programming related to scroll bar and menu functions.

- *Interface.* The interface is what a user sees. Examples of interfaces include SUN's OpenLook, HP's OpenView, OSF's Motif, and NeXT's interface, to name a few.

- *Applications.* X applications can be defined as client applications that use X and conform to X programming standards that interact with the X server.

X theory of operation. X clients and X servers do not function in the way that other clients and servers do in the TCP/IP environment. What is considered the normal operation of a client is that it *initiates* something, and servers *serve* or *answer* the requests of clients. In X the concept is skewed.

An *X display manager* exists in the X environment. Its basic function is starting the X server and keeping it operating. The X display manager itself can be started manually or automatically. With respect to X, the display manager (also referred to as *Xdm*) is a client application.

An *X display server* (Xds) is a go-between for hardware components (such as a keyboard or mouse) and X client applications. The Xds operates by caching data entered and directing it to the appropriate X client application.

The correlation of Xdm and Xds can be understood by considering the following scenario. Two windows are active on a physical display. Each window functions as a client application. With this in mind, the idea of directing data to the appropriate X client application takes on a different meaning. This architectural arrangement is required to maintain order because multiple windows may be on the display (say, four or five).

In summary, the X display manager and X server control the operations on the display, which is what a user sees. But, going one step further for clarity, most entities in an X environment function as X client applications. Examples of this are the *Xclock;* an *Xterm,* which is an emulator; or even a TN3270 emulation software package used to access a 3270 data stream in a SNA environment.

TELNET

TELNET is a TCP application. It provides the ability to perform remote logons to adjacent hosts. TELNET consists of a client and server. The majority of TCP/IP software implementations have TEL-NET, simply because it is part of the protocol suite. As previously stated, *clients* initiate something (in this case, a remote logon) and *servers* serve the requests of clients. Figure 14.20 shows the TCP/IP protocol suite with TELNET highlighted, showing its client and server.

This example of TELNET is the same on practically all TCP/IP host implementations if the protocol suite has been developed according to the RFCs. But exceptions do apply. For example, TCP/IP on a DOS-based PC cannot implement a TELNET server because of the architectural constraints of the PC; in short, the PC cannot truly multitask, and other nuances also apply. Furthermore, on some network devices this implementation cannot work. However, the point is that on most host implementations, such as UNIX, VMS, MVS, VM, VSE, and some other operating systems, the TELNET client and server will function.

Figure 14.21 shows an example of TELNET client and server interaction on different hosts. A RISC/6000 user is shown invoking TEL-NET client, native to that machine because it is in the TCP/IP protocol suite. The RISC/6000 user wants to logon to the SUN host. The SUN host has TELNET in its TCP/IP protocol suite; consequently, the TEL-NET server answers the client's request and a logical connection is

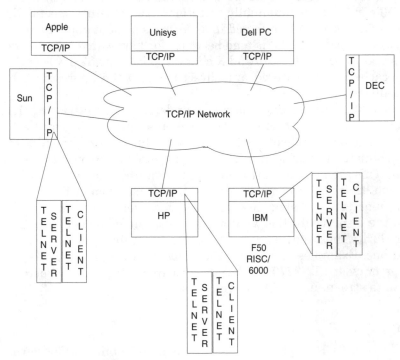

Figure 14.20   TELNET client and server.

established between the RISC/6000 and the SUN host. To the RISC/6000 user, there *appears* to be physical connection to the SUN.

This functionality of TELNET works with the majority of major vendors in the marketplace today. The key to understanding the client/server concept is to remember that clients *initiate* and servers *serve* clients' request.

File Transfer Protocol (FTP)

FTP is a file transfer application that uses TCP as a transport protocol. FTP has a client and server like TELNET; operationally, they work the same. What differs between TELNET and FTP is that TELNET enables remote logon whereas FTP permits file transfers.

FTP does not actually transfer a file from one host to another—it copies it. Hence, the original file exists and a copy of it has been put on a different machine. Figure 14.22 depicts this scenario.

Figure 14.22 shows an MVS host user invoking and moving the XYZ file to either the SUN or the MVS host. The MVS host user can use FTP client to *PUT* or *GET* a file.

Figure 14.22 shows two networks connected via a router. Any user can TELNET or perform an FTP. This type of networking scenario is powerful with regard to what can be accomplished.

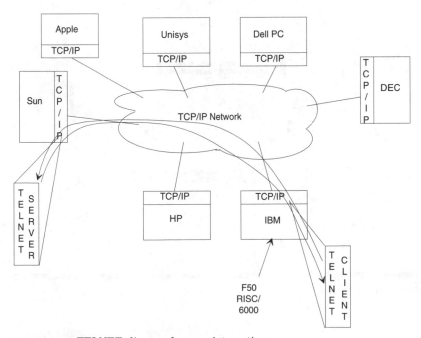

Figure 14.21   TELNET client and server interaction.

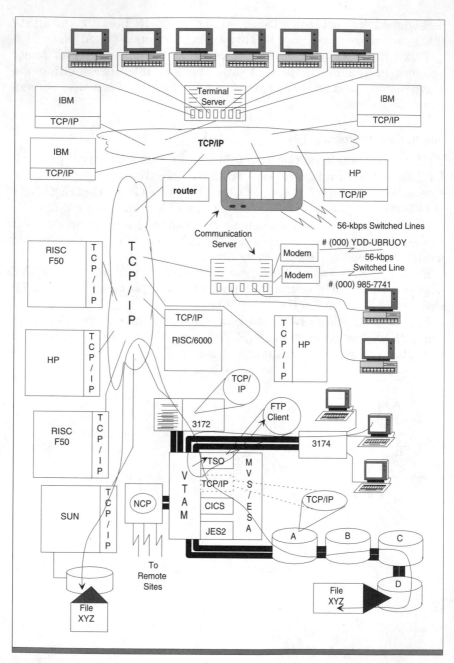

Figure 14.22   TCP/IP-based network.

Another twist with this example is that any user in either network can access the MVS host if they have privileges to do so. In this hypothetical scenario, any user could execute an FTP against the MVS host, PUT the XYZ into the MVS JES2 subsystem, and have it print or move it to the SUN system.

Examples such as this are practically as numerous as one could imagine. These are only a *few* examples to convey some simple operations.

Simple Mail Transfer Protocol (SMTP)

SMTP is another TCP application. It does not use a client and server, but the functionality is similar. SMTP utilizes what are called a *user agent* and a *message transfer agent*. Figure 14.23 shows a simple example of how SMTP operates.

Sending mail is accomplished by invoking a user agent, which, in turn, causes an editor to appear on the user's display. After the mail message is created and sent from the user agent, it is transferred to the message transfer agent. The message transfer agent is responsible for establishing communication with the message transfer agent on the destination host. Once this is accomplished, the sending message transfer agent sends the message to the receiving message transfer

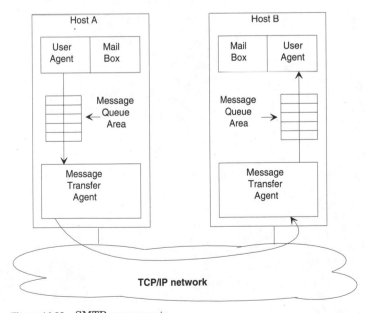

Figure 14.23   SMTP components.

agent, then stores it in the appropriate queue for the user. The recipient of the mail only needs to invoke the user agent on that machine to read the mail.

Domain Name System (DNS)

The Internet originally used *hosts* files to keep track of hosts on the Internet. This meant that when new hosts were added to the Internet, all participating hosts had to have their *hosts* file updated. As the Internet grew, this task of updating became insurmountable. The Domain Name System (DNS) grew from the need to replace such a system.

The philosophy of DNS was to replace the need to FTP updated *hosts* files throughout the entire network. Thus, the foundation of DNS was built around a distributed database architecture.

DNS structure. DNS is a hierarchical structure that conceptually appears as an upside-down tree. The root is at the top and layers are below. Figure 14.24 shows an example of how DNS is implemented in the Internet.

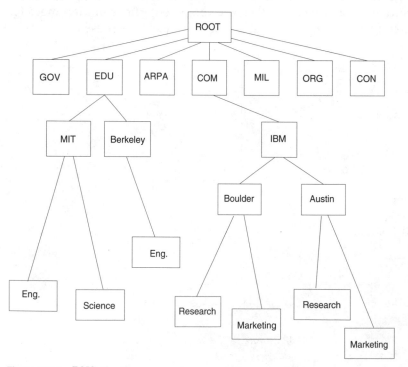

Figure 14.24 DNS structure.

The legend for the DNS structure in Fig. 14.24 is as follows:

ROOT: The root server contains information about itself and the top level domains immediately beneath it.

GOV: Refers to government entities.

EDU: Refers to any educational institutions.

ARPA: Refers to any ARPAnet (Internet) host ID.

COM: Refers to any commercial organizations.

MIL: Refers to military organizations.

ORG: Serves as a miscellaneous category for those not formally covered.

CON: Refers to countries conforming to ISO standards.

Figure 14.24 shows the Internet implementation of DNS. Three examples are shown to aid in understanding the structure. Note that IBM is under COM (which is commercial); beneath IBM are Boulder and Austin; and beneath each of them are research and marketing. The other examples are MIT and Berkeley. The example with MIT shows two *zones* beneath it, engineering and science. The Berkeley example has one layer beneath it, engineering.

At a local level, such as in a corporation, most sites follow the naming scheme and structure because it is consistent, and if a connection is ever made to the Internet, restructuring of the DNS is not necessary.

DNS components. To better understand DNS, knowing the components that make it functional is helpful. These components include the following:

DOMAIN. The last part in a domain name is considered the domain. For example, in eng.mit.edu, *edu* is the domain.

DOMAIN NAME. Defined by the DNS as being the sequence of names and domain. For example, a domain name could be eng.mit.edu.

LABEL. The DNS identifies each part of a domain name as a label. For example, eng.mit.edu has three labels.

NAME SERVER. A program operating on a host that translates names to addresses; it does this by mapping domain names to IP addresses. Also, *name server* may be used to refer to a dedicated processor running name server software.

NAME RESOLVER. This is software that functions as a client regarding its interaction with a name server. Sometimes referred to simply as the *client*.

NAME CACHE.   This is storage used by the name resolver to store information that is frequently used.

ZONE.   This is a contiguous part of a domain.

Theory of operation.   Figure 14.25 shows a TCP/IP network with five hosts. Of these five hosts, host *B* has been designated as the name server. It has a database with a list of aliases and IP addresses of participating hosts in the network. When the user on host *A* wants to communicate with host *C,* the name resolver checks its local cache. If no match is found, then the name resolver (client) sends a request (also known as a *query*) to the name server.

The name server, in turn, checks its cache for a match. If no match is found, then the name server checks its database. Though not shown in this figure, if the name server is unable to locate the name in its cache or database it will forward the request to another name server, then return the response back to host *A*.

In an internet environment that implements DNS, some givens are assumed. For example, a name resolver and a name server are required, and a foreign name server is usually part of the network.

Implementation with UDP.   The DNS provides service for both TCP and UDP; this is why the figures show DNS residing above part of TCP and part of UDP. It serves the same purpose for both transport layer protocols.

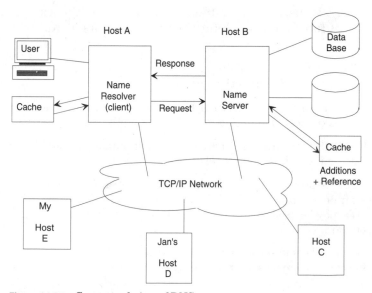

Figure 14.25   Conceptual view of DNS.

Additional information.   Additional information should be consulted on this issue if DNS is implemented. The following RFCs are a good beginning point:

RFC 882

RFC 883

RFC 920

RFC 973

RFC 974

RFC 1034

RFC 1123

RFC 1032

RFC 1033

RFC 1034

RFC 1035

14.17   Popular UDP Applications

This section presents popular UDP applications. Those covered include the following:

- Simple Network Management Protocol (SNMP)
- Trivial File Transfer Protocol (TFTP)
- Network File System (NFS)
- Remote Procedure Call (RPC)
- Custom Applications
- Packet Internet Groper (PING) and FINGER

Simple Network Management Protocol (SNMP)

SNMP is considered the de facto standard for managing TCP/IP networks as of this writing. SNMP uses *agents* and *application managers* (or simply *managers*). A user agent can reside on any node that supports SNMP, and each agent maintains status information about the node on which it operates. These nodes, which may be a host, gateway, router, or other type of network device, are called *network elements* in SNMP lingo. This term *element* is merely a generic reference to a node.

Normally, multiple elements exit in a TCP/IP network, and each has its own agent. Typically, one node is designated as a network management node. Some refer to this node as the *network manager.* This host (the network management node) has an application that communicates with each network element to obtain the status of a given element. The network management node and the element communicate via different message types. Some of these messages follow:

GET REQUEST: This type of request is used by the network manager to communicate with an element to request a variable or list about that particular network element.

GET RESPONSE: This is a reply to a GET REQUEST, SET REQUEST, or GET NEXT REQUEST.

GET NEXT REQUEST: This request is used to sequentially read information about an element.

SET REQUEST: This request enables variable values to be set in an element.

TRAP: This type of message is designed to report information such as:

- Link status

- Whether a neighbor responds

- Whether a message is received

- Element status

Information stored on elements is maintained in a *management information base* (MIB). This MIB is a database containing information about a particular element; each element has a MIB. Examples of MIB information include the following:

- Statistical information regarding segments transferred to and from the manager application

- Community name

- Interface type

- Other element-specific information

The MIB information structure is defined by the *Structure of Management Information* (SMI) language. SMI is a language used to define a data structure and methods for identifying an element for the manager application. This information identifies object variables in the MIB. At minimum, the object descriptions defined by SMI include the following:

ACCESS: Object access control is maintained via this description.

DEFINITION: This provides a textual description of an object.

NAMES: This term is also synonymous with *object identifiers*. This refers to a sequence of integers.

OBJECT DESCRIPTOR: This is a text name ascribed to the object.

OBJECT IDENTIFIER: This is a numeric ID used to identify the object.

STATUS: This describes the level of object support for status.

SNMP implementations use *ASN.1* for defining data structures in network elements. Because this language is based on a datatype definition, it can be used to define practically any element on a network.

SNMP itself is event-oriented. An *event* is generated when a change occurs to an object. SNMP operation is such that approximately every 10 to 15 minutes, the manager application communicates with each network element regarding its individual MIB data.

Additional information can be obtained from the following RFCs:

RFC 1155

RFC 1156

RFC 1157

Trivial File Transfer Protocol (TFTP)

TFTP is an application that uses UDP as a transport mechanism. The program itself is simpler than its counterpart FTP, which uses TCP as a transport mechanism. TFTP is small enough in size that it can be part of ROM on diskless workstations.

TFTP maximum packet size is 512 bytes. Because of this and the nature of operation, TFTP is popular with network devices such as routers and bridges. If implemented, it is normally used upon initial device boot.

TFTP utilizes no security provision or authentication; however, it does have some basic timing and retransmission capabilities. TFTP uses five basic types of protocol data units (PDUs):

1. Acknowledgment

2. Data

3. Error

4. Read request

5. Write request

These PDUs are used by TFTP during file transfer. The first packet TFTP establishes a session with the target TFTP program. It then requests a file transfer between the two. Next, it identifies a filename and whether or not a file will be read or written.

These five PDUs comprise the operational capability of TFTP. It is straightforward and not as complex as FTP.

Additional information can be obtained from the following RFCs:

RFC 783

RFC 1068

Remote Procedure Call (RPC)

RPC is a protocol. Technically speaking, it can operate over TCP or UDP as a transport mechanism. Applications use RPC to call a routine, thus executing like a client and making a call against a server on a remote host. This type of application programming is a high-level peer relationship between an application and a RPC server. Consequently, this means these applications are portable to the extent that RPC is implemented.

Within RPC is the *eXternal Data Representation* (XDR) protocol. XDR data description language can be used to define datatypes when heterogeneous hosts are integrated. Having the capability to overcome the inherent characteristics of different architectures lends RPC and XDR a robust solution for distributed application communication. This language permits parameter requests to be made against a file of an unlike type. In short, XDR permits datatype definition in the form of parameters and transmission of these encoded parameters.

XDR provides data transparency by way of encoding (or encapsulating) data at the application layer, so lower layers and hardware do not have to perform any conversions. A powerful aspect of XDR is automatic data conversion, performed via declaration statements and the XDR compiler. The XDR compiler generates required XDR calls, thus making the operation less manual by nature. Figure 14.26 shows an example of this type of implementation.

RPC implements what is called a *port mapper*. It starts upon RPC server initialization. When RPC services start, the operating system assigns a port number to each service. These services inform the port mapper of this port number, its program number, and other information required by the port mapper for it to match a service with a requestor.

Client applications issue a service request to a port mapper. The port mapper, in turn, identifies the requested service and returns the appropriate parameters to the requesting client application. In other words, the port mapper is similar in function to a manager—knowing what services are available and their specific addressable locations.

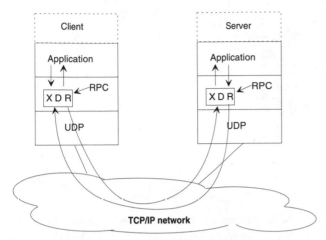

Figure 14.26   Conceptual view of RPC and XDR.

The port mapper can be used in a broadcast scenario. For example, a requesting RPC call can broadcast a call to all hosts on a network. Applicable port mappers report back the information sought after by the client. Hence, the term *Remote Procedure Call* (RPC).

Additional information on RPC and related components can be found in the following RFCs:

RFC 1057

RFC 1014

Network File System (NFS)

NFS is a product of Sun Microsystems. It permits users to execute files without knowing the location of these files. They may be local or remote with respect to the user. Users can create, read, or remove a directory. Files themselves can be written to or deleted. NFS provides a distributed file system that permits users to capitalize on access capabilities beyond their local file systems.

NFS uses RPC to make execution of a routine on a remote server possible. Conceptually, NFS, RPC, and UDP (which NFS typically uses) appear as shown in Fig. 14.27.

The idea behind NFS is having one copy of it on a server that all users on a network can access. The consequence of this is that software (and updates) can be installed on one server rather than on multiple hosts in a networked environment. NFS is based on a client/server model. However, with NFS a single NFS server can function to serve the requests of many clients.

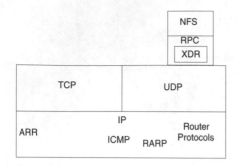

Figure 14.27 Conceptual view of NFS, RPC, and UDP.

NFS's origins are in UNIX, where it is implemented in a hierarchical (tree) structure. But NFS can operate with IBM's VM and MVS operating systems. It can also operate with Digital Equipment's VMS operating system.

NFS uses a *mount* protocol. This protocol identifies a file system and remote host to a local user's file system. NFS mount is known by the port mapper of RPC, and thus is capable of being known by requesting client applications.

NFS also uses the NFS protocol; it performs file transfers among systems. NFS uses port number 2049 in many cases; however, this is not a well-known port number (at least at the time of this writing). Consequently, the best approach to the use of NFS is to use the NFS port number with the port mapper.

In a sense, an NFS server operates with little information identified to it. A loose analogy of NFS operation is UDP. UDP assumes that a custom application (or other entity operating on top of it) will perform requirements such as retransmissions (if required) and other procedures that would otherwise be performed by a connection-oriented transport protocol such as TCP. NFS assumes that required services are implemented in other protocols.

From a user perspective, NFS is transparent. Typical user commands are entered and then passed to the NFS server, and in most cases a user does not know the physical location of a file in a networked environment.

Additional information about the Network File System and related components can be obtained from the following RFCs:

RFC 1094

RFC 1014

RFC 1057

Custom applications

Custom applications can be written that use UDP as a transport mechanism. One scenario could be where two hosts need peer program communication through a network. Writing a custom application using UDP can achieve this task, as Fig. 14.28 shows.

Packet Internet Groper (PING) and FINGER

PING is actually a protocol that uses UDP as a transport mechanism to achieve its function. It is used to send a message to a host and wait for that host to respond to the message (if the target host is *alive*). PING uses ICMP echo messages along with the echo reply messages.

PING is a helpful tool that is used on TCP/IP networks to determine if a device can be addressed. It is used in a network to determine if a network itself can be addressed. A PING can also be issued against a remote host *name*. The purpose for this function is name verification; it is generally used by individuals who troubleshoot TCP/IP networks.

FINGER is a command issued against a host that will cause the target host to return information about users logged onto that host. For example, some information retrievable via FINGER includes the user name, user interface, and job name that the user is running.

Additional information about FINGER can be obtained from RFC 1288.

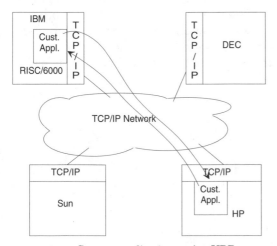

Figure 14.28   Custom applications using UDP.

14.18   Summary

TCP/IP is an upper-layer protocol that has a proven track record. It began around 1975; public demonstrations of its capabilities were presented in 1978; and in 1983 the DOD endorsed it as the protocol to use for connection to the Internet.

Many vendors supply TCP/IP products today. TCP/IP can operate on different hardware and software platforms. This flexibility, along with its cost-efficient pricing, does put it in a favorable position for those looking for a protocol that provides a variety of services such as the following:

- Remote logon
- File transfer
- E-mail
- Windowing system
- Programmatic interface support
- Network management capabilities
- Distributed processing support
- Other additional offerings

TCP/IP is dominant throughout the marketplace today; most major vendors worldwide support it to varying degrees. Its flexibility with data link layer protocols makes it attractive.

TCP/IP has two transport layer protocols, which makes usability flexible. Some need the reliability of transport like TCP, while others need a connectionless transport like UDP—TCP/IP supports both.

TCP/IP has, in many ways, become a de facto standard in many different institutions. It is used in government, in commercial business, in education, in nonprofit organizations, and for individual use, as well.

Chapter

15

TCP/IP Network Design
and IP Version 4

15.1 IP Functions

The Internet Protocol was originally designed for use in interconnected systems of packet-switched computer communication networks. This type of system has been called a *catenet*. IP provides for
transmitting blocks of data called *datagrams* from sources to destinations, where sources and destinations are hosts identified by fixed-
length addresses. IP also provides for fragmentation and reassembly
of long datagrams, if necessary, for transmission through small-packet
networks.

IP was originally limited in its purpose to provide the functions necessary to deliver a package of bits (Internet datagrams) from a source
to a destination through an interconnected group of networks. IP has
no mechanisms to augment end-to-end data reliability, flow control,
sequencing, or other services commonly found in host-to-host protocols.
However, IP can capitalize on the services of its supporting networks to
provide various types *and* qualities of service.

IP is invoked by host-to-host protocols in the Internet environment.
This protocol calls on local network protocols to carry the Internet datagram to the next gateway or destination host. In this case, a TCP module would call on the IP part to take a TCP segment (the TCP header
and user data) as the *data* portion of an Internet datagram.

IP implements two basic functions, *addressing* and *fragmentation*.
Internet modules use the addresses carried in the Internet header to
transmit Internet datagrams toward their destinations. The selection

of a path for transmission is called *routing*. Fields in the IP are used to fragment and reassemble Internet datagrams when necessary for transmission through small-packet-oriented networks.

An Internet module resides in each host engaged in Internet communication and in each router that interconnects networks. These modules share common rules for interpreting address fields and for fragmenting and assembling Internet datagrams. In addition, these modules have procedures for making routing decisions and other functions.

IP treats each Internet datagram as an independent entity unrelated to any other Internet datagram. Hence, there are no connections or logical circuits. IP uses the following four key mechanisms in providing its service:

- Type of service
- Time to live
- Options
- Header checksum

Type of service

The type of service field is used to indicate the quality of the service desired. This is an abstract or generalized set of parameters that the service choices provide in the networks that make up the Internet. This type of service indication is to be used by routers to select the actual transmission parameters for a particular network, the network for the next hop, or the next router when routing an Internet datagram.

Time to live

Time to live indicates an upper boundary of lifetime that an IP datagram has to exist. It is set by the sender of the datagram and is reduced at the points along the route where it is processed. If the time to live reaches zero before the Internet datagram reaches its destination, the Internet datagram is destroyed. The time to live can be like a self-destruct mechanism.

Options

The options field provides for control functions that are needed or useful in some situations but are unnecessary for the most common communications. This makes timestamps, security, and special routing possible.

Header checksum

The header checksum provides a verification that the information used in processing the Internet datagram has been transmitted correctly. The data may contain errors. If the header checksum fails, the Internet datagram is discarded at once by the entity that detects the error.

IP does not provide a reliable communication facility. There are no acknowledgments either end-to-end or hop-by-hop, and neither is there any error control for data, only a header checksum. IP does not perform any retransmissions and has no flow control. Any errors detected are reported via the *Internet Control Message Protocol* (ICMP). ICMP is a required component that accompanies IP.

15.2   IP Operation

Transmitting a datagram from one application program to another is illustrated by the following example.

An intermediate router is presumed in this example environment. A sending application program prepares its data and calls on its IP module to send the data as a datagram. It passes the destination address and other parameters as arguments to this call. The IP module prepares a datagram header and attaches the data to it. The IP module determines a local network address for this Internet address; in this case it is the address of a router.

It sends this datagram and the local network address to the network interface. The network interface, in turn, creates a local network header and attaches the datagram to it. It then sends the result via the local network.

The datagram arrives at a router wrapped in the local network header. The local network interface strips off this header and turns the datagram over to the Internet module. The Internet module determines from the Internet address that the datagram is to be forwarded to another host in a second network. The Internet module determines a local net address for the destination host. It calls on the local network interface for that network to send the datagram.

This local network interface creates a local network header and attaches the datagram, sending the result to the destination host. Here the destination host datagram is stripped of the local net header by the local network interface and is handed to the Internet module. The Internet module determines that the datagram is for an application program in this host. It passes the data to the application program in response to a system call, passing the source address and other parameters as a result of the call. The following diagram illustrates this process.

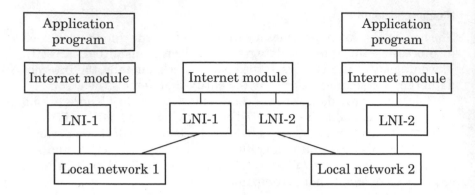

The purpose of IP is to move datagrams through a set of networks. Datagrams are passed from one Internet module to another until the destination is reached. The Internet modules reside in hosts and routers in the Internet. Datagrams are routed from one Internet module to another through individual networks on the basis of interpretation of an Internet address. Thus, one important mechanism of the Internet Protocol is the Internet address.

Because datagrams may have to traverse multiple intranetworks within the Internet, the routing of messages from one internet module to another may be achieved by *fragmentation*. Fragmentation is necessary for a datagram to traverse a network whose maximum packet size is smaller than the size of the datagram.

Fragmentation

Fragmentation of an Internet datagram is necessary when it originates in a local net that allows a large packet size and must traverse a local net that limits packets to a smaller size on its route to its destination.

An Internet datagram can be marked *don't fragment*. Any Internet datagram so marked is not to be Internet-fragmented under any circumstances. If an Internet datagram marked *don't fragment* cannot be delivered to its destination without fragmentation, it is to be discarded instead.

Fragmentation, transmission, and reassembly across a local network that is invisible to the IP module is called *intranet fragmentation* and may be used.

The Internet fragmentation and reassembly procedure needs to be able to break a datagram into an almost arbitrary number of pieces that can later be reassembled. The receiver of the fragments uses the *identification* field to ensure that fragments of different datagrams are not mixed. The *fragment offset* field tells the receiver the position of a fragment in the original datagram. The fragment offset and length determine the portion of the original datagram covered by this fragment. The *more-fragments* flag indicates (by being reset) the last fragment. These fields provide sufficient information to reassemble datagrams.

The identification field is used to distinguish the fragments of one datagram from those of another. The originating protocol module of an Internet datagram sets the identification field to a value that must be unique for that source-destination pair and protocol for the time that the datagram will be active in the internet system. The originating protocol module of a complete datagram sets the more-fragments flag to 0 and the fragment offset to 0.

To fragment a long Internet datagram, an IP module creates two new Internet datagrams and copies the contents of the Internet header fields from the long datagram into both new Internet headers. The data of the long datagram is divided into two portions on a 8-octet (64-bit) boundary (the second portion might not be an integral multiple of 8 octets, but the first must be). Call the number of 8-octet blocks in the first portion *number of fragment blocks* (NFB). The first portion of the data is placed in the first new Internet datagram, and the total length field is set to the length of the first datagram. The more-fragments flag is set to 1. The second portion of the data is placed in the second new Internet datagram, and the total length field is set to the length of the second datagram. The more-fragments flag carries the same value as the long datagram. The fragment offset field of the second new internet datagram is set to the value of that field in the long datagram plus NFB.

This procedure can be generalized for an *n*-way split, rather than the two-way split described. To assemble the fragments of an Internet datagram, an IP module (for example, at a destination host) combines Internet datagrams that all have the same value for the four following fields:

- Identification

- Source

- Destination

- Protocol

The combination is done by placing the data portion of each fragment in the relative position indicated by the fragment offset in that fragment's Internet header. The first fragment will have the fragment offset set to 0, and the last fragment will have the more-fragments flag reset to 0.

Addressing

A distinction is made between names, addresses, and routes. A `name` indicates what we seek. An `address` indicates where it is. A `route` indicates how to get there. The Internet protocol deals primarily with addresses. It is the task of higher-level protocols to make the mapping from names to addresses. The Internet module maps Internet addresses to local net addresses. It is the task of lower-level (i.e., local net or gateway) procedures to make the mapping from local net addresses to routes.

Addresses are fixed-length, of 4 octets (32 bits). An address begins with a network number, followed by a local address (called the `rest` field). There are three formats or classes of Internet addresses, as follows:

Class A. The high-order bit is 0, the next 7 bits are the network, and the last 24 bits are the local address.

Class B. The high-order 2 bits are 1-0, the next 14 bits are the network, and the last 16 bits are the local address.

Class C. The high-order 3 bits are 1-1-0, the next 21 bits are the network, and the last 8 bits are the local address.

Care must be taken in mapping Internet addresses to local net addresses—a single physical host must be able to act as if it were several distinct hosts to the extent of using several distinct Internet addresses. Some hosts will also have several physical interfaces; this is also called a *multihomed host.*

Provision must be made for a host to have several physical interfaces to the network, with each having several logical Internet addresses.

15.3   IP Terminology

IP uses terms that have specific meanings. Sometimes these terms are misunderstood; for that reason the following list is included for your reference.

ARPANET LEADER: The control information on an ARPAnet message at the host-IMP interface.

ARPANET MESSAGE: The unit of transmission between a host and an IMP in the ARPAnet. The maximum size is about 1012 octets (8096 bits).

ARPANET PACKET: A unit of transmission used internally in the ARPAnet between IMPs. The maximum size is about 126 octets (1008 bits).

DESTINATION: The destination address, an Internet header field.

DF: The Don't Fragment bit carried in the Flags field.

FLAGS: An Internet header field carrying various control flags.

FRAGMENT OFFSET: This Internet header field indicates where in the Internet datagram a fragment belongs.

GGP: Gateway-to-Gateway Protocol. The protocol primarily used between gateways to control routing and other gateway functions.

HEADER: Control information at the beginning of a message, segment, datagram, packet or block of data.

ICMP: Internet Control Message Protocol. Implemented in the Internet module, the ICMP is used from gateways to hosts and between hosts to report errors and make routing suggestions.

IDENTIFICATION: An Internet header field carrying the identifying value assigned by the sender to aid in assembling the fragments of a datagram.

IHL: The Internet Header Length field is the length of the Internet header, measured in 32-bit words.

IMP: The Interface Message Processor, the packet switch of the ARPAnet.

INTERNET ADDRESS: A 4-octet (32-bit) source or destination address consisting of a Network field and a Local Address field.

INTERNET DATAGRAM: The unit of data exchanged between a pair of Internet modules. (Includes the internet header.)

INTERNET FRAGMENT: A portion of the data of an Internet datagram with an Internet header.

LOCAL ADDRESS: The address of a host within a network. The actual mapping of an Internet local address onto the host addresses in a network is quite general, allowing for many-to-one mappings.

MF: The More-Fragments flag carried in the Internet header Flags field.

MODULE: An implementation, usually in software, of a protocol or other procedure.

MORE-FRAGMENTS FLAG: A flag indicating whether or not this Internet datagram contains the end of an Internet datagram, carried in the Internet header Flags field.

NFB: The Number of Fragments Block in the data portion of an Internet fragment. That is, the length of a portion of data, measured in 8-octet units.

OCTET: An 8-bit byte.

OPTIONS: The Internet header Options field may contain several options, and each option may be several octets in length.

PADDING: The Internet header Padding field is used to ensure that the data begins on a 32-bit word boundary. The padding is 0.

PROTOCOL: In this document, the next-higher level protocol identifier, an Internet header field.

REST: The local address portion of an Internet Address.

SOURCE: The source address, an Internet header field.

TCP: Transmission Control Protocol. A host-to-host protocol for reliable communication in Internet environments.

TCP SEGMENT: The unit of data exchanged between TCP modules (including the TCP header).

TFTP: Trivial File Transfer Protocol. A simple file transfer protocol built on UDP.

TIME TO LIVE: An Internet header field that indicates the upper bound on how long this Internet datagram may exist.

TOS: Type of Service.

TOTAL LENGTH: The Internet header Total Length field is the length of the datagram in octets, including internet header and data.

TTL: Time to Live.

TYPE OF SERVICE: An Internet header field that indicates the type (or quality) of service for this Internet datagram.

UDF: User Datagram Protocol. A user-level protocol for transaction-oriented applications.

USER: The user of the Internet protocol. This may be a higher-level protocol module, an application program, or a gateway program.

VERSION: The Version field indicates the format of the Internet header.

15.4   Routers and IP

Routers implement IP to forward datagrams between networks. Routers also implement the Gateway-to-Gateway Protocol (GGP) to coordinate routing and other internet control information. (In times past, routers were called *gateways*.)

In a router the higher-level protocols need not be implemented, and the GGP functions are added to the IP module.

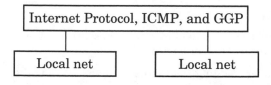

15.5   IP Header Format

The contents of the internet header are as follows:

```
0                   1                   2                   3
0 1 2 3 4 5 6 7 8 9 0 1 2 3 4 5 6 7 8 9 0 1 2 3 4 5 6 7 8 9 0 1
```

Version	IHL	Type of Service	Total Length		
Identification			Flags	Fragment Offset	
Time to Live		Protocol	Header Checksum		
Source Address					
Destination Address					
Options				Padding	

An explanation of these fields follows.

Version

4 bits.   The Version field indicates the format of the Internet header. This document describes version 4.

IHL

4 bits.   The Internet Header Length is the length of the internet header in 32-bit words, and thus points to the beginning of the data. Note that the minimum value for a correct header is 5.

Type of service

8 bits.   Type of Service provides an indication of the abstract parameters of the quality of service desired. These parameters are to be used to guide the selection of the actual service parameters when transmitting a datagram through a particular network. Several networks offer service precedence, which somehow treats high-precedence traffic as more important than other traffic (generally by accepting only traffic above a certain precedence at times of high load). The major choice is a three-way tradeoff between low delay, high reliability, and high throughput.

Bit	0–2	Precedence	
Bit	3	0 = Normal delay	1 = Low delay
Bit	4	0 = Normal throughput	1 = High throughput
Bit	5	0 = Normal reliability	1 = High reliability
Bit	6–7	Reserved for future use	

0	1	2	3	4	5	6	7
Precedence			D	T	R	0	0

Precedence

111	Network Control
110	Internetwork Control
101	CRITIC/ECP
100	Flash Override
011	Flash
010	Immediate
001	Priority
000	Routine

Delay, throughput, and reliability indications may increase the cost (in some sense) of the service. In many networks, better performance for one of these parameters is coupled with worse performance on another. Except for very unusual cases, at most two of these three indications should be set. The type of service is used to specify the treatment of the datagram during its transmission through the internet system.

The Network Control precedence designation is intended to be used only within a network. The actual use and control of that designation is up to each network. The Internetwork Control designation is intended for use only by gateway control originators. If the actual use of these precedence designations is of concern to a particular network, it is the responsibility of that network to control the access to, and use of, the precedence designations.

Total length

16 bits. Total Length is the length of the datagram, measured in octets, including the Internet header and data. This field allows the length of a datagram to be up to 65,535 octets. Such long datagrams are impractical for most hosts and networks. All hosts must be prepared to accept datagrams of up to 576 octets (whether they arrive whole or in fragments). It is recommended that hosts send datagrams larger than 576 octets only if they have assurance that the destination is prepared to accept the larger datagrams.

The number 576 is selected to allow a reasonably sized data block to be transmitted in addition to the required header information. For example, this size allows a data block of 512 octets plus 64 header octets to fit in a datagram. The maximum Internet header is 60 octets, and a typical Internet header is 20 octets, allowing a margin for headers of higher-level protocols.

Identification

16 bits.   An identifying value assigned by the sender to aid in assembling the fragments of a datagram.

Flags

3 bits.   This field provides various Control Flags.

Bit 0	Reserved	Must be 0
Bit 1	DF	0 = May Fragment 1 = Don't Fragment.
Bit 2	MF	0 = Last Fragment 1 = More Fragments.

0	1	2
0	DF	MF

Fragment offset

13 bits.   This field indicates where in the datagram this fragment belongs. The fragment offset is measured in units of 8 octets (64 bits). The first fragment has offset 0.

Time to live

8 bits.   This field indicates the maximum time that the datagram is allowed to remain in the internet system. If this field contains the value 0, then the datagram must be destroyed. This field is modified in Internet header processing. The time is measured in units of seconds, but since every module that processes a datagram must decrease the TTL by at least 1 even if it processes the datagram in less than a second, the TTL must be thought of only as an upper bound on the time a datagram may exist. The intention is to cause undeliverable datagrams to be discarded, and to bound the maximum datagram lifetime.

Protocol

8 bits.   This field indicates the next level protocol used in the data portion of the Internet datagram.

Header checksum

16 bits. A checksum on the header only. Since some header fields change (e.g., time to live), this is recomputed and verified at each point that the Internet header is processed.

The checksum algorithm is as follows:

The checksum field is the 16-bit one's complement of the one's complement sum of all 16-bit words in the header. For purposes of computing the checksum, the value of the checksum field is 0. This is a simple checksum to compute, and experimental evidence indicates that it is adequate, but it is provisional and may be replaced by a CRC procedure.

Source address

32 bits.

Destination address

32 bits.

Options

Variable. The options may or may not appear in datagrams. They must be implemented by all IP modules (host and routers). What is optional is their transmission in any particular datagram, not their implementation. In some environments the security option may be required in all datagrams.

The option field is variable in length. There may be zero or more options. There are two cases for the format of an option, a single octet of option-type. An option-type octet, an option-length octet, and the actual option-data octets.

The option-length octet counts the option-type octet and the option-length octet, as well as the option-data octets.

The option-type octet is viewed as having three fields:

1 bit	Copied flag
2 bits	Option class
5 bits	Option number

The copied flag indicates that this option is copied into all fragments on fragmentation:

0	Not copied
1	Copied

Option classes are as follows:

0   Control
1   Reserved for future use
2   Debugging and measurement
3   Reserved for future use

Internet options are defined in the following table.

Class	Number	Length	Description
0	0	—	End of Option list. This option occupies only 1 octet; it has no length octet.
0	1	—	No Operation. This option occupies only 1 octet; it has no length octet.
0	2	11	Security. Used to carry Security, Compartmentation, User Group (TCC), and Handling Restriction Codes compatible with DOD requirements.
0	3	Variable	Loose Source Routing. Used to route the Internet datagram based on information supplied by the source.
0	9	Variable	Strict Source Routing. Used to route the Internet datagram based on information supplied by the source.
0	7	Variable	Record Route. Used to trace the route an Internet datagram takes.
0	8	4	Stream ID. Used to carry the stream identifier.
2	4	Variable	Internet Timestamp.

Specific option definitions

End of option list

Type = 0

This option indicates the end of the option list. This might not coincide with the end of the Internet header according to the Internet header length. This is used at the end of all options, not the end of each option, and need only be used if the end of the options would not otherwise coincide with the end of the Internet header.

It may be copied, introduced, or deleted on fragmentation, or for any other reason.

No operation

00000001

Type = 1

This option may be used between options; for example, to align the beginning of a subsequent option on a 32-bit boundary. It may be copied, introduced, or deleted on fragmentation, or for any other reason.

Security. This option provides a way for hosts to send security, compartmentation, handling restrictions, and TCC (closed user group) parameters. The format for this option is as follows:

10000010	00001011	SSS SSS	CCC CCC	HHH HHH	TCC

Type = 130
Length = 11

Security (S field). *16 bits.* Specifies one of 16 levels of security (8 of which are reserved for future use).

00000000 00000000	Unclassified
11110001 00110101	Confidential
01111000 10011010	EFTO
10111100 01001101	MMMM
01011110 00100110	PROG

10101111 00010011	Restricted
11010111 10001000	Secret
01101011 11000101	Top Secret
00110101 11100010	Reserved for future use
10011010 11110001	Reserved for future use
01001101 01111000	Reserved for future use
00100100 10111101	Reserved for future use
00010011 01011110	Reserved for future use
10001001 10101111	Reserved for future use
11000100 11010110	Reserved for future use
11100010 01101011	Reserved for future use

Compartments (C field). *16 bits.* An all-zero value is used when the information transmitted is not compartmented. Other values for the compartments field may be obtained from the Defense Intelligence Agency.

Handling restrictions (H field). *16 bits.* The values for the control and release markings are alphanumeric digraphs and are defined in the Defense Intelligence Agency Manual DIAM 65-19, Standard Security Markings.

Transmission Control Code (TCC field). *24 bits.* Provides a means to segregate traffic and define controlled communities of interest among subscribers. The TCC values are trigraphs, and are available from HQ DCA Code 530. Must be copied on fragmentation. This option appears at most once in a datagram.

Loose source and record route

10000011	Length	Pointer	Route data

Type = 131

The loose source and record route (LSRR) option provides a means for the source of an Internet datagram to supply routing information to be used by the gateways in forwarding the datagram to the destination, and to record the route information.

The option begins with the option-type code. The second octet is the option length, which includes the option-type code and the length octet, the pointer octet, and 3 octets of route data. The third octet is the pointer into the route data indicating the octet that begins the next source address to be processed. The pointer is relative to this option, and the smallest legal value for the pointer is 4.

Route data is composed of a series of Internet addresses. Each Internet address is 32 bits, or 4 octets. If the pointer is greater than the length, the source route is empty (and the recorded route is full) and the routing is to be based on the destination address field.

If the address in the destination address field has been reached and the pointer is not greater than the length, the next address in the source route replaces the address in the destination address field. The recorded route address replaces the source address just used, and the pointer is increased by 4.

The recorded route address is the Internet module's own Internet address as known in the environment into which this datagram is being forwarded.

This procedure of replacing the source route with the recorded route (though it is in the reverse of the order it must be in to be used as a source route) means that the option (and the IP header as a whole) remains a constant length as the datagram progresses through the internet.

This option is a *loose* source route because the gateway or host IP is allowed to use any route of any number of other intermediate gateways to reach the next address in the route.

It must be copied on fragmentation, and it appears at most once in a datagram.

Strict source and record route

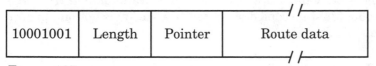

Type = 137

The strict source and record route (SSRR) option provides a means for the source of an Internet datagram to supply routing information to be used by the gateways in forwarding the datagram to the destination, and to record the route information.

The option begins with the option-type code. The second octet is the option length, which includes the option-type code and the length octet, the pointer octet, and the length—3 octets of route data. The third octet is the pointer into the route data indicating the octet that begins the next source address to be processed. The pointer is relative to this option, and the smallest legal value for the pointer is 4.

Route data is composed of a series of Internet addresses. Each internet address is 32-bits, or 4 octets. If the pointer is greater than the length, the source route is empty (and the recorded route is full) and the routing is to be based on the destination address field.

If the address in the destination address field has been reached and the pointer is not greater than the length, the next address in the source route replaces the address in the destination address field. The recorded route address replaces the source address just used, and the pointer is increased by 4.

The recorded route address is the Internet module's own Internet address as known in the environment into which this datagram is being forwarded.

This procedure of replacing the source route with the recorded route (though it is in the reverse of the order it must be in to be used as a source route) means that the option (and the IP header as a whole) remains a constant length as the datagram progresses through the internet.

This option is a *strict* source route because the gateway or host IP must send the datagram directly to the next address in the source route through only the directly connected network indicated in the next address to reach the next gateway or host specified in the route.

It must be copied on fragmentation, and it appears at most once in a datagram.

Record route

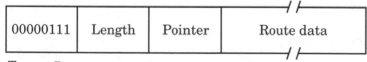

Type = 7

The record route option provides a means to record the route of an Internet datagram. The option begins with the option-type code. The second octet is the option length, which includes the option type code and the length octet, the pointer octet, and the length—3 octets of route data. The third octet is the pointer into the route data indicating the octet that begins the next area to store a route address. The pointer is relative to this option, and the smallest legal value for the pointer is 4.

A *recorded route* is composed of a series of Internet addresses. Each internet address is 32 bits, or 4 octets. If the pointer is the originating host, it must compose this option with a large enough route data area to hold all the addresses expected. The size of the option does not change due to adding addresses. The initial content of the route data area must be 0.

When an Internet module routes a datagram, it checks to see if the record route option is present. If it is, it inserts its own Internet address (as known in the environment into which this datagram is being forwarded) into the recorded route, beginning at the octet indicated by the pointer, and it increments the pointer by 4.

If the route data area is already full (the pointer exceeds the length), the datagram is forwarded without inserting the address into the recorded route. If there is some room but not enough room for a full address to be inserted, the original datagram is considered to be in error and is discarded. In either case, an ICMP parameter problem message may be sent to the source host.

It is not copied on fragmentation, and goes in only the first fragment. It appears at most once in a datagram.

Stream identifier

10001000	00000010	Stream ID

Type = 136
Length = 4

This option provides a way for the 16-bit SATNET stream identifier to be carried through networks that do not support the stream concept.

It must be copied on fragmentation, and it appears at most once in a datagram.

15.6 Internet Timestamp

01000100	Length	Pointer	Oflw	Flg
Internet Address				
Timestamp				
• • •				

Type = 68

The Internet timestamp is an integral tool in the implementation and use of IP.

The Internet timestamp appears as follows:

The option length is the number of octets in the option counting the type, length, pointer, and overflow/flag octets (maximum length 40).

The pointer is the number of octets from the beginning of this option to the end of timestamps plus 1 (i.e., it points to the octet beginning the space for next timestamp). The smallest legal value is 5. The timestamp area is full when the pointer is greater than the length.

The overflow (oflw; 4 bits) is the number of IP modules that cannot register timestamps due to lack of space.

The flag (flg; 4 bits) values are as follows:

0   Timestamps only, stored in consecutive 32-bit words.

1   Each timestamp is preceded with the Internet address of the registering entity.

3   The internet address fields are prespecified.

An IP module only registers its timestamp if it matches its own address with the next specified internet address.

The timestamp is a right-justified, 32-bit timestamp in milliseconds since midnight UT. If the time is not available in milliseconds or cannot be provided with respect to midnight UT, then any time may be inserted as a timestamp provided the high-order bit of the timestamp field is set to 1 to indicate the use of a nonstandard value.

The originating host must compose this option with a large enough timestamp data area to hold all the timestamp information expected. The size of the option does not change due to adding timestamps. The initial contents of the timestamp data area must be 0 or Internet address/0 pairs.

If the timestamp data area is already full (the pointer exceeds the length), the datagram is forwarded without inserting the timestamp, but the overflow count is incremented by 1. If there is some room but not enough room for a full timestamp to be inserted, or if the overflow count itself overflows, the original datagram is considered to be in error and is discarded. In either case, an ICMP parameter problem message may be sent to the source host.

The timestamp option is not copied upon fragmentation. It is carried in the first fragment. It appears at most once in a datagram.

The Internet header padding is used to ensure that the Internet header ends on a 32-bit boundary. The padding is 0.

Fragmentation and reassembly

The Internet identification field (ID) is used together with the source and destination address and the protocol fields to identify datagram fragments for reassembly.

The More Fragments (MF) flag bit is set if the datagram is not the last fragment. The Fragment Offset field identifies the fragment's location relative to the beginning of the original unfragmented datagram. Fragments are counted in units of 8 octets. The fragmentation strategy is designed so that an unfragmented datagram has all-zero fragmentation information (MF = 0, fragment offset = 0). If an Internet datagram is fragmented, its data portion must be broken on 8-octet boundaries.

This format allows $2^{13} = 8192$ fragments of 8 octets each, for a total of 65,536 octets. Note that this is consistent with the datagram total length field (of course, the header is counted in the total length and not in the fragments).

When fragmentation occurs, some options are copied, but others remain with only the first fragment. Every internet module must be able to forward a datagram of 68 octets without further fragmentation. This is because an internet header may be up to 60 octets, and the minimum fragment is 8 octets. Every internet destination must be able to receive a datagram of 576 octets, either in one piece or in fragments to be reassembled.

The fields that may be affected by fragmentation include the following:

1. Options field

2. More Fragments flag

3. Fragment Offset field

4. Internet Header Length field

5. Total Length field

6. Header Checksum

If the don't fragment (DF) flag bit is set, then Internet fragmentation of this datagram is *not* permitted, although it may be discarded. This can be used to prohibit fragmentation in cases where the receiving host does not have sufficient resources to reassemble Internet fragments.

One example of use of the don't fragment feature is to downline load a small host. A small host could have a bootstrap program that accepts a datagram, stores it in memory, and then executes it.

The fragmentation and reassembly procedures are most easily described by examples. The following procedures are example implementations.

This general notation is used in the following pseudoprograms:

=<   Less than or equal

Not equal

=   Equal

<–   Is set to

Also, "x to y" includes x and excludes y; for example, "4 to 7" would include 4, 5, and 6 (but not 7).

Fragmentation procedure example

The maximum-sized datagram that can be transmitted through the next network is called the *maximum transmission unit* (MTU). If the total length is less than or equal to the maximum transmission unit, then submit this datagram to the next step in datagram processing; otherwise, cut the datagram into two fragments—the first fragment being the maximum size, and the second fragment being the rest of the datagram. The first fragment is submitted to the next step in datagram processing, while the second fragment is submitted to this procedure in case it is still too large.

Notation

FO	Fragment Offset
IHL	Internet Header Length
DF	Don't Fragment flag
MF	More Fragments flag
TL	Total Length
OFO	Old Fragment Offset
OIHL	Old Internet Header Length
OMF	Old More Fragments flag
OTL	Old Total Length
NFB	Number of Fragment Blocks
MTU	Maximum Transmission Unit

Procedure

```
IF TL =< MTU THEN Submit this datagram to the next step in
datagram processing ELSE IF DF = 1 THEN discard the datagram
ELSE.
To produce the first fragment:
1    Copy the original internet header;
2    OIHL <- IHL; OTL <- TL; OFO <- FO; OMF <- MF;
3    NFB <- (MTU-IHL*4)/8;
4    Attach the first NFB*8 data octets;
5    Correct the header:
     MF <- 1; TL <- (IHL*4)+(NFB*8);
     Recompute Checksum;
6    Submit this fragment to the next step in
     datagram processing;
To produce the second fragment:
7    Selectively copy the internet header (some
     options are not copied, see option
     definitions);
```

```
8    Append the remaining data;
9    Correct the header:
     IHL <- (((OIHL*4)-(length of options not
     copied))+3)/4; TL <- OTL - NFB*8 -
     (OIHL-IHL)*4); FO <- OFO + NFB; MF <- OMF;
     Recompute Checksum;
10   Submit this fragment to the fragmentation
     test; DONE.
```

In this procedure each fragment (except the last) is made the maximum allowable size. An alternative might produce less than the maximum size datagrams. For example, one could implement a fragmentation procedure that repeatedly divided large datagrams in half until the resulting fragments were less than the maximum transmission unit size.

Reassembly procedure example

For each datagram, the buffer identifier is computed as the concatenation of the source, destination, protocol, and identification fields. If this is a whole datagram (that is, both the fragment offset and the more fragments fields are 0), then any reassembly resources associated with this buffer identifier are released and the datagram is forwarded to the next step in datagram processing.

If no other fragment with this buffer identifier is on hand, then reassembly resources are allocated. The reassembly resources consist of a data buffer, a header buffer, a fragment block bit table, a total data length field, and a timer. The data from the fragment is placed in the data buffer according to its fragment offset and length, and bits are set in the fragment block bit table corresponding to the fragment blocks received.

If this is the first fragment (that is, if the fragment offset is 0), this header is placed in the header buffer. If this is the last fragment (that is, if the more fragments field is 0), the total data length is computed. If this fragment completes the datagram (tested by checking the bits set in the fragment block table), then the datagram is sent to the next step in datagram processing; otherwise the timer is set to the maximum of the current timer value and the value of the time-to-live field from this fragment, and the reassembly routine gives up control.

If the timer runs out, then all reassembly resources for this buffer identifier are released. The initial setting of the timer is a lower bound on the reassembly waiting time. This is because the waiting time will be increased if the time to live in the arriving fragment is greater than the current timer value, but it will not be decreased if it is less. The maximum this timer value could reach is the maximum time to live (approximately 4.25 min). The current recommendation for the initial timer setting is 15 s. This may be changed as experience with this protocol accumulates. Note that the choice of this parameter value is related to the buffer capacity available and the datarate of the transmission medium—that is, datarate times timer value equals buffer size (e.g., 10 kbps × 15 s = 150 kb).

Notation

FO	Fragment Offset
IHL	Internet Header Length
MF	More Fragments flag
TTL	Time to Live
NFB	Number of Fragments Block
TL	Total Length
TDL	Total Data Length
BUFID	Buffer Identifier
RCVBT	Fragment Received Bit Table
TLB	Timer Lower Bound

Procedure

```
1    BUFID <-
     source|destination|protocol|identification;
2    IF FO = 0 and MF = 0
3    THEN IF buffer with BUFID is allocated
4    THEN flush all reassembly for this BUFID;
5    Submit datagram to next step; DONE.
6    ELSE IF no buffer with BUFID is allocated
7    THEN allocate reassembly resources
     with BUFID; TIMER <- TLB; TDL <- 0;
8    put data from fragment into data buffer with
     BUFID from octet FO*8 to octet (TL-(IHL*4))+FO*8;
9    set RCVBT bits from FO to
     FO+((TL-(IHL*4)+7)/8);
10   IF MF = 0 THEN TDL <- TL-(IHL*4)+(FO*8)
11   IF FO = 0 THEN put header in header buffer
12   IF TDL # 0
13   AND all RCVBT bits from 0 to (TDL+7)/8 are
     set
14   THEN TL <- TDL+(IHL*4)
15   Submit datagram to next step;
16   free all reassembly resources for this BUFID;
     DONE.
17   TIMER <- MAX(TIMER,TTL);
18   give up until next fragment or timer expires;
19   timer expires: flush all reassembly with this
     BUFID; DONE.
```

In the case that two or more fragments contain the same data, either identically or through a partial overlap, this procedure will use the more recently arrived copy in the data buffer and datagram delivered.

Identification

The choice of the identifier for a datagram is based on the need to provide a way to uniquely identify the fragments of a particular datagram. The protocol module assembling fragments judges fragments to belong to the same datagram if they have the same source, destination, protocol, and identifier. Thus, the sender must choose the identifier to be unique for this source, destination pair, and protocol for the time that the datagram (or any fragment of it) could be alive in the internet.

It seems, then, that a sending protocol module needs to keep a table of identifiers, one entry for each destination it has communicated with during the last maximum packet lifetime for the internet.

However, since the Identifier field allows 65,536 different values, some hosts may be able to simply use unique identifiers independent of destination.

It is appropriate for some higher-level protocols to choose the identifier. For example, TCP protocol modules may retransmit an identical TCP segment, and the probability of correct reception is enhanced if the retransmission carries the same identifier as the original transmission, since fragments of either datagram could be used to construct a correct TCP segment.

Type of service

The type of service (TOS) is for Internet service quality selection. The type of service is specified along the abstract parameters precedence, delay, throughput, and reliability. These abstract parameters are to be mapped into the actual service parameters of the particular networks that the datagram traverses.

PRECEDENCE: An independent measure of the importance of this datagram.

DELAY: Prompt delivery is important for datagrams with this indication.

THROUGHPUT: High datarate is important for datagrams with this indication.

RELIABILITY: A higher level of effort to ensure delivery is important for datagrams with this indication.

Time to live

The time to live is set by the sender to the maximum time that the datagram is allowed to be in the internet system. If the datagram is in the internet system longer than the time to live, then the datagram must be destroyed.

This field must be decreased at each point that the Internet header is processed to reflect the time spent processing the datagram. Even if no local information is available on the time actually spent, the field must be decremented by 1. The time is measured in units of seconds (i.e., the value 1 means 1 s). Thus, the maximum time to live is 255 s or 4.25 min. Since every module that processes a datagram must decrease the TTL by at least 1 even if it processes the datagram in less than a second, the TTL must be thought of as only an upper bound on the time a datagram may exist. The intention is to cause undeliverable datagrams to be discarded and to bound the maximum datagram lifetime.

Some higher-level reliable connection protocols are based on the assumption that old duplicate datagrams will not arrive after a certain time elapses. The TTL is a way for such protocols to have an assurance that their assumption is met.

Options

The options are optional in each datagram, but are required in implementations. That is, the presence or absence of an option is the choice of the sender, but each Internet module must be able to parse every option. There can be several options present in the option field.

The options might not end on a 32-bit boundary. The internet header must be filled out with octets of zeros. The first of these would be interpreted as the end-of-options option, and the remainder as Internet header padding.

Every Internet module must be able to act on every option. The Security option is required if classified, restricted, or compartmented traffic is to be passed.

Checksum

The Internet header checksum is recomputed if the Internet header is changed—for example, by a reduction of the time to live, additions or changes to Internet options, or due to fragmentation. This checksum at the Internet level is intended to protect the Internet header fields from transmission errors.

There are some applications where a few data bit errors are acceptable while retransmission delays are not. If the Internet Protocol enforced data correctness, such applications could not be supported.

Errors

Internet protocol errors may be reported via the ICMP messages.

15.7   Interfaces and IP Version 4

The functional description of user interfaces to IP is, at best, fictional, since every operating system will have different facilities. Consequently, readers must be warned that different IP implementations may have different user interfaces. However, all IPs must provide a certain minimum set of services to guarantee that all IP implementations can support the same protocol hierarchy. This section specifies the functional interfaces required of all IP implementations.

Internet protocol interfaces to the local network on one side and to either a higher-level protocol or an application program on the other side. In the following, the higher-level protocol or application program (or even a gateway program) will be called the *user* since it is using the Internet module. Since IP is a datagram protocol, there is minimal memory or state maintained between datagram transmissions, and each call on the IP module by the user supplies all information necessary for the IP to perform the service requested.

Upper level interface example

The following two example calls satisfy the requirements for the user to IP module communication (=> means *returns*):

```
SEND (src, dst, prot, TOS, TTL, BufPTR, len, Id, DF, opt =>
result)
```

where
    src = Source address
    dst = Destination address
    prot = Protocol
    TOS = Type of service
    TTL = Time to live
    BufPTR = Buffer pointer
    len = Length of buffer
    Id = Identifier
    DF = Don't fragment
    opt = Option data
    result = Response
    OK = Datagram sent OK
    Error = Error in arguments or local network error

Note that the precedence is included in the TOS and the security/compartment is passed as an option.

```
RECV (BufPTR, prot, => result, src, dst, TOS, len, opt)
```

where   BufPTR = Buffer pointer
          prot = Protocol
        result = Response
            OK = Datagram received OK
         Error = Error in arguments
           len = Length of buffer
           src = Source address
           dst = Destination address
           TOS = Type of service
           opt = Option data

When the user sends a datagram, it executes the SEND call supplying all the arguments. The IP module, on receiving this call, checks the arguments and prepares and sends the message. If the arguments are good and the datagram is accepted by the local network, the call returns successfully. If either the arguments are bad or the datagram is not accepted by the local network, the call returns unsuccessfully. On unsuccessful returns, a reasonable report must be made as to the cause of the problem, but the details of such reports are up to individual implementations.

When a datagram arrives at the IP module from the local network, either there is a pending RECV call from the user addressed or there is not. In the first case, the pending call is satisfied by passing the information from the datagram to the user. In the second case, the user addressed is notified of a pending datagram. If the user addressed does not exist, an ICMP error message is returned to the sender, and the data is discarded.

The notification of a user may be via a pseudointerrupt or similar mechanism, as appropriate in the particular operating system environment of the implementation.

A user's RECV call may then either be immediately satisfied by a pending datagram, or the call may be pending until a datagram arrives. The source address is included in the send call in case the sending host has several addresses (multiple physical connections or logical addresses). The Internet module must check to see that the source address is one of the legal addresses for this host.

An implementation may also allow or require a call to the Internet module to indicate interest in or reserve exclusive use of a class of datagrams (e.g., all those with a certain value in the protocol field).

This section functionally characterizes a user/IP interface. The notation used is similar to most procedures of function calls in high-level languages, but this usage is not meant to rule out trap-type service calls (e.g., SVCs, UUOs, EMTs), or any other form of interprocess communication.

IPv4 datagram

This is an example of the minimal data-carrying Internet datagram:

0		1	2	31
0 1 2 3 4	5 6 7 8 9 0 1 2 3 4	5 6 7 8 9 0 1 2 3 4 5 6 7 8 9 0 1		

Ver = 4	IHL = 5	Type of Service	Total Length = 21	
Identification = 111		Flg = 0	Fragment Offset = 0	
Time = 123		Protocol = 1	Header Checksum	
Source Address				
Destination Address				
Data				

Each number across the top represents one bit position.

This Internet datagram reflects version 4 of IP. The IP header consists of five 32-bit words, and the total length of the datagram is 21 octets. This datagram is a complete datagram (not a fragment).

IPv4 datagram fragment

The example below shows a moderate-size IP datagram (452 data octets), then two internet fragments that might result from the fragmentation of this datagram if the maximum-sized transmission allowed were 280 octets.

0		1	2	31
0 1 2 3 4	5 6 7 8 9 0 1 2 3 4	5 6 7 8 9 0 1 2 3 4 5 6 7 8 9 0 1		

Ver = 4	IHL = 5	Type of Service	Total Length = 472	
Identification = 111		Flg = 0	Fragment Offset = 0	
Time = 123		Protocol = 6	Header Checksum	
Source Address				
Destination Address				
Data				
Data				
Data				
Data				

IPv4 first datagram fragment

The following is an example of the first fragment that results from splitting the datagram after 256 data octets.

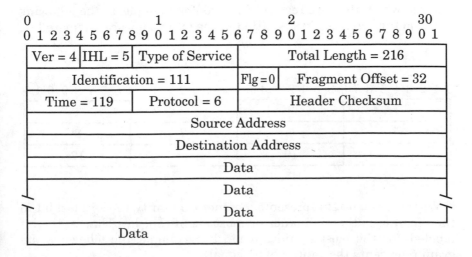

IPv4 second datagram fragment

An example of the second fragment follows.

IPv4 datagram with options

0		1	2	30

0 1 2 3 4 5 6 7 8 9 0 1 2 3 4 5 6 7 8 9 0 1 2 3 4 5 6 7 8 9 0 1

Ver = 4	IHL = 8	Type of Service	Total Length = 576	
Identification = 111			Flg = 0	Fragment Offset = 0
Time = 123		Protocol = 6	Header Checksum	
Source Address				
Destination Address				
Opt. Code = x	Opt. Len. = 3	Option Value	Opt. Code = x	
Opt. Len. = 4	Option Value		Opt. Code = 1	
Opt. Code = y	Opt. Len. = 3	Option Value	Opt. Code = 0	
Data				
Data				
Data				

Order of IP data transmission

The order of transmission of the header and data described in this document is resolved to the octet level. Whenever a diagram shows a group of octets, the order of transmission of those octets is the normal order in which they are read in English. For example, in the following diagram the octets are transmitted in the order they are numbered.

0		1	2	3

0 1 2 3 4 5 6 7 8 9 0 1 2 3 4 5 6 7 8 9 0 1 2 3 4 5 6 7 8 9 0 1

1	2	3	4
5	6	7	8
9	10	11	12

Whenever an octet represents a numeric quantity, the leftmost bit in the diagram is the high-order or most significant bit. That is, the bit labeled 0 is the most significant bit. For example, the following diagram represents the value 170 (decimal).

0 1 2 3 4 5 6 7
| 1 0 1 0 1 0 1 0 |

Whenever a multioctet field represents a numeric quantity, the left-most bit of the whole field is the most significant bit. When a multioctet quantity is transmitted, the most significant octet is transmitted first.

15.8 Summary

IP version 4 is still prevalent in the marketplace. It will most likely be prevalent for some time to come. It is deeply entrenched in the products implemented since the mid-1980s. The information provided here is helpful to those who will also work with IP version 6.

TCP/IP Network Design and IP Version 6

IP version 6 (IPv6) is a new version of the Internet Protocol, designed as a successor to IP version 4 (IPv4; RFC-791). The changes from IPv4 to IPv6 fall primarily into the following categories:

- *Expanded addressing capabilities.* IPv6 increases the IP address size from 32 bits to 128 bits, to support more levels of addressing hierarchy, a much greater number of addressable nodes, and simpler autoconfiguration of addresses. The scalability of multicast routing is improved by adding a *scope* field to multicast addresses. And a new type of address called an *anycast address* is defined, which is used to send a packet to any one of a group of nodes.

- *Header format simplification.* Some IPv4 header fields have been dropped or made optional, to reduce the common-case processing cost of packet handling and to limit the bandwidth cost of the IPv6 header.

- *Improved support for extensions and options.* Changes in the way IP header options are encoded allows for more efficient forwarding, less stringent limits on the length of options, and greater flexibility for introducing new options in the future.

- *Flow labeling capability.* A new capability is added to enable the labeling of packets belonging to particular traffic flows for which the sender requests special handling, such as nondefault quality of service or real-time service.

- *Authentication and privacy capabilities.* Extensions to support authentication, data integrity, and data confidentiality are specified for IPv6. This document specifies the basic IPv6 header and the initially defined IPv6 extension headers and options. It also discusses packet size issues, the semantics of flow labels and priority, and the effects of IPv6 on upper-layer protocols. The format and semantics of IPv6 addresses are specified separately in RFC 1884. The IPv6 version of ICMP, which all IPv6 implementations are required to include, is specified in RFC 1885.

16.1   IPv6 Terminology

NODE: A device that implements IPv6.

ROUTER: A node that forwards IPv6 packets not explicitly addressed to itself.

HOST: Any node that is not a router.

UPPER LAYER: A protocol layer immediately above IPv6. Examples are transport protocols, such as TCP and UDP; control protocols, such as ICMP; routing protocols, such as OSPF; and internet or lower-layer protocols being *tunneled* over (i.e., encapsulated in) IPv6, such as IPX, AppleTalk, or IPv6 itself.

LINK: A communication facility or medium over which nodes can communicate at the link layer, (i.e., the layer immediately below IPv6). Examples are Ethernets (simple or bridged); PPP links; X.25, Frame Relay, or ATM networks; and internet, or higher-layer *tunnels,* such as tunnels over IPv4 or IPv6 itself.

NEIGHBORS: Nodes attached to the same link.

INTERFACE: A node's attachment to a link.

ADDRESS: An IPv6-layer identifier for an interface or a set of interfaces.

PACKET: An IPv6 header plus payload.

LINK MTU: The maximum transmission unit (i.e., maximum packet size in octets), that can be conveyed in one piece over a link.

PATH MTU: The minimum link MTU of all the links in a path between a source node and a destination node.

It is possible for a device with multiple interfaces to be configured to forward non-self-destined packets arriving from some set (fewer than all) of its interfaces, and to discard non-self-destined packets arriving from its other interfaces. Such a device must obey the protocol requirements for routers when receiving packets from, and interacting with neighbors over, the former (forwarding) interfaces. It must obey the protocol requirements for hosts when receiving packets from, and interacting with neighbors over, the latter (nonforwarding) interfaces.

16.2   IPv6 Header Format

The following is a representation of the IPv6 header.

Version	Priority	Flow Label		
Payload Length			Next Header	Hop Limit
Source Address				
Destination Address				

VERSION: 4-bit Internet Protocol version number = 6.

PRIORITY: 4-bit priority value.

FLOW LABEL: 24-bit flow label.

PAYLOAD LENGTH: 16-bit unsigned integer. Length of payload (i.e., the rest of the packet following the IPv6 header), in octets. If 0, indicates that the payload length is carried in a Jumbo Payload hop-by-hop option.

NEXT HEADER: 8-bit selector. Identifies the type of header immediately following the IPv6 header. Uses the same values as the IPv4 Protocol field.

HOP LIMIT: 8-bit unsigned integer. Decremented by 1 by each node that forwards the packet. The packet is discarded if Hop Limit is decremented to 0.

SOURCE ADDRESS: 128-bit address of the originator of the packet.

DESTINATION ADDRESS: 128-bit address of the intended recipient of the packet (possibly not the ultimate recipient, if a Routing header is present).

16.3   IPv6 Extension Headers

In IPv6, optional internet-layer information is encoded in separate headers that may be placed between the IPv6 header and the upper-layer header in a packet. There are a small number of such extension headers, each identified by a distinct Next Header value. As illustrated in the following examples, an IPv6 packet may carry zero, one, or more extension headers, each identified by the Next Header field of the preceding header:

IPv6 header Next Header = TCP	TCP header + data

IPv6 header Next Header = Routing	Routing header Next Header = TCP	TCP header + data

IPv6 header Next Header = Routing	Routing header Next Header = Fragment	Fragment header Next Header = TCP	Fragment of TCP header + data

With one exception, extension headers are not examined or processed by any node along a packet's delivery path until the packet reaches the node (or each of the set of nodes, in the case of multicast) identified in the Destination Address field of the IPv6 header. There, normal demultiplexing on the Next Header field of the IPv6 header invokes the module to process the first extension header, or the upper-layer header if no extension header is present. The contents and semantics of each extension header determine whether or not to proceed to the next header. Therefore, extension headers must be processed strictly in the order they appear in the packet—a receiver must not, for example, scan through a packet looking for a particular kind of extension header and process that header prior to processing all preceding ones.

The exception referred to in the preceding paragraph is the *Hop-by-Hop Options* header, which carries information that must be examined and processed by every node along a packet's delivery path, including the source and destination nodes. The Hop-by-Hop Options header, when present, must immediately follow the IPv6 header. Its presence is indicated by the value 0 in the Next Header field of the IPv6 header.

If, as a result of processing a header, a node is required to proceed to the next header but the Next Header value in the current header is unrecognized by the node, it should discard the packet and send an ICMP Parameter Problem message to the source of the packet, with an ICMP Code value of 2 (*unrecognized Next Header type encountered*) and the ICMP Pointer field containing the offset of the unrecognized value within the original packet. The same action should be taken if a node encounters a Next Header value of 0 in any header other than an IPv6 header.

Each extension header is an integer multiple of 8 octets long, in order to retain 8-octet alignment for subsequent headers. Multioctet fields within each extension header are aligned on their natural boundaries; that is, fields of n-octet width are placed at an integer multiple of n octets from the start of the header, for $n = 1, 2, 4,$ or 8.

A full implementation of IPv6 includes implementation of the following extension headers:

Hop-by-Hop Options

Routing (Type 0)

Fragment

Destination Options

Authentication

Encapsulating Security Payload

16.4 Extension Header Order

When more than one extension header is used in the same packet, it is recommended that those headers appear in the following order:

IPv6 header

Hop-by-Hop Options header

Destination Options header

Routing header

Fragment header

Authentication header

Encapsulating Security Payload header

Destination Options header

Upper-layer header

For options to be processed by the first destination that appears in the IPv6 Destination Address they must be in the Routing header.

Each extension header should occur at most once, except for the Destination Options header, which should occur at most twice (once before a Routing header and once before the upper-layer header). If the upper-layer header is another IPv6 header (in the case of IPv6 being tunneled over or encapsulated in IPv6), it may be followed by its own extension headers, which are separately subject to the same ordering recommendations.

If and when other extension headers are defined, their ordering constraints relative to the preceding listed headers must be specified.

IPv6 nodes must accept and attempt to process extension headers in any order and occurring any number of times in the same packet, except for the Hop-by-Hop Options header, which is restricted to appear only immediately after an IPv6 header. Nonetheless, it is strongly advised that sources of IPv6 packets adhere to the preceding recommended order until and unless subsequent specifications revise that recommendation.

Options

Two of the currently defined extension headers—the Hop-by-Hop Options header and the Destination Options header—carry a *variable* number of *type-length-value* (TLV) encoded options, of the following format:

Option Type	Opt Data Len	Option Data

OPTION TYPE: 8-bit identifier of the type of option.

OPTIONAL DATA LENGTH (OPT DATA LEN):   8-bit unsigned integer identifying the length of the Option, and the data field of this option, in octets.

OPTION DATA: Variable-length field of Option-Type specific data.

The sequence of options within a header must be processed strictly in the order they appear in the header; a receiver must not, for example, scan through the header looking for a particular kind of option and process that option prior to processing all preceding ones.

The Option Type identifiers are internally encoded such that their two highest-order bits specify the action that must be taken if the processing IPv6 node does not recognize the Option Type:

00   Skip over this option and continue processing the header.

01   Discard the packet.

10   Discard the packet and, regardless of whether the packet's Destination Address was a multicast address, send an *ICMP Parameter Problem,* Code 2, message to the packet's Source Address, pointing to the unrecognized Option Type.

11   Discard the packet and, only if the packet's Destination Address was not a multicast address, send an *ICMP Parameter Problem,* Code 2, message to the packet's Source Address, pointing to the unrecognized Option Type.

The third highest-order bit of the Option Type specifies whether the Option Data of that option can change en route to the packet's final destination. When an Authentication header is present in the packet, the entire Option Data field for any option whose data may change enroute must be treated as zero-valued octets when computing or verifying the packet's authenticating value.

0   Option Data does not change enroute.

1   Option Data may change en route.

Individual options may have specific alignment requirements, to ensure that multioctet values within Option Data fields fall on natural boundaries. The alignment requirement of an option is specified using the notation $xn + y$, meaning the Option Type must appear at an integer multiple of x octets from the start of the header, plus y octets. For example:

$2n$ Any 2-octet offset from the start of the header

$8n + 2$ Any 8-octet offset from the start of the header, plus 2 octets

Padding

There are two padding options that are used when necessary to align subsequent options and to pad out the containing header length to a multiple of 8 octets. These padding options must be recognized by all IPv6 implementations:

- *Pad1* option (alignment requirement: none)

```
┌─────────────────┐
│        0        │
└─────────────────┘
```

The format of the Pad1 option is a special case—it does not have length and value fields. Pad 1 option is used to insert 1 octet of padding into the Options area of a header. If more than 1 octet of padding is required, the PadN option, described next, should be used, rather than multiple Pad1 options.

- *PadN* option (alignment requirement: none)

```
┌─────────────────┬───────────────┬───────────────
│        1        │  Opt Data Len │  Option Data
└─────────────────┴───────────────┴───────────────
```

The PadN option is used to insert 2 or more octets of padding into the Options area of a header. For N octets of padding, the Opt Data Len field contains the value $N - 2$, and the Option Data consists of $N - 2$ zero-valued octets.

16.5   IPv6 Options Header (Hop-by-Hop)

The Hop-by-Hop Options header is used to carry optional information that must be examined by every node along a packet's delivery path.

The Hop-by-Hop Options header is identified by a Next Header value of 0 in the IPv6 header and has the following format:

Next Header	Hdr Ext Len	
	Options	

NEXT HEADER: 8-bit selector. Identifies the type of header immediately following the Hop-by-Hop Options header. Uses the same values as the IPv4 protocol field.

HEADER EXTENSION LENGTH (HDR EXT LEN):   8-bit unsigned integer. Length of the Hop-by-Hop Options header in 8-octet units, not including the first 8 octets.

OPTIONS: Variable-length field, of length such that the complete Hop-by-Hop Options header length is an integer multiple of 8 octets. Contains one or more TLV-encoded options.

In addition to the Pad1 and PadN options, the following hop-by-hop option is defined:

- *Jumbo Payload* option (alignment requirement: $4n + 2$)

194	Opt Data Len = 4
Jumbo Payload Length	

The Jumbo Payload option is used to send IPv6 packets with payloads longer than 65,535 octets. The Jumbo Payload Length is the length of the packet in octets, excluding the IPv6 header but including the Hop-by-Hop Options header; it must be greater than 65,535. If a packet is received with a Jumbo Payload option containing a Jumbo Payload Length less than or equal to 65,535, an *ICMP Parameter Problem* message, Code 0, should be sent to the packet's source, pointing to the high-order octet of the invalid Jumbo Payload Length field.

The Payload Length field in the IPv6 header must be set to 0 in every packet that carries the Jumbo Payload option. If a packet is received with a valid Jumbo Payload option present and a nonzero IPv6 Payload Length field, an *ICMP Parameter Problem* message, Code 0, should be sent to the packet's source, pointing to the Option Type field of the Jumbo Payload option. The Jumbo Payload option must not be used in a packet that carries a Fragment header. If a Fragment header is encountered in a packet that contains a valid Jumbo Payload option, an *ICMP Parameter Problem* message, Code 0, should be sent to the packet's source, pointing to the first octet of the Fragment header.

An implementation that does not support the Jumbo Payload option cannot have interfaces to links whose link MTU is greater than 65,575 (40 octets of IPv6 header plus 65,535 octets of payload).

16.6   IPv6 Routing Header

The Routing header is used by an IPv6 source to list one or more intermediate nodes to be visited on the way to a packet's destination. This function is very similar to IPv4's Source Route options. The Routing header is identified by a Next Header value of 43 in the immediately preceding header, and has the following format:

Next Header	Hdr Ext Len	Routing Type	Segments Left
•	Type-specific data		•

NEXT HEADER: 8-bit selector. Identifies the type of header immediately following the Routing header. Uses the same values as the IPv4 Protocol field.

HEADER EXTENSION LENGTH (HDR EXT LEN):   8-bit unsigned integer. Length of the Routing header in 8-octet units, not including the first 8 octets.

ROUTING TYPE: 8-bit identifier of a particular Routing header variant.

SEGMENTS LEFT: 8-bit unsigned integer. Number of route segments remaining; that is, number of explicitly listed intermediate nodes still to be visited before reaching the final destination.

TYPE-SPECIFIC DATA: Variable-length field, of format determined by the Routing Type, and of length such that the complete Routing header length is an integer multiple of 8 octets.

If, while processing a received packet, a node encounters a Routing header with an unrecognized Routing Type value, the required behavior of the node depends on the value of the Segments Left field, as follows.

If Segments Left is 0, the node must ignore the Routing header and proceed to process the next header in the packet, whose type is identified by the Next Header field in the Routing header. If Segments Left is nonzero, the node must discard the packet and send an *ICMP Parameter Problem,* Code 0, message to the packet's Source Address, pointing to the unrecognized Routing Type.

The Type 0 Routing header has the following format:

Next Header	Hdr Ext Len	Routing Type = 0	Segments Left
Reserved	Strict/Loose Bit Map		
Address 1			
Address 2			

. . .   .

| Address [n] | | | |

NEXT HEADER: 8-bit selector. Identifies the type of header immediately following the Routing header. Uses the same values as the IPv4 Protocol field.

HEADER EXTENSION LENGTH (HDR EXT LEN):   8-bit unsigned integer. Length of the Routing header in 8-octet units, not including the first 8 octets. For the Type 0 Routing header, Hdr Ext Len is equal to 2 times the number of addresses in the header, and must be an even number less than or equal to 46.

ROUTING TYPE: 0.

SEGMENTS LEFT: 8-bit unsigned integer. Number of route segments remaining; that is, number of explicitly listed intermediate nodes still to be visited before reaching the final destination. Maximum legal value = 23.

RESERVED: 8-bit reserved field. Initialized to zero for transmission; ignored on reception.

STRICT/LOOSE BIT MAP: 24-bit bit map, numbered 0 to 23, left to right. Indicates, for each segment of the route, whether or not the next destination address must be a neighbor of the preceding address: 1 means strict (must be a neighbor), 0 means loose (need not be a neighbor).

ADDRESS [1 ... N]:   Vector of 128-bit addresses, numbered 1 to n.

Multicast addresses must not appear in a Routing header of Type 0, or in the IPv6 Destination Address field of a packet carrying a Routing header of Type 0. If bit number 0 of the Strict/Loose Bit Map has value 1, the Destination Address field of the IPv6 header in the original packet must identify a neighbor of the originating node. If bit number 0 has value 0, the originator may use any legal, nonmulticast address as the initial Destination Address.

Bits numbered greater than n, where n is the number of addresses in the Routing header, must be set to 0 by the originator and ignored by receivers.

A Routing header is not examined or processed until it reaches the node identified in the Destination Address field of the IPv6 header. In that node, dispatching on the Next Header field of the immediately preceding header causes the Routing header module to be invoked, which, in the case of Routing Type 0, performs the following algorithm:

```
if Segments Left = 0
{
proceed to process the next header in the packet, whose
type is identified by the Next Header field in the
Routing header
}
else if Hdr Ext Len is odd or greater than 46
{
send an ICMP Parameter Problem, Code 0, message to the
Source Address, pointing to the Hdr Ext Len field, and
discard the packet
}
else
{
compute n, the number of addresses in the Routing header,
by dividing Hdr Ext Len by 2 if Segments Left is greater
than n
{
send an ICMP Parameter Problem, Code 0, message to the
Source Address, pointing to the Segments Left field, and
discard the packet
}
else
{
decrement Segments Left by 1; compute i, the index of
the next address to be visited in the address vector, by
```

```
subtracting Segments Left from n if Address [i] or the
IPv6 Destination Address is multicast
{
discard the packet
}
else
{
swap the IPv6 Destination Address and Address[i] if bit
i of the Strict/Loose Bit map has value 1 and the new
Destination Address is not the address of a neighbor of
this node
{
send an ICMP Destination Unreachable—Not a Neighbor
message to the Source Address and discard the packet
}
else if the IPv6 Hop Limit is less than or equal to 1
{
send an ICMP Time Exceeded—Hop Limit Exceeded in
Transit message to the Source Address and discard the
packet
}
else
{
decrement the Hop Limit by 1 resubmit the packet to the
IPv6 module for transmission to the new destination
                }
         }
      }
  }
```

Consider the case of a source node S sending a packet to destination node D, using a Routing header to cause the packet to be routed via intermediate nodes $I1$, $I2$, and $I3$. The values of the relevant IPv6 header and Routing header fields on each segment of the delivery path would be as follows:

```
As the packet travels from S to I1:
Source Address = S                 Hdr Ext Len = 6
Destination Address = I1           Segments Left = 3
                                   Address[1] = I2
(if bit 0 of the Bit Map is 1,     Address[2] = I3
S and I1 must be neighbors;        Address[3] = D
this is checked by S)
As the packet travels from I1 to I2:
Source Address = S                 Hdr Ext Len = 6
Destination Address = I2           Segments Left = 2
                                   Address[1] = I1
```

```
(if bit 1 of the Bit Map is 1,        Address[2] = I3
I1 and I2 must be neighbors;          Address[3] = D
this is checked by I1)
As the packet travels from I2 to I3:
Source Address = S                    Hdr Ext Len = 6
Destination Address = I3              Segments Left = 1
                                      Address[1] = I1
(if bit 2 of the Bit Map is 1,        Address[2] = I2
I2 and I3 must be neighbors;          Address[3] = D
this is checked by I2)
As the packet travels from I3 to D:
Source Address = S                    Hdr Ext Len = 6
Destination Address = D               Segments Left = 0
                                      Address[1] = I1
(if bit 3 of the Bit Map is 1,        Address[2] = I2
I3 and D must be neighbors;           Address[3] = I3
this is checked by I3)
```

16.7   IPv6 Fragment Header

The Fragment header is used by an IPv6 source to send packets larger than would fit in the path MTU to their destinations. (Note that unlike IPv4, fragmentation in IPv6 is performed only by source nodes, not by routers along a packet's delivery path.) The Fragment header is identified by a Next Header value of 44 in the immediately preceding header, and it has the following format:

Next Header	Reserved	Fragment Offset	Res	M
Identification				

NEXT HEADER: 8-bit selector. Identifies the initial header type of the Fragmentable Part of the original packet. Uses the same values as the IPv4 Protocol field.

RESERVED: 8-bit reserved field. Initialized to 0 for transmission; ignored on reception.

FRAGMENT OFFSET: 13-bit unsigned integer. The offset, in 8-octet units, of the data following this header, relative to the start of the Fragmentable Part of the original packet.

RES: 2-bit reserved field. Initialized to 0 for transmission; ignored on reception.

M FLAG: 1 = more fragments; 0 = last fragment.

IDENTIFICATION: 32 bits. See following below.

In order to send a packet that is too large to fit in the MTU of the path to its destination, a source node may divide the packet into fragments and send each fragment as a separate packet, to be reassembled at the receiver.

For every packet that is to be fragmented, the source node generates an Identification value. The Identification must be different than that of any other fragmented packet sent recently* with the same Source Address and Destination Address. If a Routing header is present, the Destination Address of concern is that of the final destination.

The initial, unfragmented packet is referred to as the *original packet,* and it is considered to consist of two parts, as shown:

Unfragmentable Part	Fragmentable Part

The Unfragmentable Part consists of the IPv6 header plus any extension headers that must be processed by nodes en route to the destination—that is, all headers up to and including the Routing header if present; else the Hop-by-Hop Options header if present; else no extension headers.

The Fragmentable Part consists of the rest of the packet—that is, any extension headers that need be processed only by the final destination nodes, plus the upper-layer header and data.

The Fragmentable Part of the original packet is divided into fragments, each, except possibly the last (*rightmost*) one, being an integer multiple of 8 octets long. The fragments are transmitted in separate *fragment packets,* as illustrated.

- Original packet

Unfragmentable Part	First fragment	Second fragment	• • • •	Last fragment

---

* *Recently* means within the maximum likely lifetime of a packet, including transit time from source to destination and time spent awaiting reassembly with other fragments of the same packet. However, it is not required that a source node know the maximum packet lifetime. Rather, it is assumed that the requirement can be met by maintaining the Identification value as a simple, 32-bit, wrap-around counter, incremented each time a packet must be fragmented. It is an implementation choice whether to maintain a single counter for the node or multiple counters, for example, one for each of the node's possible source addresses, or one for each active (source address, destination address) combination.

■ Fragment packets

Unfragmentable Part	Fragment Header	First fragment

Unfragmentable Part	Fragment Header	Second fragment

.
.
.

Unfragmentable Part	Fragment Header	Last fragment

Each fragment packet is composed of the following parts:

1. The Unfragmentable Part of the original packet, with the Payload Length of the original IPv6 header changed to contain only the length of this fragment packet (excluding the length of the IPv6 header itself), and the Next Header field of the last header of the Unfragmentable Part changed to 44.

2. A Fragment header containing the following parts:

   The Next Header value that identifies the first header of the Fragmentable Part of the original packet

   A Fragment Offset containing the offset of the fragment, in 8-octet units, relative to the start of the Fragmentable Part of the original packet

   A Fragment Offset of the first (leftmost) fragment of 0

   An M flag value of 0 if the fragment is the last rightmost one; else an M flag value of 1

   The Identification value generated for the original packet

3. The fragment itself. The lengths of the fragments must be chosen such that the resulting fragment packets fit within the MTU of the path to the packets' destinations.

At the destination, fragment packets are reassembled into their original, unfragmented form, as illustrated:

Unfragmentable Part	Fragmentable Part

The following rules govern reassembly:

- An original packet is reassembled only from fragment packets that have the same Source Address, Destination Address, and Fragment Identification.
- The Unfragmentable Part of the reassembled packet consists of all headers up to, but not including, the Fragment header of the first fragment packet (that is, the packet whose Fragment Offset is 0), with the following two changes:
  1. The Next Header field of the last header of the Unfragmentable Part is obtained from the Next Header field of the first fragment's Fragment header.
  2. The Payload Length of the reassembled packet is computed from the length of the Unfragmentable Part and the length and offset of the last fragment. For example, a formula for computing the Payload Length of the reassembled original packet is:

```
PL.orig = PL.first - FL.first - 8 + (8 * FO.last) +
FL.last
```

   where $PL.orig$ = Payload Length field of reassembled packet
   $PL.first$ = Payload Length field of first fragment packet
   $FL.first$ = Length of fragment following Fragment header of first fragment packet
   $FO.last$ = Fragment Offset field of Fragment header of last fragment packet
   $FL.last$ = Length of fragment following Fragment header of last fragment packet

- The Fragmentable Part of the reassembled packet is constructed from the fragments following the Fragment headers in each of the fragment packets. The length of each fragment is computed by subtracting from the packet's Payload Length the length of the headers between the IPv6 header and fragment itself; its relative position in the Fragmentable Part is computed from its Fragment Offset value.

The Fragment header is not present in the final, reassembled packet. The following error conditions may arise when reassembling fragmented packets:

- If insufficient fragments are received to complete reassembly of a packet within 60 s of the reception of the first-arriving fragment of that packet, reassembly of that packet must be abandoned and all the fragments that have been received for that packet must be discarded. If the first fragment (i.e., the one with a Fragment Offset of 0) has been received, an *ICMP Time Exceeded—Fragment Reassembly Time Exceeded* message should be sent to the source of that fragment.

- If the length of a fragment, as derived from the fragment packet's Payload Length field, is not a multiple of 8 octets and the M flag of that fragment is 1, then that fragment must be discarded and an *ICMP Parameter Problem,* Code 0, message should be sent to the source of the fragment, pointing to the Payload Length field of the fragment packet.

- If the length and offset of a fragment are such that the Payload Length of the packet reassembled from that fragment would exceed 65,535 octets, then that fragment must be discarded and an *ICMP Parameter Problem,* Code 0, message should be sent to the source of the fragment, pointing to the Fragment Offset field of the fragment packet.

The following conditions are not expected to occur, but are not considered errors if they do:

- The number and content of the headers preceding the Fragment header of different fragments of the same original packet may differ. Whatever headers are present that precede the Fragment header in each fragment packet are processed when the packets arrive, prior to queueing the fragments for reassembly. Only those headers in the Offset 0 fragment packet are retained in the reassembled packet.

- The Next Header values in the Fragment headers of different fragments of the same original packet may differ. Only the value from the Offset 0 fragment packet is used for reassembly.

16.8   IPv6 Destination Options Header

The Destination Options header is used to carry optional information that need be examined only by a packet's destination nodes. The Destination Options header is identified by a Next Header value of 60 in the immediately preceding header, and it has the following format:

Next Header	Hdr Ext Len	
	Options	

NEXT HEADER: 8-bit selector. Identifies the type of header immediately following the Destination Options header. Uses the same values as the IPv4 Protocol field.

HEADER EXTENSION LENGTH (HDR EXT LEN):   8-bit unsigned integer. Length of the Destination Options header in 8-octet units, not including the first 8 octets.

OPTIONS: Variable-length field, of length such that the complete Destination Options header length is an integer multiple of 8 octets. Contains one or more TLV-encoded options.

The only destination options defined in this document are the Pad1 and PadN options specified in Sec. 16.4.

Note that there are two possible ways to encode optional destination information in an IPv6 packet: either as an option in the Destination Options header, or as a separate extension header. The Fragment header and the Authentication header are examples of the latter approach. Which approach can be used depends on what action is desired of a destination node that does not understand the optional information.

If the desired action is for the destination node to discard the packet and, only if the packet's Destination Address is not a multicast address, send an *ICMP Unrecognized Type* message to the packet's Source Address, then the information may be encoded either as a separate header or as an option in the Destination Options header whose Option Type has the value 11 in its two highest-order bits. The choice may depend on such factors as which takes fewer octets or yields better alignment or more efficient parsing.

If any other action is desired, the information must be encoded as an option in the Destination Options header whose Option Type has the value 00, 01, or 10 in its two highest-order bits, specifying the desired action (see Sec. 16.4).

16.9   IPv6 No Next Header

The value 59 in the Next Header field of an IPv6 header or any extension header indicates that there is nothing following that header. If the Payload Length field of the IPv6 header indicates the presence of octets past the end of a header whose Next Header field contains 59, those octets must be ignored and passed on unchanged if the packet is forwarded.

16.10   IPv6 Packet Size Considerations

IPv6 requires that every link in the internet have an MTU of 576 octets or greater. On any link that cannot convey a 576-octet packet in one piece, link-specific fragmentation and reassembly must be provided at a layer below IPv6. From each link to which a node is directly attached, the node must be able to accept packets as large as that link's MTU.

Links that have a configurable MTU (e.g., PPP links) must be configured to have an MTU of at least 576 octets; it is recommended that a larger MTU be configured, to accommodate possible encapsulations (i.e., tunneling) without incurring fragmentation.

It is strongly recommended that IPv6 nodes implement Path MTU Discovery, in order to discover and take advantage of paths with MTU greater than 576 octets. However, a minimal IPv6 implementation (e.g., in a boot ROM) may simply restrict itself to sending packets no larger than 576 octets and omit implementation of Path MTU Discovery.

In order to send a packet larger than a path's MTU, a node may use the IPv6 Fragment header to fragment the packet at the source and have it reassembled at the destinations. However, the use of such fragmentation is discouraged in any application that is able to adjust its packets to fit the measured path MTU (i.e., down to 576 octets).

A node must be able to accept a fragmented packet that, after reassembly, is as large as 1500 octets, including the IPv6 header. A node is permitted to accept fragmented packets that reassemble to more than 1500 octets. However, a node must not send fragments that reassemble to a size greater than 1500 octets unless it has explicit knowledge that the destinations can reassemble a packet of that size.

In response to an IPv6 packet that is sent to an IPv4 destination (i.e., a packet that undergoes translation from IPv6 to IPv4), the originating IPv6 node may receive an *ICMP Packet Too Big* message reporting a Next-Hop MTU less than 576. In that case, the IPv6 node is not required to reduce the size of subsequent packets to less than 576, but must include a Fragment header in those packets so that the IPv6-to-IPv4 translating router can obtain a suitable Identification value to use in resulting IPv4 fragments. Note that this means the payload may have to be reduced to 528 octets (576 minus 40 for the IPv6 header and 8 for the Fragment header), and smaller still if additional extension headers are used.

The Path MTU Discovery must be performed even in cases where a host thinks a destination is attached to the same link as itself.

Unlike IPv4, it is unnecessary in IPv6 to set a Don't Fragment flag in the packet header in order to perform Path MTU Discovery; that is an implicit attribute of every IPv6 packet. Also, those parts of the RFC 1191 procedures that involve use of a table of MTU plateaus do not apply to IPv6, because the IPv6 version of the *Datagram Too Big* message always identifies the exact MTU to be used.

16.11   IPv6 Flow Labels

The 24-bit Flow Label field in the IPv6 header may be used by a source to label those packets for which it requests special handling by the IPv6 routers, such as nondefault quality of service or *real-time* service. This aspect of IPv6 is, at the time of writing, still experimental and subject to change as the requirements for flow support in the Internet become clearer. Hosts or routers that do not support the functions of the Flow Label field are required to set the field to 0 when originating a packet, to pass the field on unchanged when forwarding a packet, and to ignore the field when receiving a packet.

A *flow* is a sequence of packets sent from a particular source to a particular (unicast or multicast) destination for which the source desires special handling by the intervening routers. The nature of that special handling might be conveyed to the routers by a control protocol, such as a resource reservation protocol, or by information within the flow's packets themselves; for example, in a hop-by-hop option.

The details of such control protocols or options are beyond the scope of this document.

There may be multiple active flows from a source to a destination, as well as traffic that is not associated with any flow. A flow is uniquely identified by the combination of a source address and a nonzero flow label. Packets that do not belong to a flow carry a flow label of 0.

A flow label is assigned to a flow by the flow's source node. New flow labels must be chosen (pseudo-)randomly and uniformly from the range 1 to FFFFFF hex. The purpose of the random allocation is to make any set of bits within the Flow Label field suitable for use as a hash key by routers, for looking up the state associated with the flow.

All packets belonging to the same flow must be sent with the same source address, destination address, priority, and flow label. If any of those packets includes a Hop-by-Hop Options header, then they all must be originated with the same Hop-by-Hop Options header contents (excluding the Next Header field of the Hop-by-Hop Options header). If any of those packets includes a Routing header, then they all must be originated with the same contents in all extension headers up to and including the Routing header (excluding the Next Header field in the Routing header). The routers or destinations are permitted, but not required, to verify that these conditions are satisfied. If a violation is detected, it should be reported to the source by an *ICMP Parameter Problem* message, Code 0, pointing to the high-order octet of the Flow Label field (i.e., offset 1 within the IPv6 packet).

Routers are free to opportunistically set up the flow-handling state for any flow, even when no explicit flow establishment information has been provided to them via a control protocol, a hop-by-hop option, or other means. For example, upon receiving a packet from a particular source with an unknown, nonzero flow label, a router may process its IPv6 header and any necessary extension headers as if the flow label

were 0. That processing would include determining the next-hop interface and possibly other actions, such as updating a hop-by-hop option,
advancing the pointer and addresses in a Routing header, or deciding
on how to queue the packet based on its Priority field. The router may
then choose to "remember" the results of those processing steps and
cache that information, using the source address plus the flow label as
the cache key. Subsequent packets with the same source address and
flow label may then be handled by referring to the cached information
rather than by examining all those fields that, according to the requirements of the previous paragraph, can be assumed to be unchanged
from the first packet seen in the flow.

A cached flow-handling state that is set up opportunistically, as discussed in the preceding paragraph, must be discarded no more than
6 s after it is established, regardless of whether packets of the same
flow continue to arrive. If another packet with the same source address
and flow label arrives after the cached state has been discarded, the
packet undergoes full, normal processing (as if its flow label were 0),
which may result in the recreation of a cached flow state for that flow.

The lifetime of a flow-handling state that is set up explicitly, for
example by a control protocol or a hop-by-hop option, must be specified
as part of the specification of the explicit setup mechanism; it may
exceed 6 s. A source must not reuse a flow label for a new flow within
the lifetime of any flow-handling state that might have been established for the prior use of that flow label. Since a flow-handling state
with a lifetime of 6 s may be established opportunistically for any flow,
the minimum interval between the last packet of one flow and the first
packet of a new flow using the same flow label is 6 s. Flow labels used
for explicitly setup flows with longer flow-state lifetimes must remain
unused for those longer lifetimes before being reused for new flows.

When a node stops and restarts as the result of a *crash,* it must be
careful not to use a flow label that it might have used for an earlier
flow whose lifetime may not have expired yet. This may be accomplished by recording flow-label usage on stable storage so that it can
be remembered across crashes or by refraining from using any flow
labels until the maximum lifetime of any possible previously established flows has expired (at least 6 s; more if explicit flow setup mechanisms with longer lifetimes have been used). If the minimum time for
rebooting the node is known (often more than 6 s), that time can be
deducted from the necessary waiting period before starting to allocate
flow labels.

There is no requirement that all, or even most, packets belong to
flows, that is, carry nonzero flow labels. This observation is placed here
to remind protocol designers and implementers not to assume other-

wise. For example, it would be unwise to design a router whose performance would be adequate only if most packets belonged to flows, or to
design a header compression scheme that worked only on packets that
belonged to flows.

16.12   IPv6 Packet Priority

The 4-bit Priority field in the IPv6 header enables a source to identify
the desired delivery priority of its packets, relative to other packets
from the same source. The Priority values are divided into two ranges.
Values 0 through 7 are used to specify the priority of traffic for which
the source is providing congestion control; that is, traffic that backs off
in response to congestion, such as TCP traffic. Values 8 through 15 are
used to specify the priority of traffic that does not back off in response
to congestion; that is, real-time packets being sent at a constant rate.

For congestion-controlled traffic, the following Priority values are
recommended for particular application categories:

0   Uncharacterized traffic

1   Filler traffic (e.g., netnews)

2   Unattended data transfer (e.g., e-mail)

3   Reserved

4   Attended bulk transfer (e.g., FTP and NFS)

5   Reserved

6   Interactive traffic (e.g., Telnet and X)

7   Internet control traffic (e.g., routing protocols and SNMP)

For non-congestion-controlled traffic, the lowest Priority value (8)
should be used for those packets that the sender is most willing to have
discarded under conditions of congestion (e.g., high-fidelity video traffic), and the highest value (15) should be used for those packets that
the sender is least willing to have discarded (e.g., low-fidelity audio
traffic). There is no relative ordering implied between the congestion-
controlled priorities and the non-congestion-controlled priorities.

16.13   IPv6 and Upper-Layer Protocols

Upper-layer checksums

Any transport or other upper-layer protocol that includes the addresses
from the IP header in its checksum computation must be modified for
use over IPv6, in order to include the 128-bit IPv6 addresses instead of
32-bit IPv4 addresses. In particular, the following illustration shows the
TCP and UDP *pseudoheader* for IPv6:

Source Address
Destination Address
Payload Length

0	Next Header

- If the packet contains a Routing header, the Destination Address used in the pseudoheader is that of the final destination. At the originating node, that address will be in the last element of the Routing header; at the recipients, that address will be in the Destination Address field of the IPv6 header.

- The Next Header value in the pseudoheader identifies the upper-layer protocol (6 for TCP or 17 for UDP). It will differ from the Next Header value in the IPv6 header if there are extension headers between the IPv6 header and the upper-layer header.

- The Payload Length used in the pseudoheader is the length of the upper-layer packet, including the upper-layer header. It will be less than the Payload Length in the IPv6 header (or in the Jumbo Payload option) if there are extension headers between the IPv6 header and the upper-layer header.

- Unlike IPv4, when UDP packets are originated by an IPv6 node, the UDP checksum is not optional. That is, whenever originating a UDP packet, an IPv6 node must compute a UDP checksum over the packet and the pseudoheader, and, if that computation yields a result of 0, it must be changed to hex FFFF for placement in the UDP header. IPv6 receivers must discard UDP packets containing a zero checksum, and should log the error.

The IPv6 version includes the preceding pseudoheader in its checksum computation; this is a change from the IPv4 version of ICMP, which does not include a pseudoheader in its checksum. The reason for the change is to protect ICMP from misdelivery or corruption of those fields of the IPv6 header on which it depends, which, unlike IPv4, are not covered by an internet-layer checksum. The Next Header field in the pseudoheader for ICMP contains the value 58, which identifies the IPv6 version of ICMP.

Maximum packet lifetime

Unlike IPv4, IPv6 nodes are not required to enforce maximum packet lifetime. That is the reason why the IPv4 Time-to-Live field was renamed *Hop Limit* in IPv6. In practice, very few, if any, IPv4 implementations conform to the requirement that they limit packet lifetime, so this is not a change in practice. Any upper-layer protocol that relies on the internet layer (whether IPv4 or IPv6) to limit packet lifetime ought to be upgraded to provide its own mechanisms for detecting and discarding obsolete packets.

Maximum upper-layer payload size

When computing the maximum payload size available for upper-layer data, an upper-layer protocol must take into account the larger size of the IPv6 header relative to the IPv4 header. For example, in IPv4, TCP's MSS option is computed as the maximum packet size (a default value or a value learned through Path MTU Discovery) minus 40 octets (20 octets for the minimum-length IPv4 header and 20 octets for the minimum-length TCP header). When using TCP over IPv6, the MSS must be computed as the maximum packet size minus 60 octets, because the minimum-length IPv6 header (i.e., an IPv6 header with no extension headers) is 20 octets longer than a minimum-length IPv4 header.

Formatting guidelines for options

This subsection gives some advice on how to lay out the fields when designing new options to be used in the Hop-by-Hop Options header or the Destination Options header, as described in Sec. 16.4. These guidelines are based on the following assumptions:

- One desirable feature is that any multioctet fields within the Option Data area of an option be aligned on their natural boundaries; that is, fields of n-octet width should be placed at an integer multiple of n octets from the start of the Hop-by-Hop or Destination Options header, for $n = 1, 2, 4,$ or 8.

- Another desirable feature is that the Hop-by-Hop or Destination Options header take up as little space as possible, subject to the requirement that the header length be an integer multiple of 8 octets.

- It may be assumed that when either of the option-bearing headers are present, they carry a very small number of options—usually, only one.

These assumptions suggest the following approach to laying out the fields of an option: order the fields from smallest to largest, with no interior padding, then derive the alignment requirement for the entire option based on the alignment requirement of the largest field (up to a maximum alignment of 8 octets). This approach is illustrated in the following examples.

If an option X required two data fields, of 8-, 4-octet lengths, it would be laid out as follows:

Option Type = X	Opt Data Len = 12
4-octet field	
8-octet field	

Its alignment requirement is $8n + 2$, to ensure that the 8-octet field starts at a multiple-of-8 offset from the start of the enclosing header. A complete Hop-by-Hop or Destination Options header containing this one option would look as follows:

Next Header	Hdr Ext Len = 1	Option Type = X	Opt Data Len = 12
4-octet field			
8-octet field			

If an option Y required three data fields, of 4-, 2-, and 1-octet lengths, it would be laid out as follows:

Option Type = Y		
Opt Data Len = 7	1-octet field	2-octet field
4-octet field		

Its alignment requirement is $4n + 3$, to ensure that the 4-octet field starts at a multiple-of-4 offset from the start of the enclosing header. A complete Hop-by-Hop or Destination Options header containing this one option would look as follows:

Next Header	Hdr Ext Len = 1	Pad1 Option = 0	Option Type = Y
Opt Data Len = 7	1-octet field	2-octet field	
4-octet field			
PadN Option = 1	Opt Data Len = 2	0	0

A Hop-by-Hop or Destination Options header containing both options X and Y from the preceding examples would have one of the two following formats, depending on which option appeared first.

Next Header	Hdr Ext Len = 3	Option Type = X	Opt Data Len = 12
4-octet field			
8-octet field			
PadN Option = 1	Opt Data Len = 1	0	Option Type = Y
Opt Data Len = 7	1-octet field	2-octet field	
4-octet field			
PadN Option = 1	Opt Data Len = 2	0	0

Next Header	Hdr Ext Len = 3	Pad1 Option = 0	Option Type = Y
Opt Data Len = 7	1-octet field	2-octet field	
4-octet field			
PadN Option = 1	Opt Data Len = 4	0	0
0	0	Option Type = X	Opt Data Len = 12
4-octet field			
8-octet field			

16.14   IPv6 Address Types

IPv6 addresses are 128-bit. There are three types of addresses:

1. *Unicast.*   An identifier for a single interface. A packet sent to a unicast address is delivered to the interface identified by that address.

2. *Anycast.*   An identifier for a set of interfaces (typically belonging to different nodes). A packet sent to an anycast address is delivered to

one of the interfaces identified by that address (the *nearest* one, according to the routing protocol's measure of distance).

3. *Multicast.*   An identifier for a set of interfaces (typically belonging to different nodes). A packet sent to a multicast address is delivered to all interfaces identified by that address.

There are no broadcast addresses in IPv6. This type of address is superseded by a multicast address. Here address fields are given a specific name; for example, *subscriber.* When this name is used with the *ID* for identifier after the name *subscriber ID,* it refers to the contents of that field. When it is used with the term *prefix,* it refers to all of the address up to and including this field.

In IPv6, all zeros and ones are legal values for any field unless specifically excluded. Specifically, prefixes may contain zero-valued fields or end in zeros.

16.15   IPv6 Addressing

IPv6 addresses of all types are assigned to *interfaces,* not *nodes.* Since each interface belongs to a single node, any of that node's interfaces' unicast addresses may be used as an identifier for the node.

An IPv6 unicast address refers to a single interface. A single interface may be assigned multiple IPv6 addresses of any type (unicast, anycast, and multicast). There are two exceptions to this model:

1. A single address may be assigned to multiple physical interfaces if the implementation treats the multiple physical interfaces as one interface when presenting it to the internet layer.

2. Routers may have unnumbered interfaces on point-to-point links to eliminate the necessity to manually configure and advertise the addresses.

Addresses are not required for point-to-point interfaces on routers if those interfaces are not to be used as the origins or destinations of any IPv6 datagrams.

IPv6 continues the IPv4 subnet model that is associated with one link. Multiple subnets may be assigned to that link. There are three conventional forms for representing IPv6 addresses as text strings:

1. The preferred form is *x:x:x:x:x:x:x:x,* where the *x*s are the hexadecimal values of the eight 16-bit pieces of the address. For example, the following addresses:

    FEDC:BA98:7654:3210:FEDC:BA98:7654:3210
    1080:0:0:0:8:800:200C:417A

2. Due to the method of allocating certain styles of IPv6 addresses, it is common for addresses to contain long strings of zero bits. In order to make writing addresses containing zero bits easier, a special syntax is available to compress the zeros. The use of :: indicates multiple groups of 16 bits of zeros. The :: can only appear once in an address. The :: can also be used to compress the leading and/or trailing zeros in an address. For example, the following addresses:

1080:0:0:0:8:800:200C:417A	A unicast address
FF01:0:0:0:0:0:0:43	A multicast address
0:0:0:0:0:0:0:1	The loopback address
0:0:0:0:0:0:0:0	The unspecified addresses

These may be represented as follows:

1080::8:800:200C:417A	A unicast address
FF01::43	A multicast address
::1	The loopback address
::	The unspecified addresses

3. An alternative form that is sometimes more convenient when dealing with a mixed environment of IPv4 and IPv6 nodes is $x:x:x:x:x:x:$ $d.d.d.d,$ where the xs are the hexadecimal values of the 6 high-order 16-bit pieces of the address, and the ds are the decimal values of the 4 low-order 8-bit pieces of the address (standard IPv4 representation). For example, the following addresses:

0:0:0:0:0:0:13.1.68.3

0:0:0:0:0:FFFF:129.144.52.38

In compressed form, these appear as follows:

::13.1.68.3

::FFFF:129.144.52.38

16.16   Address Type Representation

The specific type of an IPv6 address is indicated by the address' leading bits. The variable-length field comprising these leading bits is called the *Format Prefix* (FP). The initial allocation of these prefixes is as follows:

Allocation space	Prefix, binary	Fraction of address space
Reserved	0000 0000	1/256
Unassigned	0000 0001	1/256
Reserved for NSAP allocation	0000 001	1/128
Reserved for IPX allocation	0000 010	1/128

Unassigned	0000 011	1/128
Unassigned	0000 1	1/32
Unassigned	0001	1/16
Unassigned	001	1/8
Provider-based unicast address	010	1/8
Unassigned	011	1/8
Reserved for geographically based unicast addresses	100	1/8
Unassigned	101	1/8
Unassigned	110	1/8
Unassigned	1110	1/16
Unassigned	1111 0	1/32
Unassigned	1111 10	1/64
Unassigned	1111 110	1/128
Unassigned	1111 1110 0	1/512
Link-local-use addresses	1111 1110 10	1/1024
Site-local-use addresses	1111 1110 11	1/1024
Multicast addresses	1111 1111	1/256

The unspecified address, the loopback address, and the IPv6 addresses with embedded IPv4 addresses are assigned out of the 0000 0000 format prefix space. This allocation supports the direct provider addresses allocation, local use addresses, and multicast addresses. Space is reserved for NSAP addresses, IPX addresses, and geographic addresses. The remainder of the address space is unassigned for future use. This can be used for expansion of existing uses or for new uses. Fifteen percent of the address space is initially allocated. The remaining 85 percent is reserved for future use.

Unicast addresses are distinguished from multicast addresses by the value of the high-order octet of the addresses: a value of FF (11111111) identifies an address as a multicast address; any other value identifies an address as a unicast address. Anycast addresses are taken from the unicast address space, and are not syntactically distinguishable from unicast addresses.

16.17 Unicast Addresses

The IPv6 unicast address is contiguous bitwise maskable, similar to IPv4 addresses under Classless Interdomain Routing (CIDR). There are several forms of unicast address assignment in IPv6, including the global provider-based unicast address, the geographic-based unicast address, the NSAP address, the IPX hierarchical address, the site-local-use address, the link-local-use address, and the IPv4-capable host address. Additional address types can be defined in the future.

IPv6 nodes may have considerable or little knowledge of the internal structure of the IPv6 address, depending on what the host does. Remember, a host is not necessarily a computer in the sense of one that a user works on; it could be any valid network device. At a minimum, a node may consider that unicast addresses (including its own) have no internal structure, as shown in the following illustration:

128 bits
node address

A slightly sophisticated (but still rather simple) host may additionally be aware of subnet prefixes for the links it is attached to, and different addresses can have different n values, as follows:

n bits	$128 - n$ bits
Subnet prefix	Interface ID

More sophisticated hosts may be aware of other hierarchical boundaries in the unicast address. Though a very simple router may have no knowledge of the internal structure of IPv6 unicast addresses, routers will more generally have knowledge of one or more of the hierarchical boundaries for the operation of routing protocols. The known boundaries will differ from router to router, depending on what positions the router holds in the routing hierarchy.

An example of a unicast address format that will likely be common on LANs and other environments where IEEE 802 MAC addresses are available is as follows:

n bits	$80 - n$ bits	48 bits
Subscriber prefix	Subnet ID	Interface ID

The 48-bit Interface ID is an IEEE-802 MAC address. The use of IEEE 802 MAC addresses as an interface ID is expected to be very common in environments where nodes have an IEEE 802 MAC address. In other environments, where IEEE 802 MAC addresses are not available, other types of link layer addresses, such as E.164 addresses, can be used for the interface ID.

The inclusion of a unique global interface identifier, such as an IEEE MAC address, makes possible a very simple form of autoconfiguration of addresses. A node may discover a subnet ID by listening to router advertisement messages sent by a router on its attached link(s), and then fabricate an IPv6 address for itself by using its IEEE MAC address as the interface ID on that subnet.

Another unicast address format example is where a site or organization requires additional layers of internal hierarchy. In this example the subnet ID is divided into an area ID and a subnet ID. Its format is as follows:

s bits	n bits	m bits	$128 - s - n - m$ bits
Subscriber prefix	Area ID	Subnet ID	Interface ID

This technique can be continued to allow a site or organization to add additional layers of internal hierarchy. It may be desirable to use an interface ID smaller than a 48-bit IEEE 802 MAC address to allow more space for the additional layers of internal hierarchy. These could be interface IDs that are administratively created by the site or organization.

The address 0:0:0:0:0:0:0:0 is called the *unspecified address*. It must never be assigned to any node. It indicates the absence of an address. One example of its use is in the Source Address field of any IPv6 datagram sent by an initializing host before it has learned its own address.

The unspecified address must not be used as the destination address of IPv6 datagrams or in IPv6 Routing Headers.

The unicast address 0:0:0:0:0:0:0:1 is called the *loopback address*. It may be used by a node to send an IPv6 datagram to itself. It may never be assigned to any interface.

The loopback address must not be used as the source address in IPv6 datagrams that are sent outside of a single node. An IPv6 datagram with a destination address of *loopback* must never be sent outside of a single node.

16.18   IPv6 Addresses and IPv4 Addresses

The IPv6 transition mechanisms include a technique for hosts and routers to dynamically tunnel IPv6 packets over IPv4 routing infrastructure. IPv6 nodes that utilize this technique are assigned special IPv6 unicast addresses that carry an IPv4 address in the 32 low-order bits. This type of address is termed an *IPv4-compatible IPv6 address,* and it has the following format:

80 bits	16	32 bits
0000 0000	00 00	IPv4 address

A second type of IPv6 address that holds an embedded IPv4 address is also defined. This address is used to represent the addresses of IPv4-only nodes (those that *do not* support IPv6) as IPv6 addresses. This type of address is termed an *IPv4-mapped IPv6 address,* and it has the following format:

80 bits	16	32 bits
0000 0000	FFFF	IPv4 address

NSAP addresses

This mapping of NSAP addresses into IPv6 addresses is as follows:

7	121 bits
0000001	To be defined

IPX addresses

This mapping of IPX addresses into IPv6 addresses is as follows:

7	121 bits
0000010	To be defined

Global unicast addresses

This initial assignment plan for these unicast addresses is similar to assignment of IPv4 addresses under the CIDR scheme. The IPv6 global provider-based unicast address format is as follows:

3	n bits	m bits	o bits	$125 - n - m - o$ bits
010	Registry ID	Provider ID	Subscriber ID	Intrasubscriber

The high-order-bit part of the address is assigned to registries, which assign portions of the address space to providers, which assign portions of the address space to subscribers, and so on.

The *registry ID* identifies the registry that assigns the provider portion of the address. The term *registry prefix* refers to the high-order part of the address up to and including the registry ID.

The *provider ID* identifies the specific provider that assigns the subscriber portion of the address. The term *provider prefix* refers to the high-order part of the address up to and including the provider ID.

The *subscriber ID* distinguishes among multiple subscribers attached to the provider identified by the provider ID. The term *subscriber prefix* refers to the high-order part of the address up to and including the subscriber ID.

The *intrasubscriber* portion of the address is defined by an individual subscriber and is organized according to the subscriber's local internet topology. It is likely that many subscribers will choose to divide the intrasubscriber portion of the address into a subnet ID and an interface ID. In this case, the subnet ID identifies a specific physical link and the interface ID identifies a single interface on that subnet.

IPv6 unicast addresses

There are two types of local-use unicast addresses defined, link-local and site-local. The *link-local* is for use on a single link, and the *site-local* is for use in a single site. Link-local addresses have the following format:

10 bits	n bits	$118 - n$ bits
1111111010	0	Interface ID

Link-local addresses are designed to be used for addressing on a single link for purposes such as autoaddress configuration, neighbor discovery, or when no routers are present. Routers are not permitted to forward any packets with link-local source addresses.

Site-local addresses have the following format:

10 bits	n bits	m bits	$118 - n - m$ bits
1111111011	0	Subnet ID	Interface ID

Site-local addresses may be used for sites or organizations that are not yet connected to the global Internet. They do not need to request or "steal" an address prefix from the global Internet address space. IPv6 site-local addresses can be used instead. When the organization connects to the global Internet, it can then form global addresses by replacing the site-local prefix with a subscriber prefix.

Routers *must not* forward any packets with site-local source addresses outside of the site.

16.19 Anycast Addresses

An IPv6 anycast address is an address that is assigned to more than one interface (typically belonging to different nodes), with the property that a packet sent to an anycast address is routed to the *nearest* interface having that address, according to the routing protocol's measure of distance.

Anycast addresses are allocated from the unicast address space, using any of the defined unicast address formats. Thus, anycast addresses are syntactically indistinguishable from unicast addresses. When a unicast address is assigned to more than one interface, thus turning it into an anycast address, the nodes to which the address is assigned must be explicitly configured to know that it is an anycast address.

For any assigned anycast address, there is a longest address prefix P that identifies the topological region in which all interfaces belonging to that anycast address reside. Within the region identified by P, each member of the anycast set must be advertised as a separate entry in the routing system (referred to as a *host route*); outside the region identified by P, the anycast address may be aggregated into the routing advertisement for prefix P.

Note that in the worst case, the prefix P of an anycast set may be the null prefix; that is, the members of the set may have no topological locality. In that case, the anycast address must be advertised as a separate routing entry throughout the entire Internet, which presents a severe scaling limit on how many such "global" anycast sets may be supported. Therefore, it is expected that support for global anycast sets may be unavailable or very restricted.

One expected use of anycast addresses is to identify the set of routers belonging to an Internet service provider. Such addresses could be used as intermediate addresses in an IPv6 Routing header, in order to cause a packet to be delivered via a particular provider or sequence of providers. Some other possible uses are to identify the set of routers attached to a particular subnet, or the set of routers providing entry into a particular routing domain.

There is little experience with widespread, arbitrary use of Internet anycast addresses, and there are some known complications and hazards when using them in their full generality [ANYCST]. Until more experience has been gained and solutions have been agreed upon for those problems, the following restrictions are imposed on IPv6 anycast addresses:

- An anycast address *must not* be used as the source address of an IPv6 packet.

- An anycast address *must not* be assigned to an IPv6 host; that is, it may be assigned to an IPv6 router only.

The subnet-router anycast address is predefined. Its format is as follows:

n bits	128 – *n* bits
Subnet prefix	00000000000000

The *subnet prefix* in an anycast address is the prefix that identifies a specific link. This anycast address is syntactically the same as a unicast address for an interface on the link with the interface identifier set to 0.

Packets sent to the subnet-router anycast address will be delivered to one router on the subnet. All routers are required to support the subnet-router anycast addresses for the subnets with which they have interfaces.

The subnet-router anycast address is intended to be used for applications where a node needs to communicate with one of a set of routers on a remote subnet; for example, when a mobile host needs to communicate with one of the mobile agents on its home subnet.

16.20   Multicast Addresses

An IPv6 multicast address is an identifier for a group of nodes. A node may belong to any number of multicast groups. Multicast addresses have the following format:

8	4	4	112 bits
11111111	Flgs	Scop	Group ID

11111111 at the start of the address identifies the address as being a multicast address.

Flags is a set of 4 flags having the following format:

0 0 0 T

The 3 high-order flags are reserved, and must be initialized to 0. T = 0 indicates a permanently assigned (well-known) multicast address, assigned by the global internet numbering authority. T = 1 indicates a nonpermanently assigned multicast address (also referred to as *transient*).

Scope is a 4-bit multicast scope value used to limit the scope of the multicast group. The values are listed following.

0   Reserved
1   Node-local scope
2   Link-local scope

3   Unassigned

4   Unassigned

5   Site-local scope

6   Unassigned

7   Unassigned

8   Organization-local scope

9   Unassigned

A   Unassigned

B   Unassigned

C   Unassigned

D   Unassigned

E   Global scope

F   Reserved

Multicast group addresses

Group ID identifies the multicast group, either permanent or transient, within the given scope. The *meaning* of a permanently assigned multicast address is independent of the scope value. For example, if the NTP servers group is assigned a permanent multicast address with a group ID of 43 hex, then:

FF01:0:0:0:0:0:0:43 means all NTP servers on the same node as the sender.

FF02:0:0:0:0:0:0:43 means all NTP servers on the same link as the sender.

FF05:0:0:0:0:0:0:43 means all NTP servers at the same site as the sender.

FF0E:0:0:0:0:0:0:43 means all NTP servers in the internet.

Nonpermanently assigned multicast addresses are meaningful only within a given scope. For example, a group identified by the nonpermanent, site-local multicast address FF15:0:0:0:0:0:0:43 at one site bears no relationship to a group using the same address at a different site, nor to a nonpermanent group using the same group ID with different scope, nor to a permanent group with the same group ID.

Multicast addresses must not be used as source addresses in IPv6 datagrams or appear in any routing header.

Predefined multicast addresses

The following well-known multicast addresses are predefined:

Reserved multicast addresses

FF00:0:0:0:0:0:0:0

FF01:0:0:0:0:0:0:0

FF02:0:0:0:0:0:0:0

FF03:0:0:0:0:0:0:0

FF04:0:0:0:0:0:0:0

FF05:0:0:0:0:0:0:0

FF06:0:0:0:0:0:0:0

FF07:0:0:0:0:0:0:0

FF08:0:0:0:0:0:0:0

FF09:0:0:0:0:0:0:0

FF0A:0:0:0:0:0:0:0

FF0B:0:0:0:0:0:0:0

FF0C:0:0:0:0:0:0:0

FF0D:0:0:0:0:0:0:0

FF0E:0:0:0:0:0:0:0

FF0F:0:0:0:0:0:0:0

The preceding multicast addresses are reserved and shall never be assigned to any multicast group.

All nodes addresses

FF01:0:0:0:0:0:0:1

FF02:0:0:0:0:0:0:1

The preceding multicast addresses identify the group of all IPv6 nodes, within scope 1 (node-local) or 2 (link-local).

All routers addresses

FF01:0:0:0:0:0:0:2

FF02:0:0:0:0:0:0:2

The preceding multicast addresses identify the group of all IPv6 routers, within scope 1 (node-local) or 2 (link-local).

DHCP Server/Relay-Agent

FF02:0:0:0:0:0:0:C

The preceding multicast addresses identify the group of all IPv6 · DHCP Servers and Relay Agents within scope 2 (link-local).

Solicited-node address

FF02:0:0:0:0:1:XXXX:XXXX

The preceding multicast address is computed as a function of a node's unicast and anycast addresses. The solicited-node multicast address is formed by taking the 32 low-order bits of the address (unicast or anycast) and appending those bits to the 96-bit prefix FF02:0:0:0:0:1, resulting in a multicast address in the range FF02:0:0:0:0:1:0000:0000 to FF02:0:0:0:0:1:FFFF:FFFF.

For example, the solicited node multicast address corresponding to the IPv6 address 4037::01:800:200E:8C6C is FF02::1:200E:8C6C. IPv6 addresses that differ only in the high-order bits (e.g., due to multiple high-order prefixes associated with different providers) will map to the same solicited-node address, thereby reducing the number of multicast addresses that a node must join.

A node is required to compute and support a solicited-node multicast address for every unicast and anycast address it is assigned.

16.21   Node address requirement

A host is required to recognize the following addresses as identifying itself:

- Its link-local address for each interface
- Assigned unicast addresses
- Loopback address
- All-nodes multicast address
- Solicited-node multicast address for each of its assigned unicast and anycast addresses
- Multicast addresses of all other groups to which the host belongs

A router is required to recognize the following addresses as identifying itself:

- Its link-local address for each interface
- Assigned unicast addresses
- Loopback address
- The subnet-router anycast addresses for the links with which it has interfaces

- All other anycast addresses with which the router has been configured
- All-nodes multicast address
- All-router multicast address
- Solicited-node multicast address for each of its assigned unicast and anycast addresses
- Multicast addresses of all other groups to which the router belongs

The only address prefixes that should be predefined in an implementation are the following:

- Unspecified address
- Loopback address
- Multicast prefix (FF)
- Local-use prefixes (link-local and site-local)
- Predefined multicast addresses
- IPv4-compatible prefixes

Implementations should assume that all other addresses are unicast unless specifically configured (e.g., anycast addresses).

16.22 Summary

IPv6 is more robust than its predecessor. The ability to accommodate many more entities in the addressing scheme is but one of the improved abilities it has over IPv4. The information presented here is to assist the detailed planning functions that go into network design.

17

Designing Networks
That Use DHCP

The *Dynamic Host Configuration Protocol* (DHCP) is a way to pass configuration information to hosts on a TCPIP network. It is based on the *Bootstrap Protocol* (BOOTP). DHCP adds the capability of automatic allocation of reusable network addresses and additional configuration options. DHCP functions with BOOTP relay agents.

17.1 Introduction

DHCP provides configuration parameters to Internet hosts. It consists of two components: a protocol for delivering host-specific configuration parameters from a DHCP server to a host and a mechanism for allocation of network addresses to hosts.

DHCP is built on a client/server model, where designated DHCP server hosts allocate network addresses and deliver configuration parameters to dynamically configured hosts. Use of the term *server* here refers to a host providing initialization parameters through DHCP; the term *client* refers to a host requesting initialization parameters from a DHCP server.

A host should not act as a DHCP server unless explicitly configured to do so by a system administrator. The diversity of hardware and protocol implementations in the Internet would preclude reliable operation if random hosts were allowed to respond to DHCP requests.

For example, IP requires the setting of many parameters within the protocol implementation software. Because IP can be used on many dissimilar kinds of network hardware, values for those parameters cannot be guessed or assumed to have correct defaults. Also, distributed address allocation schemes depend on a polling/defense mechanism for discovery of addresses that are already in use. IP hosts may not always be able to defend their network addresses, so such a distributed address allocation scheme cannot be guaranteed to avoid allocation of duplicate network addresses.

Address allocation

DHCP supports three mechanisms for IP address allocation. *Automatic allocation* is where DHCP assigns a permanent IP address to a client. *Dynamic allocation* means that DHCP assigns an IP address to a client for a limited period of time (or until the client explicitly relinquishes the address). *Manual allocation* is where a client's IP address is assigned by the network administrator, and DHCP is used simply to convey the assigned address to the client. A particular network will use one or more of these mechanisms, depending on the policies of the network administrator.

Dynamic allocation is the only one of the three mechanisms that allows automatic reuse of an address that is no longer needed by the client to which it was assigned. Thus, dynamic allocation is particularly useful for assigning an address to a client that will be connected to the network only temporarily or for sharing a limited pool of IP addresses among a group of clients that do not need permanent IP addresses. Dynamic allocation may also be a good choice for assigning an IP address to a new client being permanently connected to a network where IP addresses are sufficiently scarce that it is important to reclaim them when old clients are retired.

Manual allocation allows DHCP to be used to eliminate the error-prone process of manually configuring hosts with IP addresses in environments where (for whatever reasons) it is desirable to manage IP address assignment outside of the DHCP mechanisms.

DHCP message format

The DHCP message format is based on the format of BOOTP messages, in order to capture the BOOTP relay agent behavior described as part of the BOOTP specification and to allow interoperability of existing BOOTP clients with DHCP servers. Using BOOTP relay agents eliminates the necessity of having a DHCP server on each physical network segment.

Recent DHCP additions

The DHCP message type, *DHCPINFORM,* has been recently added to the protocol specification. Also, the classing mechanism for identifying DHCP clients to DHCP servers has been extended to include vendor classes. The minimum lease time restriction has been removed. Finally, many editorial changes have been made to clarify the text as a result of experience gained in DHCP interoperability tests.

DHCP information

Several Internet protocols and related mechanisms address some parts of the dynamic host configuration problem. The *Reverse Address Resolution Protocol* (RARP) explicitly addresses the problem of network address discovery and includes an automatic IP address assignment mechanism. The *Trivial File Transfer Protocol* (TFTP) provides for transport of a boot image from a boot server. The *Internet Control Message Protocol* (ICMP) provides for informing hosts of additional routers via ICMP redirect messages; ICMP also can provide subnet mask information by way of the ICMP mask request message, and additional information can be obtained by the ICMP information request message. Network hosts can locate routers through the ICMP router discovery mechanism.

BOOTP is a transport mechanism for a collection of configuration information. The *Network Information Protocol* (NIP), used by Athena at MIT, is a distributed mechanism for dynamic IP address assignment. The *Resource Location Protocol* (RLP) provides for location of higher-level services. Sun Microsystems diskless workstations use a boot procedure that employs RARP, TFTP, and a RPC mechanism called *bootparams*. These bootparams deliver configuration information and operating system code to diskless network hosts. Some SUN networks also use DRARP and an autoinstallation mechanism to automate the configuration of new hosts in an existing, functional network.

In other related work, the path *minimum transmission unit* (MTU) discovery algorithm can determine the MTU of an arbitrary internet path. The *Address Resolution Protocol* (ARP) has been proposed as a transport protocol for resource location and selection.

DHCP considerations

DHCP was designed to supply DHCP clients with the configuration parameters defined in the Host Requirements RFCs. After obtaining parameters via DHCP, a DHCP client should be able to exchange packets with any other host in the Internet.

Not all of these parameters are required for a newly initialized client. A client and server may negotiate transmission of those parameters required by the client or specific to a particular subnet.

DHCP allows but does not require the configuration of client parameters not directly related to the IP protocol. DHCP also does not address registration of newly configured clients with the Domain

Name System. The DHCP original design intent is not intended to configure routers.

17.2   DHCP Terms

DHCP CLIENT: An Internet host using DHCP to obtain configuration parameters such as a network address.

DHCP SERVER: An Internet or internet host that returns configuration parameters to DHCP clients.

BOOTP RELAY AGENT: An Internet host or router that passes DHCP messages between DHCP clients and DHCP servers. DHCP is designed to use the same relay agent behavior as is specified in the BOOTP protocol specification.

BINDING: A collection of configuration parameters, including at least an IP address, associated with or bound to a DHCP client. Bindings are managed by DHCP servers.

DHCP design intent

The original design intent of DHCP includes the following points:

- DHCP should be a mechanism rather than a policy. DHCP must allow local system administrators control over configuration parameters where desired; this means that local system administrators should be able to enforce local policies concerning allocation and access to local resources where desired.

- Clients should require no manual configuration. Each client should be able to discover appropriate local configuration parameters without user intervention and be able to incorporate those parameters into its own configuration.

- Networks should require no manual configuration for individual clients. Under normal circumstances a network manager should not have to manually enter any per-client configuration parameters.

- DHCP should not require a server on each subnet. To allow for scale and economy, DHCP must work across routers or through the intervention of BOOTP relay agents.

- A DHCP client must be prepared to receive multiple responses to a request for configuration parameters. Some installations may include multiple, overlapping DHCP servers to enhance reliability and increase performance.

- DHCP must coexist with statically configured, nonparticipating hosts and with existing network protocol implementations.

- DHCP must work with the BOOTP relay agent behavior as described by RFCs 951 and 1542.
- DHCP must provide service to existing BOOTP clients.

DHCP requirements

DHCP requirements include the following, specific to the transmission of network layer parameters:

- Guarantee that any network address will not be in use by more than one DHCP client at a time.
- Retain DHCP client configuration across DHCP client reboot. A DHCP client should, whenever possible, be assigned the same configuration parameters (e.g., network address) in response to each request.
- Retain DHCP client configuration across server reboots.
- Assign a DHCP client the same configuration parameters despite restarts of the DHCP mechanism.
- Allow automated assignment of configuration parameters to new clients to avoid hand configuration for new clients.
- Support fixed or permanent allocation of configuration parameters to specific clients.

17.3 DHCP Protocol

From the client's point of view, DHCP is an extension of the BOOTP mechanism. This behavior allows existing BOOTP clients to interoperate with DHCP servers without requiring any changes to the clients' initialization software. RFC 1542 details the interactions between BOOTP and DHCP clients and servers.

DHCP message format

The following DHCP message format describes each of the fields in the DHCP message. The numbers in parentheses indicate the size of each field in octets. Two primary differences between DHCP and BOOTP exist. First, DHCP defines mechanisms through which clients can be assigned a network address for a finite lease, allowing for serial reassignment of network addresses to different clients.

Second, DHCP provides the mechanism for a client to acquire all of the IP configuration parameters that it needs in order to operate. DHCP introduces a small change in terminology intended to clarify the meaning of one of the fields. What was at one time referred to as the *vendor extensions* field in BOOTP is now referred to as the *options* field in DHCP. *Tagged* data items that were used inside the BOOTP vendor extensions field, which were formerly referred to as *vendor extensions,* are now termed *options.*

Consider the following representation of the DHCP message format.

```
0                   1                   2                   3
0 1 2 3 4 5 6 7 8 9 0 1 2 3 4 5 6 7 8 9 0 1 2 3 4 5 6 7 8 9 0 1
```

op (1)	htype (1)	hlen (1)	hops (1)
xid (4)				
secs (2)		flags (2)	
ciaddr (4)			
yiaddr (4)			
siaddr (4)			
giaddr (4)			
chaddr (16)			
sname (64)			
file (128)			
options (variable)			

DHCP defines a new *client identifier* option that is used to pass an explicit client identifier to a DHCP server. This change eliminates the overloading of the *chaddr* field in BOOTP messages, where *chaddr* is used both as a hardware address for transmission of BOOTP reply messages and as a client identifier. The client identifier is an opaque key, not to be interpreted by the server. It may contain a hardware address, identical to the contents of the chaddr field, or it may contain another type of identifier, such as a DNS name. The client identifier chosen by a DHCP client *MUST* be unique to that client within the subnet to which the client is attached. If a client uses a client identifier in one message, it MUST use that same identifier in all subsequent messages, to ensure that all servers correctly identify the client.

DHCP clarifies the interpretation of the *siaddr* field as the address of the server to use in the next step of the client's bootstrap process. A DHCP server can return its own address in the siaddr field if the server is prepared to supply the next bootstrap service; for example, the delivery of an operating system executable image. A DHCP server always returns its own address in the *server identifier* option.

DHCP message field explanation

Consider Table 17.1, explaining the fields in a DHCP message.

The options field is now of variable length. A DHCP client must be prepared to receive DHCP messages with an options field length of at least 312 octets. This requirement implies that a DHCP client must be prepared to receive a message of up to 576 octets, the minimum IP datagram size an IP host must accept. It is possible, however, that DHCP clients can negotiate the use of larger DHCP messages through the *maximum DHCP message size* option. The options field may be further extended into the *file* and *sname* fields.

When DHCP is used in initial configuration (prior to the client's TCP/IP software complete configuration), it requires mental agility on behalf of the user. The TCP/IP software installed should accept and *forward* any IP packets to the IP layer delivered to the client's hardware address before the IP address is configured. DHCP servers and BOOTP relay agents may not be able to deliver DHCP messages to clients that cannot accept hardware unicast datagrams before the TCP/IP software is configured. So, be aware of this when you find yourself in this scenario.

In order to work around some clients that cannot accept IP unicast datagrams before the TCP/IP software is configured, DHCP uses the *flags* field. Here, the leftmost bit is defined as the BROADCAST (B) flag.

TABLE 17.1 Explanation of Fields in a DHCP Message

Field	Octets	Description
op	1	Message op code / message type, 1 = BOOTREQUEST, 2 = BOOTREPLY.
htype	1	Hardware address type.
hlen	1	Hardware address length.
hops	1	Client sets to zero; optionally used by relay agents when booting via a relay agent.
xid	4	Transaction ID; a random number chosen by the client, used by the client and server to associate messages and responses between a client and a server.
secs	2	Filled in by client; seconds elapsed since client began address acquisition or renewal process.
flags	2	Flags.
ciaddr	4	Client IP address; filled in only if client is in BOUND, RENEW, or REBINDING state and can respond to ARP requests.
yiaddr	4	Your (client) IP address.
siaddr	4	IP address of next server to use in bootstrap; returned in DHCPOFFER, DHCPACK by server.
giaddr	4	Relay agent IP address; used in booting via a relay agent.
chaddr	16	Client hardware address.
sname	64	Optional server host name, null terminated string.
file	128	Boot file name, null terminated string; generic name or null in DHCPDISCOVER, fully qualified directory path name in DHCPOFFER.
options	Variable	Optional parameters field.

DHCP flags field format

The flags field format is as follows:

```
                    1 1 1 1 1 1
0 1 2 3 4 5 6 7 8 9 0 1 2 3 4 5
┌─┬─────────────────────────────┐
│B│           MBZ               │
└─┴─────────────────────────────┘
```

B: BROADCAST flag

MBZ: Must be zero

17.4   DHCP Configuration Parameters Repository

The first service provided by DHCP is to provide persistent storage of network parameters for network clients. The model of DHCP persistent storage is this: the DHCP service stores a key-value entry for each client (a unique identifier, such as an IP subnet number and a unique identifier within the subnet), and the value contains the configuration parameters for the client.

For example, in this case the key might be the IP subnet number and hardware address. Alternatively, the key might be the pair (IP subnet number, hostname), thus allowing the server to intelligently assign parameters to a DHCP client that has moved to a different subnet or that has had a hardware address change. The protocol defines that the key will be the IP subnet number and hardware address unless the client explicitly supplies an identifier using the client identifier option. A client can query the DHCP service to retrieve its configuration parameters. The client interface to the configuration parameters repository consists of protocol messages to request configuration parameters and responses from the server carrying the configuration parameters.

17.5   Network Address Dynamic Allocation

The second service provided by DHCP is the allocation of temporary or permanent network (IP) addresses to clients. The basic mechanism for the dynamic allocation of network addresses is simple: a client requests the use of an address for some period of time. The allocation mechanism (the collection of DHCP servers) guarantees not to reallocate that address within the requested time and attempts to return the same network address each time the client requests an address. In this document, the period over which a network address is allocated to a client is referred to as a *lease*. The client may extend its lease with subsequent requests. The client may issue a message to release the address back to the server when it no longer needs the address. The client may ask for a permanent assignment by asking for an infinite lease. Even when assigning *permanent* addresses, a server may choose to give out lengthy but noninfinite leases to allow detection of the fact that the client has been retired.

Some environments will require reassignment of network addresses due to exhaustion of available addresses. In such environments, the allocation mechanism will reuse addresses whose leases have expired. The server should use whatever information is available in the configuration information repository to choose an address to reuse. For example, the server may choose the least recently assigned address. As a consistency check, the allocating server should probe the reused address before allocating the address (for example, with an ICMP echo request), and the client should probe the newly received address with ARP.

17.6 Client/Server Protocol

DHCP uses the BOOTP message format shown following.

0	1	2	3
0 1 2 3 4 5 6 7	8 9 0 1 2 3 4 5	6 7 8 9 0 1 2 3	4 5 6 7 8 9 0 1
op (1)	htype (1)	hlen (1)	hops (1)
xid (4)			
secs (2)		flags (2)	
ciaddr (4)			
yiaddr (4)			
siaddr (4)			
giaddr (4)			
chaddr (16)			
sname (64)			
file (128)			
options (variable)			

The *op* field of each DHCP message sent from a client to a server contains a *BOOTREQUEST.* The *BOOTREPLY* is used in the op field of each DHCP message sent from a server to a client.

The first 4 octets of the *options* field of the DHCP message contain decimal values. The remainder of the options field consists of a list of tagged parameters that are called *options.* All *vendor extensions* are also DHCP options. For additional information, RFC 1533 provides a complete set of options defined for use with DHCP.

Some options included in the RFC are presented here. One particular option, the DHCP message type option, must be included in each DHCP message. This option defines the *type* of the DHCP message. Additional options may be allowed, required, or not allowed, depending on the DHCP message type.

17.7   DHCP Messages and Meanings

DHCPDISCOVER: Client broadcast to locate available servers.

DHCPOFFER: Server to client in response to DHCPDISCOVER with offer of configuration parameters.

DHCPREQUEST: Client message to servers either requesting offered parameters from one server and implicitly declining offers from all others or confirming correctness of previously allocated addresses after their receipt. For example, a system reboot or extending the lease on a particular network address.

DHCPACK: Server to client with configuration parameters, including committed network address.

DHCPNAK: Server to client indicating that the client's notion of the network address is incorrect (e.g., client has moved to new subnet) or that the client's lease has expired.

DHCPDECLINE: Client to server indicating that the network address is already in use.

DHCPRELEASE: Client to server relinquishing the network address and cancelling the remaining lease.

DHCPINFORM: Client to server, asking only for local configuration parameters; client already has externally configured network address.

DHCP message timeline

The following is an example of the timeline concept between a DHCP client and a DHCP server when a new address allocation is performed.

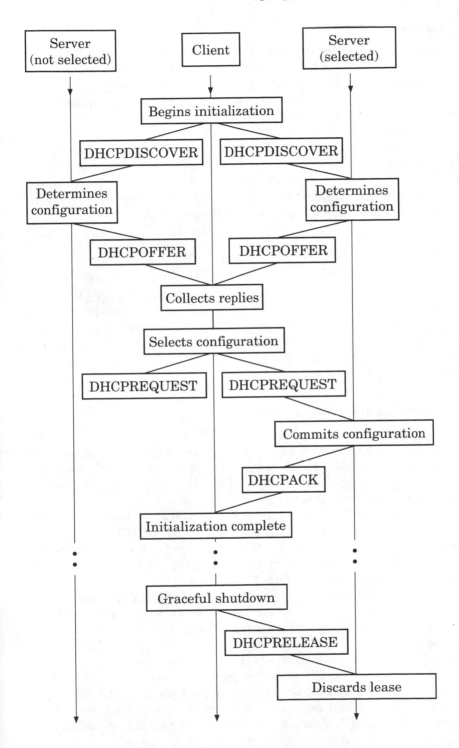

DHCP client usage

A client SHOULD use DHCP to reacquire or verify its IP address and network parameters whenever the local network parameters may have changed; for example, at system boot time or after a disconnection from the local network, as the local network configuration may change without the client's or user's knowledge.

If a client has knowledge of a previous network address and is unable to contact a local DHCP server, the client may continue to use the previous network address until the lease for that address expires. If the lease expires before the client can contact a DHCP server, the client must immediately discontinue use of the previous network address and may inform local users of the problem.

17.8   DHCP Client/Server Protocol Specification

It is important to understand the DHCP client/server specification. This section makes basic assumptions to provide helpful insights. The first assumption is that a DHCP server has a block of network addresses it can use to satisfy requests for new addresses. Another assumption is that each server maintains a database of allocated addresses and leases in its local permanent storage.

Constructing and Sending DHCP Messages

DHCP clients and servers construct DHCP messages by filling in fields in the fixed format section of the message and appending tagged data items in the variable length option area. The options area includes, first, a 4-octet *magic cookie,* followed by the options. The last option must always be the *end* option.

DHCP uses UDP as its transport protocol. Its messages from client to server are sent to the DHCP server port 67. DHCP messages are sent from a server to a client on the DHCP client port 68. A server with multiple network addresses (multihomed host) can use any of its network addresses in outgoing DHCP messages.

The *server identifier* field is used both to identify a DHCP server in a DHCP message and as a destination address from clients to servers. A server with multiple network addresses MUST be prepared to accept any of its network addresses as identifying that server in a DHCP message. To accommodate potentially incomplete network connectivity, a server is required to choose an address as a server identifier. This address is reachable from the client. For example, if the DHCP server and the DHCP client are connected to the same subnet, the server should select the IP address the server is using for communication on that subnet as the server identifier. If the server is using multiple IP addresses on that subnet, any such address may be used. If the server has received a message through a DHCP relay agent, the server should choose an address from the interface on which the message was received as the server identifier. DHCP clients are required to use the IP address provided in the server identifier option for any unicast requests to the DHCP server.

DHCP messages broadcast by a client prior to that client obtaining its IP address must have the source address field in the IP header set to 0.

If the *giaddr* field in a DHCP message from a client is nonzero, the server sends any return messages to the *DHCP server* port on the BOOTP relay agent whose address appears in giaddr. If the giaddr field is zero and the *ciaddr* field is nonzero, then the server unicasts DHCPOFFER and DHCPACK messages to the address in ciaddr. If giaddr is zero and ciaddr is zero, and the broadcast bit is set, then the server broadcasts DHCPOFFER and DHCPACK messages to 0xffffffff. If the broadcast bit is not set and giaddr is zero and ciaddr is zero, then the server unicasts DHCPOFFER and DHCPACK messages to the client's hardware address and *yiaddr* address. In all cases, when giaddr is zero, the server broadcasts any DHCPNAK messages to 0xffffffff.

If the options in a DHCP message extend into the *sname* and *file* fields, the *option overload* option is required to appear in the options field, with value 1, 2, or 3. If the option overload option is present in the options field, the options in the options field MUST be terminated by an *end* option, and MAY contain one or more *pad* options to fill the options field. The options in the sname and file fields are required to begin with the first octet of the field, are also required to be terminated by an end option, and be followed by pad options to fill the remainder of the field. Any individual options in the options, sname, and file fields are required to be entirely contained in the field. The options in the options field must be interpreted first, so that any option overload options may be interpreted. The file field must be interpreted next, followed by the sname field.

The values to be passed in an option tag may be too long to fit in the 255 octets available to a single option. Options may appear only once, unless otherwise specified in the options document. The client concatenates the values of multiple instances of the same option into a single parameter list for configuration.

DHCP clients are responsible for all message retransmission. The client MUST adopt a retransmission strategy that incorporates a randomized exponential backoff algorithm to determine the delay between retransmissions. The delay between retransmissions should be chosen to allow sufficient time for replies from the server to be delivered, based on the characteristics of the internetwork between the client and the server.

For example, in a 10-Mbps Ethernet network the delay before the first retransmission should be 4 s randomized by the value of a uniform random number chosen from the range −1 to +1. Clients with clocks that provide resolution granularity of less than 1 s may choose a noninteger randomization value. The delay before the next retransmission should be 8 s randomized by the value of a uniform number chosen from the range −1 to +1. The retransmission delay should be doubled with subsequent retransmissions, up to a maximum of 64 s. The client can provide an indication of retransmission attempts to the user as an indication of the progress of the configuration process.

The *xid* field is used by the client to match incoming DHCP messages with pending requests. A DHCP client must choose xids in such a way as to minimize the chance of using an xid identical to one used by another client. For example, a client may choose a different, random initial xid each time the client is rebooted, and subsequently use sequential xids until the next reboot. Selecting a new xid for each retransmission is an implementation decision. A client may choose to reuse the same xid or select a new xid for each retransmitted message.

Normally, DHCP servers and BOOTP relay agents attempt to deliver DHCPOFFER, DHCPACK, and DHCPNAK messages directly to the client using unicast delivery. The IP destination address is set to the DHCP yiaddr address and the link layer destination address is set to the DHCP chaddr address. Unfortunately, some client implementations are unable to receive such unicast IP datagrams until the implementation has been configured with a valid IP address.

A client that cannot receive unicast IP datagrams until its protocol software has been configured with an IP address should set the BROADCAST bit in the *flags* field to 1 in any DHCPDISCOVER or DHCPREQUEST messages that the client sends. The BROADCAST bit will provide a hint to the DHCP server and BOOTP relay agent to broadcast any messages to the client on the client's subnet. A client that can receive unicast IP datagrams before its protocol software has been configured SHOULD clear the BROADCAST bit to 0. The BOOTP clarifications document discusses the ramifications of the use of the BROADCAST bit.

A server or relay agent sending or relaying a DHCP message directly to a DHCP client should examine the BROADCAST bit in the flags field. If this bit is set to 1, the DHCP message should be sent as an IP broadcast using an IP broadcast address (preferably 0xffffffff) as the IP destination address and the link layer broadcast address as the link layer destination address. If the BROADCAST bit is cleared to 0, the message should be sent as an IP unicast to the IP address specified in the yiaddr field and the link layer address specified in the chaddr field. If unicasting is not possible, the message can be sent as an IP broadcast using an IP broadcast address (preferably 0xffffffff) as the IP destination address and the link layer broadcast address as the link layer destination address.

DHCP server administrative controls

DHCP servers are not required to respond to every DHCPDISCOVER and DHCPREQUEST message they receive. For example, for a network administrator to retain control over the clients attached to the network configuration of DHCP servers requires the server to respond only to clients that have been previously registered through some external mechanism. The DHCP specification describes only the interactions between clients and servers when the clients and servers choose to interact; it is beyond the scope of the DHCP specification to describe all of the administrative controls that system administrators might want to use. Specific DHCP server implementations may incorporate any controls or policies desired by a network administrator.

In some environments, a DHCP server will have to consider the values of the vendor class options included in DHCPDISCOVER or DHCPRE-QUEST messages when determining the correct parameters for a particular client.

A DHCP server needs to use some unique identifier to associate a client with its lease. The client MAY choose to explicitly provide the identifier through the client identifier option. If the client supplies a client identifier, the client MUST use the same client identifier in all subsequent messages, and the server must use that identifier to identify the client. If the client does not provide a client identifier option, the server MUST use the contents of the chaddr field to identify the client. It is important for a DHCP client to use an identifier that is unique within the subnet to which the client is attached in the client identifier option. Use of chaddr as the client's unique identifier may cause unexpected results, as that identifier may be associated with a hardware interface that could be moved to a new client. Some sites may choose to use a manufacturer's serial number as the client identifier, to avoid unexpected changes in a client's network address due to transfer of hardware interfaces among computers. Sites may also choose to use a DNS name as the client identifier, causing address leases to be associated with the DNS name rather than with a specific hardware box.

DHCP clients are free to use any strategy in selecting a DHCP server among those from which the client receives a DHCPOFFER message. The client implementation of DHCP should provide a mechanism for the user to directly select the *vendor class identifier* values.

17.9 DHCP Server Function

A DHCP server processes incoming DHCP messages from a client based on the current state of the binding for that client. The following messages can be received by a DHCP server from a client:

- DHCPDISCOVER
- DHCPREQUEST
- DHCPDECLINE
- DHCPRELEASE
- DHCPINFORM

Table 17.2 shows the correlation between use of the fields and options in a DHCP message by a server. A description of the DHCP server action for each possible incoming message is also presented.

DHCPDISCOVER message

When a server receives a DHCPDISCOVER message from a client, the server chooses a network address for the requesting client. If no address is available, the server may choose to report the problem to the system administrator. If an address is available, the new address should be selected as follows:

- The client's current address as recorded in the client's current binding, ELSE
- The client's previous address as recorded in the client's binding, if that address is in the server's pool of available addresses and not already allocated, ELSE
- The address requested in the *Requested IP Address* option, if that address is valid and not already allocated, ELSE
- A new address allocated from the server's pool of available addresses; the address is selected based on the subnet from which the message was received (if *giaddr* is 0) or on the address of the relay agent that forwarded the message (*giaddr* when not 0).

A server can assign an address other than the one requested or refuse to allocate an address to a particular client even though free addresses are available. In some network architectures (internets with more than one IP subnet assigned to a physical network segment) it may be that the DHCP client should be assigned an address from a different subnet than the address recorded in giaddr. Hence, DHCP does not require that the client be assigned an address from the subnet in giaddr. However, a server is free to choose some other subnet.

TABLE 17.2   Fields and Options Used by DHCP Servers

Field	DHCPOFFER	DHCPACK	DHCPNAK
op	BOOTREPLY	BOOTREPLY	BOOTREPLY
htype			
hlen	Hardware address length, octets		
hops	0	0	0
xid	xid from client DHCPDISCOVER message 0	xid from client DHCPREQUEST message 0	xid from client DHCPREQUEST message *secs* 0
ciaddr	0	ciaddr from DHCPREQUEST or 0	0
yiaddr	IP address offered to client	IP address assigned to client	0
siaddr	IP address of next bootstrap server	IP address of next bootstrap server	0
flags	flags from client DHCPDISCOVER message	flags from client DHCPREQUEST message	flags from client DHCPREQUEST message
giaddr	giaddr from client DHCPDISCOVER message	giaddr from client DHCPREQUEST message	giaddr from client DHCPREQUEST message
chaddr	chaddr from client HCPDISCOVER message	chaddr from client DHCPREQUEST message	chaddr from client DHCPREQUEST message
sname	Server host name or options	Server host name or options	Unused
file	Client boot file name or options	Client boot file name or options	Unused

Option	DHCPOFFER	DHCPACK	DHCPNAK
Requested IP address	MUST NOT	MUST NOT	MUST NOT
IP address lease time	MUST	MUST (DHCPREQUEST) MUST NOT (DHCPINFORM)	MUST NOT Use
file/sname fields	MAY	MAY	MUST NOT DHCP
Message type	DHCPOFFER	DHCPACK	DHCPNAK
Parameter request list	MUST NOT	MUST NOT	MUST
NOT Message	SHOULD	SHOULD	SHOULD
Client identifier	MUST NOT	MUST NOT	MAY
Vendor class identifier	MAY	MAY	MAY
Server identifier	MUST	MUST	MUST
Maximum message size	MUST NOT	MUST NOT	MUST NOT
All others	MAY	MAY	MUST NOT

While not required for correct operation of DHCP, the server should not reuse the selected network address before the client responds to the server's DHCPOFFER message. The server may choose to record the address as offered to the client.

The server must also choose an expiration time for the lease, as follows:

- IF the client has not requested a specific lease in the DHCPDISCOVER message and the client already has an assigned network address, the server returns the lease expiration time previously assigned to that address (note that the client must explicitly request a specific lease to extend the expiration time on a previously assigned address), ELSE

- IF the client has not requested a specific lease in the DHCPDISCOVER message and the client does not have an assigned network address, the server assigns a locally configured default lease time, ELSE

- IF the client has requested a specific lease in the DHCPDISCOVER message (regardless of whether the client has an assigned network address), the server may choose either to return the requested lease (if the lease is acceptable to local policy) or select another lease.

Once the network address and lease have been determined, the server constructs a DHCPOFFER message with the offered configuration parameters. It is important for all DHCP servers to return the same parameters (with the possible exception of a newly allocated network address) to ensure predictable client behavior regardless of which server the client selects. The configuration parameters must be selected by applying the following rules in the order given. The network administrator is responsible for configuring multiple DHCP servers to ensure uniform responses from those servers. The server MUST return to the client:

- The client's network address, as determined by the rules given earlier in this section.

- The expiration time for the client's lease, as determined by the rules given earlier in this section.

- Parameters requested by the client, according to the following rules:

    IF the server has been explicitly configured with a default value for the parameter, the server MUST include that value in an appropriate option in the *option* field, ELSE

    IF the server recognizes the parameter as a parameter defined in the Host Requirements Document, the server MUST include the default value for that parameter as given in the Host Requirements Document in an appropriate option in the *option* field, ELSE

The server MUST NOT return a value for that parameter, the server MUST supply as many of the requested parameters as possible and must omit any parameters it cannot provide.

- Any parameters from the existing binding that differ from the Host Requirements Document defaults.

- Any parameters specific to this client (as identified by the contents of *chaddr* or *client identifier* in the DHCPDISCOVER or DHCPRE-QUEST message); for example, as configured by the network administrator.

- Any parameters specific to this client's class (as identified by the contents of the *vendor class identifier* option in the DHCPDISCOVER or DHCPREQUEST message); for example, as configured by the network administrator. The parameters must be identified by an exact match between the client's vendor class identifiers and the client's classes identified in the server.

- Parameters with nondefault values on the client's subnet.

The server MAY choose to return the vendor class identifier used to determine the parameters in the DHCPOFFER message to assist the client in selecting which DHCPOFFER to accept. The server inserts the xid field from the DHCPDISCOVER message into the xid field of the DHCPOFFER message and sends the DHCPOFFER message to the requesting client.

DHCPREQUEST message

A DHCPREQUEST message may come from a client responding to a DHCPOFFER message from a server, from a client verifying a previously allocated IP address, or from a client extending the lease on a network address. If the DHCPREQUEST message contains a *server identifier* option, the message is in response to a DHCPOFFER message. Otherwise, the message is a request to verify or extend an existing lease. If the client uses a *client identifier* in a DHCPREQUEST message, it must use that same client identifier in all subsequent messages. If the client includes a list of requested parameters in a DHCPDISCOVER message, it MUST include that list in all subsequent messages.

Any configuration parameters in the DHCPACK message SHOULD NOT conflict with those in the earlier DHCPOFFER message to which the client is responding. The client SHOULD use the parameters in the DHCPACK message for configuration.

Clients send DHCPREQUEST messages like the following in the states they are in.

DHCPREQUEST generated during SELECTING. Client inserts the address of the selected server in *server identifier; ciaddr* must be zero; *requested IP address* must be filled in with the *yiaddr* value from the chosen DHCPOFFER.

The client may choose to collect several DHCPOFFER messages and select the best. A client indicates its selection by identifying the offering server in the DHCPREQUEST message. If the client receives no acceptable offers, the client may choose to try another DHCPDIS-COVER message. Therefore, the servers may not receive a specific DHCPREQUEST from which they can decide whether the client has accepted the offer. Because the servers have not committed any network address assignments on the basis of a DHCPOFFER, servers are free to reuse offered network addresses in response to subsequent requests. As an implementation detail, servers should not reuse offered addresses and may use an implementation-specific timeout mechanism to decide when to reuse an offered address.

DHCPREQUEST generated during INIT-REBOOT. *Server identifier* must not be filled in; *requested IP address* option must be filled in with the client's notion of its previously assigned address; *ciaddr* must be zero. The client is seeking to verify a previously allocated, cached configuration. The server should send a DHCPNAK message to the client if the requested IP address is incorrect, or is on the wrong network.

Determining whether a client in the INIT-REBOOT state is on the correct network is done by examining the contents of giaddr, the requested IP address option, and a database lookup. If the DHCP server detects that the client is on the wrong net, then the server should send a DHCPNAK message to the client.

If the network is correct, then the DHCP server should check if the client's notion of its IP address is correct. If not, then the server should send a DHCPNAK message to the client. If the DHCP server has no record of this client, then it must remain silent and can output a warning to the network administrator. This behavior is necessary for the peaceful coexistence of noncommunicating DHCP servers on the same wire.

If giaddr is 0x0 in the DHCPREQUEST message, the client is on the same subnet as the server. The server must broadcast the DHCPNAK message to the 0xffffffff broadcast address because the client may not have a correct network address or subnet mask, and the client may not be answering ARP requests.

If giaddr is set in the DHCPREQUEST message, the client is on a different subnet. The server MUST set the broadcast bit in the DHCP-NAK so that the relay agent will broadcast the DHCPNAK to the client, because the client may not have a correct network address or subnet mask, and the client may not be answering ARP requests.

DHCPREQUEST generated during RENEWING. A *server identifier* must not be filled in; *requested IP address* option must not be filled in; *ciaddr* must be filled in with the client's IP address. In this situation, the client is completely configured and is trying to extend its lease. This message will be unicast, so no relay agents will be involved in its transmission. Because giaddr is, therefore, not filled in, the DHCP server will trust the value in ciaddr and use it when replying to the client.

A client MAY choose to renew or extend its lease prior to T1. The server may choose not to extend the lease, but should return a DHCPACK message regardless.

DHCPREQUEST generated during REBINDING. The *server identifier* must not be filled in; *requested IP address* option must not be filled in; *ciaddr* must be filled in with the client's IP address. In this situation, the client is completely configured and is trying to extend its lease. This message must be broadcast to the 0xffffffff IP broadcast address. The DHCP server should check ciaddr for correctness before replying to the DHCPREQUEST.

The DHCPREQUEST from a REBINDING client is intended to accommodate sites that have multiple DHCP servers and a mechanism for maintaining consistency among leases managed by multiple servers. A DHCP server MAY extend a client's lease only if it has local administrative authority to do so.

DHCPDECLINE message

If the server receives a DHCPDECLINE message, the client has discovered through some other means that the suggested network address is already in use. The server MUST mark the network address as not available and SHOULD notify the local system administrator of a possible configuration problem.

DHCPRELEASE message

Upon receipt of a DHCPRELEASE message, the server marks the network address as not allocated. The server SHOULD retain a record of the client's initialization parameters for possible reuse in response to subsequent requests from the client.

DHCPINFORM message

The server responds to a DHCPINFORM message by sending a DHCPACK message directly to the address given in the *ciaddr* field of the

DHCPINFORM message. The server must not send a lease expiration time to the client and should not fill in *yiaddr*.

Client messages

Consider the following example of differences between messages from clients in various states.

	INIT-REBOOT	SELECTING	RENEWING	REBINDING
broad/unicast	broadcast	broadcast	unicast	broadcast
server-ip	MUST NOT	MUST	MUST NOT	MUST NOT
requested-ip	MUST	MUST	MUST NOT	MUST NOT
ciaddr	zero	zero	IP address	IP address

17.10   DHCP Client Function

A DHCP client can receive the following messages from a server:

- DHCPOFFER
- DHCPACK
- DHCPNAK

The remainder of this section describes the action of the DHCP client for each possible incoming message.

The client begins in INIT state and forms a DHCPDISCOVER message. The client SHOULD wait a random time between 1 and 10s to desynchronize the use of DHCP at startup. The client sets *ciaddr* to 0x00000000. The client MAY request specific parameters by including the *parameter request list* option. The client may suggest a network address and/or lease time by including the *requested IP address* and *IP address lease time* options. The client must include its hardware address in the *chaddr* field, if necessary for delivery of DHCP reply messages. The client can include a different unique identifier in the *client identifier* option. If the client included a list of requested parameters in a DHCPDISCOVER message, it must include the list in all subsequent messages.

The client generates and records a random transaction identifier and inserts that identifier into the *xid* field. The client records its own local time for later use in computing the lease expiration. The client then broadcasts the DHCPDISCOVER on the local hardware broadcast address to the 0xffffffff IP broadcast address and *DHCP server* UDP port.

If the xid of an arriving DHCPOFFER message does not match the xid of the most recent DHCPDISCOVER message, the DHCPOFFER message must be silently discarded. Any arriving DHCPACK messages must be silently discarded.

The client collects DHCPOFFER messages over a period of time, selects one DHCPOFFER message from the incoming DHCPOFFER messages, and extracts the server address from the server identifier option in the DHCPOFFER message. The time over which the client collects messages and the mechanism used to select one DHCPOFFER are implementation-dependent.

If parameters are acceptable, the client records the address of the server that supplied the parameters from the server identifier field and sends that address in the server identifier field of a DHCPRE-QUEST broadcast message. Once the DHCPACK message from the server arrives, the client is initialized and moves to BOUND state. The DHCPREQUEST message contains the same xid as the DHCPOFFER message. The client records the lease expiration time as the sum of the time at which the original request was sent and the duration of the lease from the DHCPACK message. The client should perform a check on the suggested address to ensure that the address is not already in use. For example, if the client is on a network that supports ARP, the client may issue an ARP request for the suggested request. When broadcasting an ARP request for the suggested address, the client must fill in its own hardware address as the sender's hardware address, and 0 as the sender's IP address, to avoid confusing ARP caches in other hosts on the same subnet. If the network address appears to be in use, the client MUST send a DHCPDECLINE message to the server. The client SHOULD broadcast an ARP reply to announce the client's new IP address and clear any outdated ARP cache entries in hosts on the client's subnet.

Initialization with a known network address

The client begins in INIT-REBOOT state and sends a DHCPRE-QUEST message. The client must insert its known network address as a *requested IP address* option in the DHCPREQUEST message. The client may request specific configuration parameters by including the *parameter request list* option. The client generates and records a random transaction identifier and inserts that identifier into the *xid* field. The client records its own local time for later use in computing the lease expiration. The client must not include a *server identifier* in the DHCPREQUEST message. The client then broadcasts the DHCPRE-QUEST on the local hardware broadcast address to the *DHCP server* UDP port.

Once a DHCPACK message with an xid field matching that in the client's DHCPREQUEST message arrives from any server, the client is initialized and moves to BOUND state. The client records the lease expiration time as the sum of the time at which the DHCPREQUEST message was sent and the duration of the lease from the DHCPACK message.

Initialization with external assigned network addresses

The client sends a DHCPINFORM message. The client may request specific configuration parameters by including the *parameter request list* option. The client generates and records a random transaction identifier and inserts that identifier into the *xid* field. The client places its own network address in the *ciaddr* field. The client should not request lease time parameters.

The client then unicasts the DHCPINFORM to the DHCP server if it knows the server's address; otherwise, it broadcasts the message to the limited (all ones) broadcast address. DHCPINFORM messages must be directed to the *DHCP server* UDP port.

Once a DHCPACK message with an xid field matching that in the client's DHCPINFORM message arrives from any server, the client is initialized.

Use of broadcast and unicast

The DHCP client broadcasts DHCPDISCOVER, DHCPREQUEST, and DHCPINFORM messages, unless the client knows the address of a DHCP server. The client unicasts DHCPRELEASE messages to the server. Because the client is declining the use of the IP address supplied by the server, the client broadcasts DHCPDECLINE messages.

When the DHCP client knows the address of a DHCP server, in either INIT or REBOOTING state, the client may use that address in the DHCPDISCOVER or DHCPREQUEST rather than the IP broadcast address. The client may also use unicast to send DHCPINFORM messages to a known DHCP server. If the client receives no response to DHCP messages sent to the IP address of a known DHCP server, the DHCP client reverts to using the IP broadcast address.

Reacquisition and expiration

The client maintains two times, T1 and T2, that specify the times at which the client tries to extend its lease on its network address. *T1* is the time at which the client enters the RENEWING state and attempts to contact the server that originally issued the client's network address. *T2* is the time at which the client enters the REBINDING state and attempts to contact any server. T1 must be earlier than T2, which, in turn, MUST be earlier than the time at which the client's lease will expire.

To avoid the need for synchronized clocks, T1 and T2 are expressed in options as relative times. At time T1 the client moves to RENEWING state and sends (via unicast) a DHCPREQUEST message to the server to extend its lease. The client sets the *ciaddr* field in the DHCPRE-QUEST to its current network address. The client records the local time at which the DHCPREQUEST message is sent for computation of the lease expiration time. The client MUST NOT include a *server iden-tifier* in the DHCPREQUEST message.

Any DHCPACK messages that arrive with an *xid* that does not match the xid of the client's DHCPREQUEST message are silently dis-carded. When the client receives a DHCPACK from the server, the client computes the lease expiration time as the sum of the time at which the client sent the DHCPREQUEST message and the duration of the lease in the DHCPACK message. The client has successfully reacquired its network address, returns to BOUND state and may con-tinue network processing.

If no DHCPACK arrives before time T2, the client moves to REBINDING state and sends (via broadcast) a DHCPREQUEST mes-sage to extend its lease. The client sets the ciaddr field in the DHCPREQUEST to its current network address. The client MUST NOT include a server identifier in the DHCPREQUEST message.

Times T1 and T2 are configurable by the server through options. T1 defaults to (0.5 * duration_of_lease). T2 defaults to (0.875 * dura-tion_of_lease). Times T1 and T2 should be chosen with some random fuzz around a fixed value, to avoid synchronization of client reacqui-sition.

A client can choose to renew or extend its lease prior to T1. The server can choose to extend the client's lease according to policy set by the network administrator. The server SHOULD return T1 and T2, and their values SHOULD be adjusted from their original values to take account of the time remaining on the lease.

In both RENEWING and REBINDING states, if the client receives no response to its DHCPREQUEST message, the client SHOULD wait one-half of the remaining time until T2 (in RENEWING state) and one-half of the remaining lease time (in REBINDING state), down to a min-imum of 60 s, before retransmitting the DHCPREQUEST message.

If the lease expires before the client receives a DHCPACK, the client moves to INIT state, MUST immediately stop any other network pro-cessing and requests network initialization parameters as if the client were uninitialized. If the client then receives a DHCPACK allocating that client its previous network address, the client should continue network processing. If the client is given a new network address, it must not continue using the previous network address and should notify the local users of the problem.

DHCPRELEASE

If the client no longer requires the use of its assigned network address, the client sends a DHCPRELEASE message to the server. Note that the correct operation of DHCP does not depend on the transmission of DHCPRELEASE messages.

17.11   Summary

This chapter presents information for those who require detail in the planning and design of TCP/IP networks. The information can also be used in the detailed planning of Windows NT networks.

Network Design and
the Domain Name System

The original motive for the development of the domain system was the growth in the Internet, and the following were considerations:

1. Host name to address mappings were maintained by the Network Information Center (NIC) in a single file (HOSTS.TXT) that was FTPed by all hosts (RFC 952 and 953).

2. The bandwidth consumed in distributing a new version by this scheme is proportional to the square of the number of hosts in the network, and even when multiple levels of FTP are used, the outgoing FTP load on the NIC host is considerable. Explosive growth in the number of hosts didn't lend itself to ease of distribution.

3. The network population was also changing in character. The time-shared hosts that made up the original ARPAnet were being replaced with local networks of workstations.

4. Local organizations were administering their own names and addresses, but had to wait for the NIC to change HOSTS.TXT to make changes visible to the Internet at large. Organizations also wanted some local structure on the name space.

5. The applications on the Internet were getting more sophisticated, creating a need for general-purpose name service.

6. The result was several ideas about name spaces and their management (IEN 116; RFCs 799, 819, and 830). Proposals varied, but a common thread was the idea of a hierarchical name space, with the hierarchy roughly corresponding to organizational structure, and names using "." as the character to mark the boundary between

hierarchy levels. A design using a distributed database and generalized resources was described in RFCs 882 and 883. Based on experience with several implementations, the system evolved into the scheme described here.

The terms *domain* or *domain name* are used in many contexts beyond the DNS explained in this text. Often, the term *domain name* refers to a name with the structure indicated by dots, but bears no relation to the DNS.

18.1 DNS Design Goals

The design goals of the DNS influence its structure. They are as follows:

- The primary goal is a consistent name space that will be used for referring to resources. In order to avoid the problems caused by ad hoc encodings, names should not be required to contain network identifiers, addresses, routes, or similar information as part of the name.

- The sheer size of the database and the frequency of updates suggest that the database must be maintained in a distributed manner, with local caching to improve performance. Approaches that attempt to collect a consistent copy of the entire database will become more and more expensive and difficult; hence, they should be avoided. The same principle holds for the structure of the name space, and in particular for mechanisms for creating and deleting names; these should also be distributed.

- Where there are tradeoffs between the cost of acquiring data, the speed of updates, and the accuracy of caches, the source of the data should control the tradeoff.

- The costs of implementing such a facility dictate that it be generally useful, and not restricted to a single application. We should be able to use names to retrieve host addresses, mailbox data, and other as yet undetermined information. All data associated with a name is tagged with a type, and queries can be limited to a single type.

- Because the purpose is to use the naming wisely, across dissimilar networks and applications, we provide the ability to use the same name space with different protocol families or management. For example, host address formats differ between protocols, though all protocols have the notion of address. The DNS tags all data with a class as well as the type, so that we can allow parallel use of different formats for data of type address.

- We want name server transactions to be independent of the communications system that carries them. Some systems may wish to use datagrams for queries and responses, and establish virtual circuits only for transactions that need the reliability (e.g., database updates and long transactions); other systems will use virtual circuits exclusively.

- The system should be useful across a wide spectrum of host capabilities. Both personal computers and large timeshared hosts should be able to use the system, though perhaps in different ways.

18.2 Assumptions About DNS Usage

The organization of the domain system derives from some assumptions about the needs and usage patterns of its user community and is designed to avoid many of the complicated problems found in general-purpose database systems. Assumptions here include the following:

1. The size of the total database will initially be proportional to the number of hosts using the system, but will eventually grow to be proportional to the number of users on those hosts as mailboxes and other information are added to the domain system.

2. Most of the data in the system will change very slowly (e.g., mailbox bindings and host addresses), but the system should be able to deal with subsets that change more rapidly (on the order of seconds or minutes).

3. The administrative boundaries used to distribute responsibility for the database will usually correspond to organizations that have one or more hosts. Each organization that has responsibility for a particular set of domains will provide redundant name servers, either on the organization's own hosts or on other hosts that the organization arranges to use.

4. Clients of the domain system should be able to identify trusted name servers they prefer to use before accepting referrals to name servers outside of this trusted set.

5. Access to information is more critical than instantaneous updates or guarantees of consistency. Hence, the update process allows updates to percolate out through the users of the domain system rather than guaranteeing that all copies are simultaneously updated. When updates are unavailable due to network or host failure, the usual course is to believe old information while continuing efforts to update it. The general model is that copies are distributed with timeouts for refreshing. The distributor sets the timeout value, and the recipient of the distribution is responsible for performing the refresh. In special situations, very short intervals can be specified, or the owner can prohibit copies.

6. In any system that has a distributed database, a particular name server may be presented with a query that can be answered only

by some other server. The two general approaches to dealing with this problem are *recursive,* in which the first server pursues the query for the client at another server, and *iterative,* in which the server refers the client to another server and lets the client pursue the query. Both approaches have advantages and disadvantages, but the iterative approach is preferred for the datagram style of access. The domain system requires implementation of the iterative approach, but allows the recursive approach as an option.

7. The domain system assumes that all data originates in master files scattered through the hosts that use the domain system. These master files are updated by local system administrators. Master files are text files that are read by a local name server and, hence, become available through the name servers to users of the domain system. The user programs access name servers through standard programs called *resolvers.*

8. The standard format of master files allows them to be exchanged between hosts (via FTP, mail, or some other mechanism); this facility is useful when an organization wants a domain, but doesn't want to support a name server. The organization can maintain the master files locally using a text editor, transfer them to a foreign host that runs a name server, and then arrange with the system administrator of the name server to get the files loaded.

9. Each host's name servers and resolvers are configured by a local system administrator (RFC 1033). For a name server, this configuration data includes the identity of local master files and instructions on which nonlocal master files are to be loaded from foreign servers. The name server uses the master files or copies to load its zones. For resolvers, the configuration data identifies the name servers that should be the primary sources of information.

10. The domain system defines procedures for accessing the data and for referrals to other name servers. The domain system also defines procedures for caching retrieved data and for periodic refreshing of data defined by the system administrator.

    A system administrator provides the following:

    - The definition of zone boundaries
    - Master files of data
    - Updates to master files
    - Statements of the refresh policies desired

    The domain system provides the following:

    - Standard formats for resource data
    - Standard methods for querying the database

- Standard methods for name servers to refresh local data from foreign name servers

18.3 Elements of DNS

The DNS has three major components: domain name space and resource records, name servers, and resolvers.

Domain name space and resource records. These are specifications for a tree-structured name space and the data associated with the names. Conceptually, each node and leaf of the domain name space tree names a set of information, and *query operations* are attempts to extract specific types of information from a particular set. A query names the domain name of interest and describes the type of resource information that is desired. For example, the Internet uses some of its domain names to identify hosts; queries for address resources return Internet host addresses.

Name servers. These are server programs that hold information about the domain tree's structure and set information. A name server may cache structure or set information about any part of the domain tree, but, in general, a particular name server has complete information about a subset of the domain space and *pointers* to other name servers that can be used to lead to information from any part of the domain tree. Name servers know the parts of the domain tree for which they have complete information; a name server is said to be an *authority* for these parts of the name space. Authoritative information is organized into units called *zones,* and these zones can be automatically distributed to the name servers that provide redundant service for the data in a zone.

Resolvers. These are programs that extract information from name servers in response to client requests. Resolvers must be able to access at least one name server and use that name server's information to answer a query directly or be able to pursue the query using referrals to other name servers. A resolver will typically be a system routine that is directly accessible to user programs; hence, no protocol is necessary between the resolver and the user program.

These three components roughly correspond to the three layers or views of the domain system. Consider the following detailed explanation that correlates this:

- From the *user's* point of view, the domain system is accessed through a simple procedure or OS call to a local resolver.

- The domain space consists of a single tree, and the user can request information from any section of the tree.

- From the *resolver's* point of view, the domain system is composed of an unknown number of name servers. Each name server has one or more pieces of the whole domain tree's data, but the resolver views each of these databases as essentially static.

- From a *name server's* point of view, the domain system consists of separate sets of local information called *zones*. The name server has local copies of some of the zones. The name server must periodically refresh its zones from master copies in local files or foreign name servers. The name server must concurrently process queries that arrive from resolvers.

In the interests of performance, implementations may couple these functions. For example, a resolver on the same machine as a name server might share a database consisting of the zones managed by the name server and the cache managed by the resolver.

18.4   Domain Name Space and Resource Records

The domain name space is a tree structure. Each node and leaf on the tree corresponds to a resource set (which may be empty). The domain system makes no distinctions between the uses of the interior nodes and leaves, and this memo uses the term *node* to refer to both. Each node has a label, which is 0 to 63 octets in length. Brother nodes may not have the same label, although the same label can be used for nodes that are not brothers. One label is reserved, and that is the null (i.e., zero length) label used for the *root*.

The domain name of a node is the list of the labels on the path from the node to the root of the tree. By convention, the labels that compose a domain name are printed or read left to right, from the most specific (lowest, farthest from the root) to the least specific (highest, closest to the root).

Internally, programs that manipulate domain names should represent them as sequences of labels, where each label is a length octet followed by an octet string. Because all domain names end at the root, which has a null string for a label, these internal representations can use a length byte of 0 to terminate a domain name.

By convention, domain names can be stored with arbitrary case, but domain name comparisons for all present domain functions are done in a case-insensitive manner, assuming an ASCII character set and a high-order zero bit. This means that you are free to create a node with label *A* or a node with label *a,* but not both as brothers; you could refer to either using *a* or *A.* When you receive a domain name or label, you should preserve its case. The rationale for this choice is that we may someday need to add full binary domain names for new services; existing services would not be changed.

When a user needs to type a domain name, the length of each label is omitted and the labels are separated by dots (.). Since a complete domain name ends with the root label, this leads to a printed form that ends in a dot. We use this property to distinguish between the following:

- A character string that represents a complete domain name (often called *absolute*). For example, *joejones.ISI.EDU.*

- A character string that represents the starting labels of a domain name that is incomplete and should be completed by local software using knowledge of the local domain (often called *relative*). For example, *joejones* used in the ISI.EDU domain.

Relative names are taken relative to either a well-known origin or to a list of domains used as a search list. Relative names appear mostly at the user interface, where their interpretation varies from implementation to implementation, and in master files, where they are relative to a single origin domain name. The most common interpretation uses the root "." as either the single origin or as one of the members of the search list, so a multilabel relative name is often one where the trailing dot has been omitted to save typing.

To simplify implementations, the total number of octets that represent a domain name (i.e., the sum of all label octets and label lengths) is limited to 255. A domain is identified by a domain name, and consists of that part of the domain name space that is at or below the domain name that specifies the domain. A domain is a subdomain of another domain if it is contained within that domain. This relationship can be tested by seeing if the subdomain's name ends with the containing domain's name. For example, *A.B.C.D* is a subdomain of *B.C.D, C.D, D,* and " ".

DNS technical specifications do not mandate a particular tree structure or rules for selecting labels; DNS's goal is to be as general as possible, so that it can be used to build arbitrary applications. In particular, the system was designed so that the name space does not have to be organized along the lines of network boundaries, name servers, and so on. The rationale for this is not that the name space should have no implied semantics, but rather that the choice of implied semantics should be left open to be used for the problem at hand and that different parts of the tree can have different implied semantics. For example, the *IN-ADDR.ARPA* domain is organized and distributed by network and host address because its role is to translate from network or host numbers to names; *NetBIOS* domains (RFCs 1001 and 1002) are flat because that is appropriate for that application.

However, there are some guidelines that apply to the normal parts of the name space used for hosts, mailboxes, and so on that will make the name space more uniform, provide for growth, and minimize problems as software is converted from the older host table. The political decisions about the top levels of the tree originated in RFC 920. Current policy for the top levels is discussed in RFC 1032. MILNET conversion issues are covered in RFC 1031.

Lower domains that will eventually be broken into multiple zones should provide branching at the top of the domain so that the eventual decomposition can be done without renaming. Node labels that use special characters, leading digits, and so on are likely to break older software that depends on more restrictive choices.

Before the DNS can be used to hold naming information for some kind of object, two needs must be met:

1. A convention for mapping between object names and domain names. This describes how information about an object is accessed.

2. RR types and data formats for describing the object.

These rules can be quite simple or fairly complex. Very often, the designer must take into account existing formats and plan for upward compatibility for existing usage. Multiple mappings or levels of mapping may be required. For hosts, the mapping depends on the existing syntax for host names, which is a subset of the usual text representation for domain names, together with RR formats for describing host addresses and so on. Because we need a reliable inverse mapping from address to host name, a special mapping for addresses into the IN-ADDR.ARPA domain is also defined.

For mailboxes, the mapping is slightly more complex. The usual mail address *<local-part>@<mail-domain>* is mapped into a domain name by converting *<local-part>* into a single label (regardless of dots it contains), converting <mail-domain> into a domain name using the usual text format for domain names (dots denote label breaks), and concatenating the two to form a single domain name. Thus, the mailbox *HOSTMASTER@SRI-NIC.ARPA* is represented as a domain name by *HOSTMASTER.SRI-NIC.ARPA*. An appreciation for the reasons behind this design also must take into account the scheme for mail exchanges (RFC 974).

A typical user is not concerned with defining these rules, but should understand that they are usually the result of numerous compromises between desires for upward compatibility with old usage, interactions between different object definitions, and the inevitable urge to add new features when defining the rules. The way the DNS is used to support some object is often more crucial than the restrictions inherent in the DNS.

The following figure shows a part of the current domain name space and is used in many examples in this RFC. Note that the tree is a very small subset of the actual name space.

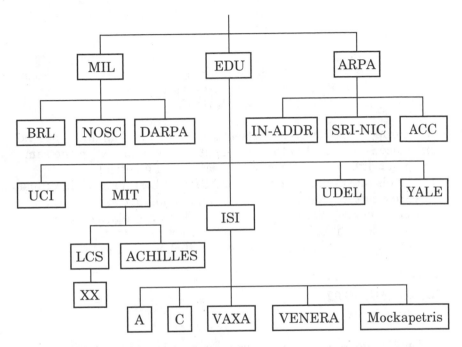

In this example, the root domain has three immediate subdomains: *MIL, EDU,* and *ARPA*. The LCS.MIT.EDU domain has one immediate subdomain, named *XX.LCS.MIT.EDU*. All of the leaves are also domains.

18.5   DNS Name Syntax

The DNS specifications attempt to be as general as possible in the rules for constructing domain names. The idea is that the name of any existing object can be expressed as a domain name with minimal changes. However, when assigning a domain name for an object, the prudent user will select a name that satisfies both the rules of the domain system and any existing rules for the object, whether these rules are published or implied by existing programs. For example, when naming a mail domain, the user should satisfy both the rules presented here and those in RFC 822. When creating a new host name, the old rules for HOSTS.TXT should be followed. This avoids problems when old software is converted to use domain names.

The following syntax will result in fewer problems with many applications that use domain names (e.g., mail and TELNET).

```
<domain> ::= <subdomain> | " "
<subdomain> ::= <label> | <subdomain> "." <label>
<label> ::= <letter> [ [ <ldh-str> ] <let-dig> ]
<ldh-str> ::= <let-dig-hyp> | <let-dig-hyp> <ldh-str>
<let-dig-hyp> ::= <let-dig> | "-"
<let-dig> ::= <letter> | <digit>
<letter> ::= Any one of the 52 alphabetic characters A through
             Z in uppercase and a through z in lowercase
<digit> ::= Any one of the 10 digits 0 through 9
```

While upper- and lowercase letters are allowed in domain names, no significance is attached to the case. That is, two names with the same spelling but different case are to be treated as if identical.

The labels must follow the rules for ARPAnet host names. They must start with a letter, end with a letter or digit, and have as interior characters only letters, digits, and hyphens. There are also some restrictions on the length. Labels must be 63 characters or less.

For example, the following strings identify hosts in the Internet:

A.ISI.EDU

XX.LCS.MIT.EDU

SRI-NIC.ARPA

A domain name identifies a node. Each node has a set of resource information, which may be empty. The set of resource information associated with a particular name is composed of separate resource records (RRs). The order of RRs in a set is not significant, and need not be preserved by name servers, resolvers, or other parts of the DNS.

When we talk about a specific RR, we assume that it has the following:

OWNER: The domain name where the RR is found.

TYPE: An encoded 16-bit value that specifies the type of the resource in this resource record. Types refer to abstract resources.

18.6   DNS Queries

Queries are messages that may be sent to a name server to provoke a response. In the Internet, queries are carried in UDP datagrams or over TCP connections. The response by the name server either answers the question posed in the query, refers the requester to another set of name servers, or signals some error condition.

In general, the user does not generate queries directly, but instead makes a request to a resolver, which, in turn, sends one or more queries to name servers and deals with the error conditions and referrals that may result. Of course, the possible questions that can be asked in a query do shape the kind of service a resolver can provide.

DNS queries and responses are carried in a standard message format. The message format has a *header*, containing a number of fixed fields that are always present, and four *sections*, which carry query parameters and RRs.

The most important field in the header is a 4-bit field called an *opcode*, which separates different queries. Of the possible 16 values, 1 (standard query) is part of the official protocol, 2 (inverse query and status query) are options, 1 (completion) is obsolete, and the rest are unassigned.

The four sections are as follow:

Question.   Carries the query name and other query parameters.

Answer.   Carries RRs that directly answer the query.

Authority.   Carries RRs that describe other authoritative servers. May optionally carry the SOA RR for the authoritative data in the answer section.

Additional.   Carries RRs that may be helpful in using the RRs in the other sections.

18.7   Standard DNS Queries

A standard query specifies a target *domain name* (QNAME), *query type* (QTYPE), and *query class* (QCLASS) and asks for RRs that match. This type of query makes up such a vast majority of DNS queries that we use the term *query* to mean standard query unless otherwise specified. The QTYPE and QCLASS fields are each 16 bits long, and are a superset of defined types and classes.

The QTYPE field may contain the following:

<any type>	Matches just that type. (e.g., A, and PTR)
AXFR	Special zone transfer QTYPE
MAILB	Matches all mailbox-related RRs (e.g. MB and MG)
*	Matches all RR types

The QCLASS field may contain the following:

<any class>	Matches just that class (e.g., IN, and CH)
*	Matches all RR classes.

The query domain name, QTYPE, and QCLASS use the name server to look for matching RRs. In addition to relevant records, the name server may return RRs that point toward a name server that has the desired information or RRs that are expected to be useful in interpreting the relevant RRs. For example, a name server that doesn't have the requested information may know a name server that does; a name server that returns a domain name in a relevant RR may also return the RR that binds that domain name to an address.

For example, a mailer trying to send mail to joejones@ISI.EDU might ask the resolver for mail information about ISI.EDU, resulting in a query for QNAME=ISI.EDU, QTYPE=MX, QCLASS=IN. The response's answer section would be:

```
ISI.EDU.   MX  10  VENERA.ISI.EDU.
           MX  10  VAXA.ISI.EDU.
```

An additional section might be:

```
VAXA.ISI.EDU.     A  10.2.0.27
                  A  128.9.0.33
VENERA.ISI.EDU.   A  10.1.0.52
                  A  128.9.0.32
```

This is because the server assumes that if the requester wants mail exchange information, it will probably want the addresses of the mail exchanges soon afterward. The QCLASS=* construct requires special interpretation regarding authority. Since a particular name server may not know all of the classes available in the domain system, it can never know if it is authoritative for all classes. Hence, responses to QCLASS=* queries can never be authoritative.

18.8   DNS Name Servers

Name servers are the repositories of information that make up the domain database. The database is divided up into sections called *zones,* which are distributed among the name servers. While name servers can have several optional functions and sources of data, the essential task of a name server is to answer queries using data in its zones. By design, name servers can answer queries in a simple manner; the response can always be generated using only local data, and contains either the answer to the question or a referral to other name servers that are closer to the desired information.

A given zone will be available from several name servers to ensure its availability in spite of host or communication link failure. By administrative fiat, we require every zone to be available on at least two servers, and many zones have more redundancy than that.

A given name server will typically support one or more zones, but this gives it authoritative information about only a small section of the domain tree. It may also have some cached nonauthoritative data about other parts of the tree. The name server marks its responses to queries so that the requester can tell whether the response comes from authoritative data or not.

DNS Database zone division

The domain database is partitioned in two ways: by *class,* and by *cuts* made in the name space between nodes. The class partition is simple. The database for any class is organized, delegated, and maintained separately from all other classes. Since, by convention, the name spaces are the same for all classes, the separate classes can be thought of as an array of parallel namespace trees. Note that the data attached to nodes will be different for these different parallel classes. The most common reasons for creating a new class are the necessity for a new data format for existing types or a desire for a separately managed version of the existing name space. Within a class, cuts in the name space can be made between any two adjacent nodes. After all cuts are made, each group of connected name space is a separate zone. The zone is said to be authoritative for all names in the connected region. Note that the cuts in the name space may be in different places for different classes, the name servers may be different, and so forth.

This means that every zone has at least one node—and, hence, domain name—for which it is authoritative, and all of the nodes in a particular zone are connected. Given the tree structure, every zone has a highest node that is closer to the root than any other node in the zone. The name of this node is often used to identify the zone.

It would be possible, though not particularly useful, to partition the name space so that each domain name was in a separate zone or so that all nodes were in a single zone. Instead, the database is partitioned at points where a particular organization wants to take over control of a subtree. Once an organization controls its own zone it can unilaterally change the data in the zone, grow new tree sections connected to the zone, delete existing nodes, or delegate new subzones under its zone.

If the organization has substructure, it may want to make further internal partitions to achieve nested delegations of name space control. In some cases, such divisions are made purely to make database maintenance more convenient.

The data that describes a zone has four major parts:

1. Authoritative data for all nodes within the zone

2. Data that defines the top node of the zone (can be thought of as part of the authoritative data)

3. Data that describes delegated subzones (i.e., cuts around the bottom of the zone)

4. Data that allows access to name servers for subzones, sometimes called *glue* data

All of this data is expressed in the form of RRs, so a zone can be completely described in terms of a set of RRs. Whole zones can be transferred between name servers by transferring the RRs, either carried in a series of messages or by FTPing a master file that is a textual representation. The authoritative data for a zone is simply all of the RRs attached to all of the nodes, from the top node of the zone down to leaf nodes or nodes above cuts around the bottom edge of the zone.

Though logically part of the authoritative data, the RRs that describe the top node of the zone are especially important to the zone's management. These RRs are of two types: name server RRs that list, one per RR, all of the servers for the zone, and a single SOA RR that describes zone management parameters. The RRs that describe cuts around the bottom of the zone are NS RRs that name the servers for the subzones. Since the cuts are between nodes, these RRs are *not* part of the authoritative data of the zone, and should be exactly the same as the corresponding RRs in the top node of the subzone. Since name servers are always associated with zone boundaries, NS RRs are only found at nodes that are the top node of some zone.

The data that makes up a zone, NS RRs are found at the top node of the zone (and are authoritative) and at cuts around the bottom of the zone (where they are not authoritative), but never in between. One of the goals of the zone structure is that any zone must have all the data required to set up communications with the name servers for any subzones. That is, parent zones have all the information needed to access servers for their children zones. The NS RRs that name the servers for subzones are often not enough for this task, since they name the servers but do not give their addresses. In particular, if the name of the name server is itself in the subzone, we could be faced with the situation where the NS RRs tell us that in order to learn a name server's address, we should contact the server using the address we wish to learn. To fix this problem, a zone contains *glue* RRs, which are not part of the authoritative data and are address RRs for the servers. These RRs are only necessary if the name server's name is below the cut, and they are only used as part of a referral response.

DNS administration considerations

When some organization wants to control its own domain, the first step is to identify the proper parent zone and get the parent zone's owners to agree to the delegation of control. While there are no particular technical constraints dealing with where in the tree this can be done, there are some administrative groupings discussed in RFC 1032 that deal with top-level organization, and middle-level zones are free to create their own rules. For example, one university might choose to use a single zone, while another might choose to organize by subzones dedicated to individual departments or schools. RFC 1033 catalogs available DNS software and discusses administration procedures.

Once the proper name for the new subzone is selected, the new owners should be required to demonstrate redundant name server support. Note that there is no requirement that the servers for a zone reside in a host that has a name in that domain. In many cases, a zone will be more accessible to the internet at large if its servers are widely distributed rather than being within the physical facilities controlled by the same organization that manages the zone. For example, in the current DNS, one of the name servers for the United Kingdom, or UK domain, is found in the United States. This allows US hosts to get UK data without using limited transatlantic bandwidth.

As the last installation step, the delegation NS RRs and glue RRs necessary to make the delegation effective should be added to the parent zone. The administrators of both zones should ensure that the NS and glue RRs that mark both sides of the cut are consistent and remain so.

The principal activity of name servers is to answer standard queries. Both the query and its response are carried in a standard message format, which is described in RFC 1035. The query contains a QTYPE, QCLASS, and QNAME, that describe the types and classes of desired information and the name of interest.

The way that the name server answers the query depends upon whether it is operating in recursive mode or not, as follows:

- The simplest mode for the server is *nonrecursive,* since it can answer queries using only local information: the response contains an error, the answer, or a referral to some other server that is closer to the answer. All name servers must implement nonrecursive queries.

- The simplest mode for the client is *recursive,* since in this mode the name server acts in the role of a resolver and returns either an error or the answer, but never referrals. This service is optional in a name server, and the name server may also choose to restrict the clients that can use recursive mode.

Recursive service is helpful in several situations, as follows:

- A relatively simple requester that lacks the ability to use anything other than a direct answer to the question

- A request that needs to cross protocol or other boundaries and can be sent to a server that can act as intermediary

- A network where we want to concentrate the cache rather than having a separate cache for each client

Nonrecursive service is appropriate if the requester is capable of pursuing referrals and is interested in information that will aid future requests. The use of recursive mode is limited to cases where both the client and the name server agree to its use. The agreement is negotiated through the use of two bits in query and response messages, as follows:

- The *recursion available,* or RA bit, is set or cleared by a name server in all responses. The bit is *true* if the name server is willing to provide recursive service for the client, regardless of whether the client requested recursive service. That is, RA signals availability rather than use.

- Queries contain a bit called *recursion desired,* or RD. This bit specifies whether the requester wants recursive service for this query. Clients may request recursive service from any name server, though they should depend upon receiving it only from servers that have previously sent an RA, or from servers that have agreed to provide service through private agreement or some other means outside of the DNS protocol.

The recursive mode occurs when a query with RD set arrives at a server that is willing to provide recursive service; the client can verify that recursive mode was used by checking that both RA and RD are set in the reply. Note that the name server should never perform recursive service unless asked via RD, since this interferes with troubleshooting of name servers and their databases.

If recursive service is requested and available, the recursive response to a query will be one of the following:

- The answer to the query, possibly prefaced by one or more CNAME RRs that specify aliases encountered on the way to an answer.

- A name error indicating that the name does not exist. This may include CNAME RRs that indicate that the original query name was an alias for a name that does not exist.

- A temporary error indication.

If recursive service is not requested or is not available, the nonrecursive response will be one of the following:

- An authoritative name error indicating that the name does not exist

- A temporary error indication

- Some combination of the following:

   RRs that answer the question, together with an indication whether the data comes from a zone or is cached

   A referral to name servers that have zones that are closer ancestors to the name than the server sending the reply

   RRs that the name server thinks will prove useful to the requester

18.9   DNS Resolvers

Resolvers are programs that interface user programs to domain name servers. In the simplest case, a resolver receives a request from a user program (e.g., mail programs, TELNET, and FTP) in the form of a subroutine call, system call, and so on, and returns the desired information in a form compatible with the local host's data formats.

The resolver is located on the same machine as the program that requests the resolver's services, but it may need to consult name servers on other hosts. Because a resolver may need to consult several name servers, or may have the requested information in a local cache, the amount of time that a resolver will take to complete can vary quite a bit, from milliseconds to several seconds.

Functions

One important goal of the resolver is to eliminate network delay and name server load from most requests by answering them from its cache of prior results. It follows that caches that are shared by multiple processes, users, machines, and so on are more efficient than nonshared caches.

The client-resolver interface to the resolver is influenced by the local host's conventions, but the typical resolver-client interface has three functions:

1. *Host name to host address translation.* This function is often defined to mimic a previous HOSTS.TXT-based function. Given a character string, the caller wants one or more 32-bit IP addresses. Under the DNS, this translates into a request for type A RRs. Since the DNS does not preserve the order of RRs, this function may choose to sort the returned addresses or select the "best" address if the service returns only one choice to the client. Note that a multiple address return is recommended, but a single address may be the only way to emulate prior HOSTS.TXT services.

2. *Host address to host name translation.* This function will often follow the form of previous functions. Given a 32-bit IP address, the caller wants a character string. The octets of the IP address are

reversed, used as name components, and suffixed with *IN-ADDR.ARPA*. A type PTR query is used to get the RR with the primary name of the host. For example, a request for the host name corresponding to IP address 1.2.3.4 looks for PTR RRs for domain name *4.3.2.1.IN-ADDR.ARPA*.

3. *General lookup function.*   This function retrieves arbitrary information from the DNS, and has no counterpart in previous systems. The caller supplies a QNAME, QTYPE, and QCLASS and wants all of the matching RRs. This function will often use the DNS format for all RR data instead of the local host's, and returns all RR content (e.g., TTL) instead of a processed form with local quoting conventions.

When the resolver performs the indicated function, it usually has one of the following results to pass back to the client:

- *One or more RRs giving the requested data.*   In this case, the resolver returns the answer in the appropriate format.

- *A name error (NE).*   This happens when the referenced name does not exist. For example, a user may have mistyped a host name.

- *A data not found error.*   This happens when the referenced name exists, but data of the appropriate type does not. For example, a host address function applied to a mailbox name would return this error since the name exists, but no address RR is present.

The functions for translating between host names and addresses may combine the *name error* and *data not found* error conditions into a single type of error return, but the general function should not. One reason for this is that applications may ask first for one type of information about a name followed by a second request to the same name for some other type of information; if the two errors are combined, then useless queries may slow the application.

Resources

In addition to its own resources, the resolver may also have shared access to zones maintained by a local name server. This gives the resolver the advantage of more rapid access, but the resolver must be careful to never let cached information override zone data. In this discussion the term *local information* is meant to mean the union of the cache and such shared zones, with the understanding that authoritative data is always used in preference to cached data when both are present.

The following resolver algorithm assumes that all functions have been converted to a general lookup function, and uses the following data structures to represent the state of a request in progress in the resolver:

SNAME: The domain name we are searching for.

STYPE: The QTYPE of the search request.

SCLASS: The QCLASS of the search request.

SLIST: A structure that describes the name servers and the zone that the resolver is currently trying to query. This structure keeps track of the resolver's current best guess about which name servers hold the desired information; it is updated when arriving information changes the guess. This structure includes the equivalent of a zone name, the known name servers for the zone, the known addresses for the name servers, and history information that can be used to suggest which error is likely to be the best one to try next. The zone name equivalent is a match count of the number of labels, from the root down, that SNAME has in common with the zone being queried; this is used as a measure of how close the resolver is to SNAME.

SBELT: A "safety belt" structure of the same form as SLIST, which is initialized from a configuration file and lists servers that should be used when the resolver doesn't have any local information to guide name server selection. The match count will be –1 to indicate that no labels are known to match.

CACHE: A structure that stores the results from previous responses. Since resolvers are responsible for discarding old RRs whose TTL has expired, most implementations convert the interval specified in arriving RRs to some sort of absolute time when the RR is stored in the cache. Instead of counting the TTLs down individually, the resolver just ignores or discards old RRs when it runs across them in the course of a search or discards them during periodic sweeps to reclaim the memory consumed by old RRs.

18.10   DNS Summary

The purpose of this chapter is to provide detailed information to those who are working with network design and need detailed information on the DNS. DNS is complex. Its design goal was to eliminate much of the work of updating the databases used in the 1980s. This chapter presents an overview of the DNS.

18.11   DNS References

Further information can be obtained from the following sources.

RFC 742   K. Harrenstien, "NAME/FINGER," Network Information Center, SRI International, December 1977.

RFC 768   J. Postel, "User Datagram Protocol," USC/Information Sciences Institute, August 1980.

RFC 793   J. Postel, "Transmission Control Protocol," USC/Information Sciences Institute, September 1981.

RFC 799   D. Mills, "Internet Name Domains," COMSAT, September 1981. Suggests introduction of a hierarchy in place of a flat name space for the Internet.

RFC 805   J. Postel, "Computer Mail Meeting Notes," USC/Information Sciences Institute, February 1982.

RFC 810   E. Feinler, K. Harrenstien, Z. Su, and V. White, "DOD Internet Host Table Specification," Network Information Center, SRI International, March 1982. (Obsolete; see RFC 952.)

RFC 811   K. Harrenstien, V. White, and E. Feinler, "Hostnames Server," Network Information Center, SRI International, March 1982. (Obsolete; see RFC 953).

RFC 812   K. Harrenstien and V. White, "NICNAME/WHOIS," Network Information Center, SRI International, March 1982.

RFC 819   Z. Su and J. Postel, "The Domain Naming Convention for Internet User Applications," Network Information Center, SRI International, August 1982. Early thoughts on the design of the domain system. The current implementation is completely different.

RFC 821   J. Postel, "Simple Mail Transfer Protocol," USC/Information Sciences Institute, August 1980.

RFC 830   Z. Su, "A Distributed System for Internet Name Service," Network Information Center, SRI International, October 1982. Early thoughts on the design of the domain system. The current implementation is completely different.

RFC 882   P. Mockapetris, "Domain Names—Concepts and Facilities," USC/Information Sciences Institute, November 1983.

RFC 883   P. Mockapetris, "Domain Names—Implementation and Specification," USC/Information Sciences Institute, November 1983.

RFC 920   J. Postel and J. Reynolds, "Domain Requirements," USC/Information Sciences Institute, October 1984. This explains the naming scheme for top-level domains.

RFC 952   K. Harrenstien, M. Stahl, and E. Feinler, "DOD Internet Host Table Specification," SRI, October 1985. Specifies the format of HOSTS.TXT, the host/address table replaced by the DNS.

RFC 953   K. Harrenstien, M. Stahl, and E. Feinler, "HOSTNAME Server," SRI, October 1985. This RFC contains the official specification of the hostname server protocol, which is obsoleted by the DNS. This TCP-based protocol accesses information stored in the RFC 952 format, and is used to obtain copies of the host table.

RFC 973   P. Mockapetris, "Domain System Changes and Observations," USC/Information Sciences Institute, January 1986.

Describes changes to RFC 882 and RFC 883 and the reasons for them. (Now obsolete).

RFC 974   C. Partridge, "Mail Routing and the Domain System," CSNET CIC BBN Labs, January 1986. Describes the transition from HOSTS.TXT-based mail addressing to the more powerful MX system used with the domain system.

RFC 1001   NetBIOS Working Group, "Protocol Standard for a NetBIOS Service on a TCP/UDP Transport: Concepts and Methods," March 1987. This RFC and RFC 1002 are a preliminary design for NETBIOS on top of TCP/IP that proposes to base NetBIOS name service on top of the DNS.

RFC 1002   NetBIOS Working Group, "Protocol Standard for a NetBIOS Service on a TCP/UDP Transport: Detailed Specifications," March 1987.

RFC 1010   J. Reynolds and J. Postel, "Assigned Numbers," USC/Information Sciences Institute, May 1987. Contains socket numbers and mnemonics for host names, operating systems, and so on.

RFC 1031   W. Lazear, "MILNET Name Domain Transition," November 1987. Describes a plan for converting the MILNET to the DNS.

RFC 1032   M. K. Stahl, "Establishing a Domain—Guidelines for Administrators," November 1987. Describes the registration policies used by the NIC to administer the top-level domains and delegate subzones.

RFC 1033   M. K. Lottor, "Domain Administrators Operations Guide," November 1987. A cookbook for domain administrators.

M. Solomon, L. Landweber, and D. Neuhengen, "The CSNET Name Server," *Computer Networks,* vol. 6, no. 3, July 1982. This describes a name service for CSNET that is independent from the DNS and from DNS use in the CSNET.

19

Designing NetWare Networks

NetWare is an upper-layer network protocol. It has grown into a mature, reputable network protocol that is capable of working with some of the largest systems available. Examples of how NetWare can operate with such large systems is covered in this chapter, but first a look at its past provides intriguing angles about the network protocol that may not be commonly known. Even today, with Windows 95, Windows 98, and Windows NT, Netware is supported.

19.1 Perspective

Novell was organized in 1983, according to the 1990 *NetWare Buyer's Guide.* In 11 years the company went from just being started (and being, in many ways, a pioneer in the industry) to buying the WordPerfect Corporation. Not bad, in anybody's book. During that timeframe, Novell made strategic moves. Quite simply, it kept changing and enhancing its product along with the rest of the industry; however, in many ways it charted its own course. For example, it was one of the first to provide media independence for its file server. This kind of thinking brought the company from its origins in the PC industry to its present compatability with some of the largest systems available in the industry.

A historical look

Novell has made many milestones in the past 14 years. These milestones had the cumulative effect of bringing the corporation to the prominence it realizes today. Based on a number of sources, including personal memory, the following recounts some of these early advancements.

1983 The *industry first* file server software is shipped.

1983 Media independent support is announced.

1985 Novell supports DOS 3.1 and NetBIOS.

1986 Protected mode support for LAN operation is provided.

1986 Novell announces a fault-tolerant LAN.

1986 Novell announces support for Token Ring.

1988 NetWare for VMS is announced.

1988 Novell support for Macintosh is available.

1988 Novell support for OS/2 is available.

1989 NetWare operating system is announced.

1989 Portable NetWare is available.

1989 Novell announces 32-bit support.

1989 Novell announces 80386 chip support.

This list of achievements could continue, but the impact that Novell made in the 1980s is clear. Currently, NetWare operates with a large program that runs under MVS and VM in the IBM environment—that is, LANRES. More information is provided on LANRES later in this chapter. Beyond this, NetWare operates with IBM's SAA, RISC/6000, and AS/400 environments. NetWare is also available on many UNIX platforms. NetWare has a dominant position among networking protocols.

Forces driving NetWare

Multiple forces have been behind NetWare's growth over the past decade. It is clear that the company made strategic business decisions when necessary and advanced its technology in parallel with other technology, but other forces seem to have factored into NetWare's success story.

Personal computer growth. During the 1980s, personal computer (PC) growth was unprecedented in the history of computers. Discounting the personal computers of the 1970s, which are not a fair comparison to those of the 1980s anyway, explaining the growth of PCs in the 1980s is simple: they went from infancy to maturity in about a decade.

So many different vendors entered the personal computer market that the list would consume the rest of the space alloted for this chapter. Compaq, Dell, AST, Zero, Packard Bell, HP, Epson, and literally dozens of other vendors entered the market and were dubbed *clones,* a term denoting systems that copied the IBM PC. Not only did many copy the PC, but some made enhancements to the PC itself. This explosive growth of a new industry split open a new market, pulling in banks, insurance companies, educational institutions, individuals, and companies of all sizes. One example sums up this explanation. The IBM PC had 64 kilobytes of memory at its introduction; now some IBM PCs can have 64 megabytes. *Kilo* is for thousand; *mega* is for million! Think about it.

Ethernet. Another driving force that contributed to the growth of NetWare and its acceptance in the marketplace was Local Area Network (LAN) growth. Ethernet became a dominant lower-layer protocol in the 1980s. NetWare and Ethernet were a good match. Together, the sum seemed to outweigh the parts.

Since NetWare could operate with Ethernet, it was practically a shoe-in success. Ethernet products began appearing in companies everywhere. This was an added plus for the growth of NetWare. Since Ethernet was growing in notoriety and becoming dominant, it was simple for a customer to see the rationale behind using a network protocol such as NetWare.

Token Ring. Another factor in the growth and acceptance of NetWare was the impact of Token Ring. When IBM marshalled its forces behind Token Ring, the user community knew it would be a significant protocol in its own right. Novell began supporting Token Ring as soon as possible. This was a plus for NetWare.

Business community. The 1980s could be considered a decade of downsizing and restructuring from a corporate viewpoint. Because of this, alternatives were required. Many corporations sought to move much data off their traditional mainframes and to support departmental LANs. This was additional fuel for the growth of NetWare. NetWare was designed with a solid infrastructure, and that design paved the way for enhancements to be made without recreating the wheel. Consequently, as a product it was solid enough to deliver the requirements of corporations of significant size and scalable enough to be implemented in small companies. These factors seemed to help propel NetWare in a positive direction.

As a spin-off of downsizing and restructuring, a need for distributed file storage emerged. NetWare was designed to acommodate just such a need. The timing of NetWare and the marketplace merged to strengthen a product that continues to grow and adapt now, some 14 years later.

19.2 NetWare Protocols: An Orientation

NetWare incorporates multiple protocols as a product. This section explores those protocols to orient the reader for in-depth details later in the chapter.

To consider NetWare as simply a PC-oriented network protocol is to totally miss the point. Even to consider the protocol as a success story from an implementation point of view is a mistake.

NetWare is a complex network protocol. It can be implemented with DOS-based systems, Macintosh, AS/400s, UNIX-based systems, DEC, MVS, and VM-based systems. Consequently, it is anything but simple. In fact, its installation and configuration varies with each host that it operates within. This section, and the remainder of this chapter, explains some of the core components and operations of NetWare.

To date, at least a dozen books have been written about the topic. The complexity of NetWare cannot be understated. However, this complexity brings forth diversity and performance. Not all the systems that NetWare operates with are covered in this chapter; rather, the focus is upon an explanation of the protocol itself.

NetWare by layers

NetWare can be evaluated by comparing its layers to those of the OSI model. Figure 19.1 best exemplifies this.

At the lowest layer is support for adapter cards. NetWare supports multiple adapter cards, including the following:

- Ethernet
- Token Ring
- ARCnet
- 802.3

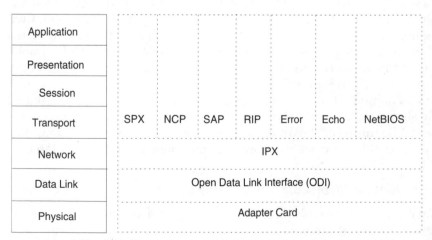

Figure 19.1   OSI and NetWare.

- FDDI
- Others

The next layer is called the *Open Data Link Interface* (ODI). This is a specification for the data link layer providing hardware and, thus, media protocol independence. Some drawings of the NetWare protocol stack do not show this layer, but it nevertheless is there. The standard was the fruition of joint work among multiple corporations, including Apple and Novell. Technically, the specification is more than just a data link specification; it defines four independent yet cohesive subcomponents. Before examining the details of ODI, consider Fig. 19.2, which shows the sublayers.

Figure 19.2 shows the sublayers where ODI operates. ODI is shown compared to the OSI layers, particularly the data link layer as it is broken into the MAC and LLC sublayers.

Internet packet exchange (IPX)

IPX operates at layer 3 as compared to the OSI model. It is a datagram protocol based upon a best-effort delivery system. As Fig. 19.1 depicts, the correlation with the network layer is direct. It operates as a best-effort delivery system where packet delivery is accomplished on a best-effort delivery mechanism. In other words, packet delivery has no

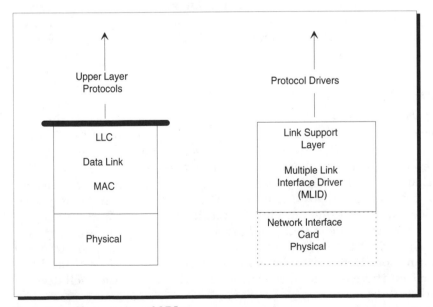

Figure 19.2   Close-up view of ODI.

relationship to other packets. This means there is no logical order of delivery.

IPX is connectionless. This means that no acknowledgments are sent from the receiving hosts to the originating host to indicate receipt of packets. Because of this connectionless nature, acknowledgment and related topics are left to higher-level protocols or programs to perform. Hence, the deduction is obvious that this protocol is faster than those above it, as shown in Fig. 19.1.

Even though IPX operates at the network layer 3 compared to the OSI model, it does perform transport layer functions. In this sense, a one-to-one correlation between NetWare and the OSI model is not accurate.

Sequenced packet exchange (SPX)

SPX operates above IPX. It is a connection-oriented protocol. Specialized applications can be built using this as the base protocol. Characteristics of SPX include ensured packet delivery; it is capable of recovering from lost data and errors that may occur in the data being passed from origin to destination. Another characteristic that makes the protocol robust is that it does not acknowledge each and every packet but waits until the maximum number of outstanding packets is reached. In NetWare lingo, this is referred to as a *window*. Operationally, SPX performs some functions that are similar to those of the transport layer in the OSI model, and after it is finished, it makes a program call to IPX for packet delivery. In short, SPX and IPX operate together to some degree. A perspective of SPX's relationship to the NetWare model is shown in Fig. 19.1.

NetWare Core Protocol (NCP)

NetWare's NCP is a defined protocol that is the procedure that file servers' operating systems utilize to accept and respond to requests. Functionally, NCP controls client and server operations by defining interactions between them. The NCP provides a similar service to SPX in that it performs some packet error checking. It also has session control between entities built into it. The NCP uses a number placed inside the *request* field of an NCP packet to request a given service. The reason for this is that NetWare services are given a number by a NetWare file server. Details of this protocol are Novell proprietary information. Hence, few details can be provided. It does seem, however, that there is general consensus that the NCP is the shell used on workstations.

Service Advertising Protocol (SAP)

Positionally, this protocol resides on top of IPX. It uses IPX to perform its function. SAP does as its name implies—it functions with nodes that provide services to *advertise* available services. Examples of available services include print and file servers. Gateway servers could be included in this as well. Those nodes that provide services broadcast SAP information periodically.

Router Information Protocol (RIP)

RIP is the routing information protocol used on NetWare networks. Functions performed by RIP include location of the best (fastest) route from a workstation to a network. RIP is used by routers to exchange information about routes, respond to requests from routers and workstations, and perform periodic routing table broadcasts among routers.

Error protocol

This protocol is operationally used among peer protocols. Programs that attempt to communicate with a host on a different network use NCP and IPX to attempt to reach that network. If for some reason that network is unreachable, an error packet regarding the state of the route to the target host is generated by a router and sent back to the requesting host. Interestingly, this function is portrayed in Fig. 19.1 as being above the IPX layer, but functionally it seems that it operates at the IPX layer.

Echo protocol

Understanding echo is similar to understanding PING in TCP/IP. This protocol is used in order to check a path en route to a target destination. If the path is functional and the target node is accessible, the echo protocol in the target node is architected such that it literally echos the packet back to the destination.

Review

NetWare is complex. It consists of multiple parts that perform different functions. Some are used in special situations, whereas others are used in most installations. Many variations on the NetWare protocol stack exist. This is a solid representation of those constituent components of NetWare. This section does not address NetWare functionality in different environments, because those are discussed later.

19.3   Open Data Interface (ODI) Concepts

ODI is a concept for protocol independence. Its roots are in the philosophy of providing a consistent interface to multiple transport layer protocols. Hence, network hardware independence can be achieved. When this is achieved, greater implementation and flexibility is realized.

ODI actually consists of the following three parts, or subcomponents:

- Multiple protocol interface
- Link support layer
- Multiple link interface driver

The protocol part of the specification calls for support for a diverse blend of protocols. In fact, if any protocol is coded against this OSI specification, then independence is achievable. These protocol drivers, however, must operate at the network layer and above.

The next part of the specification is the link support layer. The primary purpose of this layer is routing. The routing referred to here is

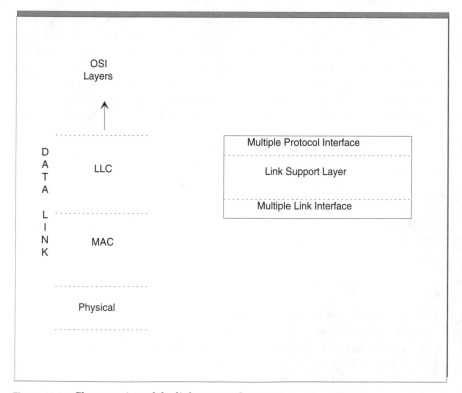

Figure 19.3   Close-up view of the link support layer.

between protocol drivers and multiple link interface drivers. Figure 19.3 provides a closer view of the link support layer and its interaction with the layers above and below it.

Figure 19.3 shows two interfaces. One provides a connectivity point with the network layer; it is called the *multiple protocol interface*. As its name implies, the interface is designed to operate with multiple protocols at the network layer and above. This interface was designed for developers creating program code so that they would have a standard interface to program into, regardless of the protocol.

The *multiple link interface* has the same philosophy behind it as the multiple protocol interface. This interface was designed as a common ground for data link layer protocol developers so that they would have a common standard to code against. A number of functions are performed at the link support layer, including coordinating numbers assigned to multiple link interface drivers after these interface drivers have been identified with the link support layer; managing the protocol stack identification assigned to network protocol drivers; managing individual network protocol drivers via their identification numbers, even though frames can be grouped according to MAC frame type; and manipulating media identification using specific frame formatting.

The fundamental purpose for having media identification and protocol identification is so the packets can be routed from a given upper-layer protocol stack to the correct lower-layer protocol interface. Basic to this idea is that this be possible without rebooting the system.

The purpose of the multiple link interface driver (MLID) is to pass data to and from the network media. The specification calls for these drivers to be protocol-independent.

Implementing ODI

ODI is implemented differently according to the operating system, device driver, network protocol, and NetWare version. The functionality behind it is a threefold concept. Figure 19.4 shows an example of the first concept behind the implementation.

Figure 19.4 shows multiple upper-layer protocol drivers against one network interface card. This is possible because of the ODI concept. This is an example of one of the possible functions that can be performed.

Figure 19.5 shows a different example of how ODI functionality occurs.

Figure 19.5 is the converse of Fig. 19.4. In Fig. 19.5, one network protocol driver is used against the link support layer and three multiple link interface drivers are used. This is an ODI converse implementation.

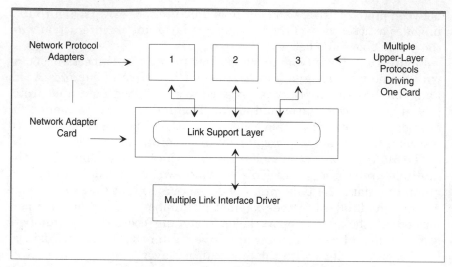

Figure 19.4   Multiple upper-layer protocols—one network adapter.

Figure 19.6 shows another example of how the ODI concept is implemented.

In Fig. 19.6, multiple network protocol drivers are hooked into the link support layer to drive three multiple link interface drivers. Three is not a magic number with this concept; it could be two or four just as easily.

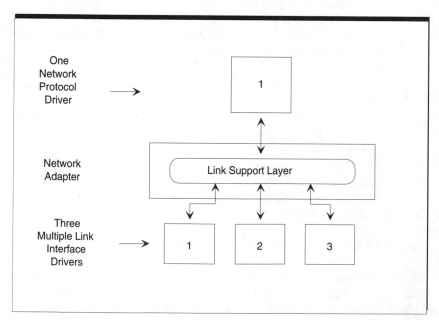

Figure 19.5   ODI converse implementation.

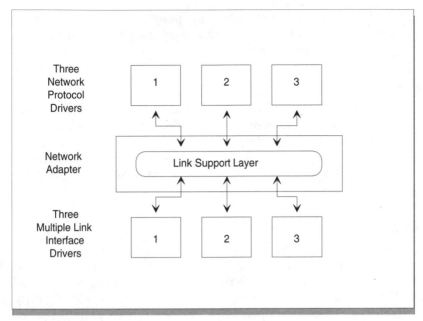

Figure 19.6   Multiple NPDs and MLIDs.

Management of ODI

The functionality of an ODI implementation is managed through a *configuration file*. This file consists, basically, of the following three components:

- Protocol
- Link support
- Link driver

These components contain parameters that control the ODI operating environment. The protocol parameters are used in the logical *BIND* that is created between the upper-layer network protocol and the multiple link interface driver. Link support reflects storage used at this part of the layer. The link driver parameters reflect the characteristics of the interface board used. Other configuration parameters may be required by different environments, and because of that variety the environment manuals need to be consulted.

19.4   Internet Packet Exchange (IPX)

IPX is used to define addressing schemes used in internetwork and intranetwork environments. NetWare network segments use numbers to identify them, primarily for routing purposes. This section explores IPX packet structure and provides additional information concerning its function in a NetWare network.

IPX packet structure

IPX packets are carried in the data portion of a MAC frame. Details about MAC frames have been provided previously in this book, and the focus here is upon the IPX protocol—specifically, its structure and contents. Figure 19.7 illustrates the IPX packet structure, components, and its relationship to a MAC frame. Inside the IPX packet are field names.

Sockets and ports

Novell refers to destination and source *sockets*. However, practically speaking, these sockets are better understood by their function, and that function is as a port. Henceforth, where Novell makes reference to a socket the term *port* is used, unless the meaning is significantly changed; then clarification is provided. The term *socket* actually refers to a network, host, and port number, just as in TCP/IP protocols.

IPX field explanation

Each field in the IPX packet has significant meaning. The following is a brief explanation of those meanings.

CHECKSUM: This field is responsible for performing packet-level checking.

PACKET LENGTH: This field contains the internetwork packet length, including the header and the data section.

TRANSPORT CONTROL: This field is used by routers between internetworks. This is primarily used by NetWare-based routers.

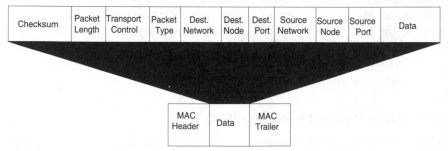

Checksum	Packet Length	Transport Control	Packet Type	Dest. Network	Dest. Node	Dest. Port	Source Network	Source Node	Source Port	Data

MAC Header	Data	MAC Trailer

Figure 19.7   IPX packet structure.

PACKET TYPE: This field indicates the service provided by the packet, regardless of whether this service is required or merely offered.

The packet type is indicated by a value. The value indicates the specific service provided. Some of the noted values and corresponding services include the following:

0	Unknown type of packet
1	Routing Information Packet (RIP)
2	Echo Packet
3	Error Packet
4	Packet Exchange Packet
5	Sequenced Packet Protocol Packet
16–31	Designated experimental protocols
17	NetWare Core Protocol (NCP)

DESTINATION NETWORK: This field identifies the target network. Each network in a NetWare networking environment requires unique network numbers.

DESTINATION NODE: This address identifies nodes on a given network.

DESTINATION PORT: This address indicates a *process* or *function* address.

SOURCE NETWORK: This field identifies the network (by number) upon which the source host is located.

SOURCE NODE: This address indicates a given node address. In any given instance, a host may function as either a source or a destination host.

SOURCE PORT: This is the port number that originally submitted the packet onto the network.

DATA: This field includes user data and other information from higher layers.

IPX is the heart of NetWare. All protocols operating above it move down the protocol stack and are enveloped into this packet. Actually, it is similar to TCP/IP in this regard; for example, regardless if TCP or UDP protocols are used, either are enclosed into an IP packet.

IPX addressing

IPX uses an addressing scheme similar to that of TCP/IP. A network address is assigned to a NetWare network, node addresses are assigned to each node on a given network, and the network protocol used by nodes on the network has identifiable ports or access points. In TCP/IP the combination of a network, host, and port address create what is called a *socket*. In NetWare, the term *socket* refers to the parallel concept of a port.

In NetWare, the network address is comprised of a 4-byte value. Host addresses use 6 bytes for an address. The socket address is a 2-byte address. The socket address reflects that address on which a server will listen and receive requests. The following is an example of some identified sockets:

File servers

451h   NetWare Core Protocol

Routers

452h   Service Advertising Protocol

453h   Routing Information Protocol

Workstations

4000h–6000h   Used for the interaction
with file servers and
other network
communications

455h   NetBIOS

456   Diagnostics

Additional addressing is used in such environments as with the LANRES product, but these addresses affect those aspects of communications with NetWare that are actually located in a different network. The addressing affects NetWare indirectly.

19.5   Sequence Packet Exchange (SPX)

SPX is a connection-oriented protocol that applications requiring such services can use to operate in a NetWare network. By default, SPX uses IPX. However, SPX has a completely different set of functions.

SPX packet structure

The SPX packet has its own fields that perform functions differently from IPX, but SPX utilizes IPX as it goes down the protocol stack (see Fig. 19.8).

Figure 19.8 shows the SPX datagram behind an IPX header inside a MAC frame. This is how it appears at the data link layer.

SPX field contents

The following lists the fields in an SPX packet with the purpose of each.

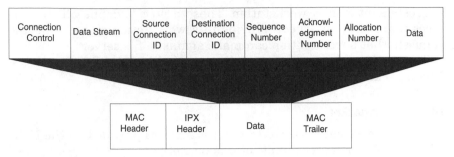

Figure 19.8   SPX packet structure.

CONNECTION CONTROL: This field controls bidirectional data flow between connections.

DATASTREAM: This field indicates the type data found in the packet.

SOURCE CONNECTION ID: This field identifies the originating point of the packet. This field is also responsible for multiplexing packets of data as they leave the node if this function is required.

DESTINATION CONNECTION ID: This field identifies the target point for the packet. The destination point may perform demultiplexing if required.

SEQUENCE NUMBER: This field is responsible for maintaining a packet count on each side of the connection. The sending side maintains a count and the receiving side maintains a count.

ACKNOWLEDGMENT NUMBER: This field performs packet orientation functions. It indicates sequence numbers of the expected SPX packets that should be received.

ALLOCATION NUMBER: This is a number that is used to indicate the number of outstanding receive buffers in a given direction at one time.

DATA: This field contains data used by the application requiring the SPX protocol.

This packet—namely, SPX itself—is considered to be a transport protocol that uses IPX as a delivery service from origin to destination. Packets exchanged between origin and destination SPX points have sequence numbers assigned to them. By these numbers determinations can be made to check for out-of-sequence, duplicate, or missing packets.

Not all applications require SPX, but specialized ones such as gateways and applications requiring session-oriented services do.

19.6   NetWare Core Protocol (NCP)

The NCP is similar to a shell. NCP procedures must be followed by a file server's operating system in order to receive and respond to requests sent from a workstation. These protocols define all the services that a file server can provide to a workstation and also all the requests that a workstation can make against a file server.

Two NCP packets exist, according to NetWare Application Notes. These packets and their field explanations follow.

NCP request packet

The request packet is issued to request services provided by the NCP. Figure 19.9 shows an example of this packet.

Request packets are issued by a workstation against a server. In a sense, the request and response packets are how workstations and the server exchange information. Details of this are considered proprietary by Novell; hence, limited information is available. The details of the fields of both of these packets are available, however.

NCP request packet field contents

Like SPX, NCP is inserted into the IPX packet when it passes down the protocol stack. The field contents and their meanings include the following:

REQUEST TYPES: According to Novell, there are seven categories. These categories and their functions include the following:

1111	Create a service connection.
2222	File service request.
3333	File service response.
5555	Destroy a service connection.
7777	Packet Burst.
8888	A private NCP request issued to a process on the same host.
9999	Indicates that the previous requests are still being processed.

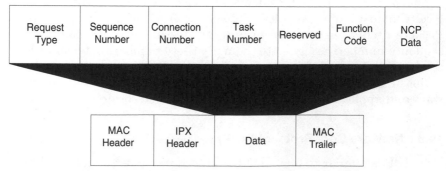

Figure 19.9 NCP request packet.

SEQUENCE NUMBER: Once a connection is established and packets begin to flow, packets are issued numbers in sequential order to indicate their sequence. When a server is finished processing these packets, it puts the sequence numbers in the response packets so the client knows that its receipt from the server is correct.

CONNECTION NUMBER: This number is used by a file server and the clients that connect to it. Each connecting client has a connection number assigned to it, and, as a result, this number identifies the clients to the server.

TASK NUMBER: Multitasking hosts can conceivably have multiple tasks operating at one time. Servers use a task number to associate *clients* with opened files, so the server may close these files as the clients finish with them.

FUNCTION CODE: This number identifies the NCP function required.

NCP DATA: This part of the packet includes data from the workstation.

These fields represent a client's or workstation's requests against a server. One field differs from this type packet and the response packet format.

NCP response packet structure

The NCP response packet is issued in *response* to the request packets it receives. The structure of this packet is shown in Fig. 19.10.

These packets are issued by the server. Note the similarities, but also the one field difference, between Fig. 19.10 and Fig. 19.9.

NCP response field contents

REQUEST TYPES: According to Novell, there are seven categories. These categories and their functions include the following:

1111   Create a service connection.

2222   File service request.

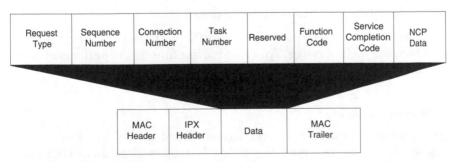

Figure 19.10   NCP response packet.

3333   File service response.

5555   Destroy a service connection.

7777   Packet Burst.

8888   A private NCP request issued to a process on the same host.

9999   Indicates that the previous requests are still being processed.

SEQUENCE NUMBER: Once a connection is established and packets begin to flow, packets are issued numbers in sequential order to indicate their sequence. When a server is finished processing these packets it puts the sequence numbers in the response packets so the client knows that its receipt from the server is correct.

CONNECTION NUMBER: This number is used by a file server and the clients that connect to it. Each connecting client has a connection number assigned to it, and, as a result, this number identifies the clients to the server.

TASK NUMBER: Multitasking hosts can conceivably have multiple tasks operating at one time. Servers use a task number to associate *clients* with opened files, so the server may close these files as the clients finish with them.

FUNCTION CODE: This number identifies the NCP function required.

SERVICE COMPLETION CODE: This field includes a value indicating whether an error occurred during processing. Any value other than 0 indicates that an error of some type occurred. Novell documentation provides additional details concerning this.

NCP DATA: This part of the packet includes data from the workstation.

Some additional detail can be obtained about NCP from Novell's Application Notes.

19.7   Service Advertising Protocol (SAP)

This protocol is used by such servers as file, print, and gateway servers to advertise their services. This advertising function is performed periodically on the network.

SAP packet structure

SAP packet structure has considerable detail inside (see Fig. 19.11). Figure 19.11 shows numerous fields, but upon close inspection, the

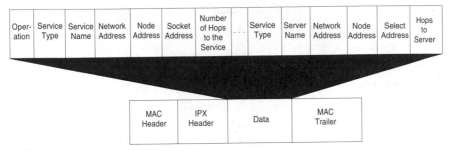

Oper-ation	Service Type	Service Name	Network Address	Node Address	Socket Address	Number of Hops to the Service	- - -	Service Type	Server Name	Network Address	Node Address	Select Address	Hops to Server

MAC Header	IPX Header	Data	MAC Trailer

Figure 19.11   SAP packet structure.

packet actually has two groups of the same information. The variables differ because of the information reflected by them.

SAP field contents

Each host that provides a service contains a SAP agent. Each agent acquires information reflected in the fields of this packet and keeps the information in a table.

OPERATION: This field defines packet operation.

SERVICE TYPE: This field identifies the service type that the server provides.

SERVICE NAME: This identifies the server name based upon network number.

NETWORK ADDRESS: This is the network address the server is located upon.

NODE ADDRESS: This is the address of where the server is located.

SOCKET NUMBER: This number is the process identifier to which packets must be sent.

NUMBER OF HOPS TO THE SERVER: This indicates the number of hops to the host where the server is located.

The remaining part of the packet may have additional information about other servers on the network.

Service type

Servers have a hex number that identifies the service they provide. This number is present in the service field of the SAP packet. Some examples of service types include the following:

Service Type	Value
User	1
User Group	2
Print Queue	3
File Server	4
Job Server	5
Gateway	6
Print Server	7
Archive Server	9
Archive Queue	8
Job Queue	A
Administration	B
SNA Gateway	21
NAS Gateway	29
TCP/IP Gateway	27
Time Synchronization Server	2D
Print Queue User	53
Network Access Server	98
Portable Netware	9E
Wildcard	FFFF
NNS Domain	133
NetWare 386 Print Server	137
NetWare 386	107
Communication Execution	130
Advertising Print Server	47

19.8   Routing Information Protocol (RIP)

Routing Information Protocol is used in a NetWare environment to route packets from one host to another, or from one network to another. Routers that operate with NetWare protocols keep a table with a list of network segments and hosts. Information is exchanged among routers via RIP packets.

RIP packet structure

The RIP packet structure is shown in Fig. 19.12. This packet structure is required support for NetWare-based networks. The packet provides information about networks, hosts, and other routers.

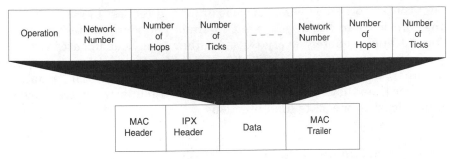

Figure 19.12   RIP packet.

RIP field contents

The RIP packets contain few fields, but they may be repeated to meet the needs of a network. The following explains these fields.

> OPERATION: This is the first field in the packet and indicates whether the packet is a response or a request. Following this field the maximum number of information sets is 50. These information sets include three components: *network number, number of hops,* and *number of ticks.*

> NETWORK NUMBER: This uniquely identifies a network segment.

> NUMBER OF HOPS: This refers to the number of routers a packet must pass to reach a given network number.

> NUMBER OF TICKS: This is an estimated reference to the amount of time it takes for a packet to reach a given network number.

When multiple routes are possible to a given network, this information is important. For example, two routes may exist between target and destination networks, but the amount of time between the two routes varies greatly.

Routing information

Routing information is maintained throughout a network in tables in routers—information such as the number of network segments that a router is aware of, the number of hops to a given network, the number of ticks it takes for a packet to reach a given network segment, and other information, such as network interface card identifications and the addresses of an additional router that can be used if the primary route is not possible.

Routing information is spread throughout a network at different times and in different ways. For example, the initial broadcast of routing segments occurs immediately after initialization. Another time that routing occurs is when there is an initial request to receive routing information. From this point in time, periodic updates are performed approximately every 60 s. Another time that updates can be performed is when routers send broadcasts to other routers connected to other networks, thus notifying other networks of the updates. Another time that broadcasts occur is when a router is powered down; a broadcast is one of its final functions.

19.9   Error, Echo, and NetBIOS Protocols

These three protocols reside on top of IPX and are explained here. These are peer protocols used by NetWare hosts.

Error

Error protocol is used when a destination cannot be reached. For example, when a packet leaves a host and reaches a router, and the router does not know the destination, it may generate a *network unreachable* message.

Echo

Echo protocol is also a peer protocol. Applications can use this protocol to check and determine if a path to a destination is reachable. In this respect, the echo protocol is similar to the Packet Internet Groper (PING). It works by simply echoing back to the originating point once it reaches the target.

NetBIOS

NetBIOS is merely an application programming interface between a network adapter card and applications (programs). Its origins predate LAN operating systems to a significant degree. It is a product of IBM and was introduced with IBM's PC network. NetBIOS is implemented in the Novell environment on top of IPX, much like SPX. In fact, Novell NetBIOS is more of an emulator to the original NetBIOS than a complete clone, because its frames are not compatible with IBM's NetBIOS.

Early on in the industry, NetBIOS was a protocol that vendors could use for application porting. However, a problem with NetBIOS is the lack of continuity between multiple vendor communication protocols. Ironically, what was meant to be a standard has, at this point in time, become so diverse that a lack of continuity exists among the many vendors implementing the protocol.

19.10   System Fault Tolerance (SFT)

System Fault Tolerance (SFT) emerged in 1987 with NetWare version 2.1. Included with this was the File Server Console (FCONSOLE), resource accounting, and security.

Version 2.1 at a glance

One of the features added to this version was the FCONSOLE. This gave individuals (namely, system administrators) the ability to monitor a network from any host on the network. This is parallel to the function of NetView in SNA. The resource accounting function was added to, so that data could be gathered about users and their groups. This function was particularly advantageous because it meant that the protocol was making strides toward becoming a well-rounded network protocol. The security introduced with this version improved conditions so that greater control could be obtained over resources and data itself. A number of different levels of security was implemented. For example, file, directory, account, internetwork connections, and groups could all have security through a password system. However, the greatest enhancement was the fault tolerance.

SFT example

System fault tolerance can best be explained by example (see Fig. 19.13). In Fig. 19.13, multiple disks exist. In fact, the same data on disk 1 is stored on disk 2. This notion of *disk mirroring* is to ensure that there is no loss of data in case of disk failure. Disk mirroring is the ability of either disk to be online at any given instant.

Should a problem arise when a disk is being read, SFT detects it and reads the backup disk. After reading the backup disk it marks the primary disk sector as bad, then restores information on the primary disk by copying data from the backup disk onto the primary disk. This is referred to as a *hot-fix*. In short, a hot-fix is the capability to detect and correct media errors while data is being moved.

The notion of *disk duplexing* also exists. This is the duplication of the entire disk, disk channel, power supply, and disk controllers. Disk duplexing is shown in Fig. 19.14.

Disk duplexing provides a default advantage; that is, it provides two possible paths for the CPU to access data. This means that whichever disk system responds first can serve the CPU—a defacto speed enhancer.

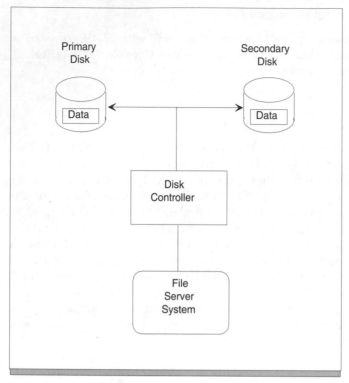

Figure 19.13 SFT example.

19.11 NetWare Implementations

NetWare can be implemented in a variety of environments. NetWare can operate on multivendor equipment all in one environment, or NetWare can be used to provide seamless connectivity between heterogeneous systems. Some example implementations are provided here.

LANRES

LANRES is an application that operates in MVS and VM environments. According to IBM, it brings the power behind the S/390 architecture to a NetWare environment. LANRES achieves this by making DASD available to NetWare servers and S/390-based printers available to NetWare clients.

LANRES also permits authorized MVS users to move data to and from a NetWare server. In addition, NetWare server files and directories can be listed, created, and deleted.

LANRES also makes LAN printers available to MVS users. In effect, it seamlessly brings together NetWare environments and S/390 to take

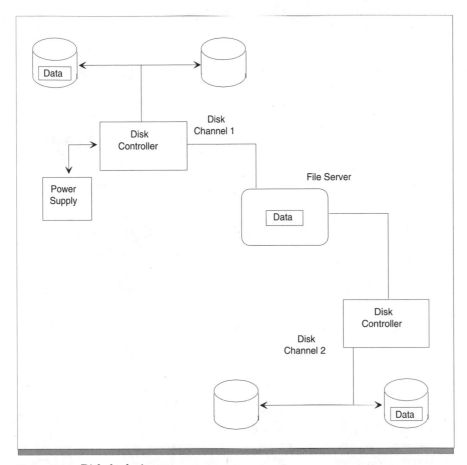

Figure 19.14 Disk duplexing.

advantage of right-positioning of work loads. Another function LAN-RES offers is centralization of LAN management to the MVS host, if desired. It also permits MVS users to send Postscript files to a Postscript printer on a LAN.

Conceptually, a LANRES environment would look like Fig. 19.15.

LANRES is versatile because of the connectivity solutions it supports. The following connectivity solutions are supported by LANRES:

- ESCON
- Parallel Channel
- APPC connection
- Host TCP/IP connection
- VM Programmable Workstation Services (VM PWSCS)

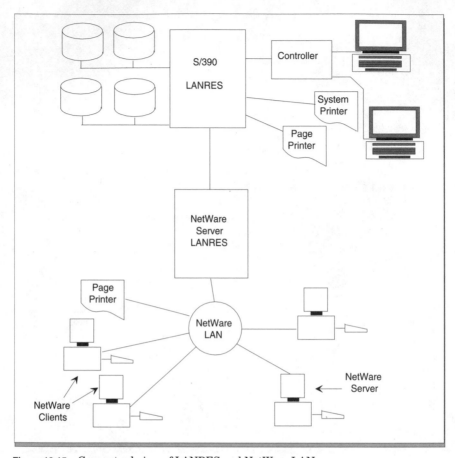

Figure 19.15   Conceptual view of LANRES and NetWare LANs.

The method of connection dictates how LANRES is configured on the host. Because of the breadth of support for connectivity solutions, the requirements, installation, and definitions are site-dependent and are directly related to how the product is used. For example, if the product is used with TCP/IP under MVS, LANRES uses sockets and TCP for connectivity. However, if APPC is used, then it connects to APPC MVS via CPI-C, conforming to SAA standards.

NetWare in UNIX

NetWare for UNIX is supported under NetWare version 3.11 for UNIX. Unlike NetWare operation in a DOS environment, in UNIX NetWare works with the UNIX operating system, file system, memory management schemes, and scheduling resources. In fact, a C programming interface makes NetWare services possible in a UNIX operating system environment. However, NetWare for UNIX is actually C source code NetWare; it has been ported to popular variations of UNIX. Figure 19.16 shows an example of this scenario.

Multiple-vendor UNIX operating environments are supported with NetWare for UNIX. UNISYS and the RISC/6000 are shown here. Beyond this example NetWare is integrated into a multiple operating system environment.

NetWare for VMS and multivendor operating systems

NetWare is supported under VMS from Digital Equipment. This is another port of NetWare. Such an environment can create flexibility, particularly if the VMS hosts are operating with UNIX and other operating systems as well. Figure 19.17 shows an example of this concept.

Figure 19.17 shows VAX and AXP hosts, but UNIX and DOS hosts also operate on the network. Because of the independence achieved

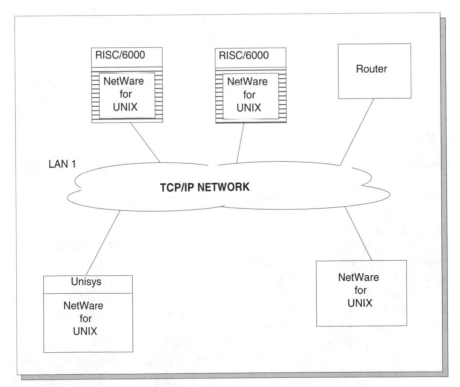

Figure 19.16   NetWare for UNIX.

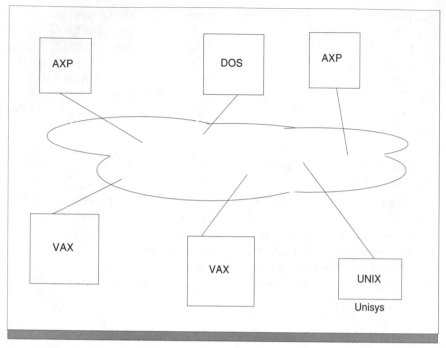

Figure 19.17   NetWare for VMS and multiple operating systems.

through NetWare, communication and file sharing can be achieved within such a diverse environment.

19.12   Summary

NetWare is a true success story from a protocol standpoint. It began in the early 1980s with the personal computer market and grew as the personal computer architecture grew. The protocol was enhanced to keep pace with network competition and continues to be refined. It is through version 4.0 now.

NetWare operates not only on PCs, but also on UNIX-based hosts with diverse backgrounds, such as IBM's RISC/6000 and AS/400 and UNISYS's version of UNIX. NetWare can also participate with two of IBM's largest operating systems—namely, MVS and VM. By leveraging upon the LANRES product, enterprise connectivity and seamlessness can be achieved with NetWare.

Novell introduced its first product in 1983. In 12 years it advanced to become an extremely robust netware operating system. Many milestones were made in the 1980s. Some of those are mentioned in the first section of this chapter. A number of forces attributed to NetWare growth named here include personal computer growth, growth in Ethernet, Token Ring announcement and growth, and factors in the business community.

NetWare is evaluated by layers, as compared to the OSI model. The components of NetWare are explained. Details are provided on IPX, SPX, NCP, SAP, RIP, the Error and Echo protocols, and NetBIOS.

The open data interface is explained and it is shown how upper-layer protocols and applications realize considerable independence from hardware. Implementing ODI is explained, along with how it is managed.

Field level details are provided on the following packets:

- IPX

- SPX

- NCP

- SAP

- RIP

IPX sockets and ports are explained, and a detailed view of the packet type field is presented. IPX addressing is explained and examples of some identifiable sockets are provided for the reader. SPX is explained and the fields inside its packet are described. NCP is discussed and both the request and response packets are explained at a field level. Request types are explained. SAP packet structure is presented and its fields are explained. SAP service types are also listed along with the hex values associated with each service type. RIP is discussed, including its packet structure. RIP routing information is also presented.

Error, Echo, and NetBIOS are discussed. The System Fault Tolerance (SFT) feature is presented. A brief look at version 2.1 when SFT was introduced is provided. SFT is discussed, along with disk duplexing and multiple disk implementation. The hot-fix is explained.

NetWare implementations are provided to give the reader an insight into the diversity of implementations that can be realized with NetWare. LANRES, NetWare in UNIX, and NetWare for VMS and multivendor operating systems are presented.

Netware is a powerful network protocol. It is used in systems of all sizes. The protocol itself is powerful enough to accommodate even enterprise networks with thousands of users.

The information provided in this chapter is helpful for those who design networks. This information is also very helpful for those who maintain networks on a daily basis.

Designing Networks with Windows NT

The purpose of this chapter is to introduce the reader to Windows NT. This chapter does not intend to replace Microsoft's documentation; neither does it attempt to condense all the material about NT covered in well-written books on this topic. The singular purpose here is to provide the reader with a snapshot of what NT is, of the power within it, and of some aspects of it. Windows NT is a Microsoft product. Its origins date back to 1988. Some characteristics included with the original design intent were to be compatible among a variety of hardware platforms and operating systems, to be easily adaptable to internationalization, to be portable, and to meet high security standards.

20.1 Perspective

Windows NT originally started with a version number of 3.1. Some sources believe that this was to provide an identity with Windows version 3.1. The fact is, applications that ran under Windows version 3.1 would also run under Windows NT version 3.1. Another characteristic of Windows NT's first release was that it was brought to market as two components; that is, Windows NT 3.1 and Windows NT Advanced Server 3.1.

Windows NT version 3.5 was released in the fall of 1994. The major advantages this version had over its predecessor include the following:

- Less memory requirement
- Point-to-Point Protocol Support
- Changes to the TCP/IP Protocol Suite

Other enhancements were included in this revision as well. For example, IPX/SPX support was included, and the restrictions that kept file naming to 11 characters were removed by implementing the NT File System.

Windows NT version 4 was released during the 1995 to 1996 timeframe. Most opinions seem to agree that this version of NT could be the standard by which other operating systems are judged. From appearances, it has the look-and-feel interface of Windows 95. This version of NT has robust features. It is separated into the *NT Server* and the *NT Workstation*.

Some common characteristics between them are the following:

- Advanced file handling systems

- Backup capabilities

- C2 security

- Graphical user interface tools

- Network capabilities

- Remote access capabilities

- TCP/IP

Other similarities exist between them. Specifics are presented in forthcoming sections.

20.2   NT architecture

The physical architecture of NT consists of the separate components that it is divided into. These components are the Workstation and the Server. Though they share commonalities, they operate independently of each other.

The NT Workstation is basically a standalone operating system. It does not require NT Server to operate (see Fig. 20.1). It can function in different modes to support a variety of software applications. NT Workstation does come with the networking component. It can easily be configured to operate in a networked environment.

NT Server is software that is capable of supporting a variety of workstations in a networked environment. Consider Fig. 20.2. In this example two segments of a hypothetical corporate intranet are shown. Here each department can operate independently from the other. However, they are connected via a fiber connection. If required, workstations in segment 1 can access the NT Server in Segment 2 and vice-versa. In addition, each NT workstation can operate independent of others.

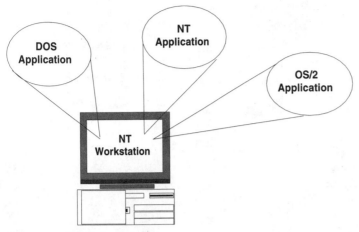

Figure 20.1   NT Workstation.

Generally speaking, NT is capable of supporting a significant amount of resources. For example, NT currently supports 4 GB of RAM per system. It also supports 2 GB of virtual memory and can address up to 402 million TB of storage.

Windows NT architecture is considered to be modular because it contains multiple components. Figure 20.3 shows NT in its entirety. The following four distinct components can be identified:

1. Application Environment Subsystems

2. Hardware Abstraction Layer (HAL)

3. Kernel

4. NT Executive Services

The Application Environment Subsystem is that part above the *WIN 32 Subsystem,* as shown in Fig. 20.3. The WIN 32 Subsystem is the main subsystem for NT. It includes WIN 32-bit Application Program Interfaces (APIs). Beyond support for 32-bit programs, the WIN 32 Subsystem supports application programs for other operating environments as well.

20.3   Architectural Analysis

The previous section briefly describes NT architecture. This section explores some of the NT components and what roles they play in the operating system.

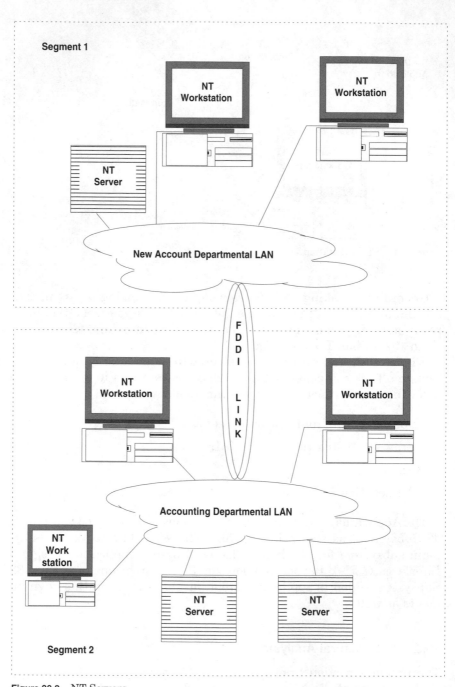

Figure 20.2 NT Servers.

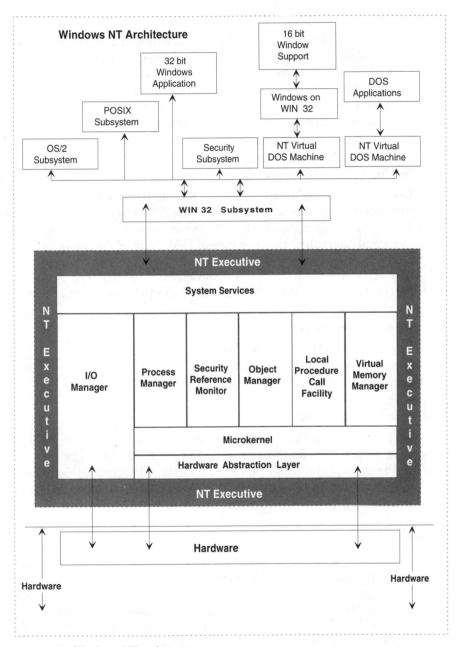

Figure 20.3 Windows NT architecture.

NT executive

The NT executive is the highest order of control within the operating system. In addition, the NT kernel is part of the executive as well. The kernel basically dispatches and schedules threads used in the operating system. For those new to the terminology of *thread* as used in this context, the following definition is adequate: a *thread* is an executable object that belongs to a process. An *object* can be something as concrete as a device port or an application.

Hardware Abstraction Layer (HAL)

The HAL is a Dynamic Load Library (DLL) used between a system's hardware and the operating system software. The purpose of HAL is to keep NT from being concerned with I/O interrupts, and to thereby make NT easily portable. It is because of HAL that NT is considered to be portable between different types of operating systems. It also provides support for Symmetrical Multiprocessing (SMP). The result is that NT can be used on Intel, MIPS, and Alpha processors and others.

Input/Output (I/O) manager

This part of NT handles input and output processing. The I/O manager coordinates all system I/O—drivers, installable file systems, network directors, and caching memory management.

Local Procedure Call (LPC) facility

This part of NT functions as an interface between all clients and servers on an NT system. Functionality of LPC is similar to that of the Remote Program Call (RPC) facility. However, LPC and RPC are not equals, because LPC permits the exchange of information between two thread processes on a local machine.

Microkernel

The microkernel is part of the NT Executive. It operates in kernel mode. The microkernel runs in kernel mode and communicates with the NT Executive via very low level primitives. In a crude way, one could think of the microkernel as that part that controls the entire system. Because NT is based around preemptive multitasking, it controls time slices and manages to pass control to other processes.

Object manager

The NT executive uses the object manager to manage objects. The object manager creates, deletes, and modifies objects. *Objects* are nothing more than abstract data types used as operating system resources. Objects can be ports (physical) or threads (logical). The object manager also works in the system to clean up stray objects that could exist if a program crashes.

Process manager

The process manager is involved in all processes and threads. General consensus defines a *process* as that which has an identifiable virtual address space, one or more threads, some system resources, and executable program code. In NT, when an application is started, the object manager is called to create a process which sequentially creates an initial thread.

Security reference monitor

The security reference monitor is the core of NT security. A logon process and a local security authority process is used in the implementation of security with NT.

Virtual Memory Manager (VMM)

The VMM translates a system's process memory address into actual memory addresses. In short, it manages virtual memory. Virtual memory in personal computers operates on the same principles as in large computers. Some aspects may be augmented or enhanced, but the foundation of the idea is the same.

NT's modular design makes it robust. It has a great degree of hardware independence. Some of the hardware platforms NT can operate on include the following:

- X86 uniprocessor computers
- X86 multiprocessor computers
- AXP RISC architecture
- AXP RISC multiprocessor computers
- MIPS RISC architecture
- MIPS RISC multiprocessor architecture
- Motorola PowerPC

Another powerful aspect of NT is its use of *unicode* rather than ASCII for a character set. Unicode is based on 16 bits, which means that this character set can represent 65,536 characters. Hence, unicode is more powerful than its ASCII counterpart, which uses 8 bits that yield only 256 characters. The inherent meaning of this is that multinational characters are supported, such as Japanese, Chinese, Russian, Swedish, and others.

20.4   Workstation and Server Commonalities

Windows NT is clearly delineated into two distinct parts. This section highlights those aspects and parts that the workstation and the server have in common.

Both the NT workstation and the server use what are considered advanced file systems. NT supports the NT file system (NTFS) and the file allocation table (FAT). NTFS supports long file names, file level compression, file data forking support (required for Macintosh systems), international filenames, software level sector support for fault tolerance, and file level security permissions.

FAT support makes NT backwards-compatible with DOS. Floppy drives use FAT, and RISC systems using NT use FAT in the boot partition.

Both workstation and server support TCP/IP. NetBIOS is supported also, as defined in RFCs 1001 and 1002. This means that logical naming at a session level is possible. The NetBIOS interface also supports Dynamic Data Exchange (DDE). DDE enables sharing data embedded within documents.

The NT workstation and server also share Dynamic Host Configuration Protocol (DHCP) clients. This means that NT stations can participate in an environment to obtain DNS addresses, IP addresses, gateway addresses, and netmasks.

NT provides support for SNMP. This makes workstations and servers capable of participating in environments that use such management tools as OpenView, SunNet Manager, and SystemView.

Both support Remote Access Service (RAS). NT version 4 supports the point-to-point tunneling protocol. This function of NT enables a virtual network to be created over a wide distance. NT data encryption makes this part of NT popular.

Both workstation and server provide support for C2-level security. Data protection on a system is achieved by Access Control Lists (ACLs). This enables directory- and file-level security maintenance.

NT workstation and server are administered in the same way. Some of the tools with which this is done include the following:

- DHCP manager
- Disk manager
- Event viewer
- Performance monitor

- RAS administrator
- Server manager
- User manager
- WINS manager

The *DHCP manager* is used to configure the station to obtain required information upon startup. In addition to the DHCP manager is the DHCP server service; this permits remote control of DHCP servers.

The *disk manager* is the tool with which disk partitions, mirrored disks, and volume set disk partitions are created.

The *event viewer* enables a user to view events on local and remote systems. Information such as the system log, security log, and application log can be obtained.

The *performance monitor* provides a method for real-time monitoring. The performance monitor also makes possible sending administrative alerts to remote systems, monitoring performance counters, and maintaining performance logs.

The *Remote Access Service administrator* is a configuration tool used to designate certain users privileges to gain access to a network node. RAS administrator can also be used to configure remote stations.

The *server manager* tool is used to create domain systems for workstations (NT), standalone servers, and domain controllers. It is also used to determine the status of servers and users that are logged on.

The *user manager* enables the creation and management of user accounts. When used on a domain controller, interdomain trust relationships are set up with this tool. It is the tool used to set up user rights, systemwide passwords, and auditing functions.

The *Windows Internet Name Service (WINS) manager* is used to manage the WINS server service. This function of NT can be used to manage a local host or remote host. The basic purpose of WINS is dynamic name resolution.

20.5   Topics of Interest

Windows NT should not be considered a trivial topic to try to understand. Some topics are presented in this section for your consideration. They are definitely core topics that are constantly discussed in NT environments.

NT security

More than one method can be used with NT security. One basic way to implement security in NT is with a logon and password; this is commonly referred to as *simple system access*. The next level, or way, of implementing security is through *resource access* security. This method of security implementation is a double-edged sword; that is, security can be tight, but then it is equally difficult to maintain. The next level, or way, of implementing security is by creating *groups*. For example, users is ABC group can access all files and programs in ABC group; on the other hand, they cannot access files or programs in, say, group DEF.

NT security is powerful and flexible. I recommend that once a site is set up with whatever security policy is in place, you make records of the way it is set up and document changes as they are made to the system.

Domains

If your background has been in TCP/IP, then you may find this topic easier to understand. Microsoft considers a *domain* to be a secure workgroup with centralized maintenance. With a little thought it is easy to understand how this can become complex, if a site is large.

Within the *Microsoft* domain, as some say, there are domain controllers. These are systems that maintain critical information to keep the domain operational; for example, such information as resources, security access privileges, passwords, logins, and other information. Many sites run the primary domain controller and the secondary or backup domain controller. A thought one needs to remember with NT and domains is that the primary domain controller is actually *made* at the time of installation and cannot be changed later. The reason for this is because the domain controller must be configured during installation. This means that on any given network only one primary domain controller can exist. Should two or more domain controllers each *think* they are the primary controller, a contention scenario will ensue. This means that the domain controller with the most trust relationships on the network will win the contention and will thus be considered the primary domain controller.

A *trust* relationship among domains simply means that two or more domains trust each other. This does not inherently mean that in this relationship all users in one domain will have automatic access to resources in the other domain. Further definition of access is required. In addition, the notion of a *global domain* is required for operations wherein multiple domains exist. One could think of this loosely as *the great global domain in the sky*. The purpose behind it is to facilitate the coordination of domains and users within various domains.

Another concept to remember about domains is that trust relationships among them are one-way, not two-way. For example, user *A* in domain *A* may trust resource *B* in domain *B;* this does not, however, mean that resource *B* in domain *B* trusts user *A* in domain *A*.

The simplest way to think of trust and domains is with three example scenarios. First, where a master domain has domains that have trust relationships with it. Second, where two domains have bidirectional trust relationships. This could loosely be called *peer-to-peer*. Third, where three or more domains have multiple trust relationships among more than one domain.

User attributes

NT users have attributes associated with them. The following list reflects the attributes generally associated with a user:

- Account
- Password
- Application access
- Logon capabilities
- Home directory
- Group memberships
- Profile
- Rights
- Remote access service capabilities
- Policies

This information is used by administrators to customize a wide variety of user profiles. Some users may have much broader abilities than others, due to their work requirements. This degree of information in user profiles enables great control over user access and provides system security.

20.6   The Registry

Windows NT employs what is called the *registry*. There is no way to do justice to this topic in detail here. Many books are available on NT that include literally dozens of pages on the registry. Simply put, the registry is the replacement for the .ini files of times past. Actually, the registry is much more than this. Data in the registry encompasses everything from device adapters to software configuration and system configuration.

The registry is actually a database. It can be divided into six subtrees. In addition, there are global and user-preferred values. Global registry entries affect hardware settings, local machine settings, systemwide software settings, and other systemwide parameters. User preferred values focus on individual settings or preferences.

The bottom of the subtree contains what are called *root keys*. There are six root keys, as follows:

```
HKEY_CLASSES_ROOT
HKEY_CURRENT_USER
HKEY_LOCAL_MACHINE
HKEY_USERS
HKEY_CURRENT_CONFIG
HKEY_DYN_DATA
```

The registry root keys naming convention was designed to make future reference to these components easy for NT programmers. Each root key maintains data about different system functions or components. For example, *classes_root* contains information about object linking and embedding, files, class, and various associations. This information is used by system and application components. The *current_user* root key maintains user settings and profiles for the user that is currently logged on. The *local_machine* root key maintains local machine hardware, memory, display, hard drives, network adapters, and so forth. The *users* root key maintains data about all user profiles. The *current_config* root key contains data about the actual configuration of the system as it is operating; this includes device setup, control values, and so forth. The *dyn_data* root key contains dynamic data required by internal registry functions.

One thing I want to mention is that the registry is not intuitively obvious. In fact, it is somewhat obscure. It is also available in Windows 95. To invoke the editor and the registry, type *regedit* at a DOS prompt or on the *RUN* command line under the pop-up menu. If you do this the registry editor will pop up on the screen. However, I do not recommend that anyone edit this unless they have a very good understanding of the consequences. If you do this, more trouble could be incurred than you anticipate.

I have found from experience that some changes are required in various parts of the registry. Changes must be made with surgical precision. If you encounter trouble in the network as you set up and configure it, it is possible that some changes will be required in the registry.

20.7   Network Configuration

Configuring NT networks is pretty straightforward. This is subjective, however. This section includes information from experience.

Configuring NT networking presupposes that it has been set up during the installation phase. If your systems have been preconfigured with NT, you may need to obtain the diskettes and CD. I recommend that you get a copy of Windows NT anyway. I would bet there will come a time in your use of NT when you will need the original manufacturer's CD to either install options or add a component.

The *Control Panel* window is the place to begin to access NT networking. Within the Control Panel is the *Network* icon. Double-click on it and the Network parameter options panel appears. Within this panel are the Identification, Services, Protocols, Adapters, and Bindings options.

The *Identification* option is where one identifies a system by name and workgroup. The *Services* option is where actual services are added or deleted from system use. *Protocols* is where protocols are added or deleted as well. In the Protocol option selection, TCP/IP can be added or deleted; other protocols can also be added or deleted. The *Adapter* option is where one identifies the network adapters used on any given system. The *Bindings* option shows the bindings as the various software components are logically mapped to hardware options and services are mapped to software components.

Tips from experience

My experience in the installation and configuration of systems using NT has taught me some things. First, I recommend that you obtain your own copy of NT Server or Workstation (with diskettes and CD). I am not implying here that you obtained an illegal copy—quite the contrary; many systems today are shipped preloaded with the operating system of your choice. Those systems that are shipped this way typically do come with the media you need or give you the option to create backups on initial system use. My recommendation is one step beyond that. It is to go ahead and obtain the manufacturer's copy of the software. Here's why: during setup, and later during the normal use, addition, and changing of equipment in the network, some parameters are required to change. Therefore, having the software in advance to make these changes is the best way to work with networks.

More specific advice comes from my experience in NT system configuration and setup of networks. The focus here is on addressing. I strongly recommend that you assign IP addresses during the setup phase of your network and write down the names given to your systems and the corresponding addresses. Documentation of these names and addresses is important. This method of initial setup provides flexibility.

First, this method of IP address setup will enable you to track and plan which systems will be located in a given domain. For example, one could assign a set of IP addresses to certain workstations in different domains to represent some logical organization of these workstations. Second, manual IP assignment in the initial phase of network configuration will enable much easier isolation of problems that could arise. Also, if your network is not extremely large, manual assignment of addresses could make future changes easier.

Configuring dual-boot systems

It is possible to install Windows 95 and Windows NT on the same system. Why would one want to do this? In order to run given applications. For example, I have some applications that are designed for Windows 95 that will not operate under NT. To solve this problem, I have Windows NT and Windows 95 installed on the same system. I select which one I want to run at boot-up.

A dual-boot approach is a good way to phase from Windows 95 to NT from an application viewpoint. It does provide the best of both worlds. Configuration with both operating systems on a single workstation is straightforward.

This is all that is required for a dual boot system: if your system has Windows 95 on it, install Windows NT as you would if no operating system were loaded on it. On the other hand, if your system has NT loaded on it, then install Windows 95 on it as if no operating system were loaded on it.

20.8   High-speed Server Connections

NT-based networks typically have one or more NT servers. I designed my network with three NT servers. An important part of server use is each server's ability for transfer utilization. For example, during the design phase of the network, one should consider data (video, voice, or multimedia) transfer from the server to each user. This consideration includes server connectivity to the network.

During the design phase of the network I decided to include three NT-based servers. I decided to use Adaptec's *Quad cards,* as I call them. Adaptec refers to these interface boards as *Cogent Quartet Series network adapters.* Both *Cogent* and *Quartet* are trademarked names and are the property of the Adaptec corporation. Their names are registered trademarks and are not just words to be used casually. Technically, these are known as *ANA-6944A.* Figure 20.4 illustrates how I implemented these interface boards into the servers in the network shown throughout this book.

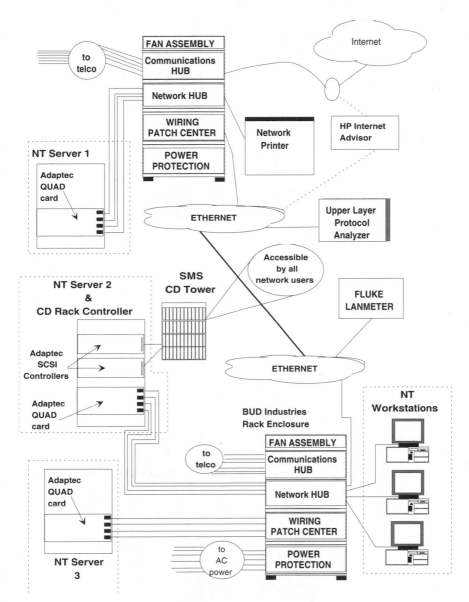

Figure 20.4 High-speed server connectivity.

The figure shows three servers. Note that each of them has an Adaptec interface board with four ports. Technically, these network interface cards are model number ANA-6944. They include four ports for actual physical connection to the network, as the illustration shows. Note that NT Server 2 includes two CD tower interface adapters. These adapters are required for the server to function with the CD server.

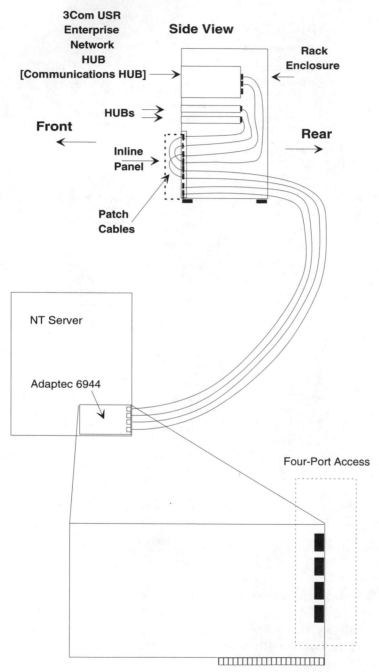

Figure 20.5 Adaptec four-port Ethernet adapter.

Figure 20.5 shows a close-up of the Adaptec board. It has four ports for network connectivity. This provides a high level of redundancy. Furthermore, this level of throughput is required to realize the potential benefit of the high-end servers on the market today.

Figure 20.6 further illustrates the implementation of NT Servers utilizing Adaptec Quartet boards in this network.

Adaptec has many products other than four-port network adapters. In fact, this corporation is really a pioneer in the area of SCSI device control. Today it has a wide range of products for desktop computers, networking, and telecommunication equipment. Adaptec is not just located in the United States. It has international locations and can be found at the following Internet address. Personally, I recommend that you contact Adaptec during the planning phase of your network and let its technical support division assist you. You may contact the Adaptec corporation to obtain more information at:

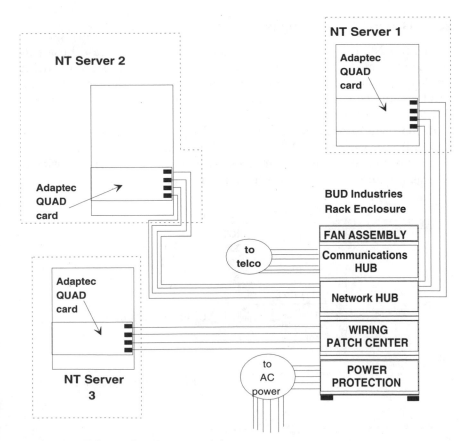

Figure 20.6 High-speed server connectivity.

Adaptec, Inc.
Phone: (800) 442-7274
Internet: www.adaptec.com

Implementing network servers involves more than just connectivity considerations. Since these servers are mission critical, they need to be protected with power protection equipment. Figure 20.7 illustrates how these servers are protected.

The network interface boards provide redundancy and greater throughput for network reliability, and it is important to provide power protection for each server. In Fig. 20.7, each server is protected and can provide full operation even with a complete power failure.

Figure 20.7 shows multiple uninterruptible power supplies, line conditioners, and spike and surge protection equipment. The servers shown in Fig. 20.6 are protected from spikes, surges, sags, transients, and waveform distortions.

20.9   General Considerations

Designing NT networks should include other aspects than those presented previously. For example, one should be aware of load balancing applications on servers, segmenting the network so that maintenance can be achieved with minimal impact to the overall network, and methods for network management.

Beyond the information provided so far in this chapter, be aware of any different versions of NT that could be used in the network. This is important because of the differences between the Enterprise Edition of NT Server and NT Server 4.0. The differences between these two ver-

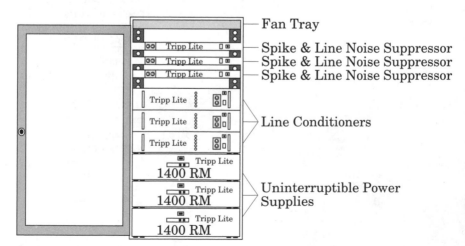

Figure 20.7   Server power protection.

sions are significant. A major difference is in the memory capabilities, regarding use, between version 4 and the Enterprise Edition.

20.10 Summary

NT has become a popular operating system. Its design has two powerful characteristics. First, the design of HAL with NT makes portability much easier than with many operating systems and thus makes integration into diverse environments easier. Second, built-in support for DOS, OS/2, and 32-bit Windows applications make it a good common ground to use where different software technologies have been deployed but require integration.

Windows NT is a powerful product. The abilities it possesses from security to multitasking and other features make it attractive for small and large installations alike. However, I recommend further research into this topic in proportion to the depth that NT will be used. The purpose of this chapter is to orient the reader to NT network design. This information should be used in conjunction with prior chapters to assist you in planning for your NT network. I suggest that you obtain original equipment manuals and site-planning information guides during the planning phase. Most vendors are happy to supply information to those who are making network plans.

21

Designing Networks with Bridges

Many networks today require connectivity at some level. Increasingly, workgroups in companies and various entities require individuality yet wholistic connectivity. Bridges operate at Layers 1 and 2, as compared to the OSI model. They work with lower-layer protocols. Bridges are more complex than repeaters, if for no other reason than the fact that they function with two layers of protocols. This chapter focuses on what bridges do and how they do it.

21.1 Functionality Within a Network

Bridges can serve multiple functions in a network environment. Some functions that bridges perform are vendor-specific; however, companies that sell bridges typically offer products that perform most basic functions. However, because of the diversity in what a bridge can do, vendors differ in their offerings. This almost sounds like a circular conversation, but there is hope! The point is that all bridges I have worked with have certain commonalities, but some are capable of performing specialized functions.

Conceptual view of operation

As mentioned previously, bridges operate at the physical and data link layer. Figure 21.1 shows an example of where this occurs.

Figure 21.1 shows an example of two hosts and a bridge connecting them together. Figure 21.2 shows a detailed view of a bridge with two physical interfaces, one for host A and the other for host B. Note that there is one data link layer, because that is where bridging is performed.

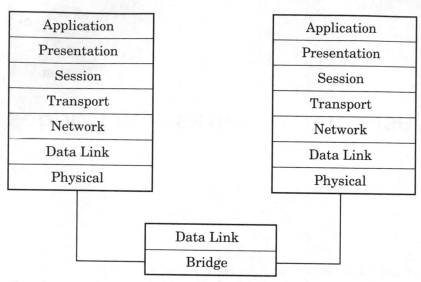

Figure 21.1 Conceptual view of a bridge.

Functional advantages

Many real-world scenarios have multiple LANs throughout an entity, be that a corporation, government agency, or whatever. When this is the case it is not uncommon for multiple higher-level protocols to be implemented at higher levels in the networks. Since some upper-layer protocols have limited capability with others, a bridge can be advantageous to use to connect multiple networks, assuming they use the same lower-layer protocol. Another advantage of bridges is that in certain situations a bridge may be a better choice than a router. Bridges are also relatively cheaper and easier to install. Other advantages of bridges include the following:

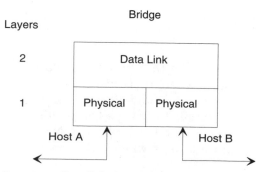

Figure 21.2 Detailed view of a bridge.

- Many bridges can connect networks of different speeds.
- They are easily managed.
- Many can be adapted to an environment as it grows.

In fairness, bridges have some disadvantages. Common ones include the following:

- Bridges can be physically installed in such a way that in reality the net result is one logical network; consequently, sometimes troubleshooting can be difficult when problems arise.
- In some implementations, such as a cascaded topology, a problem can occur with fast protocols because of delay factors.
- Bridges are transparent to end systems. Because of this fact and the potential delays encountered relative to the number of bridges, the actual limit could be indirectly imposed on the number of bridges utilized.
- The potential exists that bridges could impede the use of some applications over the Internet. An example of this scenario could be multiple copies of an application operating and, unfortunately, using the same naming or addressing scheme.

Practically speaking, bridges are good network devices when used for the right need.

21.2 Theory of Operation

Bridges can be described in different ways. Three of those ways are the focus of this section. Bridges can perform forwarding, filtering, and learning functions. *Forwarding* is passing a frame toward its ultimate destination. *Filtering* operates by discarding frames when their destination is not in a connecting network. *Learning* is a function a bridge performs when it does not receive a positive response in return when comparing a frame to its *hosts* table. The following explains these functions.

Forwarding

Forwarding is best explained by examining Fig. 21.3.

Here are two LANs, *LAN 1* and *LAN 2*. LAN 1 has three PCs connected to it. They are known on the LAN as *D1, D2,* and *D3,* respectively. A bridge connects both LANs. LAN 2 has two PCs connected to it, named *D4* and *D5*. Note the highlighted table aside from the bridge that is used to *know* which hosts are located on which LAN. In the

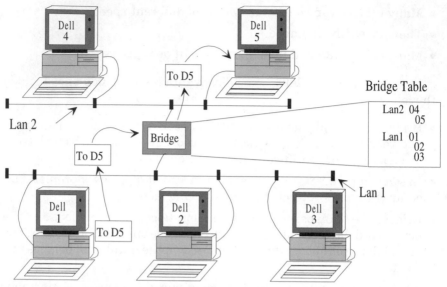

Figure 21.3 Conceptual view of forwarding frames.

bridge's table, host D5 is shown to be on LAN 2. The bridge intercepts the frame because it knows its target is on LAN 2. The packet is still broadcast on LAN 1 as well, but it is *spent* timewise in a matter of fractions of a second; therefore, it does not stay on LAN 1.

Filtering

Figure 21.4 shows two LANs, a bridge connecting them, and two PCs on LAN 1 and two PCs on LAN 2.

Figure 21.4 shows an example of the filtering function of a bridge. Note the frame leaving *host 4* destined for *host 3*. The frame is captured by the bridge and is compared against the bridge's table. After the bridge performs its compare function, it discards the frame. Host 3 receives the frame destined for it.

Learning

Bridges are said to *learn* about a host (be that a computer or other device) when a frame is received by a bridge and the bridge does not have the address of that device in its table. If it does not, the bridge dynamically updates its table and then it *knows* about this device; therefore, the bridge is considered to have learned of a device (see Fig. 21.5).

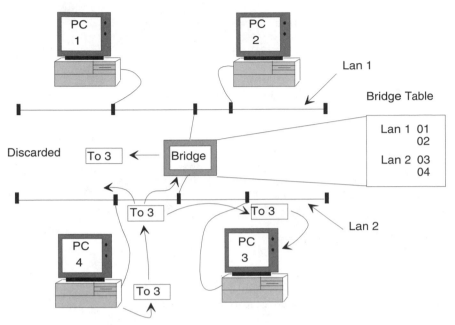

Figure 21.4 Conceptual view of filtering frames.

Figure 21.5 shows two LANs and a bridge connecting them. Assume that *host 3* has recently been added to the LAN. Now assume that host 3 wants to communicate with *host 5* on the other LAN. The bridge knew the location of host 5 before, and now it knows the location of host 3 because it has *learned* its addresses, both its host and network address. Now, any of the hosts on *LAN 2* can communicate with any hosts on *LAN 1*.

21.3   Bridges by Protocol

Bridges can also be characterized by protocol. This is sensible because they work with lower-layer protocols. The simplist approach to understanding how bridges work with different protocols is focusing upon the ways a bridge operates with these protocols.

Like protocols

Different vendors support varying protocols with their bridges. Some of the popular ones include Ethernet and Token Ring.

Ethernet.   Ethernet is a popular lower-layer protocol and is widely used throughout the marketplace. It is common for LANs to be created in

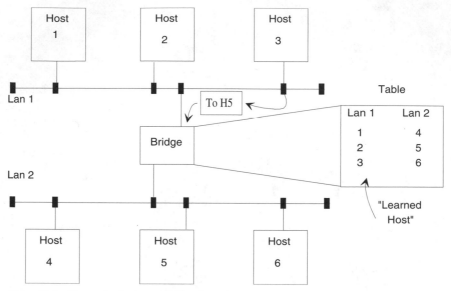

Figure 21.5 Conceptual view of bridge learning.

departments; then, over time, the realization of multiple disparate LANs becomes apparent. Multiple LANs can be connected together by bridges, thereby creating one logical network while still permitting independence of departments (see Fig. 21.6).

Figure 21.6 shows three departments that perform distinctly different functions. But these departments need to share files for purposes of creating documents, informing potential customers of products soon to be released, and general communication. Figure 21.6 shows an example where this is possible.

Token Ring.   Token Ring is another popular lower-layer protocol. Like Ethernet, multiple upper-layer protocols can operate on top of it. Figure 21.7 shows an example of how multiple Token Rings can be connected, thus making a single logical network.

Note in Fig. 21.7 that both 4- and 16-MBps Token Ring speeds are used. Many popular bridge vendors offer solutions that fit such a scenario.

Figure 21.7 shows three floors of a corporation. Each floor is a different department. The first floor is the collection department, the second floor is the billing department, and the third floor is the central data center for the corporation. Each floor has considerable flexibility. Token Ring is considered to be a self-healing technology; therefore, hosts can be inserted and removed from the network at will. Likewise, any given

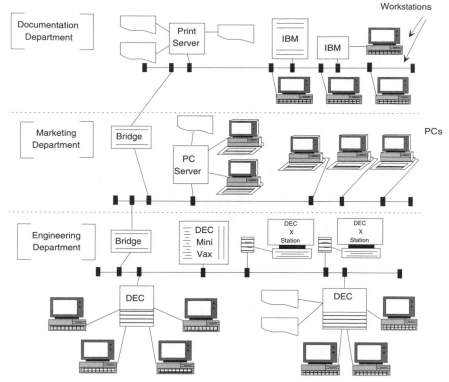

Figure 21.6   Extended Ethernet LAN bridging.

floor can be removed from the 16-MBps corporate backbones. This scenario provides independence and flexibility and is characteristically
very dynamic.

Unlike protocols

Bridges can also perform lower-layer protocol conversion. Many reputable vendors have such devices. In fact, these devices have become a
commodity in a comparatively short amount of time.

An Ethernet to Token Ring bridge operates bidirectionally. Users on
an Ethernet network can communicate with users on a Token Ring network and vice-versa. Figure 21.8 shows an example of such an environment.

Figure 21.8 shows three Ethernet-based LANs, a 16-MB Token Ring
backbone, a 4-MB Token Ring LAN with multiple hosts, and two large
SNA environments connected to another 16-MB Token Ring. This configuration makes interoperability among all hosts possible. Granted,

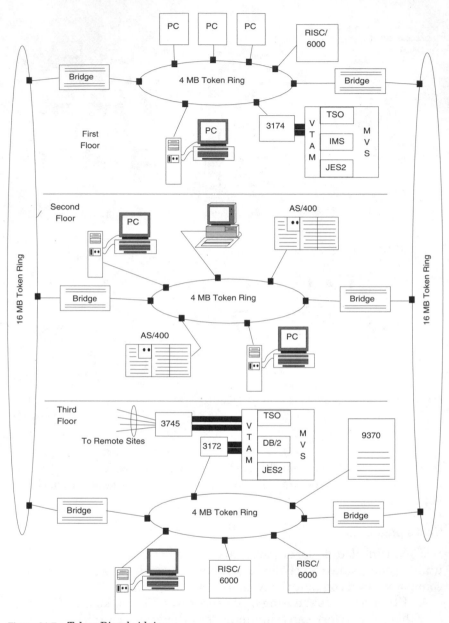

Figure 21.7   Token Ring bridging.

some additional components, such as software, and possible configuration changes may be required.

Some bridges support protocols beyond those shown here. However, most bridge vendors support these protocols. These sample implementations are examples of real installations.

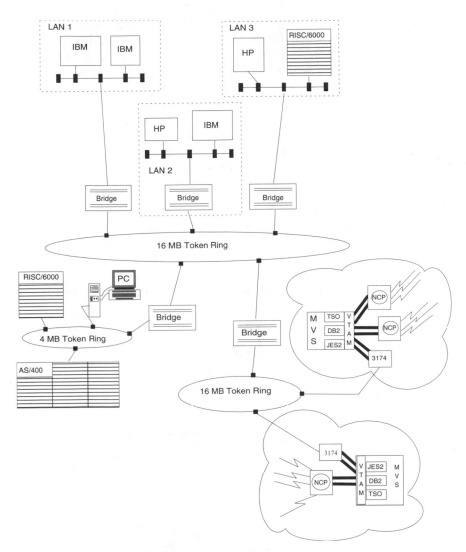

Figure 21.8 Multiprotocol bridging.

21.4 Bridges by Geographic Location

Another way bridges can be examined is with respect to their support for local and remote operations. Some examples of various bridge implementations are presented here.

Local bridging

Bridges are good devices to use in this type of environment, as a general rule. They permit segmentation of LANs while providing connectivity of them at the same time (see Fig. 21.9).

Figure 21.9 shows engineering, marketing, and documentation departments. They each have a LAN and each is connected via a bridge—one between engineering and marketing and the other between marketing and documentation. A twofold benefit is realized.

First, all three departments can communicate with any hosts in any of the other departments; thus, enterprisewide connectivity is achieved. Second, isolation of departmental computing can be maintained on each network LAN because of the way bridges operate (this aspect of bridges is explained shortly). Third, a degree of load balancing can be realized as a result of this scenario.

Remote bridging

Remote bridging does as its name implies; that is, it bridges geographically remote networks (see Fig. 21.10).

Figure 21.10 shows two sites. The need exists for both LANs to communicate. Now, with the advent of remote Ethernet bridging, these LANs can communicate. The connectivity between the two sites could

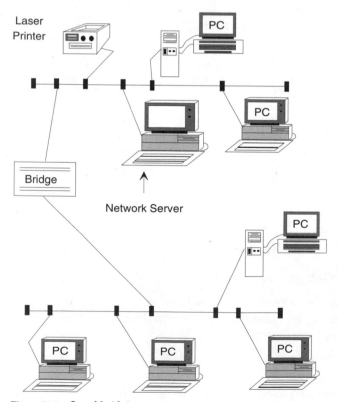

Figure 21.9 Local bridging.

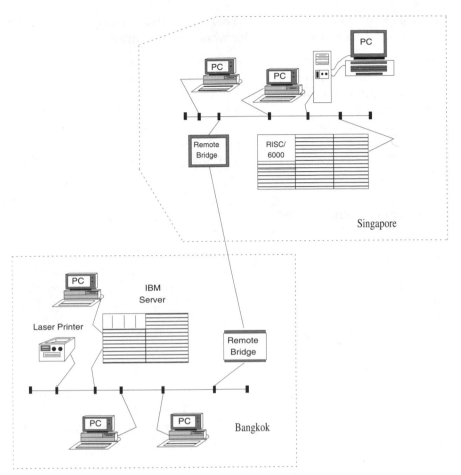

Figure 21.10   Remote bridging.

be a switched or a leased line, generally with speeds of 56 kbps or higher. However, if a switched line is used, this implies bandwidth on demand; consequently, some requirements for bridging this type of environment exist. The result is that users on both networks view all hosts as located on one LAN.

Both local and remote bridging can be performed with Token Ring networks. Bridges supporting the respective protocols are required. Depending upon the vendor offering, other network protocols may be supported as well.

Some vendors offer redundant line support for remote bridges. Others offer data compression on the fly; depending upon the vendor, some algorithms can achieve approximately a 4:1 ratio. This is effective utilization of bandwidth. Some vendors also offer network management support for their devices. These and other aspects of a bridge should be discussed with a vendor whose forte is bridges.

Author's note: Remote bridging is similar to other aspects of internetworking technology. One question always remains: "Where is the bottleneck?" I am not implying that remote Ethernet, Token Ring, or other protocol bridging will result in a bottleneck; however, I do intend to raise the question because in datacommunications a bottleneck always exists. The question is where and to what degree. It may or may not have anything to do with bridging, routing, or gateways; but it nevertheless is present.

21.5   Source Routing and Transparent Bridges

Attention is required to the way bridges obtain routing information. This is a misnomer in a sense. Bridges do not *route* in the sense that a router does, but they do have to pass frames from a source toward their destination points, wherever that may be. The transparent bridge function has been discussed briefly in Sec. 21.2, but additional details are provided here. First, source routing needs explanation.

Source routing

Source routing is an IBM function. It is a method whereby the route to the destination is determined before data leaves the originating point. Sometimes this function is called *SRB*, short for Source Route Bridging. This type of routing is dominant among IBM Token Ring networks.

Frame contents

Understanding source routing is easily achieved by understanding the contents of the IBM Token Ring frame. Figure 21.11 shows the structure and contents of the MAC frame.

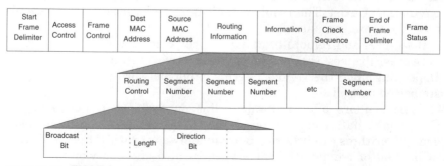

Figure 21.11   IBM Token Ring frame.

Figure 21.11 shows the IBM Token Ring frame, the highlights of the routing control field, and the highlights at bit level of the routing control field.

This frame itself differs from the IEEE 802.5 frame in that the Token Ring frame has a routing information field. Here we explore that field and its contents.

Segment numbers

The first component in the routing information field is the routing control subfield. It contains information that is used in the routing function and is explained in greater detail shortly. Segment number subfields follow the routing control subfield.

Each segment number reflects two pieces of information. Segment numbers are comprised of a *ring number* and a *bridge number*. Each ring is a LAN, and each LAN has a number associated with each ring. Each bridge used is assigned a number. The combination of the ring and bridge number creates the segment number. If multiple rings are connected via bridges, then multiple segment subfields exist, as shown in Fig. 21.11.

Routing control subfield

The routing control subfield has two significant pieces of information, the broadcast bit and the direction bit. The *broadcast bit* indicates what type of frame it is; that is, a broadcast or nonbroadcast frame. The *direction bit* indicates which way the frame is going. It is either en route from original source to destination or vice-versa. This is important, because the setting of this bit dictates how the segment number bits are interpreted.

Transparent bridges

The working definition of *transparent bridges* is that they learn those hosts that are reachable according to data link by observing frames as they pass. Another helpful term for this type of bridge is that it is considered a *spanning tree bridge*.

This type of bridge forwards frames, as discussed in Sec. 21.2. It also maintains and updates a table of MAC addresses of those hosts that are reachable across the link used to attach multiple rings. Another name sometimes given to this type of bridge is a *learning bridge*.

A transparent bridge implementation has already been shown in an earlier figure, but for the convenience of the reader it is also shown here in Fig. 21.12. This illustration also shows how power protection is implemented to cover all equipment in the various network segments.

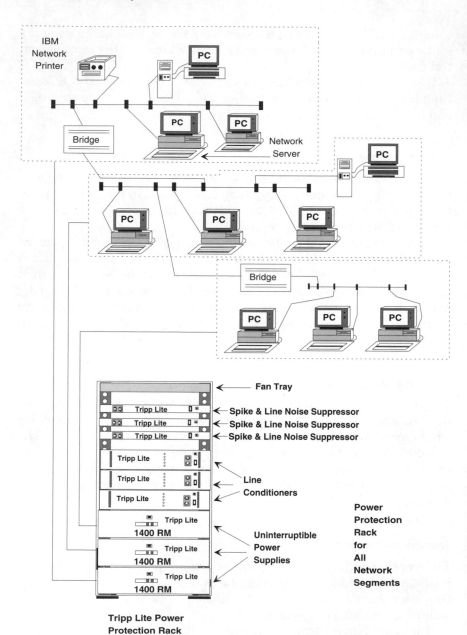

Figure 21.12   Conceptual view of a transparent bridge and power protection.

21.6   Source Routing Theory of Operation

Now that the preceding information has been covered, an explanation of how IBM source routing operates is provided. Two types of frames can exist in an IBM Token Ring network, nonbroadcast and broadcast frames.

Nonbroadcast frames

The term *nonbroadcast* means virtually the same as multicast. If there is a difference it is minimal. What is important is how nonbroadcast frames are handled in a multiring environment (see Fig. 21.13).

A nonbroadcast frame reveals the significance of the segment numbers previously discussed. Assume that *host A* on *ring 1* is the source host and the destination host is *host G* on *ring 2*. Note that *bridge X* connects rings 1 and 2 directly. In this case bridge X recognizes its bridge number and ring number. The bridge simply copies the frame

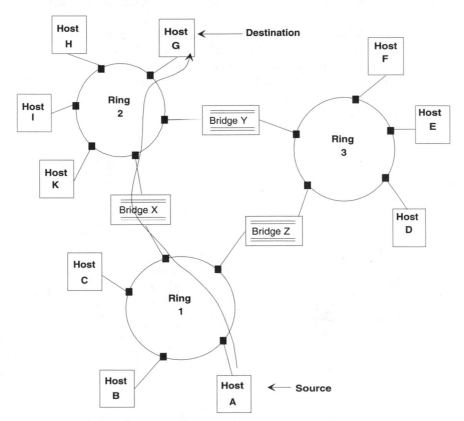

Figure 21.13   Nonbroadcast operation.

from ring 1 onto ring 2. At the same time, *bridge Z* receives the same frame. It examines its bridge number and its ring number; no match is made, so the frame is discarded.

Broadcast frames

Source routing is implemented by two types of MAC addresses via broadcast frames, according to IBM. One type of MAC frame contains a certain value that is received by all hosts on the ring on which that host exists. This frame contains a special hex value (see Fig. 21.14).

Figure 21.14 shows the frame—the box labeled *H6*—being received by all hosts on the ring where it originated. The H6 label indicates its destination, *host 6*. However, note that two rings exist, connected by a bridge. Note that the H6 frame is not repeated onto *ring 2*.

The other type of MAC frame contains an address that is considered to be a broadcast address. It has a different hex value than the example shown in Fig. 21.14. The broadcast frame is sent to all hosts, to all rings, and to all bridges connecting them. Figure 21.15 shows this environment.

Assume that *host 8* on *ring 8* sends a broadcast frame. It is received by all hosts, by each ring, and, consequently, by each bridge. Operationally it works like this: *host 8* sends the frame. *Bridge D* copies the frame and adds its bridge number and the number associated with *ring C*. At the same time, the frame reaches *bridge T*. Bridge T copies the frame and adds its bridge number along with the number for *ring*

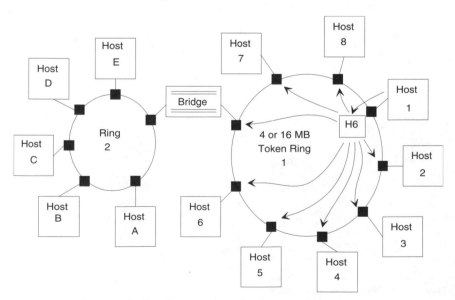

Figure 21.14   Conceptual view of a frame contained on one ring.

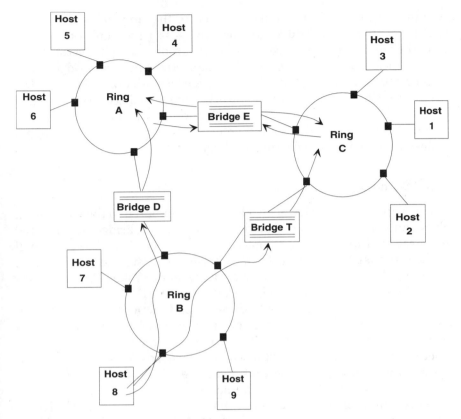

Figure 21.15   Example of a broadcast frame.

A. The frame then passes to *bridge E,* where bridge E copies it and adds its bridge number and ring C's number. The process is complete, but a question remains: why do this?

   When many hosts exist and isolation of networks needs to be achieved, but total connectivity between LANS is required, Fig. 21.15 shows an example solution. It provides multiple paths to any given ring—and the more rings, the more reason to have redundancies in paths.

Discovering routes

The process of discovering routes is twofold. First, assume that a source wants to communicate with a destination host. The first attempt the source host will make is to send a frame on the ring that it (the source host) is located upon. If no positive response is encountered, then another process is used.

   A source host sends a route discovery frame to a destination host. The source knows the destination's address; the question is how to get there.

Assume that multiple rings are attached to the ring where the source host is located. Each bridge attached to these rings copies the frame from the source, inserts its segment information, then passes the frame on. Once the frames have reached all connected rings and bridges, they begin returning to the source host. If the destination host is located, it inserts routing information into the original route discovery frame and sends it back to the source. Multiple frames may return to the source. When this happens, the source determines the route for additional frames to be sent to the destination host.

21.7 Summary

Bridges operate at the lower two layers, as compared to the OSI model. They can serve a variety of functions. For example, bridges can be used to merge multiple LANs into one *virtual* network. Another strength of bridges is that they can perform protocol conversion on LANs at the lower two layers. Bridges can convert Ethernet to Token Ring and vice-versa. Some vendors offer bridges that support FDDI bridging.

Transparent bridges perform three basic functions: forwarding, filtering, and learning. This simply means that a transparent bridge forwards frames it receives; it filters those that are not destined for another ring to which it is attached; and it learns of hosts throughout the networks on which it operates and stores this information in tables that it uses, in turn, for routing purposes.

Source routing is a function of another type of bridge. IBM uses source routing, and a field exists in the MAC frame for the insertion of routing information. This type of bridge operates by including the destination address into the frame along with the source address. Other functions that source routing bridges perform are different types of frame broadcasting.

Bridges can be used to effectively manage sites where multiple Token Ring networks exist and the need for redundancy also exists. Because Token Ring technology is considered to be self-healing, it is easy to remove and add hosts and devices to these networks.

Bridges also offer advantages to Ethernet-based LANs, particularly where multiple Ethernet LANs are geographically dispersed. Remote bridges can create a virtual LAN environment where users *think* they are all attached to the same network in the same physical location.

Implementing bridges remotely should be tempered and evaluated in light of the load at respective sites, the bandwidth available through the link, and other operational considerations.

Many well-known vendors have good products to achieve a desired result.

Chapter 22

Network Design with Routers

Routers operate at Layer 3, as compared to the OSI model. Routers route upper-layer protocols. They do not perform protocol conversion, assuming that they are routers in the classical sense. Routers, like bridges, can be examined from different angles. This chapter explores those angles.

22.1 Understanding Routers

An explanation is in order concerning the term *router*. This is especially true for those who may be new to networking devices. Sometimes different groups and individuals use terms in loose ways, and confusion can be the result.

The routing function can be defined as getting data from point *A* to point *B*, wherever that may be. This concept can be traced back to the 1970s when networking began to sprout. Those working in the Internet community were involved with networks that were sometimes located in different cities. At any rate multiple networks existed, and the desire arose to connect to networks and to connect networks together.

As an outgrowth of this desire, devices began to be used to perform this function. At the time they were generally referred to as *gateways*. Yes, gateways. An obvious question is, why? According to the *American Heritage Dictionary, gateway* is defined as: "1. An opening, as in a wall or fence, that may be closed by a gate. 2. A means of access." I believe the informal consensus on the meaning at the time probably was for the latter part of the definition provided here.

Taking a number of points into consideration, it is reasonable that devices that performed a routing function were called gateways. And, unfortunately, the confusion of this terminology still exists today. Taking the definition of *gateway* as a means of access to explain the function of a device that permitted connectivity of networks *was* reasonable. They did, in fact, provide such a function. And beyond that, these devices routed information to various networks and locations. With this in mind, coupled with the mind-set of the day during the 1970s, it was a plausible use for the term *gateway*. But, technology changes.

Today an entire industry exists around network devices. In fact, a part of this book is devoted to explaining some of these devices. I do not believe that in the 1970s most technically oriented individuals could envision the explosive technological growth in such specialized devices of the 1980s. It might have been conceivable, but not to the detailed level that hindsight provides today. Hence, the dilemma exists.

The terms *routers* and *gateways* are constantly used in various mediums, and, at best, their meaning is skewed. For the record, routers *route*—period. They may perform other peripheral functions, but the focus of routers is simply on routing data.

Gateways, on the other hand, perform protocol conversion between heterogeneous networks at Layer 3 and above at a minimum and can perform protocol conversion at all seven layers between two networks. Gateways perform protocol conversion; routers do not. Interestingly, some gateways can perform routing functions because of their architecture, but they do not necessarily have to. In fact, this is a vendor-specific offering.

The point of this section is to point out to the reader that discussing internetworking with different people can result in confusion if a clarification of terms is not agreed upon. Many who have worked for years with TCP/IP-, UNIX-, and Internet-related issues still use the term *gateway* to convey the function of a router. I have often wondered what term they use to name the device used to integrate heterogeneous networks. It would seem that a catch-22 exists.

Another comment about routers and terminology is valuable: different types of routers exist and are explained in this chapter, and not all routers perform the same functions—many functions are vendor-specific. Their are a number of prominent router vendors in the market today that sell good equipment. The point is understanding your needs and obtaining the appropriate fit so that those needs are met.

22.2 Types of Routers

Multiple types of routers exist, and they perform different functions. In some instances the names given to router functions tend to overlap to other identified functions. Routers can be explained by the geographic distance they support; that is, *local* or *remote*. They can also be explained by the upper-layer protocols supported and by their interface support.

Router operation is based upon tables of possible networks and routes. These tables are utilized to indicate the path to a given network. Router tables do not locate device addresses, as some types of bridges can. Functionally, routers exploit the information available to them to determine the most expedient route. Another unique aspect of routers is that they receive data addressed to them by hosts or other routers. Route determination is somewhat contingent upon the upper-layer protocol. For example, TCP/IP uses routing algorithms that differ from those of SNA-based networks. In this respect, routers are protocol-dependent. Some routers are simple and function with one protocol; however, other types of routers can manipulate multiple protocols—hence, the name *multiprotocol routers*.

The remainder of this chapter explores various aspects about routers and specifics of how they operate in certain environments. And, like bridges, routers have become a basic commodity in internetworking technology.

22.3 Router Function

Routers are protocol-dependent. They operate at network Layer 3, as compared to the OSI model (see Fig. 22.1).

Figure 22.1 presents an example of two hosts, shown by layers and showing where a router operates between them.

As the figure shows, the physical and data link layers are also part of the router; therefore, these aspects must be taken into consideration.

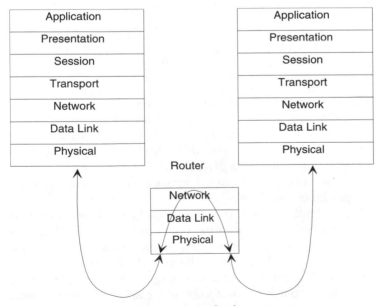

Figure 22.1   Router operation as compared to layer structure.

Some large routers (in the sense of what they support) offer a wider variety of physical layer interface support. More than a few reputable router vendors offer fine products that support such interfaces as the following:

- RS-232
- V.35
- AUI
- X.21
- HISSI
- RS-449
- Serial
- Others

In addition, lower-layer protocols must be supported as well. These, too, are contingent upon the vendor and the router. Some examples of popular protocols supported include the following:

- Ethernet
- Token Ring
- SDLC
- HDLC
- FDDI
- X.25
- Others

The network layer is where routing occurs. If you have read the other chapters in this book, you are aware that upper-layer network protocols operate differently. For example, the way that TCP/IP performs routing is different from the way SNA or, say, APPN performs routing. Consequently, these upper-layer protocols drive the router decision to a certain degree. This is so because multiprotocol routers exist and support routing multiple upper-layer protocols.

When routing is implemented, it brings together two or more networks. The consequence of this from the user's standpoint is that it is transparent, except for possible time-zone inconveniences, but those issues are easily overcome. In essence, the use of routers provides an end-to-end solution. The remainder of this chapter focuses upon some examples of different upper-layer protocol routing and also some aspects of routing in general.

22.4   Reasons to Use Routers

Routers can be implemented locally or used in an environment where multiple networks exist in different geographic locations and need the ability to exchange data.

Local implementation

Figure 22.2 shows an example of a scenario where routers are used within the same physical facility.

Figure 22.2 shows a single physical site with three distinct Ethernet LANs. Note that a router is the common denominator of them. The result of this configuration is that any of the LANs can communicate directly with any of the hosts shown via the internet protocol. Note that all the LAN hosts have TCP/IP as their upper-layer protocol. By removing the router, connectivity between all three LANs would not be achieved or other means would have to be implemented to achieve the same results.

This particular implementation is straightforward, flexible, and relatively inexpensive. In addition, the router fits into the management method that is common among TCP/IP networks.

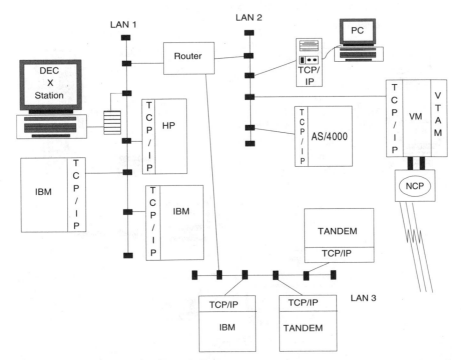

Figure 22.2   Local router implementation.

This example can take on many variations because of the flexibility with routers. In a sense, they can be customized to meet site-specific needs fairly easily. The primary reason for this is because routers maintain routing tables within them that can be customized to be a diversity of situations.

Metropolitan implementation

The notion of a metropolitan implementation may not be popular, but it is frequently a solution that meets many needs (see Fig. 22.3).

Figure 22.3 shows the Walton Insurance Agency headquarters in Dallas, where master files, statements, accounts receivable, and other

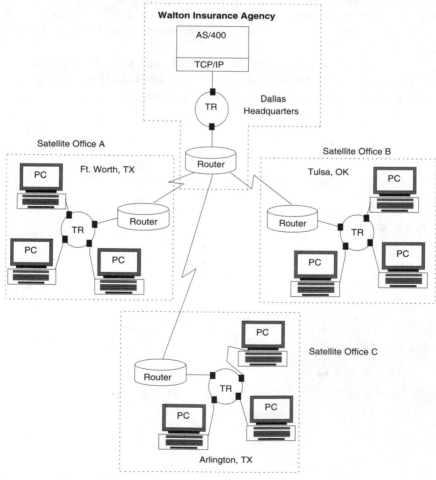

Figure 22.3 Metropolitan router implementation.

operational functions are performed. However, because the agency has prospered it also has offices in Fort Worth, Arlington, and Tulsa. Each of these three satellite offices are within 35 miles of the headquarters in Dallas.

Because data needs to be sent to and from the satellite office and headquarters, this router solution meets the needs. In fact, the router in the Dallas office can route data from Tulsa to the Fort Worth office, if configured appropriately.

Like the example of a local implementation of a router, this metropolitan router implementation is popular because the links between all sites are not considered long-distance; therefore, significant savings result.

Remote continental U.S. routing

Remote routing is a popular solution for many corporations that are geographically dispersed and in different time zones. Figure 22.4 shows an example of this idea.

Figure 22.4 shows facilities in Chicago, Memphis, Dallas, and San Francisco. Each site differs in function and, to some degree, type of equipment. But through the use of routers, the site in San Francisco can send data to Memphis or to any of the sites connected in this virtual network.

International Routing

International routing is similar in theory to routing among multiple sites in the United States. However, time considerations need attention, as does understanding the type of work to be done between all connected sites. It is also important to know the peak traffic times at all locations and to correlate them; this will help in performance tuning (see Fig. 22.5).

The significance of the international scenario versus the local, metropolitan, or even the continental U.S. scenario is the issue of time-zone differences. Merely coordinating a contact time for the staff representing each site is difficult because of the time difference.

Another reason for routing is a business reason. If a company performs significant amounts of processing, the best place to do this is where it is most cost-effective while achieving the original goals. With distributed processing and exploitation of network devices such as routers, this can be accomplished.

22.5 Types of Routing

Multiple methods are used in routing. Technically, routing schemes can be categorically defined. Different vendor network protocols tend to

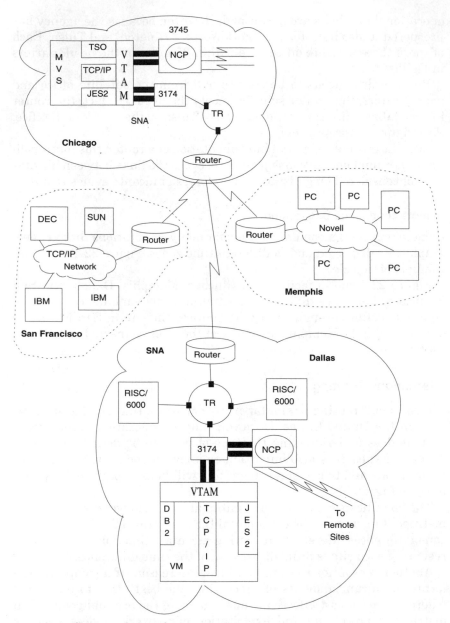

Figure 22.4 Conceptual view of remote routing.

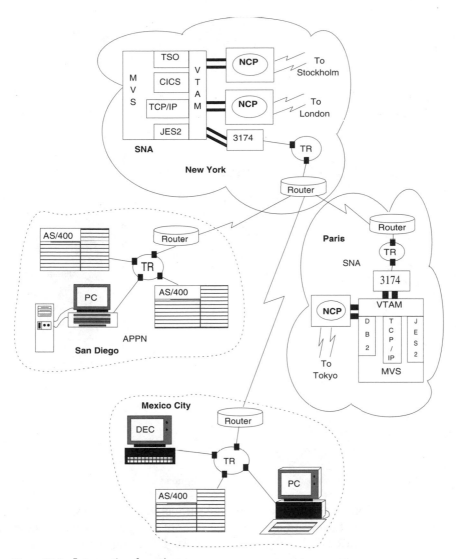

Figure 22.5 International routing.

route differently, but some common threads among the different protocols remain.

Centralized routing

Centralized routing is a scenario where a central repository of routing information is maintained. Conceptually, this appears as shown in Fig. 22.6.

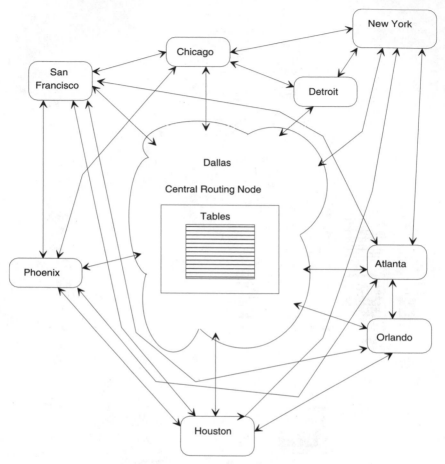

Figure 22.6 Conceptual view of a centralized routing node.

Figure 22.6 shows multiple locations connected in a myriad of combinations. Moving data from one location to another can be accomplished via multiple routes. However, the centralized routing node in Dallas maintains the routing tables.

Here, each router informs the centralized node of the potential routing of a local environment. This information is arranged into tables and distributed to each router participating within the network, and the central routing node determines the route capabilities.

Noncentralized routing

Noncentralized routing is as its name implies. The routing algorithm is not located in a central routing node. Figure 22.7 shows a conceptual view of this.

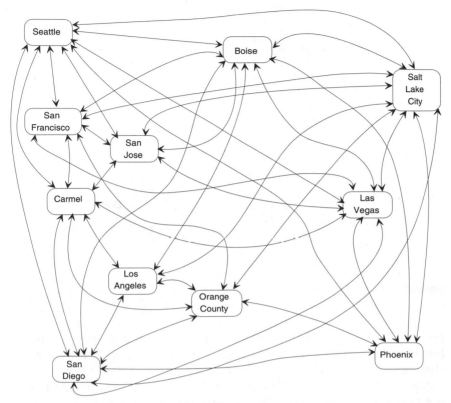

Figure 22.7   Conceptual view of noncentralized routing.

Figure 22.7 is interesting, to say the least. However, it does convey the notion of noncentralized routing. In this environment each router informs its *neighbor* of valid routes. The significant point of the figure is that each router determines the route as the packet arrives. Also, this type of implementation is constantly changing as changes are made to individual routes. Each time a change is made, updates occur.

Static routing

This type of routing is where tables and routes are made via network management functions. By definition, this means it must be performed when the network is nonoperational from a user perspective. The simple way to explain this is that no changes are performed while the network is operational. This means that the routes are, therefore, *fixed* (see Fig. 22.8).

Interpretation of the notion of static routing is easy when considering Fig. 22.8. As the lines drawn between the cities indicate, a routing

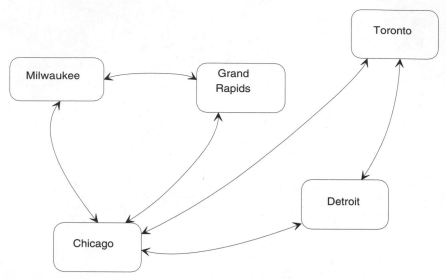

Figure 22.8   Conceptual view of static routing.

path is available. Note the paths that are *not* available. It is not possible to route directly to Toronto from Grand Rapids without going
through Chicago, and this implies that a routing table for this configuration is predetermined. Also, routing from Detroit to Grand Rapids is
not possible without going through Chicago.

This example can be changed once the network is taken offline, but
while the network is operational no changes can be made. Hence, it
derives its name—*static routing*.

These are examples of routing technology. Other methods of routing
are possible. Some ways are protocol-dependent. In order to provide an
example, two different protocols are shown in light of their routing
schemes.

SNA routing

To a considerable degree, routing in SNA is performed on the front end
(the communications controller). The Network Control Program (NCP)
inside has the routes defined, and it utilizes this software to exploit the
hardware and gear involved in the routing process (see Fig. 22.9).

Figure 22.9 shows an example of predefined routes. Each city—Boise,
Idaho; Orange County, California; Chicago, Illinois; and Houston,
Texas—has its hosts configured to route data through the indicated con-
nections. For example, note that no direct connection exists between
Chicago and Orange County. Does this mean they cannot pass data? Not

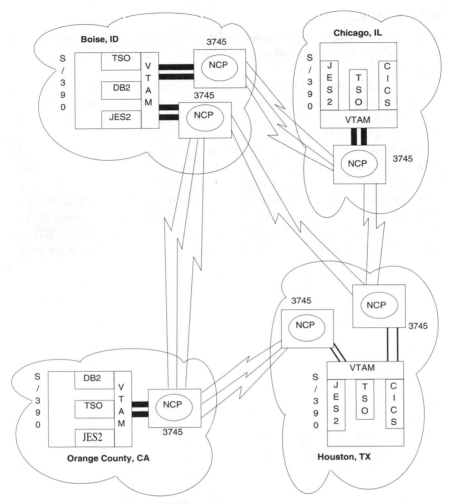

Figure 22.9 Conceptual view of SNA routing.

necessarily—because Boise and Houston are connected to both Chicago and Orange County, they could be configured to route data between those two destinations as well as the ones to which they are physically attached.

In this example, line speed, data compression, type of line (dedicated or switched), and other datacommunication issues are relatively unimportant, because the point is that even though a physical connection may or may not exist directly between two entities does not mean that routing to them cannot be achieved. This is a matter of software, and obviously some physical route must exist, but beyond that it is a matter of configuration.

TCP/IP routing

Routing in TCP/IP is performed by IP, as is explained in Chap. 14. Figure 22.10 shows an example of TCP/IP networks and routers connecting them.

Figure 22.10 shows TCP/IP networks in Columbus, Ohio; Pittsburgh, Pennsylvania; Norfolk, Virginia; and Nashville, Tennessee. These locations are connected via routers. Note that all routers have a physical link with one another. Note also that each LAN's hosts have the same names, and they could be given the same addresses. What differentiates them is the fact that they are located on different networks; therefore, there are no naming or addressing conflicts.

In this example, it is the Internet Protocol (IP) software in conjunction with one of the routing protocols that makes routing possible. The routing protocols could be either Router Information Protocol (RIP) or Open Shortest Path First (OSPF) or others. Obviously, a routing-type

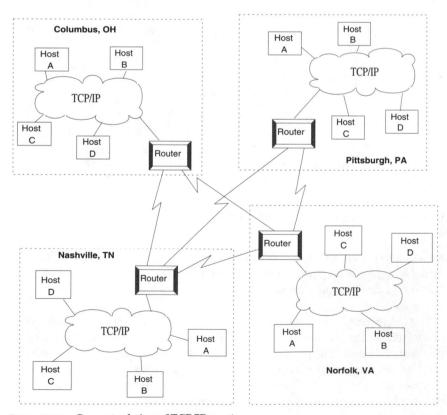

Figure 22.10   Conceptual view of TCP/IP routing.

device is required, but it is nevertheless the combination of IP and the routing protocol that makes this process happen.

Maintaining routing tables is a separate issue here. This could be done via the /etc/networks and /etc/hosts files or via the Domain Name System (DNS). Most likely it will be the latter, because of the power behind how it operates.

These examples of how different network protocols perform routing is enough to show that in a heterogeneous networking environment, routing is not a simple matter. Consider the routing issues involved in the Internet!

22.6 Bandwidth-on-demand Routing

This topic has moved into the forefront of routing in the past few years. The idea of bandwidth-on-demand routing is as its name implies—in plain English, it means that the router uses the line when it needs it and does not keep it *dedicated*. Consider the following examples showing the three phases of this routing.

Figure 22.11 shows two networks, one in Monterey, California and the other in Birmingham, Alabama.

Figure 22.11 shows two multivendor networks with multiple hosts attached to each. It also indicates that no link is established between the two locations. This is important, because it means that *no* dedicated line exists, and that means some degree of money is involved—typically savings.

Figure 22.12, on the other hand, shows a different scenario.

Figure 22.12 shows the same environment as the previous figure, but this time a link is established between the routers.

Figure 22.13 shows how the environment appears once communication is complete.

This example of a bandwidth-on-demand router may well fit the needs of many situations. More than one or two vendors have such devices available today. A consideration regarding this is weighing the consequences of purchasing such a device verses having a router with a dedicated line. Determining the amount of usage should dictate which would be the better solution; my philosophy is that the *customer* should make the decision.

22.7 Router Advantages in Brief

Routers provide a variety of capabilities that are advantageous to networking of different types. With the growth of LANs in the past decade, routers are sometimes the best solution to meet the needs of a given situation.

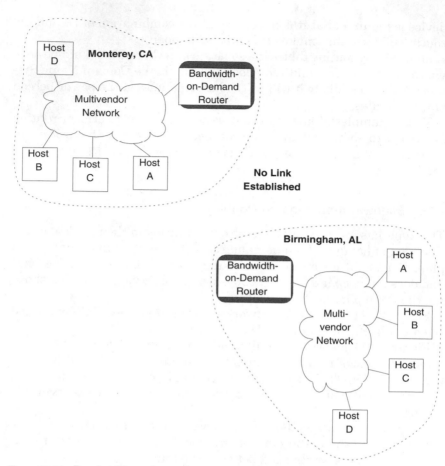

Figure 22.11 Bandwidth-on-demand routing before communication.

Segment isolation

A major advantage routers provide is the ability to split a large network into smaller, more easily manageable ones. This is important because both the number of LANs and the number of specialized devices attached to them are increasing. Figure 22.14 shows an example of how routers can be used to create a more manageable LAN environment.

Figure 22.14 portrays a single-backbone LAN. It is apparent that it is crowded and is difficult to manage. Many different types of traffic are all passed across a single backbone. This puts a load on the network and consequently causes performance degradation.

Figure 22.15 shows an example of the same equipment implemented differently.

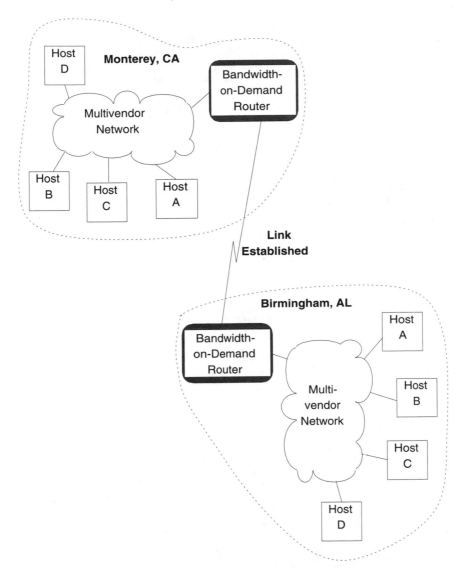

Figure 22.12   Bandwidth-on-demand routing during communication.

In Fig. 22.15, multiple LAN segments have been created, and a real sense of load balancing is the result. Note the three routers that tie the segments together. They are able to control the passing of packets to the correct segment or keep packets on a given segment and thus not impede performance. Another advantage is the capability this configuration provides. With this arrangement, a given segment can be removed from

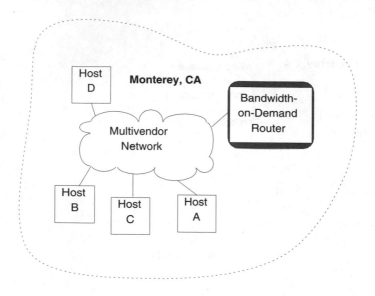

**No Link
Established**

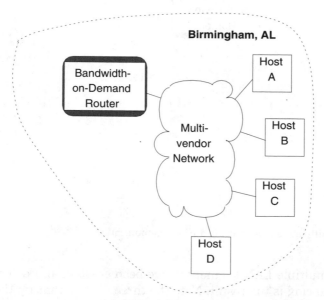

Figure 22.13   Bandwidth-on-demand routing after communication is completed.

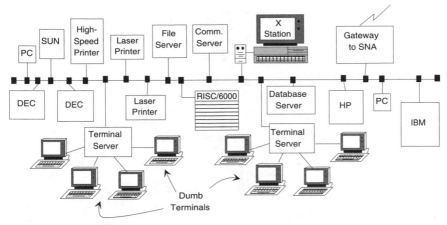

Figure 22.14   Single-backbone LAN.

other segments if changes need to be made or other management-related functions that would affect other LAN segments need to be done.

Multiprotocol support

Many vendors who sell routers have routers that support multiple lower-layer protocols quite effectively. Since the IEEE 802.X protocols call for delineation of the data link layer, it is possible to mix and match a variety of lower-layer protocols (see Fig. 22.16).

Figure 22.16 demonstrates different networks with unlike lower-layer protocols and interface connections. However, because of the versatility of routers they can be merged into the router, as shown in this sketch.

Scalable architecture

Another feature offered by some router vendors is a scalable architecture. For example, some routers can provide basic needs for, say, one protocol while being capable of being upgraded to support other types of lower-layer protocols. Network topologies are a factor in routers. Some router vendors offer routers that have the flexibility to change and expand to interoperate with topologies that change over time.

Other advantages of routers include price-performance, flexibility to support local and remote sites simultaneously, and manageability by network management technologies such as Simple Network Management Protocol (SNMP). Routers also provide what is considered an intelligent link between networks. They can also protect against network failures by their ability to isolate networks. These and other fea-

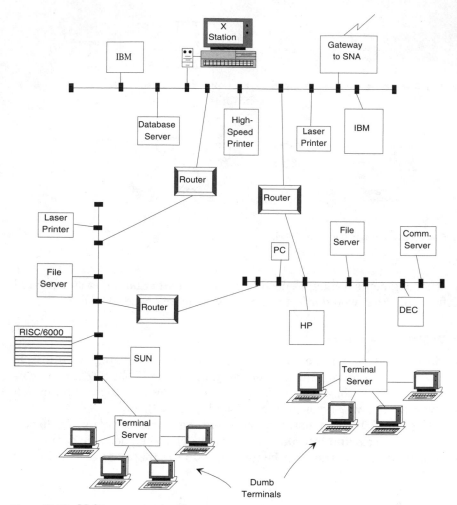

Figure 22.15   Multisegment network.

tures offered by router vendors make routers an attractive solution for meeting internetworking requirements.

22.8   Multiprotocol Routers

Much attention has been given to multiprotocol routers in the past few years. Many vendors have brought such devices to the market.

Perspective

A multiprotocol router supports multiple upper- and lower-layer protocols. By definition, this is complex for one device to do. Also, regardless

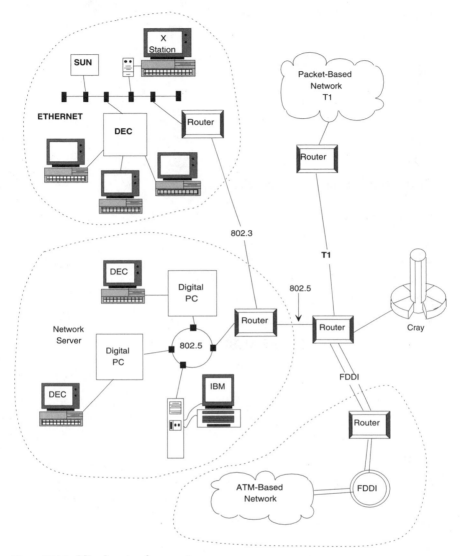

Figure 22.16 Mixed protocol support.

of who the vendor is that supplies a multiprotocol router, it must be a *robust* device to function when multiple protocols are being routed at the same time. These are technical facts, not opinion. Think of it. One device that can route IP, IPX, SNA, DECnet, and AppleTalk must be a powerful, well-architected machine.

Some of the following protocols are supported by various multiprotocol routers. After reading the list, it is reasonably conclusive that multiprotocol routers must be robust.

Physical layer protocols

RS-232

RS-422

RS-449

V.24

V.35

V.36

X.21

Physical layers specified by IEEE 802.X

Data link protocols

SDLC by IBM

ETHERNET V.2 by DIX

X.25 by CCITT

PPP as in RFCs 1171 and 1172

MAC and LLC IEEE protocols

Frame Relay by CCITT and ANSI

Upper-layer protocols

SNA

TCP/IP

AppleTalk

NetWare

OSI

DECnet

XNS

NetBIOS

Routing layer–protocol specific

Internet Protocol (IP)—TCP/IP

Internetwork Datagram Protocol (IDP)—XNS

Datagram Delivery Protocol (DDP)—AppleTalk

Connectionless Network Protocol (CNLP)—OSI

SNA

DECnet

Conceptual view examples

Based on the preceding information, some examples showing multiprotocol routing follow (see Fig. 22.17).

Figure 22.17 shows an example of three multiprotocol routers, three networks, and the backbone Frame Relay network. Since the multiprotocol routers support data layer protocol, connectivity among networks 1, 2, and 3 is possible.

Figure 22.18 shows a different example of a multiprotocol router implementation.

In Fig. 22.18, mixed lower-layer protocol networks are supported by multiprotocol routers, thus making data exchange among them possible.

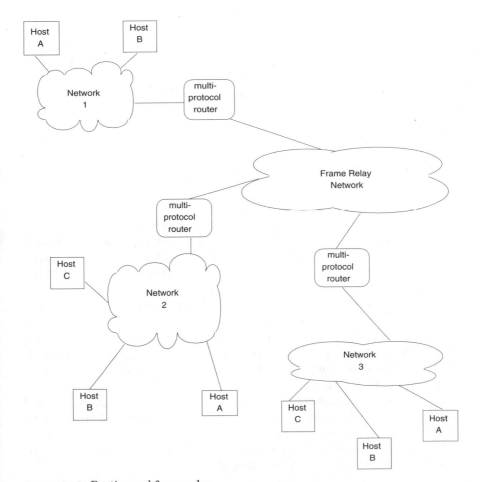

Figure 22.17 Routing and frame relay.

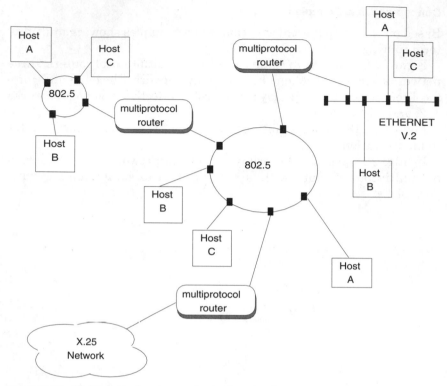

Figure 22.18   Multiprotocol routers and mixed protocols.

Figure 22.19 portrays still a different arrangement.

Figure 22.19 shows an example of multiple networks using different upper- and lower-layer protocols. This example shows the routing capabilities of multiprotocol routing among DECnet networks and TCP/IP networks.

Figure 22.20 shows an example of two NetWare and TCP/IP networks integrated using a multiprotocol router.

In this figure the routers are interconnected together, thus making the NetWare and TCP/IP networks physically and logically connected. Since NetWare supports TCP/IP, a degree of interoperability can be achieved via this arrangement.

A variety of implementations can be achieved with multiprotocol routers. The number of permutations that can be obtained with multiprotocol routers is considerably large.

IBM, Bay Networks, Cisco, and a variety of other vendors offer multiprotocol routers in the marketplace today.

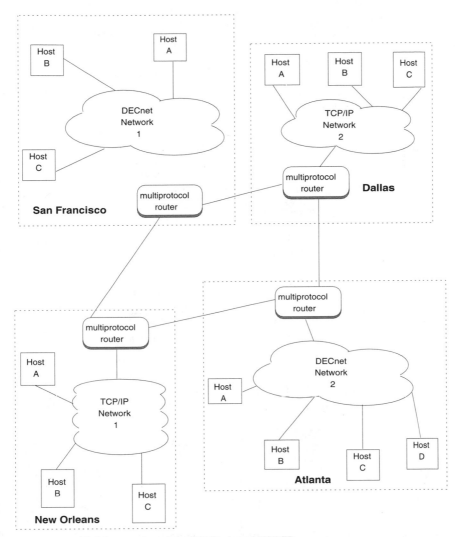

Figure 22.19 Multiprotocol routers, DECnet, and TCP/IP.

22.9 Summary

Routers are complex devices and have been around in some form or other for at least two decades. In the late 1960s and 1970s the device that performed router functions was called a *gateway*, and to this day some still use that term to refer to a router. In the networking community today, legitimate devices that perform router functions exist and are called routers. Likewise, devices called *gateways* exist; they, too, perform a specific function which is generally not routing.

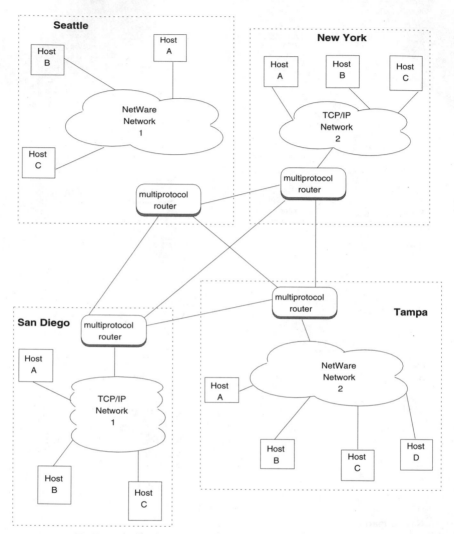

Figure 22.20   NetWare, TCP/IP, and multiprotocol routers.

Multiple types of routers exist. Some support different upper-layer protocols and are protocol-specific in their implementation. Others support different lower-layer protocols and are specific to that end. Any given router generally supports multiple physical layer interfaces, as well as multiple data link layer protocols.

Multiple reasons for routers exist. From a geographical perspective, routers can be used to meet internetworking needs. Some routers are focused upon what is considered a *metropolitan* implementation, where a major facility exists and satellite offices exist within reasonable proximity. *Remote* routers can be used to resolve the integration issues of geographically dispersed networks. The same holds true for what is considered *internal* routing.

Different types of routing are possible. *Centralized* routing focuses the routing tables within a centralized processing device. *Noncentralized* routing implements a strategy where routers exchange information about those routers with which they operate. In *static* routing the routing tables are predetermined. In other words, the tables and paths for routing are determined and configured when the network is nonoperational from a user's perspective.

Two examples of different approaches to routing are presented. SNA routes data primarily via its front-end processor by way of the network control program, but this appears to be changing. This seems to be the case because of recent announcements and because products are now capable of performing functions that not too long ago were considered to be front-processor-type functions. In addition, with the SNA networking blueprint many areas are in a state of flux.

TCP/IP is used as an example of how routing is achieved. Explanation of the software components that are involved in this process is provided. The versatility of the TCP/IP protocol stack makes it possible to consider multiple possibilities for implementation.

In the past few years a type of router has arrived on the market that is differentiated from some of its predecessors. The *bandwidth-on-demand* router is explained. It offers an alternative to a dedicated line for two geographically distant sites that need a router for intermittent connectivity; that is, on demand.

Multiple advantages are realized for those sites where routers are implemented. For example, segment isolation is possible with the implementation of a router. This is significant because troubleshooting and maintenance are easier with a segmented network than with a single-backbone network where crowding exits. Those routers that offer multiprotocol support at the upper and lower layers offer greater flexibility for growing environments. Some scalable routers are on the market today. For example, they can meet immediate needs and have the ability to expand and increase support as further needs arise.

A multiprotocol router has a tall order to achieve many functions at the same time. As in the example presented, a router that supports so many different protocols at the physical interface, data link, and upper-layer protocol layers must be vigorous in its processing capabilities.

Routers may be a part of an integration equation when multiple protocols are used, but they may not meet all possible needs. As is said early on in this chapter, routers *route*.

Network Architecture Study Questions

Network architecture is a difficult topic to teach. It is equally difficult to understand. The vocation of network design requires that many different skills be understood. These questions are helpful for those who desire to sharpen their understanding. I have not provided you with answers because the purpose is for you to benefit. Benefit in any area is not without pain. Take your time to work through these questions if you are serious about learning network design. If, after you have spent some time working with them, you are not satisfied with what you think are the answers, contact me at Edtaylor@aol.com. I will help you—but on the condition that you must be serious, for I have no time for unnecessary questions. You may find *The McGraw-Hill Internetworking Handbook* (ISBN 0-07-063263-4) helpful, for it supplies a much broader presentation of technology used today.

The questions themselves do not *teach* architecture. They do help one to rethink facts. It is the synthesis of compounded facts that creates a repository of knowledge to use in any network design.

Chapter 1

1. Explain some reasons why understanding network architecture is difficult.

2. What happened in 1981 in the technology business?

3. What is network design similar to? Explain why.

4. List at least four common fallacies that some people accept about network design. Explain some possible ramifications regarding the outcome of each.

5. What is a bus topology?

6. Explain how connection-oriented technology can work in a star-configured network.

7. Why are the terms *physical* and *logical* used with computers and networking?

8. How is ring technology implemented? How does it appear?

9. How would you explain to someone why network design is so complex a task?

10. What is the difference between digital and analog signals?

11. How would you explain a digital signal to someone?

12. What is amplitude?

13. What is frequency?

14. What is phase?

15. What is a period (beyond the English use)?

16. What is the fundamental difference between a sine wave and a square wave?

17. What is binary representation of data? Where is it used?

18. What is another way to represent a data value than binary form?

19. Calculate and show the binary values for the following:

A

8

x

(

+

M

m

T

t

20. Calculate and show the hex values for the following:

T

t

N

o

O

i

I

1

D

21. Convert the following hex values into binary:
    E7
    1E
    A2
    2B
    3C
    4D

Chapter 2

1. Is there such a thing as asynchronous transmission? Why or why not?

2. What is parity?

3. How is synchronous transmission obtained?

4. Why is discussion about bandwidth sometimes deceptive and misleading as to actual performance?

5. What is simplex transmission?

6. Explain Frequency Division Multiplexing.

7. What is the difference between a DCE and DTE?

8. What is the purpose of a UART?

9. How do bit and baud rates differ?

10. Explain amplitude, frequency, phase-shift key, and differential phase-shift key modulation.

11. What is encoding? What does it mean?

12. What is a link?

13. Explain signal distortion. List some examples of signal distortion and explain what they mean.

14. What is the difference between hard and soft media? Name and explain two examples of each.

15. Is it possible to use microwave technology to transmit a signal 400 miles? If so, explain how. If not, explain why not.

16. Is there any merit to the argument that rain can distort signals in transmission? If so, explain how this could be true.

Chapter 3

1. What contribution did Herman Hollerith make?

2. What contribution did George Boole make?

3. What contribution did Charles Babbage make?

4. What contribution did John von Neumann make?

5. What is the basic difference between the ideas of centralized computing and decentralized computing.

6. Explain the basic difference between a LAN and a WAN.

7. Comparatively speaking, are technological advances made faster today than some 50 years ago? If so, why? If not, why not?

Chapter 4

1. Explain the general timeframe for when personal computing began. Who were the primary vendors providing equipment?

2. Illustrate early PC architecture.

3. Illustrate PC architecture today.

4. What does the reference *ISA cards* mean?

5. Explain the difference between ISA, EISA, PNP, and PCMCIA.

6. Draw and explain the primary network architectures of the 1970s, 1980s, and 1990s.

Chapter 5

1. What should factor into the equation of network design?

2. List at least eight considerations that one should make prior to ordering any network equipment.

3. Explain, generally, the electrical considerations that should be part of any network design.

4. List at least 10 technical factors that should be part of your network planning.

Chapter 6

1. What is the significance of buying computers that can be upgraded?

2. What is the significance of having electrical and telephone testing equipment?

3. What is the significance of obtaining Ethernet HUBs that can be expanded?

4. Why is power protection equipment needed?

Chapter 7

1. What are some of the advantages to having a device that can provide information at a HUB level in a network?

2. Why should operating system–level information be considered during the network design phase?

3. Explain the major printer data streams. Which ones are significant to your site? How significant are the rest?

4. What are some ways to ensure secure operating environments where you are located?

5. What are some possible products that can be used to secure your environment?

6. What considerations should be included in your site if multimedia needs exist?

7. Why are network analyzers important?

8. What could the network analyzer do in the network described in this text?

9. What miscellaneous equipment was used during the planning and implementation of this network?

Chapter 8

1. What is a benefit from designing a network that can run dual protocols?

2. What benefit is shown in the illustration where two rack enclosures of duplicate equipment is provided (Fig. 8.3)?

3. What advantage does the Enterprise network HUB offer?

4. What four characteristics should be considered in your network at the earliest phases? List and explain examples of these.

5. What meters, analyzers, and scopes are considered a must for maintenance?

6. What advantages does the HP Internet Advisor provide?

7. What one item is critical to network maintenance? Explain how this fits your network design.

8. List at least 10 items to build your network plans around.

9. How will the Y2K problem affect you?

10. A list of things was provided for you to include in your maintenance plan in order to avoid problems. What are they?

Chapter 9

1. What is ATM?

2. Why is ATM popular?

3. What advantage does ATM have over other switching technologies?

4. List some functions that the ATM physical layer performs.

5. List some ATM functions.

6. List some functions that the ATM adaptation layer performs.

7. What fields comprise the ATM header, and what do they do?

8. What is the difference between a private network interface and a public network interface?

9. What are the protocol categories defined at the ATM adaptation layer?

10. Explain the meaning of a transmission path.

11. Explain the meaning of a virtual path.

12. Explain the meaning of a virtual circuit (channel).

13. List at least two interfaces used at the physical level of ATM. Explain their data rate transfer speeds.

14. List some of the functions that occur at the transmission convergence sublayer.

15. Explain some characteristics of a local router and ATM backbone.

16. What does it mean to say "ATM backbone?"

17. Draw and explain a diagram of ATM LANs connected to an ATM backbone.

18. Define ATM link, segment, ATM, and symmetric connection.

19. Briefly explain SONET.

20. Briefly explain DS3.

Chapter 10

1. Explain the basic meaning of ISDN.

2. What are some of the services derived from ISDN implementations?

3. List and briefly explain the CCITT recommendations presented that relate to ISDN technology.

4. What is a B channel?

5. What is a D channel?

6. What functions does a D channel perform?

7. What does an H channel provide?

8. What is SS7?

9. What are some characteristics of SS7?

10. What are the three SS7 protocol components?

11. List some additional references for SS7.

12. What is a basic rate interface?

13. What is a primary rate interface?

14. For what purposes are interfaces used?

15. List and explain at least two practical uses of services provided as a result of ISDN technology.

Chapter 11

1. What are some basic characteristics of frame relay?

2. What is frame relay *not?*

3. What three groups have contributed standards or recommendations to the refinement of frame relay?

4. Explain the concept of a virtual connection and the meaning of mapping tables.

5. Explain the purpose of the data link connection identifier.

6. List some considerations of peripheral costs when implementing frame relay.

7. Draw a frame relay frame. Explain the components of each field.

8. List and explain the three types of virtual circuits (connections).

9. Explain the basic difference between a switch, a network device, and a frame relay access device.

10. List at least two consumer tips related to frame relay.

Chapter 12

1. Why is network management a difficult topic to explore and discuss?

2. List at least six items that require management in a network.

3. List and explain the different major management philosophies.

4. How does poll-driven management differ from event-driven management?

5. What is the typical way in which TCP/IP has been managed in the past?

6. Explain the role that managing a network plays with regard to resource utilization requirements.

7. Explain how link bandwidth can be managed.

8. Explain the meaning that can be obtained when the response time of a certain device is monitored.

9. What are some possible interpretations that could generally be made if a device had only resource monitor management performed on it?

10. What type of information could be obtained by managing an application? List some examples.

11. Should any consideration be made regarding management for data networks that might not be applicable for multimedia networks? Explain your reasoning.

Chapter 13

1. Explain the reason why it is important to be aware of different file structures.

2. What is the difference between MVS PDSs and UNIX files?

3. Explain why one needs to know the difference between files on Apple computers and on MVS systems.

4. Which file structures will you have in your network?

Chapter 14

1. Briefly explain the history of TCP/IP.

2. Draw a diagram of the basic TCP/IP components.

3. Explain the basic function of each TCP/IP component in the drawing.

4. What functions does IP perform?

5. What function does ICMP perform?

6. Explain ARP and RARP operations. Then explain typical implementations where they are used.

7. What is TCP? List its major characteristics.

8. What is UDP? List its major characteristics.

9. What is RIP? What does it do, and how does it do it?

10. What is OSPF? What does it do, and how does it do it?

11. What is SNMP?

12. List and explain the basic functions of the components that work with SNMP so it can function.

13. What is X?

14. List and explain the layers of X.

15. What is the difference between a raw Telnet client and a TN3270 client?

16. What is FTP? What functions does it provide?

17. Define and explain the operation of SMTP.

18. What is RPC? How does it operate?

19. What is XDR? What function does it perform?

20. What is NFS? How does it operate?

21. Why would an individual want to write a custom application and use UDP as a transport mechanism?

22. What is DNS?

23. Explain the theory of operation of DNS.

24. What is the current addressing scheme of IP? Explain the classifications and what they mean with regard to networks and hosts.

25. For what is PING used?

Chapter 15

1. IP Version 4 implements two basic functions. What are they?

2. What is a type of service?

3. What is the meaning of *time to live*?

4. Explain by example your understanding of how IP operation works.

5. Explain why fragmentation is necessary.

6. Explain the basic difference between a *name,* an *address,* and a *route.*

7. Define the following terms:
   ARPA packet
   Fragment offset
   ICMP
   IHL
   IMP
   Local address
   MF
   Module
   NFB
   Rest
   Type of service

8. What is a recorded route?

9. Give an overview of the reassembly procedure.

Chapter 16

1. What is the major difference between IP version 6 and IP version 4?
2. Explain the following terms:
   Upper layer
   Link
   Neighbors
   Link MTU
   Path MTU
3. What is the hop-by-hop Options Header function?
4. What is the purpose of the IP version 6 routing header?
5. What is the purpose of the fragment header?
6. The destinations option header is used for what purpose?
7. What significant information should be considered concerning packet size and IP version 6?
8. What is the purpose of IP Flow labels in version 6?
9. Explain the packet priority field in IP version 6.
10. Explain IP version 6 in light of upper-layer protocols.
11. What are the three types of IP version 6 addressing?
12. Explain a Unicast Address.
13. Explain a Anycast Address.
14. Explain a Multicast Address.
15. Explain a Global Unicast Address.
16. Explain the notion of a Node Address Requirement.

Chapter 17

1. What is the basic idea behind DHCP operation?
2. How does the address allocation function work?
3. Define and explain the following terms:
   DHCP Client
   DHCP Server
   BOOTP Relay Agent
   Binding
4. What were some of the basic ideas behind the original design intent of DHCP?
5. Discuss and explain the DHCP Message Format.

6. What are some DHCP Configuration Parameters?

7. Define the following terms:
   DHCPDISCOVER
   DHCPOFFER
   DHCPREQUEST
   DHCPACK
   DHCPNACK
   DHCPRELEASE
   DHCPINFORM

8. Briefly discuss the DHCP server function.

9. Discuss the DHCP Discover Message.

10. Briefly explain the DHCP Client function.

Chapter 18

1. What is the basic idea behind the Domain Name System?

2. What were the original design goals of the DNS?

3. List and explain three assumptions about DNS usage.

4. List and explain the three major components of the DNS.

5. What are DNS queries, and how do they work?

6. Discuss and explain DNS Name Servers.

7. Explain database zone division.

8. Discuss DNS administration.

9. What is a DNS Resolver? How do they work?

Chapter 19

1. List and explain some of NetWare's historical roots.

2. Explain the operation of NetWare according to its layers.

3. Explain IPX and its operation.

4. Explain SPX and its operation.

5. What is ODI?

6. What is NCP?

7. What is SAP?

8. How is ODI implemented?

9. How is ODI managed?

10. What is the IPX packet structure?

11. Show and explain the SPX packet structure.

12. Explain the idea of service type in light of SPX.

13. Explain the basic idea behind the following protocols:
ERROR
ECHO
NetBIOS

14. Explain System Fault Tolerance.

15. Explain the power behind the LANRES product. Why should this product be considered during the planning phase of the network?

Chapter 20

1. To what point in time do the origins of NT reach?

2. What are some characteristics of NT version 3.5?

3. List and explain some characteristics of NT version 4 Workstation and Server.

4. List and explain the four identifiable components of NT version 4.

5. What is the significance of the HAL?

6. Discuss and briefly explain the Virtual Memory Manager.

7. List and explain in detail at least five commonalities between NT Workstation and Server.

8. Describe a domain.

9. Describe trust relationships with regard to Windows NT.

10. What is the registry? What are some of its purposes?

11. Are there any advantages to manual IP address assignment in smaller networks? If so, what do you think they are?

12. Explain why high-speed server connections are necessary with NT Server. What components are used in the example network presented here in this book? What is the significance of the example?

13. What are some advantages of using four-port network interface boards?

Chapter 21

1. At which layers in a network does a bridge operate?

2. What are some functional advantages of implementing a bridge?

3. Explain the filtering function of a bridge.

4. What is the learning function of a bridge?

5. What is the forwarding function of a bridge?

6. Explain why a company with multiple departments and multiple LANs might want to put them together via a bridge.

7. What function does a remote Token Ring bridge perform?

8. What would be some justifying premises for installing a bridge to merge a Token Ring and an Ethernet-based network?

9. What does the term *local bridge* mean?

10. Explain the functional difference between a source routing bridge and a transparent bridge.

11. Draw and explain an IBM Token Ring frame.

12. Explain the contents of the routing information field down to the bit level according to the explanation provided in this chapter.

13. What is a segment number?

14. What is a nonbroadcast frame?

15. What is a broadcast frame?

16. Explain the functional nature of a nonbroadcast frame.

17. Briefly explain route discovery.

Chapter 22

1. At what layers do routers function?

2. Briefly explain some of the confusion concerning the terminology of *routers* and *gateways*.

3. List and explain at least two reasons for routing.

4. List and explain the different types of routing covered in this chapter.

5. What is the difference between static routing and centralized routing?

6. Explain the fundamental concept behind SNA routing.

7. Explain the fundamental concept behind TCP/IP routing.

8. What role does the NCP perform in SNA routing?

9. What role does IP perform in TCP/IP routing?

10. Based upon information in this chapter and that in previous chapters, explain the fundamental difference in RIP and OSPF routing.

11. Explain the concept of bandwidth-on-demand routing.

12. Explain the idea of segment isolation and the use of a router in such environment.

13. Why would any potential router buyer be interested in scalable architecture?

14. Explain the basic concept behind a multiprotocol router as if you were explaining the benefits to a potential customer.

15. Based upon information provided about the multiprotocol routers, draw a valid implementation with at least two networks and explain the functionality provided because of multiprotocol routing.

80386, 80486, 80386SX, and 80486SX are trademarks of Intel Corporation.

ACF/VTAM, AS/400, CICS, CICS/ESA, CICS/MVS, DATABASE 2, DB2, DFSMS, DFSMS.MVS, Enterprise System/3090, Enterprise System/4381, Enterprise System/9000, Enterprise Systems Architecture/370, Enterprise Systems Architecture/390, Enterprise Systems Connection Architecture, ES/3090, ES/4381, ES/9000, ESA/370, ESA/390, ESCON, ESCON XDF, GDDM, Hardware Configuration Definition, Hiperspace, Hiperbatch, IBM, IBMLink, IMS, IMS/ESA, Information Warehouse, MVS, MVS/DFP, MVS/ESA, MVS/SP, MVS/XA, NCP, NetView, OS/2, OpenEdition, PR/SM, Presentation Manager, Processor Resource/Systems Manager, PSF, PS/2, RACF, RS6000, SDLC, SNA, Sysplex Timer, System/370, SystemView, VM/ESA, VM/XA, VTAM, and 3090 are registered trademarks of International Business Machines Corporation.

ACMS, ALL-IN-1, Alpha AXP, AXP, Bookreader, CDA, CDD, CDD/REpository, CI COHESION, DEC, DEC ACCESSWORKS, DEC MAILworks, DEC GKS, DEC PHIGS, DEC Rdb for Open VMS, DEC RTR, DEC VTX, DEC VUIT, DECalert, DECamds, DECdecision, DECdesign, DECdtm, DECforms, DECmcc, DECmessageQ, DECnet, DECNIS, DECperformance Solution, DECplan, DECprint, DECquery, DECram, DECscheduler, DECserver, DECset, DECtalk, DEC term, DECthreads, DECtp, DECtrace, DECwindows, DECwrite, Digital, DNA, EDT, eXcursion, HSC, Lat, LinkWorks, MSCP, OpenVMS, PATHWORKS, POLYCENTER, Reliable Transaction router, rtVAX, TMSCP, Trellis, TURBOchannel, ULTRIX, VAX, VAX Ada, VAX APL, VAX BASIC, VAX BLISS-32, VAX C, VAX COBOL, VAX DBMS, VAX DIBOL, VAX DOCUMENT, VAX DATATRIEVE, VAX DSM, VAX

FORTRAN, VAX LISP, VAX MACRO, VAX Notes, VAX OPS5, VAX Pascal, VAX RALLY, VAX RMS, VAX SCAN, VAX SQL, VAX TEAM-DATA, VAXcluster, VAXELN, VAXft, VAXmail, VAXshare, VAXsim-PLUS, VAXstation, VIDA, VMS, VT100, VT220, VT330, WPS, WPS-PLUS, XUI, the AXP logo, and the DIGITAL logo are trademarks of Digital Equipment Corporation.

AIXwindows, PC-AT, PS/2, Proprinter, RISC System/6000, and RT are trademarks of International Business Machines Corporation.

APDA, AppleColor, Apple Disktop Bus, AppleShare, AppleTalk, Finder, KanjiTalk, LaserWriter, Macintosh, MPW, MultiFinder, and Switcher are trademarks of Apple Computers, Inc.

Apollo, NCS, and Network Computing System are registered trademarks of Apollo Computer, Inc.

Apple, the Apple logo, AppleShare, AppleTalk, Apple IIGS, A/UX, HyperCard, ImageWrite, LaserWriter, Lisa, MacApp, Macintosh, MacWorks, and SANE are registered trademarks of Apple Computers, Inc.

Cisco is a registered trademark of Cisco Systems, Inc.

DEC, DECnet, and VAX are registered trademarks of Digital Equipment Corporation.

EtherCard PLUS is a trademark of Western Digital Corporation.

Etherlink is a trademark of 3Com Corporation.

Ethernet is a registered trademark of Xerox Corporation.

Ethernet, Xerox, and XNS are trademarks of Xerox Corporation.

HP is a registered trademark of Hewlett-Packard Company.

HP is a trademark of Hewlett-Packard Company.

HYPERchannel is a registered trademark of Network Systems Corporation.

Intel is a registered trademark of Intel Corporation.

IPX is a registered trademark of Novell Corporation.

Kerberos and XWindow are registered trademarks of the Massachusetts Institute of Technology.

LattisNet is a registered trademark of SynOptics Communications, Inc.

MacDraw, MacPaint, and MacWrite are registered trademarks of Claris Corporation.

Madge is a trademark of Madge Networks Ltd.

Microsoft C, Microsoft Windows, and MS-DOS are registered trademarks of Microsoft Corporation.

Microsoft, Windows, and Word for Windows are trademarks of Microsoft Corporation.

NAP is a registered trademark of Automated Network Management, Inc.

NETMAP is a registered trademark of SynOptics Communications, Inc.

NetWare, Novell, Internetwork Packet eXchange, and IPX are registered trademarks of Novell, Inc.

NetWare, Novell, and IPX are trademarks of Novell, Inc.

Network File System, NFS, PC-NFS, Portmapper, Sun, and SunOS are registered trademarks of Sun Microsystems, Inc.

NuBus is a trademark of Texas Instruments.

OSF and OSF/Motif are registered trademarks of the Open Software Foundation, Inc.

POSIX is a trademark of the Institute of Electrical and Electronic Engineers.

PostScript is a registered trademark of Adobe Systems, Inc.

PostScript is a trademark of Adobe Systems, Inc.

SUN and NFS are trademarks of Sun Microsystems, Inc.

UNIX is licensed by and is a registered trademark of UNIX System Laboratories, Inc.

UNIX is a registered trademark of AT&T Information Systems.

UNIX is a trademark of Unix System Laboratories, Inc.

X/Open is a registered trademark of X.Open Company Ltd.

X-Windows is a trademark of the Massachusetts Institute of Technology.

Network Architecture Acronyms and Abbreviations

10base-T	Technical name for Ethernet implemented on twisted wire
3270	Reference to a 3270 Data Stream Supporting Entity
3770	Reference to Remote Job Entry
370/XA	370/ eXtended Architecture
5250	Reference to a 5250 Data Stream Supporting Entity
576	The minimum datagram size ALL hosts, including routers, must accommodate
AAA	Autonomous Administrative Area
AAI	Administration Authority Identifier
AAL	ATM Adaptation Layer
AARP	AppleTalk Address Resolution Protocol
ABOM	A-bis Operations and Maintenance
ACB	Access Method Control Block
ACB	Application Control Block
ACCS	Automated Calling Card Service
ACD	Automatic Call Distribution
ACDF	Access Control Decision Function
ACE	Access Control List Entry
ACF	Access Control Field
ACF	Advanced Communications Function
ACIA	Access Control Inner Areas
ACID	Atomicity, Consistency, Isolation, and Durability
ACK	Positive Acknowledgement

ACL	Access Control List
ACP	Ancillary Control Process
ACS	Access Control Store
ACSA	Access Control Specific Area
ACSE	Association Control Service Element
ACSP	Access Control Specific Point
ACTLU	Activate Logical Unit
ACTPU	Activate Physical Unit
ACU	Auto Calling Unit
AD	Addendum Document to an OSI Standard
ADF	Adapter Description File
ADMD	Administrative Management Domain
ADP	Adapter Control Block
ADPCM	Adaptive Differential Pulse Code Modulation
ADSP	AppleTalk Data Stream Protocol
AE	Application Entity
AEI	Application Entity Invocation
AEP	AppleTalk Echo Protocol
AET	Application Entity Title
AF	Auxiliary Facility
AFI	Authority and Format Identifier
AFP	AppleTalk Filing Protocol
AI	Artificial Intelligence
AIFF	Audio Interchange File Format
AIX	Advanced Interactive Executive
ALS	Application Layer Structure
ALU	Application Layer User
AMI	Alternating Mark Inversion
ANI	Automatic Number Identification
ANS	American National Standard
ANSI	American National Standards Institute
AP	Application Process
AP	Argument Pointer
APB	Alpha Primary Bootstrap
APD	Avalanche Photodiode
APDU	Application Protocol Data Unit
API	Application Program Interface; Application Programming Interface

APIC	Advanced Programming Interrupt Controller
APLI	ACSE/Presentation Library Interface
APP	Applications Portability Profile
APPC	Advanced Peer-to-Peer Communications
APPC	Advanced Program-to-Program Communications
APPL	Application Program
APPN	Advanced Peer-to-Peer Networking
APT	Application Process Title
ARP	Address Resolution Protocol
ARPA	Advanced Research Projects Agency
ARQ	Automatic Repeat Request
ARS	Automatic Route Selection
AS/400	Application System/400
ASC	Accredited Standard Committee
ASCII	American Standard Code for Information Interchange
ASDC	Abstract Service Definition Convention
ASE	Application Service Element
ASN	Abstract Syntax Notation
ASN.1	Abstract Syntax Notation One
ASO	Application Service Object
ASP	Abstract Service Primitive; AppleTalk Session Protocol
AST	Asynchronous System Trap
ASTLVL	Asynchronous System Trap Level
ASTSR	Asynchronous System Trap Summary Register
ATM	Asynchronous Transfer Mode; Abstract Text Method
ATP	AppleTalk Transaction Protocol
ATS	Abstract Test Suite
AU	Access Unit
AVA	Attribute Value Assertion
B8ZS	Bipolar 8-Zeros Substitution
BACM	Basic Access Control Model
BAR	Base Address Register
BAS	Basic Activity Subset
BASIC	Beginners All-purpose Instruction Code
BB	Begin Bracket
BBS	Bulletin Board System
BC	Begin Chain
BCC	Block Check Character

BCS	Basic Combined Subset
BCVT	Basic Class Virtual Terminal
Bellcore	Bell Communications Research, Inc.
BER	Bit Error Rate
BER	Box Event Records
BGP	Border Gateway Protocol
BIB	Backward Indicator Bit
BIS	Bracket Initiation Stopped
B-ISDN	Broadband ISDN
BISUP	Broadband ISUP
BITNET	Because It's Time Network
BITS	Building Integrated Timing Systems
BIU	Basic Information Unit
BMS	Basic Mapping Support
BMU	Basic Measurement Unit
BNN	Boundary Network Node
BOC	Bell Operating Company
BOM	Beginning of Message
bps	Bits per second
BRI	Basic Rate Interface
BSC	Binary Synchronous Communications
BSS	Basic Synchronization Subset; Base Station Subsystem
BSSMAP	Base Station Subsystem Mobile Application Part
BTAM	Basic Telecommunications Access Method
BTU	Basic Transmission Unit
CA	Certification Authority
CA	Channel Adapter
CAD	Computer-aided design
CAE	Common Applications Environment
CAF	Channel Auxiliary Facility
CAI	Computer-Assisted Instruction
CASE	Common Application Service Elements
CATV	Community Antenna Television
CBD	Changeback Declaration
CBEMA	Computer & Business Equipment Manufacturers Association
CCA	Conceptual Communication Area
CCAF	Call Control Agent Function

CCAF+	Call Control Agent Function Plus
CCB	Channel Control Block
CCB	Connection Control Block
CCIRN	Coordinating Committee for Intercontinental Research Networking
CCIS	Common Channel Interoffice Signaling
CCITT	Consultative Committee for International Telephone & Telegraph
CCO	Context Control Object
CCR	Commitment, Concurrency, and Recovery
CCS	Common Channel Signaling
CCS	Common Communications Support
CCU	Central Control Unit
CCU	Communications Control Unit
CCW	Channel Command Word
CD	Committee Draft
CD	Countdown Counter
CDF	Configuration Dataflow
CDI	Change Direction Indicator
CDRM	Cross Domain Resource Manager
CDRSC	Cross-Domain Resource
CDS	Conceptual Data Storage
CDS	Conceptual Data Store
CEBI	Conditional End Bracket Indicator
CEI	Connection Endpoint Identifier
CEN/ELEC	Committee European de Normalization Electrotechnique
CEP	Connection-endpoint
CEPT	Conference of European Postal and Telecommunications Administrations
CESID	Caller Emergency Service Identification
CF	Control Function
CGM	Computer Graphics Metafile
CHILL	CCITT High-Level Language
CICS	Customer Information Control System
CIDR	Classless Inter-Domain Routing
CIGOS	Canadian Interest Group on Open Systems
CIM	Computer Integrated Manufacturing
CIS	Card Information Structure
CLI	Connectionless Internetworking

CLIST	Command List
CLNP	Connectionless Network Protocol
CLNS	Connectionless Network Service
CLSDST	Close Destination
CLTP	Connectionless Transport Protocol
CLTS	Connectionless Transport Service
CMC	Communications Management Configurations
CMIP	Common Management Information Protocol
CMIS	Common Management Information Service
CMISE	Common Management Information Service Element
CMOL	CMIP Over Logical Link Control
CMOT	CMIP Over TCP/IP
CMS	Conversational Monitor System
CMT	Connection Management
CN	Composite Node
CNM	Communication Network Management
CNMA	Communication Network for Manufacturing Applications
CNMI	Communication Network Management Interface
CNOS	Change Number of Sessions
CNT	Communications Name Table
CO	Central Office
COCF	Connection-Oriented Convergence Function
CODEC	Coder/Decoder
COI	Connection-Oriented Internetworking
COM	Continuation-of-Message DMPDU
CONF	Confirm
CONS	Connection-Oriented Network Service
CORBA	Common Object-Oriented Request Broker Architecture
COS	Class of Service
COS	Corporation for Open Systems
COTP	Connection Oriented Transport Protocol
COTS	Connection Oriented Transport Service
CP	Control Point
CP	Control Program
CPE	Customer Premises Equipment
CPH	Call Party Handling
CPF	Control Program Facility
CPI	Common Programming Interface

CPI-C	Common Programming Interface with C Language
CPMS	Control Point Management Services
CRACF	Call-Related Radio Access Control Function
CRC	Cyclical Redundancy Check
CRST	Cluster-Route-Set-Test
CRT	Cathode Ray Tube
CRV	Call Reference Value
CSm	Call Segment Model
CSMA/CA	Carrier Sense Multiple Access with Collision Avoidance
CSMA/CD	Carrier Sense Multiple Access with Collision Detection
CS-MUX	Circuit Switching Multiplexer
CSP	Communications Scanner Processor
CSN	Card Select Number Register
CSNET	Computer and Science Network
CSS	Control, Signaling, and Status Store
CSU	Channel Service Unit
CTC	Channel-to-Channel
CTCA	Channel-to-Channel Adaptor
CTCP	Communication and Transport Control Program
CTS	Clear-to-Send
CUA	Channel Unit Address; Common User Access
CURACF	Call Unreleated Service Function
CUT	Control Unit Terminal
CVS	Connection View State
CVT	Communications Vector Table
DACD	Directory Access Control Domain
DAD	Draft Addendum
DAF	Distributed Architecture Framework; Framework for Distributed Applications; Destination Address Field
DAP	Directory Access Protocol
DAS	Dual Attachment Station; Dynamically Assigned Sockets
DAT	Dynamic Address Translation
dB	Decibels
DCA	Document Content Architecture
DCC	Data Country Code
DCE	Data Communications Equipment; Distributed Computing Environment; Data Circuit-Terminating Equipment; Distributed Computing Environment
DCS	Defined Context Set

DDCMP   Digital Data Communication Message Protocol
DDIM   Device Driver Initialization Model
DDM   Distributed Data Management
DDN   Data Defense Network
DDP   Datagram Delivery Protocol
DDS   Digital Data Service
DES   Data Encryption Standard
DFC   Data Flow Control
DECNET   Digital Equipment's Network Architecture
DFI   DSP Format Identifier
DFT   Distributed Function Terminal
DHCP   Dynamic Host Configuration Protocol
DH   DMPDU Header
DIA   Document Interchange Architecture
DIB   Directory Information Base
DIS   Draft International Standard
DISP   Draft International Standardized Profile
DISP   Directory Information Shadowing Protocol
DIT   Directory Information Tree
DIU   Distribution Interchange Unit
DL   Distribution List
DLC   Data Link Control; Data Link Connection
DLCEP   Data Link Connection Endpoint
DLCI   Data Link Connection Identifier
DLPDU   Data Link Protocol Data Unit
DLS   Data Link Service
DLSAP   Data Link Service Access Point
DLSDU   Data Link Service Data Unit
DLU   Dependent Logical Unit
DMA   Direct Memory Access
DMD   Directory Management Domain
DMI   Digital Multiplexed Interface; Definition of Management
           Information; Desktop Management Interface
DMO   Domain Management Organization
DMPDU   Derived MAC Protocol Data Unit
DMTF   Desktop Management Task Force
DMUX   Double Multiplexer
DN   Distinguished Name

DNHR	Dynamic Nonhierarchical Routing
DNS	Domain Name System
DoD	U.S. Department of Defense
DOP	Directory Operational Binding Management Protocol
DOS	Disk Operating System
DP	Draft Proposal
DPG	Dedicated Packet Group
DPI	Dots per Inch
DQDB	Distributed Queue Dual Bus
DR	Definite Response
DS	Directory Services
DS3	Telephony classification of leased line speed
DS-n	Digital Signaling Level n
DSA	Directory Service Agent
DSAP	Destination Service Access Point
DSD	Data Structure Definition
DSE	DSA Specific Entries
DSL	Digital Subscriber Line
DSP	Directory Service Protocol
DSP	Domain Specific Part
DSS 1	Digital Subscriber Signaling System No. 1
DSTINIT	Data Services Task Initialization
DSU	Digital Services Unit
DSUN	Distribution Services Unit Name
DT	DMPDU Trailer
DTE	Data Terminal Equipment
DTMF	Dual-Tone Multifrequency
DTR	Data Terminal Ready
DU	Data Unit
DUA	Directory User Agent
DUP	Data User Port
DVMRP	Distance Vector Multicast Routing Protocol
E.164	An ATM address format speficied by the ITU-TS
EACK	Extended Acknowledgement
EARN	European Academic Research
EAS	Extended Area Service
EB	End Bracket
EBCDIC	Extended Binary-Coded Decimal Interchange Code

ECA	Event Detection Point
ECC	Enhanced Error Checking and Correction
ECH	Echo Canceller with Hybrid
ECMA	European Computer Manufacturers' Association
ECO	Echo Control Object
ECSA	Exchange Carriers Standards Association
EDI	Electronic Data Interchange
EDIFACT	EDI for Administration, Commerce, and Transport
EDIM	EDI Message
EDIME	EDI Messaging Environment
EDI-MS	EDI Message Store
EDIMS	EDI Messaging System
EDIN	EDI Notification
EDI-UA	EDI-User Agent
EEI	External Environment Interface
EGP	Exterior Gateway Protocol
EIA	Electronic Industries Association
EISA	Extended Industry Standard Architecture
EIT	Encoded Information type
E-Mail	Electronic Mail
EN	End Node
ENA	Extended Network Addressing
ENV	European Prestandards
EOM	End-of-Message DMPDU
EOT	End of Transmission
EP	Emulation Program
ER	Exception Response
ER	Explicit Route
EREP	Environmental Recording, Editing, and Printing
ES	End System
ESA	Enhanced Subarea Addressing
ESA	Enterprise Systems Architecture
ESCON	Enterprise System Connectivity
ESF	Extended Superframe Format
ESH	End System Hello
ES-IS	End System Intermediate System
ESS	Electronic Switching System
ESTELLE	Extended State Transition Language

ETB	End-of-Text Block
ETR	Early Token Release
ETX	End of Text
EUnet	European UNIX network
EUUG	European UNIX User's Group
EWOS	European Workshop on Open Systems
FA	Framework Advisory
FADU	File Access Data Unit
FARNET	Federation of American Research Networks
FAS	Frame Alignment Sequence
FAT	File Allocation Table
FC	Frame Control Field
FCC	Federal Communications Commission
FCS	Frame Check Sequence
FDCO	Field Definition Control Object
FDDI	Fiber Distributed Data Interface
FDDI-FO	FDDI Follow-On
FDM	Frequency Division Multiplexing
FDR	Field Definition Record
FDT	Formal Description Technique
FDX	Full Duplex
FEC	Field Entry Condition
FEE	Field Entry Event
FEI	Field Entry Instruction
FEICO	Field Entry Instruction Control Object
FEIR	Field Entry Instruction Record
FEP	Front End Processor
FEPCO	Field Entry Pilot Control Object
FEPR	Field Entry Pilot Record
FER	Field Entry Reaction
FFOL	FDDI Follow-on LAN
FID	Format Identification
FIPS	Federal Information Processing Standard
FISU	Fill In Signal Unit
FM	Function Management
FMH	Function Management Header
FOD	Office Document Format
FOR	Forward Transfer

FNC	Federal Networking Council
FR	Family of Requirement
FRICC	Federal Research Internet Coordinating Committee
FRMR	Frame Reject
FS	Frame Status Field
FSG	SGML Interchange Format
FSM	Finite State Machine
FTAM	File Transfer and Access Management
FTP	File Transfer Protocol in TCP/IP
FYI	For Your Information
FX	Foreign Exchange Service
Gb	Gigabit
Gbps	Gigabits per second
GDMO	Guidelines for the Definition of Managed Objects
GDS	Generalized Data Stream
GFI	General Format Indicator
GFP	Global Functional Plane
GGP	Gateway-to-Gateway Protocol
GMT	Greenwich Mean Time
GPS	Global Positioning System
GOSIP	Government OSI Protocol
GSA	General Services Administration
GTF	Generalized Trace Facility
GWNCP	Gateway NCP
GWSSCP	Gateway SSCP
HAL	Hardware Abstraction Layer
HCL	Hardware Compatibility List
HCS	Header Check Sequence
HDB3	High-Density Bipolar—3 zeros
HDLC	High Level Data Link Control
HDX	Half Duplex
HI-SAP	Hybrid Isochronous-MAC Service Access Point
HLR	Home Location Register
HMP	Host Monitoring Protocol
H-MUX	Hybrid Multiplexer
HOB	Head of Bus
HP-SAP	Hybrid Packet-MAC Service Access Point
HRC	Hybrid Ring Control

HSLN	High-Speed Local Network
HTML	Hypertext Markup Language
HTTP	Hypertext Transfer Protocol
Hz	Hertz (cycles per second)
IAB	Internet Architecture Board
IADCS	Interactivity Defined Context Set
IAN	Integrated Analog Network
IANA	Internet Assigned Number Authority
IAP	Inner Administrative Point
IBM	International Business Machines Corporations
IC	Interexchange Carrier
ICD	International Code Designator
ICF	Isochronous Convergence Function
ICI	Interface Control Information
ICMP	Internet Control Message Protocol
ICV	Integrity Check Value
IDI	Initial Domain Identifier
IDN	Integrated Digital Network
IDN	Interface Definition Notation
IDP	Initial Domain Part
IDP	Internetwork Datagram Packet
IDU	Interface Data Unit
IEC	Interexchange Carrier
IEC	International Electrotechnical Commission
IEEE	Institute of Electrical and Electronic Engineers
IEN	Internet Engineering Notes
IETF	Internet Engineering Task Force
IESG	Internet Engineering Steering Group
IF	Information Flow
IGMP	Internet Group Management Protocol
IGP	Interior Gateway Protocol
IGRP	Internet Gateway Routing Protocol
ILD	Injection Laser Diode
ILU	Independent Logical Unit
IMAC	Isochronous Media Access Control
IMIL	International Managed Information Library
IML	Initial Microcode Load
IMPDU	Initial MAC Protocol Data Unit

IMS	Information Management System
IN	Intelligent Network
IND	Indication
INN	Intermediate Network Node
INTAP	Interoperability Technology Association for Information Processing
IOC	Input/Output Control
IOCP	Input/Output Control Program
IONL	Internal Organization of Network Layer
IP	Internet Protocol
IPng	IP Next Generation
IPv4	IP version 4
IPv6	IP version 6
IPC	Interprocess Communication
IPDS	Intelligent Printer Data Stream
IPI	Initial Protocol Identifier
IPICS	ISP Implementation Conformance Statement
IPL	Initial Program Load
IPM	Interpersonal Message
IPMS	Interpersonal Messaging System
IPM-UA	Interpersonal Messaging User Agent
IPN	Interpersonal Notification
IPR	Isolated Pacing Response
IPX	Internetwork Packet Exchange
IR	Internet Router
IRN	Intermediate Routing Node
IRQ	Interrupt Request Lines
IRTF	Internet Research Task Force
IS	International Standard
ISA	Industry Standard Architecture
ISAM	Index-Sequential Access Method
ISC	Intersystem Communications in CICS
ISCF	Intersystems Control Facility
ISDN	Integrated Services Digital Network
ISH	Intermediate System Hello
IS-IS	Intermediate System to Intermediate System
ISO	International Standards Organization
ISODE	ISO Development Environment

ISP	International Standard Profile
ISPBX	Integrated Services Private Branch Exchange
ISPSN	Initial Synchronization Point Serial Number
ISSI	Interswitching System Interface
ISUP	ISDN User Part
IT	Information Technology
ITC	Independent Telephone Company
ITU	International Telecommunication Union
ITU-TS	International Telecommunication Union—Telecommunication Section
IUT	Implementation Under Test
IVDT	Integrated Voice/Data Terminal
IWU	Interworking Unit
IXC	Interexchange Carrier
JCL	Job Control Language
JES	Job Entry Subsystem
JTC	Joint Technical Committee
JTM	Job Transfer and Manipulation
KA9Q	TCP/IP implementation for amateur radio
kb	Kilobit
kbps	Kilobits per second
kHz	Kilohertz
km	Kilometer
LAB	Latency Adjustment Buffer
LAB	Line Attachment Base
LAN	Local Area Network
LANSUP	LAN Adapter NDIS Support
LAP	Link Access Procedure
LAPB	Link Access Procedure Balanced
LAPD	Link Access Procedures on the D channel
LAPS	LAN Adapter and Protocol Support
LATA	Local Access and Transport Area
LCF	Log Control Function
LCN	Logical Channel Number
LE	Local Exchange
LEC	Local Exchange Carrier
LED	Light-Emitting Diode
LEN	Low-Entry Networking

LI	Length Indicator
LIB	Line Interface Base
LIC	Line Interface Coupler
LIDB	Line Information Database
LIS	Logical IP Subnet
LLAP	LocalTalk Link Access Protocol
LLC	Logical Link Control
LME	Layer Management Entity
LMI	Layer Management Interface
LOCKD	Lock Manager Daemon
LOTOS	Language of Temporal Ordering Specifications
LPD	Line Printer Daemon
LPDA	Link Problem Determination Application
LPR	Line Printer
LRC	Longitudinal Redundancy Check
LSE	Local System Environment
LSL	Link Support Layer
LSS	Low-speed Scanner
LSSU	Link Status Signal Unit
LT	Local Termination
LU	Logical Unit
m	Meter
MAC	Media Access Control
MAC	Medium Access Control
MACE	Macintosh Audio Compression and Expansion
MACF	Multiple Association Control Function
MAN	Metropolitan Area Network
MAP	Manufacturing Automation Protocol
MAU	Media Access Unit
MAU	Multistation Access Unit
Mb	Megabit
MBA	MASSBUS Adapter
MBONE	Multicast Backbone
Mbps	Megabits per second
MBZ	Must Be Zero
MCA	Microchannel Architecture
MCF	MAC Convergence Function
MCI	Microwave Communications, Inc.

MCP	MAC Convergence Protocol
MCR	Monitor Console Routine
MD	Management Domain
MFA	Management Functional Areas
MFJ	Modified Final Judgment
MFS	Message Formatting Services in IMS
MH	Message Handling Package
MHS	Message Handling Service
MHS	Message Handling System
MHz	Megahertz
MIB	Management Information Base
MIC	Media Interface Connector
MID	Message Identifier
MILNET	Military Network
MIM	Management Information Model
MIME	Multipurpose Internet Mail Extension
MIN	Mobile Identification Number; Multiple Interaction Negotiation
MIPS	Million Instructions per Second
MIS	Management Information Systems
MIT	Managed Information Tree
MLID	Multiple Link Interface Driver
MMF	Multimode Fiber
MMI	Man Machine Interface
MMS	Manufacturing Message Specification
MOSS	Maintenance and Operator Subsystem
MOT	Means of Testing
MOTIS	Message Oriented Text Interchange System
MPAF	Mid-Page Allocation Field
MRO	Multiregion Operation in CICS
ms	Millisecond
MS	Management Services
MS	Message Store
MSC	Mobile Switching Center
MSCP	Mass Storage Control Protocol
MSN	Multiple Systems Networking
MSNF	Multiple Systems Networking Facility
MSS	MAN Switching System; Maximum Segment Size

MST	Multiplexed Slotted and Token Ring
MSU	Management Services Unit
MTA	Message Transfer Agent
MTACP	Magnetic Tape Ancillary Control Process
MTBF	Mean Time between Failures
MTTD	Mean Time of Diagnosis
MTOR	Mean Time of Repair
MTP	Message Transfer Part
MTS	Message Transfer System
MTSE	Message Transfer Service Element
MTU	Maximum Transfer Unit
MVS/370	Multiple Virtual Storage/370
MVS/XA	Multiple Virtual Storage/Extended Architecture
MVS	Multiple Virtual Systems
NAK	Negative Acknowledgment in BSC
NAP	Network Access Provider
NAU	Network Addressable Unit
NBP	Name-Binding Protocol
NC	Network Connection
NC	Numerical Controller
NCB	Node Control Block
NCCF	Network Communications Control Facility
NCEP	Network Connection Endpoint
NCP	Network Control Program
NCP	Network Core Protocol
NCS	Network Computing System
NCTE	Network Channel-Terminating Equipment
NDIS	Network Driver Interface Specification
NFS	Network File System
NIB	Node Identification Block
NIC	Network Interface Card
NIF	Network Information File
NIS	Names Information Socket
NISDN	Narrowband ISDN
NIST	National Institute of Standards and Technology
NIUF	North American ISDN Users' Forum
NJE	Network Job Entry
NLM	NetWare Loadable Module

NLDM	Network Logical Data Manager
nm	Nanometer
NM	Network Management
NMP	Network Management Process
NMVT	Network Management Vector Transport
NMS	Network Management Station
NN	Network Node
NOC	Network Operations Center
NPA	Numbering Plan Area
NPAI	Network Protocol Control Information
NPDA	Network Problem Determination Application
NPDU	Network Protocol Data Unit
NPM	Netview Performance Monitor
NPSI	NCP Packing Switching Interface
NRN	Nonreceipt Notification
NRZ	Non–Return to Zero
NRZI	Non–Return to Zero Inverted
ns	Nanosecond
NS	Network Service
NSAP	Network Service Access Points
NSDU	Network Service Data Unit
NSF	National Science Foundation
NTFS	Windows NT File System
NTO	Network Terminal Option
NVLAP	National Voluntary Accreditation Program
OAF	Origination Address Field
OAM	Operations, administration, and maintenance
OAM&P	Operations, Administration, Maintenance and Provisioning
OC3	Optical carrier level 3, 155 Mbps over fiber
OCA	Open Communication Architectures
OCC	Other Common Carrier
OC-n	Optical Carrier level n
ODA	Office Document Architecture
ODI	Open Data-Link Interface
ODIF	Office Document Interchange Format
ODINSUP	ODI NSIS Support
ODP	Open Distributed Processing
OIT	Object Identifier Tree

OIW	OSI Implementation Workshop
OLRT	Online Real-time
OLU	Originating Logical Unit
OM	Object Management
ONA	Open Network Architecture
ONC	Open Network Computing
OPNDST	Open Destination
O/R	Originator/Recipient
OS	Operating System
OS/400	Operating System/400 for the AS/400 Computer
OSE	Open Systems Environment
OSF	Open Software Foundation
OSI	Open Systems Interconnection
OSI/CS	OSI Communications Subsystem
OSIE	Open System Interconnection Environment
OSILL	Open Systems Interconnection Lower Layers
OSIUL	Open Systems Interconnection Upper Layers
OSNS	Open Systems Network Services
OSPF	Open Shortest Path First
PA	Prearbitrated
PABX	Private Automatic Branch Exchange
PAD	Packet Assembler/Disassembler
PAF	Prearbitrated Function
PAI	Protocol Address Information
PAM	Pass Along Message
PANS	Pretty Amazing New Stuff
PAP	Printer Access Protocol
PBX	Private Branch Exchange
PC	Path Control
PC	Personal Computer
PCCU	Physical Communications Control Unit
PCEP	Presentation Connection Endpoint
PCI	Protocol Control Information; Presentation Context Identifier; Peripheral Component Interconnect bus
PCM	Pulse Code Modulation
PCO	Points of Control and Observation
PCIR	Protocol Conformance Test Report
PDAD	Proposed Draft Addendum

PDAU	Physical Delivery Access Unit
PDC	Packet Data Channel
pDISP	Proposed Draft International Standard Profile
PDN	Public Data Network
PDU	Protocol Data Unit
PDV	Presentation Data Value
PELS	Picture Elements
PEM	Privacy Enhanced Mail
PEP	Partition Emulation Program
PETS	Parameterized Executable Test Suite
PH	Packet Handler or Packet Handling
PhC	Physical Layer Connection
PhCEP	Physical Connection Endpoint
PhL	Physical Layer
PhPDU	Physical Layer Protocol Data Unit
PhS	Physical Layer Service
Ph-SAP	Physical Layer SAP
PhSAP	Physical Layer Service Access Point
PhSDU	Physical Layer Service Data Unit
PHY	Physical Layer
PICS	Protocol Information Conformance Statement
PIN	Positive-Intrinsic Negative Photodiode
PING	Packet Internet Groper
PIP	Program Initialization Parameters
PIU	Path Information Unit
PIXIT	Protocol Implementation eXtra Information for Testing
PKCS	Public Key Cryptosystems
PLC	Programmable Logic Controller
PLCP	Physical Layer Convergence Protocol
PLMN	Public Land Mobile Network
PLP	Packet Layer Protocol
PLS	Primary Link Station; Physical Signaling
PLU	Primary Logical Unit
PM	Protocol Machine
P-MAC	Packet Switched Media Access Control
PMD	Physical layer Medium Dependent
POI	Point of Initiation; Program Operator Interface
POP	Point of Presence

POSI	Promoting Conference for OSI
POSIX	Portable Operating System Interface
POTS	Plain Old Telephone Service
PPDU	Presentation Protocol Data Unit
PPO	Primary Program Operator
PPP	Point-to-Point Protocol
PPSDN	Public Packet Switched Data Network
PRI	Primary Rate Interface
PRMD	Private Management Domain
PS	Presentation Services
PSAP	Public Safety Answering Point
PSC	Public Service Commission
PSDN	Packet Switched Data Network
PSN	Packet Switched Network
PSPDN	Packet Switched Public Data Network
PSTN	Public Switched Telephone Network
PTF	Program Temporary Fix
PTLXAU	Public Telex Access Unit
PTN	Public Telephone Network
PTT	Post, Telegraph, and Telephone
PU	Physical Unit
PUC	Public Utility Commission
PUCP	Physical Unit Control Point
PUMS	Physical Unit Management Services
PUP	Parc Universal Packet
PUT	Program Update Tape
PVC	Private Virtual Circuit
PVN	Private Virtual Network
P 1	Protocol 1 (message transfer protocol/MHS/X.400)
P 2	Protocol 2 (interpersonal messaging MHS/X.400)
P 3	Protocol 3 (submission and delivery protocol/MHS/X.400)
P 5	Protocol 5 (teletext access protocol)
P 7	Protocol 7 (message store access protocol in X.400)
QA	Queued Arbitrated
QAF	Queued Arbitrated Function
QC	Quiesce Complete
QEC	Quiesce at End of Chain
QMF	Query Management Facility

QOS	Quality of Service
QPSX	Queued Packet and Synchronous Switch
QUIPU	X.500 Conformant Directory Services in ISODE
RAM	Random Access Memory
RARE	Reseaux Associes poir la Recherche Europeenne; European Association of Research Networks
RARP	Reverse Address Resolution Protocol
RAS	Remote Access Service
RBOC	Regional Bell Operating Company
RD	Route Redirection
RD	Routing Domain
RDA	Remote Database Access
RDI	Restricted Digital Information
RDN	Relative Distinguished Name
RDP	Reliable Datagram Protocol
RDT	Resource Definition Table
RECFMS	Record Formatted Maintenance Statistics
REJ	Reject
REQ	Request
RESP	Response
RESYNC	Resynchronization
RFC	Request for Change
RFP	Request for Proposal
RFQ	Request for Price Quotation
RH	Request Header
RH	Response Header
RIB	Routing Information Base
RIF	Routing Information Field
RIM	Request Initialization Mode
RIP	Router Information Protocol
RIPE	Reseaux IP Europeens; European continental TCP/IP network operated by EUnet
RISC	Reduced Instruction Set Computer
RJE	Remote Job Entry
RM	Reference Model
RMT	Ring Management
RN	Receipt Notification
RNAA	Request Network Address Assignment

RNR	Receiver Not Ready
ROSE	Remote Operations Service Element
RPC	Remote Procedure Call in OSF/DCE; Remote Procedure Call
RPL	Request Parameter List; Remote Program Load
RPOA	Recognized Private Operating Agency
RQ	Request Counter
RR	Receiver Ready
RS	Relay System
RSF	Remote Support Facility
RSP	Response
RTM	Response Time Monitor
RTMP	Routing Table Maintenance Protocol
RTO	Round Trip Time-Out
RTR	Ready to Receive
RTS	Request to Send
RTSE	Reliable Transfer Service Element
RTT	Round Trip Time
RU	Request Unit
RU	Response Unit
S/390	IBM's System/390 Hardware Architecture
s	Second
SA	Sequenced Application
SA	Source Address Field
SA	Subarea
SAA	Specific Administrative Areas
SAA	System Applications Architecture
SABM	Set Asynchronous Mode Balanced
SACF	Single Association Control Function
SACK	Selective Acknowledgment
SAF	SACF Auxiliary Facility
SALI	Source Address Length Indicator
SAM	Security Accounts Manager
SAMBE	Set Asynchronous Mode Balanced Extended
SAO	Single Association Object
SAP	Service Access Point
SAP	Service Advertising Protocol
SAPI	Service Access Point Identifier
SAS	Single-Attachment Station

SAS	Statically Assigned Sockets
SASE	Specific Application Service Element
SATS	Selected Abstract Test Suite
SAW	Session Awareness Data
SBA	Set Buffer Address
SBI	Stop Bracket Initiation
SC	Session Connection
SC	Subcommittee
SCC	Specialized Common Carrier
SCCP	Signaling Connection Control Part
SCEP	Session Connection Endpoint
SCP	Service Control Point
SCS	System Conformance Statement
SCSI	Small Computer System Interface
SCTR	System Conformance Test Report
SDH	Synchronous Digital Hierarchy
SDIF	Standard Document Interchange Format
SDL	System Description Language
SDLC	Synchronous Data Link Control
SDN	Software Defined Network
SDSE	Shadowed DSA Entries
SDU	Service Data Unit
SE	Session Entity
SG	Study Group
SGFS	Special Group on Functional Standardization
SGML	Standard Generalized Markup Language
SIA	Stable Implementation Agreements
SID	Security ID
SIM	Set Initialization Mode
SIO	Start I/O
SIP	SMDS Interface Protocol
SLU	Secondary Logical Unit
SMAE	System Management Application Entity
SMASE	Systems Management Application Service Element
SMB	Server Message Block
SMDR	Station Message Detail Recording
SMDS	Switched Multimegabit Data Service
SMF	Single Mode Fiber

SMF	System Management Facility
SMFA	Systems Management Functional Area
SMI	Structure of the OSI Management Information Service
SMIB	Stored Message Information Base
SMP	System Modification Program
SMS	Service Management System
SMS	Station Management Standard
SMTP	Simple Mail Transfer Protocol
SNA	System Network Architecture
SNAcF	Subnetwork Access Function
SNAcP	Subnetwork Access Protocol
SNADS	SNA Distribution Services
SNAP	Subnetwork Attachment Point
SNARE	Subnetwork Address Routing Entity
SNCP	Single Node Control Point
SNDCP	Subnetwork Dependent Convergence Protocol
SNI	Subscriber-Network Interface
SNI	SNA Network Intercommection
SNI	SNA Network Interface
SNICP	Subnetwork Independent Convergence Protocol
SNMP	Simple Network Management Protocol
SNPA	Subnetwork Point of Attachment
SNRM	Set Normal Response Mode
SOA	Start of Authority
SONET	Synchronous Optical Network
SP	Signaling Point
SPAG	Standards Promotion and Applications Group
SPC	Signaling Point Code
SPDU	Session Protocol Data Unit
SPE	Synchronous Payload Envelope
SPF	Shortest Path First
SPI	Subsequent Protocol Identifier
SPM	FDDI to SONET Physical Layer Mapping Standard
SPSN	Synchronization Point Serial Number
SQL	Structured Query Language
SRH	SNARE Request Hello
SS	Session Service
SS	Switching System

SS6	Signaling System No. 6
SS7	Signaling System No. 7
SSA	Subschema Specific Area
SSAP	Session Service Access Point
SSAP	Source Service Access Point
SSCP	System Services Control Point
SSDU	Session Service Data Unit
SSM	Single Segment Message DMPDU
ST	Sequenced Terminal
STA	Spanning Tree Algorithms
STD	Standard
STM	Station Management
STM	Synchronous Transfer Mode
STM-n	Synchronous Transport Module level n
STP	Service Transaction Program in LU 6.2
STP	Shielded Twisted Pair
STP	Signal Transfer Point
STS-n	Synchronous Transport Signal level n
SUERM	Signal Unit Error Rate Monitor
SUT	System Under Test
SVA	Shared Virtual Area
SVC	Switched Virtual Circuit
SWS	Silly Window Syndrome
SYN	Synchronizing Segment; Synchronous Character in IBM's Bisync Protocol
SYNC	Synchronization
T3	A designation of telephony used over DS3 speed lines
T	Transport
TA	Terminal Adaptor
TAG	Technology Advisory Group
TAP	Trace Analysis Program
TC	Technical Committee
TC	Transport Connection or Technical Committee
TCAM	Telecommunications Access Method
TCB	Task Control Block
TCEP	Transport Connection Endpoint
TCM	Time Compression Multiplexing
TCP	Transmission Control Protocol

TCP/IP	Transmission Control Protocol/Internet Protocol
TCT	Terminal Control Table in CICS
TDM	Time Division Multiplexing
TDMA	Time Division Multiple Access
TE	Terminal Equipment
TELNET	Remote Logon in TCP/IP
TEP	Transport Endpoint
TFTP	Trivial File Transfer Protocol
TG	Transmission Group
TH	Transmission Header
THT	Token Holding Timer
TIC	Token-Ring Interface Coupler
TINA	Telecommunications Information Network Architecture
TINA-C	Telecommunication Information Network Architecture Consortium
TI RPC	Transport Independent RPC
TLI	Transport Layer Interface
TLMAU	Telematic Access Unit
TLV	Type, Length, and Value
TLXAU	Telex Access Unit
TMP	Text Management Protocol
TMS	Time Multiplexed Switching
TN3270	A version of TELNET that implements IBM 3270 data stream
TOP	Technical and Office Protocol
TOS	Type of Service
TP	Transaction Processing
TP	Transaction Program
TP	Transport Protocol
TP 0	TP class 0—simple
TP 1	TP class 1—basic error recovery
TP 2	TP class 2—multiplexing
TP 3	TP class 3—error recovery and multiplexing
TP 4	TP class 4—error detection and recovery
TPDU	Transport Protocol Data Unit
TP-PMD	Twisted Pair PMD
TPS	Two-Processor Switch
TPSP	Transaction Processing Service Provider

TPSU	Transaction Processing Service User
TPSUI	TPSU Invocation
TR	Technical Report
TR	Token Ring
TRA	Token Ring Adapter
TRPB	Truncated Reverse Path Broadcast
TRSS	Token-Ring Subsystem
TRT	Token Rotation Timer
TS	Transaction Services
TS	Transport Service
TSAP	Transport Service Access Point
TSC	Transmission Subsystem Controller
TSCF	Target System Control Facility
TSDU	Transport Service Data Unit
TSI	Time Slot Interchange
TSO	Time Sharing Option
TSR	Terminate and Stay Resident Program
TSS	Transmission Subsystem
TTCN	Tree and Tabular Combined Notation
TTL	Time to Live
TTP	Timed Token Protocol
TTP	Transport Test Platform
TTRT	Target Token Rotation Time
TTY	Teletype
TUP	Telephone User Part
TVX	Valid Transmission Timer (FDDI)
TWX	Teletypewriter Exchange Service
UA	Unnumbered Acknowledgment
UA	User Agent; Unsequenced Application
UART	Universal Asynchronous Receiver and Transmitter
UDI	Unrestricted Digital Information
UDP	User Datagram Protocol
UOW	Unit of Work
UPS	Uninterruptible Power Supply
URL	Universal Resource Locator
User-ASE	User Application Service Element
USS	Unformatted System Services
UT	Unsequenced Terminal

UTC	Coordinated Universal Time
UTP	Unshielded Twisted Pair
UUCP	UNIX-to-UNIX Copy Program
VAC	Value Added Carrier
VAN	Value Added Network
VAS	Value Added Service
vBNS	A reference to the 155 Mbps deployment of an Internet backbone to have been implemented in 1995
VCI	Virtual Channel Identifier (DQDB)
VDT	Video Display Terminal
VESA	Video Electronics Standards Association
VLR	Visitor Location Register
VLSI	Very Large Scale Integration
VPI/VCI	Virtual Path Identifier and a Virtual Call Identifier
VM	Virtual Machine
VMD	Virtual Manufacturing Device
VM/SP	Virtual Machine System Product
VPN	Virtual Private Network
VR	Virtual Route
VRPWS	Virtual Route Pacing Window Size
VS	Virtual Storage
VSAM	Virtual Storage Access Method
VSE	Virtual Storage Extended
VT	Virtual Terminal
VTAM	Virtual Telecommunications Access Method
VTE	Virtual Terminal Environment
VTP	Virtual Terminal Protocol
VTPM	Virtual Terminal Protocol Machine
VTSE	Virtual Terminal Service Element
WACA	Write Access Connection Acceptor
WACI	Write Access Connection Initiator
WAN	Wide Area Network
WAVAR	Write Access Variable
WBC	Wideband Channel
WD	Working Document
WG	Working Group
WNM	Workgroup Node Manager
WP	Working Party

WWW	World Wide Web
X	X Window System
X.25	An ITU-TX standard; a transport layer service
X.400	The ITU-TS protocol for electronic mail
XAPIA	X.400 API Association
XDR	External Data Representation
XDS	X/Open Directory Services API
XI	SNA X.25 Interface
XID	Exchange Identification
XNS	Xerox Network Standard
XTI	X/Open Transport Interface
XUDTS	Extended Unitdata Service
ZIP	Zone Information Protocol
ZIS	Zone Information Socket

D

Network Architecture: TCP/IP
Well-Known Ports

TCP and UDP transport mechanisms use Well-Known Ports. These port names reflect specific applications of wide implementation and usage. Ports are the endpoints—an addressable entity to create a logical connection. Also known as *service contact ports,* these ports provide services to callers (requestors) of a particular service. The following list includes the port's decimal number as it is known, the name of the reference associated with a specific port, and a brief description of what each port provides. The list is not exhaustive; it is intended to provide the reader with a reference for common ports used in TCP/IP networks.

Decimal	Name	Description
0		Reserved
1	TCPMUX	TCP port service multiplexer
2–4		Unassigned
5	RJE	Remote job entry
7	ECHO	Echo
9	DISCARD	Discard
11	USERS	Active users
13	DAYTIME	Daytime
15		Unassigned
17	Quote	Quote of the day
19	CHARGEN	Character generator
20	FTP-DATA	File transfer (data)
21	FTP	File transfer (control)
23	TELNET	TELNET

25	SMTP	Simple mail transfer
27	NSW-FE	NSW user system FE
29	MSG-ICP	MSG-ICP
31	MSG-AUTH	MSG authentication
33	DSP	Display support protocol
35		Any private printer server
37	TIME	Time
39	RLP	Resource location protocol
41	GRAPHICS	Graphics
42	NAMESERVER	Host name server
43	NICNAME	Who is
49	LOGIN	Login host protocol
53	DOMAIN	Domain name server
67	BOOTPS	Bootstrap protocol server
68	BOOTPC	Bootstrap protocol client
69	TFTP	Trivial file transfer
79	FINGER	Finger
101	HOSTNAME	NIC host name server
102	ISO-TSAP	ISO TSAP
103	X400	X.400
104	X400SND	X.400 SND
105	CSNET-NS	CSNET mailbox name server
109	POP2	Post Office Protocol version 2
110	POP3	Post Office Protocol version 3
111	SUNRPC	SUNRPC portmap
137	NETBIOS-NS	NETBIOS name service
138	NETBIOS-DGM	NETBIOS datagram service
139	NETBIOS-SSN	NETBIOS session service
146	ISO-TPO	ISO TPO
147	ISO-IP	ISO IP
150	SQL-NET	SQL-NET
153	SGMP	SGMP
156	SQLSRV	SQL service
160	SGMP-TRAPS	SGMP TRAPS
161	SNMP	SNMP
162	SNMPTRAP	SNMPTRAP
163	CMIP-MANAGE	CMIP/TCP manager
164	CMIP-AGENT	CMIP/TCP agent
165	XNS-COURIER	Xerox
179	BGP	Border gateway protocol

Network Architecture: TCP/IP RFC Reference

Note: Where NOL is used in this text, it means *not online.*

RFC	Title
2200	Internet Official Protocol Standards. 12 June 1997.
2177	IMAP4 IDLE Command. 2 July 1997.
2176	IPv4 over MAPOS Version 1. 25 June 1997.
2175	MAPOS 16—Multiple Access Protocol over SONET/SDH with 16-Bit Addressing. 25 June 1997.
2174	A MAPOS Version 1 Extension—Switch-Switch Protocol. 25 June 1997.
2173	MAPOS Version 1 Extension—Node Switch Protocol. 25 June 1997.
2172	MAPOS Version 1 Assigned Numbers. 25 June 1997.
2171	MAPOS—Multiple Access Protocol over SONET/SDH Version 1. 25 June 1997.
2170	Application REQuested IP over ATM (AREQUIPA). 2 July 1997.
2169	A Trivial Convention for Using HTTP in URN Resolution. 23 June 1997.
2168	Resolution of Uniform Resource Identifiers Using the Domain Name System. 23 June 1997.
2167	Referral Whois (RWhois) Protocol V1.5. 20 June 1997.
2166	APPN Implementer's Workshop Closed Pages Document DLSw v2.0 Enhancements. 19 June 1997.
2165	Service Location Protocol. 20 June 1997.
2155	Definitions of Managed Objects for APPN Using SMIv2. 16 June 1997.

2154   OSPF with Digital Signatures. 16 June 1997.

2153   PPP Vendor Extensions. 3 June 1997.

2152   A Mail-Safe Transformation Format of Unicode. 3 June 1997.

2151   A Primer On Internet and TCP/IP Tools and Utilities. 10 June 1997.

2149   Multicast Server Architectures for MARS-based ATM Multicasting. 23 May 1997.

2147   TCP and UDP over IPv6 Jumbograms. 23 May 1997.

2146   U.S. Government Internet Domain Names. 23 May 1997.

2145   Use and Interpretation of HTTP Version Numbers. 23 May 1997.

2144   The CAST-128 Encryption Algorithm. 21 May 1997.

2143   Encapsulating IP with the Small Computer System Interface. 14 May 1997.

2142   Mailbox Names for Common Services and Functions. 6 May 1997.

2141   URN Syntax. 5 May 1997.

2140   TCP Control Block Interdependence. 29 April 1997.

2139   RADIUS Accounting. 18 April 1997.

2138   Remote Authentication Dial In User Service (RADIUS). 18 April 1997.

2137   Secure Domain Name System Dynamic Update. 21 April 1997.

2136   Dynamic Updates in the Domain Name System. 21 April 1997.

2135   Internet Society "Internet Society By-Laws." 30 April 1997.

2134   Internet Society "Articles of Incorporation of the Internet Society." 1 May 1997.

2133   Basic Socket Interface Extensions for IPv6. 21 April 1997.

2132   DHCP Options and BOOTP Vendor Extensions. 7 April 1997.

2131   Dynamic Host Configuration Protocol. 7 April 1997.

2130   The Report of the IAB Character Set Workshop Held 29 February–1 March 1996. 21 April 1997.

2129   Toshiba's Flow Attribute Notification Protocol (FANP) Specification. 21 April 1997.

2128   Dial Control Management Information Base Using SMIv2. 31 March 1997.

2127   ISDN Management Information Base. 31 March 1997.

2126   ISO Transport Service on Top of TCP (ITOT). 28 March 1997.

2125   The PPP Bandwidth Allocation Protocol (BAP) and the PPP Bandwidth Allocation Control Protocol (BACP). 31 March 1997.

2124   Light-weight Flow Admission Protocol Specification Version 1.0. 28 March 1997.

2123   Traffic Flow Measurement: Experiences with NeTraMet. 28 March 1997.

2122   VEMMI URL Specification. 28 March 1997.

2121   Issues affecting MARS Cluster Size. 28 March 1997.

2120   Managing the X.500 Root Naming Context. 28 March 1997.

2119   Key Words for Use in RFCs to Indicate Requirement Levels.
       26 March 1997.

2118   Microsoft Point-To-Point Compression (MPPC) Protocol. 20 March
       1997.

2117   Protocol Independent Multicast—Sparse Mode (PIM-SM) Protocol
       Specification. 16 June 1997.

2116   X.500 Implementations Catalog—96. 24 April 1997.

2114   Data Link Switching Client Access Protocol. 3 March 1997.

2113   IP Router Alert Option. 28 February 1997.

2112   The MIME Multipart/Related Content-Type. 12 March 1997.

2111   Content-ID and Message-ID Uniform Resource Locators. 12 March
       1997.

2110   MIME E-mail Encapsulation of Aggregate Documents, Such as
       HTML (MHTML). 12 March 1997.

2109   HTTP State Management Mechanism. 18 February 1997.

2108   Definitions of Managed Objects for IEEE 802.3 Repeater Devices
       Using SMIv2. 12 February 1997.

2107   Ascend Tunnel Management Protocol—ATMP. 6 February 1997.

2106   Data Link Switching Remote Access Protocol. 3 March 1997.

2105   Cisco Systems' Tag Switching Architecture Overview. 6 February
       1997.

2104   HMAC: Keyed-Hashing for Message Authentication. 5 February
       1997.

2103   Mobility Support for Nimrod: Challenges and Solution Approaches.
       6 February 1997.

2102   Multicast Support for Nimrod: Requirements and Solution
       Approaches. 20 February 1997.

2101   IPv4 Address Behaviour Today. 4 February 1997.

2100   The Naming of Hosts. 1 April 1997.

2099   Request for Comments Summary RFC Numbers 2000–2099.
       13 March 1997.

2098   Toshiba's Router Architecture Extensions for ATM: Overview.
       4 February 1997.

2097   The PPP NetBIOS Frames Control Protocol (NBFCP). 30 January
       1997.

2096   IP Forwarding Table MIB. 30 January 1997.

2095   IMAP/POP AUTHorize Extension for Simple Challenge/Response.
       30 January 1997.

2094   Group Key Management Protocol (GKMP) Architecture. 2 July 1997.

2093   Group Key Management Protocol (GKMP) Specification. 2 July 1997.

2092   Protocol Analysis for Triggered RIP. 24 January 1997.

2091   Triggered Extensions to RIP to Support Demand Circuits. 24 January 1997.

2090   TFTP Multicast Option. 4 February 1997.

2089   V2ToV1 Mapping SNMPv2 onto SNMPv1 Within a Bilingual SNMP Agent. 28 January 1997.

2088   IMAP4 Nonsynchronizing Literals. 22 January 1997.

2087   IMAP4 QUOTA Extension. 22 January 1997.

2086   IMAP4 ACL Extension. 22 January 1997.

2085   HMAC-MD5 IP Authentication with Reply Prevention. 5 February 1997.

2084   Considerations for Web Transaction Security. 22 January 1997.

2083   PNG Portable Network Graphics Specification Version 1.0. 16 January 1997.

2082   RIP-2 MD5 Authentication. 10 January 1997.

2081   RIPng Protocol Applicability Statement. 10 January 1997.

2080   RIPng for IPv6. 10 January 1997.

2079   Definition of X.500 Attribute Types and an Object Class to Hold Uniform Resource Identifiers (URIs). 10 January 1997.

2078   Generic Security Service Application Program Interface Version 2. 10 January 1997.

2077   The Model Primary Content Type for Multipurpose Internet Mail Extensions. 10 January 1997.

2076   Common Internet Message Headers. 24 February 1997.

2075   IP Echo Host Service. 8 January 1997.

2074   Remote Network Monitoring MIB Protocol Identifiers. 16 January 1997.

2073   An IPv6 Provider-Based Unicast Address Format. 8 January 1997.

2072   Router Renumbering Guide. 8 January 1997.

2071   Network Renumbering Overview: Why Would I Want It and What Is It Anyway? 8 January 1997.

2070   Internationalization of the Hypertext Markup Language. 6 January 1997.

2069   An Extension to HTTP: Digest Access Authentication. 3 January 1997.

2068   Hypertext Transfer Protocol—HTTP/1.1. 3 January 1997.

2067   IP over HIPPI. 3 January 1997.

2066   TELNET CHARSET Option. 3 January 1997.

2065   Domain Name System Security Extensions. 3 January 1997.

2064   Traffic Flow Measurement: Meter MIB. 3 January 1997.

2063   Traffic Flow Measurement: Architecture. 3 January 1997.

2062   Internet Message Access Protocol—Obsolete Syntax. 4 December 1996.

2061   IMAP4 Compatibility with IMAP2BIS. 5 December 1996.

2060   Internet Message Access Protocol—V4 Rev1. 4 December 1996.

2059   RADIUS Accounting. 3 January 1997.

2058   Remote Authentication Dial In User Service (RADIUS). 3 January 1997.

2057   Source Directed Access Control on the Internet. 11 November 1996.

2056   Uniform Resource Locators for Z39.50. 5 November 1996.

2055   WebNFS Server Specification. 31 October 1996.

2054   WebNFS Client Specification. 31 October 1996.

2053   The AM (Armenia) Domain. 31 October 1996.

2052   A DNS RR for Specifying the Location of Services (DNS SRV). 31 October 1996.

2051   Definitions of Managed Objects for APPC. 30 October 1996.

2050   Internet Registry IP Allocation Guidelines. 5 November 1996.

2049   Multipurpose Internet Mail Extensions (MIME) Part Five: Conformance Criteria and Examples. 2 February 1996.

2048   Multipurpose Internet Mail Extensions (MIME) Part Four: Registration Procedures. 28 January 1997.

2047   Multipurpose Internet Mail Extensions (MIME) Part Three: Message Header Extensions for Non-ASCII Text. 2 December 1996.

2046   Multipurpose Internet Mail Extensions (MIME) Part Two: Media Types. 2 December 1996.

2045   Multipurpose Internet Mail Extensions (MIME) Part One: Format of Internet Message Bodies. 2 December 1996.

2044   UTF-8, a Transformation Format of Unicode and ISO 10646. 30 October 1996.

2043   The PPP SNA Control Protocol (SNACP). 30 October 1996.

2042   Registering New BGP Attribute Types. 3 January 1997.

2041   Mobile Network Tracing. 30 October 1996.

2040   The RC5, RC5-CBC, RC5-CBC-Pad, and RC5-CTS Algorithms. 30 October 1996.

2039   Applicability of Standards Track MIBs to Management of World Wide Web Servers. 6 November 1996.

2038   RTP Payload Format for MPEG1/MPEG2 Video. 30 October 1996.

2037   Entity MIB. 30 October 1996.

2036   Observations on the Use of Components of the Class A Address Space Within the Internet. 30 October 1996.

2035   RTP Payload Format for JPEG-Compressed Video. 30 October 1996.

2034   SMTP Service Extension for Returning Enhanced Error Codes. 30 October 1996.

2033   Local Mail Transfer Protocol. 30 October 1996.

2032   RTP Payload Format for H.261 Video Streams. 30 October 1996.

2031   IETF-ISOC Relationship. 29 October 1996.

2030   Simple Network Time Protocol (SNTP) Version 4 for IPv4 IPv6 and OSI. 30 October 1996.

2029   RTP Payload Format of Sun's CellB Video Encoding. 30 October 1996.

2028   The Organizations Involved in the IETF Standards Process. 29 October 1996.

2027   IAB and IESG Selection, Confirmation, and Recall Process: Operation of the Nominating and Recall Committees. 29 October 1996.

2026   The Internet Standards Process—Rev. 3. 29 October 1996.

2025   The Simple Public-Key GSS-API Mechanism. (SPKM). 22 October 1996.

2024   Definitions of Managed Objects for Data Link Switching Using SNMPv2. 22 October 1996.

2023   IP Version 6 over PPP. 22 October 1996.

2022   Support for Multicast over UNI 3.0/3.1 Based ATM Networks. 5 November 1996.

2021   Remote Network Monitoring Management Information Base Version 2 Using SMIv2. 16 January 1997.

2020   Definitions of Managed Objects for IEEE 802.12 Interfaces. 17 October 1996.

2019   Transmission of IPv6 Packets over FDDI. 17 October 1996.

2018   TCP Selective Acknowledgment Options. 17 October 1996.

2017   Definition of the URL MIME External-Body Access-Type. 14 October 1996.

2016   Uniform Resource Agents (URAs). 31 October 1996.

2015   MIME Security with Pretty Good Privacy (PGP). 14 October 1996.

2014   IRTF Research Group Guidelines and Procedures. 17 October 1996.

2013   SNMPv2 Management Information Base for the User Datagram Protocol Using SMIv2. 12 November 1996.

2012   SNMPv2 Management Information Base for the Transmission Control Protocol. 12 November 1996.

2011   SNMPv2 Management Information Base for the Internet Protocol Using SMIv2. 12 November 1996.

2010   Operational Criteria for Root Name Servers. 14 October 1996.

2009   GPS-Based Addressing and Routing. 8 November 1996.

2008   Implications of Various Address Allocation Policies for Internet
Routing. 14 October 1996.

2007   Catalogue of Network Training Materials. 14 October 1996.

2006   The Definitions of Managed Objects for IP Mobility Support Using
SMIv2. 22 October 1996.

2005   Applicability Statement for IP Mobility Support. 22 October 1996.

2004   Minimal Encapsulation Within IP. 22 October 1996.

2003   IP Encapsulation Within IP. 22 October 1996.

2002   IP Mobility Support. 22 October 1996.

2001   TCP Slow Start, Congestion Avoidance, Fast Retransmit, and Fast
Recovery Algorithms. 24 January 1997.

2000   Internet Official Protocol Standards. 24 February 1997.

1999   Request for Comments Summary RFC Numbers 1900–1999.
6 January 1997.

1998   An Application of the BGP Community Attribute in Multi-home
Routing 30 August 1996.

1997   BGP Communities Attribute. 30 August 1996.

1996   A Mechanism for Prompt Notification of Zone Changes. 28 August
1996.

1995   Incremental Zone Transfer in DNS. 28 August 1996.

1994   PPP Challenge Handshake Authentication Protocol (CHAP).
30 August 1996.

1993   PPP Gandalf FZA Compression Protocol. 30 August 1996.

1992   The Nimrod Routing Architecture. 30 August 1996.

1991   PGP Message Exchange Formats. 16 August 1996.

1990   The PPP Multilink Protocol (MP). 16 August 1996.

1989   PPP Link Quality Monitoring. 16 August 1996.

1988   Conditional Grant of Rights to Specific Hewlett-Packard Patents in
Conjunction with the Internet Engineering Task Force's Internet-
Standard Network Management Framework. 16 August 1996.

1987   Ipsilon's General Switch Management Protocol Specification
Version 1.1. 16 August 1996.

1986   Experiments with a Simple File Transfer Protocol for Radio Links
Using Enhanced Trivial File Transfer Protocol (ETFTP). 16 August
1996.

1985   SMTP Service Extension for Remote Message Queue Starting.
14 August 1996.

1984   IAB and IESG Statement on Cryptographic Technology and the
Internet. 20 August 1996.

1983   Internet Users' Glossary. 16 August 1996.

1982   Serial Number Arithmetic. 3 September 1996.

1981   Path MTU Discovery for IP Version 6. 14 August 1996.

1980   A Proposed Extension to HTML: Client-Side Image Maps.
14 August 1996.

1979   PPP Deflate Protocol. 9 August 1996.

1978   PPP Predictor Compression Protocol. 28 August 1996.

1977   PPP BSD Compression Protocol. 9 August 1996.

1976   PPP for Data Compression in Data Circuit-Terminating Equipment
(DCE). 14 August 1996.

1975   PPP Magnalink Variable Resource Compression. 9 August 1996.

1974   PPP Stac LZS Compression Protocol. 13 August 1996.

1973   PPP in Frame Relay. 19 June 1996.

1972   A Method for the Transmission of IPv6 Packets over Ethernet
Networks. 16 August 1996.

1971   IPv6 Stateless Address Autoconfiguration. 16 August 1996.

1970   Neighbor Discovery for IP Version 6 (IPv6). 16 August 1996.

1969   The PPP DES Encryption Protocol (DESE). 19 June 1996.

1968   The PPP Encryption Control Protocol (ECP). 19 June 1996.

1967   PPP LZS-DCP Compression Protocol (LZS-DCP). 13 August 1996.

1966   BGP Route Reflection: An Alternative to Full Mesh IBGP.
19 June 1996.

1965   Autonomous System Confederations for BGP. 19 June 1996.

1964   The Kerberos Version 5 GSS-API Mechanism. 19 June 1996.

1963   PPP Serial Data Transport Protocol (SDTP). 14 August 1996.

1962   The PPP Compression Control Protocol (CCP). 19 June 1996.

1961   GSS-API Authentication Method for SOCKS Version 5. 19 June
1996.

1960   A String Representation of LDAP Search Filters. 19 June 1996.

1959   An LDAP URL Format. 19 June 1996.

1958   Architectural Principles of the Internet. 6 June 1996.

1957   Some Observations on Implementations of the Post Office Protocol
(POP3). 6 June 1996.

1956   Registration in the MIL Domain. 6 June 1996.

1955   New Scheme for Internet Routing and Addressing (ENCAPS) for
IPN. 6 June 1996.

1954   Transmission of Flow Labelled IPv4 on ATM Data Links Ipsilon
Version 1.0. 22 May 1996.

1953   Ipsilon Flow Management Protocol Specification for IPv4 Version
1.0. 23 May 1996.

1952   GZIP File Format Specification Version 4.3. 23 May 1996.

1951   DEFLATE Compressed Data Format Specification V1.3. 23 May 1996.

1950   ZLIB Compressed Data Format Specification V3.3. 23 May 1996.

1949   Scalable Multicast Key Distribution. 17 May 1996.

1948   Defending Against Sequence Number Attacks. 17 May 1996.

1947   Greek Character Encoding for Electronic Mail Messages. 17 May 1996.

1946   Native ATM Support for ST2+. 17 May 1996.

1945   Hypertext Transfer Protocol—HTTP V1.0. 17 May 1996.

1944   Benchmarking Methodology for Network Interconnect Devices. 17 May 1996.

1943   Building an X.500 Directory Service in the U.S. 15 May 1996.

1942   HTML Tables. 15 May 1996.

1941   Frequently Asked Questions for Schools. 15 May 1996.

1940   Source Demand Routing: Packet Format and Forwarding Specification (V1). 14 May 1996.

1939   Post Office Protocol V3. 14 May 1996.

1938   A One-Time Password System. 14 May 1996.

1937   Local/Remote Forwarding Decision in Switched Data Link Subnetworks. 8 May 1996.

1936   Implementing the Internet Checksum in Hardware. 10 April 1996.

1935   What Is the Internet, Anyway? 10 April 1996.

1934   Ascend's Multilink Protocol Plus (MP+). 8 April 1996.

1933   Transition Mechanisms for IPv6 Hosts and Routers. 8 April 1996.

1932   IP over ATM: A Framework Document. 8 April 1996.

1931   Dynamic RARP Extensions and Administrative Support for Automatic Network Address Allocation. 3 April 1996.

1930   Guidelines for Creation, Selection, and Registration of an Autonomous System (AS). 3 April 1996.

1929   Username/Password Authentication for SOCKS V5. 3 April 1996.

1928   SOCKS Protocol V5. 3 April 1996.

1927   Suggested Additional MIME Types for Associating Documents. 1 April 1996.

1926   An Experimental Encapsulation of IP Datagrams on Top of ATM. 1 April 1996.

1925   The Twelve Networking Truths. 1 April 1996.

1924   A Compact Representation of IPv6 Addresses. 1 April 1996.

1923   RIPv1 Applicability Statement for Historic Status. 25 March 1996.

1922   Chinese Character Encoding for Internet Messages. 26 March 1996.

1921   TNVIP Protocol. 25 March 1996.

1920   Internet Official Protocol Standards. 22 March 1996.

1919   Classical Versus Transparent IP Proxies. 28 March 1996.

1918   Address Allocation for Private Internets. 29 February 1996.

1917   An Appeal to the Internet Community to Return Unused IP Networks (Prefixes) to the IANA. 29 February 1996.

1916   Enterprise Renumbering: Experience and Information Solicitation. 28 February 1996.

1915   Variance for the PPP Connection Control Protocol and the PPP Encryption Control Protocol. 28 February 1996.

1914   How to Interact with a Whois++ Mesh. 28 February 1996.

1913   Architecture of the Whois++ Index Service. 28 February 1996.

1912   Common DNS Operational and Configuration Errors. 28 February 1996.

1911   Voice Profile for Internet Mail. 19 February 1996.

1910   User-Based Security Model for SNMPv2. 28 February 1996.

1909   An Administrative Infrastructure for SNMPv2. 28 February 1996.

1908   Coexistence Between V1 and V2 of the Internet-Standard Network Management Framework. 22 January 1996.

1907   Management Information Base for V2 of the Simple Network Management Protocol (SNMPv2). 22 January 1996.

1906   Transport Mappings for V2 of the Simple Network Management Protocol (SNMPv2). 22 January 1996.

1905   Protocol Operations for V2 of the Simple Network Management Protocol (SNMPv2) 22 January 1996.

1904   Conformance Statements for V2 of the Simple Network Management Protocol (SNMPv2). 22 January 1996.

1903   Textual Conventions for V2 of the Simple Network Management Protocol (SNMPv2). 22 January 1996.

1902   Structure of Management Information for Version 2 of the Simple Network Management Protocol (SNMPv2). 22 January 1996.

1901   Introduction to Community-Based SNMPv2 22 January 1996.

1900   Renumbering Needs Work. 28 February 1996.

1899   RFC Summary Numbers 1800–1899. 6 January 1997.

1898   CyberCash Credit Card Protocol Version 0.8. 19 February 1996.

1897   IPv6 Testing Address Allocation. 25 January 1996.

1896   The Text/Enriched MIME Content-Type. 19 February 1996.

1895   The Application/CALS-1840 Content-Type. 15 February 1996.

1894   An Extensible Message Format for Delivery Status Notifications. 15 January 1996.

1893   Enhanced Mail System Status Codes. 15 January 1996.

1892   The Multipart/Report Content Type for the Reporting of Mail System Administrative Messages. 15 January 1996.

1891   SMTP Service Extension for Delivery Status Notifications. 15 January 1996.

1890   RTP Profile for Audio and Video Conferences with Minimal Control. 25 January 1996.

1889   RTP: A Transport Protocol for Real-Time Applications. 25 January 1996.

1888   OSI NSAPs and IPv6. 16 August 1996.

1887   An Architecture for IPv6 Unicast Address Allocation. 4 January 1996.

1886   DNS Extensions to Support IP V6. 4 January 1996.

1885   Internet Control Message Protocol (ICMPv6) for the Internet Protocol Version 6 (IPv6). 4 January 1996.

1884   IP V6 Addressing Architecture. 4 January 1996.

1883   Internet Protocol, Version 6 (IPv6) Specification. 4 January 1996.

1882   The 12 Days of Technology Before Christmas. 26 December 1995.

1881   IPv6 Address Allocation Management. 26 December 1995.

1880   Internet Official Protocol Standards. 29 November 1995.

1879   Class A Subnet Experiment Results and Recommendations. 15 January 1996.

1878   Variable Length Subnet Table For IPv4. 26 December 1995.

1877   PPP Internet Protocol Control Protocol Extensions for Name Server Addresses. 26 December 1995.

1876   A Means for Expressing Location Information in the Domain Name System. 15 January 1996.

1875   UNINETT PCA Policy Statements. 26 December 1995.

1874   SGML Media Types. 26 December 1995.

1873   Message/External-Body Content-ID Access Type. 26 December 1995.

1872   The MIME Multipart/Related Content-Type. 26 December 1995.

1871   Addendum to RFC 1602—Variance Procedure. 29 November 1995.

1870   SMTP Service Extension for Message Size Declaration. 6 November 1995.

1869   SMTP Service Extensions. 6 November 1995.

1868   ARP Extension—UNARP. 6 November 1995.

1867   Form-Based File Upload in HTML. 7 November 1995.

1866   Hypertext Markup Language—2.0. 3 November 1995.

1865   EDI Meets the Internet: Frequently Asked Questions about Electronic Data Interchange (EDI) on the Internet. 4 January 1996.

1864   The Content-MD5 Header Field. 24 October 1995.

1863   A BGP/IDRP Route Server Alternative to a Full Mesh Routing. 20 October 1995.

1862   Report of the IAB Workshop on Internet Information Infrastructure 1994. 3 November 1995.

1861   Simple Network Paging Protocol—V3—Two-Way-Enhanced. 19 October 1995.

1860   Variable Length Subnet Table For IPv4. 20 October 1995.

1859   ISO Transport Class 2 Non-Use of Explicit Flow Control over TCP RFC1006 Extension. 20 October 1995.

1858   Security Considerations for IP Fragment Filtering. 25 October 1995.

1857   A Model for Common Operational Statistics. 20 October 1995.

1856   The Opstat Client-Server Model for Statistics Retrieval. 20 October 1995.

1855   Netiquette Guidelines. 20 October 1995.

1854   SMTP Service Extension for Command Pipelining. 4 October 1995.

1853   IP in IP Tunneling. 4 October 1995.

1852   IP Authentication Using Keyed SHA. 2 October 1995.

1851   The ESP Triple DES-CBC Transform. 2 October 1995.

1850   OSPF V2 Management Information Base. 3 November 1995.

1848   MIME Object Security Services. 3 October 1995.

1847   Security Multiparts for MIME: Multipart/Signed and Multipart/Encrypted. 3 October 1995.

1846   SMTP 521 Reply Code. 2 October 1995.

1845   SMTP Service Extension for Checkpoint/Restart. 2 October 1995.

1844   Multimedia E-mail (MIME) User Agent Checklist. 24 August 1995.

1843   HZ—A Data Format for Exchanging Files of Arbitrarily Mixed Chinese and ASCII Characters. 24 August 1995.

1842   ASCII Printable Characters-Based Chinese Character Encoding for Internet Messages. 24 August 1995.

1841   PPP Network Control Protocol for LAN Extension. 29 September 1995.

1838   Use of the X.500 Directory to Support Mapping Between X.400 and RFC 822 Addresses. 22 August 1995.

1837   Representing Tables and Subtrees in the X.500 Directory. 22 August 1995.

1836   Representing the O/R Address Hierarchy in the X.500 Directory Information Tree. 22 August 1995.

1835   Architecture of the WHOIS++ Service. 16 August 1995.

1834   Whois and Network Information Lookup Service Whois++. 16 August 1995.

1833   Binding Protocols for ONC RPC V2. 9 August 1995.

1832   XDR: External Data Representation Standard. 9 August 1995.

1831   RPC: Remote Procedure Call Protocol Specification V2. 9 August 1995.

1830   SMTP Service Extensions for Transmission of Large and Binary MIME Messages. 16 August 1995.

1829   The ESP DES-CBC Transform. 9 August 1995.

1828   IP Authentication Using Keyed MD5. 9 August 1995.

1827   IP Encapsulating Security Payload (ESP). 9 August 1995.

1826   IP Authentication Header. 9 August 1995.

1825   Security Architecture for the Internet Protocol. 9 August 1995.

1824   The Exponential Security System TESS: An Identity-Based Cryptographic Protocol for Authenticated Key-Exchange (EISS-Report 1995/4). 11 August 1995.

1823   The LDAP Application Program Interface. 9 August 1995.

1822   A Grant of Rights to Use a Specific IBM Patent with Photuris. 14 August 1995.

1821   Integration of Real-Time Services in an IP-ATM Network Architecture. 11 August 1995.

1820   Multimedia E-mail (MIME) User Agent Checklist. 22 August 1995.

1819   Internet Stream Protocol V2 (ST2) Protocol Specification—Version ST2+. 11 August 1995.

1818   Best Current Practices. 4 August 1995.

1817   CIDR and Classful Routing. 4 August 1995.

1816   U.S. Government Internet Domain Names. 3 August 1995.

1815   Character Sets ISO-10646 and ISO-10646-J-1. 1 August 1995.

1814   Unique Addresses are Good. 22 June 1995.

1813   NFS V3 Protocol Specification. 21 June 1995.

1812   Requirements for IP V4 Routers. 22 June 1995.

1811   U.S. Government Internet Domain Names. 21 June 1995.

1810   Report on MD5 Performance. 21 June 1995.

1809   Using the Flow Label Field in IPv6. 14 June 1995.

1808   Relative Uniform Resource Locators. 14 June 1995.

1807   A Format for Bibliographic Records. 21 June 1995.

1806   Communicating Presentation Information in Internet Messages: The Content-Disposition Header. 7 June 1995.

1805   Location-Independent Data/Software Integrity Protocol. 7 June 1995.

1804   Schema Publishing in X.500 Directory. 9 June 1995.

1803   Recommendations for an X.500 Production Directory Service. 7 June 1995.

1802   Introducing Project Long Bud: Internet Pilot Project for the Deployment of X.500 Directory Information in Support of X.400 Routing. 12 June 1995.

1801   MHS Use of the X.500 Directory to Support MHS Routing. 9 June 1995.

1800   Internet Official Protocol Standards. 11 July 1995.

1799   Request for Comments Summary RFC Numbers 1700–1799. 6 January 1997.

1798   Connectionless Lightweight Directory Access Protocol. 7 June 1995.

1797   Class A Subnet Experiment. 25 April 1995.

1796   Not All RFCs Are Standards. 25 April 1995.

1795   Data Link Switching: Switch-to-Switch Protocol AIW DLSw RIG: DLSw Closed Pages, DLSw Standard V1. 25 April 1995.

1794   DNS Support for Load Balancing. 20 April 1995.

1793   Extending OSPF to Support Demand Circuits. 19 April 1995.

1792   TCP/IPX Connection MIB Specification. 18 April 1995.

1791   TCP and UDP over IPX Networks with Fixed Path MTU. 18 April 1995.

1790   An Agreement Between the Internet Society and Sun Microsystems, Inc. in the Matter of ONC RPC and XDR Protocols. 17 April 1995.

1789   INETPhone: Telephone Services and Servers on Internet. 17 April 1995.

1788   ICMP Domain Name Messages. 14 April 1995.

1787   Routing in a Multi-Provider Internet. 14 April 1995.

1786   Representation of IP Routing Policies in a Routing Registry (RIPE-81++). 28 March 1995.

1785   TFTP Option Negotiation Analysis. 28 March 1995.

1784   TFTP Timeout Interval and Transfer Size Options. 28 March 1995.

1783   TFTP Blocksize Option. 28 March 1995.

1782   TFTP Option Extension. 28 March 1995.

1781   Using the OSI Directory to Achieve User Friendly Naming. 28 March 1995.

1780   Internet Official Protocol Standards. 28 March 1995.

1779   A String Representation of Distinguished Names. 28 March 1995.

1778   The String Representation of Standard Attribute Syntaxes. 28 March 1995.

1777   Lightweight Directory Access Protocol. 28 March 1995.

1776   The Address Is the Message. 1 April 1995.

1775   To Be "On" the Internet. 17 March 1995.

1774   BGP-4 Protocol Analysis. 21 March 1995.

1773   Experience with the BGP-4 Protocol. 21 March 1995.

1772   Application of the Border Gateway Protocol in the Internet. 21 March 1995.

1771   A Border Gateway Protocol 4 (BGP-4). 21 March 1995.

1770   IPv4 Option for Sender Directed Multi-Destination Delivery. 28 March 1995.

1769   Simple Network Time Protocol (SNTP). 17 March 1995.

1768   Host Group Extensions for CLNP Multicasting. 3 March 1995.

1767   MIME Encapsulation of EDI Objects. 2 March 1995.

1766   Tags for the Identification of Languages. 2 March 1995.

1765   OSPF Database Overflow. 2 March 1995.

1764   The PPP XNS IDP Control Protocol (XNSCP). 1 March 1995.

1763   The PPP Banyan Vines Control Protocol (BVCP). 1 March 1995.

1762   The PPP DECnet Phase IV Control Protocol (DNCP). 1 March 1995.

1761   Snoop V2 Packet Capture File Format. 9 February 1995.

1760   The S/KEY One-Time Password System. 15 February 1995.

1759   Printer MIB. 28 March 1995.

1758   NADF Standing Documents: A Brief Overview. 9 February 1995.

1757   Remote Network Monitoring Management Information Base. 10 February 1995.

1756   Remote Write Protocol—V1. 19 January 1995.

1755   ATM Signaling Support for IP over ATM. 17 February 1995.

1754   IP over ATM Working Group's Recommendations for the ATM Forum's Multiprotocol BOF V1. 19 January 1995.

1753   IPng Technical Requirements of the Nimrod Routing and Addressing Architecture. 5 January 1995.

1752   The Recommendation for the IP Next Generation Protocol. 18 January 1995.

1751   A Convention for Human-Readable 128-Bit Keys. 29 December 1994.

1750   Randomness Recommendations for Security. 29 December 1994.

1749   IEEE 802.5 Station Source Routing MIB Using SMIv2. 29 December 1994.

1748   IEEE 802.5 MIB Using SMIv2. 29 December 1994.

1747   Definitions of Managed Objects for SNA Data Link Control: SDLC. 11 January 1995.

1746   Ways to Define User Expectations. 30 December 1994.

1745   BGP4/IDRP for IP-OSPF Interaction. 27 December 1994.

1744   Observations on the Management of the Internet Address Space. 23 December 1994.

1743   IEEE 802.5 MIB Using SMIv2. 27 December 1994.

1742   AppleTalk Management Information BaseII. 5 January 1995.

1741   MIME Content Type for BinHex Encoded Files. 22 December 1994.

1740   MIME Encapsulation of Macintosh Files—MacMIME. 22 December 1994.

1739   A Primer on Internet and TCP/IP Tools. 22 December 1994.

1738   Uniform Resource Locators (URL). 20 December 1994.

1737   Functional Requirements for Uniform Resource Names. 20 December 1994.

1736   Functional Requirements for Internet Resource Locators. 9 February 1995.

1735   NBMA Address Resolution Protocol (NARP). 15 December 1994.

1734   POP3 AUTHentication Command. 20 December 1994.

1733   Distributed Electronic Mail Models in IMAP4. 20 December 1994.

1732   IMAP4 Compatibility with IMAP2 and IMAP2BIS. 20 December 1994.

1731   IMAP4 Authentication Mechanisms. 20 December 1994.

1730   Internet Message Access Protocol—V4. 20 December 1994.

1729   Using the Z39.50 Information Retrieval Protocol in the Internet Environment. 16 December 1994.

1728   Resource Transponders. 16 December 1994.

1727   A Vision of an Integrated Internet Information Service. 16 December 1994.

1726   Technical Criteria for Choosing IP: The Next Generation (IPng). 20 December 1994.

1725   Post Office Protocol—V3. 23 November 1994.

1724   RIP V2 MIB Extension. 15 November 1994.

1723   RIP V2 Carrying Additional Information. 15 November 1994.

1722   RIP V2 Protocol Applicability Statement. 15 November 1994.

1721   RIP V2 Protocol Analysis. 15 November 1994.

1720   Internet Official Protocol Standards. 23 November 1994.

1719   A Direction for IPng. 16 December 1994.

1718   The Tao of IETF—A Guide for New Attendees of the Internet Engineering Task Force. 23 November 1994.

1717   The PPP Multilink Protocol (MP). 21 November 1994.

1716   Towards Requirements for IP Routers. 4 November 1994.

1715   The H Ratio for Address Assignment Efficiency. 3 November 1994.

1714   Referral Whois Protocol (RWhois). 15 December 1994.

1713   Tools for DNS Debugging. 3 November 1994.

1712   DNS Encoding of Geographical Location. 1 November 1994.

1711   Classifications in E-mail Routing. 26 October 1994.

1710   Simple Internet Protocol Plus White Paper. 26 October 1994.

1709   K-12 Internetworking Guidelines. 23 December 1994.

1708   NTP PICS PROFORMA for the Network Time Protocol V3.
        26 October 1994.

1707   CATNIP: Common Architecture for the Internet. 2 November 1994.

1706   DNS NSAP Resource Records. 26 October 1994.

1705   Six Virtual Inches to the Left: The Problem with IPng. 26 October
        1994.

1704   On Internet Authentication. 26 October 1994.

1703   Principles of Operation for the TPC.INT Subdomain: Radio
        Paging—Technical Procedures. 26 October 1994.

1702   Generic Routing Encapsulation over IPv4 networks. 21 October
        1994.

1701   Generic Routing Encapsulation (GRE). 21 October 1994.

1700   Assigned Numbers. 20 October 1994.

1699   Request for Comments Summary RFC Numbers 1600–1699.
        6 January 1997.

1698   Octet Sequences for Upper-Layer OSI to Support Basic Communi-
        cations Applications. 26 October 1994.

1697   Relational Database Management System (RDBMS) Management
        Information Base (MIB) Using SMIv2. 23 August 1994.

1696   Modem Management Information Base (MIB) Using SMIv2.
        25 August 1994.

1695   Definitions of Managed Objects for ATM Management Version 8.0
        Using SMIv2. 25 August 1994.

1694   Definitions of Managed Objects for SMDS Interfaces Using SMIv2.
        23 August 1994.

1693   An Extension to TCP: Partial Order Service. 1 November 1994.

1692   Transport Multiplexing Protocol (TMux). 17 August 1994.

1691   The Document Architecture for the Cornell Digital Library.
        17 August 1994.

1690   Introducing the Internet Engineering and Planning Group (IEPG).
        17 August 1994.

1689   A Status Report on Networked Information Retrieval: Tools and
        Groups. 17 August 1994.

1688   IPng Mobility Considerations. 11 August 1994.

1687   A Large Corporate User's View of IPng. 11 August 1994.

1686   IPng Requirements: A Cable Television Industry Viewpoint.
        11 August 1994.

1685   Writing X.400 O/R Names. 11 August 1994.

1684   Introduction to White Pages Services Based on X.500. 11 August
        1994.

1683   Multiprotocol Interoperability In IPng. 11 August 1994.

1682   IPng BSD Host Implementation Analysis. 11 August 1994.

1681   On Many Addresses per Host. 8 August 1994.

1680   IPng Support for ATM Services. 8 August 1994.

1679   HPN Working Group Input to the IPng Requirements Solicitation. 8 August 1994.

1678   IPng Requirements of Large Corporate Networks. 8 August 1994.

1677   Tactical Radio Frequency Communication Requirements for IPng. 8 August 1994.

1676   INFN Requirements for an IPng. 11 August 1994.

1675   Security Concerns for IPng. 8 August 1994.

1674   A Cellular Industry View of IPng. 8 August 1994.

1673   Electric Power Research Institute Comments on IPng. 8 August 1994.

1672   Accounting Requirements for IPng. 8 August 1994.

1671   IPng White Paper on Transition and Other Considerations. 8 August 1994.

1670   Input to IPng Engineering Considerations. 8 August 1994.

1669   Market Viability as a IPng Criteria. 8 August 1994.

1668   Unified Routing Requirements for IPng. 8 August 1994.

1667   Modeling and Simulation Requirements for IPng. 8 August 1994.

1666   Definitions of Managed Objects for SNA NAUs Using SMIv2. 11 August 1994.

1665   Definitions of Managed Objects for SNA NAUs Using SMIv2. 22 July 1994.

1664   Using the Internet DNS to Distribute RFC1327 Mail Address Mapping Tables. 11 August 1994.

1663   PPP Reliable Transmission. 21 July 1994.

1662   PPP in HDLC-like Framing. 21 July 1994.

1661   The Point-to-Point Protocol (PPP). 21 July 1994.

1660   Definitions of Managed Objects for Parallel-Printer-like Hardware Devices Using SMIv2. 20 July 1994.

1659   Definitions of Managed Objects for RS-232-like Hardware Devices Using SMIv2. 20 July 1994.

1658   Definitions of Managed Objects for Character Stream Devices Using SMIv2. 20 July 1994.

1657   Definitions of Managed Objects for the Fourth Version of the Border Gateway Protocol (BGP-4) Using SMIv2. 21 July 1994.

1656   BGP-4 Protocol Document Roadmap and Implementation Experience. 21 July 1994.

1655   Application of the Border Gateway Protocol in the Internet. 21 July 1994.

1654   A Border Gateway Protocol 4 (BGP-4). 21 July 1994.

1653   SMTP Service Extension for Message Size Declaration. 18 July 1994.

1652   SMTP Service Extension for 8bit-MIMEtransport. 18 July 1994.

1651   SMTP Service Extensions. 18 July 1994.

1650   Definitions of Managed Objects for the Ethernet-like Interface Types Using SMIv2. 23 August 1994.

1649   Operational Requirements for X.400 Management Domains in the GO-MHS Community. 18 July 1994.

1648   Postmaster Convention for X.400 Operations. 18 July 1994.

1647   TN3270 Enhancements. 15 July 1994.

1646   TN3270 Extensions for LUname and Printer Selection. 14 July 1994.

1645   Simple Network Paging Protocol—V2. 14 July 1994.

1644   T/TCP—TCP Extensions for Transactions Functional Specification. 13 July 1994.

1643   Definitions of Managed Objects for the Ethernet-like Interface Types. 13 July 1994.

1642   UTF-7—A Mail-Safe Transformation Format of Unicode. 13 July 1994.

1641   Using Unicode with MIME. 13 July 1994.

1640   The Process for Organization of Internet Standards Working Group (POISED). 9 June 1994.

1639   FTP Operation Over Big Address Records (FOOBAR). 9 June 1994.

1638   PPP Bridging Control Protocol (BCP). 9 June 1994.

1637   DNS NSAP Resource Records. 9 June 1994.

1636   Report of IAB Workshop on Security in the Internet Architecture— February 8–10, 1994. 9 June 1994.

1635   How to Use Anonymous FTP. 25 May 1994.

1634   Novell IPX over Various WAN Media (IPXWAN). 24 May 1994.

1633   Integrated Services in the Internet Architecture: An Overview. 9 June 1994.

1632   A Revised Catalog of Available X.500 Implementations. 20 May 1994.

1631   The IP Network Address Translator (NAT). 20 May 1994.

1630   Universal Resource Identifiers in WWW: A Unifying Syntax for the Expression of Names and Addresses of Objects on the Network as Used in the World-Wide Web. 9 June 1994.

1629   Guidelines for OSI NSAP Allocation in the Internet. 19 May 1994.

1628   UPS Management Information Base. 19 May 1994.

1627   Network 10 Considered Harmful (Some Practices Shouldn't Be Codified). 1 July 1994.

1626   Default IP MTU for Use over ATM AAL5. 19 May 1994.

1625   WAIS over Z39.50-1988. 9 June 1994.

1624   Computation of the Internet Checksum via Incremental Update. 20 May 1994.

1623   Definitions of Managed Objects for the Ethernet-like Interface Types. 24 May 1994.

1622   Pip Header Processing. 20 May 1994.

1621   Pip Near-Term Architecture. 20 May 1994.

1620   Internet Architecture Extensions for Shared Media. 20 May 1994.

1619   PPP over SONET/SDH. 13 May 1994.

1618   PPP over ISDN. 13 May 1994.

1617   Naming and Structuring Guidelines for X.500 Directory Pilots. 20 May 1994.

1616   X.400 (1988) for the Academic and Research Community in Europe. 19 May 1994.

1615   Migrating from X.400(84) to X.400(88). 19 May 1994.

1614   Network Access to Multimedia Information. 20 May 1994.

1613   Cisco Systems X.25 over TCP (XOT). 13 May 1994.

1612   DNS Resolver MIB Extensions. 17 May 1994.

1611   DNS Server MIB Extensions. 17 May 1994.

1610   Internet Official PROtocol Standards. 8 July 1994.

1609   Charting Networks in the X.500 Directory. 25 March 1994.

1608   Representing IP Information in the X.500 Directory. 25 March 1994.

1607   A View from the 21st Century. 1 April 1994.

1606   A Historical Perspective on the Usage of IP Version 9. 1 April 1994.

1605   SONET to Sonnet Translation. 1 April 1994.

1604   Definitions of Managed Objects for Frame Relay Service. 25 March 1994.

1603   IETF Working Group Guidelines and Procedures. 24 March 1994.

1602   The Internet Standards Process—R2. 24 March 1994.

1601   Charter of the Internet Architecture Board (IAB). 22 March 1994.

1600   Internet Official Protocol Standards. 14 March 1994.

1599   Request for Comments Summary RFC Numbers 1500–1599. 6 January 1997.

1598   PPP in X.25. 17 March 1994.

1597   Address Allocation for Private Internets. 17 March 1994.

1596   Definitions of Managed Objects for Frame Relay Service. 17 March 1994.

1595 Definitions of Managed Objects for the SONET/SDH Interface Type. 11 March 1994.

1594 FYI on Questions and Answers to Commonly Asked New Internet User Questions. 11 March 1994.

1593 SNA APPN Node MIB. 10 March 1994.

1592 Simple Network Management Protocol Distributed Protocol Interface V2. 3 March 1994.

1591 Domain Name System Structure and Delegation. 3 March 1994.

1590 Media Type Registration Procedure. 2 March 1994.

1589 A Kernel Model for Precision Timekeeping. 3 March 1994.

1588 White Pages Meeting Reports. 25 February 1994.

1587 The OSPF NSSA Option. 24 March 1994.

1586 Guidelines for Running OSPF over Frame Relay Networks. 24 March 1994.

1585 MOSPF: Analysis and Experience. 24 March 1994.

1584 Multicast Extensions to OSPF. 24 March 1994.

1583 OSPF Version 2. 23 March 1994.

1582 Extensions to RIP to Support Demand Circuits. 18 February 1994.

1581 Protocol Analysis for Extensions to RIP to Support Demand Circuits. 18 February 1994.

1580 Guide to Network Resource Tools. 22 March 1994.

1579 Firewall-Friendly FTP. 18 February 1994.

1578 FYI on Questions and Answers: Answers to Commonly Asked Primary and Secondary School Internet User Questions. 18 February 1994.

1577 Classical IP and ARP over ATM. 20 January 1994.

1576 TN3270 Current Practices. 20 January 1994.

1575 An Echo Function for CLNP (ISO 8473). 18 February 1994.

1574 Essential Tools for the OSI Internet. 18 February 1994.

1573 Evolution of the Interfaces Group of MIB-II. 20 January 1994.

1572 Telnet Environment Option. 14 January 1994.

1571 Telnet Environment Option Interoperability Issues. 14 January 1994.

1570 PPP LCP Extensions. 11 January 1994.

1569 Principles of Operation for the TPC.INT Subdomain: Radio Paging—Technical Procedures. 7 January 1994.

1568 Simple Network Paging Protocol—V1(b). 7 January 1994.

1567 X.500 Directory Monitoring MIB. 11 January 1994.

1566 Mail Monitoring MIB. 11 January 1994.

1565 Network Services Monitoring MIB. 11 January 1994.

1564   DSA Metrics (OSI-DS 34 (v3)). 14 January 1994.

1563   The Text/Enriched MIME Content-Type. 10 January 1994.

1562   Naming Guidelines for the AARNet X.500 Directory Service. December 1993.

1561   Use of ISO CLNP in TUBA Environments. December 1993.

1560   The MultiProtocol Internet. December 1993.

1559   DECnet Phase IV MIB Extensions (Obsoletes RFC 1289). December 1993.

1558   A String Representation of LDAP Search Filters. December 1993.

1557   Korean Character Encoding for Internet Messages. December 1993.

1556   Handling of Bi-Directional Texts in MIME. December 1993.

1555   Hebrew Character Encoding for Internet Messages. December 1993.

1554   ISO-2022-JP-2: Multilingual Extensions of ISO-2022-JP. December 1993.

1553   Compressing IPX Headers over WAN Media (CIPX). December 1993.

1552   The PPP Internetwork Packet Exchange Control Protocol. December 1993.

1551   Novell IPX over Various WAN Media (IPXWAN) (Obsoletes RFC 1362). December 1993.

1550   IP: Next Generation (IPng) White Paper Solicitation. December 1993.

1549   PPP in HDLC Framing. December 1993.

1548   The Point-to-Point Protocol (PPP) (Obsoletes RFC 1331). December 1993.

1547   Requirements for an Internet Standard Point-to-Point Protocol. December 1993.

1546   Host Anycasting Service. November 1993.

1545   FTP Operation Over Big Address Records (FOOBAR). November 1993.

1544   The Content-MD5 Header Field. November 1993.

1543   Instructions to RFC Authors (Obsoletes RFC 1111). October 1993.

1542   Clarifications and Extensions for the Bootstrap Protocol (Obsoletes RFC 1532). October 1993.

1541   Dynamic Host Configuration Protocol (Obsoletes RFC 1531). October 1993.

1540   Internet Official Protocol Standards (Obsoletes RFC 1500). October 1993.

1539   The Tao of IETF: A Guide for New Attendees of the Internet Engineering Task Force (Obsoletes RFC 1391). October 1993.

1538   Advanced SNA/IP: A Simple SNA Transport Protocol. October 1993.

1537   Common DNS Data File Configuration Errors. October 1993.

1536 Common DNS Implementation Errors and Suggested Fixes. October 1993.

1535 A Security Problem and Proposed Correction with Widely Deployed DNS Software. October 1993.

1534 Interoperation Between DHCP and BOOTP. October 1993.

1533 DHCP Options and BootP Vendor Extensions (Obsoletes RFC 1497). October 1993.

1532 Clarifications and Extensions for the Bootstrap Protocol (Obsoleted by RFC 1542). October 1993.

1531 Dynamic Host Configuration Protocol (Obsoleted by RFC 1541). October 1993.

1530 Principles of Operation for the TPC.INT Subdomain: General Principles and Policy. October 1993.

1529 Principles of Operation for the TPC.INT Subdomain: Remote Printing—Administrative Policies (Obsoletes RFC 1486). October 1993.

1528 Principles of Operation for the TPC.INT Subdomain: Remote Printing—Technical Procedures (Obsoletes RFC 1486). October 1993.

1527 What Should We Plan Given the Dilemma of the Network? September 1993.

1526 Assignment of System Identifiers for TUBA/CLNP Hosts. September 1993.

1525 Definitions of Managed Objects for Source Routing Bridges (Obsoletes RFC 1286). September 1993.

1524 A User Agent Configuration Mechanism for Multimedia Mail Format Information. September 1993.

1523 The Text/Enriched MIME Content-Type. September 1993.

1522 MIME (Multipurpose Internet Mail Extensions) Part Two: Message Header Exensions for Non-ASCII Text (Obsoletes RFC 1342). September 1993.

1521 MIME (Multipurpose Internet Mail Extensions) Part One: Mechanisms for Specifying and Describing the Format of Internet Message Bodies (Obsoletes RFC 1341). September 1993.

1520 Exchanging Routing Information Across Provider Boundaries in the CIDR Environment. September 1993.

1519 Classless Inter-Domain Routing (CIDR): An Address Assignment and Aggregation Strategy (Obsoletes RFC 1338). September 1993.

1518 An Architecture for IP Address Allocation with CIDR. September 1993.

1517 Applicability Statement for the Implementation of Classless Inter-Domain Routing (CIDR). September 1993.

1516 Definitions of Managed Objects for IEEE 802.3 Repeater Devices (Obsoletes RFC 1368). September 1993.

1515 Definitions of Managed Objects for IEEE 802.3 Medium Attachment Units (MAUs). September 1993.

1514   Host Resources MIB. September 1993.

1513   Token Ring Extensions to the Remote Network Monitoring MIB (Obsoletes RFC 1271). September 1993.

1512   FDDI Management Information Base (Updates RFC 1285). September 1993.

1511   Common Authentication Technology Overview. September 1993.

1510   The Kerberos Network Authentication Service (V5). September 1993.

1509   Generic Security Service API: C-Bindings. September 1993.

1508   Generic Security Service Application Program Interface. September 1993.

1507   DASS Distributed Authentication Security Service. September 1993.

1506   A Tutorial on Gatewaying Between X.400 and Internet Mail. August 1993.

1505   Encoding Header Field for Internet Messages (Obsoletes RFC 1154). August 1993.

1504   Appletalk Update-Based Routing Protocol: Enchanced Appletalk Routing. August 1993.

1503   Algorithms for Automating Administration in SNMPv2 Managers. August 1993.

1502   X.400 Use of Extended Character Sets. August 1993.

1501   OS/2 User Group. August 1993.

1500   Internet Official Protocol Standards (Obsoletes RFC 1410; Obsoleted by RFC 1540). August 1993.

1499   Not yet issued.

1498   On the Naming and Binding of Network Destinations. August 1993.

1497   BOOTP Vendor Information Extensions (Obsoletes RFC 1395; Obsoleted by RFC 1533; Updates RFC 951). August 1993.

1496   Rules for Downgrading Messages from X.400/88 to X.400/84 When MIME Content-Types Are Present in the Messages (Updates RFC 1328). August 1993.

1495   Mapping Between X.400 and RFC-822 Message Bodies (Obsoletes RFC 1327). August 1993.

1494   Equivalences Between 1988 X.400 and RFC-822 Message Bodies. August 1993.

1493   Definitions of Managed Objects for Bridges (Obsoletes RFC 1286). July 1993.

1492   An Access Control Protocol. Sometimes Called TACACS. July 1993.

1491   A Survey of Advanced Usages of X.500. July 1993.

1490   Multiprotocol Interconnect over Frame Relay (Obsoletes RFC 1294). July 1993.

1489   Registration of a Cyrillic Character Set. July 1993.

1488   The X.500 String Representation of Standard Attribute Syntaxes. July 1993.

1487   X.500 Lightweight Directory Access Protocol. July 1993.

1486   An Experiment in Remote Printing (Obsoleted by RFC 1528, RFC 1529). July 1993.

1485   A String Representation of Distinguished Names (OSI-DS 23 v5). July 1993.

1484   Using the OSI Directory to Achieve User Friendly Naming (OSI-DS 24 v1.2). July 1993.

1483   Multiprotocol Encapsulation over ATM Adaptation Layer 5. July 1993.

1482   Aggregation Support in the NSFNET Policy-Based Routing Database. June 1993.

1481   IAB Recommendation for an Intermediate Stratgegy to Address the Issue of Scaling. July 1993.

1480   The US Domain (Obsoletes RFC 1386). June 1993.

1479   Inter-Domain Policy Routing Protocol Specification: Version 1. July 1993.

1478   An Architecture for Inter-Domain Policy Routing. June 1993.

1477   IDPR as a Proposed Standard. July 1993.

1476   RAP: Internet Route Access Protocol. June 1993.

1475   TP/IX: The Next Internet. June 1993.

1474   The Definitions of Managed Objects for the Bridge Network Control Protocol of the Point-to-Point Protocol. June 1993.

1473   The Definitions of Managed Objects for the IP Network Control Protocol of the Point-to-Point Protocol. June 1993.

1472   The Definitions of Managed Objects for the Security Protocols of the Point-to-Point Protocol. June 1993.

1471   The Definitions of Managed Objects for the Link Control Protocol of the Point-to-Point Protocol. June 1993.

1470   FYI on a Network Management Tool Catalog: Tools for Monitoring and Debugging PCT/IP Internets and Interconnected Devices (Obsoletes RFC 1147). June 1993.

1469   IP Multicast over Token-Ring Local Area Networks. June 1993.

1468   Japanese Character Encoding for Internet Messages. June 1993.

1467   Status of CIDR Deployment in the Internet (Obsoletes RFC 1367). August 1993.

1466   Guidelines for Management of IP Address Space (Obsoletes 1366). May 1993.

1465   Routing Coordination for X.400 MHS Service Within a Multi-Protocol/Multi-Network Environment Table Format V3 for Static Routing. May 1993.

1464　Using the Domain Name System To Store Arbitrary String Attributes. May 1993.

1463　FYI on Introducing the Internet—A Short Bibliography of Introductory Internetworking Readings for the Network Novice (FYI 19). May 1993.

1462　FYI on "What is the Internet?" (Also FYI 20). May 1993.

1461　SNMP MIB Extension for Multiprotocol Interconnect over X.25. May 1993.

1460　Post Office Protocol V3 (Obsoletes RFC 1225). May 1993.

1459　Internet Relay Chat Protocol. May 1993.

1458　Requirements for Multicast Protocols. May 1993.

1457　Security Label Framework for the Internet. May 1993.

1456　Conventions for Encoding the Vietnamese Language VISCII: Vietnamese Standard code for Information Interchange and VIQR: Vietnamese Quoted-Readable Specification Revision 1.1. May 1993.

1455　Physical Link Security Type of Service. May 1993.

1454　Comparison of Proposals for Next Version of IP. May 1993.

1453　A Comment on Packet Video Remote Conferencing and the Transport/Network Layers. April 1993.

1452　Coexistence Between v1 and v2 of the Internet-Standard Network Management Framework. April 1993.

1451　Manager-to-Manager Management Information Base. April 1993.

1450　Management Information Base for v2 of the Simple Network Management Protocol (SNMPv2). April 1993.

1449　Transport Mappings for v2 of the Simple Network Management Protocol (SNMPv2). April 1993.

1448　Protocol Operations for v2 of the Simple Network Management Protocol (SNMPv2). April 1993.

1447　Party MIB for v2 of the Simple Network Management Protocol (SNMPv2). April 1993.

1446　Security Protocols for v2 of the Simple Network Management Protocol (SNMPv2). April 1993.

1445　Administrative Model for v2 of the Simple Network Management Protocol SNMPv2). April 1993.

1444　Conformance Statements for v2 of the Simple Network Management Protocol (SNMPv2). April 1993.

1443　Textual Conventions for v2 of the Simple Network Management Protocol (SNMPv2). April 1993.

1442　Structure of Management Information for v2 of the Simple Network Management Protocol (SNMPv2). April 1993.

1441　Introduction to v2 of the Internet-Standard Network Management Framework. April 1993.

1440   SIFT/UFT: Sender-Initiated/Unsolicited File Transfer. July 1993.

1439   The Uniqueness of Unique Identifiers. March 1993.

1438   Internet Engineering Task Force Statements of Boredom (SOBs). April 1993.

1437   The Extension of MIME Content-Types to a New Medium. April 1993.

1436   The Internet Gopher Protocol (A Distributed Document Search and Retrieval Protocol). March 1993.

1435   IESG Advice from Experience with Path MTU Discovery. March 1993.

1434   Data Link Switching: Switch-to-Switch Protocol. March 1993.

1433   Directed ARP. March 1993.

1432   Recent Internet Books. March 1993.

1431   DUA Metrics. February 1993.

1430   A Strategic Plan for Deploying an Internet X.500 Directory Service. February 1993.

1429   Listserv Distributed Protocol. February 1993.

1428   Transition of InternetMail from Just-Send-8 to 8bit-SMTP/MIME. February 1993.

1427   SMTP Service Extension for Message Size Declaration. February 1993.

1426   SMTP Service Extension for 8bit-MIMEtransport. February 1993.

1425   SMTP Service Extensions. February 1993.

1424   Privacy Enhancement for Internet Electronic Mail: Part IV: Key Certification and Related Service. February 1993.

1423   Privacy Enchancement for Internet Electronic Mail: Part III: Algorithms, Modes, and Identifiers (Obsoletes RFC 1115). February 1993.

1422   Privacy Enhancement for Internet Electronic Mail: Part II: Certificate-Based Key Management (Obsoletes RFC 1114). February 1993.

1421   Privacy Enhancement for Internet Electronic Mail: Part I: Message Encryption and Authentication Procedures (Obsoletes RFC 1113). February 1993.

1420   SNMP over IPX (Obsoletes 1298). March 1993.

1419   SNMP over AppleTalk. March 1993.

1418   SNMP over OSI (Obsoletes 1161). March 1993.

1417   The North American Directory Forum NADF Standing Documents: A Brief Overview (Obsoletes RFCs 1295, 1255, and 1218). February 1993.

1416   Telnet Authentication Option (Obsoletes RFC 1409). February 1993.

1415   FTP-FTAM Gateway Specification. January 1993.

1414   Identification MIB. February 1993.

1413   Identification Protocol (Obsoletes RFC 931). February 1993.

1412   Telnet Authentication: SPX. January 1993.

1411   Telnet Authentication: Kerberos V4. January 1993.

1410   IAB Official Protocol Standards (Obsoletes RFCs 1360, 1280, 1250, 1200, 1100, 1083, 1130, and 1140; Obsoleted by RFC 1500). March 1993.

1409   Telnet Authentication Option (Obsoleted by RFC 1416). January 1993.

1408   Telnet Environment Option. January 1993.

1407   Definitions of Managed Objects for the DS3/E3 Interface Type (Obsoletes RFC 1233). January 1993.

1406   Definitions of Managed Objects for the DS1 and E1 Interface Types (Obsoletes RFC 1232). January 1993.

1405   Mapping Between X.400 (1984/1988) and Mail-11 (DECnet Mail). January 1993.

1404   Model for Common Operational Statistics. January 1993.

1403   BGP OSPF Interaction (Obsoletes RFC 1364). January 1993.

1402   There's Gold in Them Thar Networks! or Searching for Treasure in All the Wrong Places (Also FYI 10; Obsoletes RFC 1290). January 1993.

1401   Correspondence Between the IAB and DISA on the Use of DNS Throughout the Internet. January 1993.

1400   Transition and Modernization of the Internet Registration Service. March 1993.

1399   Not yet issued.

1398   Definitions of Managed Objects for the Ethernet-like Interface Types (Obsoletes RFC 1284). January 1993.

1397   Default Route Advertisement in BGP2 And BGP3 Versions of the Border Gateway Protocol. January 1993.

1396   The Process for Organization of Internet Standards—Working Group (POISED). January 1993.

1395   BOOTP Vendor Information Extensions. (Obsoletes RFC 1084, RFC 1048; Obsoleted by RFC 1497; Updates RFC 951). January 1993.

1394   Relationship of Telex Answerback Codes to Internet Domains. January 1993.

1393   Traceroute Using an IP Option. January 1993.

1392   Internet Users' Glossary (Also FYI 18). January 1993.

1391   The Tao of IETF—A Guide for New Attendees of the Internet Engineering Task Force (Also FYI 17; Obsoleted by RFC 1539). January 1993.

1390   Transmission of IP and ARP over FDDI Networks. January 1993.

1389   RIP Version 2 MIB Extension. January 1993.

1388   RIP Version 2—Carrying Additional Information (Updates RFC 1058). January 1993.

1387   RIP Version 2 Protocol Analysis. January 1993.

1386   The US Domain (Obsoleted by RFC 1480). December 1992.

1385   EIP: The Extended Internet Protocol: A Framework for Maintaining Backward Compatibility. November 1992.

1384   Naming Guidelines for Directory Pilots. January 1992.

1383   An Experiment in DNS-Based IP Routing. December 1992.

1382   SNMP MIB Extension for the X.25 Packet Layer. November 1992.

1381   SNMP MIB Extension for X.25 LAPB. November 1992.

1380   IESG Deliberations on Routing and Addressing. November 1992.

1379   Extending TCP for Transactions—Concepts. November 1992.

1378   The PPP AppleTalk Control Protocol (ATCP). November 1992.

1377   The PPP OSI Network Layer Control Protocol (OSINLCP). November 1992.

1376   The PPP DECnet Phase IV Control Protocol (DNC). November 1992.

1375   Suggestion for New Classes of IP Addresses. November 1992.

1374   IP and ARP on HIPPI. October 1992.

1373   Portable DUAs. October 1992.

1372   Telnet Remote Flow Control Option (Obsoletes RFC 1080). October 1992.

1371   Choosing a "Common IGP" for the IP Internet (The IESG's Recommendation to the IAB). October 1992.

1370   Applicability Statement for OSPF. October 1992.

1369   Implementation Notes and Experience for the Internet Ethernet MIB. October 1992.

1368   Definitions of Managed Objects for IEEE 802.3 Repeater Devices (Obsoleted by RFC 1516). October 1992.

1367   Schedule for IP Address Space Management Guidelines (Obsoleted by RFC 1467). October 1992.

1366   Guidelines for Management of IP Address Space (Obsoleted by RFC 1466). October 1992.

1365   An Address Extension Proposal. September 1992.

1364   BGP OSPF Interaction (Obsoleted by RFC 1403). September 1992.

1363   A Proposed Flow Specification. September 1992.

1362   Novell IPX over Various WAN Media (IPXWAN) (Obsoleted by RFC 1551). September 1992.

1361   Simple Network Time Protocol (SNTP). August 1992.

1360   IAB Official Protocol Standards (Obsoletes RFCs 1280, 1250, 1100, 1083, 1130, 1140, and 1200; Obsoleted by RFC 1410). September 1992.

1359   Connecting to the Internet: What Connecting Institutions Should Anticipate (Also FYI 16). August 1992.

1358   Charter of the Internet Architecture Board (IAB). August 1992.

1357   A Format for E-mailing Bibliographic Records. July 1992.

1356   Multiprotocol Interconnect on X.25 and ISDN in the Packet Mode (Obsoletes RFC 877). August 1992.

1355   Privacy and Accuracy Issues in Network Information Center Databases. August 1992.

1354   IP Forwarding Table MIB. July 1992.

1353   Definitions of Managed Objects for Administration of SNMP Parties. July 1992.

1352   SNMP Security Protocols. July 1992.

1351   SNMP Administrative Model. July 1992.

1350   The TFTP Protocol (Revision 2) (Obsoletes RFC 783). July 1992.

1349   Type of Service in the Internet Protocol Suite (Updates RFCs 1248, 1247, 1195, 1123, 1122, 1060, and 791). July 1992.

1348   DNS NSAP RRs. (Updates RFCs 1034, 1035). July 1992.

1347   TCP and UDP with Bigger Addresses (TUBA): A Simple Proposal for Internet Addressing and Routing. June 1992.

1346   Resource Allocation, Control, and Accounting for the Use of Network Resources. June 1992.

1345   Character Mnemonics and Character Sets. June 1992.

1344   Implications of MIME for Internet Mail Gateways. June 1992.

1343   A User Agent Configuration Mechanism For Multimedia Mail Format Information. June 1992.

1342   Representation of Non-ASCII Text in Internet Message Headers (Obsoleted by 1522). June 1992.

1341   MIME (Multipurpose Internet Mail Extensions) Mechanisms for Specifying and Describing the Format of Internet Message Bodies (Obsoleted by RFC 1521). June 1992.

1340   Assigned Numbers (Obsoletes RFCs 1060, 1010, 990, 960, 943, 923, 900, 870, 820, 790, 776, 770, 762, 758, 755, 750, 739, 604, 503, 433, and 349; IENs 127). July 1992.

1339   Remote Mail Checking Protocol. June 1992.

1338   Supernetting: An Address Assignment and Aggregation Strategy (Obsoleted by RFC 1519). June 1992.

1337   TIME-WAIT Assassination Hazards in TCP. May 1992.

1336   Who's Who in the Internet—Biographies of IAB, IESG, and IRSG Members (Obsoletes RFC 1251, FYI 9). May 1992.

1335   A Two-Tier Address Structure for the Internet: A Solution to the Problem of Address Space Exhaustion. May 1992.

1334   PPP Authentication Protocols. October 1992.

1333   PPP Link Quality Monitoring. May 1992.

1332   The PPP Internet Protocol Control Protocol (IPCP) (Obsoletes RFC 1172). May 1992.

1331   The Point-to-Point Protocol (PPP) for the Transmission of Multi-Protocol Datagrams over Point-to-Point Links (Obsoletes RFC 1171, RFC 1172; Obsoleted by RFC 1548). May 1992.

1330   Recommendations for the Phase I Deployment of OSI Directory Services (X.500) and OSI Message Handling Services (X.400) Within the ESnet Community. May 1992.

1329   Thoughts on Address Resolution for Dual MAC FDDI Networks. May 1992.

1328   X.400 1988 to 1984 Downgrading (Updated by RFC 1496). May 1992.

1327   Mapping Between X.400(1988)/ISO 10021 and RFC 822 (Obsoletes RFCs 987, 1026, 1138, and 1148; Obsoleted by RFC 1495; Updates RFC 822). May 1992.

1326   Mutual Encapsulation Considered Dangerous. May 1992.

1325   FYI on Questions and Answers—Answers to Commonly Asked "New Internet User" Questions (Obsoletes RFC 1206, FYI 4). May 1992.

1324   A Discussion on Computer Network Conferencing. May 1992.

1323   TCP Extensions for High Performance (Obsoletes RFC 1072, RFC 1185). May 1992.

1322   A Unified Approach to Inter-Domain Routing. May 1992.

1321   The MD5 Message-Digest Algorithm. April 1992.

1320   The MD4 Message-Digest Algorithm (Obsoletes RFC 1186). April 1992.

1319   The MD2 Message-Digest Algorithm. April 1992.

1318   Definitions of Managed Objects for Parallel-Printer-like Hardware Devices. April 1992.

1317   Definitions of Managed Objects for RS-232-like Hardware Devices. April 1992.

1316   Definitions of Managed Objects for Character Stream Devices. April 1992.

1315   Management Information Base for Frame Relay DTEs. April 1992.

1314   A File Format for the Exchange of Images in the Internet. April 1992.

1313   Today's Programming for KRFC AM 1313 Internet Talk Radio. April 1992.

1312   Message Send Protocol 2 (Obsoletes RFC 1159). April 1992.

1311   Introduction to the STD Notes. March 1992.

1310   The Internet Standards Process. March 1992.

1309   Technical Overview of Directory Services Using the X.500 Protocol (Also FYI 14). March 1992.

1308   Executive Introduction to Directory Services Using the X.500 Protocol (Also FYI 13). March 1992.

1307   Dynamically Switched Link Control Protocol. March 1992.

1306   Experiences Supporting By-Request Circuit-Switched T3 Networks. March 1992.

1305   Network Time Protocol (Version 3) Specification, Implementation, and Analysis (Obsoletes RFCs 1119, 1059, and 958). March 1992.

1304   Definitions of Managed Objects for the SIP Interface Type. 1992 February.

1303   A Convention for Describing SNMP-Based Agents. February 1992.

1302   Building a Network Information Services Infrastructure (Also FYI 12). February 1992.

1301   Multicast Transport Protocol. February 1992.

1300   Remembrances of Things Past. February 1992.

1299   Not yet issued.

1298   SNMP over IPX (Obsoleted by RFC 1420). February 1992.

1297   NOC Internal Integrated Trouble Ticket System Functional Specification Wishlist ("NOC TT Requirements"). January 1992.

1296   Internet Growth (1981–1991). January 1992.

1295   User Bill of Rights for Entries and Listings in the Public Directory (Obsoleted by RFC 1417). January 1992.

1294   Multiprotocol Interconnect over Frame Relay (Obsoleted by RFC 1490). January 1992.

1293   Inverse Address Resolution Protocol. January 1992.

1292   A Catalog of Available X.500 Implementations (Also FYI 11). January 1992.

1291   Mid-Level Networks—Potential Technical Services. December 1991.

1290   There's Gold in Them Thar Networks! or Searching for Treasure in All the Wrong Places (Also FYI 10; Obsoleted by RFC 1402). December 1991.

1289   DECnet Phase IV MIB Extensions (Obsoleted by RFC 1559). December 1991.

1288   The Finger User Information Protocol (Obsoletes RFCs 1196, 1194, and 742). December 1991.

1287   Towards the Future Internet Architecture. December 1991.

1286   Definitions of Managed Objects for Bridges (Obsoleted by RFC 1493, RFC 1525). December 1991.

1285   FDDI Management Information Base (Updated by RFC 1512). January 1991.

1284   Definitions of Managed Objects for the Ethernet-like Interface Types (Obsoleted by RFC 1398). December 1991.

1283   SNMP over OSI (Obsoletes RFC 1161; Obsoleted by RFC 1418). December 1991.

1282   BSD Rlogin (Obsoletes RFC 1258). December 1991.

1281   Guidelines for the Secure Operation of the Internet. November 1991.

1280   IAB Official Protocol Standards (Obsoletes RFCs 1250, 1100, 1083, 1130, 1140, and 1200; Obsoleted by RFC 1360). March 1991.

1279   X.500 and Domains. November 1991.

1278   A String Encoding of Presentation Address. November 1991.

1277   Encoding Network Addresses to Support Operation over Non-OSI Lower Layers. November 1991.

1276   Replication and Distributed Operations Extensions to Provide an Internet Directory Using X.500. November 1991.

1275   Replication Requirements to Provide an Internet Directory Using X.500. November 1991.

1274   The COSINE and Internet X.500 Schema. November 1991.

1273   A Measurement Study of Changes in Service-Level Reachability in the Global TCP/IP Internet. November 1991.

1272   Internet Accounting: Background. November 1991.

1271   Remote Network Monitoring Management Information Base (Obsoleted by RFC 1513). November 1991.

1270   SNMP Communications Services. October 1991.

1269   Definitions of Managed Objects for the Border Gateway Protocol (Version 3). October 1991.

1268   Application of the Border Gateway Protocol in the Internet (Obsoletes RFC 1164). October 1991.

1267   A Border Gateway Protocol 3 (BGP-3). (Obsoletes RFC 1105, RFC 1163). October 1991.

1266   Experience with the BGP protocol. October 1991.

1265   BGP Protocol Analysis. October 1991.

1264   Internet Routing Protocol Standardization Criteria. October 1991.

1263   TCP Extensions Considered Harmful. October 1991.

1262   Guidelines for Internet Measurement Activities. October 1991.

1261   Transition of NIC Services. September 1991.

1260   Not yet issued.

1259   Building the Open Road: The NREN as Test-Bed for the National Public Network. September 1991.

1258   BSD Rlogin (Obsoleted by RFC 1282). September 1991.

1257   Isochronous Applications Do Not Require Jitter-Controlled Networks. September 1991.

1256   ICMP Router Discovery Messages. September 1991.

1255   Naming Scheme for c=US (Obsoletes RFC 1218; Obsoleted by RFC 1417). September 1991.

1254   Gateway Congestion Control Survey. August 1991.

1253   OSPF Version 2: Management Information Base (Obsoletes RFC 1252). August 1991.

1252   OSPF Version 2: Management Information Base (Obsoletes RFC 1248; Obsoleted by RFC 1253). August 1991.

1251   Who's Who in the Internet: Biographies of IAB, IESG, and IRSG members (Also FYI 9; Obsoleted by RFC 1336). August 1991.

1250   IAB official protocol standards (Obsoletes RFC 1200; Obsoleted by RFC 1360). August 1991.

1249   DIXIE Protocol Specification. August 1991.

1248   OSPF Version 2: Management Information Base (Obsoleted by RFC 1252; Updated by RFC 1349). July 1991.

1247   OSPF Version 2 (Obsoletes RFC 1131; Updated by RFC 1349). July 1991.

1246   Experience with the OSPF Protocol. July 1991.

1245   OSPF Protocol Analysis. July 1991.

1244   Site Security Handbook (Also FYI 8). July 1991.

1243   Appletalk Management Information Base. July 1991.

1242   Benchmarking Terminology for Network Interconnection Devices. July 1991.

1241   Scheme for an Internet Encapsulation Protocol: Version 1. July 1991.

1240   OSI Connectionless Transport Services on Top of UDP: Version 1. June 1991.

1239   Reassignment of Experimental MIBs to Standard MIBs (Updates RFCs 1229, 1230, 1231, 1232, and 1233). June 1991.

1238   CLNS MIB for Use with Connectionless Network Protocol (ISO 8473) and End System to Intermediate System (ISO 9542) (Obsoletes RFC 1162). June 1991.

1237   Gudeline for OSI NSAP Allocation in the Internet. July 1991.

1236   IP to X.121 Address Mapping for DDN. June 1991.

1235   Coherent File Distribution Protocol. June 1991.

1234   Tunneling IPX Traffic Through IP Networks. June 1991.

1233   Definitions of Managed Objects for the DS3 Interface type (Obsoleted by RFC 1407; Updated by RFC 1239). May 1991.

1232   Definitions of Managed Objects for the DS1 Interface Type (Obsoleted by RFC 1406; Updated by RFC 1239). May 1991.

1231   IEEE 802.5 Token Ring MIB (Updated by RFC 1239). May 1991.

1230   IEEE 802.4 Token Bus MIB (Updated by RFC 1239). May 1991.

1229   Extensions to the Generic-Interface MIB (Updated by RFC 1239). May 1991.

1228   SNMP-DPI: Simple Network Management Protocol Distributed Program Interface. May 1991.

1227   SNMP MUX Protocol and MIB. May 1991.

1226   Internet Protocol Encapsulation of X.25 Frames Internet Protocol Encapsulation of X.25 Frames. May 1991.

1225   Post Office Protocol: Version 3 (Obsoletes RFC 1081; Obsoleted by RFC 1460). May 1991.

1224   Techniques for Managing Asynchronously Generated Alerts. May 1991.

1223   OSI CLNS and LLC1 Protocols on Network Systems HYPERchannel. May 1991.

1222   Advancing the NSFNET Routing Architecture. May 1991.

1221   Host Access Protocol (HAP) Specification: Version 2 (Updates RFC 907). April 1991.

1220   Point-to-Point Protocol Extensions for Bridging. April 1991.

1219   On the Assignment of Subnet Numbers. April 1991.

1218   Naming Scheme for c=US (Obsoleted by RFC 1417). April 1991.

1217   Memo from the Consortium for Slow Commotion Research (CSCR). April 1991.

1216   Gigabit Network Economics and Paradigm Shifts. April 1991.

1215   Convention for Defining Traps for Use with the SNMP. March 1991.

1214   OSI Internet Management: Management Information Base. April 1991.

1213   Management Information Base for Network Management of TCP/IP-Based Internets: MIB-II (Obsoletes RFC 1158). March 1991.

1212   Concise MIB Definitions. March 1991.

1211   Problems with the Maintenance of Large Mailing Lists. March 1991.

1210   Network and Infrastructure User Requirements for Transatlantic Research Collaboration: Brussels, July 16–18, and Washington, July 24–25 1990. March 1991.

1209   Transmission of IP Datagrams over the SMDS Service. March 1991.

1208   Glossary of Networking Terms. March 1991.

1207   FYI on Questions and Answers: Answers to Commonly Asked "Experienced Internet User" Questions. February 1991.

1206   FYI on Questions and Answers: Answers to Commonly Asked "New Internet User" Questions (Obsoletes RFC 1177; Obsoleted by RFC 1325). February 1991.

1205   5250 Telnet Interface. February 1991.

1204   Message Posting Protocol (MPP). February 1991.

1203   Interactive Mail Access Protocol: Version 3 (Obsoletes RFC 1064). February 1991.

1202   Directory Assistance Service. February 1991.

1201   Transmitting IP Traffic over ARCNET Networks (Obsoletes RFC 1051). February 1991.

1200   Defense Advanced Research Projects Agency, Internet Activities Board; DARPA IAB Official Protocol Standards (Obsoletes RFC 1104; Obsoleted by RFC 1360). April 1991.

1199   RFC Numbers 1100–1199. December 1991.

1198   FYI on the X Window System (Also FYI 6). January 1991.

1197   Using ODA for Translating Multimedia Information. December 1990.

1196   Finger User Information Portocol (Obsoletes RFC 1194; Obsoleted by RFC 1288). December 1990.

1195   Use of OSI IS-IS for Routing in TCP/IP and Dual Environments (Updated by RFC 1349). December 1990.

1194   Finger User Information Protocol (Obsoletes RFC 742; Obsoleted by RFC 1288). November 1990.

1193   Client Requirements for Real-Time Communication Services. November 1990.

1192   Commercialization of the Internet Summary Report. November 1990.

1191   Path MTU discovery (Obsoletes RFC 1063). November 1990.

1190   Experimental Internet Stream Portocol: Version 2 (ST-11) (Obsoletes IEN 119). October 1990.

1189   Common Management Information Services and Protocols for the Internet (CMOT and CMIP) (Obsoletes RFC 1095). October 1990.

1188   Proposed Standard for the Transmission of IP Datagrams over FDDI Networks (Obsoletes RFC 1103). October 1990.

1187   Bulk Table Retrieval with the SNMP. October 1990.

1186   MD4 Message Digest Algorithm (Obsoleted by RFC 1320). October 1990.

1185   TCP Extension for High-Speed Paths (Obsoleted by RFC 1323). October 1990.

1184   Telnet Linemode Option (Obsoletes RFC 1116). October 1990.

1183   New DNS RR Definitions (Updates RFC 1034, RFC 1035). October 1990.

1182   Not yet issued.

1181   RIPE Terms of Reference. September 1990.

1180   TCP/IP Tutorial. January 1991.

1179   Line Printer Daemon Protocol. August 1990.

1178   Choosing a Name for Your Computer (Also FYI 5). August 1990.

1177   FYI on Questions and Answers: Answers to Commonly Asked "New Internet User" Questions (Obsoleted by RFC 1206). August 1990.

1176   Interactive Mail Access Protocol: Version 2. (Obsoletes RFC 1064). August 1990.

1175   FYI on Where to Start: A Bibliography of Internetworking Information (Also FYI 3). August 1990.

1174   IAB Recommended Policy on Distributing Internet Identifier Assignment and IAB Recommended Policy Change to Internet "Connected" Status. August 1990.

1173   Responsibilities of Host and Network Managers: A Summary of the "Oral Tradition" of the Internet. August 1990.

1172   Point-to-Point Protocol (PPP) Initial Configuration Options (Obsoleted by RFC 1332). July 1990.

1171   Point-to-Point Protocol for the Transmission of Multi-Protocol Datagrams over Point-to-Point Links (Obsoletes RFC 1134; Obsoleted by RFC 1331). July 1990.

1170   Public Key Standards and Licenses. January 1991.

1169   Explaining the Role of GOSIP. August 1990.

1168   Intermail and Commercial Mail Relay Services. July 1990.

1167   Thoughts on the National Research and Education Network. July 1990.

1166   Internet Numbers (Obsoletes RFCs 1117, 1062, and 1020). July 1990.

1165   Network Time Protocol (NTP) over the OSI Remote Operations Service. June 1990.

1164   Application of the Border Gateway Protocol in the Internet (Obsoleted by RFC 1268). June 1990.

1163   Border Gateway Protocol (BGP) (Obsoletes RFC 1105; Obsoleted by RFC 1267). June 1990.

1162   Connectionless Network Protocol (ISO 8473) and End System to Intermediate System (ISO 9542) Management Information Base (Obsoleted by RFC 1238). June 1990.

1161   SNMP over OSI (Obsoleted by RFC 1283). June 1990.

1160   Internet Activities Board (Obsoletes RFC 1120). May 1990.

1159   Message Send Protocol (Obsoleted by RFC 1312). June 1990.

1158   Management Information Base for Network Management of TCP/IP-Based Internets: MIB-II (Obsoleted by RFC 1213). May 1990.

1157   Simple Network Management Protocol (SNMP) (Obsoletes RFC 1098). May 1990.

1156   Management Information Base for Network Management of TCP/IP-Based Internets (Obsoletes RFC 1066). May 1990.

1155   Structure and Identification of Management Information for TCP/IP-Based Internets (Obsoletes RFC 1065). May 1990.

1154   Encoding Header Field for Internet Messages (Obsoleted by RFC 1505). April 1990.

1153   Digest Message Format. April 1990.

1152   Workshop Report: Internet Research Steering Group Workshop on Very-High-Speed Networks. April 1990.

1151   Version 2 of the Reliable Data Protocol (RDP) (Updates RFC 908). April 1990.

1150   FYI on FYI: Introduction to the FYI notes (Also FYI 1). March 1990.

1149   Standard for the Transmission of IP Datagrams on Avian Carriers. April 1990.

1148   Mapping Between X.400(1988)/ISO 10021 and RFC 822 (Obsoleted by RFC 1327; Updates RFCs 822, 987, 1026, and 1138). March 1990.

1147   FYI on a Network Management Tool Catalog: Tools for Monitoring and Debugging TCP/IP Internets and InterConnected Devices (Also FYI 2; Obsoleted by RFC 1470). April 1990.

1146   TCP Alternate Checksum Options (Obsoletes RFC 1145). March 1990.

1145   TCP Alternate Checksum Options (Obsoleted by RFC 1146). February 1990.

1144   Compressing TCP/IP Headers for Low-Speed Serial Links. February 1990.

1143   Q Method of Implementing Telnet Option Negotiation. February 1990.

1142   OSI IS-IS Intra-Domain Routing Protocol. February 1990.

1141   Incremental Updating of the Internet Checksum (Updates RFC 1071). January 1990.

1140   DARPA IAB Official Protocol Standards (Obsoletes RFC 1130; Obsoleted by RFC 1360). May 1990.

1139   Echo Function for ISO 8473. January 1990.

1138   Mapping Between X.400(1988)/ISO 10021 and RFC 822 (Obsoleted by RFC 1327; Updates RFCs 822, 987, and 1026; Updated by RFC 1148). December 1989.

1137   Mapping Between Full RFC 822 and RFC 822 with Restricted Encoding (Updates RFC 976). December 1989.

1136   Administrative Domains and Routing Domains: A Model for Routing in the Internet. December 1989.

1135   Helminthiasis of the Internet. December 1989.

1134   Point-to-Point Protocol: A Proposal for Multi-Protocol Transmission of Datagrams over Point-to-Point Links (Obsoleted by RFC 1171). November 1989.

1133   Routing Between the NSFNET and the DDN. November 1989.

1132   Standard for the Transmission of 802.2 Packets over IPX Networks. November 1989.

1131   OSPF Specification (Obsoleted by RFC 1247). October 1989.

1130   Defense Advanced Research Projects Agency, Internet Activities Board: DARPA IAB IAB Official Protocol Standards (Obsoletes RFC 1100; Obsoleted by RFC 1360). October 1989.

1129   Internet Time Synchronization: The Network Time Protocol. October 1989.

1128   Measured Performance of the Network Time Protocol in the Internet System. October 1989.

1127   Perspective on the Host Requirements RFCs. October 1989.

1126   Goals and Functional Requirements for Inter-Autonomous System Routing. October 1989.

1125   Policy Requirements for Inter–Administrative Domain Routing. November 1989.

1124   Policy Issues in Interconnecting Networks. September 1989.

1123   Requirements for Internet Hosts—Application and Support (Updated by RFC 1349). October 1989.

1122   Requirements for Internet Hosts Communication Layers (Updated by RFC 1349). October 1989.

1121   Act One—The Poems. September 1989.

1120   Internet Activities Board (Obsoleted by RFC 1160). September 1989.

1119   Network Time Protocol (Version 2) Specification and Implementation (Obsoletes RFC 1059, RFC 958; Obsoleted by RFC 1305). September 1989.

1118   Hitchhikers Guide to the Internet. September 1989.

1117   Internet numbers (Obsoletes RFCs 1062, 1020, and 997; Obsoleted by RFC 1166). August 1989.

1116   Telnet Linemode Option (Obsoleted by RFC 1184). August 1989.

1115   Privacy Enhancement for Internet Electronic Mail: Part III— Algorithms, Modes, and Identifiers [Draft] (Obsoleted by RFC 1423). August 1989.

1114   Privacy Enhancement for Internet Electronic Mail: Part II—Certificate-Based Key Management [Draft] (Obsoleted by RFC 1422). August 1989.

1113   Privacy Enhancement for Internet Electronic Mail: Part I—Message Encipherment and Authentication Procedures [Draft] (Obsoletes RFC 989, RFC 1040; Obsoleted by RFC 1421). August 1989.

1112   Host Extensions for IP Multicasting (Obsoletes RFC 988, RFC 1054). August 1989.

1111   Request for Comments on Request for Comments: Instructions to RFC Authors (Obsoletes RFC 825; Obsoleted by RFC 1543). August 1989.

1110   Problem with the TCP Big Window Option. August 1989.

1109   Report of the Second Ad Hoc Network Management Review Group. August 1989.

1108   Security Option for the Internet Protocol (Obsoletes RFC 1038). November 1991.

1107   Plan for Internet Directory Services. July 1989.

1106   TCP Big Window and NAK Options. June 1989.

1105   Border Gateway Protocol (BGP) (Obsoleted by RFC 1267). June 1989.

1104   Models of Policy-Based Routing. June 1989.

1103   Proposed Standard for the Transmission of IP Datagrams over FDDI Networks (Obsoleted by RFC 1188). June 1989.

1102   Policy Routing in Internet Protocols. May 1989.

1101   DNS Encoding of Network Names and Other Types (Updates RFC 1034, RFC 1035). April 1989.

1100   Defense Advanced Research Projects Agency, Internet Activities Board; DARPA IAB Official Protocol Standards (Obsoletes RFC 1083; Obsoleted by RFC 1360). April 1989.

1099   Request for Comments Summary RFC Numbers 1000–1099. December 1991.

1098   Simple Network Management Protocol (SNMP) (Obsoletes RFC 1067; Obsoleted by RFC 1157). April 1989.

1097   Telnet Subliminal-Message Option. April 1989.

1096   Telnet X Display Location Option. March 1989.

1095   Common Management Information Services and Protocol over TCP/IP (CMOT) (Obsoleted by RFC 1189). April 1989.

1094   NFS: Network File System Protocol Specification. March 1989.

1093   NSFNET Routing Architecture. February 1989.

1092   EGP and Policy-Based Routing in the New NSFNET Backbone. February 1989.

1091   Telnet Terminal-Type Option (Obsoletes RFC 930). February 1989.

1090   SMTP on X.25. February 1989.

1089   SNMP over Ethernet. February 1989.

1088   Standard for the Transmission of IP Datagrams over NetBIOS Networks. February 1989.

1087   Defense Advanced Research Projects Agency, Internet Activities Board; DARPA IAB Ethics and the Internet. January 1989.

1086   ISO-TP0 Bridge between TCP and X.25. December 1988.

1085   ISO Presentation Services on Top of TCP/IP-Based Internets. December 1988.

1084   BOOTP Vendor Information Extensions (Obsoletes RFC 1048; Obsoleted by RFC 1395). December 1988.

1083   Defense Advanced Research Projects Agency, Internet Activities Board; DARPA IAB Official Protocol standards (Obsoletes RFC 1011; Obsoleted by RFC 1360). December 1988.

1082   Post Office Protocol: Version 3: Extended Service Offerings. December 1988.

1081   Post Office Protocol: Version 3 (Obsoleted by RFC 1225). November 1988.

1080   Telnet Remote Flow Control Option (Obsoleted by RFC 1372). November 1988.

1079   Telnet Terminal Speed Option. December 1988.

1078   TCP Port Service Multiplexer (TCPMUX). November 1988.

1077   Critical Issues in High Bandwidth Networking. November 1988.

1076   HEMS Monitoring and Control Language (Obsoletes RFC 1023). November 1988.

1075   Distance Vector Multicast Routing Protocol. November 1988.

1074   NSFNET Backbone SPF-Based Interior Gateway Protocol. October 1988.

1073   Telnet Window Size Option. October 1988.

1072   TCP Extensions for Long-Delay Paths (Obsoleted by RFC 1323). October 1988.

1071   Computing the Internet Checksum (Updated by RFC 1141). September 1989.

1070   Use of the Internet as a Subnetwork for Experimentation with the OSI Network Layer. February 1989.

1069   Guidelines for the Use of Internet-IP Addresses in the ISO Connectionless-Mode Network Protocol (Obsoletes RFC 986). February 1989.

1068   Background File Transfer Program (BFTP). August 1988.

1067   Simple Network Management Protocol (Obsoleted by RFC 1098). August 1988.

1066   Management Information Base for Network Management of TCP/IP-Based Internets (Obsoleted by RFC 1156). August 1988.

1065   Structure and Identification of Management Information for TCP/IP-Based Internets (Obsoleted by RFC 1155). August 1988.

1064   Interactive Mail Access Protocol: Version 2 (Obsoleted by RFC 1176, RFC 1203). July 1988.

1063   IP MTU Discovery Options (Obsoleted by RFC 1191). July 1988.

1062   Internet Numbers (Obsoletes RFC 1020; Obsoleted by RFC 1117). August 1988.

1061   Not yet issued.

1060   Assigned Numbers (Obsoletes RFC 1010; Obsoleted by RFC 1340; Updated by RFC 1349). March 1990.

1059   Network Time Protocol (Version 1) Specification and Implementation (Obsoleted by RFC 1305). July 1988.

1058   Routing Information Protocol (Updated by RFC 1388). June 1988.

1057   RPC: Remote Procedure Call Protocol Specification: Version 2 (Obsoletes RFC 1050). June 1988.

1056   PCMAIL: A Distributed Mail System for Personal Computers (Obsoletes RFC 993). June 1988.

1055   Nonstandard for Transmission of IP Datagrams over Serial Lines: SLIP. June 1988.

1054   Host Extensions for IP Multicasting (Obsoletes RFC 988; Obsoleted by RFC 1112). May 1988.

1053   Telnet X.3 PAD Option. May 1988.

1052   IAB Recommendation for the Development of Internet Network Management Standards. April 1988.

1051   Standard for the Transmission of IP Datagrams and ARP Packets over ARCNET Networks (Obsoleted by RFC 1201). March 1988.

1050   RPC: Remote Procedure Call Protocol Specification (Obsoleted by RFC 1057). April 1988.

1049   Content-Type Header Field for Internet Messages. April 1988.

1048   BOOTP Vendor Information Extensions (Obsoleted by RFC 1395). February 1988.

1047   Duplicate Messages and SMTP. February 1988.

1046   Queuing Algorithm to Provide Type-of-Service for IP Links. February 1988.

1045   VMTP: Versatile Message Transaction Protocol: Protocol Specification. February 1988.

1044   Internet Protocol on Network System's HYPERchannel: Protocol Specification. February 1988.

1043   Telnet Data Entry Terminal option: DODIIS implementation (Updates RFC 732). February 1988.

1042   Standard for the Transmission of IP Datagrams over IEEE 802 networks (Obsoletes RFC 948). February 1988.

1041   Telnet 3270 Regime Option. January 1988.

1040   Privacy Enhancement for Internet Electronic Mail: Part I: Message Encipherment and Authentication Procedures (Obsoletes RFC 989; Obsoleted by RFC 1113). January 1988.

1039   DoD Statement on Open Systems Interconnection Protocols (Obsoletes RFC 945). January 1988.

1038   Draft Revised IP Security Option (Obsoleted by RFC 1108). January 1988.

1037   NFILE—A File Access Protocol. December 1987.

1036   Standard for Interchange of USENET Messages (Obsoletes RFC 850). December 1987.

1035   Domain Names—implementation and specification (Obsoletes RFCs 973, 882, and 883; Updated by RFCs 1348, 1183, and 1101). November 1987.

1034   Domain Names—Concepts and Facilities (Obsoletes RFCs 973, 882, and 883; Updated by RFCs 1348, 1183, and 1101). November 1987.

1033   Domain Administrators Operations Guide. November 1987.

1032   Domain Administrators Guide. November 1987.

1031   MILNET Name Domain Transition. November 1987.

1030   On Testing the NETBLT Protocol over Diverse Networks. November 1987.

1029   More Fault Tolerant Approach to Address Resolution for a Multi-LAN System of Ethernets. May 1988.

1028   Simple Gateway Monitoring Protocol. November 1987.

1027   Using ARP to Implement Transparent Subnet Gateways. October 1987.

1026   Addendum to RFC 987: Mapping between X.400 and RFC-822 (Obsoleted by RFC 1327; Updates RFC 987; Updated by RFC 1138, RFC 1148). September 1987.

1025   TCP and IP Bake Off. September 1987.

1024   HEMS Variable Definitions. October 1987.

1023   HEMS Monitoring and Control Language (Obsoleted by RFC 1076). October 1987.

1022   High-Level Entity Management Protocol (HEMP). October 1987.

1021   High-Level Entity Management System (HEMS). October 1987.

1020   Internet Numbers (Obsoletes RFC 997; Obsoleted by RFC 1062, RFC 1117). November 1987.

1019   Report of the Workshop on Environments for Computational Mathematics. September 1987.

1018   Some Comments on SQuID. August 1987.

1017   Network Requirements for Scientific Research: Internet Task Force on Scientific Computing. August 1987.

1016   Something a Host Could Do with Source Quench: The Source Quench Introduced Delay (SQuID). July 1987.

1015   Implementation Plan for Interagency Research Internet. July 1987.

1014   XDR: External Data Representation Standard. June 1987.

1013   X Window System Protocol, Version 11: Alpha Update. April 1987, June 1987.

1012   Bibliography of Request for Comments 1 through 999. June 1987.

1011   Official Internet Protocols (Obsoletes RFC 997; Obsoleted by RFC 1083). May 1987.

1010   Assigned numbers (Obsoletes RFC 990; Obsoleted by RFC 1340). May 1987.

1009   Requirements for Internet gateways (Obsoletes RFC 985). June 1987.

1008   Implementation Guide for the ISO Transport Protocol. June 1987.

1007   Military Supplement to the ISO Transport Protocol. June 1987.

1006   ISO Transport Services on top of the TCP: Version 3 (Obsoletes RFC 983). May 1987.

1005   ARPANET AHIP-E Host Access Protocol (Enhanced AHIP). May 1987.

1004   Distributed-Protocol Authentication Scheme. April 1987.

1003   Issues in Defining an Equations Representation Standard. March 1987.

1002   Defense Advanced Research Projects Agency, Internet Activities Board, End-to-End Services Task Force, NetBIOS Working Group; DARPA IAB End to End Services Task Force NetBIOS Working Group Protocol Standard for a NetBIOS Service on a TCP/UDP Transport: Detailed Specifications. March 1987.

1001   Defense Advanced Research Projects Agency, Internet Activities Board, End-to-End Services Task Force, NetBIOS Working Group; DARPA IAB End-to-End Services Task Force NetBIOS Working Group Protocol Standard for a NetBIOS Service on a TCP/UDP Transport: Concepts and Methods. March 1987.

1000   The Request for Comments Reference Guide (Obsoletes RFC 999). August 1987.

999   Request for Comments Summary Notes: 900–999 (Obsoleted by RFC 1000). April 1987.

998   NETBLT: A Bulk Data Transfer Protocol (Obsoletes RFC 969). March 1987.

997   Internet Numbers (Obsoleted by RFC 1020, RFC 1117; Updates RFC 990). March 1987.

996   Statistics server. February 1987.

995   International Organization for Standardization; ISO End System to Intermediate System Routing Exchange Protocol for Use in Conjunction with ISO 8473. April 1986.

994   International Organization for Standardization; ISO Final Text of DIS 8473, Protocol for Providing the Connectionless-Mode Network Service (Obsoletes RFC 926). March 1986.

993   PCMAIL: A Distributed Mail System for Personal Computers (Obsoletes RFC 984; Obsoleted by RFC 1056). December 1986.

992   On Communication Support for Fault Tolerant Process Groups. November 1986.

991   Official ARPA-Internet Protocols (Obsoletes RFC 961; Obsoleted by RFC 1011). November 1986.

990   Assigned Numbers (Obsoletes RFC 960; Obsoleted by RFC 1340; Updated by RFC 997). November 1986.

989   Privacy Enhancement for Internet Electronic Mail: Part I: Message Encipherment and Authentication Procedures (Obsoleted by RFC 1040, RFC 1113). February 1987.

988   Host Extensions for IP Multicasting (Obsoletes RFC 966; Obsoleted by RFC 1054, RFC 1112). July 1986.

987   Mapping Between X.400 and RFC 822 (Obsoleted by RFC 1327; Updated by RFCs 1026, 1138, and 1148). June 1986.

986   Guidelines for the Use of Internet-IP Addresses in the ISO Connectionless-Mode Network Protocol [Working draft] (Obsoleted by RFC 1069). June 1986.

985   National Science Foundation, Network Technical Advisory Group; NSF NTAG Requirements for Internet Gateways—Draft Requirements for Internet Gateways [Draft] (Obsoleted by RFC 1009). May 1986.

984   PCMAI: A Distributed Mail System for Personal Computers (Obsoleted by RFC 993). May 1986.

983   ISO Transport Arrives on Top of the TCP (Obsoleted by RFC 1006). April 1986.

982   Guidelines for the Specification of the Structure of the Domain Specific Part (DSP) of the ISO Standard NSAP Address. April 1986.

981   Experimental Multiple-Path Routing Algorithm. March 1986.

980   Protocol Document Order Information. March 1986.

979   PSN End-to-End Functional Specification. March 1986.

978   Voice File Interchange Protocol (VFIP). February 1986.

977   Network News Transfer Protocol. February 1986.

976   UUCP Mail Interchange Format Standard (Updated by RFC 1137). February 1986.

975   Autonomous Confederations. February 1986.

974   Mail Routing and the Domain System. January 1986.

973   Domain System Changes and Observations (Obsoleted by RFC 1034, RFC 1035; Updates RFC 882, RFC 883). January 1986.

972   Password Generator Protocol. January 1986.

971   Survey of Data Representation Standards. January 1986.

970   On Packet Switches with Infinite Storage. December 1985.

969   NETBLT: A Bulk Data Transfer Protocol (Obsoleted by RFC 998). December 1985.

968   Twas the Night Before Start-Up. December 1985.

967   All Victims Together. December 1985.

966   Host Groups: A Multicast Extension to the Internet Protocol (Obsoleted by RFC 988). December 1985.

965   Format for a Graphical Communication Protocol. December 1985.

964   Some Problems with the Specification of the Military Standard Transmission Control Protocol. November 1985.

963   Some Problems with the Specification of the Military Standard Internet Protocol. November 1985.

962   TCP-4 Prime. November 1985.

961   Official ARPA-Internet Protocols (Obsoletes RFC 944; Obsoleted by RFC 991). December 1985.

960   Assigned Numbers (Obsoletes RFC 943; Obsoleted by RFC 1340). December 1985.

959   File Transfer Protocol (Obsoletes RFC 765 [IEN 149]). October 1985.

958   Network Time Protocol (NTP) (Obsoleted by RFC 1305). September 1985.

957   Experiments in Network Clock Synchronization. September 1985.

956   Algorithms for Synchronizing Network Clocks. September 1985.

955   Towards a Transport Service for Transaction Processing Applications. September 1985.

954   NICNAME/WHOIS (Obsoletes RFC 812). October 1985.

953   Hostname Server (Obsoletes RFC 811). October 1985.

952   DoD Internet Host Table Specification (Obsoletes RFC 810). October 1985.

951   Bootstrap Protocol (Updated by RFCs 1497, 1395, 1532, and 1542). September 1985.

950   Internet Standard Subnetting Procedure (Updates RFC 792). August 1985.

949   FTP Unique-Named Store Command. July 1985.

948   Two Methods for the Transmission of IP Datagrams over IEEE 802.3 Networks (Obsoleted by RFC 1042). June 1985.

947   Multi-Network Broadcasting Within the Internet. June 1985.

946   Telnet Terminal Location Number Option. May 1985.

945   DoD Statement on the NRC Report (Obsoleted by RFC 1039). May 1985.

944   Official ARPA-Internet Protocols (Obsoletes RFC 924; Obsoleted by RFC 961). April 1985.

943   Assigned Numbers (Obsoletes RFC 923; Obsoleted by RFC 1340). April 1985.

942   National Research Council; NRC Transport Protocols for Department of Defense Data Networks. February 1985.

941   International Organization for Standardization; ISO Addendum to the Network Service Definition Covering Network Layer Addressing. April 1985.

940   Gateway Algorithms and Data Structures Task Force; GADS Toward an Internet Standard Scheme for Subnetting. April 1985.

939   National Research Council; NRC Executive Summary of the NRC Report on Transport Protocols for Department of Defense Data Networks. February 1985.

938   Internet Reliable Transaction Protocol Functional and Interface Specification. February 1985.

937   Post Office Protocol: Version 2 (Obsoletes RFC 918). February 1985.

936   Another Internet Subnet Addressing Scheme. February 1985.

935   Reliable Link Layer Protocols. January 1985.

934   Proposed Standard for Message Encapsulation. January 1985.

933   Output Marking Telnet Option. January 1985.

932   Subnetwork Addressing Scheme. January 1985.

931   Authentication Server (Obsoletes RFC 912; Obsoleted by RFC 1413). January 1985.

930   Telnet Terminal Type Option (Obsoletes RFC 884; Obsoleted by RFC 1091). January 1985.

929   Proposed Host-Front End Protocol. December 1984.

928   Introduction to Proposed DoD Standard H-FP. December 1984.

927   TACACS User Identification Telnet Option. December 1984.

926   International Organization for Standardization; ISO Protocol for Providing the Connectionless Mode Network Services (Obsoleted by RFC 994). December 1984.

925   Multi-LAN Address Resolution. October 1984.

924   Official ARPA-Internet Protocols for Connecting Personal Computers to the Internet (Obsoletes RFC 901; Obsoleted by RFC 944). October 1984.

923   Assigned Numbers (Obsoletes RFC 900; Obsoleted by RFC 1340). October 1984.

922   Broadcasting Internet Datagrams in the Presence of Subnets. October 1984.

921   Domain Name System Implementation Schedule—Revised (Updates RFC 897). October 1984.

920   Domain Requirements. October 1984.

919   Broadcasting Internet Datagrams. October 1984.

918   Post Office Protocol (Obsoleted by RFC 937). October 1984.

917   Internet Subnets. October 1984.

916   Reliable Asynchronous Transfer Protocol (RATP). October 1984.

915   Network Mail Path Service. December 1984.

914   Thinwire Protocol for Connecting Personal Computers to the Internet. September 1984.

913   Simple File Transfer Protocol. September 1984.

912   Authentication Service (Obsoleted by RFC 931). September 1984.

911   EGP Gateway under Berkeley UNIX 4.2. August 1984.

910   Multimedia Mail Meeting Notes. August 1984.

909   Loader Debugger Protocol. July 1984.

908   Reliable Data Protocol (Updated by RFC 1151). July 1984.

907   Bolt Beranek and Newman, Inc; BBN Host Access Protocol Specification (Updated by RFC 1221). July 1984.

906   Bootstrap Loading Using TFTP. June 1984.

905   ISO Transport Protocol Specification ISO DP 8073 (Obsoletes RFC 892). April 1984.

904   Exterior Gateway Protocol Formal Specification (Updates RFC 827, RFC 888). April 1984.

903   Reverse Address Resolution Protocol. June 1984.

902   ARPA Internet Protocol Policy. July 1984.

901   Official ARPA-Internet Protocols (Obsoletes RFC 880; Obsoleted by RFC 924). June 1984.

900   Assigned Numbers (Obsoletes RFC 870; Obsoleted by RFC 1340). June 1984.

899   Requests for Comments Summary Notes: 800–899. May 1984.

898   Gateway Special Interest Group Meeting Notes. April 1984.

897   Domain Name System Implementation Schedule (Updates RFC 881; Updated by RFC 921). February 1984.

896   Congestion Control in IP/TCP Internetworks. January 1984.

895   Standard for the Transmission of IP Datagrams over Experimental Ethernet Networks. April 1984.

894   Standard for the Transmission of IP Datagrams over Ethernet Networks. April 1984.

893   Trailer Encapsulations. April 1984.

892   International Organization for Standardization; ISO Transport Protocol Specification [Draft] (Obsoleted by RFC 905). December 1983.

891   DCN Local-Network Protocols. December 1983.

890   Exterior Gateway Protocol Implementation Schedule. February 1983.

889   Internet Delay Experiments. December 1983.

888   "STUB" Exterior Gateway Protocol (Updated by RFC 904). January 1983.

887   Resource Location Protocol. December 1983.

886   Proposed Standard for Message Header Managing. December 1983.

885   Telnet End of Record Option. December 1983.

884   Telnet Terminal Type Option (Obsoleted by RFC 930). December 1983.

883   Domain names: Implementation Specification (Obsoleted by RFC 1034, RFC 1035; Updated by RFC 973). November 1983.

882 Domain names: Concepts and facilities (Obsoleted by RFC 1034, RFC 1035; Updated by RFC 973). November 1983.

881 Domain Names Plan and Schedule (Updated by RFC 897). November 1983.

880 Official Protocols (Obsoletes RFC 840; Obsoleted by RFC 901). October 1983.

879 TCP Maximum Segment Size and Related Topics. November 1983.

878 ARPANET 1822L Host Access Protocol (Obsoletes RFC 851). December 1983.

877 Standard for the Transmission of IP Datagrams over Public Data Networks (Obsoleted by RFC 1356). September 1983.

876 Survey of SMTP Implementations. September 1983.

875 Gateways, Architectures, and Heffalumps. September 1982.

874 A Critique of X.25. September 1982.

873 Illusion of Vendor Support. September 1982.

872 TCP-on-a-LAN. September 1982.

871 Perspective on the ARPANET Reference Model. September 1982.

870 Assigned Numbers (Obsoletes RFC 820; Obsoleted by RFC 1340). October 1983.

869 Host Monitoring Protocol. December 1983.

868 Time Protocol. May 1983.

867 Daytime Protocol. May 1983.

866 Active Users. May 1983.

865 Quote of the Day Protocol. May 1983.

864 Character Generator Protocol. May 1983.

863 Discard Protocol. May 1983.

862 Echo Protocol. May 1983.

861 Telnet Extended Options: List option (Obsoletes NIC 16239). May 1983.

860 Telnet Timing Mark Option (Obsoletes NIC 16238). May 1983.

859 Telnet Status Option (Obsoletes RFC 651). May 1983.

858 Telnet Supress Go Ahead Option (Obsoletes NIC 15392). May 1983.

857 Telnet Echo Option (Obsoletes NIC 15390). May 1983.

856 Telnet Binary Transmission (Obsoletes NIC 15389). May 1983.

855 Telnet Option Specifications (Obsoletes NIC 18640). May 1983.

854 Telnet Protocol Specification (Obsoletes RFC 765, NIC 18639). May 1983.

853 Not issued.

852 ARPANET Short Blocking Feature. April 1983.

851   ARPANET 1822L Host Access Protocol (Obsoletes RFC 802; Obsoleted by RFC 878). April 1983.

850   Standard for Interchange of USENET Messages (Obsoleted by RFC 1036). June 1983.

849   Suggestions for Improved Host Table Distribution. May 1983.

848   Who Provides the "Little" TCP Services? March 1983.

847   Summary of Smallberg Surveys (Obsoletes RFC 846). February 1983.

846   Who Talks TCP?—Survey of 22 February 1983 (Obsoletes RFC 845; Obsoleted by RFC 847). February 1983.

845   Who Talks TCP? Survey of 15 February 1983 (Obsoletes RFC 843; Obsoleted by RFC 846). February 1983.

844   Who Talks ICMP, Too?—Survey of 18 February 1983 (Updates RFC 843). February 1983.

843   Who talks TCP? Survey of 8 February 83 (Obsoletes RFC 842; Obsoleted by RFC 845; Updated by RFC 844). February 1983.

842   Who talks TCP? Survey of 1 February 83 (Obsoletes RFC 839; Obsoleted by RFC 843). February 1983.

841   National Bureau of Standards; NBS Specification for Message Format for Computer-Based Message Systems. January 1983.

840   Official Protocols (Obsoleted by RFC 880). April 1983.

839   Who talks TCP? (Obsoletes RFC 838; Obsoleted by RFC 842). January 1983.

838   Who Talks TCP? (Obsoletes RFC 837; Obsoleted by RFC 839). January 1983.

837   Who Talks TCP? (Obsoletes RFC 836; Obsoleted by RFC 838). January 1983.

836   Who Talks TCP? (Obsoletes RFC 835; Obsoleted by RFC 837). January 1983.

835   Who Talks TCP? (Obsoletes RFC 834; Obsoleted by RFC 836). December 1982.

834   Who Talks TCP? (Obsoletes RFC 833; Obsoleted by RFC 835). December 1982.

833   Who Talks TCP? (Obsoletes RFC 832; Obsoleted by RFC 834). December 1982.

832   Who Talks TCP? (Obsoleted by RFC 833). December 1982.

831   Backup Access to the European Side of SATNET. December 1982.

830   Distributed System for Internet Name Service. October 1982.

829   Packet Satellite Technology Reference Sources. November 1982.

828   Data Communications: IFIP's International "Network" of Experts. August 1982.

827   Exterior Gateway Protocol (EGP) (Updated by RFC 904). October 1982.

826   Ethernet Address Resolution Protocol: On Converting Network Protocol Addresses to 48.bit Ethernet Addresses for Transmission on Ethernet Hardware. November 1982.

825   Request for Comments on Requests for Comments (Obsoleted by RFC 1111). November 1982.

824   CRONUS Virtual Local Network. August 1982.

823   DARPA Internet Gateway (Updates IEN 109, IEN 30). September 1982.

822   Standard for the Format of ARPA Internet Text Messages (Obsoletes RFC 733; Updated by RFCs 1327, 1148, and 1138). August 1982.

821   Simple Mail Transfer Protocol (Obsoletes RFC 788). August 1982.

820   Assigned Numbers (Obsoletes RFC 790; Obsoleted by RFC 1340). August 1982.

819   Domain Naming Convention for Internet User Applications. August 1982.

818   Remote User Telnet Service. November 1982.

817   Modularity and Efficiency in Protocol Implementation. July 1982.

816   Fault Isolation and Recovery. July 1982.

815   IP Datagram Reassembly Algorithms. July 1982.

814   Name, Addresses, Ports, and Routes. July 1982.

813   Window and Acknowledgment Strategy in TCP. July 1982.

812   NICNAME/WHOIS (Obsoleted by RFC 954). March 1982.

811   Hostnames Server (Obsoleted by RFC 953). March 1982.

810   DoD Internet Host Table Specification (Obsoletes RFC 608; Obsoleted by RFC 852). March 1982.

809   UCL Facsimile System. February 1982.

808   Summary of Computer Mail Services Meeting Held at BBN on 10 January 1979. March 1982.

807   Multimedia Mail Meeting Notes. February 1982.

806   National Bureau of Standards; NBS Proposed Federal Information Processing Standard: Specification for Message Format for Computer-Based Message Systems (Obsoleted by RFC 841). September 1981.

805   Computer Mail Meeting Notes. February 1982.

804   International Telecommunication Union, International Telegraph and Telephone Consultative Committee; ITU CCITT CCITT Draft Recommendation T.4 [Standardization of Group 3 Facsimile Apparatus for Document Transmission]. 1981.

803   Dacom 450/500 Facsimile Data Transcoding. November 1981.

802   ARPANET 1822L Host Access Protocol (Obsoleted by RFC 851). November 1981.

801   NCP/TCP Transition Plan. November 1981.

800   Requests for Comments Summary Notes 700–799. November 1981.

799   Internet Name Domains. September 1981.

798   Decoding Facsimile Data from the Rapicom 450. September 1981.

797   Format for Bitmap Files. September 1981.

796   Address Mappings (Obsoletes IEN 115). September 1981.

795   Service Mappings. September 1981.

794   Pre-emption (Updates IEN 125). September 1981.

793   Transmission Control Protocol. September 1981.

792   Internet Control Message Protocol (Obsoletes RFC 777; Updated by RFC 950). September 1981.

791   Internet Protocol (Obsoletes RFC 760; Updated by RFC 1349). September 1981.

790   Assigned Numbers (Obsoletes RFC 776; Obsoleted by RFC 1340). September 1981.

789   Vulnerabilities of Network Control Protocols: An example. July 1981.

788   Simple Mail Transfer Protocol (Obsoletes RFC 780; Obsoleted by RFC 821). November 1981.

787   Connectionless Data Transmission Survey/Tutorial. July 1981.

786   Mail Transfer Proocol: ISI TOPS20 MTP-NIMAIL Interface. July 1981.

785   Mail Transfer Protocol: ISI TOPS20 File Definitions. July 1981.

784   Mail Transfer Protocol: ISI TOPS20 Implementation. July 1981.

783   TFTP Protocol (Revision 2) (Obsoletes IEN 133; Obsoleted by RFC 1350). June 1981.

782   Virtual Terminal Management Model. 1981.

781   Specification of the Internet Protocol (IP) Timestamp Option. May 1981.

780   Mail Transfer Protocol. (Obsoletes RFC 772; Obsoleted by RFC 788). May 1981.

779   Telnet Send-Location Option. April 1981.

778   DCNET Internet Clock Service. April 1981.

777   Internet Control Message Protocol (Obsoletes RFC 760; Obsoleted by RFC 792). April 1981.

776   Assigned Numbers (Obsoletes RFC 770; Obsoleted by RFC 1340). January 1981.

775   Directory Oriented FTP Commands. December 1980.

774   Internet Protocol Handbook (Obsoletes RFC 766). October 1980.

773   Comments on NCP/TCP Mail Service Transition Strategy. October 1980.

772   Mail Transfer Protocol (Obsoleted by RFC 780). September 1980.

771   Mail Transition Plan. September 1980.

770   Assigned Numbers (Obsoletes RFC 762; Obsoleted by RFC 1340). September 1980.

769   Rapicom 450 Facsimile File Format. September 1980.

768   User Datagram Protocol. August 1980.

767   Structured Format for Transmission of Multi-Media Documents. August 1980.

766   Internet Protocol Handbook: Table of Contents (Obsoleted by RFC 774). July 1980.

765   File Transfer Protocol Specification (Obsoletes RFC 542; Obsoleted by RFC 959). June 1980.

764   Telnet Protocol Specification (Obsoleted by RFC 854). June 1980.

763   Role Mailboxes. May 1980.

762   Assigned Numbers (Obsoletes RFC 758; Obsoleted by RFC 1340). January 1980.

761   DoD Standard Transmission Control Protocol. January 1980.

760   DoD Standard Internet Protocol (Obsoletes IEN 123; Obsoleted by RFC 791, RFC 777). January 1980.

759   Internet Message Protocol. August 1980.

758   Assigned Numbers (Obsoletes RFC 755; Obsoleted by RFC 1340). August 1980.

757   Suggested Solution to the Naming, Addressing, and Delivery Problem for ARPANET Message Systems. September 1979.

756   NIC Name Server—A Datagram-Based Information Utility. July 1979.

755   Assigned Numbers (Obsoletes RFC 750; Obsoleted by RFC 1340). May 1979.

754   Out-of-Net Host Addresses for Mail. April 1979.

753   Internet Message Protocol. May 1979.

752   Universal Host Table. January 1979.

751   Survey of FTP Mail and MLFL. December 1978.

750   Assigned Numbers (Obsoletes RFC 739; Obsoleted by RFC 1340). September 1978.

749   Telnet SUPDUP-Output Option. September 1978.

748   Telnet Randomly-Lose Option. April 1978.

747   Recent Extensions to the SUPDUP Protocol. March 1978.

746   SUPDUP Graphics Extension. March 1978.

745   JANUS Interface Specifications. March 1978.

744   A Message Archiving and Retrieval Service. January 1978.

743   FTP Extension: XRSQ/XRCP. December 1977.

742   NAME/FINGER Protocol (Obsoleted by RFC 1288). December 1977.

741   Specifications for the Network Voice Protocol (NVP). November 1977.

740   NETRJS Protocol (Obsoletes RFC 599). November 1977.

739   Assigned Numbers (Obsoletes RFC 604, RFC 503; Obsoleted by RFC 1340). November 1977.

738   Time server. October 1977.

737   FTP Extension: XSEN. October 1977.

736   Telnet SUPDUP Option. October 1977.

735   Revised Telnet Byte Macro Option (Obsoletes RFC 729). November 1977.

734   SUPDUP Protocol. October 1977.

733   Standard for the Format of ARPA Network Text Messages (Obsoletes RFC 724; Obsoleted by RFC 822). November 1977.

732   Telnet Data Entry Terminal option (Obsoletes RFC 731; Updated by RFC 1043). September 1977.

731   Telnet Data Entry Terminal option (Obsoleted by RFC 732). June 1977.

730   Extensible Field Addressing. May 1977.

729   Telnet Byte Macro Option (Obsoleted by RFC 735). May 1977.

728   Minor Pitfall in the Telnet Protocol. April 1977.

727   Telnet Logout Option. April 1977.

726   Remote Controlled Transmission and Echoing Telnet Option. March 1977.

725   RJE Protocol for a Resource Sharing Network. March 1977.

724   Proposed Official Standard for the Format of ARPA Network Messages (Obsoleted by RFC 733). May 1977.

723   Not issued.

722   Thoughts on Interactions in Distributed Services. September 1976.

721   Out-of-Band Control Signals in a Host-to-Host Protocol. September 1976.

720   Address Specification Syntax for Network Mail. August 1976.

719   Discussion on RCTE. July 1976.

718   Comments on RCTE from the Tenex Implementation Experience. June 1976.

717   Assigned Network Numbers. July 1976.

716   Interim Revision to Appendix F of BBN 1822. May 1976.

715   Not issued.

714   Host-Host Protocol for an ARPANET-Type Network (NOL). April 1976.

713   MSDTP-Message Services Data Transmission Protocol. April 1976.

712   Distributed Capability Computing System (DCCS) (NOL). February 1976.

711   Not issued.

710   Not issued.

709   Not issued.

708   Elements of a Distributed Programming System. January 1976.

707   High-Level Framework for Network-Based Resource Sharing. December 1975.

706   On the Junk Mail Problem. November 1975.

705   Front-End Protocol B6700 Version. November 1975.

704   IMP/Host and Host/IMP Protocol Change (Obsoletes RFC 687). September 1975.

703   July, 1975 Survey of New-Protocol Telnet Servers (NOL). July 1975.

702   September, 1974, Survey of New-Protocol Telnet Servers (NOL). July 1974.

701   August, 1974 Survey of New-Protocol Telnet Servers. August 1974.

700   Protocol Experiment. August 1974.

699   Request for Comments Summary Notes: 600–699. November 1982.

698   Telnet Extended ASCII Option. July 1975.

697   CWD Command of FTP (NOL). July 1975.

696   Comments on the IMP/Host and Host/IMP Protocol Changes (NOL). July 1975.

695   Official Change in Host-Host Protocol. July 1975.

694   Protocol Information (NOL). June 1975.

693   Not issued.

692   Comments on IMP/Host Protocol Changes (RFC 687, RFC 690). June 1975.

691   One More Try on the FTP. May 1975.

690   Comments on the Proposed Host/IMP Protocol Changes (NOL; Updates RFC 687; Updated by RFC 692). June 1975.

689   Tenex NCP Finite State Machine for Corrections. May 1975.

688   Tentative Schedule for the New Telnet Implementation for the TIP (NOL). June 1975.

687   IMP/Host and Host/IMP Protocol Changes (Obsoleted by RFC 704; Updated by RFC 690). June 1975.

686   Leaving Well Enough Alone (NOL). May 1975.

685   Response Time in Cross Network Debugging. April 1975.

684   Commentary on Procedure Calling as a Network Protocol. April 1975.

683   FTPSRV—Tenex Extension for Paged Files. April 1975.

682   Not issued.

681   Network UNIX. March 1975.

680   Message Transmission Protocol (NOL). April 1975.

679   February, 1975, Survey of New-Protocol Telnet Servers (NOL). February 1975.

678   Standard File Formats. December 1974.

677   Maintenance of Duplicate Databases (NOL). January 1975.

676   Not issued.

675   Specification on Internet Transmission Control Program (NOL). December 1974.

674   Procedure Call Documents: Version 2. December 1974.

673   Not issued.

672   Multi-Site Data Collection Facility. December 1974.

671   Note on Reconnection Prococol (NOL). December 1974.

670   Not issued.

669   November, 1974, Survey of New-Protocol Telnet Servers (NOL). December 1974.

668   Not issued.

667   BBN Host Ports (NOL). December 1974.

666   Specification of the Unified User-Level Protocol (NOL). November 1974.

665   Not issued.

664   Not issued.

663   Lost Message Detection and Recovery Protocol. November 1974.

662   Performance Improvement in ARPANET File Transfers from Multics. November 1974.

661   Protocol Information (NOL). November 1974.

660   Some Changes to the IMP and the IMP/Host Interface. October 1974.

659   Announcing Additional Telnet Options (NOL). October 1974.

658   Telnet Output Linefeed Disposition. October 1974.

657   Telnet Output Vertical Tab Disposition Option. October 1974.

656   Telnet Output Vertical Tabstops Option. October 1974.

655   Telnet Output Formfeed Disposition Option. October 1974.

654   Telnet Output Horizontal Tab Disposition Option. October 1974.

653   Telnet Output Horizontal Tabstops Option. October 1974.

652   Telnet Output Carriage-Return Disposition Option. October 1974.

651   Revised Telnet Status Option (Obsoleted by RFC 859). October 1974.

650   Not issued.

649   Not issued.

648   Not issued.

647   Proposed Protocol for Connecting Host Computers to ARPA-like Networks via Front End Processors (NOL). November 1974.

646   Not issued.

645   Network Standard Data Specification Syntax (NOL). June 1974.

644   On the Problem of Signature Authentication for Network mail. July 1974.

643   Network Debugging Protocol. July 1974.

642   Ready Line Philosophy and Implementation (NOL). July 1974.

641   Not issued.

640   Revised FTP Reply Codes. June 1974.

639   Not issued.

638   IMP/TIP Preventive Maintenance Schedule (NOL). April 1974.

637   Change of Network Address for SU-DSL (NOL). April 1974.

636   TIP/Tenex Reliability Improvements. June 1974.

635   Assessment of ARPANET Protocols (NOL). April 1974.

634   Change in Network Address for Haskins Lab (NOL). April 1974.

633   IMP/TIP Preventive Maintenance Schedule (NOL). April 1974.

632   Throughput Degradations for Single Packet Messages (NOL). May 1974.

631   International Meeting on Minicomputers and Data Communication: Call for Papers (NOL). April 1974.

630   FTP Error Code Usage for More Reliable Mail Service (NOL). April 1974.

629   Scenario for Using the Network Journal (NOL). March 1974.

628   Status of RFC Numbers and a Note on Preassigned Journal Numbers (NOL). March 1974.

627   ASCII Text File of Hostnames (NOL). March 1974.

626   On a Possible Lockup Condition in IMP Subnet Due to Message Sequencing. March 1974.

625   On-line Hostnames Service (NOL). March 1974.

624   Comments on the File Transfer Protocol (Obsoletes RFC 607). February 1974.

623   Comments on On-Line Host Name Service (NOL). February 1974.

622   Scheduling IMP/TIP Down Time (NOL). February 1974.

621   NIC User Directories at SRI ARC (NOL). March 1974.

620   Request for Monitor Host Table Updates. March 1974.

619   Mean Round-Trip Times in the ARPANET (NOL). March 1974.

618   Few Observations on NCP Statistics. February 1974.

617   Note on Socket Number Assignment. February 1974.

616   Latest Network Maps. February 1973.

615   Proposed Network Standard Data Pathname Syntax. March 1974.

614   Response to RFC 607: "Comments on the File Transfer Protocol" (Updates RFC 607). January 1974.

613   Network Connectivity: A Response to RFC 603 (NOL; Updates RFC 603). January 1974.

612   Traffic Statistics (December 1973) (NOL). January 1974.

611   Two Changes to the IMP/Host Protocol to Improve User/Network Communications (NOL). February 1974.

610   Further Datalanguage Design Concepts (NOL). December 1973.

609   Statement of Upcoming Move on NIC/NLS Service (NOL). January 1974.

608   Host Names On-Line (NOL; Obsoleted by RFC 810). January 1974.

607   Comments on the File Transfer Protocol (Obsoleted by RFC 624; Updated by RFC 614). January 1974.

606   Host Names On-Line. December 1973.

605   Not issued.

604   Assigned Link Numbers (NOL; Obsoletes RFC 317; Obsoleted by RFC 1340). December 1973.

603   Response to RFC 597: Host status (NOL; Updates RFC 597; Updated by RFC 613). December 1973.

602   "The Stockings Were Hung By the Chimney with Care." December 1973.

601   Traffic Statistics (November 1973) (NOL). December 1973.

600   Interfacing an Illinois Plasma Terminal to the ARPANET (NOL). November 1973.

599   Update on NetRJS (Obsoletes RFC 189; Obsoleted by RFC 740). December 1973.

598   Network Information Center; SRI NIC RFC Index—December 5, 1973 (NOL). December 1973.

597   Host status (NOL; Updated by RFC 603). December 1973.

596   Second Thoughts on Telnet Go-Ahead (NOL). December 1973.

595   Second Thoughts in Defense of the Telnet Go-Ahead (NOL). December 1973.

594   Speedup of Host-IMP Interface (NOL). December 1973.

593   Telnet and FTP Implementation Schedule Change (NOL). November 1973.

592   Some Thoughts on System Design to Facilitate Resource Sharing (NOL). November 1973.

591   Addition to the Very Distant Host Specifications (NOL). November 1973.

590   MULTICS Address Change (NOL). November 1973.

589   CCN NETRJS Server Messages to Remote User (NOL). November 1973.

588   London Node is Now Up (NOL). October 1973.

587   Announcing New Telnet Options (NOL). October 1973.

586   Traffic Statistics (October 1973) (NOL). November 1973.

585   ARPANET Users Interest Working Group Meeting (NOL). November 1973.

584   Charter for ARPANET Users Interest Working Group (NOL). November 1973.

583   Not issued.

582   Comments on RFC 580: Machine Readable Protocols (NOL) (Updates RFC 580). November 1973.

581   Corrections to RFC 560: Remote Controlled Transmission and Echoing Telnet Option (NOL). November 1973.

580   Note to Protocol Designers and Implementers (Updated by RFC 582). October 1973.

579   Traffic Statistics (September 1973). November 1973.

578   Using MIT-Mathlab MACSYMA from MIT-DMS Muddle (NOL). October 1973.

577   Mail Priority (NOL). October 1973.

576   Proposal for Modifying Linking (NOL). September 1973.

575   Not issued.

574   Announcement of a Mail Facility at UCSB (NOL). September 1973.

573   Data and File Transfer: Some Measurement Results (NOL). September 1973.

572   Not issued.

571   Tenex FTP Problem (NOL). November 1973.

570   Experimental Input Mapping Between NVT ASCII and UCSB On Line System (NOL). October 1973.

569   NETED: A Common Editor for the ARPA Network. October 1973.

568   Response to RFC 567—Cross Country Network Bandwidth (NOL) (Updated by RFC 568). September 1973.

567   Cross Country Network Bandwidth (Updated by RFC 568). September 1973.

566   Traffic Statistics (August 1973) (NOL). September 1973.

565   Storing Network Survey Data at the Datacomputer (NOL). August 1973.

564   Not issued.

563   Comments on the RCTE Telnet Option (NOL). August 1973.

562   Modifications to the Telnet Specification (NOL). August 1973.

561   Standardizing Network Mail Headers (Updated by RFC 680). September 1973.

560   Remote Controlled Transmission and Echoing Telnet Option (NOL). August 1973.

559   Comments on the new Telnet Protocol and Its Implementation (NOL). August 1973.

558   Not issued.

557   Revelations in Network Host Measurements (NOL). August 1973.

556   Traffic Statistics (July 1973) (NOL). August 1973.

555   Responses to Critiques of the Proposed Mail Protocol (NOL). July 1973.

554   Not issued.

553   Draft Design for a Text/Graphics Protocol (NOL). July 1973.

552   Single Access to Standard Protocols (NOL). July 1973.

551   Letter from Feinroth re: NYU, ANL, and LBL Entering the Net, and FTP Protocol (NOL). August 1973.

550   NIC NCP Experiment (NOL). August 1973.

549   Minutes of Network Graphics Group Meeting, 15–17 July 1973 (NOL). July 1973.

548   Hosts Using the IMP Going Down Message (NOL). August 1973.

547   Change to the Very Distant Host Specification (NOL). August 1973.

546   Tenex Load Averages for July 1973 (NOL). August 1973.

545   Of What Quality Be the UCSB Resources Evaluators? (NOL). July 1973.

544   Locating On-Line Documentation at SRI-ARC (NOL). July 1973.

543   Network Journal Submission and Delivery (NOL). July 1973.

542   File Transfer Protocol (Obsoletes RFC 354; Obsoleted by RFC 765). July 1973.

541   Not issued.

540   Not issued.

539   Thoughts on the Mail Protocol Proposed in RFC 524 (NOL). July 1973.

538   Traffic Statistics (June 1973) (NOL). July 1973.

537   Announcement of NGG Meeting July 16–17 (NOL). June 1973.

536   Not issued.

535   Comments on File Access Protocol (NOL). July 1973.

534   Lost Message Detection (NOL). July 1973.

533   Message-ID Numbers (NOL). July 1973.

532   UCSD-CC Server-FTP Facility (NOL). July 1973.

531   Feast or Famine? A Response to Two Recent RFCs About Network Information (NOL). June 1973.

530   Report on the Survey Project (NOL). June 1973.

529   Note on Protocol Synch Sequences (NOL). June 1973.

528   Software Checksumming in the IMP and Network Reliability (NOL). June 1973.

527   ARPAWOCKY. May 1973.

526   Technical Meeting: Digital Image Processing Software Systems (NOL). June 1973.

525   MIT-MATHLAB Meets UCSB-OLS—An Example of Resource Sharing (NOL). June 1973.

524   Proposed Mail Protocol (NOL). June 1973.

523   SURVEY Is in Operation Again (NOL). June 1973.

522   Traffic Statistics (May 1973) (NOL). June 1973.

521   Restricted Use of IMP DDT (NOL). May 1973.

520   Memo to FTP Group: Proposal for File Access Protocol (NOL). June 1973.

519   Resource Evaluation (NOL). June 1973.

518   ARPANET Accounts (NOL). June 1973.

517   Not issued.

516   Lost Message Detection (NOL). May 1973.

515   Specifications for Datalanguage: Version 0/9 (NOL). June 1973.

514   Network Make-Work (NOL). June 1973.

513   Comments on the New Telnet Specifications (NOL). May 1973.

512   More on Lost Message Detection (NOL). May 1973.

511   Enterprise Phone Service to NIC from ARPANET Sites (NOL). May 1973.

510   Request for Network Mailbox Addresses (NOL). May 1973.

509   Traffic Statistics (April 1973) (NOL). May 1973.

508   Real-Time Data Transmission on the ARPANET (NOL). May 1973.

507   Not issued.

506   FTP Command Naming Problem (NOL). June 1973.

505   Two Solutions to a File Transfer Access Problem (NOL). June 1973.

504   Distributed Resources Workshop (NOL). April 1973.

503   Socket Number List (NOL; Obsoletes RFC 433; Obsoleted by RFC 1340). April 1973.

502   Not issued.

501   Un-muddling "Free File Transfer" (NOL). May 1973.

500   Integration of Data Management Systems on a Computer Network (NOL). April 1973.

499   Harvard's Network RJE (NOL). April 1973.

498   On Mail Service to CCN (NOL). April 1973.

497   Traffic Statistics (March 1973) (NOL). April 1973.

496   TNLS Quick Reference Card Is Available (NOL). April 1973.

495   Telnet Protocol Specifications (NOL; Obsoletes RFC 158). May 1973.

494   Availability of MIX and MIXAL in the Network (NOL). April 1973.

493   Graphics Protocol (NOL). April 1973.

492   Response to RFC 467 (NOL; Updates RFC 467). April 1973.

491   What is "Free"? (NOL). April 1973.

490   Surrogate RJS for UCLA-CCN (NOL). March 1973.

489   Comment on Resynchronization of Connection Status Proposal (NOL). March 1973.

488   NLS Classes at Network Sites (NOL). March 1973.

487   Free File Transfer (NOL). April 1973.

486   Data Transfer Revisited (NOL). March 1973.

485   MIX and MIXAL at UCSB (NOL). March 1973.

484   Not issued.

483   Cancellation of the Resource Notebook Framework Meeting (NOL). March 1973.

482   Traffic Statistics (February 1973) (NOL). March 1973.

481   Not issued.

480   Host-Dependent FTP Parameters (NOL). March 1973.

479   Use of FTP by the NIC Journal (NOL). March 1973.

478   FTP Server-Server Interaction—II (NOL). March 1973.

477   Remote Job Service at UCSB (NOL). May 1973.

476   IMP/TIP Memory Retrofit Schedule (rev.2) (NOL; Obsoletes RFC 447). March 1973.

475   FTP and Network Mail System (NOL). March 1973.

474   Announcement of NGWG Meeting: Call for papers (NOL). March 1973.

473   MIX and MIXAL? (NOL). February 1973.

472   Illinois' Reply to Maxwell's Request for Graphics Information (NIC 14925) (NOL). March 1973.

471   Workship on Multi-Site Executive Programs (NOL). March 1973.

470   Change in Socket for TIP News Facility (NOL). March 1973.

469   Network Mail Meeting Summary (NOL). March 1973.

468   FTP Data Compression (NOL). March 1973.

467   Proposed Change to Host-Host Protocol: Resynchronization of Connection Status (NOL; Updated by RFC 492). February 1973.

466   Telnet Logger/Server for Host LL-67 (NOL). February 1973.

465   Not issued.

464   Resource Notebook Framework (NOL). February 1973.

463   FTP Comments and Response to RFC 430 (NOL). February 1973.

462   Responding to User Needs (NOL). February 1973.

461   Telnet Protocol Meeting Announcement (NOL). February 1973.

460   NCP Survey (NOL). February 1973.

459   Network Questionnaires (NOL). February 1973.

458   Mail Retrieval via FTP (NOL). February 1973.

457   TIPUG (NOL). February 1973.

456   Memorandum: Date Change of Mail Meeting (NOL). February 1973.

455   Traffic Statistics for January 1973 (NOL). February 1973.

454   File Transfer Protocol—Meeting Announcement and a New
       Proposed Document (NOL). February 1973.

453   Meeting Announcement to Discuss a Network Mail System (NOL).
       February 1973.

452   Not issued.

451   Tentative Proposal for a Unified User Level Protocol (NOL). Febru-
       ary 1973.

450   MULTICS Sampling Timeout Change (NOL). February 1973.

449   Current Flow-Control Scheme for IMPSYS (NOL; Updates RFC
       442). January 1973.

448   Print Files in FTP (NOL). February 1973.

447   IMP/TIP Memory Retrofit Schedule (NOL; Obsoletes RFC 434;
       Obsoleted by RFC 476). January 1973.

446   Proposal to Consider a Network Program Resource Notebook
       (NOL). January 1973.

445   IMP/TIP Preventive Maintenance Schedule (NOL). January 1973.

444   Not issued.

443   Traffic Statistics (December 1972) (NOL). January 1973.

442   Current Flow-Control Scheme for IMPSYS (NOL; Updated by RFC
       449). January 1973.

441   Inter-Entity Communication—An Experiment (NOL). January 1973.

440   Scheduled Network Software Maintenance (NOL). January 1973.

439   PARRY Encounters the DOCTOR (NOL). January 1973.

438   FTP Server-Server Interaction (NOL). January 1973.

437   Data Reconfiguration Service at UCSB (NOL). January 1973.

436   Announcement of RJS at UCSB (NOL). January 1973.

435   Telnet issues (NOL; Updates RFC 318). January 1973.

434   IMP/TIP Memory Retrofit Schedule (NOL). January 1973.

433   Socket number list (NOL; Obsoletes RFC 349; Obsoleted by RFC
       1340). December 1972.

432   Network Logical Map (NOL). December 1972.

431   Update on SMFS Login and Logout (NOL; Obsoletes RFC 399). December 1972.

430   Comments on File Transfer Protocol (NOL). February 1972.

429   Character Generator Process (NOL). December 1972.

428   Not issued.

427   Not issued.

426   Reconnection Protocol (NOL). January 1973.

425   But My NCP Costs $500 a Day . . . December 1972.

424   Not issued.

423   UCLA Campus Computing Network Liaison Staff for ARPANET (NOL; Obsoletes RFC 389). December 1972.

422   Traffic Statistics (November 1972) (NOL). December 1972.

421   Software Consulting Service for Network Users (NOL). November 1972.

420   CCA ICCC Weather Demo (NOL). January 1973.

419   To: Network Liaisons and Station Agents (NOL). December 1972.

418   Server File Transfer under TSS/360 at NASA Ames (NOL). November 1972.

417   Link Usage Violation (NOL). December 1972.

416   ARC System Will Be Unavailable for Use During Thanksgiving Week (NOL). November 1972.

415   Tenex Bandwidth (NOL). November 1972.

414   File Transfer Protocol (FTP) Status and Further Comments (NOL; Updates RFC 385). December 1972.

413   Traffic Statistics (October 1972) (NOL). November 1972.

412   User FTP Documentation (NOL). November 1972.

411   New MULTICS Network Software Features (NOL). November 1972.

410   Removal of the 30-Second Delay When Hosts Come Up (NOL). November 1972.

409   Tenex Interface to UCSB's Simple-Minded File System (NOL). December 1972.

408   NETBANK (NOL). October 1972.

407   Remote Job Entry Protocol (Obsoletes RFC 360). October 1972.

406   Scheduled IMP Software Releases (NOL). October 1972.

405   Correction to RFC 404 (NOL; Obsoletes RFC 404). October 1972.

404   Host Address Changes Involving Rand and ISI (NOL; Obsoleted by RFC 405). October 1972.

403   Desirability of a Network 1108 Service (NOL). January 1973.

402   ARPA Network Mailing Lists (NOL; Obsoletes RFC 363). October 1972.

401   Conversion of NGP-0 Coordinates to Device Specific Coordinates (NOL). October 1972.

400   Traffic Statistics (September 1972) (NOL). October 1972.

399   SMFS Login and Logout (NOL; Obsoleted by RFC 431; Updates RFC 122). September 1972.

398   ICP Sockets (NOL). September 1972.

397   Not issued.

396   Network Graphics Working Group Meeting—Second Iteration (NOL). November 1972.

395   Switch Settings on IMPs and TIPs (NOL). October 1972.

394   Two Proposed Changes to the IMP-Host Protocol (NOL). September 1972.

393   Comments on Telnet Protocol Changes (NOL). October 1972.

392   Measurement of Host Costs for Transmitting Network Data (NOL). September 1972.

391   Traffic Statistics (August 1972) (NOL; Obsoletes RFC 378). September 1972.

390   TSO Scenario (NOL). September 1972.

389   UCLA Campus Computing Network Liaison Staff for ARPA Network (NOL; Obsoleted by RFC 423). August 1972.

388   NCP Statistics (NOL; Updates RFC323). August 1972.

387   Some Experiences in Implementing Network Graphics Protocol Level 0 (NOL). August 1972.

386   Letter to TIP Users-2 (NOL). August 1972.

385   Comments on the File Transfer Protocol (NOL; Updates RFC 354; Updated by RFC 414). August 1972.

384   Official Site Idents for Organizaions in the ARPA Network (NOL; Obsoletes RFC 289). August 1972.

383   Not issued.

382   Mathematical Software on the ARPA Network (NOL). August 1972.

381   Three Aids to Improved Network Operation (NOL). July 1972.

380   Not issued.

379   Using TSO at CCN (NOL). August 1972.

378   Traffic Statistics (July 1972) (NOL; Obsoleted by RFC 391). August 1972.

377   Using TSO via ARPA Network Virtual Terminal (NOL). August 1972.

376   Network Host Status (NOL; Obsoletes RFC 370). August 1972.

375   Not issued.

374   IMP System Announcement (NOL). July 1972.

373   Arbitrary Character Sets (NOL). July 1972.

372   Notes on a Conversation with Bob Kahn on the ICCC (NOL). July 1972.

371   Demonstration at International Computer Communications Conference (NOL). July 1972.

370   Network Host Status (NOL; Obsoletes RFC 367; Obsoleted by RFC 376). July 1972.

369   Evaluation of ARPANET services January–March, 1972 (NOL). July 1972.

368   Comments on "Proposed Remote Job Entry Protocol" (NOL). July 1972.

367   Network Host Status (NOL; obsoletes RFC 366; Obsoleted by RFC 370). July 1972.

366   Network Host Status (NOL; Obsoletes RFC 362; Obsoleted by RFC 367). July 1972.

365   Letter to All TIP Users (NOL). July 1972.

364   Serving Remote Users on the ARPANET (NOL). July 1972.

363   Stanford Research Institute, Network Information Center; SRI NIC ARPA Network Mailing Lists (NOL; Obsoletes RFC 329; Obsoleted by RFC 402). August 1972.

362   Network Host Status (NOL; Obsoletes RFC 353; Obsoleted by RFC 366). June 1972.

361   Daemon Processes on Host 106 (NOL). July 1972.

360   Proposed Remote Job Entry Protocol (NOL; Obsoleted by RFC 407). June 1972.

359   Status of the Release of the New IMP System (3600) (NOL; Obsoletes RFC 343). June 1972.

358   Not issued.

357   Echoing Strategy for Satellite Links (NOL). June 1972.

356   ARPA Network Control Center (NOL). June 1972.

355   Response to NWG/RFC 346 (NOL). June 1972.

354   File Transfer Protocol (NOL; Obsoletes RFC 264, RFC 265; Obsoleted by RFC 542; Updated by RFC 385). July 1972.

353   Network Host Status (NOL; Obsoletes RFC 344; Obsoleted by RFC 362). June 1972.

352   TIP Site Information from (NOL). June 1972.

351   Graphics Information Form for the ARPANET Graphics Resources Notebook (NOL). June 1972.

350   User Accounts for UCSB On-Line System (NOL). May 1972.

349   Proposed Standard Socket Numbers (NOL; Obsoleted by RFC 1340). May 1972.

348   Discard Process (NOL). May 1972.

347   Echo Process (NOL). May 1972.

346   Satellite Considerations (NOL). May 1972.

345   Interest in Mixed Integer Programming (MPSX on NIC 360/91 at CCN) (NOL). May 1972.

344   Network Host Status (NOL; Obsoletes RFC 342; Obsoleted by RFC 353). May 1972.

343   IMP System Change Notification (NOL; Obsoletes RFC 331; Obsoleted by RFC 359). May 1972.

342   Network Host Status (NOL; Obsoletes RFC 332; Obsoleted by RFC 344). May 1972.

341   Not issued.

340   Proposed Telnet Changes (NOL). May 1972.

339   MLTNET: A "Multi Telnet" Subsystem for Tenex (NOL). May 1972.

338   EBCDIC/ASCII Mapping for Network RJE (NOL). May 1972.

337   Not issued.

336   Level 0 Graphic Input Protocol (NOL). May 1972.

335   New Interface—IMP/360 (NOL). May 1972.

334   Network Use on May 8 (NOL). May 1972.

333   Proposed Experiment with a Message Switching Protocol (NOL). May 1972.

332   Network Host Status (NOL; Obsoletes RFC 330; Obsoleted by RFC 342). April 1972.

331   IMP System Change Notification (NOL; Obsoleted by RFC 343). April 1972.

330   Network Host Status (NOL; Obsoletes RFC 326; Obsoleted by RFC 332). April 1972.

329   Stanford Research Institute, Network Information Center; SRI NIC ARPA Network Mailing Lists (NOL; Obsoletes RFC 303; Obsoleted by RFC 363). May 1972.

328   Suggested Telnet Protocol Changes (NOL). April 1972.

327   Data and File Transfer Workshop Notes (NOL). April 1972.

326   Network Host Status (NOL; Obsoletes RFC 319; Obsoleted by RFC 330). April 1972.

325   Network Remote Job Entry Program—NETRJS (NOL). April 1972.

324   RJE Protocol Meeting (NOL). April 1972.

323   Formation of Network Measurement Group (NMG) (NOL; Updated by RFC 388). March 1972.

322   Well Known Socket Numbers (NOL). March 1972.

321   CBI Networking Activity at MITRE (NOL). March 1972.

320   Workshop on Hard Copy Line Printers (NOL). March 1972.

319   Network Host Status (NOL; Obsoletes RFC 315; Obsoleted by RFC 326). March 1972.

318   Ad hoc Telnet Protocol (NOL; Updates RFC 158; Updated by RFC 435). April 1972.

317   Official Host-Host Protocol Modification: Assigned Link Numbers (NOL; Obsoleted by RFC 604). March 1972.

316   ARPA Network Data Management Working Group (NOL). February 1972.

315   Network Host Status (NOL; Obsoletes RFC 306; Obsoleted by RFC 319). March 1972.

314   Network Graphics Working Group Meeting (NOL). March 1972.

313   Computer-Based Instruction (NOL). March 1972.

312   Proposed Change in IMP-to-Host Protocol (NOL). March 1972.

311   New Console Attachments to the USCB Host (NOL). February 1972.

310   Another Look at Data and File Transfer Protocols (NOL). April 1972.

309   Data and File Transfer Workshop Announcement (NOL). March 1972.

308   ARPANET Host Availability Data (NOL). March 1972.

307   Using Network Remote Job Entry (NOL). February 1972.

306   Network Host Status (NOL; Obsoletes RFC 298; Obsoleted by RFC 315). February 1972.

305   Unknown Host Numbers (NOL). February 1972.

304   Data Management System Proposal for the ARPA Network (NOL). February 1972.

303   Stanford Research Institute, Network Information Center; SRI NIC ARPA Network Mailing Lists (NOL; Obsoletes RFC 300; Obsoleted by RFC 329). February 1972.

302   Exercising the ARPANET (NOL). February 1972.

301   BBN IMP (#5) and NCC Schedule March 4, 1971 (NOL). February 1972.

300   ARPA Network Mailing Lists (NOL; Obsoletes RFC 211; Obsoleted by RFC 303). January 1972.

299   Information Management System (NOL). February 1972.

298   Network Host Status (NOL; Obsoletes RFC 293; Obsoleted by RFC 306). February 1972.

297   TIP Message Buffers (NOL). January 1972.

296   DS-1 Display System (NOL). January 1972.

295   Report of the Protocol Workshop (NOL). January 1972.

294   On the Use of "Set Data Type" Transaction in File Transfer Protocol (NOL; Updates RFC 265). January 1972.

293   Network Host Status (NOL; Obsoletes RFC 288; Obsoleted by RFC 298). January 1972.

292   Graphics Protocol: Level 0 Only (NOL). January 1972.

291   Data Management Meeting Announcement (NOL). January 1972.

290   Computer Networks and Data Sharing: A Bibliography (NOL; Obsoletes RFC 243). January 1972.

289   What We Hope Is an Official List of Host Names (NOL; Obsoleted by RFC 384). December 1971.

288   Network Host Status (NOL; Obsoletes RFC 287; Obsoleted by RFC 293). January 1972.

287   "Status of Network Hosts" (NOL; Obsoletes RFC 267; Obsoleted by RFC 288). December 1971.

286   Network Library Information System (NOL). December 1971.

285   Network Graphics (NOL). December 1971.

284   Not issued.

283   NETRJT: Remote Job Service Protocol for TIPS (NOL; Updates RFC 189). December 1971.

282   Graphics Meeting Report (NOL). December 1971.

281   Suggested Addition to File Transfer Protocol (NOL). December 1971.

280   Draft of Host Names (NOL). November 1971.

279   Not issued.

278   Revision of the Mail Box Protocol (NOL; Obsoletes RFC 221). November 1971.

277   Not issued.

276   NIC Course (NOL). November 1971.

275   Not issued.

274   Establishing a Local Guide for Network Usage (NOL). November 1971.

273   "More on Standard Host Names" (NOL; Obsoletes RFC 237). October 1971.

272   Not issued.

271   IMP System Change Notifications (NOL). January 1972.

270   Correction to BBN Report No. 1822 (NIC NO 7958) (NOL; Updates NIC 7959). January 1972.

269   Some Experience with File Transfer (NOL; Updates RFC 122, RFC 238). December 1971.

268   Graphics Facilities Information (NOL). November 1971.

267   Network Host Status (NOL; Obsoletes RFC 266; Obsoleted by RFC 287). November 1971.

266   "Network Host Status" (NOL; Obsoletes RFC 255; Obsoleted by RFC 267). November 1971.

265   File Transfer Protocol (NOL; Obsoletes RFC 172; Obsoleted by RFC 354; Updated by RFC 294). November 1971.

264   Data Transfer Protocol (NOL; Obsoletes RFC 171; Obsoleted by RFC 354). December 1971.

263   "Very Distant" Host Interface (NOL). December 1971.

262   Not issued.

261   Not issued.

260   Not issued.

259   Not issued.

258   Not issued.

257   Not issued.

256   IMPSYS Change Notification (NOL). November 1971.

255   "Status of Network Hosts" (NOL). (Obsoletes RFC 252; Obsoleted by RFC 266). October 1971.

254   Scenarios for Using ARPANET Computers (NOL). October 1971.

253   Second Network Graphics Meeting Details (NOL). October 1971.

252   Network Host Status (NOL; Obsoletes RFC 240; Obsoleted by RFC 255). October 1971.

251   Weather Data (NOL). October 1971.

250   Some Thoughts on File Transfer (NOL). October 1971.

249   Coordination of Equipment and Supplies Purchase (NOL). October 1971.

248   Not issued.

247   Proffered Set of Standard Host Names (NOL; Obsoletes RFC 226). October 1971.

246   Network Graphics Meeting (NOL). October 1971.

245   Reservations for Network Group Meeting (NOL). October 1971.

244   Not issued.

243   "Network and Data Sharing Bibliography" (NOL; Obsoleted by RFC 290). October 1971.

242   Data Descriptive Language for Shared Data (NOL). July 1971.

241   Connecting Computers to MLC Ports (NOL). September 1971.

240   Site Status (NOL; Obsoletes RFC 235; Obsoleted by RFC 252). September 1971.

239   Host Mnemonics Proposed in RFC 226 (NIC 7625) (NOL). September 1971.

238   "Comments on DTP and FTP Proposals" (NOL; Updates RFC 171, RFC 172; Updated by RFC 269). September 1971.

237   NIC View of Standard Host Names (NOL; Obsoleted by RFC 273). September 1971.

236   Standard Host Names (NOL; Obsoleted by RFC 240). September 1971.

235   Site Status (NOL; Obsoleted by RFC 240). September 1971.

234   Network Working Group Meeting Schedule (NOL; Updates RFC 222, RFC 204). October 1971.

233   Standardization of Host Call Letters (NOL). September 1971.

232   Postponement of Network Graphics Meeting (NOL). September 1971.

231   Service Center Standards for Remote Usage: A User's View (NOL). September 1971.

230   Toward Reliable Operation of Minicomputer-Based Terminals on a TIP (NOL). September 1971.

229   "Standard Host Names" (NOL; Updates RFC 70). September 1971.

228   "Clarification" (NOL; Updates RFC 70). September 1971.

227   Data Transfer Rates (Rand/UCLA) (NOL; Updates RFC 113). September 1971.

226   "Standardization of Host Mnemonics" (NOL; Obsoleted by RFC 247). September 1971.

225   Rand/UCSB Network Graphics Experiment (NOL; Updates RFC 74). September 1971.

224   Comments on Mailbox Protocol (NOL). September 1971.

223   Network Information Center Schedule for Network Users (NOL). September 1971.

222   Subject: System Programmer's Workshop (NOL; Updates RFC 212; Updated by RFC 234). September 1971.

221   Mail Box Protocol: Version 2 (NOL; Obsoletes RFC 196; Obsoleted by RFC 278). August 1971.

220   Not issued.

219   User's View of the Datacomputer (NOL). September 1971.

218   Changing the IMP Status Reporting Facility (NOL). September 1971.

217   Specifications Changes for OLS, RJE/RJOR, and SMFS (NOL; Updates RFCs 74, 105, and 122). September 1971.

216   Telnet Access to UCSB's On-Line System (NOL). September 1971.

215   NCP, ICP, and Telnet: The Terminal IMP Implementation (NOL). August 1971.

214   "Network Checkpoint" (NOL; Obsoletes RFC 198). August 1971.

213   IMP System Change Notification (NOL). August 1971.

212   University of Southern California, Information Sciences Institute; USC ISI NWG Meeting on Network Usage (NOL; Obsoletes RFC 207; Updated by RFC 222). August 1971.

211   ARPA Network Mailing Lists (NOL; Obsoletes RFC 168; Obsoleted by RFC 300). August 1971.

210   Improvement of Flow Control (NOL). August 1971.

209   Host/IMP Interface Documentation (NOL). August 1971.

208   Address Tables (NOL). August 1971.

207   "September Network Working Group Meeting" (NOL; Obsoleted by RFC 212). August 1971.

206   User Telnet—Description of an Initial Implementation (NOL). August 1971.

205   NETCRT—A Character Display Protocol (NOL). August 1971.

204   Sockets in Use (NOL; Updated by RFC 234). August 1971.

203   Achieving Reliable Communication (NOL). August 1971.

202   Possible Deadlock in ICP (NOL). July 1971.

201   Not issued.

200   RFC List by Number (NOL; Obsoletes RFC 170, RFC 160; Obsoleted by MIC 7724). August 1971.

199   Suggestions for a Network Data-Tablet Graphics Protocol (NOL). July 1971.

198   Site Certification—Lincoln Labs 360/67 (NOL; Obsoletes RFC 193; Obsoleted by RFC 214). July 1971.

197   Initial Connection Protocol—Reviewed (NOL). July 1971.

196   "Mail Box Protocol" (NOL; Obsoleted by RFC 221). July 1971.

195   Data Computers—Data Descriptions and Access Language (NOL). July 1971.

194   Data Reconfiguration Service—Compiler/Interpreter Implementation Notes (NOL). July 1971.

193   Network Checkout (NOL; Obsoleted by RFC 198). July 1971.

192   Some Factors Which a Network Graphics Protocol Must Consider (NOL). July 1971.

191   Graphics Implementation and Conceptualization at Augmentation Research Center (NOL). July 1971.

190   DEC PDP-10-IMLAC Communication System (NOL). July 1971.

189   Interim NETRJS Specifications (Obsoletes RFC 88; Obsoleted by RFC 599; Updated by RFC 283). July 1971.

188   Data Management Meeting Announcement (NOL). January 1971.

187   Network/440 Protocol Concept (NOL). July 1971.

186   Network Graphics Loader (NOL). July 1971.

185   NIC Distribution of Manuals and Handbooks (NOL). July 1971.

184   Proposed Graphic Display Modes (NOL). July 1971.

183   EBCDIC Codes and Their Mapping to ASCII (NOL). July 1971.

182   Compilation of List of Relevant Site Reports (NOL). June 1971.

181   Modifications to RFC 177 (NOL; Updates RFC 177). July 1971.

180   File System Questionnaire (NOL). June 1971.

179   Link Number Assignments (Updates RFC 107). June 1971.

178   Network Graphic Attention Handling (NOL). June 1971.

177   Device Independent Graphical Display Description (NOL; Updates RFC 125; Updated by RFC 181). June 1971.

176   Comments on "Byte Size for Connections" (NOL). June 1971.

175   Socket Conventions Reconsidered (NOL). June 1971.

174   UCLA Computer Science Graphics Overview (NOL). June 1971.

173   Network Data Management Committee Meeting Announcement (NOL). June 1971.

172   File Transfer Protocol (NOL; Obsoleted by RFC 265; Updates RFC 114; Updated by RFC 238). June 1971.

171   Data Transfer Protocol (NOL; Obsoleted by RFC 264; Updates RFC 114; Updated by RFC 238). June 1971.

170   Stanford Research Institute, Network Information Center; SRI NIC. RFC List by Number (NOL; Obsoleted by RFC 200). June 1971.

169   Computer Networks (NOL). May 1971.

168   ARPA Network Mailing Lists (NOL; Obsoletes RFC 155; Obsoleted by RFC 211). May 1971.

167   Socket Conventions Reconsidered (NOL). May 1971.

166   Data Reconfiguration Service: An Implementation Specification (NOL). May 1971.

165   Proffered Official Initial Connection Protocol (NOL; Obsoletes RFCs 145, 143, and 123; Updated by NIC 7101). May 1971.

164   Minutes of Network Working Group Meeting, May 16–19, 1971 (NOL). May 1971.

163   Data Transfer Protocols (NOL). May 1971.

162   NETBUGGERS3 (NOL). May 1971.

161   Solution to the Race Condition in the ICP (NOL). May 1971.

160   Stanford Research Institute, Network Information Center; SRI NIC RFC Brief (NOL; Obsoleted by RFC 200; Updates NIC 6716). May 1971.

159   Not issued.

158   Telnet Protocol: A Proposed Document (NOL; Obsoleted by RFC 495; Updates RFC 139; Updated by RFC 318). May 1971.

157   Invitation to the Second Symposium on Problems in the Optimization of Data Communications Systems (NOL). May 1971.

156   Status of the Illinois Site: Response to RFC 116 (NOL; Updates RFC 116). April 1971.

155   ARPA Network Mailing Lists (NOL; Obsoletes RFC 95; Obsoleted by RFC 168). May 1971.

154   Exposition Style (NOL). May 1971.

153   SRI ARC-NIC Status (NOL). May 1971.

152   SRI Artificial Intelligence Status Report (NOL). May 1971.

151   Comments on a Proffered Official ICP: RFC 123, RFC 127 (NOL; Updates RFC 127). May 1971.

150   Use of IPC Facilities: A Working Paper (NOL). May 1971.

149   Best Laid Plans (Updates RFC 140). May 1971.

148   Comments on RFC 123 (NOL; Updates RFC 123). May 1971.

147   Definition of a Socket (NOL; Updates RFC 129). May 1971.

146   Views on Issues Relevant to Data Sharing on Computer Networks (NOL). May 1971.

145   Initial Connection Protocol Control Commands (NOL; Obsoletes RFC 127; Obsoleted by RFC 165). May 1971.

144   Data Sharing on Computer Networks (NOL). April 1971.

143   Regarding Proffered Official ICP (NOL; Obsoleted by RFC 165). May 1971.

142   Time-Out Mechanism in the Host-Host Protocol (NOL). May 1971.

141   Comments on RFC 114: A File Transfer Protocol (NOL; Updates RFC 114). April 1971.

140   Agenda for the May NWG Meeting (NOL; Updated by RFC 149). May 1971.

139   Discussion of Telnet Protocol (NOL; Updates RFC 137; Updated by RFC 158). May 1971.

138   Status Report on Proposed Data Reconfiguration Service (NOL). April 1971.

137   Telnet Protocol—A Proposed Document (NOL; Updated by RFC 139). April 1971.

136   Host Accounting and Administrative Procedures (NOL). April 1971.

135   Response to NWG/RFC 110 (NOL; Updates RFC 110). April 1971.

134   Network Graphics Meeting (NOL). April 1971.

133   File Transfer and Recovery (NOL). April 1971.

132   Typographical Error in RFC 107 (NOL; Obsoleted by RFC 154; Updates RFC 107). April 1971.

131   Response to RFC 116: May NWG Meeting (NOL; Updates RFC 116). April 1971.

130   Response to RFC 111: Pressure from the Chairman (NOL; Updates RFC 111). April 1971.

129   Request for Comments on Socket Name Structure (NOL; Updated by RFC 147). April 1971.

128   Bytes (NOL). April 1971.

127   Comments on RFC 123 (NOL; Obsoleted by RFC 145; Updates RFC 123; Updated by RFC 151). April 1971.

126   Graphics Facilities at Ames Research Center (NOL). April 1971.

125   Response to RFC 86: Proposal for Network Standard Format for a Graphics Data Stream (NOL; Updates RFC 86; Updated by RFC 177). April 1971.

124   Typographical Error in RFC 107 (NOL; Updates RFC 107). April 1971.

123   Proffered Official ICP (NOL; Obsoletes RFC 66, RFC 80; Obsoleted by RFC 165; Updates RFC 98, RFC 101; Updated by RFC 127, RFC 148). April 1971.

122   Network Specifications for UCSB's Simple-Minded File System (NOL; Updated by RFCs 217, 269, and 399). April 1971.

121   Network On-Line Operators (NOL). April 1971.

120   Network PL1 Subprograms (NOL). April 1971.

119   Network Fortran Subprograms (NOL). April 1971.

118   Recommendations for Facility Documentation (NOL). April 1971.

117   Some Comments on the Official Protocol (NOL). April 1971.

116   Structure of the May NWG Meeting (NOL; Updates RFC 99;
       Updated by RFC 131, RFC 156). April 1971.

115   Some Network Information Center Policies on Handling Documents
       (NOL). April 1971.

114   File Transfer Protocol (NOL; Updated by RFCs 141, 172, and 171).
       April 1971.

113   Network Activity Report: UCSB Rand (NOL; Updated by RFC 227).
       April 1971.

112   User/Server Site Protocol: Network Host Questionnaire Responses
       (NOL). April 1971.

111   Pressure from the Chairman (NOL; Updates RFC 107; Updated by
       RFC 130). March 1971.

110   Conventions for Using an IBM 2741 Terminal as a User Console for
       Access to Network Server Hosts (NOL; Updated by RFC 135).
       March 1971.

109   Level III Server Protocol for the Lincoln Laboratory NIC 360/67
       Host (NOL). March 1971.

108   Attendance List at the Urbana NWG Meeting, February 17–19,
       1971 (NOL; Updates RFC 101). March 1971.

107   Output of the Host-Host Protocol Glitch Cleaning Committee
       (NOL; Updates RFC 102; Updated by RFCs 179, 132, 124, and 111,
       and NIC 7147). March 1971.

106   User/Server Site Protocol Network Host Questionnaire (NOL).
       March 1971.

105   Network Specifications for Remote Job Entry and Remote Job
       Output Retrieval at UCSB (NOL; Updated by RFC 217). March
       1971.

104   Link 191 (NOL). February 1971.

103   Implementation of Interrupt Keys (NOL). February 1971.

102   Output of the Host-Host Protocol Glitch Cleaning Committee
       (NOL; Updated by RFC 107). February 1971.

101   Notes on the Network Working Group Meeting, Urbana, Illinois,
       February 17, 1971 (NOL; Updated by RFC 108, RFC 123). February
       1971.

100   Categorization and Guide to NWG/RFCs (NOL). February 1971.

99   Network Meeting (NOL; Updated by RFC 116). February 1971.

98   Logger Protocol Proposal (NOL; Updated by RFC 123). February
       1971.

97   First Cut at a Proposed Telnet Protocol (NOL). February 1971.

96   Interactive Network Experiment to Study Modes of Access to the Network Information Center (NOL). February 1971.

95   Distribution of NWG/RFCs Through the NIC (NOL; Obsoleted by RFC 155). February 1971.

94   Some Thoughts on Network Graphics (NOL). February 1971.

93   Initial Connection Protocol (NOL). January 1971.

92   Not issued.

91   Proposed User-User Protocol (NOL). December 1970.

90   CCN as a Network Service Center (NOL). January 1971.

89   Some Historic Moments in Networking (NOL). January 1971.

88   NETRJS: A Third Level Protocol for Remote Job Entry (NOL; Obsoleted by RFC 189). January 1971.

87   Topic for Discussion at the Next Network Working Group Meeting (NOL). January 1971.

86   Proposal: Network Standard Format for Data Stream Control Graphics Display (NOL; Updated by RFC 125). January 1971.

85   Network Working Group Meeting (NOL). December 1970.

84   List of NWG/RFCs 1–80 (NOL). December 1970.

83   Language-Machine for Data Reconfiguration (NOL). December 1970.

82   Network Meeting Notes (NOL). December 1970.

81   Request for Reference Information (NOL). December 1970.

80   Protocols and Data Formats (NOL; Obsoleted by RFC 123). December 1970.

79   Logger Protocol Error (NOL). November 1970.

78   NCP Status Report: UCSB/Rand (NOL). October 1970.

77   Network Meeting Report (NOL). November 1970.

76   Connection by Name: User Oriented Protocol (NOL). October 1970.

76A   Syntax and Semantics for the Terminal User Control Language for the Proposed PDP-11 ARPA Network Terminal System (NOL). October 1970.

75   Network Meeting (NOL). October 1970.

74   Specifications for Network Use of the UCSB On-Line System (NOL; Updated by RFC 217, RFC 225). October 1970.

73   Response to NWG/RFC 67 (NOL). September 1970.

72   Proposed Moratorium on Changes to Network Protocol (NOL). September 1970.

71   Reallocation in Case of Input Error (NOL). September 1970.

70   Note on Padding (NOL; Updated by RFC 228). October 1970.

69   Distribution List Change for MIT (NOL; Updates RFC 52). September 1970.

68   Comments on Memory Allocation Control Commands: CEASE, ALL, GVB, RET, and RFNM (NOL). August 1970.

67   Proposed Change to Host/IMP Spec to Eliminate Marking (NOL). 1970.

66   NIC—Third Level Ideas and Other Noise (NOL; Obsoleted by RFC 123). August 1970.

65   Comments on Host/Host Protocol Document #1 (NOL). August 1970.

64   Getting Rid of Marking (NOL). July 1970.

63   Belated Network Meeting Report (NOL). July 1970.

62   Systems for Interprocess Communication in a Resource Sharing Computer Network (NOL; Obsoletes RFC 61). August 1970.

61   Note on Interprocess Communication in a Resource Sharing Computer Network (NOL; Obsoleted by RFC 62). July 1970.

60   Simplified NCP Protocol (NOL). July 1970.

59   Flow Control—Fixed Versus Demand Allocation (NOL). June 1970.

58   Logical Message Synchronization (NOL). June 1970.

57   Thoughts and Reflections on NWG/RFC 54 (NOL; Updates RFC 54). June 1970.

56   Third Level Protocol: Logger Protocol (NOL). June 1970.

55   Prototypical Implementation of the NCP (NOL). June 1970.

54   Official Protocol Proffering (NOL; Updated by RFC 57). June 1970.

53   Official Protocol Mechanism (NOL). June 1970.

52   Updated Distribution List (NOL; Updated by RFC 69). July 1970.

51   Proposal: A Network Interchange Language (NOL). May 1970.

50   Comments on the Meyer Proposal (NOL). April 1970.

49   Conversations with S. Crocker (UCLA) (NOL). April 1970.

48   Possible Protocol Plateau (NOL). April 1970.

47   BBN's Comments on NWG/RFC #33 (NOL; Updates RFC 33). April 1970.

46   ARPA Network Protocol Notes (NOL). April 1970.

45   New Protocol Is Coming (NOL). April 1970.

44   Comments: NWG/RFC 33 and 36 (NOL; Updates RFC 36). April 1970.

43   Proposed Meeting (NOL). April 1970.

42   Message Data Types (NOL). March 1970.

41   IMP-IMP Teletype Communication (NOL). March 1970.

40   More Comments on the Forthcoming Protocol (NOL). March 1970.

39   Comments on Protocol re: NWG/RFC #36 (NOL; Updates RFC 36). March 1970.

38   Comments on Network Protocol from NWG/RFC #36 (NOL). March 1970.

37   Network Meeting Epilogue, Etc. (NOL). March 1970.

36   Protocol Notes (NOL; Updates RFC 33; Updated by RFC 39, RFC 44). March 1970.

35   Network Meeting (NOL). March 1970.

34   Some Brief Preliminary Notes on the Augmentation Research Center Clock (NOL). February 1970.

33   New Host-Host Protocol (NOL; Obsoletes RFC 11; Updated by RFC 36, RFC 47). February 1970.

32   Connecting M.I.T. Computers to the ARPA Computer-to-Computer Communication Network (NOL). January 1969.

31   Binary Message Forms in Computer (NOL). February 1968.

30   Documentation Conventions (Obsoletes RFC 27). February 1970.

29   Response to RFC 28. January 1970.

28   Time Standards. January 1970.

27   Documentation conventions (Obsoletes RFC 24; Obsoleted by RFC 30). December 1969.

26   Not issued.

25   No High Link Numbers. October 1969.

24   Documentation Conventions (Obsoletes RFC 16; Obsoleted by RFC 27). November 1969.

23   Transmission of Multiple Control Messages. October 1969.

22   Host-Host Control Message Formats (NOL). October 1969.

21   Network Meeting. October 1969.

20   ASCII Format for Network Interchange (NOL). October 1969.

19   Two Protocol Suggestions to Reduce Congestion at Swap Bound Nodes. October 1969.

18   Link Assignments. September 1969.

17   Some Questions re: Host-IMP Protocol. August 1969.

16   M.I.T. (Obsoletes RFC 10; Obsoleted by RFC 24). September 1969.

15   Network Subsystem for Time Sharing Hosts (NOL). September 1969.

14   Not issued.

13   Referring to NWG/RFC 11 (NOL). August 1969.

12   IMP-Host Interface Flow Diagrams (NOL). August 1969.

11   Implementation of the Host-Host Software Procedures in GORDO (NOL; Obsoleted by RFC 33). August 1969.

10   Documentation Conventions (Obsoletes RFC 3; Obsoleted by RFC 16). July 1969.

9   Host Software (NOL). May 1969.

8   Functional Specifications for ARPA Network. May 1969.

7   Host-IMP Interface (NOL). May 1969.

6   Conversation with Bob Kahn. April 1969.

5   Decode Encode Language. June 1969.

4   Network Timetable (NOL) March 1969.

3   Documentation Conventions (Obsoleted by RFC 10). April 1969.

2   Host Software (NOL). April 1969.

1   Host Software (NOL). April 1969.

Open Shortest Path First (OSPF) with Digital Signatures

Signing routing information as a routing function is not new. In other words, identification of routing information did not emerge overnight. A need for greater security in routing protocols exists and is widely recognized.

F.1 OSPF and Current Operation

OSPF currently provides *simple password* authentication. In this method, the password travels in the clear. The simple password authentication method is vulnerable because any listener can discover and use the password. Put another way, one using a network analyzer in promiscuous mode can intercept this information. The *Keyed MD5* authentication is useful for protection of protocol packets passed between neighboring hosts, but it does not address the authentication of routing data that is flooded from source to eventual destination, through routers that may themselves be susceptible to breaches.

Fundamental to the idea of digital signatures are OSPF Link State Acknowledgment (LSA) data, distributed certified router information, keys, and a neighbor-to-neighbor authentication algorithm to protect local protocol exchanges. Hello packet content, Link State Requests, Link State Updates, or Database Descriptions are protected by the neighbor-to-neighbor algorithm. However, the LSAs that are flooded inside the Link State Update packets are individually protected by a digital signature. Consequently, each LSA is signed by the originator of the information and stays with the data it travels with via OSPF flooding. This provides end-to-end integrity and authentication for LSA data. Hence, the digital signature attached to an LSA by the source router provides assurance that the data comes from the advertising router. This also ensures that the data has not been modified by a router in the course of a flooding scenario. In the case where incorrect routing data is originated by a faulty router, the signature identifies the source of the problem.

F.2   Implementation of Digital Signatures

Digital signatures are implemented using public key cryptography. An overview of this design is presented here. Public key cryptography operates where each router has a pair of keys, a *public key* and a *private key*. The private key, in turn, is used to generate a unique signature of a block of data (the LSA). Each router signs its own LSA by first running a one-way algorithm on the data, then using its private key to sign the digest. A signature of an LSA is appended to the LSA.

The public key can be used by any router to verify the signature. However, the private key must be kept secret by one router and the public key must be distributed to all routers that receive link state information from the signer. The distribution of this is achieved by creating a new LSA, the *Public Key LSA* (PKLSA), and then distributing it by the standard OSPF flood procedure. Flooding ensures that a router's public key is sent everywhere that the router's signed LSAs are sent.

Any router can send out a public key and claim to be a given router. Consequently, the public key itself provides no assurance of the actual identity of the sender. In order to achieve this, assurance has to be provided by a Trusted Entity.

A *Trusted Entity* (TE) is a system that generates certificates for routers. A *certificate* is a packet of information about a router that identifies a router and supplies a public key. Certified router information includes a router id, its role, the address ranges the router may advertise, a timestamp, and the router's public key. The certificate is signed by the TE. Each router must be configured with a certificate and a TE public key to use in verifying other routers' certificates. Router PKLSAs contain a certificate for that router. A router receiving a PKLSA verifies the certificate using the TE public key, and then verifies the whole LSA using the router public key contained in the certificate. Verification provides assurance that the PKLSA is from the correct router, and that it has not been altered by any other router in the flood path.

Digital Signatures in OSPF is backward-compatible with the standard OSPF V2 in a limited way. Digital signatures for OSPF LSAs can be implemented with the following functions:

1. Support for a digital signature algorithm
2. Support for a signed version of all routing information LSAs

3. Support for a new LSA: Router Public Key LSA (PKLSA)

4. A mechanism for key certification and certificate distribution

5. Extra configuration data, such as the following:

   Trusted Entity (TE) information and key(s)

   Router certification data and key

   Area environment flag (signed/unsigned)

   Timing intervals

An implementation of this design that is based on the OSPF in Gated V.3.5 Beta 3 current exists. This implementation is available for use and experimentation. Please contact the authors for information.

F.3   Signed LSA Processing

A signed LSA contains a standard OSPF V2 header and data in addition to key identification information, a signature length, and a signature. The top bit of the LS type field is set to indicate the presence of a signature. The signature covers the LSA header, LSA data, the key identification information, and the signature length that must be appended to the LSA data.

Two exceptions to this coverage exist. First, an LSA created with an *age=MaxAge* has a signature that begins with the age field. Second, the LSA header checksum is set to 0 for the generation of the signature. To assist in parsing the message, key id information and signature length fields are placed at the end of the LSA, following the signature. However, the message must be signed. In addition, these fields must be immediately appended to LSA data. This is accomplished either by doing the *sign and verify* in parts, or by storing the LSA data with appended fields and the LSA signature separately in the link state database (LSDB).

When a signed LSA is received, the signature can be verified using the public key from the advertising router contained in the advertising router's PKLSA. If verification of the signature is verified, then the signed LSA is stored for use in routing calculations. If the signature verification is not verified, the LSA must be discarded. However, if the identified key is not available, then the signed LSA must be stored for a period of time defined by the configurable *MAX_TRANSIT_DELAY* interval. If the key arrives within the allotted time interval, the LSA will be processed. If the key does not arrive within this interval, the LSA will be discarded. This delay period prevents loss of routing information due to LSAs arriving prior to their associated PKLSAs; this is not normally the case, but it can happen.

If the LSA is a Router Link's LSA, then the router's advertised link is required to check for address ranges stored in the PKLSA for the advertising router. All network links, including link types 2 and 3, must have an IP address that fits in one of the ranges defined by the list of address ranges in the PKLSA. If a link does not fit into one of these ranges, then an error must be logged and the LSA must be discarded.

A less restrictive, but still useful, level of control can be obtained by defining allowed address ranges for an area, so that all routers in an area can be configured with the same set. One method of control is to use a zero address and mask that can be defined to contain all IP addresses.

Link State Acknowledgments must be sent for all LSAs that are discarded due to verification failures, that are stored waiting for keys, and that are discarded because they are advertising a link that they are not allowed to advertise.

F.4   Router Public Key LSA

A Router Public Key LSA (PKLSA) is sent in the same manner as all other LSAs. This LSA contains the router's public key and identifying information that has been certified by a Trusted Entity. A router public key is used to verify signatures produced by this router. Only one PKLSA is stored per router in the LSDB for a given area, so the Router ID and LS type can be used to retrieve a given PKLSA.

To assist in parsing the message, the router signature length and certification length fields reside at the end of the LSA, following the signature. The message must be signed and verified with these fields that are immediately appended to the LSA data. The router signature of the PKLSA is verified in the same manner as other signed LSAs. Certification must be verified using the referenced TE public key. If either verification fails, for any reason, the PKLSA is discarded.

A successfully verified PKLSA is stored for use in verifying signed LSAs from the advertising router. For each router to which this is logically connected, one PKLSA can be stored at any given time. Each PKLSA is uniquely identified by the values (*TE ID* and *RTR KEY ID*) in the certified data. When a PKLSA arrives for a given router, and there is already a PKLSA stored for that router, the PKLSA with the most recent *Create Time* is the one kept.

Whenever groups of LSAs are sent by a router, such as when synchronizing databases or sending updates, PKLSAs must be sent or requested before other LSAs to minimize the time spent processing LSAs that arrive prior to their associated keys. The PKLSA is sent at intervals like all other LSAs, and it is sent immediately if a router obtains a new key to distribute. A PKLSA is sent via OSPF flooding within an OSPF area. PKLSAs are not flooded outside an area, with the exception of an Autonomous System Border Router's PKLSAs, which must be flooded wherever AS external LSAs are flooded. The decision to flood or not flood can be implemented by checking the router role stored in the certified part of the PKLSA.

A router may flush its keys from routing tables by flooding a PKLSA for that key with age=MaxAge. This is called *premature aging* of the PKLSA. A key can also be removed from routing tables by a PKLSA from the same router that contains a valid certificate for a new key with a more recent Create Time. If a key is superseded by a more recent key it is not necessary to flush the old key with a MaxAge PKLSA.

When a new key is received, the LSAs stored in the LSDB that are signed with the old key must be replaced within MAX_TRAN-SIT_DELAY if the sending router is working properly. This is because a router distributing a new key sends all of its self-originated LSAs signed with the new key immediately after sending the new PKLSA. To ensure that data signed with an old (possibly subverted) key does not persist in the LSDB in error, all LSAs signed with a flushed or superseded key are aged to within MAX_TRANSIT_DELAY of MaxAge. This should allow time for the new LSAs signed with the new key to arrive. If new LSAs do not arrive, or if the key has been flushed and not replaced, then the old LSA data will disappear from the LSDB in a timely fashion.

Link State Acknowledgments must be sent for PKLSAs that are discarded due to verification failures or because the PKLSA was less recent than the one already stored.

F.5 MaxAge Processing

The age field in the OSPF LSA header is used to keep track of how long a given LSA has been in the system. When the age field reaches Max-Age, a router stops using the LSA for routing, and it floods the MaxAge LSA to make sure that all routers stop using this LSA. In the normal course of the OSPF protocol, an LSA is always replaced by an updated version before the age reaches MaxAge, unless the advertising router fails, or changes in the autonomous system (AS) have made the routing information in the LSA inaccurate. An LSA with age=MaxAge is either of the following:

1. An LSA that is intentionally flushed from the AS by the advertising router because the information in it is no longer accurate

2. An orphan LSA that has aged to MaxAge because its originating router has not refreshed it at the normal refresh intervals

The age field cannot generally be included in the signature, because it must be updated by routers other than the originating router. For the same reason, the age field is not included in the checksum computation. The age field must be protected, because if a faulty router started to age out other routers' LSAs, it would effectively deny service to those other routers.

To protect the age field, the signature must include the age field if and only if the originating router creates an LSA with age=MaxAge. Verification of the signature on a signed LSA must include the age field if and only if the age field value is MaxAge. In this manner, the originating router can flush an LSA, but other routers cannot.

An LSA that ages to MaxAge in the LSDB of any router is still discarded by that router, but it is not synchronously flushed from the AS.

An LSA will be removed from a router's Link State Database in one of the two following ways:

1. The router receives a version of the LSA with the age field set to MaxAge and a valid signature that covers the age field.

2. The LSA incrementally reaches MaxAge while it is stored by the router.

If a standard OSPF V2 router goes down, an LSA from that router will age in the LSDBs of each remaining router until it reaches Max-Age somewhere. As soon as it reaches MaxAge in some router's LSDB it is flooded, and this causes it to be flushed from the AS in a synchronized fashion. If a router running OSPF with digital signatures goes down, its signed LSAs will be aged out by each remaining router individually. This will slow database convergence, but the databases will still converge, and a fairly obvious security hole will be closed.

F.6   Identifying Keys

A router key is identified by the *Router ID,* and the identifiers associated with the particular key in its certificate: *TE ID* and *Router Key ID.* All three of these values are stored in a PKLSA. The Router ID is the standard LSA header Advertising Router. The TE ID and RTR KEY ID are stored in the PKLSA certified data area. The TE ID is a number assigned to a Trusted Entity that must uniquely identify one TE in the AS. The TE ID in a certificate identifies the TE that produced the certificate. The RTR KEY ID is associated with a key by the Trusted Entity that produced the certificate. The Trusted Entity must produce a stream of RTR KEY IDs for one router such that the router will not reuse a key ID until all references to the last key having that ID are gone from the AS. If a key is replayed, or reused too soon, the Create Time in the key certification will determine which key is current. RTR KEY IDs do not have to be sequential.

F.7   Identification of TE Public Keys

Each TE public key has an associated *TE ID, TE KEY ID*. The combination of the TE ID and TE KEY ID uniquely identifies one TE public key in the AS. The TE ID is a number assigned to a Trusted Entity that uniquely identifies one TE in the AS. The TE KEY ID must identify one particular key for a TE at any given time. The TE KEY ID distinguishes between a new key and an old key for the same TE. The TE KEY ID also differentiates between keys for different signature algorithms if one TE serves multiple algorithms. Each TE can have at most one current key per signature algorithm.

There can be multiple TE keys stored on each router. A TE public key is used to verify the certificates issued by other routers, and in an AS with several TEs, any given router may need several TE public keys. TE KEY IDs do not have to be used sequentially, and they can be reused. There is no timestamp for TE keys because these are not certified. Configuration Management is responsible for ensuring that TE KEY IDs are not reused before all references to a previously used key with the same TE ID and TE KEY ID are gone from the AS, that a given TE ID and TE KEY ID on one router identifies the same key as it does on any other router, and that the rules for TE Key Replacement are followed.

F.8   Signing Keys

A router is configured with a pair of keys. The private key is protected from disclosure and is used for signing. The public key is flooded in a PKLSA and is used for verifying signatures. A router may have one key per area to use for signing at any given time. A router may use the same key for several or all areas.

There are three uses of signature verification in this design:

1. The signature in a signed LSA can be verified with the public key distributed by the advertising router in a Public Key LSA. A signed LSA contains the TE ID and RTR KEY ID of the key used to sign it. The signed LSA's Advertising Router ID is used to retrieve the router's PKLSA, and the TE ID and RTR KEY ID indicate if the router key in the PKLSA is the same as the one used to generate the signature.

2. The router's signature in a PKLSA is verified with the public key contained in that PKLSA.

3. The PKLSA contains data certified with a signature generated by a TE. The PKLSA certified data contains the TE ID and TE KEY ID

for the TE key that can be used to verify the certificate. The TE public keys must be configured on each router.

F.9 Trusted Entity (TE) Requirements

This design does not specify how the Trusted Entity (TE) must be implemented, where it must reside, or how it must communicate with routers. There are several very different possible approaches to the implementation of a Trusted Entity. This design does mandate certain requirements for what a Trusted Entity must do. A Trusted Entity must generate a certificate for each signing router that contains individualized information about that router and is signed with the Trusted Entity private key. The Trusted Entity must have a unique TE ID for itself, it must create a RTR KEY ID for each router key that is unique for the given Router for this TE at this time, and it must timestamp certificates with a Create Time that is consistent for itself and for any other Trusted Entities operating in the AS. Note that routers do not have to be time-synched, but TEs do.

Create Time is used by routers as a relative measure to determine which key is more recent.

The TE Public Key, TE ID, TE Key ID and Signature Algorithm must be made available to each router processing certificates from this TE. A TE can theoretically create certificates for more than one signature algorithm. The TE key and the router public key certified do not have to be of the same signature algorithm.

There can be more than one TE in an AS, but the TE ID must identify a unique TE.

The concept of *scope* relates to Router Keys, TE Keys, and Signature Algorithms. The scope of a PKLSA, and, therefore, a router key, is defined to be the set of routers that will receive and store that PKLSA in the course of OSPF flooding. A router produces a PKLSA for each attached area. In a router with more than one area, the PKLSAs for each area may match, or each may contain a different key. The scope of PKLSA for an internal router is all the routers in that area. An Area Border Router (ABR) has multiple PKLSAs, each having a scope of one attached area. The scope of an Autonomous System Border Router's (ASBR's) PKLSA is the same as the scope of the ASBR's AS externals (ASEs)—all the routers in all the nonstub areas in the AS. An ASBR that is an ABR produces multiple PKLSAs that each have a scope of all the routers in all the nonstub areas in the AS. (This last case results in some situations that require special management.)

The scope of a TE key is defined as the set of routers that are configured with this key. If a system is configured properly, then a TE public key will be configured on all the routers that will receive PKLSAs certified by that TE key. The minimum scope for a TE key is an area. If one router distributes a key certified with a given TE key, then all the routers in the area must be able to verify the certificate. A TE key certifying an ASBR's key must have a scope of all nonstub areas in the AS. If the TE key is not on some router that receives PKLSAs certified by that TE key, then those PKLSAs and all the LSAs that require them will be discarded. A TE key gets to all the routers in its scope via out-of-band configuration.

The scope of a signature algorithm is defined as the set of routers that are capable of verifying the given algorithm's signatures. The minimum scope for a signature algorithm is an area. All routers in an area must be able to verify any signature algorithm used for signing by any router in the area. The algorithm used to certify an ASBR's key must have a scope of all nonstub areas in the AS if the ASEs are to be accessible everywhere. If a signature algorithm is not available to verify an LSA, then the LSA must be discarded. If a signature algorithm is not available to verify the certification in a PKLSA, then the PKLSA must be discarded.

Router keys should be changed periodically, and immediately if a key is found to be compromised. The regular period for changing a key is some locally determined function of the size of the key and the level of security needed.

Each router can have *one* valid key per area at any given time. Restricting the number of keys at a given time to one key per router per area allows key replacement to also serve the purpose of key revocation, without having a revocation list and without routers having synchronized time. Each key for the router/area revokes the last key, provided the *new* key has a more recent Create Time than the last key. The Create Time in each certificate is used to prevent an old key from being reused, but this Create Time is used only for comparing the relative ages of certificates and does not require the router to run a time synchronization protocol itself. An ABR can use the same key for all its attached areas, or it can have a unique key for each area. This allows an AS to be managed by area, with each area potentially having a different TE, signature algorithm, key size, and/or key.

When a new key replaces an old key, the router must quickly replace LSAs signed with the old key with LSAs signed with the new key. To change a router key, the following steps must be followed:

1. A valid certificate for the new key must be obtained for the router.

2. The router builds and sends a new PKLSA with the new certificate.

3. The router signs each self-originated LSA with the new key and sends them.

When a PKLSA is received, one or more of the following occur:

1. If the PKLSA's age = MaxAge, remove the PKLSA from the LSDB and age LSAs signed with this key to be MaxAge – MAX_TRANSIT_DELAY, if they were not already older than this. This is a way to get rid of a key that should no longer be used.

2. If the PKLSA is a refresh LSA for an existing key, update the LSDB.

3. If the PKLSA contains a different key than the one currently stored for this router, compare the certificate Create Time. If the PKLSA key is less recent, discard it. If the PKLSA key is more recent, install it in the LSDB and remove the old key from the LSDB. If an old key was deleted from the LSDB, age LSAs signed with this key to be MaxAge – MAX_TRANSIT_DELAY, if they were not already older than this.

F.10   Trusted Entity Key Replacement

It is necessary to change a TE public key periodically. It is recommended that the TE public key be relatively large, so that it does not frequently require replacement. A router may store multiple TE public keys. Each key is uniquely identified by TE ID and TE KEY ID. TE keys are used to verify certificates received from other routers in their PKLSAs. When a router sends a new certificate signed with a new TE key, all the routers that receive the PKLSA containing the certificate must have that new TE key in order to verify, store, and use that PKLSA. Management of TE public keys is done outside the OSPF protocol, and a method is suggested but not mandated by this design. Initially, all routers must be configured with the TE keys they will need to verify the certificates they will receive. To prevent use of a TE key, that key must be replaced by a new TE key having the same TE ID and signature algorithm. A compromised or faulty router can continue using certificates signed with the old TE key, but none of the properly configured routers will be able to verify them.

Changing a TE public key presents a design challenge. When a TE public key is changed, all the certificates depending on that key must also change. The router keys in the certificates may or may not be changed at the same time. When the TE key and certificates change, all PKLSAs depending on them must be reissued. In order to verify these new certificates, all routers receiving the new PKLSAs must have the new TE public key. So, the TE key replacement must be a synchronized event. Routers are not required to have synchronized clocks. The TE public key may well be distributed to the routers via an out-of-band mechanism, such as a smart-card reader. It is not reasonable to require that all the routers obtain the TE public key at the same time.

F.11   Flexible Cryptographic Environments

It is likely that an AS will have one cryptographic environment in use throughout the AS, with one trusted entity, one signature algorithm in use, and one key in use per router. To allow those cases where this is not true, multiple signature algorithms, multiple trusted entities, and multiple keys per router are allowed.

It is possible to support multiple signature algorithms. Each router and TE key has a signature algorithm associated with it. All routers sending a key with a given algorithm must be capable of generating signatures of that kind, and all routers receiving keys with a given algorithm must be able to verify the signatures. If a router receives an LSA signed with a signature algorithm that it does not support, the LSA must be discarded. LSAs that cannot be verified by a router are not flooded by that router. When using multiple signature algorithms, the scope of each algorithm must be determined and routers must be configured with support for these algorithms accordingly.

If an area supports two signature algorithms and is to have full connectivity, some routers may sign with algorithm A and others with algorithm B, but all routers in the area must be able to verify signatures for A and B. In an AS that is divided into areas, it is possible for each area to have a different signature algorithm. The ABR connecting two areas would have to support both algorithms, but the internal routers in a given area would only have to know one algorithm.

ASBRs present a problem for this sort of division. ASEs flood throughout the nonstub areas of an AS. Any router that cannot verify an ASE will discard it without flooding. So, to have access to an ASE, a router—and all the routers in the flooding path—must support the algorithm used by the ASBR. One way around these difficulties is to have a lowest common denominator algorithm that is used for signing by all ASBRs and supported for verification throughout the AS. Another approach is to place ASBRs on the backbone and configure all areas using a signature algorithm different from the ASBR to have a default route to the backbone. A combined approach will allow an ASBR to be in a nonbackbone area if it uses a signature algorithm supported on the backbone, and the areas using different signature algorithms are configured with a default to the backbone.

F.12   Multiple Trusted Entities

It is possible to have multiple Trusted Entities in an AS. Each TE has a unique TE identifier. Every router receiving PKLSAs certified by a given TE must have that TE's public key. If a router receives a PKLSA certified by a TE for which it does not have a public key, the PKLSA must be discarded. When using multiple TEs, the scope of each TE must be determined, and routers in this scope must be configured with the TE key.

An ABR may have one key for each attached area. These keys may differ in size, algorithm and/or certifying TE. Generally, each key will have a scope of the attached area, and there will be no conflict between keys.

F.13   Compatibility with Standard OSPF V2

OSPF with Digital Signatures is compatible with standard OSPF V2 in an autonomous system. Within an AS, there may be *signed* areas and *unsigned* areas. There will never be both signed and unsigned LSAs used in any one area. Each area will have an environment flag indicating whether it is *signed* or *unsigned*. The environment flag is a per-area configuration value for the router. The signed areas must contain all routers running OSPF with Digital Signatures, and the unsigned areas contain routers running standard OSPF V2 code.

An area border router connecting a signed to an unsigned area must be running OSPF with Digital Signatures with one area set to be unsigned. In order to arrange this limited compatibility, a router running OSPF with Digital Signatures must be able to process both signed and unsigned LSAs. The only router that will actually be processing both kinds of LSAs is an Area Border Router connecting a signed area to an unsigned area. An ABR connecting a signed to an unsigned area will generate signed summaries for one area and unsigned summaries for the other. An ABR must not flood signed LSAs into unsigned areas. An ABR must not flood unsigned LSAs into signed areas. This will result in AS external LSAs being dropped if they reach an area that has a different environment from the one in which they were created. There are special limitations in the case of a router that is an ABR. Complete connectivity is provided within the AS because of the summarization provided by ABRs connecting signed and unsigned areas.

Limitations exist on connectivity to AS external routes in an AS with a mixture of signed and unsigned areas, depending on the location of AS border routers. An ASBR in a signed area will generate signed ASE LSAs. These LSAs will be flooded to every contiguously connected signed area. The connected signed areas are the *scope* of these ASEs. A host located in an area that is not in this scope will not have connectivity to these external routes. An ASBR in an unsigned area will generate unsigned ASE LSAs. These LSAs will have a scope of all the contiguously connected unsigned areas, and will be available to hosts in this scope.

F.14   Special Considerations and Restrictions for the ABR/ASBR

There are special restrictions and configuration considerations for a router running OSPF with Digital Signatures that is both an Area Border Router and an Autonomous System Border Router. An ASBR produces AS external LSAs that are flooded throughout the nonstub areas of the AS. An ABR that is generating digital signatures may be using a different key, certifying Trusted Entity, or signature algorithm for each of its attached areas, or it might be signing in some areas and not in others.

An ABR/ASBR with no restrictions on its configuration could produce multiple versions of an ASE that would all be flooded throughout the nonstub areas of the AS. The results of this production of multiple versions of LSAs would be detrimental to performance, and could produce unpredictable routing behavior.

The PKLSA of an ASBR is also flooded throughout the nonstub areas of the AS, and in the case of an ABR/ASBR there could be multiple, distinct PKLSAs for a given router, one per attached area, all being flooded throughout the AS. If two distinct PKLSAs from one ABR/ASBR router were present in one area, the key with the most recent Create Time would be stored, and all LSAs signed with a less recent key would be unverifiable.

F.15   LSA Formats

This LSA is the vehicle for distribution of a router public key. The PKLSA is sent by one router and stored by all the other routers in the flooding scope. The PKLSA contains the public key that other routers will use to verify the signatures created by this router. A Router PKLSA will be communicated in the usual database exchange and via flooding mechanisms. The regular period for sending this LSA is *LSRefreshTime*. The Router PKLSA will also be sent when there is a new key, or a key to be flushed from the system.

The flooding scope of a PKLSA is the area, except in the case of ASBRs. The flooding scope of an ASBR's PKLSA is the same as that of the ASEs. The *role* of the router (RTR, ABR, ASBR, ABR/ASBR) is stored in the PKLSA inside the certificate, and can be checked during flooding (See Fig. F.1).

F.16   Router Public Key Certificate

A router public key certificate is a package of data signed by a Trusted Entity. This certificate is included in the router PKLSA and in the router

| 0 1 1 1 1 1 1 1 1 1 2 2 2 2 2 2 2 2 2 2 3 3 | | |
| 0 1 2 3 4 5 6 7 8 9 0 1 2 3 4 5 6 7 8 9 0 1 2 3 4 5 6 7 8 9 0 1 | | |

LS Age	Options	LS Type
Link State ID		
Advertising Router		
LS Sequence Number		
LS Checksum	Length	
Certificate		
Signature		
Cert Length	Sign Length	

Figure F.1   Router public key LSA.

configuration information. To change any of the values in the certificate, a new certificate must be obtained from a TE. For example, see Fig. F.2.

F.17   Signed LSA

A signed LSA is an OSPF LSA with signature data and a digital signature attached. The first bit of the *LSA Type* field is set to indicate the presence of a signature. The signature follows the *LSA Data*. Signature length and ID fields are positioned at the end of the signed LSA. For example, see Fig. F.3.

Router Id			
TE Id	TE Key Id	Rtr Key Id	Sig Alg
Create Time			
Key Field Length		Router Role	#Net Ranges
IP Address			
Address Mask			
IP Address/Address Mask for each Net Range ...			
...			
Router Public Key			
Certification			

Figure F.2   Router public key certificate.

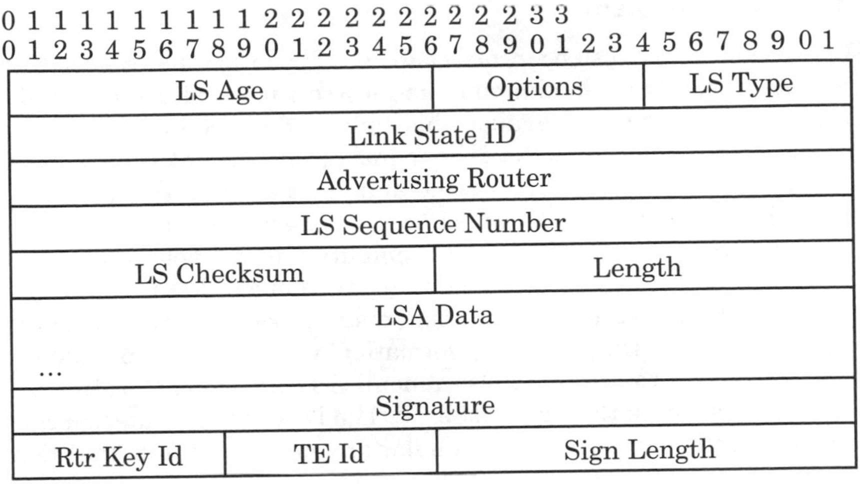

```
0 1 1 1 1 1 1 1 1 1 2 2 2 2 2 2 2 2 2 2 3 3
0 1 2 3 4 5 6 7 8 9 0 1 2 3 4 5 6 7 8 9 0 1 2 3 4 5 6 7 8 9 0 1
```

LS Age		Options	LS Type
Link State ID			
Advertising Router			
LS Sequence Number			
LS Checksum		Length	
LSA Data			
...			
Signature			
Rtr Key Id	TE Id	Sign Length	

Figure F.3   Any signed LSA.

F.18   Area Border Routers (ABRs)

Area border routers can inject incorrect routing information into their attached areas about the backbone and the other areas in Summary LSAs. They can also inject incorrect routing information into the backbone about their attached areas.

Because all the area border routers in one area work from the same database of LSAs received in their common area, it would be possible for the area border routers to corroborate each other. Any area border router for an area could double check the Summary LSAs received over the backbone from the other ABRs for the area, and could double-check the Summary LSAs flooded through the area from the other area border routers. The other routers in the area or backbone should be warned of a failure of this check. The warning could be a signed message from the area border router detecting the failure, flooded by the usual mechanism.

Another possibility would be that the area border routers in an area could originate multiple sets of Summary LSAs—one for itself containing its own information and one for each of the area border routers in the area containing the information that each of them should originate. Each router in the area or backbone could then determine for itself whether the area border routers agreed. This distribution of information but coordination of processing is in keeping with the paradigm of link state protocols, where information and processing are duplicated in each router. Both alternatives mean much additional processing and additional message transmission, over and above the additional processing required for signature generation and verification. Because the vulnerability is isolated to a few points in each area, the source of incorrect information is detectable.

F.19   Internal Routers

The internal routers can be incorrect about information they themselves originate. A router could announce an incorrect metric for a valid link. There is no way to guard against this, but the damage would be small and localized even if the router is announcing that the link is up when it is down, or vice-versa. A router could announce a connection that does not, in fact, exist. If a router announces a nonexistent connection to a transit network, the OSPF Dijkstra computation will not consider the connection without a similar announcement from another router at the other end. Therefore, no damage would result (above network impact to transmit and store the incorrect information) without the cooperation of another router. A router could also announce a connection to a stub network or a host route that does not exist. The Dijkstra computation cannot perform the same check for a similar announcement from the other end, because no other end exists.

A faulty router announcing a nonexistent connection to a stub network or host could result in the faulty router receiving IP packets bound for that network or host. Unless the faulty router then forwarded the packets to the correct destination by source routing, the failure of packet delivery could expose the incorrect routing. To exploit the vulnerability deliberately, the faulty router would have to be able to handle and pass on the received traffic for the incorrectly announced destination. Furthermore, if the incorrect routing were discovered, the signatures on the routing information would identify the faulty router as the source of the incorrect information. Finally, this design checks router advertisements against allowed address ranges certified by a trusted entity. A faulty router could announce nonexistent host or stub network routes, but only to addresses within its allowed ranges.

F.20   Autonomous System
Border Routers (ASBRs)

The autonomous system border routers can produce incorrect routing information in the external route information they originate. There is no way to double-check or corroborate this information as there is with area border routers. No authority exists within an autonomous system to authorize the networks that an autonomous system boundary router can announce, as is the case for the internal networks that an internal router can announce. Consequently, the autonomous system boundary routers remain an unprotected vulnerability. With this in mind, special care should be taken to protect the autonomous system boundary routers through other means.

Glossary

7.0-compatible According to Apple documentation, an application that runs without problems in System Software version 7.0.

7.0-dependent According to Apple documentation, an application that requires the existence of features that are present only in System Software version 7.0.

7.0-friendly According to Apple documentation, an application that is 7.0-compatible and takes advantage of some of the special features of System Software version 7.0, but is still able to perform all its principal functions when operating in version 6.0.

abend Abnormal end of task.

Abstract Syntax Machine-independent types and values, defined using an ASN.1.

Abstract Syntax Notation One The OSI language used to describe abstract entities or concepts in a machine.

ACB In VTAM, access method control block. In NCP, adapter control block.

ACB name The name of a micro instruction. A name typically specified on the VTAM APPL definition statement.

accept In a VTAM application program, to establish a session with a logical unit in response to a CINIT request.

Access Control Entry Specifies identifiers and access rights to granted or denied holders of the identifiers, default protection for directories, or security alarms.

Access Control List A list defining the kinds of access granted or denied to users of an object.

access method A technique for moving data between main storage and input/output devices. Also a technique used in telecommunications.

Access Method Control Block (ACB) A control block that links an application program to VSAM or VTAM.

ACF/VTAM Advanced Communications Function for the Virtual Telecommunications Access Method.

acknowledgment A positive response sent to indicate successful reception of information.

acquire In VTAM, to take over resources that were formerly controlled by an access method in another domain.

activate   To initialize a resource.

active   Operational. The state of a resource when it has been activated and is operational.

active application   An application currently capable of being used by a user.

active window   The terminal window where current operations are in the foreground.

ACTLU   In SNA, a command used to start a session with a logical unit.

ACTPU   In SNA, a command used to start a session with a physical unit.

Adapter Control Block (ACB)   In NCP, a control block that contains line control information and the states of I/O operations. In an I/O database, a definition describing an adapter or device controller and the I/O interconnect.

Adaptive Session-Level Pacing   Pacing where session components exchange pacing windows that may vary in size during the course of a session.

address   In data communication, this is a designated identifier.

Address Descriptor Record   Information that reflects the address of an Apple event.

addressing   In datacommunication, the way in which a station selects the station to which it is to send data.

Address Mask   A bit mask used to select bits from an IP address for subnet addressing.

Address Resolution   Conversion of an IP address into a corresponding physical address, such as Ethernet or Token Ring.

Address Resolution Protocol (ARP)   A TCP/IP protocol used to dynamically bind a high-level IP address to low-level physical hardware addresses. ARP works across single physical networks and is limited to networks that support hardware broadcast.

Address Space   Addresses used to uniquely identify network accessible units, sessions, adjacent link stations, and links in a node for each network in which the node participates.

adjacent control point   A control point directly connected to an APPN, LEN, or composite node.

adjacent NCPs   Network control programs connected by subarea links with no intervening NCPs.

adjacent nodes   Two nodes connected by at least one path that connects no other node.

adjacent SSCP table   A table identifying SSCPs that VTAM can enter into a session with.

adjacent subareas   Subareas connected by one or more links with no intervening subareas.

Advanced Communications Function (ACF)   A group of IBM licensed programs.

Advanced Peer-to-Peer Network (APPN)   An upper-layer networking protocol based on peer technology. The fundamental difference between APPN and SNA is that VTAM is not required for session establishment after initial download of parameters.

Advanced Peer-to-Peer Network (APPN) END node   A node that can register its local LUs with its network node server. It can also have links to multiple nodes, but can have only one CP-CP session with a network node at a time. CP-CP sessions can never be established between END nodes.

Advanced Peer-to-Peer Network (APPN) Interchange node   This type of node can characteristically be described by its functions, which include controlling network resources, performing CDRM functions in subarea networks, and it can own NCPs. This type of node appears to be an APPN type node to an APPN network, and it appears to be a subarea node to a subarea network. It can reside between an APPN network and a subarea network, thus providing integration of the two.

Advanced Peer-to-Peer Network (APPN) LEN node   This type of node is different from an END node, because it supports functions not supported by an END node. For example, an LEN node supports ILU protocols but not CP-CP sessions.

Advanced Peer-to-Peer Network (APPN) NETWORK node   An APPN NETWORK node performs the following functions:

- Distributed directory services
- Intermediate routing services in an APPN network
- Network services for specific end nodes
- Intermediate session routing
- Management service focal point

The APPN network node cooperates with other network nodes to maintain a network topology database, which is used to select optimal routes for LU-LU sessions based on requested classes of service. An APPN network node can also attach to a subarea network as a peripheral node or to other end nodes.

Advanced Program-to-Program Communication (APPC)   A protocol architecture based on T2.1 architecture utilizing LU6.2 to accomplish peer communications. Many references to APPC are simply LU6.2. The basic meaning of APPC is communication between programs—that is, transactions programs. This type of protocol permits communication between programs written in different languages.

Advanced Research Projects Agency (ARPA)   Formerly named DARPA, which was the government agency that funded the ARPANET.

alert   In SNA, a message sent to a management subsystem, typically using network management vector transport (NMVT) protocol.

Alertable   In DECnet architecture, a synchronous alert that delivers data to specific points.

Alertsafe   According to Digital Equipment documentation, a routine that can be called without risk of triggering an alert while asynchronous delivery of alerts is enabled.

Alias File   A file that contains a pointer to another file, directory, or volume.

Alias Name   A naming convention sometimes used to refer to a different name that means the same as the alias, or refers to another name which may be used as a pointer.

allocate   A LU6.2 verb that assigns a session to a conversation.

Allocation Class   According to Digital Equipment documentation, this is a unique number between 0 and 255 that the system manager assigns to a pair of hosts and to the dual-pathed devices that the hosts make available to other nodes in a VMS cluster.

Alpha Primary Bootstrap   According to Digital Equipment documentation, the primary bootstrap program that initializes an AXP system with OpenVMS AXP.

alternate route   A route which is not the primary method of moving data from one point to another point.

ampersand (&)   When used in a command in most UNIX operating systems, it places the task or tasks in background operation.

Ancillary Control Process   A process acting as an interface between software and an I/O driver.

APAR   Authorized Program Analysis Report.

API   Application Program Interface.

APPC   Advanced Program-to-Program Communication.

APPL   Application program.

Apple Event   According to Apple documentation, a high-level event that adheres to the Apple Event Interprocess Messaging Protocol.

Apple Event Handler   According to Apple documentation, this is a defined function that extracts pertinent data from an Apple event.

Apple Event Interprocess Messaging Protocol   A standard defined by Apple Computer, Inc., for communication among applications. According to Apple documentation, high-level events that adhere to this protocol are called *Apple events*.

Apple Event parameter   According to Apple documentation, this is a keyword specifying a descriptor record containing data which the target application of an Apple event must use.

Apple File Exchange   A program that permits file transfer between Apple computers and DOS-based computers.

AppleShare File Server   Software that permits users to perform tasks in AppleTalk networks.

AppleShare Print Server   A Macintosh computer and software that manages network printing.

AppleTalk Data Stream Protocol (ADSP) An AppleTalk protocol that provides the capability for maintaining a connection-oriented session between entities on an internet.

AppleTalk Echo Protocol (AEP) A response-oriented protocol whereby a response is sent when a packet is received.

AppleTalk Filing Protocol (AFP) The protocol used between an application and a file server. AFP is a client of ASP.

AppleTalk Internet Router Router software operating on an Apple computer supporting up to eight AppleTalk networks.

AppleTalk Phase 2 Introduced in June of 1989, it extended the capability of AppleTalk Phase 1; for example, it supports Token Ring and provides more efficient routing techniques. It is included in System/7 software.

AppleTalk Session Protocol (ASP) An AppleTalk session protocol used to establish and maintain logical connections between a workstation and a server.

AppleTalk Transaction Protocol (ATP) An AppleTalk protocol that functions in many ways like a connection-oriented protocol. For example, it orients the packets into the order in which they need to be received, and if any packets have been lost, automatic retransmission of those packets is performed.

AppleTalk Transition A message containing information indicating specific occurences that relate to the AppleTalk Transition Queue.

AppleTalk Transition Queue An operating system queue.

Application Layer According to the ISO OSI model, this is layer 7. It provides application services.

application program Software that provides functions needed by a user. A user may be defined as a human, an API, a transaction program, or other logical entity.

Application Program Interface (API) An addressable point that serves the function to bring together two or more entities.

application program major node According to IBM documentation, in VTAM this is a group of application program minor nodes.

Application Result Handler A program designed to perform predefined functions of results generated from applications.

application server A computer used solely to provide processing power for application programs.

Application Service Element (ASE) A definition explaining the capabilities of an application entity.

Application Service Object A subobject of an application entity; it may contain ASE elements or service objects as subobjects.

application transaction program The program built around LU6.2 protocols.

apply A System Modification Program (SMP) command, used in certain SNA environments, whereby programs and/or program fixes are added to system libraries.

APPN   Advanced Peer-to-Peer Network.

APPN Intermediate Routing Network   An APPN network consisting of network nodes and their interconnections.

Argument List   According to Digital Equipment, a vector of entries representing a procedure parameter list and possibly a function value.

Argument Pointer   According to Digital Equipment, General Register 12 on VAX systems. By convention, AP contains the address of the base of the argument list for procedures initiated using CALL instructions.

ARP   Address Resolution Protocol. A TCP/IP protocol that maps IP addresses to hardware addresses.

ARPA   Advanced Research Projects Agency. A participant in the early development of TCP/IP.

ARPANET   Served as the central backbone for the IN during the seventies and most of the eighties.

ASCII (American Standard Code for Information Interchange)   A standard code using a character set based on binary digits (1s and 0s). This character set is the foundation whereby letters, numbers, and specialized control functions are defined.

Assignment Statement   In Digital Command Language (DCL), the association of a symbol name to use with a character string or numeric value. In Digital Equipment implementations, symbols can define synonyms for system commands or can be used for variables in command procedures.

Association Control Service Element   Used to establish and terminate associations between applications.

asynchronous (ASYNC)   In datacommunication, the transmission of data without synchronous protocol.

Asynchronous System Trap   A method whereby a specific event can be identified via a software-simulated interrupt.

Asynchronous Transfer Mode (ATM)   A CCITT standard defining cell relay. This is where data of multiple types of services, such as data, voice, and/or video, are moved in fixed-size cells throughout a network.

attenuation   A term used in fiberoptics to refer to the reduction of signal loss, measured in decibels.

attribute   From a security perspective, an identifier or a holder of an identifier. When used in a conversation concerning threads, it specifies detailed properties about the objects to be created.

Attributes Object   Describes details of the objects to be created.

authentication   A process of establishing identity.

authorized path   In VTAM under MVS, a facility that enables an application program to specify that a data transfer or related operation be carried out in a privileged and more efficient manner.

automatic logon In SNA, a process by which VTAM automatically creates a session-initiation request to establish a session between two logical units (LUs). The result of this request is the SNA BIND command from the Primary Logical Unit (PLU) to the Secondary Logical Unit (SLU). Hence, a LU-LU session is established if the BIND image is correct and other parameters are accurate.

Automatic Record Locking According to Digital Equipment documentation, a capability provided in Open VMS Record Management Services that allows a user to lock only one record in a specific shared file at any given time.

A/UX Toolbox According to Apple documentation, a library that enables a program running under the A/UX operating system to call Macintosh User Interface Toolbox and operating system routines.

Background Process In most UNIX environments, a process not requiring the total attention of the system for operation.

Backplane Interconnect According to Digital Equipment documentation, VAX systems have an internal processor bus that allows I/O device controllers to communicate with main memory and the central processor. These I/O controllers may reside on the same bus as memory and the central processor, or they may be on a separate bus.

BASE disk In SNA, and specifically the VM operating system, this is the disk containing text decks and macroinstructions for VTAM, NetView, and VM/SNA console support (VSCS).

Base Priority Priority a VM system assigns to a process when it is created. Normally, it comes from the authorization file.

Basic Logical Object An object in a specific logical structure that has no subordinate.

baud The number of times per second a signal can change on a transmission line.

begin bracket In SNA, the value of the begin-bracket indicator in the request header (RH). It is the first request in the first chain of a bracket. Its value denotes the start of a bracket.

BER Bit Error Rate.

Berkeley broadcast A nonstandard IP broadcast address using all zeros in the host portion instead of all ones.

best-effort delivery A description of network technologies that do not provide reliability at link levels.

Bezier curve A curve defined by three outline points—two outline points on a curve that serve as endpoints and one not on the curve point. These determine the degree of curvature.

BF Boundary Function.

Big Endian A format for storage or transmission of binary data in which the most significant byte comes first.

Binary Synchronous Communication (BSC) A telecommunication protocol using a standard set of transmission control characters and control character sequences.

BIND In SNA, a request for session activation between logical units.

BIND command In SNA, the command used to start a session and define the characteristics thereof.

BIND image In SNA, the session parameters used to establish and govern the session between logical units. In VTAM, the BIND image is located in the LOG-MODE table in the form of entries—one entry per type of image required to define the LU.

BIND pacing In SNA, BIND pacing can be used to prevent a BIND standoff. It is a technique used by the Address Space Manager (ASM).

bitmap Generally speaking, an array of data bits used for graphic images.

bitmap device A device that displays bitmaps.

bitmap font A bitmap font is made from a matrix of dots.

BIU segment In SNA, data contained within a Path Information Unit (PIU). It consists of either a Request/Response Header (RH) followed by all or part of a Request/Response unit (RU), or only part of an RU.

blocking AST An AST that can be requested by a process using the lock management system services. A blocking AST is delivered to the requesting process when it is preventing another process from accessing a resource.

Boot Server According to Digital Equipment documentation, the management center for a VMScluster system and its major source provider. The boot server provides disk access and downline loads satellite nodes.

Bootstrap Block That part of the index file on a system disk that contains a program which loads the operating system into memory.

Boundary Function In SNA, protocol support for attached peripheral nodes.

Boundary Node (BN) Fundamentally performs the function of transforming network addresses to local addresses.

bracket In SNA, one or more chains of RUs and their responses that are exchanged between session partners.

Bracket Protocol A data flow control protocol in which session partners exchange data via IBM's SNA bracket protocol.

broadcast IN TCP/IP, a request for logical connection at layers one and two in the network. Broadcast technology is exemplified by Ethernet.

broadcast search In APPN, the simultaneous search to all network nodes in the form of a request for some type of data.

broadcast storm A situation in a network using broadcast technology where a considerable number of broadcasts are put on the medium at one time.

browse With regard to functions that can be performed on a entity, browse merely permits viewing.

BSC   Binary Synchronous Communication.

Btrieve   According to Novell documentation, a complete indexed record management system designed for high-performance data handling.

bucket   According to Digital Equipment documentation, a storage structure used for building and processing files. A bucket contains one or more records or record cells. Buckets are the unit of contiguous transfer between Open VMS Record Management Services buffers and the disk.

buffer   A temporary storage area used to hold input or output data.

Bundle Bit   The FINDER uses information in a bundle bit (BNDL Resource) to associate icons with the file.

button   A button is generally agreed to be that which is pressed on a mouse. Mice may have two or three buttons. Two-button mice are common in non-Xwindow environments. Three-button mice are common in Xwindow environments and can be used in non-Xwindow environments, depending on the mouse vendor.

CA   Channel adapter or channel attachment.

cache   A high-speed storage storage buffer.

call   To invoke a program, routine, or subroutine.

Call Connected Packet   A DTE packet transmission indicating DCE acceptance of the incoming call.

calling   The process of transmitting selection signals to establish a connection between data stations.

Call Progress Signal   Communication from the DCE to the calling DTE indicating status of a call.

Call Request Packet   In X.25 communications, a call supervision packet transmitted by a DTE to ask for a call establishment through the network.

cancel   To terminate.

carrier   In datacommunication, a continuous frequency capable of being modulated.

carrier sense   A device (transceiver, interface board, or other entity) capable of detecting a constant frequency.

Carrier Sense Multiple Access with Collision Detection (CSMA/CD)   A protocol utilizing equipment capable of detecting a carrier which permits multiple access to a common medium. This protocol also has the ability to detect a collision, because this type of technology is broadcast-oriented.

casual connection   In SNA, this type of connection is made in subarea networks with PU T5 nodes attached via a boundary function using low-entry networking capabilities.

Catalog   In SNA, a list of pointers to libraries, files, or datasets.

CCITT   *Comite Consultatif International Telegraphique et Telephonique.* The International Telegraph and Telephone Consultative Committee.

CCW In SNA, Channel Command Word.

CDRM In SNA, refers to Cross-Domain Resource Manager.

CDRSC In SNA, refers to Cross-Domain Resource.

Central Directory Server According to IBM documentation, an APPN network node that provides a repository for network resource locations.

Central Processing Unit (CPU) A CPU is the circuitry that executes instructions.

channel Generically speaking, a channel is a path over which data can move. In most IBM documentation, the word *channel* has a specific meaning. For example, IBM supports two types of channels today—parallel and serial.

channel adapter A device used to attach the communication controller to a host channel.

channel-attached In SNA terminology, connotes a serial or parallel data link protocol. IBM has other data link protocols, such as SDLC, ESCON, Token Ring, and so on.

channel link A data link connection between two devices.

character-coded An SNA term used in VTAM, meaning unformatted.

Chooser According to Apple documentation, an accessory that lets a user select shared devices, such as printers and file servers.

CICS Customer Information Control System.

CID Communication identifier or connection identifier.

CINIT A request sent from a SSCP to a primary logical unit requesting that a BIND command be issued.

CI Only VMScluster Configuration According to Digital Equipment, a type of VMScluster configuration in which the computer interconnect (CI) device is used for most interprocessor communication. In these configurations, a node may be a VAX processor or a Hierarchical Storage Controller (HSC).

circuit switching Connectivity on demand between DTEs and DCEs.

cladding The surrounding part of a cable that protect the core optical fibers. This part is between the fibers and the cable jacket.

class of service (COS) In SNA, class of service defines explicit routes, virtual routes, and priority, and is used to provide a variety of services within the network.

Class of Service Database In APPN, a database maintained independently by each network node, and optionally by APPN END nodes.

cleanup In SNA, a term referring to how sessions are terminated between LUs. Specifically, it is a network services request that causes a particular LU-LU session to be ended immediately.

clear indication packet A call supervision packet that data circuit-terminating equipment (DCE) transmits to inform data terminal equipment (DTE) that a call has been cleared.

clear request packet A call supervision packet transmitted by data terminal equipment (DTE) to ask that a call be cleared.

click To press and release a mouse button.

client A term used to connote peer technology. Clients are programs used to initiate something. In TCP/IP, clients can be found in TELENT and FTP. In the X windowing system, a client is typically a program that conforms to the X protocol and works in conjunction with an X server.

Client Application In Apple environments, an application using Apple Event Interprocess Messaging Protocol to request a service. For example, printing a list of files or spell-checking a list of words.

CLNP Connectionless Network Protocol. A protocol that does not perform retransmissions or perform error recovery at a transport layer.

clocking The use of clock pulses to control synchronization.

Closed User Group (CUG) A user group that can communicate with other users in the group, but not with users outside the group.

CLSDST Close destination.

cluster A network of computers in which only one computer has file-system disk drives attached to it.

Cluster Controller In SNA, this is the precursor to the establishment controller. It is a device to which terminals and printers attach. IBM's 3174 cluster controllers appear as a PU2.0.

CMC Communication Management Configuration.

CMOT The use of Common Management Information Services over TCP/IP. Succinctly, it is the implementation of the OSI network management specification over TCP/IP.

CMS Converational Monitor System.

CNM Communication Network Management.

CNN Composite Network Node.

CNOS Change Number of Sessions.

collision An event where two or more devices simultaneously perform a broadcast on the same medium. This term is used in Ethernet networks, and also in networks where broadcast technology is implemented.

collision detection This term is used to define a device that can determine when a simultaneous transmission attempt has been made.

command A request to execute an event. According to Digital Equipment, when used in reference to Digital Command Language (DCL) it means an instruction, generally an English-type word, entered by the user at a terminal or included in a command procedure.

Command Facility A component of IBM's NetView program that is the base for command processors that can monitor, control, automate, and improve the operation of an SNA network.

Command-Line Prompt   Generally, a place on a terminal where commands can be entered. The direction of these commands is contingent on the system or software from which the command line is generated. According to Hewlett-Packard's documentation, it is that which appears on the screen immediately after login. Usually the command-line prompt is either a $ (for Bourne and Korn shells) or a % (for C shells), but it can be modified. A popular modification is to print the current working directory and the history stack number before the $ or %. You can find the command-line prompt by pressing Return several times. Everytime you press Return, the HP-UX operating systems print the prompt.

Command List (CLIST)   In IBM's SNA, this is a list of commands and statements designed to perform a specific function for the user. A variety of CLISTs exists; for example, NetView, TSO, and REXX.

Common Management Information Protocol (CMIP)   The OSI protocol for systems management.

Common Management Information Service Element   The Application Service Element responsible for relaying systems management information.

Common Parent   The lowest level directory that appears in pathnames of multiple files or directories on the same volume.

communication adapter   Generally agreed to be a device (normally an interface) that provides a common point for a device and the datacommunication device being used.

Communication Controller   A control unit whose operations are controlled by one or more programs stored and executed in the unit. In most instances it manages lines and routing of data through a network.

communication control unit   A communication device that controls transmission of data over lines in a network.

Communication Identifier (CID)   A VTAM key for locating the control blocks that represent a session. This key is created during session establishment and is deleted when the session ends.

communication line   Deprecated term for telecommunication line.

Communication Network Management (CNM)   According to IBM documentation, as applied to SNA, the process of designing, installing, operating, and managing distribution of information and control among users of communication systems.

Communication Network Management (CNM) Application Program   According to IBM documentation, a VTAM application that issues and receives formatted management services request units for PUs. NetView is an example of a CNM application program.

Communication Network Management (CNM) Interface   A common point where applications can move data and commands to the access method. This data and these commands are associated with communication system management.

component   Generally speaking, hardware or software.

composite LEN node A group of nodes made up of a single type 5 node and subordinate type 4 nodes. To a type 2.1 node, a composite LEN node appears as one LEN node. An example of a composite LEN node is NCP and VTAM.

Composite Network Node (CNN) A group of nodes made up of a type 5 node and its subordinate type 4 nodes that appear as a single APPN Network Node to the APPN network.

Composite Node In IBM networking, specifically SNA with VTAM, a type 5 node and its owned type 4 nodes that collectively appear as a single node to other APPN nodes in an APPN network.

Computer Interconnect (CI) A fault-tolerant, dual-path bus, with a bandwidth of 70 Mbps.

Concurrency Controls Methods provided by Btrieve to resolve possible conflicts when two applications attempt to update or delete the same records at the same time.

configuration The manner in which the hardware and software of an information processing system are organized and interconnected.

Configuration Restart In SNA, the VTAM recovery facility that can be used after a failure or deactivation of a major node, VTAM, or the host processor to restore the domain to its status at the time of the failure or deactivation.

configuration services A type of network services in a control point. Configuration services activate, deactivate, and record the status of PUs, links, and link stations.

congestion loss In Digital Equipment's DECnet, a condition in which data packets transmitted over a network are lost when the DECnet for Open VMS Routing layer is unable to buffer them.

connected To have a physical path from one point to another.

connection In datacommunications two types of connections exist: physical and logical. A physical connection consists of a tangible path between two or more points. A logical connection is a capability to communicate between two or more endpoints.

Connection Control Block A data structure that is used by ADSP to store state information about the connection end.

Connection End The combination of an AppleTalk socket and the ADSP information maintained by the socket client.

connectionless internetworking A set of subnetworks connected physically whereby their nature is capable of providing connectionless network service.

connectionless service A network service that delivers data or packets as separate pieces. An example of this type of service is TCP/IP's Internet Protocol (IP).

Connection Listening Socket A socket that accepts ADSP requests to open connections and passes them on to a socket client.

Connection Network   A representation within an APPN network of a shared-access transport facility (SATF), such as a token ring, that allows nodes identifying their connectivity to the SATF by a common virtual routing node to communicate without having individually defined connections to one another.

connection-oriented internetworking   A set of subnetworks connected physically whereby their nature is capable of connection-oriented network service.

connection-oriented service   A type of service offered in some networks. This type of service has three phases: connection establishment, data transfer, and connection release.

Connection Server   A program that accepts an open connection request passed to it by a connection listener and selects a socket to respond to the request.

connectivity   The notion of device communication interchange, even if such devices are diverse.

Console Communication Services (CCS)   In SNA environments, services that act as an interface between the control program and the VSCS component of VTAM for VM.

contention   A term frequently used in SNA. It has multiple meanings, depending upon the context. One example is how a session can be explained. In this case, the network accessible units attempt to initiate the same action at the same time against each other. Another example is contention in LU6.2. Here, it is the attempt to allocate a session by two programs against each other, at the same time.

context   Information on a process maintained by the Process Manager.

context dependence   When the glyph corresponding to a character can be modified depending on the preceding and following characters.

continue-any mode   Specifies whether VTAM is to receive the data in terms of logical records or buffers.

continue-specific mode   In IBM's VTAM, the state of a session or APPC conversation permitting its input to satisfy only RECEIVE requests issued in specific-mode.

contour   A closed loop in a TrueType outline glyph, defined by a group of outline points.

control block   A storage area that holds control information.

controller   A device that coordinates and controls the operation of one or more input/output devices.

Controlling Application Program   According to IBM documentation, an application program which a secondary logical unit (other than an application program) is automatically put in session with whenever the secondary logical unit is available.

controlling logical unit   Either an application program or a device-type LU.

control logical unit (CLU)   A logical unit that resides in a Transaction Processing Facility (TPF) type 2.1 node. It is used to pass private protocol requests between the TPF type 2.1 node and the logon manager, which is a VTAM application program. Communication flow between the CLU and the logon manager enables a logical unit controlled by VTAM to establish a session with TPF.

control panel   A place that allows a user to set or "control" a feature of some sort.

Control Panels Folder   In Apple documentation, a directory located in the System Folder for storing control panels. This allows users to modify their work environments on Apple or Macintosh computers.

control point (CP)   The managing component of a type 2.1 node that manages the resources of that node. In an APPN network node, the CP can engage in CP-CP sessions with other APPN nodes.

Control Program   Normally this type of program performs system-oriented functions, such as scheduling and supervising execution of programs of a computer system. In IBM's Account Interactive eXecutive, it is that part of the operating system that determines the order in which basic functions should be performed.

Control Vector   A particular structure that is one of a general class of RU substructures, basically characterized by a variable length and having a 1-byte key that is used as an identifier.

conversation   A logical connection between two transaction programs using an LU 6.2 session.

Conversational Monitor System (CMS)   An IBM Virtual Machine (VM) operating system facility that provides interactive time sharing, problem solving, and program development capabilities. CMS operates under control of the Control Program component of a VM system.

converted command   An intermediate form of a character-coded command produced by VTAM through use of an unformatted system services definition table. Converted command format is fixed. The Unformatted System Services (USS) table must be constructed in such a manner that character-coded commands are converted into the predefined, converted command format.

Core Apple Event   According to Apple documentation, an event that nearly all applications can use to communicate.

COS   Class of service.

cost   According to Digital Equipment documentation, a numeric value assigned to a circuit that exists between two adjacent nodes. In the DECnet for Open VMS network, data packets are routed on paths with the lowest cost.

CP   Control Point or Control Program. A Control Point is a part of T2.1 architecture. A Control Program in IBM terminology is that software that runs on a VM host. The CP communicates with the hardware.

CP capabilities   One definition, according to IBM documentation, is the level of network services provided by the control point (CP) in an APPN end node or network node. Control Program capabilities are exchanged during the activation of CP-CP sessions between nodes.

CPCB   Control Program Control Block or Control Point Control Block.

CP-CP session   A parallel session between two control points, using LU 6.2 protocols and a mode name of CPSVCMG, on which network services requests and replies are exchanged.

CP name   The name of a control point (CP), consisting of a network ID qualifier identifying the network to which the CP's node belongs, and a unique name within the scope of that network ID identifying the CP. Each APPN or LEN END node has one CP name, assigned to it at system-definition time.

CPU   Central Processing Unit.

Cross-Domain   In SNA, refers to resources in a different domain. Domains, in SNA, have to do ownership.

Cross-Domain Keys   In SNA, a pair of cryptographic keys used by a System Services Control Point (SSCP) to encipher the session cryptography key that is sent to another SSCP.

Cross-Domain Link   A subarea link connecting two subareas that are in different domains. A physical link connecting two domains.

Cross-Domain Resource (CDRSC)   A term used in SNA refering to a resource (typically software) that resides in another domain, under the control of a different VTAM.

Cross-Domain Resource Manager (CDRM)   In SNA, refers to the function in the SSCP that controls initiation and termination of cross-domain sessions.

Cross-Network LU-LU Session   In SNA, a session between logical units (LUs) in different networks.

Cross-Network Session   A session whose path traverses more than one SNA network.

cryptographic   In SNA, a term pertaining to transformation of data to conceal its meaning.

Cryptographic Session   In SNA, an LU-LU session in which a Function Management Data (FMD) request may be enciphered before it is transmitted and deciphered after it is received.

CSA   Common Service Area or Common Storage Area.

CSALIMIT   Common Service Area (CSA) buffer use limit.

CSMA/CD   Carrier Sense Multiple Access with Collision Detection.

CSP   Communication Scanner Processor.

CUA   In SNA, particularly in VTAM, a term referring to the channel unit address.

currency   The previous, current, and next position of a record in a file. There are two types of currency: logical and physical. The physical previous, current, and next positions form the physical currency. The logical previous, current, and next positions form the logical currency. According to Zac, it means money.

Customer Information Control System (CICS) An IBM software program that supports realtime transactions between remote users and custom written transactions. It includes facilities for building, using, and maintaining databases.

cut buffer A memory area that holds text which has been deleted from a file.

CWALL An NCP threshold of buffer availability, below which the NCP will accept only high-priority Path Information Units (PIUs).

cycle A complete oscillation of a wave.

DARPA Defense Advanced Research Projects Agency, formerly called ARPA. The government agency that funded research and experimentation with the ARPANET.

DASD Direct Access Storage Device. This is IBM's terminology for a disk drive in mainframe environments.

database A collection of data with a given structure.

data channel An IBM term used as a synonym for input/output channel.

data circuit A pair of associated transmit and receive channels providing a means for two-way data communication.

Data Circuit-Terminating Equipment (DCE) In a data station, equipment that provides signal conversion and coding between the data terminal equipment (DTE) and the line.

datacommunication Transfer of data among functional units by means of data transmission according to a protocol. The transmission, reception, and validation of data.

Data Encryption Standard (DES) In computer security, the National Institute of Standards and Technology (NIST) Data Encryption Standard, adopted by the United States government as Federal Information Processing Standard (FIPS) Publication 46, which allows only hardware implementations of the data encryption algorithm.

Data Flow Control (DFC) In SNA, a request or response unit (RU) category used for requests and responses exchanged between the data flow control layer in one half-session and the data flow control layer in the session partner.

Datagram Delivery Protocol In AppleTalk networks, a protocol that provides socket-to-socket delivery of data packets.

Data Host Node In SNA, a host dedicated to processing applications that does not control network resources, except for its channel-attached or communication adapter-attached devices.

data link In SNA, a synonym for link.

Data Link Control (DLC) A set of rules used by nodes at a layer 2 within a network. The data link is governed by data link protocols, such as Ethernet or Token Ring.

Data Link Control (DLC) Protocol Rules used by two nodes at a data link layer to accomplish an orderly exchange of information. For example, Ethernet, Channel, FDDI, or Token Ring.

Data Link Layer   Layer 2 of the OSI Reference Model. It synchronizes transmission and handles error correction for a data link.

Data Link Level   The conceptual level of control logic between high-level logic and a data link protocol that maintains control of the data link.

Data Network   An arrangement of data circuits and switching facilities for establishing connections between data terminal equipment. A term commonly found in X.25 network implementations.

Data Packet   In X.25, a packet used for the transmission of user data on a virtual circuit at the DTE/DCE interface.

Data Server   According to a common definition in Apple documentation, an application that acts like an interface between a database extension on a Macintosh computer and a data source, which can be on the Macintosh computer or on a remote host computer. It can be a database server program that can provide an interface to a variety of different databases, or it can be the data source itself, such as a Macintosh application.

Data Set   A way that data, programs, and other representations of information are stored in IBM's MVS operating system environment.

Data Stream   In SNA, multiple data streams are identified. Generally, a continuous stream of data elements being transmitted, in character or binary-digit form, using a defined format.

Data Switching Exchange (DSE)   Equipment at a single location that provides switching functions, such as circuit switching, message switching, and packet switching.

Data Terminal Equipment (DTE)   That part of a data station which constitutes a data source, data link, or both.

Data Types   IN SNA, particularly NetView, they can be alerts, events, and statistics.

Data Unit   In the OSI environment, it is the smallest unit of a file content meaningful to an FTAM file action.

DBCS   Double-Byte Character Set.

DC   Data Chaining.

DCE   Distributed Computing Environment or Data Circuit-Terminating Equipment.

DCE Clear Confirmation Packet   A call supervision packet that a DCE transmits to confirm that a call has been cleared.

DCSS   Discontiguous Shared Segment.

DDname   Data Definition Name.

deactivate   A term frequently used in SNA environments. It means to take a resource out of service.

deallocate   A term used in APPC whereby a LU6.2 application program interface (API) terminates a conversation and makes the session free for a future conversation.

decipher   To convert enciphered data in order to restore the original data.

decrypt   In computer security, to decipher or decode. Synonym for decipher.

defacto standard   A standard that is the result of some technology that has been developed and used and has achieved some level of popularity.

default SSCP list   In VTAM, a list of SSCPs to which a session request can be routed when a cross-domain resource manager (CDRM) is not specified.

Defense Data Network (DDN)   Used loosely to refer to MILNET, ARPANET, and the TCP/IP protocols they use. More specifically, it is MILNET and associated parts of the connected Internet that connect military installations.

Defined Context Set   A set of presentation contexts negotiated between peer presentation entities.

Definite Response (DR)   According to IBM documentation, in SNA it is a protocol that requests the receiver of the request to return a response unconditionally, whether positive or negative, to that request chain.

Definition Statement   In IBM's VTAM program, this statement describes an element of the network. In IBM's NCP, it is a type of instruction that defines a resource.

de jure standard   A standard set by a body or by official concensus.

DELTA disk   In SNA, the virtual disk in a VM operating system that contains Program Temporary Fixes (PTFs) that have been installed but not yet merged.

descent line   An imaginary line usually marking the furthest distance below the base line of the descenders of glyphs in a particular font.

descriptor   A data buffer parameter passed for an Extended Get or Extended Step operation.

descriptor type   An identifier for the type of data referred to by the handle in a descriptor record.

Desktop Folder   In Apple environments, a directory, located at the root level of each volume. It is used by the Finder for storing information about the icons that appear on the desktop area of the screen. The Desktop Folder is invisible to the user. It is what the user sees on screen.

Destination Logical Unit (DLU)   The logical unit to which data is to be sent.

DEV   Device Address Field.

device   When used in networking scenarios, the term is typically used generically. For example, it could be a modem, host, terminal, or other entity.

dial-in   In most SNA environments, the notion of inbound traffic towards the host.

dial-out   In most networking environments, the notion of outbound capabilities to access resources elsewhere.

DIGITAL Command Language   According to Digital Equipment documentation, a command interpreter in the operating system. It provides a means of communication between the user and the operating system.

Digital Data Communication Message Protocol (DDCMP)   According to Digital Equipment documentation, the link level protocol that Digital Equipment Corporation uses in its network products. DDCMP operates over serial lines, delimits frames by a special character, and includes checksums at the link level. It is relevant to TCP/IP because the original NSFNET used DDCMP over its backbone lines.

DIGITAL Network Architecture   According to Digital Equipment, a set of protocols governing the format, control, and sequencing of message-exchange for all Digital network implementations. The protocols are layered, and they define rules for data exchange from the physical link level up through the user interface level. DNA controls all data that travels throughout a Digital network. DNA also defines standard network management and network generation procedures.

Digital Storage Architecture   According to Digital Equipment documentation, the specifications from Digital governing the design of and interface to mass storage products. DSA defines the functions to be performed by host computers, controllers, and drives, and specifies how they interact to manage mass storage.

Digital Storage Systems Interconnect   A data bus that uses the System Communication Architecture protocols for direct host-to-storage communications. The DSSI cable can extend to 6 m and has a peak bandwidth of 4 MB.

Direct Access Storage Device (DASD)   A device in which access time is effectively independent of the location of the data.

Direct Activation   According to IBM documentation, the activation of a resource as a result of an activation command specifically naming the resource.

Direct Deactivation   According to IBM documentation, the deactivation of a resource as a result of a deactivation command specifically naming the resource.

Directed Broadcast Address   In TCP/IP based environments, an IP address that specifies all hosts on a specific network. A single copy of a directed broadcast is routed to the specified network where it is broadcast to all machines on that network.

Directed Locate Search   A search request sent to a specific destination node known to contain a resource, such as a logical unit, to verify the continued presence of the resource at the destination node and to obtain the node's connectivity information for route calculation.

Directed Search   Synonym for Directed Locate Search.

Directory   Depending upon the environment, this term is used in different ways. For example, in UNIX environments a directory is a listing of files and the files themselves. This definition is generally the case in most environments; however, some vendors contend that a significant difference exists. In IBM's VM/SP environment, it is a control program (CP) disk file that defines each virtual machine's normal configuration: the user ID, password, normal and maximum allowable virtual storage, CP command privilege classes allowed, dispatching priority, logical editing symbols to be used, account number, and CP options desired. In APPN, it is a database that lists names of resources and records the CP name of the node where each resource is located. Another definition of a directory is the subdivision of a volume, available in the Hierarchical File System. A directory can contain files and other directories.

Directory Access Protocol The protocol used between a Directory User Agent and a Directory System Agent.

Directory Entry An object in the Directory Information Base to model information. It can be an object entry or an alias entry.

Directory Information Base A set of Directory entries. It contains objects to which the Directory provides access and which include all of the pieces of information that can be read or manipulated using the Directory operations.

Directory Information Shadowing Protocol A protocol used for shadowing between two Directory Service Agents in the Directory Services standard.

Directory Information Tree A tree structure of the Directory Information Base.

Directory Name Names for Directory entries in the Directory Information Base.

Directory Operational Binding Management Protocol A protocol used by Directory Service Agents to activate showing agreement. This allows Directory Service Agents to establish, modify, and terminate operational bindings.

Directory Service (DS) According to its use in OSI environments, an application service element that translates the symbolic names used by application processes into the complete network addresses used.

Directory Service Agent An application entity that offers the Directory services.

Directory Service Protocol The protocol used between two Directory System Agents.

Directory Services (DS) A control point component of an APPN node that maintains knowledge of the location of networks resources.

Directory User Agent An application entity that provides the Directory services.

disable In a loose sense, it is similar to deactivate.

disabled Pertaining to a state of a processing unit that prevents the occurrence of certain types of interruptions.

discarded packet A piece of data, called a *packet,* that is intentionally destroyed.

disconnection Termination of a physical connection.

Discontiguous Shared Segment (DCSS)   According to IBM documentation, an area of virtual storage outside the address range of a virtual machine. It can contain read-only data or reentrant code. It connects discontiguous segments to a virtual machine's address space so programs can be fetched.

Discretionary Controls   Security controls that are applied at the user's option.

Disjoint Network   According to IBM documentation, a network of two or more subnetworks with the same network identifier that are not directly connected, but are indirectly connected; for example, through SNA network interconnection.

Disjoint SSCP   According to IBM documentation, an SSCP that does not have a direct SSCP-SSCP session with other SSCPs in its network-ID subnetwork.

Disk Cache   A part of RAM that acts as an intermediate buffer when data is read from and written to file systems on secondary storage devices.

display   Generally, used to refer to a terminal.

Display Server   As defined in X Window System arenas, it is the software that controls the communication between client programs and the display, including the keyboard, mouse, and screen combination.

Distinguished Name   Name of a Directory entry.

Distributed Computing Environment (DCE)   An Open Software Foundation (OSF) set of standards for distributed computing. Also, DCE is distributed computing in the general sense of the term.

Distributed Directory Database   According to documentation related to IBM's APPN architecture, the complete listing of all resources in the network as maintained in individual directories scattered throughout an APPN network.

Distributed Network Directory   Synonym for distributed directory database.

DLU   Destination logical unit.

DNS   Domain Name Service. In TCP/IP environments, a protocol for matching object names and network addresses. It was designed to replace the need to update/etc/hosts files of participating entities throughout a network.

Domain   That part of a computer network in which the data processing resources are under common control. In TCP/IP environments, a part of the DNS naming hierarchy. Syntactically, a domain name consists of a sequence of names separated by periods.

Domain Name System (DNS)   The online distributed database system used to map human-readable machine names into IP addresses. DNS servers throughout the connected Internet implement a hierarchical namespace that allows sites freedom in assigning machine names and addresses. DNS also supports separate mappings between mail destinations and IP addresses.

Domain Operator   According to IBM documentation, a person or program that controls operation of resources controlled by one SSCP.

Domain Search   In the context of APPN networking, a search initiated by a network node to all of its client APPN END nodes when a search request is received by a network node and that network node does not have any entry in its database for the requested resource.

Dotted Decimal Notation   A phase typically found in TCP/IP network conversations. Specifically, this refers to the addressing scheme of the Internet Protocol (IP). It is the representation of a 32-bit address consisting of four 8-bit numbers written in base 10 with periods separating them.

Double-Byte Character Set (DBCS)   A set of characters in which each character is represented by 2 bytes. For example, languages like Japanese, Chinese, and Korean use this method to represent characters.

Downline System Load   According to Digital Equipment documentation, a DECnet for Open VMS function that permits an unattended target node to receive an operating system file image or terminal server image from another node.

DR   In SNA, dynamic reconfiguration or definite response.

drag   In Apple and X window environments, to press and hold down a mouse button while moving the mouse on the desktop. Typically, dragging is used with menu selecting, moving, and resizing operations.

drain   In APPC, to honor pending allocation requests before deactivating session with a partner logical unit.

DRDS   Dynamic Reconfiguration Data Set.

drop cable   In the IBM Cabling System, a cable that runs from a faceplate to the distribution panel in a wiring closet. In TCP/IP networking environments where thicknet cable and transceivers are used, that cable between the devices' network interface card and the transceiver.

Drop Folder   In Apple environments, a type of folder (holding place) that serves as a private mailbox for individuals. Once someone places a file in a drop folder, only the owner of the drop folder can retrieve it. According to Apple documentation, users can create drop folders by setting the appropriate Apple-Share or Macintosh file sharing access privileges.

DS   Desired state, Directory Service, or Directory Services.

DSE   Data Switching Exchange.

DSECT   Dummy Control Section.

DSname   Data Set Name.

DSRLST   Direct Search List. In SNA, a message unit that contains a search request sent throughout subarea networks to obtain information about a network resource, such as its name, routing information, and status information.

DTE   Data Terminal Equipment.

DTE/DCE interface   The physical interface and link access procedures between data terminal equipment (DTE) and data circuit-terminating equipment (DCE).

dump   A term used frequently in SNA environments. Typically, it means to obtain to the contents of some aspect of memory. Specifically, it means to record, at a particular instant, the contents of all or part of one storage device in another storage device. One noted professional in the field, namely Zelma Gandy, defines a dump as "The contents of memory used for debugging." A *core dump* refers to extracting the contents of main memory. A *VTAM dump* is used loosely to refer to reading data areas in IBM's VTAM program offering.

duplex   Pertaining to communication in which data can be sent and received at the same time.

DVT   Destination Vector Table.

dynamic   In a generic sense, to do something on the fly. A more specific explanation is to perform an operation that does not require a predetermined or fixed time.

Dynamic Node ID Assignment   According to Apple documentation, the AppleTalk addressing scheme that assigns node IDs dynamically, rather than associating a permanent address with each node. Dynamic node ID assignment facilitates addition and removal of nodes from the network by preventing conflicts between old node IDs and new node IDs.

dynamic path update   A generic reference meaning the process of changing network path parameters for sending information without regenerating complete configuration tables.

Dynamic Reconfiguration Data Set (DRDS)   According to IBM documentation, a term used in VTAM. It refers to a data set used for storing definition data that can be applied to a generated communication controller configuration at the operator's request, or can be used to accomplish dynamic reconfiguration of NCP, local SNA, and packet major nodes. This type of reconfiguration data set can be used to dynamically add PUs and LUs, delete PUs and LUs, and move PUs. It is activated with the VARY DREDS operator command.

dynamic window   A window that may change its title or reposition any of the objects within its content area.

EBCDIC   Extended Binary-Coded Decimal Interchange Code. IBM's basic character set used to represent data within the SNA environment. It consists of 8-bit coded characters.

echo   In datacommunication, a reflected signal on a communications channel.

electromagnetic interference (EMI)   A type of noise that is the result of currents induced in electric conductors.

Electronic Data Interchange (EDI)   A set of standard data formats for electronic information exchange.

element   This term has meanings in different networking environments. In SNA, the particular resource within a subarea that is identified by an element address.

element address   According to IBM documentation, a value in the element address field of the network address identifying a specific resource within a subarea.

Emulation Program (EP)   A program that simulates the functions of another program. A generic example could be a 3270 terminal emulation program. Other possibilities also exist.

EN In IBM's APPN architecture manuals, an APPN End node.

enable To make functional. In a loose sense, to activate.

enabled The state of being capable of performing work.

encapsulate Generally agreed upon in the internetworking community to mean surrounding one protocol with another protocol for the purpose of passing the foreign protocol through the native environment.

encipher According to IBM documentation, to scramble data or to convert it to a secret code that masks the meaning of the data to any unauthorized recipient. In VTAM, to convert clear data into enciphered data.

encrypt Synonym for encipher.

encryption The process of transforming data into an unintelligible form.

end bracket A term specifically used in SNA. It is the value of the end bracket indicator in the request header (RH) of the first request of the last chain of the bracket. The value denotes the end of the bracket.

END Node With reference to APPN, a node that can receive packets addressed to it and send packets to other nodes. It cannot route packets from other nodes.

END Node Domain That area defined by an END node control point, attached links, and its local LUs.

end user Defined by IBM documentation as either a program or a human.

end-user verification LU6.2 identification check of end users by means of identifiers and passwords on the attached Function Management Headers (FMHs).

Entry Mask According to Digital Equipment documentation, on VAX systems, a word where the bits represent the registers to be saved when a procedure is called with a CALLS or CALLG instruction, and restored when the procedure executes a RET instruction.

entry point According to IBM documentation, a type 2.0, 2.1, 4, or 5 node that provides distributed network management support. It sends network management data about itself and the resources it controls to a focal point for centralized processing, and it receives and executes focal-point initiated commands to manage and control its resources.

EP Emulation Program.

ER Explicit Route or Exception Response.

ERP Error recovery procedures.

ES-IS Routing An Open Systems term used to refer a routing exchange protocol that provides an automated means for ISs and ESs on a subnetwork to dynamically determine the existence of each other. It also means to permit an IS to inform an ES of a potentially better route towards a destination.

Ethernet A data link level protocol. It (version 2.0) was defined by Digital Equipment Corporation, Intel Corporation, and the Xerox Corporation in 1982. It specified a data rate of 10 Mbps, a maximum station distance of 2.8 km, maximum number of stations as 1024, a shielded coaxial cable using baseband signalling, functionality of CSMA/CD, and a best-effort delivery system.

Ethernet meltdown A term used where Ethernet protocol is used as the data link layer protocol in a network. It is an event that causes saturation or near saturation on an Ethernet data link. This scenario usually results from illegal or misrouted packets and lasts a short time.

EtherTalk A term used in Apple and Ethernet environments. It is software that enables AppleTalk protocols to run over industry-standard Ethernet technology.

event This term can mean a predefined occurance in a given network. It has a specific meaning in SNA; in NetView it is a record indicating irregularities of operation in the physical elements of a network.

Event Class According to Apple documentation, an attribute that identifies a group of related Apple events. The event class appears in the message field of the Apple event's event record. In conjunction with the event ID attribute, the event class specifies what action an Apple event performs.

Event ID According to Apple documentation, an attribute that identifies a particular Apple event within a group of related Apple events. The event class appears in the where field of the Apple event's event record. In conjunction with the event class attribute, the event ID specifies what action an Apple event performs.

exception An abnormal condition when compared to what has been predefined as a normal condition.

Exception Response (ER) According to IBM documentation, a protocol requested in the for-of-response-requested field of a Request Header that directs the receiver to return a response only if the request is unacceptable as received or cannot be processed.

Exception Service Routine According to Digital Equipment documentation, a routine by which VAX and AXP hardware initially pass control to service an exception. An exception service routine passes control to a general exception dispatcher that attempts to locate a condition handler to further service the exception.

Exchange Identification (XID) In SNA, a specific type of Basic Link Unit that is used to convey node and link characteristics between adjacent nodes. In the SNA network, XIDs are exchanged between link stations before and during link activation to establish and negotiate link and node characteristics, and after link activation to communicate changes in these characteristics.

EXEC According to IBM documentation, in a VM operating system, a user-written command file that contains CMS commands, other user-written commands, and execution control statements, such as branches.

executable image An image that can be run in a process. When run, an executable image is read from a file for execution in a process.

executive A generic name for the collection of procedures included in the operating system software that provides the operating system's basic control and monitoring functions.

Executive Mode   According to Digital Equipment documentation, the second most privileged processor access mode. The Open VMS Record Management Services and many of the operating system's system service procedures execute in executive mode.

exit   To execute an instruction within a portion of a program in order to terminate the execution of that portion.

Exit List (EXLST)   According to IBM documentation, in VTAM a control block that contains the addresses of routines that receive control when specified events occur during execution.

exit program   Synonym for exit routine.

exit routine   One of two types of routines: Installation exit routes or User exit routes.

EXLST   Exit List.

Expedited Flow   According to IBM's documentation, a data flow designated in the transmission header (TH) used to carry network control, session control, and various data flow control request/response units (RUs). Expedited flow is separate from the normal flow, which carries primarily end-user data.

Explicit Route (ER)   According to IBM's documentation, in SNA a series of one or more transmission groups that connect two subarea nodes. It is identified by an origin subarea address, a destination subarea address, an explicit route number, and a reverse explicit route number.

Explicit Route Length   The number of transmission groups in an explicit route.

EXT   External Trace File.

Extended Architecture (XA)   According to IBM documentation, an extension to System/370 architecture. It takes advantage of changing such factors as the addressability of the hardware architecture.

Extended Attribute Block   According to Digital Equipment documentation, an Open VMS Record Management Services user data structure that contains additional file attributes beyond those expressed in the file access block, such as boundary types and file protection information.

Extended Binary-Coded Decimal Interchange Code (EBCDIC)   IBM's coded character set of 256 8-bit characters and control functions.

Extended Network Addressing   In IBM's traditional subarea networking, the addressing system that splits addresses into an 8-bit subarea and a 15-bit element portion. The subarea portion of the address is used to address host processors or communication controllers. The element portion is used to permit processors or controllers to address resources.

Extended Recovery Facility (XRF)   In SNA, a facility that provides an alternate subsystem to take over sessions from the failing subsystem.

Extended Subarea Addressing   According to IBM documentation, a network addressing system used in a network with more than 255 subareas.

fan out box   A term used in local area network circles that refers to a device that functions like a hub. It provides the capability for multiple connections to make a central conection.

FDDI   Fiber Distributed Data Interface.

FDDI   Fiber Distributed Data Interface. An IEEE 802 compatible physical and data link control standard for a 100-Mbps fiber ring.

FDM   Frequency Division Multiplexing. A technique that provides for division of frequency bandwidth into smaller subbands to provide each user the exclusive use of a subband.

FH   Frame handler.

Fiber Distributed Data Interface (FDDI)   An American National Standards Institute (ANSI) standard for a 100-Mbps LAN using optical fibers. A data link protocol compatable to the IEEE 802 specification.

Field-Formatted   In SNA, this pertains to requests or responses that are encoded into fields, each having a specified format, such as binary codes, bit-significant flags, and symbolic names.

FIFO   First-in-first-out.

File Definition Language   According to Digital Equipment documentation, a special purpose language used to write specifications for data files. These specifications are written in text files called FDL files; they are then used by Open VMS Record Management Services utilities and library routines to create the actual data files.

File Filter Function   According to Apple documentation, a function supplied by the application for determining which files the user can open through a standard file dialog box.

File Header   According to Digital Equipment documentation, a block in the index file describing a file on a Files-11 disk structure. The file header contains information needed by the file system to find and use the file. Some of this information is displayed when the DCL command DIRECTORY is entered. There is at least one file header for every file on the disk.

File ID   In the Apple environment, an unchanging number assigned by the File Manager to identify a file on a volume. When it establishes a file ID, the File Manager records the filename and parent directory ID of the file.

File Identifier   According to Digital Equipment documentation, a 6-byte value used to uniquely identify a file on a Files-11 disk volume. The file number, file sequence number, and relative volume number are contained in the file identifier.

File Organization   In Digital Equipment networks, the particular file structure used as the physical arrangement of the data comprising a file on a mass storage media. The Open VMS Record Management Services file organizations are sequential, relative, and indexed.

File Access Data Unit   A subtree of the hierarchical access structure. It is used to specify a location on a file structure.

file attributes Term originating in OSI that refers to the properties of a file that do not depend on an FTAM dialogue.

File Directory The OSI equivalent of a directory in a file system.

Files-11 A Digital Equipment term used to refer to the name of the structure used by the RSX-111, IAS, and Open VMS operating systems.

Files-11 Ancillary Control Process A Digital Equipment term refering to the interface process that is the files manager for the Files-11 on-disk structure.

Files-11 On-Disk Structure Level 1 According to Digital Equipment documentation, the original Files-11 structure used by IAS, RSX-11M, and RSX-11S for disk volumes. VAX systems support structure level 1 to ensure compatibility among systems. AXP systems do not support structure level 1.

Files-11 On-Disk Structure Level 2 Digital Equipment reference to the second-generation disk file structure supported by the operating system. The Files-11 data structure prepares a volume to receive and store data in a way recognized by the operating system.

file server A generic term used to refer to a computer whose primary task is to control the storage and retrieval of data from hard disks. Any number of other computers can be linked to the file server in order to use it to access data. This means that less storage space is required on the individual computer.

File System Specification Record In Apple computer environments, a record that identifies a stored file or directory by volume reference number, parent directory ID, and name. The file system specification record is the file identification convention adopted by system software version 7.0.

File Transfer, Access, and Management An OSI application protocol standard which allows remote files to be transferred, accessed, and managed.

file translator A generic term referring to a utility program that converts a file from one computer format to another, such as from Macintosh to DOS. Apple File Exchange is a file translator that is supplied with Macintosh system software.

filter A device or program that separates data, signals, or material in accordance with specified criteria.

Flow Control In SNA, the process of managing data rate transfer between components within the network. This same concept refers to other networking environments.

FMH Function Management Header.

Focal Point According to IBM documentation, in NetView the focal point domain is the central host domain. It is the central control point for any management services element containing control of the network management data.

font size The size of the glyphs in a font in points, measured from the base line of one line of text to the base line of the next line of single-spaced text.

font style How a font (character or number) is represented.

Foreground Process A process currently interacting with the user. In the X window system, a process that has the terminal window's attention. This is in contrast to a background process.

Formatted System Services In IBM's SNA, specifically VTAM, a portion of VTAM that provides certain system services as a result of receiving a field-formatted command, such as an Initiate or Terminate command.

fragment A term used in TCP/IP network environments. One of the pieces that results when an IP router divides an IP datagram into smaller pieces for transmission across a network. Fragments use the same format as datagrams. Fields in the IP header declare whether a datagram is a fragment and, if so, the offset of the fragment in the original datagram. IP software at the receiving end must reassemble fragments into complete datagrams.

frame One definition generally agreed upon is a packet as it is transmitted across a serial line. The term originated from character-oriented protocols. In OSI environments, it is a data structure pertaining to a particular area of data. It also consists of slots that can accept values of specific attributes.

Frame Relay A protocol defined by the CCITT and ANSI that identifies how data frames are switched in higher speeds than X.25, but in packet mode.

Frame-Relay Frame Handler (FRFH) A term reflecting a router function that uses the address field in a frame-relay frame.

Frame-Relay Switching Equipment (FRSE) In Frame Relay environments, a device capable of relaying frames to the next device in a frame-relay network en route to a frame-relay terminal equipment (FRTE) destination.

Frame-Relay Switching Equipment (FRSE) Subport Set In Frame Relay technology, the set of primary and, optionally, substitute subports within an FRSE that comprise those used for a given segment set.

Frame-Relay Switching Equipment (FRSE) Support An agreed-upon set of NCP frame-relay functions that includes the frame-relay frame handler (FRFH) functions, defined by American National Standards Institute (ANSI) Standards T1.617 and T1.618.

Frame-Relay Terminal Equipment (FRTE) In Frame Relay technology based networks, a device capable of connecting to a frame-relay network. An FRTE adds a frame header when sending data to the frame-relay network and removes the frame header when receiving data from the frame-relay network.

frequency The rate of signal oscillation, expressed in hertz.

frequency division multiplexing (FDM) A method of multiplexing data on a carrier channel based upon frequency.

FRFH Frame-Relay Frame Handler.

FRSE Frame-Relay Switching Equipment.

FRTE Frame-Relay Terminal Equipment.

FTAM A term from the OSI networking protocols. It manipulates File Transfer, Access, and Management.

FTP (File Transfer Protocol) In TCP/IP based networks, a program that runs as a TCP application. It does not move a file from one place to another, rather it copies a source file to a destination file. Consequently, two files exist unless one is deleted. FTP consist of a client and server. The FTP client is used to invoke the FTP program. The FTP server is used to serve the request of the client. In normal implementations, FTP uses ports 20 and 21.

full duplex (FDX)   Synonym for duplex.

full-screen mode   Where the contents of an entire terminal screen can be displayed at once.

Function Management Header (FMH)   According to IBM documentation, one or more headers, optionally present in the leading request units (RUs) of an RU chain, that allow one LU to select a transaction program or device at the session partner. It also permits other control functions, such as changing the destination or the characteristics of the data during the session, and transmitting between session partners status or user information about the destination.

gateway   In internetworking terminology, the agreed-upon definition is to perform protocol conversion between dissimilar protocols. This may be upper-layer protocol conversion only, or it may include lower-layer protocol conversion as well; this depends upon the vendor offering and the implementation. For example, TCP/IP to SNA, DECnet to SNA, AppleTalk to TCP/IP gateways exist, to name a few. In SNA, IBM uses the term in multiple ways. One explanation, according to IBM documentation, is the combination of machines and programs that provide address translation, name translation, and SSCP rerouting between independent SNA networks. In SNA, a gateway consists of one gateway NCP and at least one gateway VTAM.

Gateway-Capable Host   According to IBM documentation, a host node that has a defined NETID and SSCPNAME but does not perform gateway control functions.

Gateway NCP   According to IBM documentation, an NCP that performs address translation permitting cross-network session traffic. In this sense the gateway NCP connects two or more independent SNA networks.

Gateway VTAM   According to IBM documentation, a SSCP capable of cross-network session initiation, termination, takedown, and session outage notification.

GCS   Group Control System.

GDDM   Graphical Data Display Manager.

Generalized Trace Facility (GTF)   In SNA, an optional program that records significant system events, such as supervisor calls and start I/O operations, for the purpose of problem determination.

generation   In SNA, the process of assembling and link editing definition statements so that resources can be identified to all the necessary programs in a network. This is the origin of the term GEN.

generation definition   According to IBM documentation, the definition statement of a resource used in generating a program.

generic unbind   Synonym for session deactivation request.

global   Affecting the entire file, the entire system, or the entire image, depending on context.

global symbol   Agreed upon as a symbol defined in a module of a program potentially available for reference by another module. The linker resolves (matches references with definitions) global symbols.

Global Symbol Table   In a library, an index of defined global symbols used to access the modules defining the global symbols. The linker also puts global symbol tables into an image.

glyph   A distinct visual representation of a character that a display device, such as a monitor or printer, can display.

Gold Key   According to Digital Equipment documentation, the upper left key on VT100 series terminal keypads. This enables alternate keypad functions.

GOSIP   Government Open Systems Interconnect Profile; a Federal Information Processing Standard that specifies a well-defined set of OSI protocols for government communications systems procurement. GOSIP was intended to eliminate the use of TCP/IP protocols on government internets, but clarifications have specified that government agencies can continue to use TCP/IP.

Government OSI Profiles   Functional standards used by government agencies in their procurement of open system equipment and software.

Graphical Data Display Manager (GDDM)   According to IBM documentation, it is used in the NetView Performance Monitor (NPM), in conjunction with the Presentation Graphics Feature (PGF), to generate online graphs in the NPM Graphic Subsystem.

Gray Region   Typically used in X Window or Apple environments, a gray region defines the desktop, or the display area of all active devices, excluding the menu bar on the main screen and the rounded corners on the outermost screens. It is the area in which windows can be moved.

group   Generically defined as a set of users in a system.

Group Control System (GCS)   A VM component that provides multiprogramming and shared memory support.

GTF   Generalized Trace Facility.

guest   In the Apple environment, a user who is logged on to an AppleShare file server without a registered user name and password. A guest connot own a directory or folder.

half-duplex (HD, HDX)   Transmission in only one direction at a time.

half-duplex operation   Data link transmission where data can be in both directions one way at a time.

half-duplex transmission   Data transmission in either direction, one direction at a time.

half-open connection   A scenario where one end of a connection is established, but the other end is unreachable or has disposed of its connection information.

Half-Session   According to IBM's documentation, a session-layer component consisting of the data flow control and transmission control components. These comprise one end of a session.

hardcopy Generally a printout.

Hardware Address Also called a *hard address*. In Ethernet networks, the 48-bit address assigned to the Ethernet network interface card. In Token Ring, the 12-digit hex address assigned to the network interface card.

Hardware Monitor In SNA, a component of NetView. It is called the Network Problem Determination Application. It is used to identify network problems, such as hardware, software, and microcode.

header Control information that precedes user data in a frame or datagram that passes through networks. Specifically, this portion of a message contains control information.

heartbeat Technically known as *signal quality error* (SQE), a voltage in a receiver that can be sent to a controller (interface board) to inform the controller that collision detection is functional.

Help Balloon Typically used in Apple environments, a rounded-type window containing explanatory information for the user.

help panel A display of information concerning a particular topic requested. This is also called a *help menu*.

hertz The number of cycles per second.

Hierarchical Routing From a TCP/IP perspective, this type of routing is based on a hierarchical addressing scheme. Most TCP/IP routing is based on a two-level hierarchy in which an IP address is divided into a network portion until the datagram reaches a gateway that can deliver it directly. The concept of subnets introduces additional levels of hierarchical routing.

Hierarchy In SNA, this type of networking is considered traditional. Traditional SNA networking requires VTAM for session establishment. In networking, the term can be contrasted with Peer networking, which does not require an intervening component for session establishment.

High Performance Option (HPO) According to IBM documentation, an extension to VM/SP. The fundamental purpose of HPO is to provide performance and operation enhancements for large system environments.

home directory Generally, this concept exists in all hosts. It is the place where a user originates operations in any system. For example, in UNIX the .profile file contains the beginning place for a user. This .profile is customized for users and the beginning place, or home base, can differ. In Digital Equipment's VMS environment, the same is true but different terms are used. So it is with IBM's MVS, VM, and VSE operating systems.

hop In APPN, a portion of a route that has no intermediate nodes. It consists of only a single transmission group connecting adjacent nodes. One definition is the moving of a packet through a router.

hop count A measure of distance between two points in the Internet. Each hop count corresponds to one router separating a source from a destination (for example, a hop count of 3 indicates that three routers separate a source from a destination).

host master key   In SNA, deprecated term for master cryptography key.

Host Node   According to Digital Equipment documentation's DECnet for Open VMS network, a node that provides services for another node. For the VAX Packetnet System Interface, a node that accesses a packet switching data network by means of an X.25 multihost connector node. It is also referred to as the node that makes a device available to other nodes in a VMScluster configuration. A host node can be either a processor that adds the device to the mass storage control protocol server database or a hierarchical storage controller server. According to IBM documentation, it is defined as a processor.

host processor   A processor that controls all or part of a user application network. Normally, the data communication access method resides on this host.

HPO   High Performance Option.

hpterm   According to Hewlett-Packard's documentation, a type of terminal window, sometimes called a *terminal emulator program,* that emulates HP2622 terminals, complete with softkeys. In the HP-UX environment, the hpterm window is the default window for the user's X environment.

IAB   Internet Architecture Board. A group related to TCP/IP protocol. Specifically, a group of people who set policy and review standards for TCP/IP and the Internet. The IAB was reorganized in 1989; technically oriented individuals moved to research and engineering subgroups. See **IRTF** and **IETF**.

ICA   Integrated Communication Adapter.

ICMP   Internet Control Message Protocol. Specific to the TCP/IP protocol suite, an integral part of the Internet Protocol. It handles error and control messages. Routers and hosts use ICMP to send reports of problems about datagrams back to the original source that sent the datagram. ICMP also includes an echo request/reply used to test whether a destination is reachable and responding.

icon   A small, graphic representation of an object on the root window. Icons are found in Apple hosts as well as in the X window system.

Icon Family   In the Apple computer family of products, the set of icons that represent an object, such as an application or document, on the desktop.

ID   Identifier or identification.

Idle State   A state in which the Macintosh Portable computer slows from its normal 16 MHz clock speed to a 1MHz clock speed. The Power Manager puts the Macintosh Portable in the idle state when the system has been inactive for 15 seconds.

IEEE   Institute of Electrical and Electronic Engineers.

IETF   Internet Engineering Task Force. A group of people concerned with short-term and medium-term problems with TCP/IP and the connected Internet. IETF is divided into six areas, which are further divided into working groups.

ILU   Independent Logical Unit.

image   Procedures and data bound together by the linker to form an executable program. This executable program is executed by the process. There are three types of images: executable, shareable, and system.

image mode   The default screen mode using multiple image planes for a single screen. The number of image planes determines the variety of colors that are available to the screen.

image name   The name of the file in which an image is stored.

image planes   The primary display planes on a device that supports two sets of planes. The other set of display planes is known as the *overlay planes*. These two sets of planes are treated as two separate screens in stacked mode and as one screen in combined mode.

image privileges   The privileges assigned to an image when it is installed.

IMS   Information Management System.

IMS/VS   Information Management System/Virtual Storage.

inactive   This term has a variety of meanings depending upon the context or environment. It is, however, generally agreed to pertain to something that is not operational or to a node or device that is not connected or is not available for connection to another node or device. In IBM's AIX operating system, pertains to a window that does not have an input focus. In SNA, particularly VTAM, pertains to the state of a resource or a major or minor node that is not activated or for which the VARY INACT command has been issued.

Incoming call packet   A call supervision packet transmitted by data circuit-terminating equipment (DCE) to inform called data terminal equipment (DTE) that another DTE has requested a call.

Independent Logical Unit (ILU)   In SNA, a type of LU that does not require VTAM for session establishment after the initial download of parameters.

index   A structure that permits retrieval of records in an indexed file by key value.

Indexed File Organization   A Digital Equipment–type file organization in which a file contains records, and a primary key index is used to process the records sequentially by index or randomly by index.

Indexed Sequential File   According to Digital Equipment documentation, a record file in which each record has one or more data keys embedded in it. Records in the file are individually accessible by specifying a key associated with the record.

Index File   According to Digital Equipment documentation, the file on the Files-11 volume that contains the access information for all files on the volume and enables the operating system to identify and access the volume.

Index File Bitmap   According to Digital Equipment documentation, a table in the index file of a Files-11 volume that indicates which file headers are in use.

Index Path   According to NetWare documentation, a logical ordering of records in a Btrieve file based on the values of an index. An index path for each index in a file exists. A file may have up to 24 separate index paths.

indirect activation   According to IBM documentation, in VTAM, the activation of a lower-level resource of the resource hierarchy as a result of SCOPE or ISTATUS specifications related to an activation command naming a higher-level resource.

indirect deactivation   According to IBM documentation, in VTAM, the deactivation of a lower-level resource of the resource hierarchy as a result of a deactivation command naming a higher-level resource.

Information (I) frame   A frame in I format used for numbered information transfer.

Information/Management   A feature of the Information/System that provides interactive systems management applications for problem, change, and configuration management.

Information Management System/Virtual Storage (IMS/VS)   A software subsystem offering by IBM. It is a database/data communication (DB/DC) system that can manage complex databases and networks.

inhibited   According to IBM, a logical unit (LU) that has indicated to its system services control point (SSCP) that it is temporarily not ready to establish LU-LU sessions. An initiate request for a session with an inhibited LU will be rejected by the SSCP. The LU can separately indicate whether this applies to its ability to act as a primary logical unit (PLU) or a secondary logical unit (SLU).

initial program load (IPL)   An IBM term, referring to the initialization procedure that causes an operating system to commence operation. The process by which a configuration image is loaded into storage at the beginning of a work day or after a system malfunction. The process of loading system programs and preparing a system to run jobs.

INITIATE   In SNA, a network services request sent from a logical unit (LU) to a system services control point (SSCP) requesting that an LU-LU session be established.

initiating LU (ILU)   In SNA, the LU that first requests a session setup. The ILU may be one of the LUs that will participate in the session, or it may be a third-party LU. If it is one of the session participants, the ILU is also called the *origin LU* (OLU).

initiator   In OSI, a file service user that requests an FTAM establishment.

inoperative   The condition of a resource that has been active but is no longer. The resource may have failed, received an INOP request, or is being suspended while a reactivate command is being processed.

Input/Output Channel   In a data processing system, a functional unit that handles transfer of data between internal and peripheral equipment. In a computing system, a functional unit, controlled by a processor, that handles transfer of data between processor storage and local peripheral devices. In IBM terminology, it refers to a specific type of path, either parallel or serial.

installation exit   The means by which an IBM software product may be modified by a customer's system programmers to change or extend the functions of the IBM software product. Such modifications consist of exit routines written to replace one or more existing modules of an IBM software product, or to add one or more modules or subroutines to an IBM software product, for the purpose of modifying or extending the functions of the IBM software product.

installation exit routine   A routine written by a user to take control at an installation exit of an IBM software product.

installationwide exit   Synonym for installation exit.

INT   Internal trace table.

integrated communication adapter (ICA)   A communication adapter that is an integral part of the host processor.

Integrity Control   According to Novell documentation, the method used to ensure the completeness of files. Specifically, Btrieve uses preimaging and Net-Ware's Transaction Tracking System to guarantee integrity.

intensive mode recording (IMR)   An NCP function that forces recording of temporary errors for a specified resource.

Interactive Problem Control System (IPCS)   According to IBM documentation, a component of VM that permits online problem management, interactive problem diagnosis, online debugging for disk-resident CP abend dumps, problem tracking, and problem reporting.

Interactive System Productivity Facility (ISPF)   An IBM licensed program that serves as a full-screen editor and dialogue manager. Used for writing application programs, it provides a means of generating standard screen panels and interactive dialogues between the application programmer and the terminal user.

Interapplication Communication (IAC)   In Apple terminology, a collection of features, provided by the Edition Manager, Apple Event Manager, Event Manager, and PPC Toolbox, that help applications work together.

interchange node   A new type of node supported by VTAM beginning in Version 4 Release 1. It is a type of node that acts as both an APPN network node and a subarea type 5 node to transform APPN protocols to subarea protocols and vice versa.

Interconnected Networks   According to IBM, SNA networks connected by gateways—gateway NCPs, that is.

interface   A shared boundary between two functional units, defined by functional characteristics, signal characteristics, or other characteristics, as appropriate. The concept includes the specification of the connection of two devices having different functions. Hardware, software, or both, that links systems, programs, or devices.

intermediate node   A node that is at the end of more than one branch.

intermediate routing node (IRN)   A node containing intermediate routing functions.

intermediate session routing (ISR)   In APPN, a type of routing function within an APPN network node that provides session-level flow control and outage reporting for all sessions that pass through the node but whose end points are elsewhere.

Intermediate SSCP   In SNA, an SSCP along a session initiation path that owns neither of the LUs involved in a cross-network LU-LU session.

International Organization for Standardization (ISO)   An organization of national standards bodies from various countries established to promote the development of standards to facilitate international exchange of goods and services and to develop cooperation in intellectual, scientific, technological, and economic activity.

Internet   According to different documents describing the Internet, it is a collection of networks, routers, gateways, and other networking devices that use the TCP/IP protocol suite and function as a single, cooperative virtual network. The Internet provides universal connectivity and three levels of network services: unreliable, connectionless packet delivery; reliable, full-duplex stream delivery; and application-level services like electronic mail that build on the first two. The Internet reaches many universities, government research labs, and military installations and over a dozen countries.

Internet Address   According to Apple documentation, an AppleTalk address that includes the socket number, node ID, and network number. According to TCP/IP documentation, the 32-bit address assigned to the host. It is a software address that on little-i internets is locally managed, but on the big-I Internet is dictated to the user (entity desiring access to the Internet).

Internet Packet Exchange (IPX)   A Novell protocol that operates at layer 3, according to the OSI model. It is used in the NetWare protocols; it is similar to IP in TCP/IP.

Internet Protocol (IP)   A protocol used to route data from its source to its destination. A part of TCP/IP protocol.

interpersonal message   According to OSI related documents, a message type used for human-to-human communication in MHS.

interpersonal messaging system   According to multiple explanations in the OSI community, a MHS system supporting the communication of interpersonal messages.

InterPoll   According to Apple documentation, software from Apple that helps administrators monitor the network and diagnose the source of problems that arise.

Interpret Table   In IBM's VTAM, an installation-defined correlation list that translates an argument into a string of eight characters. This table can translate logon data into the name of an application program for which the logon is intended.

Inter-User Communication Vehicle (IUCV)   According to IBM documentation, a VM facility for passing data between virtual machines and VM components.

I/O   Input/output.

IOPD   Input/output problem determination.

IP   Internet Protocol. The TCP/IP standard protocol that defines the IP datagram as the unit of information passed across an internet and provides the basis for connectionless, best-effort packet delivery service. IP includes the ICMP control and error message protocol as an integral part. The entire protocol suite is often referred to as TCP/IP because TCP and IP are the two fundamental protocols.

IP Address   The 32-bit dotted decimal address assigned to hosts that want to participate in a TCP/IP internet or the big-I Internet. IP addresses are software addresses. Actually, an IP address consists of a network portion and a host portion. The partition makes routing efficient.

IPCS   Interactive Problem Control System.

IP datagram   In TCP/IP networks, a basic unit of information passed across a TCP/IP internet. An IP datagram is to an internet as a hardware packet is to physical network. It contains a source and destination address along with data.

IPL   Initial program loader or initial program load.

IRN   Intermediate routing node.

IRSG   Internet Research Steering Group. A committee consisting of the IRTF research group chairpersons plus the IRTF chairperson, who direct and coordinate research related to TCP/IP and the connected Internet.

IRTF   Internet Research Task Force. A group of people working on research problems related to TCP/IP and the connected Internet.

ISDN   Integrated Services Digital Network. A set of standards being developed within ANSI, ISO, and CCITT for the delivery of various services over digital networks.

IS-IS routing   Routing between ISs within a routing domain.

ISO   International Organization for Standardization.

ISODE   ISO Development Environment. In the ISO environment, a set of public domain software subroutines that provide an interface between the GOSIP-specified session layer (ISO) and the DoD-specified transport layer (TCP/IP). Allows the development of applications that will execute over both OSI and TCP/IP protocol stacks as a migration path from TCP/IP networks to GOSIP networks.

ISPF   Interactive System Productivity Facility.

ISR   Intermediate Session Routing.

ISTATUS   According to IBM documentation, in VTAM and NCP, a definition specification method for indicating the initial status of resources.

IUCV   Inter-User Communication Vehicle.

JCL   Job Control Language.

job   A way by which an accounting unit is assigned to a process and its subprocesses, if any, and all subprocesses that they create. Jobs are classified as batch and interactive. For example, the job controller creates an interactive job to handle a user's requests when the user logs in to the system, and it creates a batch job when the symbiont manager passes a command input file to it.

Job Control Language   A language used in IBM's MVS operating system environment to identify a job to an operating system and to describe the job's requirements.

Job Controller   The system process that establishes a job's process context, starts a process running the LOGIN image for the job, maintains the accounting record for the job, manages symbionts, and terminates a process and its subprocesses.

Job Information Block   A data structure associated with a job that contains the quotas pooled by all processes in the job.

Katakana   A character set of symbols used in one of the two common Japanese phonetic alphabets, which is used primarily to write foreign words phonetically.

Keyboard Binding   In an X window environment, an association of a special key press with a window manager function. For example, pressing the special keys Shift Esc displays the system menu of the active window.

Keyboard Resources   According to Apple documentation, a category of files that are stored in a resource file by the Resource Manager and are used by the Macintosh Script Management System, including the International Utilities Package.

keyboard script   The script for keyboard input. It determines the character input method and the keyboard mapping; that is, what character codes are produced when a sequence of keys is pressed.

keyword   According to Apple documentation, a four-character code used to uniquely identify the descriptor record for either an attribute or a parameter in an Apple event. In Apple Event Manager functions, constants are typically used to represent the four-character codes. In programming languages, a lexical unit that, in certain contexts, characterizes some language construct. In some contexts, IF characterizes an if-statement. A keyword normally has the form of an identifier. One of the predefined words of an artificial language. A significant and informative word in a title or document that describes the content of that document. A name or symbol that identifies a parameter.

keyword operand   In the IBM environment, particularly with JCL, an operand that consists of a keyword followed by one or more values (such as DSNAME=HELLO).

keyword parameter   A parameter that consists of a keyword followed by one or more values.

LAN   Local area network.

LAP Manager   According to Apple documentation, a set of operating system utilities that provide a standard interface between the AppleTalk protocols and the various link access protocols, such as LocalTalk (LLAP), EtherTalk (ELAP), and TokenTalk (TLAP).

Least-Weight Route   According to IBM's documentation, in APPN, the one route calculated by topology and routing services (TRS) to have the lowest total weight after TRS compares the node characteristics and TG characteristics of each intermediate node and intermediate TG of each possible route for the class-of-service requested, and computes the total combined weight for nodes and TGs in each route. After a least-weight route is calculated between two given nodes, the result may be stored to prevent repetition of this calculation in future route selections.

LEN   Low-entry networking.

LEN connection   A link over which LEN protocols are used.

LEN node   In APPN, according to IBM documentation, a node that supports independent LU protocols but does not support CP-CP sessions. It may be a peripheral node attached to a boundary node in a subarea network, an end node attached to an APPN network node in an APPN network, or a peer-connected node directly attached to another LEN node or APPN end node.

Level 1 Router   According to Digital Equipment documentation, a DECnet for Open VMS node that can send and receive packets and route packets from one node to another node within a single area.

Level 2 Router   According to Digital Equipment documentation, a DECnet for Open VMS node that can send and receive packets and route packets from one node to another within its own area and between areas.

Lexical Function   According to Digital Equipment documentation, a command language construct that the DIGITAL Command Language command interpreter evaluates and substitutes before it parses a command string.

Librarian   According to Digital Equipment, a program that allows the user to create, update, modify, list, and maintain object library, help library, text library, and assembler macro library files.

Limited Resource   According to IBM documentation, a connection facility that causes a session traversing it to be terminated if no session activity is detected for a specified period of time.

Limited-Resource Session   According to IBM documentation, a session that traverses a limited resource link. This session is terminated if no session activity is detected for a specified period of time.

line   The portion of a data circuit external to data circuit-terminating equipment (DCE), that connects the DCE to a data switching exchange (DSE), that connects a DCE to one or more other DCEs, or that connects a DSE to another DSE.

line control   Synonym for data link control protocol.

line control discipline   Synonym for link protocol.

line discipline   Synonym for link protocol.

line group   One or more telecommunication lines of the same type that can be activated and deactivated as a unit.

line speed   The number of binary digits that can be sent over a telecommunication line in one second, expressed in bits per second (bps).

line switching   Synonym for circuit switching.

link   The combination of the link connection (the transmission medium) and two link stations, one at each end of the link connection.

Link Access Protocol   According to Digital Equipment documentation, a set of procedures used for link control on a packet switching data network. X.25 defines two sets of procedures:

- LAP—The data terminal equipment/data circuit-terminating equipment interface is defined as operating in two-way simultaneous asynchronous response mode with the DTE and DCE containing a primary and secondary function.

- LAPB—The DTE/DCE interface is defined as operating in two-way asynchronous balanced mode.

According to Apple documentation, an AppleTalk protocol that controls the access of a node to the network hardware. A link access protocol makes it possible for many nodes to share the same communications hardware.

link-attached   Pertaining to devices that are connected to a controlling unit by a data link.

link connection   The physical equipment providing two-way communication between one link station and one or more other link stations; for example, a telecommunication line and data circuit-terminating equipment (DCE).

link connection segment   A part of the configuration that is located between two resources listed consecutively in the service point command service (SPCS) query link configuration request list.

link level   A reference to the physical connection between two nodes and/or the protocols used to govern that connection.

Link Problem Determination Aid (LPDA)   According to IBM documentation, a series of procedures used to test the status of and to control DCEs, the communication line, and the remote device interface. These procedures, or a subset of them, are implemented by host programs (such as the NetView program and VTAM), communication controller programs (such as NCP), and IBM LPDA DCEs.

Link Protocol   Rules for sending and receiving data over a medium.

Link Services Layer   Routes packets between LAN boards with their MLIDs and protocol stacks. The LSL maintains LAN board, protocol stack, and packet buffer information.

Link Station   According to IBM documentation, the hardware and software components within a node representing a connection to an adjacent node over a specific link. In VTAM, a named resource within an APPN or a subarea node that represents the connection to another APPN or subarea node that is attached by an APPN or a subarea link. In the resource hierarchy in a subarea network, the link station is subordinate to the subarea link.

Little Endian   A storage format or transmission of binary data in which the least significant byte comes first.

LLC   Logical Link Control. According to OSI documentation, a sublayer in the data link layer of the OSI model. The LLC provides the basis for an unacknowledged connectionless service or connection-oriented service on the local area network.

LL2   Link Level 2.

local   Pertaining to a device accessed directly without use of a telecommunication line.

local access   The ability to execute a program on the computer to which you are attached.

Local Address   According to IBM documentation, in SNA, an address used in a peripheral node in place of a network address and transformed to or from a network address by the boundary function in a subarea node.

Local area network (LAN)   A collection of computers and other related devices connected together on the premises within a limited geographical area.

Local Area Transport   According to Digital Equipment documentation, a communications protocol that the operating system uses within a local area network to communicate with terminal servers.

Local Area VAXcluster System   According to Digital Equipment documentation, a type of VAXcluster configuration in which cluster communication is carried out over the Ethernet by software that emulates certain computer interconnect (CI) port functions. A VAXcluster node can be a VAX or a Micro VAX processor; hierarchical storage controllers (HSCs) are not used.

Local Client   In an X window environment, a program running on your local computer, the same system that is running your X server.

Local Directory Database   According to IBM documentation, a set of LUs in a network known at a particular node. The resources included are all those in the node's domain as well as any cache entries.

local management interface (LMI)   A set of operational procedures and messages, as well as DLCI 1023, are defined in Frame-Relay Specification with Extensions, a document based on proposed T1S1 standards, which are copyrighted by Digital Equipment Corporation, Northern Telecom, Inc., and StrataCom, Inc. In this context, the term local management interface (LMI) is a deprecated term for link integrity verification tests (LIVT). Current meaning: any frame-relay management interface procedures, such as DLCI 1023 or DLCI 0.

local non-SNA major node   According to IBM documentation, in VTAM, a major node whose minor nodes are channel-attached non-SNA terminals.

local SNA major node   According to IBM documentation, in VTAM, a major node whose minor nodes are channel-attached peripheral nodes.

Local Symbol   According to Digital Equipment documentation, a symbol meaningful only to the module that defines it. Symbols not identified to a language processor as global symbols are considered to be local symbols. A language processor resolves local symbols. They are not known to the linker and cannot be made available to another object module. They can, however, be passed through the linker to the symbolic debugger.

LocalTalk   According to Apple documentation, a type of AppleTalk network that is inexpensive and easy to set up. LocalTalk is commonly used to connect small to medium sized workgroups.

Local Topology Database   According to IBM documentation, a database in an APPN NN or LEN node containing an entry for each transmission group (TG) having at least one END node for an endpoint. In an APPN END node, the database has one entry for each TG connecting to the node. In a network node, the database has an entry for each TG connecting the network node to an end node. Each entry describes the current characteristics of the TG that it represents. A network node has both a local and a network topology database, while an end node has only a local topology database.

Locate Mode   According to Digital Equipment documentation, an Open VMS Record Management Services record access technique in which a program accesses records in a Open VMS RMS I/O buffer area to reduce overhead.

location name   An identifier for the network location of the computer on which a port resides. The PPC toolbox provides the location name. It contains an object string, a type string, and a zone. An application can specify an alias for its location name by modifying its type string.

logical channel   In packet mode operation, a sending channel and a receiving channel that together are used to send and receive data over a data link at the same time.

logical channel identifier   A bit string in the header of a packet that associates the packet with a specific switched virtual circuit or permanent virtual circuit.

Logical Link Control (LLC) Protocol   In a local area network, the protocol that governs the exchange of transmission frames between data stations independently of how the transmission medium is shared.

logical name   According to Digital Equipment documentation, a user-specified name for any portion or all of a file specification. For example, the logical name INPUT can be assigned to a terminal device from which a program reads data entered by a user. Logical name assignments are maintained in logical name tables for each process, each group, and the system. Logical names can be assigned translation attributes, such as terminal and concealed.

Logical Name Table   According to Digital Equipment documentation, a table that contains a set of logical names and their equivalence names for a particular process, a particular group, or the system.

logical record   A group of related fields treated as a unit.

Logical Unit (LU)   An addressable endpoint.

Logical Unit 6.2 Those protocols and that type of LU that support advanced program-to-program communication (APPC).

login directory The default directory a user is assigned to upon logon into a system.

logoff According to IBM documentation, in VTAM, an unformatted session-termination request. In general, to terminate interaction with a system; actually entering a command of some sort to close the connection.

logon According to IBM documentation, in VTAM, an unformatted session-initiation request for a session between two logical units. In general, to sign on or get to the point where work can be done.

Logon Manager A VTAM application program that provides logon services for the Transaction Processing Facility (TPF).

Logon Mode According to IBM documentation, in VTAM, a subset of session parameters specified in a logon mode table for communication with a logical unit.

Logon Mode Table According to IBM documentation, in VTAM, a set of sentries for one or more logon modes. Each logon mode is identified by a logon mode name.

Low-Entry Networking (LEN) According to IBM documentation, a capability in nodes allowing them to directly attach to one another using peer-to-peer protocols and to support multiple and parallel sessions between logical units. However, LEN does not provide all of the capabilities of APPN; for example, it does not provide CP-CP session support.

Low-Entry Networking (LEN) END Node According to IBM documentation, an END node that provides all SNA end-user services, can attach directly to other nodes using peer protocols, and derives network services implicitly from an adjacent network node when attached to an APPN network without a session between its local CP and another CP.

Low-Entry Networking (LEN) Node According to IBM documentation, a node that supports independent LU protocols but does not support CP-CP sessions.

LU Logical unit.

LU Group According to IBM documentation, in the NetView Performance Monitor (NPM), a file containing a list of related or unrelated logical units. The LU group is used to help simplify data collection and analysis.

LU-LU session A logical connection between two Logical Units in an SNA network that provides communication between two end users.

LU-Mode Pair According to IBM documentation, in the VTAM implementation of the LU 6.2 architecture, the coupling of an LU name entry and a mode name entry. This coupling allows a pool of sessions with the same characteristics to be established.

LU6.2 Session A logical connection utilizing LU6.2 protocols.

LU Type According to IBM documentation, the classification of an LU in terms of SNA protocols and options it supports for a given session.

LU Type 6.2 (LU6.2)   According to IBM documentation, a type of Logical Unit that supports general communication between programs in a distributed processing environment. LU6.2 is characterized by a peer relationship between transaction programs and efficient utilization of a session for multiple transactions.

macroinstruction   According to IBM documentation, an instruction in a source language that is to be replaced by a defined sequence of instructions in the same source language and that may also specify values for parameters in the replaced instructions.

main screen   The screen on which a menu bar appears.

Maintain System History Program (MSHP)   According to IBM documentation, a program used for automating and controlling various installation, tailoring, and service activities for a VSE system.

Maintenance and Operator Subsystem (MOSS)   According to IBM documentation, a subsystem of an IBM communication controller, such as the 3725 or the 3720, that contains a processor and operates independently of the rest of the controller. It loads and supervises the controller, runs problem determination procedures, and assists in maintaining both hardware and software.

major node   According to IBM documentation, in VTAM, a set of resources that can be activated and deactivated as a group.

Management Information Base   A collection of managed objects. A term used with the concept of SNMP-based network management.

Management Information Tree   A tree structure of the Management Information Base.

Management Services (MS)   According to IBM documentation, one of the types of network services in control points (CPs) and physical units (PUs). Management services are provided to assist in the management of SNA networks, such as problem management, performance and accounting management, configuration management, and change management.

MASSBUS Adapter   According to Digital Equipment documentation, an interface device between the backplane interconnect and the MASSBUS device.

Mass Storage Control Protocol   According to Digital Equipment documentation, the software protocol used to communicate I/O commands between a VAX processor and DSA-compliant devices on the system.

Master File Directory (MFD)   According to Digital Equipment documentation, the file directory on a disk volume that contains the names of all user file directories on a disk, including its own.

matte   In window-based environments, the border located inside the window between the client area and the frame, used to create a three-dimensional effect for the frame and window.

Media Access Control   According to OSI nomenclature, a sublayer in the Data Link Layer which controls access to the physical medium of a network.

medium   A physical carrier of electrons or photons. The medium may be hard, as in a type of cable, or soft, as in microwaves, for example.

Medium Access Control (MAC)   A protocol that comprises the lower part of the second layer in the OSI model. It governs access to the transmission medium to enable the exchange of data between nodes.

Medium Access Control (MAC) Sublayer   Supports topology-dependent functions and uses services of the physical layer to provide services to the Logical Link Control (LLC) sublayer.

menu   A list of selections from which to make a choice.

MERGE disk   According to IBM documentation, a virtual disk in the VM operating system that contains Program Temporary Fixes (PTFs) after the VMFMERGE EXEC is invoked.

message   Generically, meaningful data passed from one end user to another. The end user may be a human or a program.

message (MHS)   According to OSI documentation, a structured set of data that is sent from a user agent to one or more recipient user agents.

Message Block   According to Apple documentation, a byte stream that an open application uses. It is used to send data to and receive data from another open application. The PPC Toolbox delivers message blocks to an application in the same sequence in which they were sent.

Message Store   In a TCP/IP environment, an entity acting as an intermediary between an user agent and its local message transfer agent.

Message Transfer Agent   In TCP/IP, a subpart of the electronic mail component known as Simple Mail Transfer Protocol (SMTP). It is an object in the Message Transfer System. MTAs use a store and forward method to relay messages from originator to recipient. They interact with user agents when a message is submitted and upon delivery.

Message Unit   According to IBM documentation, in SNA, the unit of data processed by any layer; for example, a basic information unit (BIU), a path information unit (PIU), or a request-response unit (RU).

MHS   Message Handling Service. The service provided by the CCITT X.400 series of standards, consisting of a user agent to allow users to create and read electronic mail; a message transfer agent to provide addressing, sending, and receiving services; and a reliable transfer agent to provide routing and delivery services.

Migration Data Host   According to IBM documentation, a VTAM node support that acts as both an APPN END node and a SNA subarea node.

MILNET   Originally, this network was part of the ARPANET. In 1984 it was segmented for military installation usage.

minimize   To turn a window into an icon.

Minor Node   According to IBM documentation, in VTAM, a uniquely defined resource within a major node.

Mixed Interconnect VMScluster System   According to Digital Equipment documentation, any VMScluster system that utilizes more than one interconnect for SCA traffic. Mixed interconnect VMScluster systems provide maximum flexibility in combining CPUs, storage, and workstations into highly available configurations.

MMS   Manufacturing Messaging Service. According to OSI documentation, a messaging service between programmable devices.

modem (modulator/demodulator)   A device that converts digital to analog signals and vice-versa for the purpose of using computer devices in remote locations.

mode name   In SNA, a name used by the initiator of a session to designate the characteristics desired for the session.

monitor   Generally considered to be the same as display. It can also mean to watch a task, program execution, or the like.

Monitor Console Routine   According to Digital Equipment documentation, the command interpreter in an RSX-11 system; also an optional command interpreter in the operating system.

MOSS   Maintenance and Operator Subsystem.

mounting a volume   According to Digital Equipment documentation, the logical association of a volume with the physical unit on which it is loaded. Loading or placing a magnetic tape or disk pack on a drive and placing the drive on line.

Mount Verification   According to Digital Equipment documentation, a feature that suspends I/O to and from volumes while they are changing status. Mount verification also ensures that, following a suspension in disk I/O, the volume being accessed is the same as was previously mounted.

Move Mode   According to Digital Equipment documentation, an Open VMS Record Management Services record I/O access technique in which a program accesses records in its own working storage area.

MPC   Multipath channel.

MS   Management Services.

MSG   Console Messages.

MTU   Maximum Transfer Unit. The largest amount of data that can be transferred across a given physical network. For local area networks like the Ethernet, the MTU is determined by the network hardware. For long-haul networks that use aerial lines to interconnect packet switches, the MTU is determined by software.

Multicast   A technique that allows copies of a single packet to be passed to a selected subset of all possible destinations. Some hardware supports multicast by allowing a network interface to belong to one or more multicast groups. Broadcast is a special form of multicast in which the subset of machines to receive a copy of a packet consists of the entire set. IP supports an internet multicast facility.

multicast address   According to Apple documentation, an Ethernet address for which the node accepts packets just as it does for its permanently assigned Ethernet hardware address. The low-order bit of the high-order byte is set to 1. Each node can have any number of multicast addresses, and any number of nodes can have the same multicast address. The purpose of a multicast address is to allow a group of Ethernet nodes to receive the same transmission simultaneously, in a fashion similar to the AppleTalk broadcast service.

multicasting   A Directory Service Agent uses this mode to chain a request to many other Directory Service Agents.

MultiFinder   According to Apple documentation, prior to version 7.0 system software, a multitasking operating system for Macintosh computers that enables several applications to be open at the same time. In addition, processes (such as print spooling) can operate in the background so that users can perform one task while the computer performs another.

Multi-Homed Host   A TCP/IP host connected to two or more physical networks; thus, they have more than one address. They can serve as router-type devices.

Multilink Transmission Group   According to IBM documentation, a transmission group containing two or more links.

multimode   The transmission of multiple modes of light.

multipath channel (MPC)   According to IBM documentation, a channel protocol that uses multiple unidirectional subchannels for VTAM-to-VTAM bidirectional communication.

Multiple-Domain Network   According to IBM documentation, a network with more than one system services control point in traditional subarea SNA. In APPN, an APPN network with more than one network node.

Multiple Link Interface Driver   According to Novell documentation, this type of driver accepts multiple protocol packets. When an MLID device driver receives a packet, the MLID does not interpret the packet; it copies identification information and passes the packet to the Link Support Layer. MLIDs are either supplied by Novell, by the network board manufacturer, or by a third party supplier.

multipoint line   A telecommunication line or circuit that connects two or more stations.

mutex   A term used in Digital Equipment network environments. According to Digital Equipment documentation, a semaphore is used to control exclusive access to a region of code that can share a data structure or other resource. The mutex semaphore ensures that only one process at a time has write access to the region of code.

MVS   Multiple Virtual Storage.

MVS/XA   Multiple Virtual Storage/Extended Architecture. An IBM operating system.

Name-Binding Protocol (NBP)   According to Apple documentation, the AppleTalk transport level protocol that translates a character string into a network address.

Name Block   According to Digital Equipment documentation, an Open VMS Record Management Services user data structure that contains supplementary information used in parsing file specifications.

name resolution   The process of locating an entry by sequentially matching each relative distinguished name in a purported name to a vertex of the Directory Information Tree.

name translation   According to IBM documentation, an SNA network interconnection. It includes the conversion of logical unit names, logon mode table names, and class-of-service names used in one network to equivalent names for use in another network.

Naming Context   In OSI networks, a substructure of the Directory Information Tree. It starts at a vertex and extends downwards to leaf and/or non-leaf structures.

Naming Context Tree   According to popular OSI documentation, a tree structure where each node represents a naming context.

NCB   Node Control Block.

NCCF   Network Communications Control Facility. A part of IBM's NetView. It is the command that starts the NetView command facility. It is a command line in NetView whereby various commands can be offered.

NCP   Network Control Program.

NCP/EP Definition Facility (NDF)   According to IBM documentation, a program that is part of System Support Programs (SSP). It is used to generate a Partitioned Emulation Program (PEP) load module or a load module for a Network Control Program (NCP) or for an Emulation Program (EP).

NCP Major Node   According to IBM documentation, it refers to VTAM, where a set of minor nodes represent resources, such as lines and peripheral nodes, controlled by IBM's network control program.

negative response (NR)   According to IBM documentation, in SNA, a response indicating that a request did not arrive successfully or was not processed successfully by the receiver.

Negotiable BIND   According to IBM documentation, in SNA, the capability allowing two half-sessions to negotiate the parameters of a session when the session is being activated.

NetBIOS   The standard interface to networks that is used by IBM PCs and compatibles. With a TCP/IP network, NetBIOS refers to a set of guidelines that describes how to map NetBIOS operations into equivalent TCP/IP operations.

NetView   According to IBM, a program used to monitor and manage a network and diagnose network problems.

NetView Performance Monitor (NPM)   According to IBM, a program that collects, monitors, analyzes, and displays data relevant to the performance of VTAM.

NetWare Loadable Module   According to Novell documentation, a program that is part of a file server memory with NetWare. An NLM can be loaded or unloaded while the file server is running, become part of the operating system, and access NetWare directly.

network   A collection of computers and related devices connected together in such a way that collectively they can be more productive than standalone equipment.

Network Address   In general, each participating entity on a network has an address so that it can be identified when exchanging data. According to IBM documentation, in a subarea network, an address consists of subarea and element fields that identify a link, link station, PU, LU, or SSCP.

Network Address Translation   According to IBM documentation, in a SNA network interconnection, it is the conversion of the network address assigned to an LU in one network into an address in an another network.

network architecture   The logical and physical structure of a computer network.

Network Connect Block   According to Digital Equipment documentation, a user-generated data structure used in a nontransparent task to identify a remote task and optionally send user data in calls to request, accept, or reject a logical link connection. For the VAX Packetnet System Interface, a block that contains the information necessary to set up an X.25 virtual circuit or to accept or reject a request to set up an X.25 virtual circuit.

Network Control   In SNA, according to IBM documentation, a request or response unit (RU) category used for request and responses exchanged between PUs. The purpose of this is activating and deactivating explicit and virtual routes. The term is used to refer to send load modules to adjust peripheral nodes.

Network Control Program   According to Digital Equipment documentation, an interactive utility program that allows control and monitoring of a network. According to IBM documentation, a program that controls the operation of a communication controller.

Network Layer   According to OIS documentation, defined as layer 3. It is responsible for data transfer across the network. It functions independent of the network media and the topology.

Network Management Vector Transport (NMVT)   According to IBM documentation, a protocol used for management services in an SNA network.

Network Name   According to IBM documentation, in SNA, the symbolic identifier by which end users refer to a network accessible unit, a link, or a link station within a given network. Another definition by IBM is used in refernce to APPN networks; network names are also used for routing purposes. In a multidomain network, the name of the APPL statement defining a VTAM application program. This network name must be unique across domains.

Network Node Server   According to IBM documentation, an APPN network node that provides network services for its local LUs and client end nodes.

Network Number   According to Apple documentation, a 16-bit number that provides a unique identifier for a network in an AppleTalk internet.

Network Operator   A person who performs a variety of functions for a network, some of which are control functions.

Network-Qualified Name   A name that uniquely identifies a specific resource within a specific network. It consists of a network identifier and a resource name, each of which is a 1- to 8-byte symbol string.

Network Range   According to Apple documentation, a unique range of contiguous network numbers used to identify each Ethernet and Token Ring network on an AppleTalk internet.

Network Routing Facility (NRF)   According to IBM documentation, an IBM program that resides in an NCP. NRF provides a path for routing messages between terminals and routes messages over this path without going through the host processor.

Network Services   According to IBM documentation, those services within a network accessible unit that control network operation.

Network Services Header   According to IBM documentation, in traditional SNA, a 3-byte field in a function management data (FMD) request or response unit (RU) that flows in an SSCP-LU, SSCP-PU, or SSCP-SSCP session. This is used primarily to identify the network services category of the request unit (RU).

Network Services Protocol   According to Digital Equipment documentation, a formal set of conventions used in a DECnet for Open VMS network to perform network management and to exchange messages over logical links.

Network Terminal Option (NTO)   According to IBM documentation, a program used in conjunction with NCP that allows some non-SNA devices to participate in sessions with SNA application programs in the host processor.

Network Topology Database   In an APPN network, according to IBM documentation, the representation of the current connectivity between the network nodes within an APPN network. It includes entries for all network nodes and the transmission groups interconnecting them and entries for all virtual routing nodes to which network nodes are attached.

NFS   Network File System. According to Sun Microsystems, Inc., a protocol developed by Sun that uses IP to allow a set of cooperating computers to access each other's file systems as if they were local. NFS hides differences between local and remote files by placing them in the same name space. Originally designed for UNIX systems, it is now implemented on many other systems, including personal computers like the PC and Apple computers.

NIB   Node Initialization Block.

NLDM   Network Logical Data Manager. According to IBM documentation, a subset of NetView. NLDM is a command that starts the NetView sessions monitor. NLDM also identifies various panels and functions as part of the session monitor.

NMVT   Network Management Vector Transport.

NN   Network Node.

NNT   NetView-NetView Task.

node Generally, a term used to refer to a computer or related device. In IBM's SNA, node types exist that reflect certain functions they can perform. According to Digital Equipment documentation, an individual computer system in a network that can communicate with other computer systems in the network. A VAXBI interface—such as a central processor, controller, or memory subsystem—that occupies one of 16 logical locations on a VAXBI bus. A VAX processor or HSC that is recognized by system communications services software.

Node Initialization Block (NIB) According to IBM documentation, in VTAM, a control block associated with a particular node or session that contains information used by the application program. The information identifies the node or session and indicates how communication requests on a session are to be handled by VTAM.

Node Name According to IBM documentation, in VTAM, the symbolic name assigned to a specific major or minor node during network definition.

Node Number A unique number used to identify each node on a network.

Node Type According to IBM documentation, a designation of a node according to the protocols it supports and the network accessible units that it can contain. Five types are defined: 1.2.0, 2.1, 4, and 5. Within a subarea network, type 1, type 2.0, and type 2.1 nodes are peripheral nodes, while type 4 and type 5 nodes are subarea nodes.

nonclient A program that is written to run on a terminal and must be fooled by a terminal emulation window into running in the window environment.

Non-Command Image According to Digital Equipment documentation, a program not associated with a DCL command. To invoke a non-command image, use the file name containing the program as the parameter to the RUN command.

nonprivileged According to Digital Equipment documentation, an account with no privilege other than TMPMBX and NETMBX and a user identification code greater than the system parameter MAXSYSGROUP. In DECnet for Open VMS, this term means no privileges in addition to NETMBS, which is the minimal requirement for any network activity.

No Response According to IBM documentation, in SNA, a protocol requested in the for-of-response-requested field of the request header. It directs the receiver of the request not to return any response, regardless of whether or not the request is received and processed successfully.

Normal Flow According to IBM documentation referencing SNA, a data flow designated in the transmission header (TH) that is used primarily to carry end-user data. It refers to the rate at which requests flow. On normal flow, regulation can be achieved by session-level pacing. Normal and expedited flows move in both the primary-to-secondary and secondary-to-primary directions.

normalize In windowing environments, to change an icon back into its original appearance. The opposite of *iconify*.

notification An indication that something in the network requires the operator's attention.

NOTIFY   According to IBM documentation, a network services request sent by a SSCP to a LU. It is used to inform the LU of the status of a procedure requested by the LU.

NPDA   Network Problem Determination Application. According to IBM documentation, a part of NetView. Also a command that starts the NetView hardware monitor. NPDA identifies various panels and functions as part of the hardware monitor.

NPDU   Network Protocol Data Unit. In OSI terminology, a packet. A logical block of control symbols and data transmitted by the network layer protocol.

NSF   National Science Foundation. A government agency that has enabled scientists to connect to networks comprising the Internet.

NSFNET   National Science Foundation NETwork. Reference to a network that spans the United States.

Null Key   According to Novell documentation, a key field that allows the value of the field to be a user-defined null character. For this type of key, Btrieve does not index a record if the record's key value matches the null value.

NVP   Network Voice Protocol. A TCP/IP protocol for handling voice information.

Object   According to Apple documentation, the first field in the name of an AppleTalk entity. The object is assigned by the entity itself and can be anything the user or application assigns. According to Digital Equipment documentation, a passive repository of information to which the system controls access. Access to an object implies access to the information it contains. Examples of protected objects are files, volumes, global sections, and devices. A DECnet for OpenVMS process that receives a logical link request. It performs a specific network function or is a user defined image for a special purpose application. A VAX Packetnet System Interface management component that contains records to specify account information for incoming calls and to specify a command procedure that is initiated when the incoming call arrives.

Object Class   According to Digital Equipment documentation, on VAX systems, a set of protected objects with common characteristics. For example, all files belong to the FILE class whereas all devices belong to the DEVICE class.

Object Entry   In Open Systems networking, a directory entry which is the primary collection of information in the Directory Information Base about an object in the real world, not an alias entry.

Object Identifier Based Name   Reference to the names that are based on the OBJECT IDENTIFIER type.

Object Identifier Tree   In OSI terminology, a tree where edges are labeled with integers.

Object Identifier Type   In OSI and other environments that implement ASN.1, an ASN.1 type whose values are the path names of the nodes of the object identifier tree.

offline   Refers to a resource not being available.

online   Refers to a resource being available.

Open Application Event   According to Apple documentation, an Apple event that asks an application to perform the tasks—such as displaying untitled windows—associated with opening itself; one of the four required Apple events.

Open Datalink Interface   According to Novell documentation, a set of specifications defining relationships between one or more protocol stacks, the LSL, and one or more MLIDs. These specifications allow multiple communication protocols, such as IPX/SPX, TCP/IP, and AppleTalk, to share the same driver and adapter.

Open Shortest Path First. (OSPF)   A routing protocol based upon the least cost for routing.

operand   In SNA, an entity on which an operation is performed. That which is operated upon. An operand is usually identified by an address part of an instruction.

Optional Parameter   According to Apple documentation, a supplemental parameter in an Apple event used to specify data that the server application should use in addition to the data specified in the direct parameter.

oscillation   The periodic movement between two values.

Other-Domain Resource   According to IBM documentation, a representation for an LU that is owned by another domain and is referenced by a symbolic name, which can be qualified by a network identifier.

owner   According to Digital Equipment documentation, a user with the same user-identification code as the protected object. An owner always has control access to the object and can therefore modify the object's security profile. When the system processes an access request from an owner, it considers the access rights in the owner field of a protection code.

pacing   In IBM's SNA, a technique by which a receiving component controls the rate of transmission of a sending component to prevent overrun or congestion.

Pacing Response   According to IBM documentation, in SNA, an indicator that signifies the readiness of a receiving component to accept another pacing group. The indicator is carried in a response header for session-level pacing and in a transmission header for virtual route pacing.

Pacing Window   According to IBM documentation, the path information units (PIUs) that can be transmitted on a virtual route before a virtual-route pacing response is received indicating that the virtual route receiver is ready to receive more PIUs on the route.

packet   A term used generically in many instances. It is a small unit of control information and data that is processed by the network protocol.

Packet Assembly/Disassembly Facility   In packet switching technology, a device at a packet switching network permitting access from an asynchronous terminal. Terminals connect to a PAD, and a PAD puts the terminal's input data into packets, then takes the terminal's output data out of packets.

page   In virtual storage, a fixed-length block that has a virtual address and is transferred as a unit between real storage and secondary storage.

pagelet   According to Digital Equipment documentation, a 512-byte unit of memory in an AXP environment. On AXP systems, certain DCL and utility commands, system services, and system routines accept as input or provide as output memory requirements and quotas in terms of pagelets.

Page Table Base Register   According to Digital Equipment documentation, on AXP systems, the processor register or its equivalent, in a hardware privileged context block that contains the page frame number of the process's first level page table.

Panel   According to IBM documentation, an arrangement of information that is presented in a window.

Parallel Links   According to IBM documentation, in SNA, two or more links between adjacent subarea nodes.

Parallel Sessions   According to IBM documentation, two or more concurrently active sessions between the same two network accessible units (NAUs) using different pairs of network addresses or local-form session identifiers. Each session can have independent session parameters.

Parallel Transmission Groups   According to IBM documentation, multiple transmission groups (TGs) connecting two adjacent nodes.

parameter   A generic term used to refer to a given constant value for a specified application and that may denote the application.

parent window   In windowing environments, a window that causes another window to appear. Specifically, it refers to windows that "own" other windows.

Partitioned Data Set (PDS)   According to IBM documentation, a type of storage, divided into partitions, called *members*. Each member contains records that are the actual data which is stored.

Path   In a network, any route between two or more nodes.

Path Control (PC)   According to IBM documentation, the function that routes message units between network accessible units in the network and provides the paths between them. It is depicted in traditional SNA layers. PC converts the BIUs from transmission control (possibly segmenting them) into path information units (PIUs) and exchanges basic transmission units containing one or more PIUs with data link control.

Path Information Unit (PIU)   According to IBM documentation, a message unit containing only a transmission header (TH), or a TH followed by a Basic Information Unit (BIU) or a BIU segment.

pending active session   According to IBM documentation, in VTAM, the state of an LU-LU session recorded by the SSCP when it finds both LUs available and has sent a CINIT request to the primary logical unit (PLU) of the requested session.

Performance Assist   According to Digital Equipment documentation, the Open VMS Volume Shadowing uses controller performance assists to improve full copy and merge operation performance. There are two distinct types of performance assists: the full copy assist and the minimerge assist.

Peripheral Host Node   According to IBM documentation, a type of node defined in SNA terminology. It does not provide SSCP functions and is not aware of the network configuration. The peripheral host node does not provide subarea node services. It has boundary function provided by its adjacent subarea.

Peripheral Logical Unit (PLU)   A logical unit in a peripheral node found in SNA networks. It should not be confused with a Primary Logical Unit, also known as a PLU.

Peripheral LU   Peripheral Logical Unit.

Peripheral Node   According to IBM documentation, a node that uses local addresses for routing and is not affected by changes in network addresses. A peripheral node requires boundary-function assistance from an adjacent subarea node.

Peripheral Path Control   According to IBM documentation, the function in a peripheral node that routes message units between units with local addresses and provides the paths between them.

permanent virtual circuit   A term used in many different types of network environments. Generally, a permanent logical association between two DTEs, which is analogous to a leased line. Packets are routed directly by the network from one DTE to the other.

personal computer (PC)   A term becoming more vague with the passing of time. It basically refers to an individual's computer. By this definition, that means it has its own processor, memory, storage, and display.

phase   The place of a wave in an oscillation cycle.

physical connection   A link that makes transmission of data possible. Generally, agreed to mean a tangible link; it may support electron, photon, or other data type representation transfer.

Physical Layer   In OSI circles, the lowest layer defined by the OSI model. However, layer 0 would be the lowest of layers in such a model. This layer (layer 0) represents the medium (be it hard or soft).

Physical Unit (PU)   According to IBM documentation, a component (be that software or firmware) that manages and monitors specified resources associated with a node. The type of PU, indicated by number, is typically either 5, 4, 2.0, or 2.1. The type of PU dictates what supporting services are available.

Physical Unit (PU) Services   According to IBM documentation, that component within a PU that provides configuration services and maintenance services for SSCP-PU sessions.

PING   Packet InterNet Groper. A program found in TCP/IP based networks. It is the name of a program used with TCP/IP networks used to test reachability of destinations by sending them an ICMP echo request and waiting for a reply.

pixel   The smallest dot that can be drawn on the screen.

point   A unit of measurement for type.

Point-to-Point Protocol (PPP)   A type of protocol used over asynchronous and synchronous connections for router-to-router or host-to-network communications.

polling   The process whereby data stations are invited, one at a time, to transmit on a multipoint or point-to-point connection.

Port   A term used in TCP/IP based networks. In TCP/IP two transport protocols exist: TCP and UDP. Applications that reside on top of these protocols have a port number assigned to them for addressing purposes. Generally, it is an addressable point.

Port Name   In Apple documentation, that which contains a name string, a type string, and a script code.

Power Manager   According to Apple documentation, firmware that provides an interface to the power management hardware in the Macintosh portable computer.

PPDU   Presentation Protocol Data Unit. In OSI terminology, logical blocks of control symbols and data transmitted at the presentation layer protocol.

Presentation Layer   According to the OSI model for networks this is layer 6. Data representation occurs here. Syntax of data, such as ASCII or EBCDIC, is determined at this layer.

Primary Application Program   According to IBM documentation, in VTAM, an application program acting as the primary end of an LU-LU session.

primary end of a session   According to IBM documentation, the end of a session that uses primary protocols. The primary end establishes the session. For an LU-LU session, the primary end of the session is the primary logical unit.

PrimaryInit Record   According to Apple documentation, a data structure in the declaration ROM of a NuBus card that contains initialization code. The Slot Manager executes the code in the PrimaryInit record when it first locates a declaration ROM during system startup.

Primary Key   According to Digital Equipment documentation, the mandatory key within the data records of an indexed file; used by Open VMS Record Management Services to determine the placement of records within the file and to build the primary index.

Primary Logical Unit (PLU)   According to IBM documentation, the logical unit that sends the BIND to activate a session with its partner LU.

PrintMonitor   According to Apple documentation, a background print spooler that is included with the Macintosh MultiFinder.

print server   In networking, a term used in a general sense to convey that a computer controls spooling and other printer operations.

private partition   According to IBM documentation, in VSE, an allocated amount of memory for the execution of a specific program or application program. Storage in a private partion is not addressable by programs running in other virtual address spaces.

privilege   According to Digital Equipment documentation, protecting the use of certain system functions that can affect system resources and integrity. System managers grant privileges according to user's needs and deny them to users as a means of restricting their access to the system.

process   Depending upon the context, it can mean an open application or an open desk accessory.

processor   That component which interprets and executes instructions.

Processor Status   According to Digital Equipment documentation, on VAX systems, a privileged processor register, known as the processor status longword, consisting of a word of privileged processor status and the processor status word itself. The privileged processor status information includes the current interrupt priority level, the previous access mode, the current access mode, the interrupt stack bit, the trace trap pending bit, and the compatibility mode bit.

Processor Status Word   According to Digital Equipment, on VAX systems, the low order word of the processor status longword. Processor status information includes the condition codes (carry, overflow, 0, and negative), the arithmetic trap enable bits (integer overflow, decimal overflow, and floating underflow), and the trace enable bit.

Product-Set Identification (PSID)   According to IBM documentation, a technique for identifying the hardware and software products that implement a network component.

PROFILE EXEC   According to IBM documentation, in VM, a special EXEC procedure with a filename of PROFILE. The procedure is normally executed immediately after CMS is loaded into a virtual machine. It contains CP and CMS commands that are to be issued at the start of every terminal session.

Program Operator   According to IBM documentation, in SNA, a VTAM application program that is authorized to issue VTAM operator commands and receive VTAM operator awareness messages.

Program Temporary Fix (PTF)   According to IBM documentation, a temporary solution or bypass of a problem diagnosed by IBM in a current unaltered release of the program.

protocol   An agreed-upon way of doing something.

protocol data unit   A general term referring to that which is exchanged between peer layer entities.

Proxy ARP   In TCP/IP networks, a technique where one machine answers ARP requests intended for another by supplying its own physical address.

pulse dispersion   The spreading of pulses as they traverse an optical fiber.

PU-PU flow   According to IBM documentation, in SNA, the exchange between physical units (PUs) of network control requests and responses.

Queued Session   According to IBM documentation, in VTAM, a requested LU-LU session that cannot be started because one of the LUs is not available. If the session-initiation request specifies queuing, the system services control points (SSCPs) record the request and later continue with the session-establishment procedure when both LUs become available.

Quit Application Event   According to Apple documentation, an Apple event that requests that an application perform the tasks—such as releasing memory, asking the user to save documents, and so on—associated with quitting; one of the four required Apple events. The Finder sends this event to an application immediately after sending it a Print Documents event or if the user chooses Restart or Shut Down from the Finder's Special menu.

RACF   Resource Access Control Facility. An IBM security program package.

RARP   Reverse Address Resolution Protocol. A TCP/IP protocol for mapping Ethernet addresses to IP addresses. It is used by diskless workstations that do not know their IP address. In essence it asks, "Who am I?" Normally, a response occurs and is cached in the host.

read-only memory (ROM)   Memory in which stored data cannot be modified except under special conditions.

real resource   In VTAM, a resource identified by its real name and its real network identifier.

receive pacing   According to IBM documentation, the pacing of message units being received by a component.

Record Access Block   According to Digital Equipment documentation, a Open VMS Record Management Services user control block allocated at either assembly or run time to communicate with RMS. The control block describes the records in a particular file and associates with a file access block to form a record access stream. A RAB defines the characteristics needed to perform record-related operations, such as update, delete, or get.

Record Management Services   According to Digital Equipment documentation, a set of operating system procedures that is called by programs to process files and records within files. RMS allows programs to issue GET and PUT requests at the record level as well as read and write blocks. RMS is an integral part of the system software; its procedures run in executive mode.

Region Code   According to Apple documentation, a number used to indicate a particular localized version of Macintosh system software.

relative path   The path through a volume's (disk's) hierarchy from one file or directory to another.

release   A distribution of a new product or new function and APAR fixes for an existing product. Normally, programming support for the prior release is discontinued after some specified period of time following the availability of a new release.

Remote Client   In an X window environment, an X program that runs on a remote system, but allows output of the program to be viewed locally.

Remote Operations Service Element   In Open Networking environments, an application service element that provides the basis for remote requests.

Request Header (RH)   According to IBM documentation, control information that precedes a Request Unit (RU).

Request Parameter List (RPL)   According to IBM documentation, a VTAM control block that contains the parameters necessary for processing a request for data transfer, for establishing or terminating a session, or for some other operation.

Request/Response Header (RH)   According to IBM documentation, control information associated with a particular RU. The RH precedes an RU and specifies the type of RU (request unit or response unit).

request response unit (RU)   A generic term for a request unit or a response unit.

Request Unit (RU)   According to IBM documentation, a message unit that contains control information, end-user data, or both.

Required Apple Event   According to Apple documentation, one of four core Apple events that the Finder sends to applications. These events are called Open Documents, Open Application, Print Documents, and Quit Application. They are a subset of the core Apple events.

reset   Generally, a change to the original state of operation.

resource   Generally, the main storage, secondary storage, input/output devices, processing unit, files, control or processing programs, or anything else that can be used by a user directly or indirectly.

Resource Access Control Facility (RACF)   According to IBM documentation, an IBM program that provides for access control by identifying and verifying the users of the system, by authorizing access to protected resources, by logging the detected unauthorized attempts to enter the system, and by logging the detected accesses to protected resources.

Resource Definition Table (RDT)   According to IBM documentation, a VTAM table that describes characteristics of each node available to VTAM and associates each node with a network address. This is a main VTAM network configuration table.

Resource Hierarchy   According to IBM documentation, a VTAM relationship among network resources in which some resources are subordinate to others as a result of their position in the network structure and architecture; for example, the logical units (LUs) of a peripheral physical unit (PU) are subordinate to the PU, which, in turn, is subordinate to the link attaching it to its subarea node.

Resource Registration   According to IBM documentation, the process of identifying names of resources, such as LUs, to a network node server or a central directory server.

Resource Takeover   According to IBM documentation, a VTAM action initiated by a network operator to transfer control of resources from one domain to another without breaking the connections or disrupting existing LU-LU sessions on the connection.

Resource Types   According to IBM documentation, with reference to NetView, a concept to describe the organization of panels. Resource types are defined as central processing unit, channel, control unit, and I/O device for one category; and communication controller, adapter, link, cluster controller, and terminal for another category. Resource types are combined with data types and display types to describe display organization.

response   A reply to some occurance, or the lack thereof.

Response Header (RH)   According to IBM documentation, a header, optionally followed by a response unit, that indicates whether the response is positive or negative and that may contain a pacing response.

Response Time   According to IBM documentation, a term used with the product NetView. It refers to the elapsed time between the end of an inquiry or demand on a computer system and the beginning of the response; for example, the length of time between an indication of the end of an inquiry and the display of the first character of the response at a user terminal.

Response Unit (RU)   According to IBM documentation, a message unit that acknowledges a request unit. It may contain prefix information received in a request unit.

restoring   In window-based environments, changing a minimized or maximized window back to its regular size.

Restructured Extended Executor (REXX)   According to IBM documentation, a general-purpose, procedural language for end-user personal programming, designed for ease of use by both casual general users and computer professionals. It is also useful for application macros.

Result Handler   A routine that the Data Access Manager calls to convert a data item to a character string.

Return Code   A code used to identify the action or lack thereof of a program execution.

RFC   Request for Comments. Proposed and accepted TCP/IP standards.

RLOGIN   Remote LOGIN. A logon service provided by Berkeley 4BSD UNIX systems that allows users of one machine to connect to other UNIX systems.

RMS-11   According to Digital Equipment documentation, a set of routines that are linked with compatibility mode programs and provide similar functional capabilities to Open VMS Record Management Services. The file organizations and record formats used by RMS-11 are very similar to those of RMS.

root menu   That menu which could be called the main menu. That menu from which other menus originate.

root window   In the X windowing environment, what is presented on the screen once the X graphical user interface is visible to the user. It is the window that other windows are based upon.

Route Selection Services (RSS)   According to IBM documentation, a subcomponent of the topology and routing services component that determines the preferred route between a specified pair of nodes for a given class of service.

routing   The moving of data through paths in a network.

Routing Information Base   A collection of output from route calculations.

Routing Table Maintenance Protocol   According to Apple documentation, a protocol used by routers on an AppleTalk internet to determine how to forward a data packet to the network number to which it is addressed.

RTMP Stub According to Apple documentation, the portion of the Routing Table Maintenance Protocol contained in an AppleTalk node other than a router. DDP uses the RTMP stub to determine the network number of the network cable to which the node is connected and to determine the network number and node ID on one router on that network cable.

RTT Round Trip Time. A measure of delay between two hosts.

RU Chain According to IBM documentation, an SNA set of related request/response units (RUs) that are consecutively transmitted on a particular normal or expedited data flow.

RUN disk According to IBM documentation, a virtual disk that contains the VTAM, NetView, and VM/SNA console support (VSCS) load libraries, program temporary fixes (PTFs), and user-written modifications from the ZAP disk.

SACK Selective ACKnowledgement In TCP/IP, an acknowledgement mechanism used with sliding window protocols. This permits a receiver to acknowledge packets received out of order within the current sliding window.

same-domain According to IBM documentation, pertaining to communication between entities in the same SNA domain.

Satellite Node According to Digital Equipment documentation, a processor that is part of a local area VMScluster system. A satellite node is booted remotely from the system disk of the boot server in this type of VMScluster system.

screen In SAA Basic Common User Access architecture, the physical surface of a display device upon which information is shown to a user.

screen dump A screen capture capable of being routed to a file.

SCS SNA Character String.

SDLC Synchronous Data Link Control.

secondary end of a session According to IBM documentation, the end of a session that uses secondary protocols. For an LU-LU session, the secondary end of the session is the secondary logical unit (SLU).

SecondaryInit Record According to Apple documentation, a data structure in the declaration ROM of a NuBus card that contains initialization code. The Slot manager executes the code in the SecondaryInit Record after RAM patches to the Operating System have been loaded from disk during system startup.

Secondary Logical Unit (SLU) According to IBM documentation, the LU that contains the secondary half-session for a particular LU-LU session. An LU may contain secondary and primary half-sessions for different active LU-LU sessions.

Segment According to IBM documentation, with reference to a token-ring network, a section of cable between components or devices. A segment may consist of a single patch cable, several patch cables that are connected, or a combination of building cable and patch cables that are connected. In TCP/IP, this is the unit of transfer sent from TCP on one machine to TCP on another.

segmentation   According to IBM documentation, a process by which path control divides basic information units into smaller units, called *BIU segments,* to accommodate smaller buffer sizes in adjacent nodes. Both segmentation and segment assembly are optional Path Control features. The support for either or both is indicated in the BIND request and response.

Semaphore   According to Digital Equipment documentation, in a DECnet for Open VMS network, a common data structure used to control the exchange of signals between concurrent processes.

send pacing   According to IBM documentation, the pacing of message units (in SNA) that a component is sending.

Sequential Access Mode   According to Digital Equipment documentation, the retrieval or storage of records where a program reads or writes records one after the other in the order in which they appear, starting and ending at any arbitrary point in the file.

Sequential File Organization   According to Digital Equipment documentation, a file organization in which records appear in the order in which they were originally written. The records can be fixed length or variable length. Sequential file organization permits sequential record access and random access by the record's file address. Sequential file organization with fixed length records also permits random access by relative record number.

server   An entity that serves the request of a client. This may be in the context of TCP/IP applications with clients and servers, or it could refer to a print or file server.

Service Access Point (SAP)   A logical addressable point.

service primitive   Part of a service element. Four types exists: confirm, indication, request, and response.

session   A logical connection between two addressible end points.

Session Activation Request   According to IBM documentation, a request in SNA that activates a session between two network accessible units and specifies session parameters that control various protocols during session activity; for example, BIND and ACTPU.

Session Awareness (SAW) Data   According to IBM documentation, data collected by the NetView program about a session that includes the session type, the names of session partners, and information about the session activation status. It is collected for LU-LU, SSCP-LU, SSCP-PU, and SSCP-SSCP sessions and for non-SNA terminals not supported by NTO. It can be displayed in various forms, such as most recent sessions lists.

Session Connector   According to IBM documentation, a session-layer component in an APPN network node or in a subarea node boundary or gateway function that connects two stages of a session. Session connectors swap addresses from one address space to another for session-level intermediate routing, segment session message units as needed, and (except for gateway function session connectors) adaptively pace the session traffic in each direction.

Session Control (SC)   According to IBM documentation, one of the following:

- One of the components of transmission control. Session control is used to purge data flowing in a session after an unrecoverable error occurs, to resynchronize the data flow after such an error, and to perform cryptographic verification.

- A request unit (RU) category used for requests and responses exchanged between the session control components of a session and for session activation and deactivation requests and responses.

Session Control Block (SCB) According to IBM documentation, in NPM, control blocks in a common storage area for session collection.

Session Data According to IBM documentation, data about a session collected by the NetView program, consisting of session awareness data, session trace data, and session response time data.

Session Deactivation Request According to IBM documentation, in SNA, a request that deactivates a session between two network accessible units (NAUs); for example, UNBIND and DACTPU.

Session-Establishment Request According to IBM documentation, in VTAM, a request to an LU to establish a session. For the primary logical unit (PLU) of the requested session, the session-establishment request is the CINIT sent from the system services control point (SSCP) to the PLU. For the secondary logical unit (SLU) of the requested session, the session-establishment request is the BIND sent from the PLU to the SLU.

Session ID According to IBM documentation, a number that uniquely identifies a session.

Session Initiation Request According to IBM documentation, an Initiate or logon request from a logical unit (LU) to a system services control point (SSCP) that an LU-LU session be activated.

Session Layer According to the OSI reference model, layer 5. It coordinates the dialogue between two communicating application processes.

Session-Level LU-LU Verification According to IBM documentation, an LU 6.2 security service that is used to verify the identity of each logical unit when a session is established.

Session-Level Pacing According to IBM documentation, a flow control technique that permits a receiving half-session or session connector to control the data transfer rate (the rate at which it receives request units) on the normal flow. It is used to prevent overloading a receiver with unprocessed requests when the sender can generate requests faster than the receiver can process them.

Session Limit According to IBM documentation, a term used to refer to the maximum number of concurrently active LU-LU sessions that a specific LU can support.

Session Manager (SM) Typically a third-party product that permits a user on one terminal to logon to multiple applications concurrently.

Session Monitor According to IBM documentation, a component of NetView that collects and correlates session-related data and provides online access to this information.

Session Parameters   According to IBM documentation, the parameters that specify or constrain the protocols (such as bracket protocol and pacing) for a session between two network accessible units.

Session Partner   According to IBM documentation, in SNA, one of the two network accessible units (NAUs) having an active session.

Session Path   According to IBM documentation, the half-sessions delimiting a given session and their interconnection (including any intermediate session connectors).

Session Services   According to IBM documentation, one of the types of network services in the control point (CP) and in the logical unit (LU). These services provide facilities for an LU or a network operator to request that a control point aid with initiating or terminating sessions between LUs. Assistance with session termination is needed only by SSCP-dependent LUs.

Session Stage   According to IBM documentation, that portion of a session path consisting of two session-layer components that are logically adjacent and their interconnection. An example is the paired session-layer components in adjacent type 2.1 nodes and their interconnection over the link between them.

Shadow Resource   According to IBM documentation, an alternate representation of a network resource that is retained as a definition for possible future use.

Shareable Image   According to Digital Equipment documentation, an image that has all of its internal references resolved, but must be linked with one or more object modules to produce an executable image. A shareable image cannot be executed. A shareable image file can be used to contain a library of routines.

Shared-Access Transport Facility (SATF)   A transmission facility, such as a multipoint link connection or a token-ring network where multiple pairs of nodes can form concurrently active links.

Shared Image   According to Digital Equipment documentation, an image that is installed so that multiple users in a system can share the memory pages where the image is loaded.

Shared Partition   According to IBM documentation, in VSE, a partition allocated for a program such as VSE/POWER that provides services for and communicates with programs in other partitions of the system's virtual address spaces. Storage in a shared partition is addressable by programs running concurrently in other partitions.

Sibling Networks   According to Novell documentation, two or more coequal networks branching off the same node in an internetwork. Workstations on these networks that use NetWare Btrieve must have access to a file server loaded with BSERVER.

sift-down effect   According to IBM documentation, the copying of a value from a higher-level resource to a lower-level resource. The sift-down effect applies to many of the keywords and operands in NCP and VTAM definition statements. If an operand is coded on a macroinstruction or generation statement for a higher-level resource, it need not be coded for lower-level resources for which the same value is desired. The value "sifts down"—that is, becomes the default for all lower-level resources.

silly-window syndrome   In TCP/IP based networks, a scenario where a receiver keeps indicating a small "window" and a sender continues to send small segments to it.

Single-Byte Character Set (SBCS)   According to IBM documentation, a character set in which each character is represented by a 1-byte code.

Single Console Image Facility (SCIF)   According to IBM documentation, a VM facility that allows multiple consoles to be controlled from a single virtual machine console.

Single-Domain Network   According to IBM documentation, a network with one SSCP.

single mode   A type of fiberoptic cable containing just one mode.

SIO   Start I/O.

Sleep State   According to Apple documentation, a low power-consumption state of the Macintosh portable computer. In the sleep state, the Power Manager and the various device drivers shut off power or remove clocks from the computer's various subsystems, including the CPU, RAM, ROM, and I/O ports.

sliding window   A scenario where a protocol permits the transmitting station to send a stream of bytes before an acknowledgement arrives.

SLIP   Serial Line IP. A protocol to run IP protocol over serial lines. An example is using telephone lines.

SLU   Secondary Logical Unit.

SM   Session Manager.

SMF   System Management Facility.

SMP   System Modification Program.

SMS   Storage Management Subsystem.

SMTP   Simple Mail Transfer Protocol. A TCP/IP application that provides electronic mail support. The SMTP protocol specifies how two mail systems interact and the format of control messages.

SNA   Systems Network Architecture.

SNA Network   A collection of IBM hardware and software put together in such a way as to form a collective greater than the parts. The components comprising the network conform to the SNA format and protocol specifications defined by IBM.

SNA Network Interconnection (SNI)   According to IBM, the connection of two or more independent SNA networks to allow communication between logical units in those networks. The individual SNA networks retain their independence.

SNMP   Simple Network Monitoring Protocol. A de facto industry standard protocol used to manage TCP/IP networks.

Socket   A concept from Berkeley 4BSD UNIX that allows an application program to access the TCP/IP protocols. In TCP/IP networks, the internet address of the host and the port number it uses. A TCP/IP application is identified by its socket.

Solicited Message   According to IBM documentation, a response from VTAM to a command entered by a program operator.

source route   A route determined by the source. TCP/IP implements source routing by using an option field in an IP datagram.

Specific Mode   According to IBM documentation, in VTAM, the following:

- The form of a receive request that obtains input from one specific session.

- The form of an accept request that completes the establishment of a session by accepting a specific queued CINIT request.

SSCP   System Services Control Point.

SSCP-Dependent LU   An LU requiring assistance from a SSCP to establish a LU-LU session.

SSCP ID   According to IBM documentation, in SNA, a number that uniquely identifies a SSCP. The SSCP ID is used in session activation requests sent to physical units (PUs) and other SSCPs.

SSCP-Independent LU   According to IBM documentation, an LU that can activate an LU-LU session (that is, send a BIND request) without assistance from an SSCP. It does not have an SSCP-LU session. Currently, only an LU 6.2 can be an independent LU.

SSCP-LU Session   According to IBM documentation, in SNA, a session between the SSCP and a logical unit (LU). The session enables the LU to request the SSCP to help initiate LU-LU sessions.

SSCP-PU Session   According to IBM documentation, in SNA, a session between a SSCP and a PU. SSCP-PU sessions allow SSCPs to send requests to and receive status information from individual nodes in order to control the network configuration.

SSCP Rerouting   According to IBM documentation, an SNA network interconnection. A technique used by the gateway system services control point (SSCP) to send session-initiation RUs, by way of a series of SSCP-SSCP sessions, from one SSCP to another until the owning SSCP is reached.

SSCP-SSCP Session   According to IBM documentation, a session between the SSCP in one domain and the SSCP in another domain. This type of session is used to initiate and terminate cross-domain LU-LU sessions.

SSP   System Support Programs.

stack   An area of memory in the application partition that is used to store temporary variables.

start-stop (SS) transmission   Asynchronous transmission whereby each signal that represents a character is preceded by a start signal and is followed by a stop signal.

station   An input or output point.

statistic   Significant data about a defined resource.

Status   Generally speaking, a condition or state of a resource. According to Digital Equipment documentation, a display type for the Network Control Program commands SHOW and LIST. Status refers to dynamic information about a component that is kept in either the volatile or permanent database.

Status Monitor   According to IBM documentation, a component of the NetView program that collects and summarizes information on the status of resources defined in a VTAM domain.

Stream   In IBM's SNA, a structured protocol. For example, a 3270 data stream, a GDS data stream, or a LU6.2 data stream. According to Digital Equipment documentation, an access window to a file associated with a record control block, supporting record operation requests. Generally, it is a full-duplex connection between a user's task and a device.

Subarea   According to IBM documentation, a portion of the SNA network consisting of a subarea node, attached peripheral nodes, and associated resources.

Subarea Address   According to IBM documentation, a value in the subarea field of a network address that identifies a particular subarea.

Subarea Host Node   According to IBM documentation, a node that provides both subarea function and an application program interface (API) for running application programs. It provides SSCP functions and subarea node services, and is aware of the network configuration.

Subarea Link   According to IBM documentation, a link that connects two subarea nodes.

Subarea LU   According to IBM documentation, a logical unit that resides in a subarea node.

Subarea Network   According to IBM documentation, interconnected subareas, their directly attached peripheral nodes, and the transmission groups that connect them.

Subarea Node (SN)   According to IBM documentation, a node that uses network addresses for routing and maintains routing tables that reflect the configuration of the network. Subarea nodes can provide gateway function to connect multiple subarea networks, intermediate routing functions, and boundary function support peripheral nodes. Type 4 and type 5 nodes are subarea nodes.

Subarea Path Control   According to IBM documentation, the function in a subarea node that routes message units between network accessible units (NAUs) and provides the paths between them.

subdirectory   According to Digital Equipment documentation, a directory file, cataloged in a higher level directory, that lists additional files belonging to the owner of the directory.

subsystem   A secondary or subordinate software system.

summary   According to Digital Equipment documentation, the default display type for the Network Control Program commands SHOW and LIST. A summary includes the most useful information for a component, selected from the status and characteristics information.

Supervisor   According to IBM documentation, that part of a control program that coordinates the use of resources and maintains the flow of processing unit operations.

Supervisor Call (SVC)   According to IBM documentation, a request that serves as the interface into operating system functions, such as allocating storage. The SVC protects the operating system from inappropriate user entry. All operating system requests must be handled by SVCs.

switched connection   A data link connection that functions like a dial telephone.

switched line   A line where the connection is established by dialing.

Switched Major Node   According to IBM documentation, in VTAM a major node whose minor nodes are physical units and logical units attached by switched SDLC links.

switched network   A network that establishes connections by a dialing function.

Switched Network Backup   According to IBM documentation, an optional facility that allows a user to specify, for certain types of physical units (PUs), a switched line to be used as an alternate path if the primary line becomes unavailable or unusable.

switched virtual circuit   A temporary logical association between two DTEs connected to a packet switching data network.

symbiont   According to Digital Equipment documentation, a process that transfers record-oriented data to or from a device. For example, an input symbiont transfers data from card readers to disks. An output symbiont transfers data from disks to line printers.

Symbiont Manager   According to Digital Equipment documentation, the function that maintains spool queues and dynamically creates symbiont processes to perform the necessary I/O operations.

symbol   According to Digital Equipment documentation, an entity that when defined will represent a particular function or entity (for example, a command string, directory name, or file name) in a particular context.

Symbol Table   According to Digital Equipment documentation, that portion of an executable image that contains the definition of global symbols used by the debugger for images linked with the DEBUG qualifier. A table in which the DIGITAL Command Language places local symbols. DCL maintains a local symbol table for each command level.

Synchronization Point   According to IBM documentation, an intermediate or end point during processing of a transaction at which an update or modification to one or more of the transaction's protected resources is logically complete and error free.

Synchronous Backplane Interconnect   According to Digital Equipment documentation, that part of the hardware that interconnects the VAX processor, memory controllers, MASSBUS adapters, and the UNIBUS adapter.

Sync Point Services (SPS)   According to IBM documentation, the component of the sync point manager that is responsible for coordinating the managers of protected resources during sync point processing. SPS coordinates two-phase commit protocols, resync protocols, and logging.

System Communications Services   According to Digital Equipment documentation, a protocol responsible for the formation and breaking of intersystem process connections and for flow control of message traffic over those connections. System services such as the VMScluster connection manager and the mass storage control protocol, or MSCP, disk server communicate with this protocol.

System Control Block   According to Digital Equipment documentation, on VAX systems, the data structure in system space that contains all the interrupt and exception vectors known to the system.

System Definition   According to IBM documentation, the process, completed before a system is put into use, by which desired functions and operations of the system are selected from various available options.

System Disk   According to Digital Equipment documentation, the disk that contains the operating system. In a VMScluster environment, a system disk is set up so that most of the files can be shared by several processors. In addition, each processor has its own directory on the system disk that contains its page, swap, and dump files.

System File   According to Apple documentation, a file, located in the System Folder, that contains the basic system software plus some system resources, such as font and sound resources.

system generation   Synonym for system definition.

System GETVIS Area   According to IBM documentation, a storage space that is available for dynamic allocation to VSE's system control programs or other application programs.

System Image   According to Digital Equipment documentation, the image read into memory from disk when the system is started up.

System Management Facility (SMF)   According to IBM documentation, a feature of MVS that collects and records a variety of system- and job-related information.

system menu   In a windowing environment, particularly the X window environment, the menu that displays when you press the system menu button on the window manager window frame. Every window has a system menu that enables you to control the size, shape, and position of the window.

System Modification Program (SMP)   According to IBM documentation, a program used to install software changes on MVS systems.

System Services Control Point (SSCP)   According to IBM documentation, a component within a subarea network for managing the configuration, coordinating network operator and problem determination requests, and providing directory services and other session services for end users of the network. Multiple SSCPs, cooperating as peers with one another, can divide the network into domains of control, with each SSCP having a hierarchical control relationship to the physical units and logical units within its own domain.

System Services Control Point (SSCP) Domain   According to IBM documentation, the system services control point, the physical units (PUs), the logical units (LUs), the links, the link stations, and all the resources that the SSCP has the ability to control by means of activation and deactivation requests.

Systems Network Architecture (SNA)   IBM's description of the logical structure, formats, protocols, and operational sequences for its network offering.

System Support Program (SSP)   According to IBM documentation, an IBM licensed program, made up of a collection of utilities and small programs, that supports the operation of the NCP.

takeover   According to IBM documentation, the process by which the failing active subsystem is released from its extended recovery facility (XRF) sessions with terminal users and replaced by an alternate subsystem.

Task Specifier   According to Digital Equipment documentation, information provided to DECnet for Open VMS software that enables it to complete a logical link connection to a remote task. This information includes the name of the remote node on which the target task runs and the name of the task itself.

TCP   Transmission Control Protocol. The TCP/IP standard transport level protocol that provides the reliable, full-duplex, stream service on which many application protocols depend. It is connection-oriented in that before transmitting data, participants must establish a connection.

Telecommunications Access Method (TCAM)   According to IBM documentation, the access method prior to VTAM.

TELNET   The TCP/IP standard protocol for remote terminal service.

terminal   Generally agreed upon as meaning a point of entry with a display and keyboard.

Terminal Access Facility (TAF)   According to IBM documentation, in the NetView program, a facility that allows a network operator to control a number of subsystems. In a full-screen or operator control session, operators can control any combination of such subsystems simultaneously.

Terminal-Based Program   In the X window environment, a program (nonclient) written to be run on a terminal (not in a window). Terminal-based programs must be fooled by terminal-emulation clients to run on the X Window System.

Terminal Emulator   Generally, a program that performs some type of simulation; typically this simulation is of a type of terminal.

Terminal Server   A network device that is used to connect "dumb" terminals to a network medium. Consequently, these terminals have virtual terminal access to hosts and devices located on a network.

Terminal Type The type of terminal attached to your computer. UNIX uses the terminal type to set the TERM environment variable so that it can communicate with the terminal correctly. In the SNA environment, the terminal type is required in order to know how to configure the system so it can function.

TERMINATE According to IBM documentation, in SNA, a request unit that is sent by a logical unit (LU) to its system services control point (SSCP) to cause the SSCP to start a procedure to end one or more designated LU-LU sessions.

Term0 According to Hewlett Packard documentation, a level 0 terminal is a reference standard that defines basic terminal functions.

TFTP Trivial File Transfer Protocol. A TCP/IP standard protocol for file transfer that uses UDP as a transport mechanism. TFTP depends only on UDP, so it can be used on machines like diskless workstations.

TG Weight According to IBM documentation, a quantitative measure of how well the values of a transmission group's characteristics satisfy the criteria specified by the class-of-service definition, as computed during route selection for a session.

Thread According to Digital Equipment documentation, a single, sequential flow of control within a program. It is the active execution of a designated routine, including any nested routine invocations. A single thread has a single point of execution within it. A thread can be executed in parallel with other threads.

threshold Generally agreed to mean a percentage value set for a resource.

Tile In the X window environment, a rectangular area used to cover a surface with a pattern or visual texture.

time division multiplexing (TDM) A technique used to multiplex data on a channel by a time sharing of the channel.

time domain reflectometer (TDR) A device used to troubleshoot networks. It sends signals through a network medium to check for continuity.

Time Sharing Option Extensions (TSO/E) According to IBM, the base for all TSO enhancements.

timeout An event that occurs at the end of a predetermined period of time.

Title Bar In the X window environment, the rectangular area between the top of the window and the window frame. The title bar contains the title of the window object. For example, Xclock for clocks.

TN3270 A program that uses TELNET protocol but produces an EBCDIC 3270 data stream. The program is normally found as a TN3270 client application that provides access into a 3270-based environment.

token The symbol of authority passed successively from one data station to another to indicate the station temporarily in control of the transmission medium.

Token Ring A network with a ring topology that passes tokens from one attaching device to another.

Token-Ring Interface Coupler (TIC)   Interface board used to connect a device such as a 3720, 3725, or 3745 Communication Controller to a Token-Ring network.

Token-Ring network   A ring network that allows unidirectional data transmission between data stations by a token-passing procedure.

Topology and Routing Services (TRS)   According to IBM documentation, an APPN control point component that manages the topology database, computes routes, and provides a route selection control vector (RSCV) that specifies the best route through the network for a given session based on its requested class of service.

trace   A record of events captured and used to troubleshoot hardware and/or software.

Transaction   According to Apple documentation, a sequence of Apple events sent back and forth between a client and a server application, beginning with the client's initial request for a service.

Transaction Processing Facility (TPF)   A software system designed to support real-time applications.

Transaction Program   According to IBM, a program that conforms to LU6.2 protocols.

transceiver   A device that connects a host's cable from the interface board to the main cable of the network.

Translated Code   According to Digital Equipment documentation, the native AXP object code in a translated image. Translated code includes:

- AXP code that reproduces the behavior of equivalent VAX code in the original image.

- Calls to the translated image environment.

Translated Image   According to Digital Equipment documentation, an AXP executable or shareable image created by translating the object code of a VAX image. The translated image, which is functionally equivalent to the VAX image from which it was translated, includes both translated code and the original image.

Translated Image Environment   According to Digital Equipment documentation, a native AXP shareable image that supports the execution of translated images. The TIE processes all interactions with the native AXP system and provides an environment similar to VAX for the translated image by managing VAX state; by emulating VAX features such as exception processing, AST delivery, and complex VAX instructions; and by interpreting untranslated VAX instructions.

translation   According to Digital Equipment documentation, the process of converting a VAX binary image to an AXP image that runs with the assistance of the TIE on an AXP system. Translation is a static process that converts as much VAX code as possible to native Alpha AXP instructions. The TIE interprets any untranslated VAX code at run time.

translation table   A table used to replace one or more characters with alternative characters.

Transmission Group (TG)   According to IBM, a group of links between adjacent subarea nodes, appearing as a single logical link for routing of messages.

Transmission Header (TH)   According to SNA, control information, optionally followed by a basic information unit, created and used by path control to route message units and to control their flow within the network.

Transmission Priority   According to IBM documentation, a rank assigned to a message unit that determines its precedence for being selected by the path control component in each node along a route for forwarding to the next node in the route.

Transport Layer   According to the OSI model, the layer that provides a reliable end-to-end service to its users.

Transport Network   According to IBM documentation, that part of an SNA network that includes the data link control and path control layer.

trap   An event used in SNMP managed networks to send data to the network manager. A trap is sent from a SNMP Agent.

Trash Folder   According to Apple documentation, a directory at the root level of a volume for storing files that the user has moved to the Trash icon. After opening the Trash icon, the user sees the collection of all items that have been moved to the Trash icon—that is, the union of appropriate Trash directories from all mounted volumes. A Macintosh setup to share files among users in a network environment maintains separate Trash subdirectories for remote users within its shared, network Trash directory. The Finder for system software version 7.0 empties a Trash directory only when the user of that directory chooses the Empty Trash command.

TSO/E   Time Sharing Option Extensions. According to IBM documentation, a program that provides enhancements to MVS/XA users.

TTL   Time to Live. A technique used in best-effort delivery systems to avoid endlessly looping packets. For example, packets have a "time" associated with their lifetime.

Type   According to Apple documentation, the second field in the name of an AppleTalk entity. The type is assigned by the entity itself and can be anything the user or application assigns.

Type 2.1 END Node   According to IBM documentation, a type 2.1 node that provides full SNA end-user services, but no intermediate routing or network services to any other node; it is configured only as an endpoint in a network.

Type 2.1 Network   According to IBM documentation, a collection of interconnected type 2.1 network nodes and type 2.1 end nodes. A type 2.1 network may consist of nodes of just one type, namely, all network nodes or all end nodes; a pair of directly attached end nodes is the simplest case of a type 2.1 network.

Type 2.1 Node   A node that conforms to IBM's Type 2.1 architecture.

Type 5 Node   According to IBM documentation, a node that can be any one of the following:

- Advanced peer-to-peer networking (APPN) END node.
- Advanced peer-to-peer networking (APPN) network node.
- Interchange node.
- Low-entry networking (LEN) node.
- Migration data host.
- Subarea node.
  It is also a node that traditionally has the SSCP.

UDP   User Datagram Protocol. A TCP/IP standard protocol that is in contrast to TCP. UDP is connectionless and unreliable.

UNBIND   According to IBM, a request to deactivate a session between two logical units (LUs).

unformatted   According to IBM, pertaining to commands (such as LOGON or LOGOFF) entered by an end user and sent by a logical unit in character form.

Unformatted System Services (USS)   According to IBM documentation, in SNA products, a system services control point (SSCP) facility that translates a character-coded request, such as a logon or logoff request, into a field-formatted request for processing by formatted system services and that translates field-formatted replies and responses into character-coded requests for processing by a logical unit.

Unit Control Block   According to Digital Equipment documentation, structure in the I/O database that describes the characteristics of and current activity on a device unit. The unit control block also holds the fork block for its unit's device driver; the fork block is a critical part of a driver fork process. The UCB also provides a dynamic storage area for the driver.

Universal Symbol   According to Digital Equipment documentation, a global symbol in a shareable image that can be used by modules linked with that shareable image. Universal symbols are typically a subset of all the global symbols in a shareable image. When creating a shareable image, the linker ensures that universal symbols remain available for reference after symbols have been resolved.

Unsolicited Message   According to IBM documentation, a message from VTAM to a program operator, that is unrelated to any command entered by the program operator.

Upline Dump   According to Digital Equipment documentation, in DECnet for Open VMS, a function that allows an adjacent node to dump its memory to a file on a system.

User Exit   According to IBM documentation, it is a point in an IBM-supplied program at which a user exit routine may be given control.

User Exit Routine   According to IBM documentation, a user-written routine that receives control at predefined user exit points. User exit routines can be written in assemblers or a high-level language.

User File Directory   According to Digital Equipment documentation, a file that briefly catalogs a set of files stored on disk or tape. The directory includes the name, type, and version number of each file in the set. It also contains a unique number that identifies that file's actual location and points to a list of its file attributes.

User Privileges   According to Digital Equipment documentation, those privileges granted to a user by the system manager.

USS   Unformatted System Services.

UUCP   Unix to Unix Copy Program. An application program that allows one UNIX system to copy files to or from another UNIX system.

VAXBI   According to Digital Equipment documentation, the part of the VAX 8200, VAX 8250, VAX 8300, and VAX 8350 hardware that connects I/O adapters with memory controllers and the processor. In VAX 8530, VAX 8550, VAX 8700, or VAX 8800, or VAX 6200 and VAX 6300 systems, the part of the hardware that connects I/O adapters with the bus that interfaces with the processor and memory.

VAXcluster Configuration   According to Digital Equipment documentation, a highly integrated organization of Open VMS systems that communicate over a high-speed communications path. VAXcluster configurations have all the functions of single-node systems, plus the ability to share CPU resources, queues, and disk storage. Like a single-node system, the VAXcluster configuration provides a single security and management environment. Member nodes can share the same operating environment or serve specialized needs.

VAX Environment Software Translator (VEST)   According to Digital Equipment documentation, a software migration tool that translates VAX executable and shareable images into translated images that run on AXP systems. VEST is part of the DECmigrate tool set.

VAX Vector Instruction Emulation Facility (VVIEF)   According to Digital Equipment documentation, a standard feature of the operating system that allows vectorized applications to be written and debugged in a VAX system in which vector processors are not available. VVIEF emulates the VAX vector processing environment, including the nonprivileged VAX vector instructions and the vector system services. Use of VVIEF is restricted to user mode code.

Vector   According to Digital Equipment documentation, a storage location that contains the starting address of a procedure to be executed when a given interrupt or exception occurs.

Vector Present System   According to Digital Equipment documentation, a VAX system that in its hardware implementation complies with the VAX vector architecture and incorporates one or more optional vector processors.

Virtual Disk   According to IBM documentation, in VM, a physical disk storage device, or a logical subdivision of a physical disk storage device, that has its own address, consecutive storage space for data, and index or description of stored data so that the data can be accessed.

Virtual Filestore   In OSI, the OSI abstraction of a collection of files, directories, and/or references.

Virtual Machine (VM) According to IBM documentation, in VM, a functional equivalent of a computing system. On the 370 Feature of VM, a virtual machine operates in System/370 mode. On the ESA Feature of VM, a virtual machine operates in System/370, 370-XA, ESA/370, or ESA/390 mode. Each virtual machine is controlled by an operating system. VM controls the concurrent execution of multiple virtual machines on an actual processor complex.

Virtual Machine/Enterprise Systems Architecture (VM/ESA) According to IBM documentation, an IBM program that manages the resources of a single computer so that multiple computing systems appear to exist. Each virtual machine is the functional equivalent of a real machine.

Virtual Machine/Extended Architecture (VM/XA) According to IBM documentation, an operating system that facilitates conversion to MVS/XA by allowing several operating systems (a production system and one or more test systems) to run simultaneously on a single 370-XA processor.

Virtual Machine Group According to IBM documentation, in the Group Control System (GCS), two or more virtual machines associated with each other through the same named system.

Virtual Machine/System Product (VM/SP) According to IBM, a program that manages the resources of a single computer so that multiple computing systems appear to exist.

Virtual Machine/System Product High Performance Option (VM/SP HPO) According to IBM documentation, a program that can be installed and executed in conjunction with VM/SP to extend the capabilities of VM/SP with programming enhancements, support for microcode assists, and additional functions.

Virtual Route (VR) According to IBM documentation, in SNA, either of the following:

- A logical connection between two subarea nodes that is physically realized as a particular explicit route.

- A logical connection that is contained wholly within a subarea node for intranode sessions.

Virtual Route (VR) Pacing According to IBM documentation, in SNA, a flow control technique used by the virtual route control component of path control at each end of a virtual route to control the rate at which path information units (PIUs) flow over the virtual route.

Virtual Routing Node According to IBM documentation, a representation of node's connectivity to a connection network defined on a shared-access transport facility, such as a token ring.

Virtual Storage According to IBM documentation, storage space that may be regarded as addressable main storage by the user of a computer system in which virtual addresses are mapped into real addresses.

Virtual Storage Access Method (VSAM) According to IBM documentation, an access method of direct or sequential processing of fixed- and variable-length records on direct access devices.

Virtual Storage Extended (VSE)   According to IBM documentation, a program whose full name is the Virtual Storage Extended/Advanced Function. It is a software operating system controlling the execution of programs.

Virtual Telecommunication Access Method (VTAM)   According to IBM documentation, a program that controls communication and the flow of data in an SNA network. It provides single-domain, multiple-domain, and interconnected network capability.

VIT   VTAM Internal Trace.

VM   Virtual Machine.

VM/ESA   Virtual Machine/Enterprise Systems Architecture.

VMScluster Configuration   According to Digital Equipment documentation, a highly integrated organization of Open VMS AXP systems, or a combination of AXP or VAX systems, that communicate over a high-speed communications path. VMScluster configurations have all the functions of single-node systems, plus the ability to share CPU resources, queues, and disk storage. Like a single-node system, the VMScluster configuration provides a single security and management environment. Member nodes can share the same operating environment or serve specialized needs.

VM/SNA Console Support (VSCS)   According to IBM documentation, a VTAM component for the VM environment that provides Systems Network Architecture (SNA) support. It allows SNA terminals to be virtual machine consoles.

VM/SP   Virtual Machine/System Product.

VM/SP HPO   Virtual Machine/System Product High Performance Option.

VM/370 Control Program (CP)   According to IBM documentation, that component of VM/370 that manages the resources of a single computer with the result that multiple computing systems appear to exist. Each virtual machine is the functional equivalent of an IBM System/370 computing system.

VSE   Virtual Storage Extended.

VSE/Advanced Functions   According to IBM documentation, the basic operating system support needed for a VSE-controlled installation.

VSE/ESA   Virtual Storage Extended/Enterprise Systems Architecture.

VTAM   Virtual Telecommunications Access Method.

VTAM Application Program   According to IBM documentation, a program that has opened an access method control block (ACB) to identify itself to VTAM and that can therefore issue VTAM macroinstructions.

VTAM Common Network Services (VCNS)   According to IBM documentation, VTAM's support for shared physical connectivity between Systems Network Architecture (SNA) networks and certain non-SNA networks.

VTAM Definition   According to IBM documentation, the process of defining the user application network to VTAM and modifying IBM-defined characteristics to suit the needs of the user.

VTAM Definition Library According to IBM documentation, the operating system files or data sets that contain the definition statements and start options filed during VTAM definition.

VTAM Internal Trace (VIT) According to IBM documentation, a trace used in VTAM to collect data on channel I/O, use of locks, and storage management services.

VTAM Operator According to IBM documentation, a person or program authorized to issue VTAM operator commands.

VTAM Operator Command According to IBM documentation, a command used to monitor or control a VTAM domain.

waveform The representation of a disturbance as a function as it occurs in time and its relationship to space.

wavelength The distance an electromagnetic wave can travel in the amount of time it takes to oscillate through a complete cycle.

Well-Known Port A term used with TCP/IP networks. In TCP/IP, applications and programs that reside on top of TCP and UDP, respectively, have a designated port assigned to them. This agreed-upon port is known as a well-known port.

window A term used with environments such as X Windows. Generally, the term is used in contrast with line or full-screen mode.

Window-Based Program A program written for use with a windowing system; for example, with an X Window environment or the MS Window environment. The opposite of a window-based program is a terminal-based program.

Window Decoration In the X Window environment, the frame and window control buttons that surround windows managed by the Window Manager.

Window Manager A program in the X Window system that controls size, placement, and operation of windows on the root window. The window manager includes the functional window frames that surround each window object, as well as a menu for the root window.

X.21 A CCITT standard defining logical link control and media access control in X.25 networks.

X.25 A CCITT standard for packet switched network layer services.

X.400 A CCITT and ISO combination of standards for providing electronic mail services.

X.500 A CCITT and ISO combination of standards for providing directory services.

X Application An application program that conforms to X protocol standards.

Xenix A version of UNIX that can run on a PC.

X Library A collection of C language routines based upon the X protocol.

X Protocol A protocol that uses TCP as a transport mechanism. It supports asynchronous, event-driven distributed window environments; this can be across heterogeneous platforms.

X Terminal A terminal and machine specifically designed to run an X server. In this type of environment, X clients are run on remote systems.

X Toolkit A collection of high level programs based upon programming from the X library.

X Window System A software system developed at MIT whose original design intent was to provide distributed computing support for the development of programs. It supports two-dimensional bitmapped graphics.

ZAP Disk According to IBM documentation, the virtual disk in the VM operating system that contains the user-written modifications to VTAM code.

Zone According to Digital Equipment documentation, a section of a fully configured VAXft fault-tolerant computing system that contains a minimum of a CPU module, memory module, I/O module, and associated devices. A VAXft system consists of two such zones with synchronized processor operations. If one zone fails, processing continues uninterrupted through automatic failover to the other zone. In AppleTalk, a logical grouping of devices in an AppleTalk internet that makes it easier for users to locate network services. The network administrator defines zones during the router setup process. The zone is the third field in the name of an AppleTalk entity.

Zone Information Protocol An AppleTalk protocol that maintains a table in each router, called the *zone information table,* that lists the relationship between zone names and networks.

Zone Name According to Apple documentation, a name defined for each zone in an AppleTalk internet. A LocalTalk network can have just one zone name. Ethernet and Token Ring networks can have multiple zone names, called a *zone list.*

Zone of Authority In the Domain Name System, the group of names a given name server is an authority for.

Bibliography

Abbatiello, Judy, and Ray Sarch (eds.): *Telec Communications and Data Communications Factbook,* Data Communications, New York; CCMI/McGraw-Hill, Ramsey, N.J., 1987.

Apple Computer, Inc.: *Planning and Managing AppleTalk Networks,* Addison-Wesley, Menlo Park, Calif., 1991.

———: *Technical Introduction to the Macintosh Family,* 2d ed., Addison-Wesley, Menlo Park, Calif., 1992.

Ashley, Ruth, and Judi N. Fernandez: *Job Control Language,* Wiley, New York, 1984.

Aspray, William: *John Von Neumann and The Origins of Modern Computing,* MIT Press, Cambridge, Mass., 1990.

ATM Forum:*ATM User-Network Interface Specification,* Prentice-Hall, Englewood Cliffs, N.J., 1993.

Bach, Maurice J.: *The Design of The UNIX Operating System,* Prentice-Hall, Englewood Cliffs, N.J., 1986.

Baggott, Jim: *The Meaning of Quantum Theory,* Oxford University Press, New York, 1992.

Bashe, Charles J., Lyle R. Johnson, John H. Palmer, and Emerson W. Pugh: *IBM's Early Computers,* MIT Press, Cambridge, Mass., 1986.

Berson, Alex: *APPC Introduction to LU6.2,* McGraw-Hill, New York, 1990.

Black, Uyless: *Data Networks Concepts, Theory, and Practice,* Prentice-Hall, Englewood Cliffs, N.J., 1989.

———: *TCP/IP and Related Protocols,* McGraw-Hill, New York, 1992.

———: *The V Series Recommendations Protocols for Data Communications over the Telephone Network,* McGraw-Hill, New York, 1991.

———: *The X Series Recommendations Protocols for Data Communications Networks,* McGraw-Hill, New York, 1991.

Blyth, W. John, and Mary M. Blyth: *Telecommunications: Concepts, Development, and Management,* Glencoe/McGraw-Hill, Mission Hills, Calif., 1990.

Bohl, Marilyn: *Information Processing,* 3d ed., Science Research Associates, Chicago, 1971.

Bradbeer, Robin, Peter De Bono, and Peter Laurie: *The Beginner's Guide to Computers,* Addison-Wesley, Menlo Park, Calif., 1982.

Brookshear, J. Glenn: *Computer Science: An Overview,* Benjamin/Cummings, Menlo Park, Calif., 1988.

Bryant, David: *Physics,* Hodder and Stoughton, Great Britain, 1971.

Campbell, Joe: *C Programmer's Guide to Serial Communications,* Howard W. Sams, Carmel, Ind., 1987.

———: *The RS-232 Solution,* SYBEX, Alameda, Calif., 1984.

Chorafas, Dimitris N.: *Local Area Network Reference,* McGraw-Hill, New York, 1989.

Comer, Douglas: *Internetworking With TCP/IP Principles, Protocols, and Architecture,* Prentice-Hall, Englewood Cliffs, N.J., 1988.

———: *Internetworking with TCP/IP,* vol. I: *Principles, Protocols, and Architecture,* Prentice-Hall, Englewood Cliffs, N.J., 1991.

———, and David L. Stevens: *Internetworking with TCP/IP,* vol. II: *Design, Implementation, and Internals,* Prentice-Hall, Englewood Cliffs, N.J., 1991.

Dayton, Robert L.: *Telecommunications: The Transmission of Information,* McGraw-Hill, New York, 1991.

Dern, Daniel P.: *The Internet Guide for New Users,* McGraw-Hill, New York, 1994.

Digital Equipment Corp.: *DECnet Digital Network Architecture (Phase V): Network Routing Layer Functional Specification,* EK-DNA03-FS-001, Digital Equipment Corp., Maynard, Mass., 1991.

———: *DECnet / OSI for OpenVMS: Introduction and Planning,* AA-PNHTB-TE, Digital Equipment Corp., Maynard, Mass., 1993.

———: *OpenVMS DCL Dictionary: A–M,* AA-PV5LA-TK, Digital Equipment Corp., Maynard, Mass., 1993.

———: *OpenVMS DCL Dictionary: N–Z,* AA-PV5LA-TK, Digital Equipment Corp., Maynard, Mass., 1993.

———: *OpenVMS Glossary,* AA-PV5UA-TK, Digital Equipment Corp., Maynard, Mass., 1993.

———: *OpenVMS Software Overview,* AA-PVXHA-TE, Digital Equipment Corp., Maynard, Mass., 1993.

Edmunds, John J.: *SAA / LU 6.2 Distributed Networks and Applications,* McGraw-Hill, New York, 1992.

Feit, Sidnie: *TCP / IP Architecture, Protocols, and Implementation,* McGraw-Hill, New York, 1993.

Forney, James S.: *DOS Beyond 640K,* 2d ed., Windcrest/McGraw-Hill, New York, 1992.

———: *MS-DOS Beyond 640K: Working with Extended and Expanded Memory,* Windcrest, Blue Ridge Summit, Pa., 1989.

Fortier, Paul J.: *Handbook of LAN Technology,* Intertext Publications/Multiscience Press, New York, 1989.

Gasman, Lawrence: *Broadband Networking,* Van Nostrand Reinhold, New York, 1994.

Graubart-Cervone, H. Frank: *VSE / ESA JCL Utilities, Power, and VSAM,* McGraw-Hill, New York, 1994.

Groff, James R., and Paul N. Weinbert: *Understanding UNIX: A Conceptual Guide,* Que Corp., Carmel, Ind., 1983.

Hecht, Jeff: *Understanding Fiber Optics,* Howard W. Sams, Carmel, Ind., 1990.

Hewlett-Packard Co.: *HP OpenView SNMP Agent Administrator's Reference,* J2322-90002, Hewlett-Packard Co., Ft. Collins, Colo., 1992.

———: *HP OpenView SNMP Management Platform Administrator's Reference,* J2313-90001, Hewlett-Packard Co., Ft. Collins, Colo., 1992.

———: *HP OpenView Windows User's Guide,* J2316-90000, Hewlett-Packard Co., Ft. Collins, Colo., 1992.

———: *Using HP-UX: HP 9000 Workstations,* B2910-90001, Hewlett-Packard Co., Ft. Collins, Colo., 1992.

———: *Using the X Window System,* B1171-90037, Hewlett-Packard Co., Ft. Collins, Colo., 1991.

IBM Corp.: *3172 Interconnect Controller: Operator's Guide,* GA27-3970-00, IBM Corp., Research Triangle Park, N.C., 1992.

———: *3172 Interconnect Controller: Planning Guide,* GA27-3867-05, IBM Corp., Research Triangle Park, N.C., 1992.

———: *3172 Interconnect Controller: Presentation Guide,* IBM Corp., White Plains, N.Y., 1990.

———: *3174 Establishment Controller: Functional Description,* GA23-0218-08, IBM Corp., Research Triangle Park, N.C., 1991.

———: *3270 Information Display System: 3274 Control Unit Description and Programmer's Guide,* GA23-0061-2, IBM Corp., Research Triangle Park, N.C., 1985.

———: *3270 Information Display System: Data Stream Programmer's Reference,* GA23-0059-07, IBM Corp., Research Triangle Park, N.C., 1992.

———: *3270 Information Display System: Introduction,* GA27-2739-22, IBM Corp., Research Triangle Park, N.C., 1988.

———: *APPN Architecture and Product Implementations Tutorial,* GG24-3669-01, IBM Corp., Research Triangle Park, N.C., 1992.

———: *Dictionary of Computing,* SC20-1699-8, IBM Corp., Poughkeepsie, N.Y., 1991; McGraw-Hill, New York, 1994.

———: *Enterprise System / 9000 Models 120, 130, 150, and 170: Introducing the System,* GA24-4186-00, IBM Corp., Endicott, N.Y., 1990.

———: *Enterprise Systems Architecture/390 ESCON I/O Interface: Physical Layer,* SA23-0394-00, IBM Corp., Kingston, N.Y., 1991.

———: *Enterprise Systems Architecture/390: Principles of Operation,* SA22-7201-00, IBM Corp., Poughkeepsie, N.Y., 1990.

———: *Enterprise Systems Connection,* GA23-0383-01, IBM Corp., Kingston, N.Y., 1991.

———: *Enterprise Systems Connection: ESCON I/O Interface,* SA22-7202-01, IBM Corp., Poughkeepsie, N.Y., 1991.

———: *Enterprise Systems Connection Manager,* GC23-0422-01, IBM Corp., Kingston, N.Y., 1991.

———: *ES/9000 Multi-Image Processing,* vol. 1: *Presentation and Solutions Guidelines,* GG24-3920-00, IBM Corp., Poughkeepsie, N.Y., 1992.

———: *High Speed Networking Technology: An Introductory Survey,* GG24-3816-00, IBM Corp., Raleigh, N.C., 1992.

———: *The Host as a Data Server Using LANRES and Novell NetWare,* GG24-4069-00, IBM Corp., Poughkeepsie, N.Y., 1993.

———: *The IBM 6611 Network Processor,* GG24-3870-00, IBM Corp., Raleigh, N.C., 1992.

———: *IBM Enterprise Systems Architecture/370: Principles of Operation,* SA22-7200-0, IBM Corp., Poughkeepsie, N.Y., 1988.

———: *IBM Networking Systems: Planning and Reference,* SC31-6191-00, IBM Corp., Research Triangle Park, N.C., 1992.

———: *IBM Network Products Implementation Guide,* GG24-3649-01, IBM Corp., Raleigh, N.C., 1993.

———: *IBM System/370 Extended Architecture: Principles of Operation,* SA22-7085-0, IBM Corp., Research Triangle Park, N.C., 1983.

———: *IBM System/370: Principles of Operation,* GA22-7000-10, IBM Corp., Poughkeepsie, N.Y., 1987.

———: *IBM Virtual Machine Facility: Terminal User's Guide,* GC20-1810-9, IBM Corp., Poughkeepsie, N.Y., 1980.

———: *IBM VSE/ESA: System Control Statements,* SC33-6513-00, IBM Corp., Mechanicsburg, Pa., 1990.

———: *IBM VSE/Interactive Computing and Control Facility: Primer,* SC33-6561-01, IBM Corp., Charlotte, N.C., 1993.

———: *IBM VSE/POWER: Networking,* SC33-6573-00, IBM Corp., Mechanicsburg, Pa., 1990.

———: *Installation Guidelines for the IBM Token-Ring Network Products,* GG24-3291-02, IBM Corp., Research Triangle Park, N.C., 1991.

———: *JES3 Introduction,* GC23-0039-2, IBM Corp., Poughkeepsie, N.Y., 1986.

———: *LAN File Services/ESA: MVS Guide and Reference,* SH24-5265-00, IBM Corp., Endicott, N.Y., 1993.

———: *LAN File Services/ESA: VM Guide and Reference,* SH24-5264-00, IBM Corp., Endicott, N.Y., 1993.

———: *LAN Resource Extension and Services/MVS: General Information,* GC24-5625-03, IBM Corp., Endicott, N.Y., 1994.

———: *LAN Resource Extension and Services/MVS: Guide and Reference,* SC24-5623-02, IBM Corp., Endicott, N.Y., 1994.

———: *LAN Resource Extension and Services/VM: General Information,* GC24-5618-03, IBM Corp., Endicott, N.Y., 1994.

———: *LAN Resource Extension and Services/VM: Guide and Reference,* SC24-5622-01, IBM Corp., Endicott, N.Y., 1993.

———: *MVS/ESA and Data in Memory: Performance Studies,* GG24-3698-00, IBM Corp., Poughkeepsie, N.Y., 1992.

———: *MVS/ESA: General Information for MVS/ESA System Product Version 4,* GG28-1600-04, IBM Corp., Poughkeepsie, N.Y., 1992.

———: *MVS/ESA: JES2 Command Reference Summary,* GX22-0017-03, IBM Corp., Poughkeepsie, N.Y., 1993.

———: *MVS/ESA JES2 Commands,* GC23-0084-04, IBM Corp., Poughkeepsie, N.Y., 1993.

———: *MVS/ESA Operations: System Commands Reference Summary,* GX22-0013-1, IBM Corp., Poughkeepsie, N.Y., 1989.

————: *MVS/ESA SP Version 4 Technical Presentation Guide,* GG24-3594-00, IBM Corp., Poughkeepsie, N.Y., 1990.

————: *MVS/ESA: System Commands,* GC28-1626-05, IBM Corp., Poughkeepsie, N.Y., 1993.

————: *NetView: Command Quick Reference,* SX75-0090-00, IBM Corp., Research Triangle Park, N.C., 1993.

————: *NetView: Installation and Administration,* SC31-7084-00, IBM Corp., Research Triangle Park, N.C., 1993.

————: *NetView: NetView Graphic Monitor Facility Operation,* SC31-6099-1, IBM Corp., Research Triangle Park, N.C., 1991.

————: *Sockets Interface for CICS—Using TCP/IP Version 2 Release 2 for MVS: User's Guide,* GC31-7015-00, IBM Corp., Research Triangle Park, N.C., 1992.

————: *Synchronous Data Link Control: Concepts,* GA27-3093-04, IBM Corp., Research Triangle Park, N.C., 1992.

————: *System Information Architecture: Formats,* GA27-3136, IBM Corp., Research Triangle Park, N.C., 1993.

————: *Systems Network Architecture: Architecture Reference, Version 2,* SC30-3422-03, IBM Corp., Research Triangle Park, N.C., 1993.

————: *Systems Network Architecture: Concepts and Products,* GC30-3072-4, IBM Corp., Research Triangle Park, N.C., 1991.

————: *Systems Network Architecture: Technical Overview,* GC30-3073-3, IBM Corp., Research Triangle Park, N.C., 1991.

————: *Systems Network Architecture: Type 2.1 Node Reference, Version 1,* SC20-3422-2, IBM Corp., Research Triangle Park, N.C., 1991.

————: *TCP/IP Version 2 Release 2.1 for MVS: Offload of TCP/IP Processing,* SA31-7033-00, IBM Corp., Research Triangle Park, N.C., 1992.

————: *TCP/IP Version 2 Release 2.1 for MVS: Planning and Customization,* SC31-6085-02, IBM Corp., Research Triangle Park, N.C., 1992.

————: *Virtual Machine/Enterprise Systems Architecture,* GC24-5441, IBM Corp., Endicott, N.Y., 1990.

————: *Virtual Machine/Enterprise Systems Architecture,* SC24-5460-03, IBM Corp., Endicott, N.Y., 1993.

————: *Virtual Machine/Enterprise Systems Architecture: General Information,* GC24-5550-02, IBM Corp., Endicott, N.Y., 1991.

————: *VM/ESA and Related Products: Overview,* GG24-3610-00, IBM Corp., Poughkeepsie, N.Y., 1990.

————: *VM/ESA: CMS Command Reference,* SC24-5461-03, IBM Corp., Endicott, N.Y., 1993.

————: *VM/ESA: CMS Primer,* SC24-5458-02, IBM Corp., Endicott, N.Y., 1992.

————: *VM/ESA: CP Command and Utility Reference,* SC24-5519-03, IBM Corp., Endicott, N.Y., 1993.

————: *VM/ESA Release 2 Overview,* GG24-3860-00, IBM Corp., Poughkeepsie, N.Y., 1992.

————: *VSE/ESA Version 1.3: An Introduction Presentation Foil Master,* GG24-4008-00, IBM Corp., Raleigh, N.C., 1992.

————: *VTAM: Operation,* SC31-6420-00, IBM Corp., Research Triangle Park, N.C., 1993.

————: *VTAM: Resource Definition Reference Version 4 Release 1 for MVS/ESA,* SC31-6427-00, IBM Corp., Research Triangle Park, N.C., 1993.

Jain, Bijendra N., and Ashok K. Agrawala: *Open Systems Interconnection,* McGraw-Hill, New York, 1993.

Kessler, Gary C.: *ISDN,* McGraw-Hill, New York, 1990.

————, and David A. Train: *Metropolitan Area Networks Concepts, Standards, and Services,* McGraw-Hill, New York, 1992.

Killen, Michael: *SAA and UNIX IBM's Open Systems Strategy,* McGraw-Hill, New York, 1992.

————: *SAA Managing Distributed Data,* McGraw-Hill, New York, 1992.

Kochan, Stephen G., and Patrick H. Wood: *Exploring the UNIX System,* Hayden Books, Indianapolis, Ind., 1984.

Madron, Thomas W.: *Local Area Networks: The Next Generation,* Wiley, New York, 1988.

Martin, James: *Local Area Networks Architectures and Implementations,* Prentice-Hall, Englewood Cliffs, N.J., 1989.

McClain, Gary R.: *Open Systems Interconnection Handbook,* Intertext Publications/ Multiscience Press, New York, 1991.

Meijer, Anton: *Systems Network Architecture: A Tutorial,* Pitman, London; Wiley, New York, 1987.

Merrow, Bill: *VSE/ESA Concepts and Facilities,* McGraw-Hill, New York, 1994.

————: *VSE/ESA Performance Management and Fine Tuning,* McGraw-Hill, New York, 1993.

Nash, Stephen G.: *A History of Scientific Computing,* ACM Press, New York, 1990.

Naugle, Matthew G.: *Local Area Networking,* McGraw-Hill, New York, 1991.

————: *Network Protocol Handbook,* McGraw-Hill, New York, 1994.

Nemzow, Martin A. W.: *The Ethernet Management Guide: Keeping the Link,* 2d ed., McGraw-Hill, New York, 1992.

O'Dell, Peter: *The Computer Networking Book,* Ventana Press, Chapel Hill, N.C., 1989.

Parker, Sybil P.: *McGraw-Hill Dictionary of Science and Engineering,* McGraw-Hill, New York, 1984.

Pugh, Emerson W.: *Memories That Shaped an Industry,* MIT Press, Cambridge, Mass., 1984.

————, Lyle R. Johnson, and John H. Palmer: *IBM's 360 and Early 370 Systems,* MIT Press, Cambridge, Mass.

Ranade, Jay, and George C. Sackett, *Introduction to SNA Networking Using VTAM/NCP,* McGraw-Hill, New York, 1989.

Rose, Marshall T.: *The Open Book: A Practical Perspective on OSI,* Prentice-Hall, Englewood Cliffs, N.J., 1990.

————: *The Simple Book: An Introduction to Management of TCP/IP-Based Internets,* Prentice-Hall, Englewood Cliffs, N.J., 1991.

Samson, Stephen L.: *MVS Performance Management,* McGraw-Hill, New York, 1990.

Savit, Jeffrey: *VM/CMS Concepts and Facilities,* McGraw-Hill, New York, 1993.

Schatt, Stan: *Understanding Local Area Networks,* 2d ed., Howard W. Sams, Carmel, Ind., 1990.

Schlar, Serman K.: *Inside X.25: A Manager's Guide,* McGraw-Hill, New York, 1990.

Seyer, Martin D.: *RS-232 Made Easy: Connecting Computers, Printers, Terminals, and Modems,* Prentice-Hall, Englewood Cliffs, N.J., 1991.

Sidhu, Gursharan S., Richard F. Andrews, and Alan B. Oppenheimer: *Inside AppleTalk,* 2d ed., Addison-Wesley, Menlo Park, Calif., 1990.

Spohn, Darren L.: *Data Network Design,* McGraw-Hill, New York, 1993.

Stallings, William: *ISDN: An Introduction,* Macmillan, New York, 1989.

————: *Handbook of Computer-Communications Standards,* vol. 1, Macmillan, New York, 1987.

————: *Handbook of Computer-Communications Standards,* vol. 2, Macmillan, New York, 1987.

————: *Handbook of Computer-Communications Standards,* vol. 3, Macmillan, New York, 1988.

Stamper, David A.: *Business Data Communications,* Benjamin/Cummings, Menlo Park, Calif., 1986.

Tang, Adrian, and Sophia Scoggins: *Open Networking with OSI,* Prentice-Hall, Englewood Cliffs, N.J., 1992.

Umar, Amjad: *Distributed Computing: A Practical Synthesis,* Prentice-Hall, Englewood Cliffs, N.J., 1993.

White, Gene: *Internetworking and Addressing,* McGraw-Hill, New York, 1992.

Zwass, Vladimir: *Introduction to Computer Science,* Barnes & Noble Books, New York, 1981.

Index

A priori network design, 10
AAL functions, 174–175
Address Resolution Protocol, 266–267
Advanced Peer-to-Peer Networking, 48–49
Amplitude, 12
Amplitude modulation, 28–29
Analog, 10–11
Anycast address, 373–375
Apple file structure, 227
Appletalk, 49–50
Architecture, 3
   digital network, 2, 51–53
   distributed network, 75–77
   how to learn, 43
   NT, 127–128, 460–461
   personal computer, 67–72
   systems network, 2, 56–57
Asynchronous transmission, 19–20
ATM:
   cell structure, 175–176
   concepts, 177–179
   implementation, 179–181
   interface types, 177
   layer structure, 172–173
   physical layer architecture, 181–186
   technology, 171
   terminology, 186–187

B channel, 193–194
Babbage, Charles, 44
Baseband signalling, 11
Baud rate, 28
Binary, 15–16
Bit, 16
Bit-oriented, 21
Bit rate, 28
Bridge:
   filtering, 482
   forwarding, 481–482

Bridge (*Cont.*):
   learning, 482–483
   operation, 479–481
Broadband signaling, 11
Broadcast frame, 494–495
Byte, 16
Byte-oriented, 20–21

Cartesian coordinate system, 11–12
Client identifier, 386
Coaxial cable, 37
Computing:
   centralized, 45
   decentralized, 45–46
   personal, 65–67
Cross talk, 35

D channel, 192–193
Data circuit equipment, 26–27
Data link connection identifier, 204–205
Data representation, 15
Data terminal equipment, 26–27
Data, voice, and multimedia management, 213–215
Datagrams, 309
   fragments, 336
Delay, 35
Design needs, 83–84
   external, 84, 85
   internal, 83, 84
DHCP, 381–382
   client function, 402
   message format, 382–383
   messages and meanings, 390
   protocol, 385–386
   terms, 384–385
DHCPDecline, 401–402
DHCPDiscover message, 396
DHCPRequest message, 399–400

Differential phase shift key modulation, 29–30
Digital network architecture, 2, 51–53
Digital signal, 11
Distributed network architecture, 75–77
DNA, 2
DNS, 408–409
    elements, 411–412
    name servers, 418–420
    name syntax, 415–416
    queries, 416–418
    resolvers, 423–424
DS3, 184–185

Electrical:
    considerations, 86–89
    testing, 102–105
Encoding techniques, 31
External design needs, 84–85

Fading, 35
Fallacies, 2
Fiber, 100-MB, 185–186
Fiberoptic cable, 37–38
Files, 225–226
File structures:
    Apple, 227
    multiple virtual storage, 227–230
    OS/400, 232–234
    S/36, 244–247
    S/38, 243–244
    Unix, 231–232
    Virtual Machine, 235–238
    Virtual Storage Extended, 241–243
Frame relay:
    access devices, 207–210
    frame, 205–206
    support for data and voice, 201–204
Frequency, 12–13
Frequency division multiplexing, 25
Frequency modulation, 28–29
Frequency shift key modulation, 29
FTP, 295–297
Full duplex transmission, 24

Grandmother, author's, 9

H channel, 194–195
Half duplex transmission, 24
Hardware abstraction layer, 125–126
Hardware addresses, 290–291

Harmonic distortion, 35
Hexadecimal, 17
High-speed connectivity, 474–476
Hub implementation, 7

ICMP, 262–264
Infrared communication, 39
Interfaces, 26
Internal design needs, 83–84
Internet Control Message Protocol, 262–264
Internet timestamp, 316–317
Interpretation:
    of bandwidth, 22–23
    of channels, 23
IP:
    addresses, 371–372
    fragmentation, 312
    header format, 317
    and network design, 261–263
    operation, 311
    terminology, 314
    Version 4, 309
    Version 6, 341
        address types, 366–367
        addressing, 367–368
        flow labels, 359–360
        header format, 343
        routing header, 349–350
        terminology, 342
IPX, 433–434
    addressing, 441
ISDN:
    channels, 192–193
    data and voice, 189–191
    definition, 190–191
    use, 198–200

Jitter, 35
Jumbo payload, 347, 348

LANRES, 452–455
Learning tools, 61–63
Leased lines, 41–42
Links, types, 33
Logical network, 7
Logical view of a bus, 6

Management:
    of core equipment, 215–216
    information, 222–224
    philosophies, 218–220

Manchester encoding, 33–34
Microwave, 39–40
Modulation:
   amplitude, 28–29
   frequency, 28–29
   frequency shift key, 29
   phase shift key, 30–31
   techniques, 29–30
Multicast, 375–376
Multimedia and virtual circuits, 206–207
Multiple Virtual Storage file structure,
      227–230
Multiplexers, types, 25–26
Multiplexing, 24–25
   frequency division, 25
   time division, 25

NCP, 434–444
NetWare, 2, 53–54
   layers, 432, 433
   networks, 429
Network:
   architect, 1
   design considerations, 95–96
   design premises, 149–159
   maintenance, 168–169
   operation, 162–163
   planning, with IP, 261–263
   test tools, 142–143
Networking blueprint, 58–59
NFS, 305–306
Nonlinear distortion, 35
NT:
   architecture, 127–128, 460–461
   Domains, 468–469
   Disk Manager, 467
   Executive, 127–128, 464
   HAL, 464
   LPC, 464
   Registry, 469, 470
   tips, 471–472
   VMM, 465

Open Systems Interconnection, 54–56
Open/VMS, 239–241
Open Data Interface, 436–437
OS/400 file structure, 232–234
OSPF, 270–273

Parallel transmission, 23–24
Parity, 20
Period, 13

Personal computer architecture, 67–72
Personal computing, 65–67
Phase, 13
Phase shift key modulation, 30–31
Physical hub topology, 7
Planning TCP/IP networks, 258–261
Point-to-point communication, 40
Port manipulation, 290
Post hoc network design, 8
Power protection, 109–112, 491–492

Remote bridge, 488–489
Router:
   protocols, 268–270
   types, 498–499
Routing:
   SNA, 508–509
   source, 490–491
   static, 507–508
   TCP/IP, 510–511
RS-232, 31

S/36 file structures, 244–247
S/38 file structures, 243–244
SAP, 435–447
Satellite communication, 38–39
Serial transmission, 23
Signal:
   characteristics, 11
   distortion, 34, 35
   types, 10
Simple network management protocol,
      221
Simplex tranmission, 24
Sine wave, 13–14
SNA, 2
   routing, 508–509
Sockets, 290
SONET, 183–184
Source routing, 490–491
SPX, 434, 442–443
Square wave, 14
SS7, 195–196
Star:
   implementation, 8
   topology, 7
Static routing, 507–508
Syllogism, hypothetical, 47
Synchronous tranmission, 20–21
System fault tolerance, 451–452
Systems network architecture, 2,
      56–57

T1, 31
TCP:
  connection establishment, 275–278
  and data communication, 283–285
  header, 273–275
TCP/IP, 2, 57–58
  growth, 253–255
  in the 1970s, 251–252
  in the 1980s, 252
  in the 1990s, 252–253
  in the 21st century, 253
  network planning, 258–261
  routing, 510–511
  structure, 256–257
TELNET, 293–295
Thick-net, 6
Three-legged chair, 4
Time division multiplexing, 25
Transmission:
  asynchronous, 19–20
  full duplex, 24
  half duplex, 24
  parallel, 23–24
  serial, 23
  simplex, 24
  synchronous, 20–21

Transmission Control Protocol/Internet
    Protocol (see TCP/IP)
Twisted-pair media, 36–37

UDP, 286–288
  applications, 301–306
Unicast address, 369–370
Universal Synchronous/Asynchronous
    Receiver/Transmitter, 27–28
UNIX file structure, 231–232

V.35, 31
Virtual link, 203–204
Virtual Machine file structure, 235–238
Virtual Storage Extended file structure,
    241–243
von Neumann, John, 44–45

Waveform, 13–14
Well-known ports, 290
Windows NT, 59–61

X, 292–293
X.21, 32–33

Y2K problem, 164–167

ABOUT THE AUTHOR

Ed Taylor is the Founder of Information World, Inc. He is a former network architect for IBM. Mr. Taylor is responsible for contributions to the Taylor Networking Series from McGraw-Hill. He authored *Multiplatform Network Management* as well as *The McGraw-Hill Internetworking Command Reference.*

Mr. Taylor's book, *The McGraw-Hill Internetworking Handbook,* has been published in Japanese by Fuji Technosystems of Tokyo, Japan. He has other work soon to be published in Traditional Character Long Form Chinese in Taiwan.

Some of Mr. Taylor's consulting experience includes work for NEC, Orange County, CA, BASF, Chrysler, Hewlett-Packard, Dow Jones, Ore-Ida Foods, Mutual of New York (MONY), and IBM Education.